Complementing Latin American Borders

Complementing Latin American Borders

floyd merrell

Purdue University Press
West Lafayette, Indiana

Printed in the United States of America

Library of Congress Cataloging-in-Publication Data

Merrell, Floyd, 1937-
  Complementing Latin American borders / Floyd Merrell.
    p. cm.
  ISBN 1-55753-324-5 (alk. paper)
  1. Latin America--Civilization. 2. Latin America--Social life and
customs. 3. Arts, Latin American. 4. Peirce, Charles S. (Charles
Sanders), 1839-1914--Contributions in semiotics. I. Title.

  F1408.3.M466 2003
  980--dc22

2003022845

CONTENTS

FIGURES

Preface

[T]hose who still haven't crossed a border will do it very soon.

—Guillermo Gómez-Peña

One may be better able to comprehend one's relationship with other cultures upon struggling to comprehend those other cultures in terms of their relationship with yet other cultures, including one's own culture. Upon attempting to act on this twisting, self-returning assumption, I find myself distorting the customarily conceived equation for knowing the other.[1]

I distort the equation somewhat, for I try to resist the temptation of imperiously bringing sweeping generalities to my topic, as is, unfortunately, often the case of books bearing tidings from postmodernism, postcolonialism, subaltern studies, cultural studies, and other global visions. That "top-down" approach is all too familiar in the academy these days. The generalizations within the cover of this book emerge from a transdisciplinary, "top-down" approach, to be sure. But these generalizations do not issue forth from a fleshless theoretical scheme. They emerge out of my particular experiences in daily Latin American life from all walks over the past forty years. These experiences, I would like to believe, provide a "bottom-up" approach to complement "top-down" generalizations. This approach makes way for "border thinking," or thinking from within the interstices, to appropriate Walter Mignolo's (2000) enticing phrase. Thinking from within the interstices, I would suggest, brings particulars into an incongruous complementary relationship with generalities.

My evoking terms the likes of "incongruous complementarity" and "border thinking" brings into question the title of my inquiry. "Borders," when rendered "textual"—which for good or for bad is virtually inevitable in academia—can be conceived as the customary virgule between a term and its other, or better, its multiple *others*. However, when the virgule becomes a hyphen, the terms enter into complementary *interdependent, interrelated, interaction* (this italicized trio of concepts will be self-defined as the pages of this volume flow by). "Complementing borders" is appropriately ambiguous, I would suggest. Borders complement themselves, for the one side serves to fill out or complete the other side; both sides mutually supply each other's lack insofar as that may be possible. At the same time, people who inhabit cultural borders, the interstices, do not belong to either of the two sides, yet they are contained within the complementation that emerges when two or more cultures interdependently, interrelatedly, and incongruously interact. Border dwellers complement the borders' complementation.

I once thought about labeling this book *Tempering Latin American Borders*. Tempering is much like complementing insofar as it entails the process of providing a balance, a middle way between apparent extremes. Tempering entails adjusting to the needs of the two sides of the equation by tenuously counterbalancing them. It brings about a more satisfactory transitory condition by mixing cultural ingredients in a liquid, flowing manner; it puts cultures in tune with one another; it introduces attunement by altering cultural rhythms found in the two extremes such that they enter into syncopated dissonance and consonance; it mixes cultural tints and hues in such a way that a kaleidoscopic panorama emerges. Indeed, from the broad view, borders evince a tempering process. In the final analysis, however, I decided to remain with *Complementing Latin American Borders*, the reasons for which, I trust, will become evident as the reader surfs along the pages of this volume.

That much written, I wish respectfully to insist that I enjoy no privileged vantage point regarding the story I have to tell. My story is from the inside, and therein it must remain. Let me try to explain. According to a particular strain of current wisdom, we exist within a universe of marvelously magical resonances.[2] If disparate and apparently incompatible cultural phenomena are brought into resonance with each another, it means they have learned to live in tenuous harmony through consonance and dissonance, in a complementary embrace, somehow. The trick to our understanding this resonance lies in our getting a concrete feel for and a sense of the harmony, consonance, dissonance, and yes, of the incongruous complementarity contained within the resonance. This is not easy, of course. Our entire tradition mitigates against our doing so. We in academia, in that grave world of textualism, have unfortunately inherited a self-confident, presumably authoritarian, voice that is satisfied with nothing short of clear, distinct, and reductive accounts. This voice is obsessed with conserving those timeless sanctuaries from whence chants can be heard over unique and singular expressions in the arts and the humanities, and over colorless, soundless, tasteless, and scentless scientific and pseudo-scientific accounts presumably describing and exploring any and all phenomena. With respect to cultural and social matters, this monolithic voice cherishes familiar dichotomies between those who have and those who don't have, those who enjoy hegemony and those who find themselves outside the sphere of control, those who are privileged with a voice and the others. Actually, it has become increasingly apparent over the past few years that there never was any homogeneous "we," nor was there any pure, uncontaminated "other." That idea was coughed up, I suspect, as a last ditch attempt by the gasping, wheezing, faltering shibboleths of modernity as we have known them.

Nevertheless, the all-too-familiar discourse often goes on, quite obstinately and with undaunted self-confidence. Thus we often have that humdrum mapping of current cultural trends as if culture were an ideological block governed by some rational globalizing economic machine. Scholars, caught up in the euphoria and in an effort to slide along the cutting edge, write about global flows and local narratives apparently with totalizing sugarplums still dancing in their heads. At the same time, there is a lingering infatuation with pseudo-positivist discourse where words are defined by other words with no end in sight—this is strange, since in philosophy of science positivism has been a dead horse for over fifty years. As a result, there is lip service in litany fashion to "logics" of "dispersion," "alterity," "hegemony," "dissemination," "difference," "supplementarity," "simulacra," "consumption," "subalternity," and even "history," as well as to "logics" of "neo-" or "late-" or "post-capitalism," and to other various and sundry kindred "logics." We read songs of praise in honor of these "logics," as if we all knew what they were about. Now I must reveal my ignorance by confessing that I have no idea what they are about. The very use of the term "logic" within these contexts is born of a sneaky totalizing tendency, it seems to me. What I wish to attempt in this volume is place Latin America's intriguing yet unruly and alienating nonlinear, nonbinary, and inordinately vague "logics" of everyday practices under the title "alternate cultural logics," and account for them as best I can in view of certain trends on the Latin American socio-cultural scene.

There remains, then, the need to qualify properly that numbing complexity of Latin America's cultures. This presents a problem, a big problem. The very term "Latin America" becomes ambiguous. It often throws Spanish, Portuguese, and French colonial traditions into one pot of stew, discards many African and Amerindian elements as unwanted cores and peelings, and adds the presumed spices of European high culture in hopes of giving the whole concoction a bit more respectability. How can all the countries of the entire region, whether quasi-authoritarian or pseudo-democratic, rich or poor, all these ethnically and culturally kaleidoscopic societies, be jumbled into one rubric? How can any opinion regarding this whole be anything but an oversimplification?

Upon accepting his Nobel Prize for Literature in 1982, Gabriel García Márquez observed that his art was inseparable from that "monstrous reality": Latin America. He alluded to the anomalous habit Europeans and North Americans have of eagerly applauding recent Latin American literature while holding the people incapable of governing themselves. The continent's literary output itself however, presents a tenuous image. This is the image of a people whose literary expression has, over the centuries, been distorted by colonial and neocolonial patterns. These patterns are coupled with creative juices flowing from a genealogical tree fed by roots embedded deeply within the cultural soil consisting of the most heterogeneous mix of human life the world has likely ever seen. Indeed, a "monstrous reality," one might conclude. Yet, the following pages attempt somehow to afford a feel and a sense of this "monstrous reality," while eschewing the very notions of essentialism, representation, and foundations.[3]

But, it's back to the same problem. How can I generalize the ungeneralizable, say the unsayable? Myriad exceptions mock my every attempt to generalize over an area as diverse as Latin America. Recent anthropological studies defy talk about "Latin Americans" with evidence that it is impossible effectively to qualify or quantify the extraordinary multiplicity even of a single provincial town in Mexico, Guatemala, Peru, Brazil, or Bolivia. In this light, how can "Latin America" be construed in the aggregate rather than in its virtually indescribable diversity? One might wish to assert that we need more attention to details and fewer Grand Theories. Focus on specifics should give us a better feel for local enclaves within the broad cultural panorama. The trouble is that obsessive focus on particulars by social scientists and Latin American area specialists often takes refuge in the comforts of the facts and nothing but the facts. The end product is usually an encyclopedic tidal wave of particulars concocted by specialists who know little about a lot and a lot about hardly anything at all. Nevertheless, they wax ebullient over their presumed command of a tossing ocean of incoherent minutiae with the illusion that it endows them with breadth of mind and of knowledge. They carry onward and upward, confident that rigorless telephone directory accounts of names, dates, places, events, and works guarantees them immunity from wild speculation ending in groundless sweeping generalizations about the entirety of the field. This scholarly practice more often than not turns out to be hardly more than superficial newspaper reporting, with little backbone to it.

I am by no stretch of the imagination saying that saving grace may ultimately be had in Grand Theories. Take, for instance, economics, where global remedies for Latin America the likes of "dependency," "modernization," and "import substitution," pervaded the scene during the 1960s and the 1970s. These theories, the brain-children of socialism, and conservative and liberal capitalism, became great competing giants with feet of clay. They all ultimately led to naught.[4] Then, with the debt crisis of the 1980s, virtually all of Latin America—the most notable exception being Cuba—turned a favorable but uncritical eye toward the "structural adjustment programs" of "neoliberalism." As a result, government fiscal spending is now severely restricted, subsidies to the farmers and the poor have gone down the tube, labor unions have lost much of the marginal power they enjoyed, there have been cuts in corporate taxes and taxes on higher income bracket citizens have been reduced, currencies have been devalued, import tariffs have been lowered, controls on foreign investment have been loosened, and privatization has become the name of the game. Today, it is becoming increasingly obvious that "neoliberalism" is another case of grandiose visions coupled with massive applications, and the end-product will likely be overall disasters. The Grand Unified Theorists of neoliberal economics have had their say, and their day might be coming to an end.

Between those academics who can, at a moment's notice, spout out a catalogue of facts without overriding organization, and those who enthusiastically pour forth the solution to end all solutions to Latin America's problems, there is quite a void. What I attempt in this volume is to form a vague notion of the big picture without suffering alienation from the nitty-gritty affairs of everyday life in Latin American. A comprehensive view is worthless unless contextualized in a sphere of particulars; a successive grasp of particulars is of little use unless given a comprehensive setting, however vague. Striking a happy pose with the comprehensive and the contextual and generalities and particularities held together in a virtually impossible slithering embrace is not an easy matter. The one side is so cumbersome it cannot be circumscribed; the other side slides and writhes, threatening to slip free and cut loose at any moment. What ought to be according to some conceptual grasp or other rarely proves to be equal to what is, for what might be always stands at least an outside chance of becoming what will have been at some future time and place. And yet, there must be at least a few relative constants available to us, we would like to think. But more likely than not such thinking is self-defeating. We must be content with less, it would appear.

How much less? Considerably less. For we must be willing to admit that all cultural knowing is contextual knowing, and that particulars within their respective contexts are invariably always becoming something other than what they were becoming. Nothing is set in stone; everything is in a process of change. If all cultural knowing is contextual, then our agenda would surely entail making explicit those assumptions that are usually implicit in an effort to sharpen thinking, and it would avoid projecting *ad hominem* stereotypes. Each culture provides a set of guidelines, both explicit and implicit, that everybody follows upon arising in the morning and attending to their daily affairs. The citizens of each culture have a feel for the right way to live, a feel they begin internalizing at birth, and they more often than not tend to conduct their lives according to this feel—at least outside occasional rebellious moments. However, our confidence that we can tune in to these cultural feels is often hopelessly optimistic. It never fails to outrun our capacity to appraise cultural phenomena with a cool mind and a contrite heart.

Regarding Latin America, we might assume there exists a complex set of cultures with their own pliable *modus operandi*. To identify the nature of these cultures would demand a capacity for divination beyond all but very few of us. There have been numerous aborted attempts to specify the essential nature of Latin America's cultural milieu. As a case in point, a "universalist" neo-Hegelian trend became the vogue in Latin America during the 1940s and 1950s. In Mexico, for instance, it was hopefully launched into the stratosphere with a series of studies going by the name of "Colección México y lo Mexicano," published by Porrúa y Obregón, which included an early version of Octavio Paz's *Labyrinth of Solitude* (Abelardo 1960). Soon thereafter, Leopoldo Zea and some of his Mexican colleagues sought a definition of "Mexicanness" (*mexicanidad*), as a concrete expression of "humanity" (*lo humano*). The task was to account for what it is to be Mexican in the sense of concrete everyday life and how one's Mexicanness is folded into what it is to be anyone at any time and any place (Zea 1955, 1976). In the 1960s the neo-Hegelian search for what makes a particular culture unique ran into the brick wall of "functionalism" maintaining a Marxist or quasi-Marxist posture. The Hegelian strain looked inward in search of the roots of its cultural essence, while the Marxist approach tended to place the blame for the Latin American condition on the global economic struggles as they were conceived to exist at that time. Proponents of the former generally accused proponents of the latter of historical myopia, while the latter branded the former as starry-eyed utopianists with their feet firmly planted in thin air. The crux of the conundrum lies in Latin American intellectuals' gauging themselves in their relationship with the values and standards of the West by the measuring rod and by reference to intellectual canons from the West itself.

It is now quite evident that Western physical sciences and especially the social sciences are themselves and by their very nature culturally embedded. Louis Dumont (1977, 1980, 1986), for example, erects the distinction between *Homo hierarchicus,* typical of Indian and other cultures, and *Homo aequalis,* typical of the West, while availing himself of his inherited Western standards. In a comparable manner, Latin America's neo-Scholastic, Catholic legacy could conceivably be pitted against a Calvinistic Protestantism that tends to be most prevalent in many parts of the United States. Dumont's grand dichotomy might in this respect appear quite *apropos,* especially in view of the fact that "liberation theology" hardly wrought any change in this somewhat artificial distinction. Perhaps one might surmise that the recent neo-liberal wave can eventually turn the tide in favor of a more egalitarian Latin America, somewhat in line with the United States' culture—if indeed that is desirable. Frankly, I, for one, doubt it. But only time will tell. Meanwhile, back on the present Latin American scene, whenever Amerindian and Afro-American movements are given a favorable nod and encouraged to express their ethnicity and find their elusive identity, that nod is often made from within a selected set of Western ideas regarding ethnicity and identity. To make matters worse, these movements are usually knotted up in middle class values that are already chiefly Western in orientation anyway.

So it seems that I am once again back where I started. How is it possible genuinely to generalize and remain attuned to the necessary particulars? To be more specific, how can a white-anglo male like myself hope to write anything about Latin Americans with an iota of respectability? Clifford Geertz's "experiencing near" and "experiencing distant" and his "thick" and "thin" descriptions aside, the problem lies not in knowing what one is doing, that is, knowing on a cognitive, intellectual level.[5] Rather, the problem is a matter of feeling and sensing that what there is cannot legitimately be linearly displayed by way of a string of words slapped onto a blank page. If the feeling and sensing are indeed genuine at all, they are just that: feeling and sensing. Telling a story about them, even when they are given window dressing consisting of the flossiest of testimonials or the most charming of tales, cannot but be in part a lie, a fiction. That is to say, if a modicum of truth there must be, it cannot be more than a partial truth, and since at least a modicum of twisted ideas, biases, and distortions there will invariably be, whatever truth there is will be offset by untruths.

It must now appear that I'm digging a hole for myself that will soon suck me away entirely from whatever credibility I might have enjoyed thus far. But not quite, I would hope. That is, not quite, if I can entice whatever reader I may still have out there to forget distinctions of the sort that are customarily evoked. Yes. Forget binaries, insofar as that may be possible. As a first step in that direction, I would invite you to begin "thinking Peircean." I refer to that North American polymath and semiotician, Charles Sanders Peirce, author of the most developed three-way concept of the sign to date, and intrepid critic of the Cartesian mind/body split and other obstinate dualisms. I will call on the expertise of Peirce often. Evocation of Peirce's philosophy, I hope to illustrate, is a salutary move, however difficult the task of weaving his concepts into my story may be.

After spreading all the above on the table in full view, you should expect to travel a winding pathway through the narrative that follows this modest foreword. There will be frequent jumps from the particular to the general, from theoretical semiotic concerns to concrete happenings throughout Latin American history, and from close analyses to speculative flights of the imagination. There will be occasional harmony, euphony, and consonance, but there will also be moments of dissonance and discord, some of them teetering on the brink. Along the way, I expect, Peirce will give us a few hints regarding those slippery, flowing "cultural logics" of contextual complementarity as an alternative to the tight-lipped prescriptions and prohibitions of classical Aristotelian logic and other bivalent ways of thinking.

In order to give you a feel for these " cultural logics," I allude to the Latin American context in conjunction with the notions of rhythms and resonances, symmetries and asymmetries, equilibria and disequilibria, foregrounding and back-grounding, euphonies and discords, continuous flows and syncopes, all of which are found in everyday life, the arts, politics, economics, and social institutions and prac-tices. Regarding everyday life, focus rests on interhuman relations, in the arts, mu-sic, and dance above all. In politics, I make mention of the irresistible pull of foreign models and the struggle for a viable, *sui generis* expression of the tacit will of the people. In economic affairs, I allude to Latin America's attraction and the repulsion—the love-hate relationship—with Western ideologies and their applica-tion in social institutions and practices, and a host of hybrid mixes. The general theme, following Peirce's process philosophy, is that of the ebb and flow, continuity and discontinuity, fusion and diffusion, ordering and disordering, and the intermix-ing and dispersal, of wishes and desires, tendencies and compulsions, and propensi-ties and proclivities, among Latin Americans, past and present.

As I have already confessed, this is a tall order indeed. With more than twenty nations and the diversity of dialects, ethnicities, influences, and attitudes, how is it possible to fold a convincing account into the pages of a solitary volume? In four words, *it is not possible*. Entirely possible, that is. For, in light of some of my above remarks, particulars cannot simply be forgotten, especially if the task at hand is to illustrate how generalities are never fixed but are in an incessant process of becom-ing something other than what they were becoming. So neither I nor anyone else can say everything about so much as a small corner of the Latin American cultural mix. How can I, then, say anything at all and at the same time provide a glimpse of what is not in my saying? How can I select from the virtual infinity of cultural possibili-ties that which sheds more than a modicum of light on a large part of that whole? The very terms "large" and "part" are anomalous with respect to the whole. The whole is so mind-bogglingly complex that to say a "part" of it is to remain within the complexity; to say a "large portion" of it is to resort to generalities of such broad na-ture that they threaten to become airy platitudes. How can I say what I have on my mind if it is but a cloud of vagueness that yields so many particulars that the differ-ences between many of them are differences that hardly make a difference? How can I condense this cloud into a desiccated and properly sanitized machine for taxono-mizing the object under observation and for grinding out a story that will be met with an all-knowing nod by any and all onlookers? Once again, in three words: *I can not*. Not really. Yet, I should try; I must try, I will try. Upon so doing, and in order to bring some sort of coherence to my story, I have highlighted certain aspects of Bra-zilian and Mexican cultures, with frequent digressive words directed toward other areas of Latin America. It is my hope that this will help give my account some de-gree of continuity and coherence. The proof, I must say, will be in the taste the reader brings to the task of the reading. The final responsibility, then, lies with you.[6]

I begin my story with a dialogue, or better, a *polylogue,* in the form of a rather satirical play on various Jorge Luis Borges characters. It revolves around some of the issues addressed by Anglo-American analytic philosophy and its aftermath, es-pecially with the entrance of Richard Rorty into the imaginary verbal encounter. The flavor of this meeting of minds is often disrespectful, and at times it even borders on the absurd. But it moves along. Minds and mouths can't help moving along, for they are in the flux and the flow of the universe. They meander, swirl with the eddies, occasionally break into a frenzied dance upon entering a few whitewater stretches, lull around during the slow moments, and all the while they become what they were not. That is the feel I wish to convey by what at the outset might be taken as a bizarre heresy of all that is laudable about Borges.

I begin with a *polylogue* in order to leave you with a sense of the interlocutors' noncommunication. Their inability to engage in genuine dialogue patterns much textualism and would-be dialoguing in today's academic world; it also helps illuminate the dilemma we find ourselves in when attempting to understand other cultures as self-contained wholes. Consequently, in the chapters that follow I will often return to the characters in the *polylogue* and the incapacity of their words—language—to bring them together into a close-knit community. Something more than words is needed: if message I may have, this is it.

I chose some of Borges's characters for reasons that will become evident: he is, simply put, the writer that lends himself most effectively to this sort of thing.[7] Other than that, I chose Borges, the bookish and cosmopolitan Borges, the Borges who rarely really rubbed elbows with "real people," the Borges who issued a call for authoritarian leadership and even military dictatorships in Latin America, the Borges who said that with a few exceptions Latin American literature was not worth the trouble, the Borges who never fully fleshed out a single character in his prose, the cogitating, obsessively intellectualizing Borges, because I happen to think that no other writer is as "Latin American" as he is.

"Outlandish!," comes the immediate response. And so it might appear at the outset. But think about it for a moment. Who more effectively than Borges demonstrates the virtues and the *aporias* concealed in any and all metaphysical issues. Who more adequately portrays the multiple ambiguities in all private and collective cultural manifestations? Who is capable of such twists and turns of heart and mind? Who can view things as if from the "outside" with a wry grin and an occasional chuckle while remaining clearly "inside?" Whose irony is more subtle? Yes, Borges. In an abstract, intensively metaphorical way he *is* the pushes and pulls, the melodies and harmonies, the point and counterpoint, and the incessantly varying fugue, expressing Latin America. Latin Americans are supreme contemplators. When they wish to express their inner feelings it is usually through poetry, prose, and other artistic expressions. It is less commonly through metaphysical essays.[8] Yet Borges tries to express himself through a tense combination of the two narrative modes. He attempts to articulate contemplative, even mystical, experiences by way of sheer intellection. Of course, ultimately he fails. He cannot help but fail. In fact, he knew he would fail from the very beginning. But that didn't stop him for a moment. He reveled in the futile game; he enjoyed every minute of it. With this in mind, I have done what I could by initiating my inquiry with a Borges-inspired polylogue.

So, the book you have in your hands will follow this sequence. First, there is the polylogue. Then Latin America is presented as an invention, an imaginary construct. A brief essay on Peirce's concept of the sign is followed by a turn to a selection of character traits among the people of Latin America. The next few chapters present the concept of sympathetic vibrations and cultural patterning, of rhythms and their disruptions, of signs and their streaming and cascading as an expression of culture, and of vagueness and generality and alternate "logics of culture," by way of

Latin American borders and the border of borders. Finally, I develop the themes of what I call *homogeneity, heterogeneity,* and *hegemony* in the Latin American scene through signs of music and dance and literature and the arts and everyday living as cultural expression.

And there you have it in a nutshell. I resist the usual chapter by chapter rundown as a preview of coming attractions. I would suggest that we must take a leap into the semiosic maelstrom without the customary profusion of ideological, theoretical, and methodological and rhetorical preliminaries. Somehow, if we are fortunate, we might in this manner be able to feel and sense what is of utmost importance, for we can't expect adequately to know it without having first taken that initial leap followed by some sporadic floundering about while we learn to swim with the flow. (Besides, I have provided you with a brief introduction preceding each of the five parts into which this inquiry is subdivided. That should put you somewhat in tune with what is to follow.)

Acknowledgments

I wish to extend my thanks to the proudly humble people of Tepito and its surroundings, in the heart of Mexico City, which I have frequented over the years beginning in 1965. There, in Tepito, I have spent many hours walking and sitting, watching the flow of people and events, listening to the myriad rhythms and sounds, sensing the aromas, tasting the food, feeling the texture and the age and the grime of this centuries-old *barrio,* and all the while contemplating, wondering, pondering, thinking, and on occasion even talking—not as a Baudelaire *Flâneur,* mind you, but dressed like and wandering about in the manner of a street urchin with a giant question mark hovering over my head. My usual routes through the area, familiar on a map of the mushrooming metropolis, have become in terms of concrete experience progressively unfamiliar as the years went by.

My last journey through Tepito left me despondent, and even somewhat depressed; yet my usual contemplative, wondering, pondering, thinking mood prevailed. A sense of tranquillity soon began to pervade my feelings. In spite of it all, I realized these people know how to survive, to accommodate themselves to whatever life has to offer and at the same time to alter their world so as to bring it into resonance with their own form of life, and to improvise, incessantly to improvise, in order to make it through the day, and the next, and the next. Somehow I sensed that if there is any hope for us at all, to a large extent it rests with people of this sort throughout the world, the people that in academic jargon are now referred to as abstract labels such as "marginalized" and "subaltern"—that, notwithstanding all the good intentions I still find somewhat demeaning. I would suggest that we try to learn from them. They have many lessons to offer. If we continue merely theorizing about them while remaining ensconced within our comfortable university settings, I believe it is *we* who will be much the poorer as a result.

I wish to thank Professor Lúcia Santaella for her extended invitations to teach at the Pontifícia Universidade Católica (PUC) of São Paulo. I thoroughly enjoyed my seminars with some of the excellent students in the Program of Communication and Semiotics at PUC, and I have learned much from them as well. I've also learned from the classes, seminars, and lectures I've had the opportunity to give at the Universidade Federal da Bahia (UFBA) in Salvador of Bahia state at the invitation of Professor Waldomiro José da Silva Filho, and at other universities in Ilheus, Feira de Santana, and Brasília.

I cannot fail to acknowledge my debt to the people on the streets of that bustling Brazilian metropolis, São Paulo, as well as in the neighborhoods of Salvador and other cities. Along the main arteries and side streets, the markets and shopping centers and favelas, I'm grateful for what I have been able to sense of Brazil's music, her dance, her marvelous language, and the flows and rhythms of her culture. Above all, I owe more than I can say to capoeira Mestre Curió and to Mestra Jararaca. While at a bone-creaking age I struggled with the subtle art of capoeira, they taught me about learning with and through the body, and that what has been so learned resides within corporeal memory, not the textually oriented mind. They've helped me understand that textual knowing is in comparison to corporeal knowing synthetic, given its linear, fleshless yield produced by a hard-driven quest for consistency and completeness.

The problem is that I can never get enough of Brazil. There is so much to feel, sense, and understand. What I have accomplished has been no more than a beginning. If after years of contemplating Mexican life and living with my remarkable Mexican wife I remain with profound question marks regarding Mexican culture, the gaps in my knowledge of Brazilian culture at this stage seem insurmountable. However, the journey will continue; of that I have no doubt. Time may tell the enticing, enchanting tale more satisfactorily. A few perplexing questions may be answered; doubts may partially subside; like Zen koans, at least a few of Brazil's enigmas may begin to reveal their secrets. That, at least, is the hope I continue to nurture.

My thanks go to Purdue University for the freedom I have been allowed in the pursuit of my interests. As universities go, Purdue is hierarchically and bureaucratically quite inflexible. I can write what I just wrote because it is no news to anybody. Yet, I must say that after taking care of my teaching and service and administrative duties at this institution, I have been given a long and lax rein and allowed to do my own thing pretty much as I saw fit. Here at Purdue, I wish to thank my students from three graduate seminars, who patiently put up with my stuttering and stammering my way through much of what now finds itself between the covers of this book, and to Howard Mancing, whose comments after having read the first draft were helpful. My thanks also to Tom Bacher, Margaret Hunt, and the staff of Purdue University Press. I cannot disregard the great debt I owe all those scholars from whom I have drawn what few meager ideas of my own I have been able to squeeze out on the pages that follow. The list is too long to reproduce here; I will let the epigraphs, quotes, and works cited pay homage to their importance. In particular I must thank Professor Iván Almeida for granting me permission to reprint the *polylogue* that initiates this volume, which was first published in Volume 4 of *Variaciones Borges,* and Richard Lanigan of *The American Journal of Semiotics,* for permission to reprint much of what makes up chapter twelve.

Above all, I could never allow this book to see the light of day without having dedicated it to Araceli. She has been the heart and soul of my learning about, my merging with, and my creating a certain vague sense of, Latin America, and especially Mexico, over the years. Thank you.

Notes

1.   As Renato Rosaldo (1993:64) puts the problem: "[W]e ethnographers should be open to asking not only how our descriptions of others would read if applied to ourselves but how we can learn from other people's descriptions of ourselves." This book bears implicit acknowledgment to ethnography. If I were hard pressed to cite the most prominent influence of ethnography on my writing, with certain reservations I might mention Clifford Geertz (1973, 1983, 2000; also Ortner 1999), from among a host of other scholars. I write "with certain reservations," for I do not follow Geertz' or other kindred spirits' theoretical framework, methodological thrust, and analytical aplomb to the letter—for example, I am especially critical of the priority of language and textuality in Geertz and much recent ethnography (in this regard I am inclined toward the likes of Abram 1996, Classen 1993, Hastrup 1995, Howes 1991, and Stoller 1989, 1997). This is to say that Geertz' essays on culture

strike a chord that resonates with many of my experiences in Latin America, even though I do not exactly tune in to his "textualism" and "linguicentrism."

2. For representative readings along these lines, see Bateson (1979), Capra (1996), Cole (1985), Mansfield (1995), and Smith (1995).

3. I must mention at this juncture that regarding my leaving essentialism, representation, and foundationalism within the dreams of reason and complete and consistent knowledge from which we are slowly awakening, my inspiration comes not from cultural studies, postcolonial theory, or feminism, but from post-analytic philosophy. This, I trust, will become apparent in Part III of the present volume.

4. For "modernization" and "import substitution" see Johnson (1958) and Ruiz (1992), for "dependency" theory, see Cardoso and Faletto (1979), Frank (1967) and Furtado (1970).

5. Indeed, Geertz (1983:70) tells us that to understand other cultures is "more like grasping a proverb, catching an illusion, seeing a joke than it is like achieving communion." It is, in short, much like getting the gist of a Zen Koan.

6. For further on the problems inherent in these rhetorical questions, see Butler, Laclau, and Zizek (2000).

7. I should add that while knowledge of Borges's metaphysical short stories, especially those found in English translation in *Labyrinths* (1962) is a prerequisite for understanding the polylogue's allusions and innuendoes, I would hope that the reader unfamiliar with the Argentine writer will nonetheless read the polylogue as a play on the absurd, which it certainly is as well.

8. I write it is "less commonly . . . essays" with regard to expressing "their inner feelings," while maintaining mindfulness that Latin America has yielded its share of first-rate philosophers and scientists, and indeed, in many cases they deserve more respect and acclaim than they have received.

Just Waiting
(or, Looking Back on the Lines of His Face)[1]

> [T]o you whom I never chanced to meet but who inhabit border-
> lands similar to mine;
> to you for whom the borderlands is unknown territory.

—Gloria Anzaldúa

****

THE CAST OF CHARACTERS
(in the order of their appearance):

Tlöny: An inhabitant from the planet Tlön in Borges's "Tlön, Uqbar, Orbis Tertius" (1962 [1944]) all of whose citizens are incorrigible Berkeleyan subjective idealists.

Funy: The hypernominalistic Funes, of "Funes the Memorious" (1962 [1944]) who is capable of seeing only particulars and incapable of generalizations of an abstract nature.

Hladdy: Hladdik, the character of "The Secret Miracle" (1962 [1944]) who asks God to allow him time to finish a play before he meets with his death by the firing squad; his petition is granted, time is stopped for a year, he finishes his work, and then he is shot.

Lönny: The hyperlogical Lönnrot, of "Death and the Compass" (1962 [1944]) who, through his hypothetico-deductive reasoning powers, believes he has outwitted Scharlach, the author of three homicides; but in the end he becomes aware that his antagonist has trapped him within his own labyrinth and that he will become the fourth victim.

---

1. Allusion in the parenthetical clause of the title is obviously to some of Jorge Luís Borges's final lines in *Dreamtigers* (1964b [1960]). What follows is a *polylogue* by fictional characters representing characters in Borges's fictions, all of which should be immediately recognizable (for those who are not familiar with Borges's work, I include a Cast of Characters). They solipsistically and felicitously talk past each other and in the process create fictive metatheory. Their pseudodialogical encounter is the result of my own very tenuous tongue-in-cheek effort to remind us of our fallibility and fallacies with the suggestion that perhaps we need not take ourselves so seriously. So, please enjoy.

Maggie: The (female) Magician of "The Circular Ruins" (1962 [1944]) who dreams a son, and after believing she has interpolated him into reality, realizes that she, too, is a character in someone else's dream.

T'sui: T'sui Pên of "The Garden of Forking Paths" (1962 [1944]) and author of an eternally circular novel that spins a labyrinth within time rather than space.

Emmy: Emma Zunz, from a short story of the same name (1962 [1944]), who poses as a prostitute for her father's employer who was indirectly responsible for his recent death, then she kills her client and pleads self-defense, claiming he raped her.

Pierre: Pierre Menard of "Pierre Menard, Author of the Quixote" (1962 [1944]) who, without having previously reread Cervantes's work, and by sheer intuitive powers, writes a narrative fragment identical to some lines from *Don Quixote*.

Anonymous: Various characters from a diversity of Borges's short stories.

Daneri: Argentino Daneri of "The Aleph" (1970 [1949]) who enjoys the privilege of gazing, in mystical fashion, upon the Aleph, a golf-ball size sphere containing the entire universe, past, present, and future.

Averroës: The historical Arabic intellectual by that same name, from "Averroës Search" (1962 [1944]) who, while reading Aristotle's *Poetics*, becomes confounded by the terms "tragedy" and "comedy," and attempts to derive their meaning from within his own cultural mind-set which contains no counterpart to "tragedy" and "comedy."

Rorty: Richard Rorty. Enough said.

****

Tlöny: Well, here we are. The question is, who are we waiting for? Or in the language of one of my marvelous planet's hemispheres, our anticipating becoming becomes his/her appearing and delivering us from self-perpetuating entropying.

Funy: Just say what you have on your mind. And why all the gerunds. Give me a few nouns and I can without a moment's hesitation name what there is (actually I once devised an alternative number system consisting of completely arbitrarily and unordered names instead of numbers: quite ingenious, no?).

Hladdy: I agree. Tlöny, you really have no need of becoming, or of time. Forget about time. It's of no consequence. I once wrote an entire play in less than the blink of an eye—or in less than a rifle shot, if I may put it cryptically. In essence, everything is always already here and now.

Tlöny: Not so. There is essentially no essence, and matter is of no matter, for all there is is mind. And my mind is capable of bringing into existence his/her excellence for whom we lie in wait at my pleasure.

Lönny: My hyperlogical reasoning regarding the future tells me that, since our venerable savior and restorer of all that is good remains eternally outside your impoverished mental constructs, you stand nary a chance of knowing the time and place of his/her appearance. You, Tlöny, are trapped in a labyrinth of your own making. Either that, or you're dreaming.

Maggie: Life is a dream. And a dream? Nothing but a dream. I must confess that I once thought I was different, but alas, those concentric tongues of fire that approached me while meditating at my circular ruins revealed that I am of no essence whatsoever.

Funy: What garble! Who let her in?

Hladdy: Dream? If you are dreaming you can't say either "I am dreaming" or "I am awake," for there is nothing outside the dream by which to gauge your dreaming or waking state.

T'sui: Time? Dream? Essence? Mind? It's all according to the mouth of the thinker. Time is infinitely repeatable, so it is eternal, so there is no time. And essence? Who is to say what is as it is and what is mere figment. In another parallel diverging or converging time, we might all be dreaming, some of us might be dreaming and others not. Who are we to know who we are or when he/she for whom we garner tenuous anticipations will decide to make his/her grand appearance.

Emmy: I once faked a rape and shot my fictitious accoster and got off scot-free. Now that's changing your own parallel line for another one. Dream, shmeam. What I do I do, and I make no bones about it.

Funy: A woman after my own heart, that is, what was my heart a second ago, for it is now another heart, no, oh dear, I no longer know what it is—if it really is, that is.

Lönny: Ha! Spoken like a genuine Humean. Utter drivel. Combine Funy with Tlöny and you have Tweedledum and Tweedledee. Tlöny's world is a Berkeleyan fantasyland and Funy's is no more than Hume's bundles of percepts displacing each other with numbing frequency. Put them together, and if a repetition there can ever be, then that will be living proof that time is henceforth refuted.

Maggie: The pot calling the kettle black. You once waltzed to your death at the fourth corner of your woven labyrinth as if time did not exist, only to realize that your temporal repetitions were somewhat asymmetrical and hence temporalized, and you met with your death at the hands of he who was to have become your prisoner. I'm familiar with your pathetic game.

Lönny: I'll have you know my reasoning powers are beyond the pale of life and death. I suggested to my would be assassin that we should simplify our labyrinth to a one-dimensional line, that line within which so many metaphysicians have lost their way. He agreed that it would be a more parsimonious labyrinth, and then proceeded to fire his pistol in my direction. But before the slug traveled the distance between him and my heart, it had to travel half the distance, then half of that distance, *ad infinitum*, without ever piercing my chest in his or my lifetime. You see? I already had him caught in a one-dimensional Zenoesque labyrinth I subtly wove before him.

Pierre: I too disagree with Lönny's aborted refutation of time. I once wrote a few paragraphs that were identical to some fragments from the original *Don Quixote*, and the critics applauded me for my originality. My pages were a repetition, but the content differed, hence they were different at a different time. Time continues to move along quite handily, thank you.

Hladdy: Please. Let's stick to the task at hand.

Maggie: I agree. I could easily conjure up he/she for whom we are here in painful expectation at will if I wished—I once dreamed a son, by the way. But I think it behooves us to let him/her for whom we wait decide upon a time and a place to make an appearance.

T'sui: Don't deceive yourself. There's an infinity of times and places. So if he/she appears at some infinitesimal time and place, we infinitesimal beings will in all probability not even know it.

Anonymous One: Yes. We are victims of that infinite lottery the whole of which lies eternally beyond our grasp.

Maggie: Who's that guy? *Where* is he?

T'sui: I recall once having met the acquaintance of a race of people who spoke like him in some world, I believe it went by the name of Babylon.

Tlöny: No matter.

Funy: You mean no mind.

Maggie: Never mind matter, and pay no mind to mind. Essentially our duty is to . . .

Tlöny: Essentially? You're contradicting yourself again.

Maggie: The horror, the horror, suddenly realizing all is nothing but a dream.

Tlöny: Foul! Our dreamt worlds know of no continuity and no identity. Therefore there is actually no Averroës outside our thinking, dreaming, or perceiving him/her.

Funy: Ave who? Where did that name come from?

Tlöny: Oh. It must have slipped my mind. It is Averroës who is to appear before us.

Hladdy: Somehow I sensed we were waiting for Godot.

From the audience: I would have suspected it to be Gödel. After all, the stage you lunatics have created for yourselves is, if infinite, then inconsistent, and if finite, then incomplete.

Funy: And what bumbling fool said that? I have no faith in what I can't see before me clearly and distinctly.

Daneri: Who said that, you ask? It was, if I recall correctly, one of the anguish-ridden library rats in that massive aedificium housing countless books that are listed in one book which is either infinite or finite, take your pick. I saw it during that fleeting moment when I experienced the entire universe, past, present and future.

Emmy: Whoever said that needs a strong dose of reality to pick her up. Who cares about the big picture? All I want is to be whoever I need to be, at whatever time and place.

Maggie: How simple minded. Your optimism regarding your abilities is exceeded only by your self-indulgent dreams.

Emmy: You mean fictions, don't you? Unlike you, I have no need of dreams. I fabricate. Therefore my world is not the world I found, but the world I made.

Tlöny: You? Make your own world? You are hardly aware of the subtlety of the task. You simply feign, you take on the appearance of what you are not.

Emmy: I'll have you know I'm capable of convincing anyone of virtually anything. Give me a mass of shirtless workers and I'll outdo Evita Perón at her own game.

Hladdy: I insist that we attend to the issue at hand, which is our waiting for, who was it?, oh yes, Averroës.

Tlöny: Speak for yourself you hapless soul. Unlike you, I would never have suffered the humility of a death sentence in the first place, for the judge, the jury and the trial lawyers would have all been of my own mind's making from the beginning. I could have made them judge me in whichever way I wanted them to.

Funy: My world is even simpler still. Between the command given to the firing squad, their firing their rifles, and the moment the bullets reached me, I would be another me, so they would not be able to execute the person who was identical to the person they had condemned.

T'sui: I wonder. Which intricately woven time line will Averroës ride in on? Will it be ours or another one that in the past bifurcated toward who knows where and who knows when?

Tlöny: It makes no difference. When I conjure Averroës up, his/her anti-self, in fact countless Averroës anti-selves, will be around to populate each and every bifurcating world.

Emmy: I'm sorry if I sound patronizing, but you people have lost your zest for life. There's nothing like the good 'ole game of fake appearances.

Maggie: Listen! Do you hear someone coming?

Funy: It's a flickering image, vague.

Tlöny: My God! Are my mental faculties failing me? There should be empty space before me, for I have not intentionally perceived any object. But lo!, methinks there is some appearance. Let it come toward me so I can grasp it and know if it is real.

T'sui: Forget appearances. Your entire world is no more than appearances. What you need is years of meditation to cure you of your grand delusions of ontological edification.

Hladdy: Yes, there's definitely someone out there. And so soon too. I regret I have not yet completed my part in this dialogue.

Pierre: What dialogue? Everything you people have said has been written since the beginning of time. I should know.

Daneri: Time? Nothing but a pain in the essence.

Tlöny: Essence? It's of no matter, if you don't mind my saying so.

Funy: Mind? That fabled ghost in the machine? We need no such airy nothings.

Averroës: Pardon me. Can anyone tell me what Aristotle meant by "tragedy" and "comedy"?

Daneri: I've seen this fellow somewhere. Yes. Now I know, in the Aleph. He was juxtaposed with Bruno's burning at the stake, the Piltdown man's nonexistence many centuries ago, Madonna's performance as the Material Girl, Rodney King's beating in Los Angeles, a jaguar pouncing on a helpless capybara in the wilds of Brazil, and Remedio la Bella's ascension to heaven. Why he's,... he's Averroës.
In unison: AVERROËS!

Tlöny: My mind must be deceiving me, or perhaps I'm deceiving myself.

Funy: He's not who I thought he was, that is, is, no, was.

Maggie: In my wildest dreams I would never thought that he would look like no more than just another bloke.

Emmy: He's no hunk, I'll admit. But I wouldn't mind bringing a rape charge against him.

Pierre: I could write a story about this man. Perhaps I would call it "Averroës Search."

T'sui: It is my observation that your Western deities, if this strange being is any indication, are lacking in charisma.

Hladdy: Forgive me Averroës, my master, and forgive my colleagues for their impudence. Allow me to prostrate myself before you. I feel most humble, and at the same time honored.

Averroës: Do you, sir, know anything about "tragedy" and "comedy"?

Anonymous Two: He's the Antichrist! Pierce his heart with a stake, shoot him with a silver bullet, beat him over the head with a cross.

Lönny: I don't get it. My inferential powers fail to account for the fact that you can be Averroës and at the same time express a concern for such trivia as "tragedy" and "comedy."

Averroës: I can explain it all. You see? I picked up this text at a used book store and...

Anonymous Two: The incarnation of evil!

T'sui: Those barbarians over there could learn some manners?

Hladdy: My Lord, forgive me, no, forgive them, for they know not what they do, and lead me out of this temptation.

Averroës: Whew, this poor chap needs to see a shrink. Get up off your knees, will you? Anyway, the author of the book I bought wrote the whole thing with a muddled head and convoluted language—must have been a literary critic. Among other strange words, he kept referring to what he called "tragedy" and "comedy."

Maggie: Tell your story to Lönny. His tragic flaw landed him in a labyrinth at the other end of Scharlach's gun.

Lönny: It was those bloody Jews. If they had known how to compute the days of the month properly I would easily have apprehended Scharlach and he would now be in prison where he belongs.

Maggie: Anti-Semitism is no excuse for your hypercogitating fits and errors.

Anonymous Two: Heed my warning. He's surely a secret agent of The Company.

Anonymous Three: Agent 666 no doubt. The end is upon us!

Anonymous One: Either that, or he is the Man of the Book who holds the key to the Universe's, that is, the Library's, most cherished secrets.

Emmy: Hey! All you clowns out there get the hell out of here and leave us alone. Can't you see Averroës is just mixed up and needs a little comforting?

Averroës: Thank you, and I must confess that I am quite confused.

From the audience: This is all absurd. Get to the point or I want my money back.

T'sui: I agree. Let me try to get this straight. You people were in wait of someone who turned out to be Averroës who is oblivious regarding the nature of his mission. Some of my most venerable ancestors were not aware of their greatness until their life was drawing to a close. If Averroës can also be counted among such individuals who are, how do you say it? Bigger than life? Then we must aid him/her in realizing the destiny that brought him/her into our midst.

Emmy: I don't know which one of me is saying this, but I think we owe it to our newcomer to listen to his/her story.

T'sui: You drew the words from my mouth like water from a well.

Lönny: Against my better inferences, I'll go along with the proposition. Averroës, my man, er, woman?, what, pray tell, is your story?—and please don't bring up this "tragedy" and "comedy" nonsense again.

Averroës: How can I ignore it? That Greek author kept repeating those words.

Lönny: Forget the words. Just tell us what's on your mind.

Averroës: You don't understand. That *is* what's on my mind.

Hladdy: Maybe I can help. I once wrote a play...

Pierre: Yeah, we know about all that. And I once wrote some lines identical to one of the greatest novels ever written. Averroës, on the other hand, is trying to interpret what was written by some stranger from a strange land.

Rorty: In that case, I suggest that all we need to do is enter into the great Conversation of Humankind.

Anonymous Two: That vile heretic has forced his way into your midst! He is the one who secretly and contingently rolls dice in the latrines of the innumerable hexagons of the Library. Not only has he embraced that abominable philosopher who pronounced the death of God, he has impudently spelled the death of philosophy. Don't listen to him.

T'sui: Very interesting. I'm sure our newcomer would enjoy reading that Argentine writer, Jorge Luis Borges.

Daneri: Wait. I recognize this man who is now before us. Why, it's Richard Rorty, that notorious propagator of mirrorless minds incapable of representing an essenceless nature, that famous kibitzer who advocates incessant prattling without prioritizing or hierarchizing anyone or anything. When I experienced him in the Aleph he was chatting with groups of politicians, philosophers, literary theorists, graduate students, CEOs, little old ladies at Wal-Mart, and anyone else who would lend him an ear.[2]

Funy: He's my kind of person, always someone other than who he was.

Emmy: I think I've heard of him. He's that guy that doesn't like arguments, for they are not edifying. Just likes to sit around a jaw a bit.

Tlöny: But he's not one of us. Perhaps we should ban him forever.

Lönny: I suspect ulterior motives. Only criminals and politicians can change hats so often.

Hladdy: Rumor has it that he makes a hefty salary for his amiable chitchatting. It's not fair. Why couldn't I have enjoyed the same benefits after writing my play?

Maggie: I doubt that he could interpolate any of his dreamy, soporific muttering into reality. Like all those egg-headed academics, he's hardly street-wise.

Pierre: Actually, what he wrote had all been written before. Hence his work is quite inferior to my own: he read Oakeshott and other philosophers before rewriting them,

---

2. The verbal evocations surrounding Rorty here and below are based chiefly on his *Consequences of Pragmatism* (1982) and *Contingency, Irony, and Solidarity* (1988); for various interpretations of Rorty see Malachowski (1990).

while my eyes were never opened to that noble Cervantes text when I wrote my own text.

Hladdy: Our Holy Father/Mother and Savior and Spirit incorporated into a single entity, Averroës, what is your wise counsel? Should we embrace this stranger or stone him until he has expelled his last life-giving breath?

Averroës: Let he/she who is free of the tyranny of influence cast the first stone. (By the way, has he by chance ever heard of "tragedy" and "comedy"?)

Emmy: Ha! You strike out, Pierre. You can't condemn Rorty, for you admitted to having copied Russell and James.

Pierre: I admitted to no such thing. It was those pompous literary critics who had nothing more to do than find similarities between texts—intertextuality they called it. They are no better than those secret societies in Babel or Babylon.

Lönny: I suggest we allow Rorty to say his piece. I doubt he can do us any harm.

Funy: I'm game. What do you have on your mind, or I should say, what did you have on your mind that was something other that what you now have that is now becoming what you had in order to make way for what is becoming that which you now have on your mind. (Gads, it will take me at least two days to recall in my memory all that transpired today.)

Rorty: I thought I'd drop by because I sympathize with Averroës's search for the inessential essence of a couple of words once jotted down by the native of an exotic culture.

Hladdy: You, a mere sinner, claiming you sympathize with our esteemed Savior? How dare you!

Rorty: Please. I want no argument. I am quite adverse to such macho tactics. Let us sit in a circle, hold hands, put on our happy faces, and chat for a spell.

Emmy: Yeah. Give the guy a chance.

Rorty: Thank you. Say, aren't you that sly lady who once took a lover in a D. H. Lawrence novel?

Emmy: Hardly.

Rorty: I'm sorry. I must have you confused with someone else.

Hladdy: Get down to business, or I'll put you before the firing line. You probably deserve it more than I. I was merely a victim of a devastating war. Rumor has it that you are guilty of trying single-handedly to do away with philosophy as we know it and put college professors in the unemployment lines and make taxi drivers of young ABDs.

Rorty: I actually believe philosophers should plead temporary insanity every time anyone catches them at their mistakes instead of writing volumes upon volumes in an effort to expunge themselves of their wrongdoing. With such a plea, no jury would convict them, then they could go on their way spreading good will and cheer among all peoples of all ages and creeds and tongues and races and gender and sexual orientation.

Funy: Rorty, the perpetual waffler—how could I see him as a person of fixed nature anyway? Impossible!—is changing faces with the rapidity of a coin flipped into the air. I'm losing my patience.

Maggie: Me, too. Just get on with it.

Tlöny: I find Rorty quite interesting. He reminds me of my compatriots for whom philosophy is literature and hence all books must contain their own antibook.

Rorty: If you will allow me ... as I see it, Averroës's problem is this. He can't distinguish between matters of fact and matters of definition regarding a couple of words translated from an exotic language into his own.

Averroës: That's it precisely! Only God—that is, me—and Shakespeare can be everybody and nobody. So how can I ever hope to comprehend "tragedy" and "comedy" written by the pen of Aristotle, who I am not, from another time and another place? (By the way, how do you know I'm not a woman?)

Rorty: My friend Willie Quine tells me that when a native from another tribe such as Aristotle appears to agree that bachelors aren't married, we can never know whether he is forced to say so by his own language or simply because he has never experienced anything to the contrary.

T'sui: Bachelors? Where did they come from? Something has been lost in the translation, I fear.

Emmy: By the way Rorty darling, are you married?

Lönny: By Rorty's own admission, he should not even be able to know what Quine said in his own language, let alone what Aristotle said. So how can he be so smug with respect to Quine's words.

Rorty: The fact of the matter is that I don't really need to know. Knowledge is boring anyway, and besides, it endows those who think they possess it with inordinate power so that they can waylay us all and cheat us out of our rightful academic inheritance. In spite of what he thought he was doing, Quine was actually just kibitzing rather than pretending he knew something. And he did so quite effectively.

T'sui: But please tell us about bachelors, that is, tell us what Quine told you about bachelors.

Rorty: To make a long story short, Quine said a stranger in her strange language might say "Gavagai" when it appears that she is looking in the direction of a bachelor. But how can we know "Gavagai" is the equivalent of "Bachelor" in our language? It might mean "A determinate set of sex parts," "A rather chunky lad," "An ageing yuppie," or even "A particular space-time slice from the four dimensional continuum."

Funy: That's only part of our problem. Five minutes from now Averroës will be someone other than who he now is. So we could then call him "Gavagao," and in another five minutes, "Gavagau," then "Gavagoe," then "Gavagoi," and so on. It's an uncertain world you know.

Tlöny: Not only that, but I could conjure him up as a "Green Gavagai," you as a "Grue Gavagai," T'sui as a "Blue Gavagai," Lönny as a "Bleen Gavagai," Emmy as a "Grange Gavagai," Maggie as a "Oreen Gavagai." There's no end to the possible attributes we can endow him with. The language we use and the ethereal mental objects to which they refer could all become as confusing as they are in my beloved planet, Tlön.[3]

Pierre: Good Lord! With those precedents how could I ever again hope to write a few fragments identical to a previously existing text?

T'sui: Besides, "Gavagai" brings terrible memories of "Samurai." We fought those people bitterly for decades, you know.

Rorty: Oh dear. I see I've opened Pandora's box.

Anonymous Three: We warned all of you. He brings evil!

Lönny: Speaking of boxes, I just thought of a magnificent labyrinth for Scharlach the next time we meet. It consists of stairways going up or down or to the right or to the left, depending on the eye of the beholder. I'd have him coming and going.

---

3. I should point out that the apparently bizarre terms I have pecked out on the keyboard did not pop out of the clear blue. "Gavagai" is Quine's (1960) own invention, for the play on "Grue" and "Green-Blue" I pay due respects to Nelson Goodman's (1965:59-83) notorious "New Riddle of Induction," and allusion to "cats" and "cherries" a few lines down is a variation of a thought-experiment created by Hilary Putnam (1983a:1-25).

Daneri: Mavrits Escher already constructed that one you clout. It's called "Relativity." I gazed upon it in the Aleph.

Anonymous One: That's nothing. I once saw an object capable of every one of your variations on a theme. It consisted of an ordinary coin worth twenty cents, but it had been many things besides: a tiger, a blind man, an astrolabe, a compass, a vein in a marble pillar, the bottom of a well, and in fact, it had been, was, and could have been an infinity of things.

Tlöny: Elementary my dear fellow. Why, on my planet we can lose coins and then proceed to find them whenever and wherever we wish.

Emmy: Let's have a little respect for Rorty. After all, he, along with Averroës, is our guest.

T'sui: Whatever happened to Averroës anyway?

Rorty: I thank you once again, ma'am. You see? Whatever might be the meaning of "Gavagai," that meaning does not determine the reference of the word to the thing, nor does the thing cause reference to the word.

Maggie: You've lost me there.

Rorty: Oh, excuse me. I'll stick to the basics. When Averroës says, "I'd like to know the meaning of 'tragedy' and 'comedy'" it sounds like he wants hard-rock foundations of meanings fixed onto words for all time. Actually, there is no absolutely determinate reason for believing in solid physical reality any more than in Homer's gods or in figments of the imagination.

Tlöny: Here! Here!

Anonymous Four: Beware. He now spreads pagan doctrine.

Rorty: If we could all get together in good faith and engage in amiable talk with open minds it doesn't matter of what the world is made or of what, ultimately, human nature consists. Just talking the talk will ultimately make us free.

Funy: I was born free, but afterward, everywhere I went language staked out its claims.

Tlöny: Don't flatter yourself. You never tasted a morsel of freedom in your life.

Rorty: But if we could just talk for a while . . .

Emmy: Talk ends bachelor life and turns young girls' hearts from dolls to diamonds.

Pierre: Contrary to what you all probably believe, my liberating scripts are prior to talk, which is oppressively phonocentric and author of the myth of presence.

T'sui: She who knows talks not; she who talks knows not.

Rorty: My God! You're all hopelessly mad! How did I ever think I could free you of your fallacies?

Maggie: Who's there? Averroës? Is that you again? Did you once again appear out of the clear blue or am I dreaming? Why is your hair so ruffled, your eyes glazed and blood-shot.

In unison: AVERROËS!

Hladdy: Your present countenance is unbecoming of you, my Master.

Funy: Wait a minute. He can't be Averroës. I've never seen this bum in my life.

Averroës: Yes, it is I. I have been traveling far and wide in cyberspace while you've been wasting your time gassing. It gives me great pleasure to announce that I discovered a gentleman who claims he knows of Aristotle.
[Jorge Luis Borges appears, standing in the hallway that opens into the room where all are gathered.]

Pierre: I remain unimpressed.

Daneri: How can this be? This man was nowhere to be found in that golf ball sized apparition containing the entire universe I once contemplated.

Maggie: I think he's dreaming.

Rorty: The face looks familiar. If I recall correctly, he was either a fabulist who tried to write the end of philosophy or a philosopher who tried to write fables with no ending. (I hope he can talk to us in a language capable of bringing order to this mayhem.)

T'sui: End? How could there be any end? The infinitely converging and diverging bifurcating time lines double back on themselves and eat their own tail to abolish time for all time. This foreigner among us was doomed from the beginning if he ever thought time is the substance he is made of, that it is a river that sweeps him along, that it is a tiger which destroys him but that he is the tiger, that it is a fire which consumes him but that he is the fire, that the world is unfortunately real or that he, unfortunately, is who he is. This man can lay no better claim to existence or to essence than can we. As my venerable ancestors taught me: we should never trust mere appearances.

[At that moment our newly arrived guest unwittingly happens to turn his head in the direction of a mirror in the hallway, and as his expressionless eyes blankly meet themselves, he vanishes, as do Tlöny and Funy and Hladdy and Lönny and Maggie and T'sui and Emmy and Pierre and Daneri and Averroës and Rorty and those anonymous souls and the audience and the furniture and floor and walls and ceiling and the very mirror reflecting itself an infinite number of times in the adjacent mirror on the other side of the hallway. And space collapses and with it time, to leave that infamous singularity, that infinitesimally minuscule point in space, the marvelously real Aleph, that evinces premonitions of an impending Big Bang and eons upon eons of expansion and a Great Crunch and then another Big Bang and eons upon eons of expansion, ... and so on. And through it all the rip-roaring laughter of that fleet-footed dancer nimbly springing from mountain peak to mountain peak, Friedrich Nietzsche, pierces the hoary void. In the end, however, everybody had the time of their lives and the freedom to exhaust all possible repertories of nonsensical talk. And all was well that ended well.]

Part I

Chapter one argues that our world is more fabricated and fashioned than found. A supreme case is that of Christopher Columbus, who was instrumental in the "invention"—rather than "discovery"—of America, an "invention" that has culminated in numerous hard-rock stereotypes regarding Latin America's social, political, and economic makeup and the numbing complexity of her cultures and subcultures. This chapter also introduces the notion of "emptiness," and the *border of borders*, those interstices from whence everything that is emerges. We become witness to the importance of feeling and sensing in addition to intellectualizing and cognizing, since the latter pair of terms can get nowhere without their standing on the robust, albeit vague and confounding, shoulders of the former terms. Chapter two offers a brief look at C. S. Peirce's conception of signs, signs of the body (*feeling* and *sensing*) and mind (*intellectualizing* and *cognizing*); that is, of *bodymind* signs. The binary body/mind distinction and standard logical Principles of Identity, Noncontradiction, and Excluded-Middle begin giving way to triadicity and more general "logics," that embrace extralinguistic tacit knowing as well as discursive knowledge. The following chapter pays homage to signs of subversion engendered by the socially disenfranchised, the so-called unempowered "subaltern groups." This story begins during the colonial period in Latin America, with special attention to the concept of "hybridism" as a tentative step toward the idea of alternate cultural "logics." To round out this incursion, the erstwhile strictly prohibited *both-and* and *neither-nor* modes of feeling and sensing and thinking begin to take their rightful place at the side of *either/or* categories, which serves further to introduce the concept of process to these vague "logics." Chapter four presents four basic human traits as manifested in part or the whole of Latin America: *personalismo, machismo, caudillismo,* and *jeitinho.* This, I will suggest, is an additional and necessary step toward the idea that everyday living tends to resist classical logical principles. The stage is thus set for illustration in chapter five of four basic postures adopted by subservient groups in colonial Latin America, that incorporate both-and and neither-nor processes in addition to either/or categories. Signs and countersigns engendered out of these postures go beyond the sober-minded means and methods of classical logic, which serves as further preparation for the presentation of the ways and workings of Latin America's inner cultural dynamics.

Chapter One

Invented Realities

> The border almost touches the forbidden,
> just a few steps,
> just a few.
>
> —Luisa Valenzuela

> I live smack in the fissure between two worlds, in the infected
> wound.
>
> —Guillermo Gómez-Peña

> Make a run for the border.
>
> —Taco Bell ad

How It All Began to End

Nietzsche had it quite right: seeing is interpreting. His dictum has been reiterated often by what might pass as "postmodern" history, philosophy, and sociology of science.[1] This is a quite recent notion, however. Modern thought taught that science, presumably capable of setting down immutable foundations, was the model to be emulated by all disciplines. It seemed only reasonable that since science was so successful, all other human endeavors to find Truth (and even Beauty) should follow suit. Eventually, if everybody remained faithful to scientific procedures, knowledge would work itself out to its logical end. The product would be emancipation, and the good life for all.

The formula, whether in the hard sciences, the social sciences, or the humanities seemed to be: take in the relevant facts, record them, analyze them, draw up a conclusion, and tell everybody else about your venerable acts. Yet, these days we are forced to concede that perception cannot but be selective, for there is no innocent eye or ear or hand or nose or palate. Description comes only by way of language, which is laden with predispositions, presuppositions, and prejudices. And analysis and reason are no fool-proof road to Truth. Consequently, the end product is always an interpretation from within some "horizon of expectations" or other, if I may avail myself of Hans-Georg Gadamer's (1975) term. At every level, what is believed to be known is the product of some theory, the theory is motivated by an impulsive desire for professional, political, economic, or some other gain, and the motivation is supported by the theory. A vicious circle, it would appear. But actually, with more luck than management, perhaps it can turn out to be more virtuous than vicious (Toulmin 1982).

In this vein, I would hope that the preceding polylogue might help reveal our customary overconfidence regarding our capacities for logical and rational thought and the ability to manipulate people and culture and nature (Lönny, Emmy, Pierre), our blind faith in authority (Hladdy), our ignorance with respect to our severe limitations (Funy), and the absence of genuine *dialogic* interaction (Tlöny, Maggie). The inhabitants of Borges's "Library of Babel" and "Lottery in Babylon" were perhaps on the right track. At least they were aware of their own inadequacies, having resigned themselves to the equivalent of the "epistemological uncertainties" admirably outlined by Nelson Goodman (1978) and Joseph Margolis (1991), among others. That is where we perhaps should look; at least that is where I intend to look. Upon so doing, I will journey into that relatively unknown territory customarily forbidden by the West's obsession for clear and distinct solutions to all problems, for logic and reason of the most stultifying sort, and for the so-called "myth of presence."[2]

Enough gassing over preliminaries, and down to the brass tacks.

Fashioned Rather than Found

The emergence in the European—"Eurocentric"—mind of America as a hitherto unknown continent affords a prime example of interpretation prior to seeing, of construction taking precedence over *passively* internalizing what there is, of worlds made rather than ready-made and just sitting there, awaiting their discovery.

The exploits of Christopher Columbus are a case in point. Columbus obviously possessed a keen sense of observation. The catalyst that set him to the task of finding an alternative route to the Indies was endowed in him by virtue of his nature as a headstrong visionary. Whenever he confronted some unexpected features of the "reality" that spread its furniture before him, he was hardly ever deterred a whit. He harnessed his visions and rode them roughshod through the empirical labyrinth he had entered, refashioning it to fit his needs. Thus in the "marvelously real" new panorama before him in what was soon to be known as "America," he saw one-eyed men, men with dog-faces, women in the form of mermaids, men and women who engaged in anthropophagous practices, and many other exotic apparitions besides. In fact, he saw an entire menagerie of strange nonhuman and subhuman beings and beasts (Arens 1979).

Columbus, like many other voyagers during his time, was unable, or at least did not wish, to separate "reality" from fantasy. They all brought with them a world constructed with considerably more than mere rational knowledge. Merlin the Magician and Marco Polo's tales and Amadís of Gaul were apparently at times more real to them than the material landscape they contemplated. Thus, "they felt a desperate need to test their imagination, one formed by fables and books of chivalry" (Alvar 1992:167).[3] Indeed, Columbus was a far cry from that presumably enlightened, Weberian "disenchantment of the world" his successors of the West were later to enjoy and to employ in their obsession with using and abusing nature. Columbus's observations were the outcome of his mind-set and his mind-set alone, and his mind-set was aided and abetted by his loose and limber observations: his world looked sympathetically upon him just as he was in sympathetic attunement with his world. Yes, indeed. Columbus's "enchanted" world was at the outset not the Indies at all, but a New World in the full sense of the term. It was, much like a strange combination of Lönny's, Tlöny's, and Emmy's "realities" of our polylogue; it was a world of Columbus's mind's own making. And a magnificent "magical" world it was, worthy of our inveterate dreamer from the polylogue, Maggie (Greenblat 1991).[4]

Columbus's running into this "enchanting" New World had a profound impact on European life and thought. In fact, it eventually shattered the reigning Western conception of the world. Mexican historian and philosopher Edmundo O'Gorman (1961 [1958]) argues that neither Columbus nor other Europeans of the time could have genuinely *discovered* America, because they could not yet fathom the idea of another continent and another collection of human beings. The general notion had it that God created the world and endowed "man" with its stewardship, and that was that. The world as it was was all there was and all there could possibly be: three continents and three races, period. Consequently, in order for America to emerge into existence it had to be *invented*. It had to be conceived as an ontological something where nothing was supposed to have existed. As an invented, dreamt, and intersubjectively constructed ontological something, it could then gain its rightful status in the world of observed somethings. In a manner of speaking, the invented map would become coterminous with the territory (Mignolo 1989, 1997a).

Following the "invention of America" idea, O'Gorman writes that Columbus, the bred-in-the-bone citizen of medievalism tinged with a sense of the Renaissance, twisted and warped what he saw in order to jam-pack it into his original idea of things. At the outset he proclaimed that Cuba was part of the mainland of Cipango (Japan), and he proceeded to cajole his crew into signing a statement swearing that they were at the shores of the Orient. When that invention failed to bear fruit, he proposed that what he had run into was no continental mainland at all, but an elongated island and a scattering of small islands running from the far North to the far South. Such an outlandish hypothesis was destined to the trash bin of futile hopes as well. Then, during his third voyage he reached the coast of Venezuela at the Orinoco River delta. He found the water fresh rather than salty, which would have accounted for a large body of land and play havoc with his newly formed theory that this area was populated by many small islands rather than there existing a continental mass. However, using Biblical evidence, he postulated that this river poured forth from a large fountain in the center of the Garden of Eden. Blindly insisting that the Garden was in the Orient, he had no qualms about a recomputing of the Earth's circumference so as to render it considerably smaller than previously believed, and the Americas were erased and the vast distance across the Atlantic and Pacific was drastically reduced. Moreover, he claimed that, rather than round, the Earth was pear-shaped, with the Garden at the uppermost point—desperation can lead to what, during later times, may be taken as naive rhetorical manipulations. In the final analysis, however, and in spite of Columbus's efforts, the existence of a new continent, as well as its population of new peoples, was forced upon the European mind. But before this concession could be forthcoming, the medieval image of the world had to be revised, with appendages and accommodations and deletions. The amended image was not "reality" precisely as it had been observed but "reality" according to the newly constructed model: America had been invented, fashioned, and mentally fabricated rather than simply found. "Reality" could hardly hope to cope with such machinations of the human mind. (Of course, we know so much from our subjective idealist, Tlöny and the inhabitants of his strange planet, and from the hypothetico-deductive

Lönny, though "reality" finally got the better of his hopeless faith in his own objective reasoning.)

O'Gorman uses a Heideggerian approach to his conception of Columbus and the Europeans' construction, that is, invention, of the New World. Perhaps in this vein we could attach the label "ontological idealism" to the entire process. But that would not tell the whole story. "Idealism" can't get far unless there is some collective—call it dialogic if you wish—give and take between minds, and between minds and the world.[5] Otherwise, some form of solipsism would surely prevail; this evokes images of Tlöny. A solipsistic "hypothetical objectivism" of the Lönny type would hardly fare any better, since, like "ontological idealism," from within it, genuine dialogue would be virtually out of the question. The meeting of minds between Columbus and Europeans at the turn of the fifteenth century whose hands were put to work refashioning the world entailed means and methods, ways of getting things done, and pragmatic interaction between citizens of the community and between them and their world. This interaction, I would submit, is quite akin to what we might dub "methodological realism" as a complementary counterpart to "ontological idealism" and "hypothetical objectivism." Methodological realism is not necessarily any more real than ontological idealism, mind you. Rather than merely solipsistic, it is a community effort, the process of human interaction: in their Rortyan talk, but even more importantly in their nonverbal interrelations with each other and with their environment. "Methodological realism" has to do with what is fashioned for the time being, coupled with presentiments of what possibly lies in the future. And presentiments there certainly were prior to and during the time of Columbus. There were purportedly signs of the existence of a fourth region or continent with a fourth race of people. This particular presentiment came in the form of the ideal space of a Golden Age. The Golden Age consisted of a pagan or Christian Paradise, a Promised Land, a nostalgia for a mythical space where the trials and tribulations of the present would be alleviated and the good life would be waiting for all.

In this respect, America, writes Mexican intellectual Alfonso Reyes (1960:29), was desired before it was found, and as Leopoldo Zea (1970) put it, Europe discovered America because she needed to. Consequently:

> This desire and necessity turned the spirit of invention from its classical origin toward the construction of spaces that were essentially the *counter-image,* the inverse of European reality . . . .On this virgin soil without history, even though millenary civilizations ostensibly proved the contrary, one *could* (or better, *should*) remake the western world. As soon as America was integrated into universal history, its future was colored with the nostalgia of the European past. (Ainsa 1989:103,106)

The ontologically ideal and hypothetically objective complemented the methodologically real, and in the process a New World emerged. What was in the mind brought about the doing and what was done was done because the doing was in the mind. Invention, it would appear, is intrinsic to humankind's very thinking and doing (Bruner 1956, 1986, 1987; Varela, Thompson, Rosch 1993).

In this vein, let us put the ontologically ideal, hypothetically objective, and methodically real into one package. And what do we have here? The makings of what philosopher Charles S. Peirce labeled "objective idealism," which, in Rescher and Brandom's (1979) words, is just that: ontological idealism coupled with "methodological realism."[6] In this manner, America as invented is of a nature outside the grasp of our Borgesian characters from the polylogue, for they barely communicate with one another. Each is wrapped up in her/his own self. There is hardly any interdependent, interrelated, interactive oneness of mind and of thought that gives rise to something new. Averroës was as real for them as any other aspect of their world; he could not have been the product of a community effort in the order of the invention of America.[7]

Mexican novelist and essayist Carlos Fuentes (1976) sees the spirit of invention deeply rooted in Miguel de Cervantes's solipsistic *Don Quixote*. The problem is that *Quixote*'s fabricated rather than found world, like the worlds of our Borgesian characters, was of individual rather than collective effort. Quixote the individual believes what he wants to believe, sees what he wants to see, and during his initial adventures he says what he believes and sees, with neither regrets nor remorse. Let us not feel so smug about our knowledge of our own world, however. Actually, Isaac Newton, author of our classical world of physics, was not as removed from the Don's "reality" concoctions as we would like to believe. Newton, John Maynard Keynes writes, was the "last of the magicians" (in Dobbs 1975:13–14, see also White 1999). He remained with a foot caught in the doorway of his enchantment with the world. In comparable fashion, the Don remained firmly embedded in a world that corresponded to the novels of chivalry he had voraciously consumed. Through the Don's correspondences, his creator, Cervantes, as Michel Foucault (1970) argues, was one of the first to perceive the fallacy of representation. The master builder of the machine age, Newton, and a demented old man, Don Quixote, lived out their wildest dreams: each in his own way told an intriguing tale. In this manner Don Quixote, like Newton, retained his enchantment of the world. At the same time, as an individual, he divorced himself from it. He entered that know-it-all universe of disenchantment.

Physicist Niels Bohr once quipped that if a theory doesn't appear outlandish enough, it has hardly any chance of passing the litmus test of scientific inquiry. Newton's story out of another pen at another place could have been written off as simply outlandish and absurd, and he could well have passed his days in an asylum; Don Quixote's spoken world was equally outlandish, and, unlike Newton, during his day he was subjected to scorn and ridicule. Both Newton and Quixote invented their worlds and found a way to relate them to what they saw. If the Don's enchantment of his world lingered, there was also some premonition of the West's waning enchantment. If Newton's partial and lingering enchantment was conveniently hidden away in the closet, he was so much the wiser for it, since thanks to his rhetorical sleight of hand, he was destined to be regarded as a giant among giants in what was to become a thoroughly disenchanted world.

Fuentes writes elsewhere that the invention of America is:

> indistinguishable from the naming of America. Indeed, [Cuban writer] Alejo Carpentier gives priority to this function of the American writer: to baptize things that without him would be nameless. To discover is to invent is to name. No one dares stop and reflect whether the names being given to things real and imagined are intrinsical to the named, or merely conventional, certainly not substantial to them. The invention of America occurs in a pre-Socratic time, that time whose disappearance Nietzsche lamented; it happens in a mythical time magically arisen in the midst of the nascent Age of Reason, as if to warn it, in Erasmian terms, that reason that knows not its limits is a form of madness. (Fuentes 1988b:186) (brackets added)

Fuentes also relates the invention to the "utopization" of America. It is the creation of an imaginary space, a timeless space. Borges's Aleph, unlike the Zahir—reference to both of which was made in the polylogue—is also timeless: the universe sucked into a "black hole" of the sort labeled a "naked singularity," virtually a point in space that contains everything, past, present, and future (merrell 1991b). A combination of the Aleph and the Zahir is a concoction of mutually incompatible objects, acts, and events compacted into an instant, which is actually comparable to Fuentes's (1990:50–71) "utopized" America (see also Ainsa 1995, Portella 1995). The invention of America, then, entailed the creation of the Amerindian, dichotomized and hierarchized, colonial culture. That invented world has managed to perpetuate itself to the present-day as an apparently dichotomized and presumably eternally hierarchized social, political, and economic form of life (Bonfil Batalla 1996:76–79).

This invention is a collective imaginary construct through and through, the result of prevailing social and cultural conventions.[8] Constructed at a time when the enchantment of the world still reigned supreme, especially through the eyes and at the hands and pens of the likes of Columbus, it can be said that in a sense America has never been entirely disenchanted. It still retains a certain aura of enchantment: its magical, mythical, mysterious, even mystical character endures, timelessly, within an imaginary space (Jara and Spadaccini 1992a:5–10). The enchanted Amadís was pure invention, product of the imaginary, in the order of Tlöny's mind-world in the polylogue. As enchantment, it was a symbol of the discovery and conquest, while the colonial image was utopian, and the national period, as we shall note in various of the sections that follow, has been pervaded by the myth of modernization, Western style. The idea of utopia is pure dream, not entirely unlike that of Maggie (Borges's Magician in "The Circular Ruins" [1962 {1944}]).[9] Modernization, moreover, follows the venerated Western tradition of logic, reason, and practice on the road toward the good life, a concoction of Lönny's bloated confidence in his mental maneuvers and Emmy's down-to-earth pragmatic answers to problems. In retrospect, however, all these worlds make up one world, which is not The World, but merely a combination of many worlds into one world, a synthetically invented world—of which neither Tlöny nor Maggie nor Lönny nor Emmy nor anybody else as individuals could have been fully aware. In this respect, between and behind the invention of America and Amadís, the idea of invention and that of utopia, and the invention of modernization in Latin America, there is only what can be called none other than emptiness. Yes, imagination and invention emerge from pure emptiness.

Now, what could I possibly have in mind with this strange interjection of the term emptiness? Admittedly a troublesome question. Proper qualification of emptiness, I fear, must await the emergence of a number of other processes to which I allude in the following chapters. But the fact remains that I brought the term up here. Perhaps it was a mistake? Perhaps. For a sense of emptiness is a difficult pill to swallow. Still, to add fuel to the all-consuming flame of the idea of invention, a sense of emptiness should become an integral part of my inquiry, however vague it may appear, at the earliest possible juncture. That much said, I might venture to suggest that a *border* separates the term's *invention, utopia,* and *modernization,* from what at a given time and place may be considered the "real." It is not a mere border, however. It is, so to speak, the *border of borders;* it is a *multiply imaginary* line of demarcation. In the case of the invention of America, the border of borders was first constructed as a result of European longings, and later reconstructed when a New World presented itself in such fantastic, magical dress that it couldn't help lending itself to the most incredible flights of the imagination motivated by dreamy desires for some other place: *utopia.* The border of borders is just that, a virtual border in want of something it can dissect into at least two somethings, a border that without that something and those somethings is nothing; it is no more than the border of borders, it is just emptiness. Pure emptiness.[10]

My liberal use of apparently loose and free-wheeling generalities cries out for qualification. So before proceeding, I suppose I should try to clarify myself regarding what I have dubbed the border of borders and related concepts as best I know how.

Fuzzy Borders Have Their Advantages

Mexican philosopher Antonio Caso (1941:105) once wrote that a history that generalizes is a history that falsifies. Philosopher of science Karl Popper would chafe at Caso's observation with the counterargument that historical generalities are not viably falsifiable, hence history cannot be scientific (Popper 1963:33–59). I would take the liberty to suggest that my generalities in the preceding section are both *vaguely* falsifiable, though in a nonlogical sense, and *generally* nonfalsifiable, for, as we shall note, they cannot be falsified according to the tenets of good classical logic.[11] Consequently, it can also be said that they are *neither* falsifiable *nor* nonfalsifiable, but rather, they are simply there. If you like them you embrace them, but at your own risk. If you don't like them, you push them aside; yet they will most likely pop up later to haunt you.

And now, what can I possibly mean by that? Another difficult question. What I have tenuously stated in the preceding paragraph contains the thesis of this entire volume in a nutshell. The problem is that I can't adequately say any of the parts without somehow saying the whole, and if I could by some stretch of the imagination blurt out the whole in a few words, I would be saying virtually nothing at all as far as the incredulous onlooker is concerned. I am caught up in a Bertrand Russell sort of dilemma: in order completely to specify the class of all humans, I must begin by specifying one human, then another, and so on, but I will never reach the end of the line, so I'll never completely specify the class of all humans; in order to specify the class of all humans by articulating the word "human," I am using a particular contextualized instantiation of a word in reference to the whole class of all possible instantiations to which the word belongs, hence I am committing a category mistake. Yet, if I can't say what I want to say, perhaps I could at least give an indication of what I want to say by saying what I don't want to say? Does this mean that at each juncture I must "falsify" what I want to say? Not really. The question "Is Popper's proposition falsifiable?" carries the seeds of its self-destruction, for there is no un-ambiguous answer. Popper's assertion cannot apply to itself without falling into an inconsistency. It says what everything else is, without the capacity to say what it is itself; nevertheless, it implicitly says what it is not.

Antonio Caso, in contrast to Popper, generalizes "falsification" to include any and all intellectual endeavors. In fact, the very act of generalization is a "falsifying" act: it falsifies its own object.[12] Yet this falsification cannot be avoided, for to talk about the past in the complete absence of generalizations would be to spout nothing but trivia and more trivia. The past consists of multiply variegated interrelatedness: everything is interdependent upon and interactive with everything else. Such interre-latedness emerges into what is taken for the "real" during what in human memory and recording devices amounted to some time and some place. Reducing interrelat-edness to disconnected atoms as historical fact dismembers everything, and the whole disintegrates into an orderless heap. The past was process, without absolutely clear and distinct parts. Yet, when the past was present and felt and sensed and per-ceived and conceived, it was broken up into parts in order that it might be made in-telligible. Now that the past is past, it cannot but be reduced to generalizations, even though they only aggravate and annoy. When so reduced, the past consists of gener-alizations generalized from past processes. We can accept this past now generalized with the acknowledgment that we will never know it explicitly. Or, we can reject a generalized past with the assumption that we can know it by knowing a few of its disjointed particulars. The problem is that disjointed particulars give us no more than a heap of quite unintelligible "facts." This simply won't do. So it's back to generali-ties, as if they represented the world as it really is. The trouble, to repeat, is that gen-eralities never directly say what *is*. When on their best behavior, they can only give us a glimpse of what *is* by revealing, at some time and place, what *is not*.

The worst sorts of generalities saying what in part *is not*, of course, are stereo-types. And it hardly needs saying, Latin America is the target of some of the most sweeping and mistaken stereotypes (generalizations) in existence. Perhaps we should look in that direction for a moment in order to know what the Latin American scene at least in part *is not*.

On the Other Hand, Stereotypes Are Stultifying

Latin American historian Fredrick Pike (1992) writes at length on U.S. stereotypes regarding Latin America. Most of them boil down to the distinction between *civilization* and *nature* (that is, *barbarism*).[13] Throughout the Americas, "civilized" people's judgment of "natural" people was in the beginning a matter of the relationships between Europeans and Amerindians and Europeans and African slaves. In the U.S., this attitude was later transferred to the whole of Latin America. "We" considered ourselves rational and tempered while "they" were passionate and child-like; "we" were in possession of all those solid "male" attributes and "they" were victims of their emotions, like "women." "We" Protestants stood on our own two feet before God; "they" were dependent on a woman, the virgin, and a collection of lesser images, the saints. "We" were born to dominate, to impose "our" will on others and on nature; "they" were the sultry temptress giving of herself to the most aggressive and most attractive takers. "We" were orderly. "We" conducted our affairs smoothly, working together in mutually cooperative efforts toward a common goal; "they" were lawless, violent, volatile, incapable of organizing themselves . . . yet they were charming and delightful, what "we" would like to be during our lightest moments. These fundamental distinctions supposedly boiled down to education, or the lack thereof. After all, "we" presumed "we" placed stress on the enlightenment of all citizens, for proper preparation of the mind domesticates the body's raw passions.[14] "They," in contrast, consisted chiefly of illiterate peoples whose savagery could not help but surface at the slightest provocation. Two of the most telling stereotypes are those of George Washington and Simón Bolívar: the first is supposed to use well-tempered reason; the second, so the story goes, is passioned and undisciplined. These two radically mythified figures illustrate the civilization/nature dichotomy condensed to a drop. Bolívar once predicted that the U.S. would wreak havoc on Latin America in the name of liberty. Actually, the havoc came "just as often in the name of civilization, virtually impossible to define except as *our* way of life, real, imagined, and mythologized" (Pike 1992:xvi).

Dualisms all! The evidence is there. Stereotypes as generalities play on binary relations, for, like Nietzschean metaphors, metonyms, anthropomorphisms, and gross generalizations, they are oversimplifications, and oversimplifications cannot but be a mere matter of a binary choice between *either* this *or* that. But the story continues, with even greater lust for thoughtless dichotomies.

In stereotypical fashion, the 1960s generation in the U.S., with long hair, lack of distinguishing features between male and female and all, was conceived by some presumably stalwart citizens to be a backward step to nature. The popular saying, "Let it all hang out," was typical not of "us" adults and reasoning people, but of "them." "We" knew better, like civilized people. This new generation, of course, contradicted "our" stereotype of "ourselves," and perhaps in part for that reason the 1960s movement met with such resistance. It was also, quite significantly, during that same period when Latin America was most desirous of "modernization," of becoming "First World" instead of remaining mired in its "Third World" status. "Modernization" meant the systematic application of "civilized" standards of material production and consumption. That rebellious sibling, Fidel Castro, cast aside the idea of "modernization" and threatened to return Cuba to its former "paradisiacal" state, which was precisely what the U.S. had always held in contempt regarding the whole of Latin America. Cuba, the disrespectful upstart, must be punished for its illicit actions. Yet Cuba, in attempting to go back to what it was, was actually falling in line with the traditional U.S. stereotype of Latin America in general: a playground in the tropics. The message seemed to be: "You Latinos should strive to become 'like us,' modern; yet as mere providers of raw goods and consumers of our manufactured goods, you should stay as you are, pre-modern." It is no wonder that "they," the Latin Americans, puzzled over just what "we" expected of "them."[15] But in order for this entire scene to be properly grasped, we must acknowledge that there was not simply a border between a binarily conceived pair of terms, "them" and "us," but a border, and a border of the border. That is, there was that infinitesimal dividing line that is not merely nothing for it is something: it is emptiness.

Yes, emptiness again, I'm afraid. However, a sense of emptiness is absolutely necessary before there can be a cut separating "this" from "that" in good binary fashion. Emptiness is also necessary in that, as a borderless border, it can give rise to imaginary space, for example, the imaginary space that was to become Latin America as invention, which now exists as a presumed dipolar opposite to the U.S. O'Gorman (1961:142–43) writes that Latin America was never a space signifying civilization in opposition to everything else signifying nature or barbarism, with a border serving to separate the two spaces—as per Frederick Jackson Turner's interpretation of U.S. history (Weber and Rausch 1994). The Latin American colonies remained rooted in tradition, depending on the patronage of centralized institutions for a guiding light. They did not strike out on their own in line with the North American rugged individualist "Go West young man" mentality. These colonies remained turned in on themselves, first in the Medieval, then in the Baroque, modes, without fully assimilating the disenchanted hell-bent-for-leather-subject-imposing-its-will-on-the-world attitude. Thus the border of imaginary space occupied by the Latin American colonies did a twisting Möbius fold into itself to become a border separating itself from itself. All this is still confusing, I would suspect. But perhaps for the time being I can do no better than I just did. The concept of an imaginary Latin America and the border of the border, emptiness, between Latin America and the U.S., is not grasped in terms of particulars or concrete images. And as a generality it can hardly be construed as anything but vacuous. The only recourse may rest in my suggesting that one must somehow get a certain feel for emptiness, a feel emerging from "between the lines," so to speak. Of course I cannot say this feel outright. Although I will have much to say about saying it at a later time, perhaps the most I can say at this juncture is that we will run across the need for acquiring a feel for Latin America time and time again as the pages of this book unfold.

For the moment, allow me to present another example—and, of necessity, indulge in a few more tenderly tenuous generalities. The Cuban exiles in the U.S., especially those who left the island during the early years of the Castro regime, were set apart, they set themselves apart, from other Latinos. They would like to consider themselves more as citizens of the world than merely Caribbeans or Latinos. They were from Cuba, the perennial crossroads—that is, border—between the continent and the colonies, the chief remaining colony after the independence movement in the

Central and South American republics, the island where justice turned its eyes else-where during the colonial period and organized racketeering made a sham of justice in the twentieth century up until 1959: Cuba the palimpsest of cultures and ethnici-ties, Cuba the epitome of imaginary space that is everywhere and nowhere, that is every part of the Latin American continent and no part of it.

Earl Shorris observes that for the self-exiled Cubans, to live in Miami is "to live in a special country, somewhere between the United States and history. Miami and Cuba have been tied together culturally and economically since Cuba dominated the hemisphere in the sixteenth century" (Shorris 1992:67). Cuban Miami is tied to Cuba. Yet it is in a certain sense nowhere in the U.S. And it is tied to the U.S. Yet in this regard it has hardly anything to do with Cuba (Perez 1999). It *both* is *and* is not Cuba, and it *both* is *and* is not the U.S.; it is *neither* the one *nor* the other but some-thing else that has not yet found itself, has as yet no characteristic identity, has not been able to express itself in terms of its identity. It is in a virtual process of emerg-ing but still can't quite get off the ground. It is *there* and it is *not there;* it is neither *here* nor *there,* neither *there* nor *not there.* In a word, it is in a sense gradually easing its way out of the void, out of emptiness.

Cuban Miami is in this sense a border between the U.S. and Cuba, what Cuba never was but nonetheless exists within the confines of an imaginary space, what Cuba is not and never will be, but nonetheless it is a virtual space in the imagination. Cuban Miami, in short, is a border of a border, a border folded into itself. It is like zero, zilch, neither actual *Zeitgeist* nor potential paradise: it is emptiness. If you gaze upon Figure 1 you will notice that Cuban Miami, a line, an imaginary infinitesimal division, is nevertheless frizzled, fuzzed, an exceedingly vague space that is at once *neither* Cuba *nor* the U.S. Yet since it is *not* exactly Cuba it at least has that much in

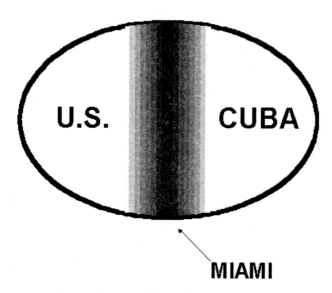

Figure 1

common with the U.S., and since it is *not* exactly the U.S. it has at least that much in common with the Cuba. So in this sense in a manner of speaking it is *both* Cuba *and* the U.S. It is *both* the one thing *and* the other, and it is *neither* the one thing *nor* the other.[16]

But, . . . I must say once again that I'm afraid all this must appear terribly confusing. How did I get myself in this mess anyway? How do I get myself out of it? How can I qualify what I have said a little better?

Talking Past Each Other

Allow me to repeat myself. In the Nietzschean sense there are no genuine, unmediated facts. There are only interpretations from particular perspectives, interpretations arising from the border of borders, the infinitesimal nonspace that might as well be a yawning void, for it is the nothing that contains the possibility of everything. So in this regard the vague line of demarcation in Figure 1 depicting the border of borders, this "emptiness," cannot lend itself to interpretations. It just *is.* It is, if I may say so without committing a heresy, like a Zen Master once said: "When I heard the temple bell ring, suddenly there was no bell and no I, just sound" (Kapleau 1976:107). In other words, at the gut level, the interpretation is the feeling, just the feeling. There is no explicit, logical, linguistically formulated interpretation.

Regarding the Latin American scene, dominance/subservience, hegemonic/subaltern, *criollos/mestizos, mestizos*/Amerindians, *mestizos*/African Americans, *criollos*/ Amerindians, *criollos*/African Americans, oligarchy/peasantry, males/females, conservatives/liberals, culture/nature, civilization/barbarism, and all the other grand dichotomizing stereotypes of Latin American cultural history just don't cut it.[17] At the level of interpretations in their most basic form, rather than binaries, there is resonance and consonance and dissonance, harmony and disequilibria, order and clutter; that is, there is hum, along with a perpetually off-beat rhythm. Juan Perón, Argentine dictator from 1945 to 1955, once said that the people don't think, they feel. It is not enough to think the resonance, the hum, and rhythm. The feel is where it's at; yet it is neither here nor there, now nor then. It simply *is,* which is to say virtually nothing at all, and which is also to say virtually everything. Nothing and everything, comparable to Borges's "Everything and Nothing" (1962 [1944]). Borges tells us that an actor and playwright, upon reaching the end of the trail, was caught up with the realization that he had been so many selves that he knew not his true self. He implored to God that his mind might be put at ease and that he might be able to know who he was. Then:

> "I who have been so many men in vain want to be one and my-
> self." The voice of the Lord answered from a whirlwind: "Neither
> am I anyone; I have dreamt the world as you dreamt your work,
> my Shakespeare, and among the forms in my dream are you, who
> like myself are many and no one." (Borges 1962:249)

Borges never ceased in his attempt to intellectualize the incognizable, to articulate the ineffable. This is a risky game. If the player can't pull it off properly it can blow up in her face and leave nothing at all. But there must be something, if no more than a feel for the sound, the hum, the resonance, the rhythm. Borges's strategy consists of creating metaphysical medleys that satirize by revealing the folly of them all. His strategy, then, features fragmentation, heterogeneity, the image of disorder and even randomness, the play of paradoxes, inversions, assymetries, disjunctions, and impossible conjunctions. He carries out his strategy supremely. It recalls the Menippean satires of antiquity. Unlike the customary satires which criticize people and practices from a presumably fixed standpoint, Menippean satires undermined any and all certainties of position and perspective. The Menippeans were usually experimental, testing high philosophical concepts against the everyday common world in order freely to mix disparate moral and psychological conditions, as in insanity, unrestrained carnivalesque practices, spontaneous creativity, and wild flights of the imagination, all of which constantly border on chaos. Like the Menippeans, Borges intellectualizes and satirizes to the nth degree, from within the comfortable confines of his high culture, his cosmopolitan tower. Yet, in spite of his un-Menippean detachment from the everyday cultural life of the people, he evinces a sense of consonance and dissonance, of feel and hum and rhythm.[18]

When Cuban writer José Lezama Lima (1981) suggests that "image" precedes and announces "possibilities," I take him to mean that the "image" creates the vision of possible alternatives, of something to fill in the erstwhile excluded middle in order to frizzle conventionally conceived dichotomies of thought and of practices. The "image," distinction between what might be and what has been and therefore might even appear to be, is by its very nature subversive. It is an expression of what might replace what is taken to be "real" with some dreamy "irreal" world where there is neither reality nor the fantastic or magical but a magically realistic reality magicalized. There is only the imagined, the invented, from nowhere, that is, from the border of borders. Hence with respect to Latin America, the "image" is *neither* a centripetal push toward the center, nature, barbarism, jungle, pampa, mountains, valleys, deserts, *nor* a centrifugal pull outward in the direction of metropolitanism, modernization, or foreign means and models. Rather, it is a third push-pull between the peaks and valleys of the wave form, between the ups and downs of the resonance, between crystalline order and the shattered emerald of chaos: this movement that doubles back on itself becomes a movement of complementation, of incongruous complementarity, with the one complementing the other in such a way that within the one lies a suggestion of the other, and vice versa.[19]

I repeat my suggestion: in view of the preceding polylogue, there are no essential essences, no matters of which mind can be totally aware, no mind that is ultimately all that matters; there are no fixed facts, but only *interdependent, interrelated, interactive* feels and sensations and perspectives and interpretations. This wipes out the content of the present and the past and hopes for the future, leaving the equivalent of what might seem like the "empty set" of set theory. But actually, it is even less than that; in fact, it is infinitely less than that. It is nothing but a single idea. . . . No, that's not right. It is no idea at all; it is more like a nonidea. . . . No, not that either, I'm afraid. It's simply—but by no means simply at all—the emptiness of any and all ideas. That is, there is nothing but vacuous perspective and a vacuous interpretation, without any perspective or interpretation of anything at all. This empty nonperspective is only available if there is a vague sense of some alternative, . . . No, . . . of an empty nonalternative, since no alternative can be actualized from within the empty nonperspective. Besides, when something is actualized, it almost immediately does a disappearing act; and there you have it again, the emptiness. Cussed emptiness. But why cussed? Without it there can be no alternatives at all. So if you remain convinced that alternatives can't exist, and that there is nothing except insofar as it is entrenched in some particular way of perceiving, then what there is is dependent upon some perspective, and that on emptiness.[20] Everything that is, shares this characteristic; it is the only characteristic shared by everything. So in the absence of anything sayable regarding emptiness, what are we to do? Wait around like a Beckett character for something that never happens to happen? Wait for someone to come who is never the same as the person who finally arrives, if indeed anyone arrives at all? Sit there in expectant anticipation that nothing will happen with high hopes that something will happen, but it doesn't happen, so you are surprised that you are not surprised that it doesn't happen? No. Nobody will jump onto the scene and deliver us from our learned unknowing. The answer, allow me to suggest, lies in our attending to what's between the *either* and the *or*.

For instance, Walter Mignolo (2000:58) criticizes Edward Said's (1978) Orientalism with the rejoinder that without Occidentalism there can be no Orientalism. The point is well taken. A positive assertion cannot be genuinely positive without its negation lurking about somewhere. There is no "beyond," no "beyond Occidentalism" (Coronil 1996), or "beyond eurocentrism" (Dussel 1998). What there is as possibility is simply there, in the line, and more deeply, in the border of borders, between one term and its *other*, between one chess piece and another. Nor can there be a possible checkmate, for the borders proliferate without end, slithering to and fro with the flows of culture. And what makes for the very possibility of borders and borders of borders? *Both-and* and *neither-nor*, I would submit, as illustrated through Figure 1.

Where am I going with all this anyway? I'm not really sure, since upon attempting to account for emptiness I've apparently stepped out into thin air. But at least I need to be clear on an important point. The edict "All 'facts' are interpretations" is not simply a concession to that poststructuralist reveling in a liberally perfumed atmosphere of words, words, and more words, the soothing idea that all we have is signifiers, so there is no need to worry our delicate heads over any other aspect of the big world out there. I write "soothing," for our invented world of books, classrooms, word processors, and conference circuits provides an attractive placebo effect. I write "reveling," since the convenient idea that there is nothing but floating signifiers allows a happy-go-lucky virtually free association play of linguistic signs from the safe confines of our sedentary swivel-chair existence at the computer terminal. And I write "words, words, and more words," because these poststructuralist practices are "linguicentric" through and through.[21] Language, contrary to the usual "linguicentric" practices, is definitely not all there is, and the sooner we face up to the genuine complexity of semiosis the better off we'll be.

So in the final analysis when I write "feeling" and "interpretations," I do not mean many of those roguishly contrived and widely disseminated texts that go by the name of poststructuralism, cultural studies, postmodernism, postcolonialism, subaltern studies, women's studies, gay studies, queer theory, and so on. Feeling and sensations and perspectives and interpretations are genuinely contextual, and contexts include extralinguistic sights and sounds and smells and tastes and touch and kinesthetic sensations, all of bodymind, that include iconic and indexical as well as linguistic signs.[22] Genuine contextuality looks with disfavor on any and all self-confident, presumably iron-clad conclusions, that one woman's interpretation is flawed because it is from a twisted perspective and another woman's interpretation is superior because her perspective is legitimate. All perspectives are to a greater or lesser degree twisted, and no perspective is absolutely true to form and a faithful mirror of the world. Perspectives may give some inkling regarding our multiple "semiotic realities" and usually by more luck than management they might even enjoy some approximation to the "actually real" world. But they are all inexorably incomplete and inadequate to the big, virtually unfathomable, task. I write that interpretations are "genuinely contextual," for they are just that: inseparable from visceral, proprioceptive feels, visual images, background noises, and haptic, tactile, corporeal sensations. An interpretation, if dressed in linguistic apparel, can be so dressed because there were prelinguistic proclivities, premonitions, presuppositions, and prejudices regarding what was supposed to be, what now is, and what the future might hold in store.

What and how one feels and senses and does is what one can slightly after the fact find oneself feeling and sensing and doing, but by the time one finds out what one is up to, one is up to something else. And now, one realizes that one felt and sensed and did in the manner in which one did because that is just what one did. At this most basic level, there was as yet no language, no necessary contrivances, manipulations, dominance, and subservience, auras of superiority and the shame of inferiority; there was as yet not necessarily any good guys and bad guys. There was only feeling and sensing and doing, before language had a chance to do its thing and erect its hierarchies. When a somewhat clumsy concoction of words is slapped into this extralinguistic feeling, sensing and doing, it always seems impoverished. This is because the words are a long step removed from concrete feeling, sensing, and doing. At this concrete level, when we resonate with the rhythms of our culture, we are part of a community. Our saying-and-doing-in-alliance-with-our-saying-with-words marks us as individuals within gangs and cliques and societies and associations and pressure groups engaged in word agonistics that periodically erupt in violent tactics. Extralinguistic interpreting while within our cultural flows, in contrast, helps us keep the resonance strong. Such interpretating, at the concrete level of feeling, sensing, and doing at extralinguistic levels implies a post-Cartesian, *participatory culture*. Before entering this theme, however, let us take a digressionary turn toward the notion of feeling and sensing and doing from a Peircean view.

Why Peirce? Peirce, because for him semiosis is radically *participatory*. It excludes neither the subject—either of the sign's taking or its making—nor the semiotic object. Peirce, because, I would submit, his notion of semiosis marks at least the beginning of a "re-enchantment" with the world. Peirce, because his sign is properly triadic rather than merely binary, and it enfolds, within itself as we shall note, the nature of what I have termed emptiness.[23]

So, I invite you to indulge with me in somewhat of a crash course on Charles Sanders Peirce.

Notes

1.   For history and philosophy, see especially Feyerabend (1975), Hanson (1958, 1969), Hesse (1966), Kuhn (1970), and Polanyi (1958); for leading studies in sociology, Barnes (1996), Barnes and Edge (1982), Bloor (1983), Brown (1994), Latour (1987, 1993, 1999), Woolgar (1988a, 1988b), and for the controversy surrounding these views, Koertge (1998).

2.   In addition to deconstruction and poststructuralism in their various incarnations, this "relatively unknown territory" has, in philosophical circles, enjoyed an increasing share of the spotlight in recent times by the likes of relativists and constructivists (Goodman 1978), post-empiricist and post-analytic philosophers (Rorty 1979, 1989, Rajchman and West 1985), somewhat "reluctant realists" (Putnam 1983a, 1990), and those who would like to tow the line between, though in a sense not really "beyond," objectivism and relativism (Bernstein 1983).

3.   See Tzvetan Todorov's *The Conquest of America* (1984). Though his book has been criticized, and justifiably so, it still gives food for thought. For diverse views and more sober evaluations, see the entire volume of which Alvar's essay is a part in Jara and Spadaccini (1992b), also Cevallos-Candau (1994b), Magasich-Airola and Beer (2000), and Rabassa (1993).

4.   It bears mentioning that in recent times much has been written by ecologically aware scholars and investigators regarding a "re-enchantment" of what Max Weber dubbed our "disenchanted world" (for example, Berman 1981, Griffin 1988b, Hayward 1987, Toulmin 1982, 1990; and regarding Columbus's lingering "enchantment," Jara and Spadaccini 1992a).

5.   Recent interpretations of the "invention of America" have tended toward the philological and rhetorical rather than O'Gorman's Heideggerian-inspired ontological interpretation (Boelhower 1988; Coronil 1989; Piedra 1989; Rabassa 1993). Given my "antilinguicentric" posture in this essay, I would prefer an interpretation of the "invention" in line with what I will shortly call "objective idealism," following the thought of C. S. Peirce.

6.   I would recommend a general survey of objective idealism in Rescher and Brandom (1979), Almeder (1980), and Hookway (1985), and perhaps, for my own ruminations on the topic, merrell (1995a, 1997, 2000b, 2001).

7.   Although limited space does not allow my pressing further on this topic, I might mention that a combination of Ainsa (1989) on the "invention" of America, Fischer (1990) on the idea of "invention" as foreign to the traditional notion of ultimate Truth, and Turner (1996) on the "invention" of the Renaissance perspective, suggests the ways and means of "inventing" worlds quite effectively.

8.   In anthropology see Geertz (1973, 1983), in philosophy, Skolimowski (1986, 1987), in psychology, Bruner (1986, 1987) and in sociology, Bloor (1976, 1983).

9. While a large number of the short stories in Borges's *Labyrinths* (1962) are found in *Ficciones* (1944), some of them are taken from other collections of stories, and the volume also includes a selection of essays from *Other Inquisitions* (1964a [1952]).

10. For a more detailed discussion of the *border of borders* from such an unexpected source as physicist John Archibald Wheeler's interpretation of the quantum universe, see merrell (1998b, 2000a).

11. I ask of your patience regarding the terms *vaguely* and *generally;* their interrelatedness will be qualified below.

12. This quandary is comparable to what is known as the *tu quoque* argument: rationalism stands tenuously on the base of an irrational leap of faith in rationalism; likewise relativism can only be embraced by faith in the unwavering truth of relativism; and so on (Bartley 1984).

13. Of course we have Lévi-Strauss's (1966) nature/culture binary (see Paz 1970b [1967]), but I am speaking of something else that is germane and rather exclusive to Latin American history. "Civilization" is used in reference to those respectable cultures of proper European vintage, and then there are those other cultures that remain close to "natural" drives and desires, those "barbarous" cultures.

14. The problematics of this assumption in our time ring loud and clear in Allan Bloom's best selling *Closing of the American Mind* (1987).

15. Wish respect to the ambivalent messages sent from U.S. to Cuba, see Louis A. Perez's excellent study, *On Becoming Cuban* (1999).

16. Shorris writes what he writes in reference to what he sees as the Cubans who cannot forget the Cuba they left, who continue to insist on exile rather than immigration or assimilation, and whose offspring exist in the *both-and* and *neither-nor* space, in a sort of Netherland. One particular Cuban recalls: "My definition is 'I am not.' I am not American and I am not Cuban. I am nothing" (Shorris 1992:141). Now, I realize my words surrounding Figure 1 appear to be hardly more than hasty, facile generalizations for which there are many exceptions. Granted, and I would especially recommend the work of multidisciplinary artist Coco Fusco (1995), whose testimony reveals the complexity of this issue. Fusco's (1995:4) observation that the Cuban children of her generation "didn't choose to leave or to stay—the wars that shaped our identities as Cuban or American are ones we inherited" is on target. Yet the ambiguity, the vagueness, of Cuban-American or American-Cuban or some mix in between, reveals the subtlety of the second generation Cubans' condition.

17. *Criollos* (creoles) are Spaniards born in the Americas, those who were born in Spain and migrated to the colonies were known as *peninsulares. Mestizos* are usually considered a mixture of Amerindian and European.

18. In a graduate seminar on the Spanish American essay I once blurted out that no writer was more closely tied to Latin American culture than Borges. My words, needless to say, fell on incredulous ears, and they immediately even grated on my own mind. After pondering over my rather unintentionally mouthed assertion, I have come to the conclusion that Borges encapsulates in intellectual form, and at the same time with references to the best of Western philosophy and literature, a sense of the feel I allude to. In this manner at least, he is, indeed, the most Latin American of Latin American writers.

19. For this general view along the lines of narrative and the idea of utopia, see once again Ainsa (1977, 1986).

20. The "perspectivism" I allude to is neither that of Nietzsche (1913) nor that of José Ortega y Gasset (1964), though it bears resemblance to both. Rather, it is more akin to philosophy of a particular "constructivist" sort. That term is loaded with many meanings. The view I have taken as a result of my previous studies is a composite of Nelson Goodman (1978), Peirce, Hilary Putnam (1981, 1983a), and Henryk Skolimowski (1986, 1987)—though I realize these philosophers are at odds on many other points. This form of "perspectivism" can to a certain extent be found in the work of Peruvian intellectual Victor Raúl Haya de la Torre (1948), who was influenced by Ortega y Gasset and Einstein's relativity. It is also found lurking in the corners of many Latin American literary works such as José María Arguedas's *El zorro de arriba y el zorro de abajo* (1971), João Guimarães Rosa's *The Devil to Pay in the Backlands* (1963 [1956]), Clarice Lispector's *The Passion According to G. H.* (1988 [1964]), José Emilio Pacheco's *You Will Die in a Distant Land* (1991 [1967]), Gabriel García Márquez's *One Hundred Years of Solitude* (1971 [1967]), Julio Cortázar's *Hopscotch* (1966 [1963]), Augusto Roa Bastos's *I the Supreme* (1986 [1974]), Alejo Carpentier's *The Kingdom of This World* (1957 [1949]), Carlos Fuentes's *The Death of Artemio Cruz* (1964 [1962]), Luisa Valenzuela's *The Lizard's Tail* (1983 [1983]), Mario Vargas Llosa's *The Green House* (1968 [1966]), and above all Borges's short stories.

21. "Linguicentrism" is a label I attach here and elsewhere to the faith and accompanying practices in human semiotic activity as reducible to language and language alone, practices that often ignore extralinguistic olfactory, gustatory, tactile, auditive, visual, and kinesthetic signs. Even some of the "antilogocentric" poststructuralists and deconstructors are guilty of "linguicentrism" insofar as they tend to focus on hardly anything but language and textuality (merrell 1997, 1998b).

22. "Kinesthetics," a term that will occasionally be called into service on the pages that follow, is a sense of bodily position, presence, or movement chiefly as a result of stimulation of nerve endings in muscles, tendons, and joints; hence it is "deeper" and "more intimate" than the stimulation received from "outside" by the basic five sensory channels. I should point out as well that "kinesthetics," in psychology considered a matter of "inner phenomenal qualities," has recently been the target of heated polemics, with neither the "qualiaphiles" nor the "qualiaphobes" definitely getting the upper hand thus far (see Flanagan 1992:61–85).

23. Along these lines, for a sense of "participation" and a "re-enchantment" of the world—though they do not all specifically use the terms—see Corrington (1994), Rochberg-Halton (1986), Neville (1992), Turley (1977), and if you are so inclined, perhaps also merrell (1995a, 1996, 1998a, 1998b).

Chapter Two

A Company of Three

> Cradled in one culture, sandwiched between two cultures, strad-
> dling all three cultures and their value systems, *la mestiza* under-
> goes a struggle of flesh, a struggle of borders, an inner war.
> —Gloria Anzaldúa

> [B]etween cultural creation and cultural suppression new borders
> arise.
> —Carlos Vélez-Ibáñez

The Magical Number Three?

The most fundamental of Peirce's sign types consists of his concept of the sign as trinary with a vengeance; it depends upon a continuity of interrelations between signs. As such, it is process, it is semiosis. We are always caught in the flow of this process, because body and mind and thought itself are inextricably bound up with and of the very nature of signs (Peirce 1931–35 *CP:*5.421).

Peirce's sign consists of a *representamen* (itself often called a sign), that relates to its respective *semiotic object.* But in order to be a genuine sign it must also inter-relate with a third term, its *interpretant* (roughly, that which is most responsible for engendering the sign's meaning). This third component of the sign mediates between the other components in such a way that it brings them into interrelation with each other and they in turn are brought into interrelation with it in the same way that they are brought into interrelation with each other. It is an ongoing three-way "democ-ratic" affair, that allows all components the possibility of equal time and the possibil-ity that any one of them can become any of the other ones (for Peirce's own descrip-tion of the sign process, see *CP:*2.227–434).

The most fundamental of Peirce's sign types consists of the trichotomy of *icons, indices,* and *symbols.* Icons resemble the objects to which they relate (a circle which is like the sun). Borges's "Aleph" (1970 [1949]), the object of Daneri's supreme contemplation, is for practical purposes not an icon, because, as a self-contained, self-sufficient whole, it *is* the entire universe and hence there can be nothing other with which it interrelates; yet it is contained within the universe, so in a sense it *is* an icon of the purest sort. Indices relate to their objects by some natural connection (smoke as an indication of fire). Maggie (the Magician) of Borges's "The Circular Ruins" thought she created an icon, a dreamt son, and then she thought she interpo-lated him into the world to render him "real." But she was mistaken, for she was the figment of yet another dream. In this manner her dreamt image, in addition to its iconic qualities, was also an index, an indication, of her own condition. The relation between symbols and their objects entails sign use according to cultural convention

21

(a national flag evincing hardly any similarity with and no natural connection to its object, or the word "horse" in relation to a certain species of quadripeds). Symbols of the best and most common sort are those of language. Lönny (Lönnrot, the detective of Borges's "Death and the Compass" [1962 {1944}]), that supreme ratiocinator, believed the symbolic, linguistic, logical, and geometrical signs he constructed were irrefutable proof that he was hot on the trail of the assassin, Scharlach. But in the end he realized they were signs of his own making, partly arbitrary and with no necessary correlation to the "real" world. As the Quixote implied long before Richard Rorty's (1979) destruction of the "mind-as-mirror-of-nature" metaphor, symbols are no faithful "representation" of the "real."

According to Peirce, the meaning of signs, and especially linguistic signs, is found in their interrelations with and dependency upon other signs. An interpretant gives purpose, direction, and meaning to a sign. But this interpretant, upon becoming an interpretant charged with meaning, becomes in the process another sign (representamen)—the sign of meaning—that comes into interrelation with the first sign in its interrelation with its object. It can then take on its own object—which can be the same object, now slightly modified—and in its turn it engenders its own interpretant. This interpretant then becomes yet another sign (representamen), and so on. The ongoing sign process has been dubbed by Umberto Eco (1976:69) "unlimited semiosis." It consists of a succession of signs along the semiosic stream that become a network of glosses, or commentaries, of signs on the signs preceding them. The process of signs becoming other signs is in principle endless. All signs are incessantly becoming something other than what they were becoming. Consequently, for Peirce there is no ultimate meaning (interpretant). The meaning of a given sign is itself a sign of that sign, which calls for its own meaning, which is in turn another sign. So there is no absolutely final meaning, for us finite, fallible, sign makers and takers at least.

This rather intense Peircean palaver might be too much too quickly. Besides, it most likely appears as of little consequence regarding the topic at hand. Yet, I would suggest that there is plenty of reason for my apparent methodological madness, however irrelevant it may seem at this juncture. I bring up Peirce's triadic concept of the sign rather abruptly not for the purpose of creating confusion, but, I hope, to set the proper mood for what is to follow. Just as we are indelibly inside semiosis, so also both you and I are at this "moment" suspended "inside" this book and "inside" the context within which we happen to find ourselves, and we must try to make heads or tails of the whole concoction. On so doing, we must cope with a nonlinear, back and forth, spiraling, self-enclosing, texts and contexts in the making, that give us pieces from a jig-saw puzzle rather than a linear *A-B-C* development. Since this book—and both you and I and our contexts besides—are inside semiosis, why should I, how could I, expect to render it of a nature any different from semiosis? The very idea would be presumptuous. The best I can do is provide a certain feel for, and if I am lucky maybe even a sense of, what this book is about.

Like this book, the universe, as I have tentatively implied above, is not that deterministic linear, cause-and-effect parade of events envisioned by classical science. It is complex, not simple; it is more chaotic than orderly; it by and large favors asymmetry over symmetry. In this light, I would suggest that we cannot simply have either linearity or nonlinearity. We need both our well-reasoned linearity and our "chaos" principle, in order effectively to negotiate the now placid, now elusive, now winding and heaving, stream of semiosis. By the same token, if we construed semiosis as we would a map we could study with the presumed detachment of a classical scientist studying bacteria under the microscope, we would be destined to deluded hopes and unfulfilled dreams. For, unlike the traditional concept of knowledge as a map or mirror of nature, we are squarely within the map, and we must find our way about by groping in the dark, by a certain element of intuition, premonition, inclination, educated guesses, and even sheer chance, as well as by using our customary faculties of reason as best we know how.

Consequently, there is little use trying by linear methods to "get the picture" of what I am trying to write. There is no picture, no picture that we are capable of seeing from some imperious outside vantage point at least. Moreover, we are, ourselves, signs among the signs around us. Like Niels Bohr once remarked with respect to the world of quantum theory, we are both spectators and actors in the great drama of existence. The traditional Western idea of a neutral spectator surveying her world and cramming it into her cognitive map that mirrors the world in all its brilliance, is rapidly becoming defunct. So if the Peircean terms, representamen, semiotic object, and interpretant at this stage remain to a large extent foreign, I would expect that at least they have etched some trace or other on your mind. Perhaps I can suggest that we let the Peircean sign components grow on us, and we on them, as we attempt to proceed through the remainder of this labyrinthine journey.

So much for the introductory salad from Peirce's semiotic menu. Now for a healthy serving of meat and potatoes, if I may.

Not a Matter of Merely Three, But of Threes

Since in the Peircean sense virtually anything can be a sign, the definition of a sign must indeed be of the most general sort. It is not simply a matter of the question "What *is* a sign?" but of the questions "What is it like to be a sign?" and "What do signs do?" Signs are not special kinds of things, but rather, anything is a sign insofar as it manifests sign functions, which I have tentatively defined in terms of *interaction, interrelatedness,* and *codependence* or *codependent emerging.* The Peircean sign is often taken as something that *stands for* something *to* someone *in* some respect or capacity (*CP:2.228*). With respect to the mind-set of our contemporary milieu, I must express my displeasure with the concept of a sign's "standing for" (as well as "referring to," "corresponding to," and "representing") something. More properly, a sign *codependently emerges,* and it *interrelates* and *interacts* and *co-participates with* something (its object). It also *codependently interrelates* and *interacts* and *co-participates with* the someone who made it and the someone processing it, and *with* whatever it is being processed into (its interpretant), which in turn becomes another sign by way of its triadic interrelations with the sign, the object, and the sign maker and interpreter.

Peirce himself once defined a sign as "anything that determines something else (its interpretant) to refer to an object to which itself refers (its object) in the same way, the interpretant becoming in turn a sign, and so on *ad infinitum*" (*CP:*2.303). A sign or representamen, say, the word "cross," interrelates with (signifies) an interpretant (roughly a concept, meaning) of the sign within a particular community regarding conventional ceremonies and the everyday Christian life.[1] But the function of the sign and its interpretant remains incomplete unless there is also interrelatedness with some semiotic object. Suppose the object of the sign "cross" is a particular *cross* in some chapel with which you are familiar during a Sunday ceremony. Upon the sign and interpretant coming into interrelation with their object, the interpretant (which mediates between the sign and its object) becomes in its own turn another sign (representamen) within *this* particular context in *this* chapel. The sign then engenders its own interpretant regarding *this* activity within *this* context. And as the ceremony proceeds, at each and every juncture the sign (representamen), its interpretant, and its object, take in a successive string of different countenances as they become something slightly *other* than what they were during the moment of their antecedent becoming as signs. In other words, with each feeling or sensation or thought of a cross, with each verbal evocation "cross," with each furtive glance or fixation on the actual *cross* standing "out there" in the chapel, the sign, whether engendered from the object (*cross*), from a previous instantiation of the word "cross," or from the interpretant (a thought or concept in the mind), becomes another sign. It cannot help but do so.

Another example, if I may. Suppose Columbus is in the Caribbean close to the Venezuelan coast. Some of his crew are pulling water up from the sea with which to wash down the deck. They are in a playful mood. One seaman tosses a bucket of water in another's face, and he immediately notices that it has no salty taste. Columbus is called over. He inspects the water and declares that it is fresh rather than briny, which is quite uncharacteristic of sea water—this could conceivably have occurred when Columbus's ship once approached the Orinoco River delta. One sign has become another sign. Of course the sign is in a certain sense the same sign: it is that familiar liquid Columbus and his crew see and taste, it is *water,* with which we would interrelate the linguistic sign in the English language, "water." But it is not the same sign: first it was *salt water* and now it is *fresh water.* The visual and tactile sign seems to be the same, but the gustatory sign reveals a difference which evokes a different semiotic object and a different interpretant. So there is Sign-Object (*salt water*)-Interpretant, and then the interpretant became another sign in the order of Sign-Object(*fresh-water*)-Interpretant. A sign became another sign among a plethora of signs in this enchanting New World the complexity of which was so mind-numbing that the intrepid adventurers hardly had any recourse but incessantly to invent new signs at each and every turn. And they did so.

In this sense, I would rephrase the customary Peircean definition of the sign as: anything that codependently interrelates with its interpretant in such a manner that that interpretant codependently interrelates with its object in the same way that the object codependently interrelates with it, such co-relations serving to engender another sign from the interpretant, and subsequently the process is re-iterated. Admittedly, that was a big mouthful. Yet it's basically the way of signs, with stress on the notions of codependency, co-relations, interrelatedness, and above all *interactive participation*. I have taken my cue once again from Peirce, who writes: "a sign is something by knowing which we know something more" (*CP*:8.332). Ideas and thoughts themselves are signs. Thus just as signs in the world and signs in the mind multiply and grow, so also does knowing.

But there is more, much more. Since semiosis implies mediation, it is deeper and more comprehensive than the ordinary expressions "derivation of meaning" or "interpretation." Engendering and processing signs and making them meaningful is more than merely getting information out of them or making sense of them. It is a matter of an interplay between what Peirce called the categories: *Firstness, Secondness,* and *Thirdness*. In schematic form, Firstness is *possibility* (what *might be*), Secondness is *actuality* (what presumably *is*), and Thirdness is *potentiality, probability,* or *necessity* (what *could be, would be,* or *should be,* given a certain set of conditions). But like all definitions, these are admittedly vague and somewhat deceptive. In reality, Firstness, in and of itself, is not an identified concrete quality of something (like, for example, the sensation of a body of *water* we might be looking at at this moment). It is nothing more than a possibility, a pure abstraction—abstracted, separated from everything else—as something enjoying its own self-presence and nothing more: it cannot (yet) be present *to* some conscious semiotic agent *as* such-and-such (*water* in this case). It is an entity without defined or definable parts, without antecedents or subsequents. It simply *is*. In this regard, it is the bare beginning of something from "emptiness," of something from the possibility of everything; it is at once everything and nothing, it simply *is what it is*.

The *whatness* or the *happens-to-be* of that which is perceived belongs to the category of Secondness. It is a matter of something actualized in the manner of *this* entity *here,* presented *for* some sign maker or taker. As such it is hardly more than a particularity, a singularity. It is what we had before us as Firstness, such as, for example, a vague "watery looking" image without there yet being any consciousness *of* it or its being identified *as* such-and-such. But now, a manifestation of Secondness, it has been set apart from the self-conscious agent, willing and ready to be seen as *salt water*. But at this point it is not (yet) salt water. That is, it is not a word-sign (symbol) identifying the entity in question and bringing with it a ponderous mass of cultural baggage regarding salt water (in the case of Columbus and his crew, setting out from Sevilla, the Mediterranean, adventurous life at sea, exploration of new horizons, etc.). At the first stage of Secondness the *salt water* is little more than the possibility of a physical entity, a "brute fact," as Peirce was wont to put it. It is just one more thing from the furniture of the self's physical world: it is mere *otherness* in the most primitive sense. If Firstness is pure affirmation of what *is as it is,* Secondness is negation insofar as it is *other*.

Thirdness can be tentatively qualified as that which brings about *mediation* between two other entities in such a manner that they are related to each other in the same way they are related to the third entity as a result of its mediary act. The mediary act is as if Firstness, Secondness, and Thirdness were twisted into an intertwined Borromean knot that clasps them together by way of a central "node," or better, "vortex," in such a way that they are "democratically" conjoined. Each of them can intermittently play the role of any of the categories, yet at a given space-time juncture, one of the three will be a First, one a Second, and one a Third (see Figure 2). In order for this "democratic" process to occur, co-relations between the three periph-eral "points" can exist only by way of the central vortex or "fourth point" (if you will, consider this vortex comparable to what I have termed "emptiness"). You might visualize the vortex as the center of an "axle" that holds the spokes of a wheel to-gether. The wheel is in constant motion, but the central point of the axle just sits there: it is the point about which the continuity of movement regarding the whole emerges. However, the vortex and the axle give relatively static images. These im-ages are false to themselves. Actually the central "point" of the sign is a scintillating, titillating, shimmering, effervescence of action. Hence: vortex, like *Yin/Yang* (☯), is the center of incessant activity in the Eastern tradition.

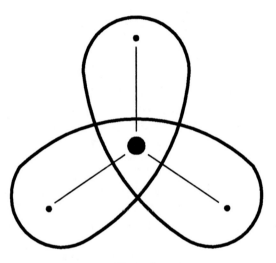

Figure 2

Since the peripheral "points" of Figure 2 can be occupied by any of the three categories, whatever at a given space-time slice happens to be a First is no more than a vague feeling. What is a Second entails bare consciousness *of* the First on the part of some sign maker or taker. What is Third brings the two together and potentially gives them some meaning as a genuine semiotic entity. That is to say, if Secondness entails the becoming of consciousness to the extent that a *salt water* image of Firstness is seen *as* a body of *salt water,* Thirdness entails the becoming of con-sciousness to the level of awareness *that* the physical entity *water* is the instantiation of a class of stuff that goes by the name of salt water (in the English language, that is). Consciousness sees *that* the salt water, like all salt water, provides a certain func-tion in one's life and in the life of one's community, given the attributes that make it salt water. Thus Thirdness has to do with a sign as *generality*—the particular instan-tiations of the sign belonging to Secondness—according to what Peirce called social *convention,* and as a result of *habit* forming tendencies to use the same sign in rela-tion to a class of similar objects in the physical world. Once again we see that the codependently interrelated interaction of sign, object, and interpretant is not a "standing for" or "representing" or "corresponding" or "referring" act. It is an act of codependent interrelating with and at the same time an interacting with, where everything participates with everything else in the bootstrapping operation of semiosis. Signs are not mere surrogates for something else. No sign component is an island unto itself, but rather, each component is dependent upon and interrelated with all other sign components (*CP:*5.474).

The story had it, nevertheless, that what Columbus and his crew originally considered "salt water" became something *other than* what it was: it became "fresh water." In this process, the Thirdness of the erstwhile sign was abruptly taken back to its quality as Firstness, the image *salt water* became an *other* image, *fresh water,* the Secondness of object also became *other,* as did the sign's Thirdness mediating between them, and a new sign was born. Now, "fresh water" interrelated and was codependent with an entirely different set of signs (rain on the parched soil of the Spanish central plains, the Guadalquivir river, barrels in the ship's hold of the precious liquid, this new sign where another sign should be, and so on). The sign of Figure 2 whirls about its axis not on the two-dimensional plane but in a nonlinear, wobbly, virtually strange attractor manner, such that at any moment the three legs can change partners, and the dance, now something *other* than what it was, goes on.

Unfortunately, Peirce's triadology is often passed off as a combination of binaries. A possible reason for this confusion is that when we think of threes, in spite of our better judgment, Euclidean triangles almost invariably come to mind. Consequently, Peirce's sign triad often finds itself diagrammed as a triangle (for example, Ogden and Richards 1923). The triangular form is not properly triadic, however. It merely consists of a set of three binary relations connecting the three corners of the triangle along its three sides, no more, no less. Figure 3, in contrast, in the form of a tripod, ties each sign component to the other two, and in addition, to the interrelation between them. The interrelation between *R* (representamen, sign) and *O* (object), for example, is no interrelation at all outside consideration of the interrelations between *R* and *I* (interpretant) and between *O* and *I*. None of the interrelations hold outside the "vortex" connecting them to one another. The vortex can in this manner be conceived as the "pre-sign" without which the sign could not have become a sign. At the same time the vortex is an infinitesimal "porthole" through which the sign in question can pass and become yet another sign. A sign might consist of the word "salt water," which can be manifested either as sound waves in the air or marks on paper. The object, the *salt water* within the visible field, is at the outset taken in much that same way it is always taken, as *water.* The interpretant, then, might be engendered in a mind in terms of the sign's signification regarding its function in the community of which that particular mind is a citizen. Subsequently, certain responses from all parties present in Columbus's sea-going vessel surrounded by *salt water* could be forthcoming. In this manner, to reiterate, the sign components are seen as appropriately codependent, interrelated, and interactive (this trio of terms will become increasingly important as this inquiry proceeds, with respect to the notion of a "cultural logics" as an alternative to standard linear, binary logic).[2]

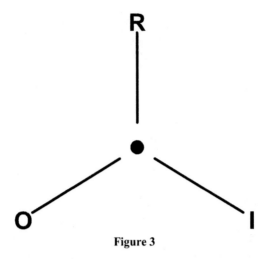

Figure 3

Unfortunately, Figures 2 and 3 as points with three lines in tripod fashion present what might threaten to become a static picture: there is no necessary indication of dynamism, movement, process, fluidity. In order to create the proper image, one must keep in mind that with each and every re-iteration of the sign, the *I* must become another *R* relating to its *O* and engendering its own *I,* which is always already in the process of becoming yet another *R,* and so on. This notion of meaning change or signs becoming signs as a trembling, effervescent, "revolving" image is not simply a circle repeating itself. Rather, an *I* is already in the process of becoming an *R* codependently interrelating with ("revolving about") its own *O* and *I,* the latter in the process becoming another *R,* and so on. All this is like a syncopated, off-balance flow. It is resonant and consonant, but at the same time it is just a little dissonant, asymmetrical, out of whack. The beat has rhythm, to be sure, but it often sort of manages to catch us off guard, for with every turn the semiotic sea within which we are sailing becomes something *other* than what it was.

How can we more properly account for this? The first step, perhaps, entails our becoming more aware of our limitations, finite, fallible human animals that we are.

The Limits of Sensing Signs

All sensed objects, acts, and events are *relative to* a perceptual field, a particular viewpoint, a specific mode of sensing. In other words, not even in the very beginning do we see things as they really are, but, as briefly suggested at the beginning of chapter one, through a culturally-dependent and partly idiosyncratic filter: feeling and sensing are always already interpreting.

Yet what we feel and sense and interpret, we do so before we have become consciously aware *of* our feeling and sensing and interpreting in terms of interrelations between signs. Unlike Funy, in spite of ourselves we abstract, generalize, and establish interrelations. From William James's "blooming, buzzing confusion," we actively select a world that is simple enough for our severely limited cerebral faculties. Yet, unlike Tlöny, our world is always to a greater or lesser degree somehow in tune with the "real," though, in the manner of Lönny, we are often more wrong than right.

We must keep in mind, then, that the senses are already quite educated in terms of what they should do upon our confronting the scintillating, vibrant, dancing ocean of possibilities within the vortex. There is no innocent eye, ear, nose, tongue, hand, or body. What we pick up with the senses is already gauged by particular biologically determined and culture-laden modes of sensing. Once our senses have selected what they are prone to select, we are in a position to see it, hear it, smell it, taste it, or feel it.[3] All this, of course, we noted regarding Columbus and the other "inventors" of America, those stalwart citizens of the world whose "reality" was a construct, whose new home was what they wanted it to be because that is what they had been predisposed to make it.

In order further to qualify this act of constructing a semiotic world, assume we have nothing more before us than a set of twelve straight lines connected at various angles, something like Figure 4. There are in the very least three possibilities open to us. John may tell us: "I see it *as* a hallway." Mary remarks: "I prefer to look at it *as* if it were a truncated pyramid seen from above." George, a geometry student, sees it "*as* quite simply a set of straight lines on a two-dimensional sheet." And they are all correct. There is no hard-core nuts-and-bolts account of how properly to see and identify the drawing. We do not put the visual grist our eyes send to the intellectual mill in our skull where identification and interpretation take place. We do not simply begin with visual sensations and later turn our interpretative capacity loose on it in two separate operations. What we see is what we have selected and constructed *a priori,* and what we have constructed is what we get. Essentially it is all one process.[4] John saw Figure 4 *as* a hallway and Mary saw it *as* a truncated pyramid. What were they thinking of when they saw the "same thing"? They might have been thinking of nothing at all. Or perhaps Mary was thinking of a date she had the previous night and John was thinking about a rapidly approaching exam. Mary might have been in a state of readiness to see pyramids because she is a student of Middle American archeology; John might have been in a state of readiness to see hallways, for he is a dormitory dweller on campus and is used to such sights.

But they certainly didn't have to be thinking about halls and pyramids respectively. At the most primitive level, that of a sort of pre-Firstness, they simply saw the "same thing" (i.e., photons of approximately the same frequency struck their retinas). But at the levels of Firstness in the process of becoming Secondness they didn't see the "same thing," for they took their respective images differently. And at the level of Secondness in the process of becoming Thirdness, different labels were slapped onto the photons received. In other words, it is like the well-known ambiguous "rabbit-duck" drawing. One person sees it *as* a "duck," the other *as* a "rabbit." The Donald Duck enthusiast might tend to see a "duck"; the Bugs Bunny fan might report that it is a "rabbit." They have a disposition for contradictory sightings of a drawing offering itself up as the depiction of two contradictory objects. Yet both of those objects' depiction is by way of two identical drawings—or the same ambiguous drawing, if you will. (Compare this situation to that of Columbus and his crew. They sensed the same visual sign, *salt water,* which was simply taken for what it was believed to be, for that is what they expected, but their gustatory sensations revealed another sign, *fresh water,* which contradicted the previous sign.)

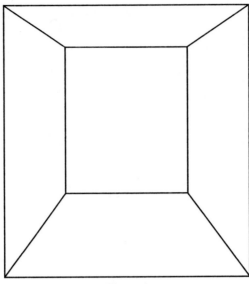

Figure 4

Such seeing *as* is the product of a readiness to see things in a certain way according to a certain set of *expectations*—a waiting for what we think we know will make its appearance *for* us, however wrong we may be, like the characters of our polylogue. Consequently, Figure 4 is seen and it is seen *as* such-and-such. There is not necessarily any willful interpretation going on, no voluntary act of cognition, no contemplation or thinking ("Now, let me see, what can that be? Ah, yes, it's . . . "). No. It is just seen and seen *as* some-*thing* in particular. This seeing is part of an ongoing, interrelated process, from Firstness to Secondness, and on toward Thirdness, from pre-linguistic feeling and sensing and perceiving to linguistic or symbolic conceptual signs. It is not an autonomous act or a set of individual acts. The drawing is seen in a particular manner because the mode of seeing is largely *habituated, sedimented, entrenched,* and *automatized.* It is the end of a long process of habituation ending in a particular style of seeing. During this process, what was once conscious has now become tacit.

For instance, as a child you learned to read with difficulty, translating marks into sounds, combining sounds into words, and doing so out loud before you could engage in the act silently. Now you simply do it, as a matter of course, while leaving your mind free to think about the implications of the words, sentences, and paragraphs that march by. By a comparable process John sees Figure 4 as a hallway, Mary sees it as a truncated pyramid. Each person sees it as s/he sees it because that is the way s/he habitually sees such drawings: to each his/her own. We all have a little bit of Maggie's dreamy Firstness, Tlöny's and Funy's nominalistic Secondness, and Lönny's hypothetico-deductive Thirdness in us, though some of us might like to believe we are a commonsensical combination of Emmy's pragmatic eclecticism and Hladdy's earthy sincerity and respect for authority.

The "object" identified *as* a "hallway," a "pyramid," or a "geometrical figure" was variously sensed in terms of codependent interrelations—two-dimensional or

three-dimensional, protruding inward or extending outward—and it was contextualized, according to particular dispositions to sense certain things in certain ways. In
this manner, Figure 4 is in Peirce's terms *vague:* it is unstable or metastable in terms
of the various possibilities it presents. But from some *habit* or *disposition* to see
things as the result of innate, culturally indoctrinated, or merely idiosyncratic *readiness* governed by a certain set of *expectations,* it is soon stabilized. The vague, unstable feel of Figure 4 is close to what at a more "primitive" level is pre-Firstness:
the scintillating, titillating, vibrating juxtaposition of many possibilities none of
which have been actualized *for* some particular sign maker and taker *as* such-and-
such. At this stage there is no more than the vague sensation, say, of dark connected
straightness on lightness. There is at most only raw seeing, without the emergence of
seeing *as.* The next moment of the process, seeing *as,* requires Secondness, something *other* than the raw image of Firstness as such. Figure 4 is not literally either a
hallway or a pyramid or a geometrical figure; it is seen *as* one of the three possibilities. Such seeing *as* entails the actualization of a sign from the range of possibilities.
As yet, we are at the level of particularities (Seconds), though the entire semiotic
process of feeling, sensing, and seeing *as* to this point is a process. In order to account for the engenderment of generalities within the process of semiosis, we must
consider the Thirdness of Figure 4. One sees it either *as* lines on a plane, a hallway,
or a pyramid, in terms of its particular attributes merging into the general category of
objects possessing those attributes upon its being cognized. According to some general category, one can then potentially see *that* the geometrical figure is of such-and-
such a sort, *that* it consists of twelve lines connected at various angles, *that* its visible portion is four-faced, *that* as a hallway it is seen from somewhere at the left side,
or *that* as a pyramid it is truncated, to mention only a few possibilities of its
cognizability. This seeing *that* constitutes knowledge about geometry, construction
of buildings, principles of archeology, and so on.

So essentially we have (1) *seeing,* (2) relatively naive seeing *as,* and (3) media-
tive seeing *that.* It would be nice if these three modes corresponded clearly and distinctly to the three Peircean categories. But life is never simple. *Seeing* is not the
whole of Firstness, for it emerges from pre-Firstness and merges into seeing *as;* seeing *as* is not simply Secondness, for the *as* of seeing overlaps with the seeing *that* of
Thirdness. At the same time, Thirdness cannot be Thirdness without the inclusion of
Firstness and Secondness in their process of emerging into the daylight of Thirdness.
Moreover, mere consciousness, consciousness *of* something *other,* and self-
consciousness, are themselves process rather than products, becoming rather than
things or essences. So they cannot simply be chopped and packed into any neat classificatory grid. The problem is that when we become conscious *of* Figure 4, it is already in the process of being interpreted. And if and when we become conscious *of*
our self-conscious self *in* the act of interpreting the drawing, we are not conscious *of*
the act in the here and now but *of* the becoming of the act a moment prior to our becoming conscious *of* it.

Hence, seeing, seeing *as,* and seeing *that* are inextricably conjoined. They constitute the filter through which we construe our "semiotic world" of work, study, and
play. They simply cannot be categorically separated. They are process.

Re-Enter Symbols

With regard to the semiosic process, Figure 4 begins its trek toward genuine sign-hood as a lonely icon seen and unrelated to anything else: it is merely the possibility of some interrelation with some *other*. After its iconicity has been made manifest and it is interrelated with, say, pyramids, its contemplator's attention has already (indexically) been drawn toward that something else seen *as* such-and-such. Then, once it has been identified, a (symbolic) label, "pyramid," may be slapped onto it. Now, there is seeing *that* it has certain attributes, and subsequently a string of sentences, "The pyramid is truncated," "has a rectangular ground plan," "is either non-symmetrical or it is viewed from above and to my left," and many other utterances as well, can be engendered. Each predicate joins an icon expressed in symbolic form to the subject or index. However, once again, just as there are no pure icons, indices, or symbols, so also there are no nonfuzzy lines of demarcation separating signs in their process of engenderment. There is no telling precisely at what point in time one sign began to merge into another one. Signs differ in degree, not in kind.

This brings up the question of language, that is, of symbolic signs, signs of the most developed sort according to Peirce. Seeing and seeing *as* are chiefly of iconic and indexical processes, while symbolicity is by and large like the operation of "seeing *that*"—though, to repeat, there are no distinct lines of demarcation here. The next step after "seeing *that*" something is so-and-so is to try to say it is so. However, the saying invariably remains *incomplete*—when it is not thoroughly inadequate—and *inconsistency* never ceases to threaten. For example, a physicist cannot effectively say what it is she sees and does in her laboratory with a few solitary sentences. Her activity entails a ponderous load of semiotic baggage that a layperson could not hope to unpack, try as our physicist may to explain it. What she sees and says and does would even tax the prepared mind at the outset. In this regard, assume she decides to take on a new lab assistant. First, she must construct an entire text and a context for him, and then he must work with her in the laboratory for some time before he can really be in tune with what she sees and says and does. Once he has been properly indoctrinated, however, there is no longer any need for preliminary discussions and exemplary moves. Each morning they can roll up their sleeves and get to work, with relatively few linguistic preliminaries. In other words, they see the laboratory apparatus *as* such-and-such and they tacitly see and know *that* it is to be used in such-and-such a way.

They can now properly play the "language game" of physics, seeing what they see, doing what they do, and saying what they say according to proper scientific habits of thought and of practice, while taking everything else in as a matter of course. They don't need to see and say "meter," but brush their perception of the instrument as an object aside and simply take a reading. The meter has an obvious meaning for them, but it presents itself as an unnoticed background. It is what is left virtually unseen and unsaid as such. Yet it is pregnant with meaning. Consequently, it would appear to a newly arrived layperson that the two scientists know more than they are actually saying to each other. That is, they are telling each other *that* such-and-such is the case, but to the novice it could be so much Greek. He can see what they see, but he is incapable of seeing *as* and seeing *that* in the same way they do. So he asks them what they are doing. Problems arise. How can they completely and consistently explain their activity, which required twenty or more years of schooling and countless hours in the laboratory? The mind-numbing conglomerate of all the signs involved in these years of experience is condensed to a drop which is *tacitly* implied in their every move. How can they describe this "drop" of semiosis unless they guide the novice in their midst through a long set of semiotic experiences? They can't, at least they can't in any completely adequate way.[5]

Take our Borgesean polylogue, for example. All the characters garnered certain expectations that Averroës would soon make his appearance, and they held a *tacit*— albeit exceedingly vague—image with respect to the nature of Averroës as a sign. When he arrived, he evinced a rather unexpected countenance. Consequently, Hladdy saw and said one Averroës, Emmy saw and said another one, for Maggie Averroës was someone else altogether, for Tlöny yet another strange being had entered the scene, and so on. Averroës was just Averroës, but he was seen, seen *as,* seen *that,* and said in diverse ways. Actually, the concoction of characters in this absurd drama comes from distinct cultures—that is, different Borges stories. So we wouldn't expect all parties involved to see and say things in the same way. In fact, the worlds they saw and said were worlds they had felt, imagined, invented, fabricated. They all lived in distinct worlds. These worlds were felt and sensed and interpreted before they were said, and when they were said the saying could not help but remain hopelessly *incomplete* and/or *inconsistent* in regard to other possible sayings. Of course, the polylogue presented textually as mere black marks on white is capable of providing little information regarding nonverbal cues and clues that accompanied the words. That is both the bane and the beauty of texts. The text, however, illustrates an important point: the characters actually *knew more than they were saying and could have said,* which is characteristic of most "seeing" when coupled with "seeing *as*" and "seeing *that.*" Consequently, they talked past each other.

What We Feel and Know and What We Can Say about It

They talked past each other because, in light of Peirce's concept of Firstness, all knowing, whether mathematical or logical, scientific or artistic, and even our knowing of the coming and going of everyday life, relies to a greater or lesser extent on personal confidence and behavioral traits, and skill and judgment: *tacit knowing.*

Consider the relatively simple case of learning to drive a car. The student in driver training class tries to assimilate the verbal instructions given her by her instructor, plus a host of visual examples put forth. But to hardly any avail. She remains inordinately clumsy the first time she finds herself behind the wheel. She must concentrate intensely on almost every move in serial fashion. The task is excruciating, and after many mistakes, she ends in a sweat. With practice, however, her driving skills gradually become second nature to her. She learns to "chunk" them into larger and larger wholes, until finally, the entire activity becomes more or less tacit, habituated, automatized. She can now drive almost "without thinking." Since she no longer need be consciously aware *of* many of her moves, having conveniently internalized them as part of her everyday activities, they become merely another movement in the ongoing symphony of her everyday living. While driving, she can now concentrate on a conversation with a friend at her side, the news report on the radio, a dinner engagement she will have with a client that evening, or whatever. It might be said that she is now "inside" her driving: it has become *habit*. She is now able to perform her driving act in a rather thoughtless, quasi-mechanical way, *habit* having relieved her of the necessity of thinking through each step.

In other words, our experienced driver has "chunked" individual signs into conglomerate (iconic) wholes that are taken virtually in automaton fashion. Instead of thinking "I'm going x miles per hour, so I should release the gas feed, push in on the clutch, and shift into y gear," it is simply done. Bodymind does it, with no further ado.[6] The signs were all there, and the desired outcome was brought to fruition, but each and every one of the signs was not consciously and intentionally carried out to its well-reasoned, cognitive end. Rather, they were all interpreted in terms of resemblance between this context now and numerous comparable contexts in the past, as if the relation were purely iconic, instead of indexical and symbolic. There is no language (symbolicity) explicitly taking place, nor are there any natural or cause-effect relations (indexicality), but merely "chunked" (iconic) signs and responses in terms of the signs' interrelations with comparable signs of the past. Her knowing how to drive has become tacit knowing.

With respect to tacit knowing, chemist and philosopher Michael Polanyi (1958) toiled for years with the idea that all of us, from the most humble human specimen behind the wheel of a car to Einstein, handle the affairs of our everyday living on the basis of two different kinds of awareness: *focal* and *subsidiary*. If you grab a hammer and nail to pound in the wall for a picture-hanging ceremony, you begin by holding the nail in one hand, trying to hit it with the hammer held in the other hand, and hoping to miss your thumb. In the process, you attend to both the hammer and the nail, but not in the same way. On the one hand, you maintain eye contact with the (indexical) effect of your strokes on the nail as you wield your hammer. You don't so much feel that the handle of the tool has struck the palm of your hand as you feel that the hammer has struck the head of the nail. On the other hand, you are alert to the (iconic) sign-feelings in your palm, your fingers and thumb on the nail, and your strokes, while striving to coordinate your actions.

In Polanyi's terms, you are *subsidiarily* (tacitly, iconically) aware of the whole of your activity, which gives you a rather vague feel, in conjunction with your eye contact *focally* (indexically) directed toward the nail's head. The vague feel is not watched directly but indirectly; the directed attention is in contrast quite precise. In another way of putting it, you focus your attention on the nail's head, but at the same time you are aware of the whole of your moves. Your general awareness of both of these processes is not directly perceived, though you rely on it in regard to your movements culminating in hitting the nail with your hammer. You possess *subsidiary awareness* of the whole of your movement and *focal awareness* of actually driving the nail into the wall. In fact, your activity proceeds *from* subsidiary awareness *to* focal awareness. In this *from-to* relationship, the latter is quite fully conscious, while the former can exist at various degrees of consciousness. Your general feeling is that of a whole taken in tacit, nonconscious, iconic fashion. Your direct attention is conscious, attuned specifically to the hammer-sign brought down with force on the nail-sign. If the nail-sign becomes slightly bent, you adjust the force and direction of your blow with the hammer-sign in order to correct the entry of the nail-sign into the drywall, which is another sign in contiguous relation with the nail-sign and hammer-sign. Your *focal* attention compels you to adjust your moves so as to coordinate them with your *subsidiary* feel for the general activity. You operate at conscious (indexical and iconic) levels as well as nonconscious (iconic) levels.

All this while, you are in charge of integrating Firstness and Secondness, and of engendering interpretants and Thirdness, for the iconic and indexical signs with which you are in *focal* and *subsidiary* contact. Your *subsidiary awareness* is chiefly iconic in nature, while your *focal awareness* is chiefly indexical, the first pertaining to Firstness and the second to Secondness. And, as a sign maker and taker, you contribute a necessary ingredient of Thirdness. If, after hanging your painting, your room comes more or less in line with your initial *image* of the final product, then you have brought about a reconstruction of a portion of your "semiotic world." Your room as a sign has come to mediate between the general *image* (icon, Firstness) and each and every particular act (index, Secondness) bringing about the approximate realization of that *image* in such a way that the finished product (symbol, Thirdness, particularly when put into words) is related to the *image* and the acts in the same way that the *image* and acts are related to themselves and to the product. In other words, like Figure 2, Firstness, Secondness, and Thirdness, and the Firsts, Seconds, and Thirds of Representamens, Objects, and Interpretants, are all clasped in a flowing hug, which includes your-*self,* your-*self* as a sign among signs.

However, the tale cannot be told quite so simply. In addition to Thirdness, I must more effectively include symbols (the linguistic function) in your hammer-and-nail activity properly to complete the sign triad, for symbols can be much more than vague feels and focal perceptual grasps. While you were pounding the nail in the wall you remained *subsidiarily* aware of your surroundings while maintaining *focal* awareness on your task. If, while in the act, someone entered the room and asked you what you were up to while standing on a chair in your living room, you might have said: "I'm hanging a painting." Well, you definitely were not hanging a painting at that moment; you were doing no more than driving a nail into the wall. The notion of hanging a painting involved your initial *image,* the task at hand, and what you expected to be the final product, all of which was *tacitly* acknowledged. You had a general model (icon) of the whole of your activity, and at the particular moment the question was asked you happened to be in the act of penetrating the drywall before you with a nail, and that's that. However, saying "I'm hanging a painting" would be most likely understood by the person having newly arrived on the scene, for the two of you share picture-hanging "language games." You know a nail and a hammer are necessary tools, and that after a certain set of activities there should be a nail-head protruding from a wall at a certain height in order to hang a painting. Your utterance is made against the background of a general conceptual scheme. (Compare this situation to the characters of our polylogue talking past each other; they hardly shared any "language games," they were from radically different cultures, they lived in other worlds in other times and other places.)

Knowing, with respect to whatever activity, is in this sense largely *tacit.* It entails a feeling, a sense, an implicit ability, for being aware of what is going on. And though some of this knowing can be made explicit in the form of language, much of it cannot. The wine-taster's taste buds, the jazz musician's finely tuned ear, the art dealer's visual clues, the cloth merchant's feel for exquisite fabric, the chef's keen sense of aromas, all these forms of expert knowledge are acquired in part from textbooks. Books and lecture hall note-taking were of little use to these experts when they were apprentices without the accompanying training of the tongue, ear, eye, nose, and hand. Only by tuning in on a wave length comparable to that of the masters' serving as examples, and by countless hours of practice getting the right hang of things, could they become adept at their profession. By such practice an expert acquires a sort of "sixth sense" enabling him to see what the novice or layperson cannot see. And she now apparently goes through his act with little effort. It has become second nature to her. There is little language here. In fact, if she were asked to explain precisely how she differentiates between good wine and poor wine, she would mention a few principles, then stutter and fumble around. She would be somewhat at a loss for words, for *she knows more than she can explicitly tell.* What she does when she tastes wine is part of her *tacit knowing.* The same applies to hanging a painting, or driving a car. In all cases, signs have been "chunked," conglomerated, such that they are made and taken as wholes (icons).

Signs, and their makers and takers, have become entangled within these conglomerates, and neither Firstness nor Secondness nor Thirdness can be effectively disentangled. They are by nature, and by their very function, interrelated; in fact, they are mutually interpenetrating, they codependently emerge. The point of all this is that, with regard to Figures 2 and 3, just as I went through the motions of discussing nonverbal icons and indices leading up to their incorporation into symbols, so also symbols themselves, acting out their role alongside icons and indices, can culminate in compound clusters of signs made and taken tacitly. The interpretants of these signs depend upon *subsidiary* as well as *focal* awareness, iconicity as well as indexicality, Firstness as well as Secondness, and feeling as well as sensing, in addition to cognition and Thirdness. The wine taster, jazz musician, and so on, get a feel for what they do through relatively nonformalized and nonarticulated channels as tacit knowing. But when called upon to verbalize what they do, they can do so only to a greater or lesser extent. Such verbalization can go only so far, because *they always know more than they can tell.* A portion of their knowledge will always remain at the levels of Firstness and Secondness, unmediated and unmediable by Thirdness.

In an attempt more adequately to qualify this nature of semiosis, let us take a more prolonged tour through the Latin American scene, especially regarding the process within which the "havenots" are engaged in their eternal interaction with the "haves."

Notes

1.   As I mentioned in passing above, the terms "sign" and "representamen" are often used interchangeably, though they are not the same. All the components of a sign (representamen, object, and interpretant), are, or can become, themselves signs in their own right. Consequently, what within one context is construed to be an object or an interpretant, in another context could be another representamen, and vice versa.

This semiotic activity forms the makings of what in the previous chapter I dubbed "methodological realism," that is, a pragmatic sort of realism that is the product of the entire community.

2. I should mention at this juncture that my conception of these alternative "logics" comes from various directions, in particular, Melhuish's (1967) "paradoxical nature of the world," Lupasco's (1947) "logic of contradiction," Brazilian logician Newton da Costa's (1974) "paraconsistent logic," Rescher and Brandom's (1979) "logic of inconsistency," "fuzzy logic" (Kosko 1993, Zadeh 1965, 1975), fractals, chaos theory, and the physics of complexity (Stewart 1989, Stewart and Golubitshy 1992), "quantum logic" (Putnam 1976, 1985; for more technical, Gibbins 1987, Redhead 1987, also Plotnitsky 1994), what I sense as the implications of the "limitative theorems" for formal systems of Gödel, Alfred Tarski, Alan Turing, Emil Post, Alonzo Church, and others (DeLong 1970), and above all, Peirce's pioneer but unfinished work on the "logic of vagueness" (Black 1937, Dozoretz 1979, Engel-Tiercelin 1992, merrell 1996, 1997, 1998a, 1998b, Nadin 1982, 1983).

3. Given the complexity of the problem of perception, and for economy of exposition, I will allude most often to sensing as "seeing." I have no particular bias against the other modes of sensing. It is simply that what the eye does is perhaps most easily discussed—though that point is debatable—and it is easiest to illustrate graphically.

4. Regarding the following paragraphs, I owe a massive debt to the work of Norwood Hanson (1958, 1969)

5. For an excellent example of this process, see Duhem (1954); for my own discussion of Duhem's importance to the general *semiosic* process, see merrell (1995b, 1997).

6. The term "bodymind," used frequently in this inquiry, follows the anti-Cartesian nondualist notion according to which (1) no sign is exclusively of the body or the mind; all signs are a flow of *interdependent, interrelated interactive* bodymind processes, and (2) bodymind processes are semiotic processes through and through; all communication is a matter of feeling and emotion as well as experience or perception and thought or conception; it is extralinguistic and nonverbal as well as linguistic. As Peirce himself puts it: "It is not a historical fact that the best thinking has been done by words, or aural images. It has been performed by means of visual images and muscular imaginations" (*NEM* 4.375).

Chapter Three

The Hedgehog Above, The Fox Below

> A bilingual writer is really two *different* writers, has two very different voices, writes in two different styles, and most important, looks at the world through two different sets of glasses. This takes a splitting of the self that doesn't come easily and can be dangerous.
>
> —Rosario Ferré

> [T]his gap between movement and word is what separates one culture from another. And that is the only border that concerns me personally. Geographical borders are by nature artificial.
>
> —Ilán Stavans

What They Don't See Can Harm Them

James Scott (1990) writes of "hidden transcripts." Such occult, silent, tacitly acknowledged informal "documents" are relevant, I would submit, with respect to the struggle in Latin America and other developing regions between the "haves" and the "havenots," those who dwell in the *inner sancta* of hegemony and those who cannot, the dominant and the subordinate, those who dictate the nature of their cultural signs' interpretants and those who do not. (That is to say, "hidden transcripts" are relevant, if we render them extralinguistic in addition to Scott's exclusively textualist interpretation of them.)

A "hidden transcript" is a text (presumably symbolicity, Thirdness) prescribing conduct on the part of the havenots. However, the text does not function at the level of genuine Peircean symbolicity as I described it in chapter two. For, during the coming and going of everyday activities, the text ordinarily rests at the level of subsidiary (iconic) attention (of Firstness). It is the motivator of tacit feeling, sensing, and knowing and saying; it allows for things to be done because that is the way they are customarily done in the give-and-take (chiefly of Secondness) of daily life. Making and taking signs of the hidden transcript comes naturally, so to speak. That is why the transcript is hidden. Using this hidden text or guide, subordinate groups, by subtle subversive acts, can get their digs in at the haves. Yet the text remains occult insofar as the official channels of communication go. That is, in the presence of the haves, the text is latently concealed within the minds of the havenots, and when the haves take their leave, the text is put to use, and the havenots can occasionally have the final say.

A hidden transcript, we are told, "represents a critique of power spoken behind the back of the dominant. The powerful, for their part, also develop a hidden transcript representing the practices and claims of their rule that cannot be openly avowed. A comparison of the hidden transcript of the weak with that of the powerful and of *both* hidden transcripts to the public transcript of power relations offers a substantially new way of understanding resistance to domination" (Scott 1990:xii). Through studies of George Eliot, George Orwell, and by a critique of orthodox Marxism, especially regarding the theory of "false consciousness," Scott embarks on a disquisition concerning the process of domination by the hegemonic power-bloc that develops a code of public conduct dictating what can and what cannot be said. At the same time, he explores the means by which the powerless use their hidden transcripts in the form of gossip, rumors, folktales, songs, gestures, jokes, theater, rituals, festivals, and carnivals, to subvert the means, the methods, and the ends of the powerful.

The havenots, by exploiting the hidden transcript, ingratiate themselves with their superiors while giving a sly wink to their peers, and then they clandestinely take measures partly to sabotage the works they are presumably carrying out in collaboration with those same superiors. This practice is not limited to any subordinate group, but is the general *modus operandi* in all cultures and at all times. Indeed, we read that rarely can we "speak of an individual slave, untouchable, serf, peasant, or worker, let alone groups of them, as being either entirely submissive or entirely insubordinate. Under what conditions, however, do veiled ideological opposition and unobstructive material resistance dare to venture forth and speak their name openly? Conversely, how is open resistance forced into increasingly furtive and clandestine expression?" (Scott 1990:192). Scott goes on to write that the most genuine metaphor for expressing this practice is that of "cultural guerrilla warfare."[1] In the best of scenarios, there is an understanding on the part of the superordinate powermongers—who are actually not as dominant as they would like to be or as they think they are—and the subordinate "cultural guerrillas." The first are plodding hedgehogs, the second nimble foxes. The first know only brute lumbering and often blundering force. They consist of bureaucratic bodies that move with the viscosity of cold molasses and of indecisive leaders who operate in constant fear of reprisals or replacement by others aggressively seeking promotion. The second inhabit that no-man's-land and engage in the equivalent of fakes, false moves, intentionally feeble attacks in order to provoke the enemy, probings to uncover weaknesses, and advances and retreats whenever they are propitious. "Cultural guerrilla" advances become increasingly assertive, except when they are met with an overpowering riposte. These "guerrilla" moves in actual practice come in the order of "poaching," a breaching of verbal hand-shake agreements, steady encroachments of land holdings, a little pilfering here and there, some verbal nuances when it is safe, and tax evasions whenever one can get away with it.[2] The limits are constantly tested in order to ascertain precisely how far one can go. The powerful try to keep on their toes, but aside from their obvious dominance regarding economic and political might, they are no match for their sprightly antagonists.

In light of the preceding chapter, and with respect to the Latin American condition, I would deem Scott quite on track. But with some reservations. The first problem is that language, and with it binarism, is prioritized in the hidden transcript concept—so, what else is new? I would suggest that Scott prioritizes language in his creation of the metaphor and the superordinate groups to which he alludes fall into the same "linguicentric" trap. Consequently, the hidden transcript is for them a means of control by the discursive power invested in them. The second problem is that the signs of the hidden transcript, as a result of this "linguicentrism," tend to be taken as relatively fixed and intransient. What actually takes place is something quite the contrary, thanks to the subordinates' creative and often disruptive activities: all signs, linguistic and otherwise, are made to be unmade, and they are taken only insofar as they can to a greater or lesser degree be mistaken and remade into other signs along the semiosic stream of signs becoming signs, as we noted in chapter two. The nimble seditious activities in the part of the subordinates implies, in addition to language, the use of nods, winks, grimaces, catcalls, whistles, and gestures with the arms and legs and shoulders and head and torso, and feigned anger and surprise and laughter and gaiety and rebellion according to what the context calls for. All this entails semiosis, process. Nothing is of permanent nature.

In short, the hidden transcript of the subordinate groups actually implies the entire gamut of signs, nonverbal as well as verbal, and iconic and indexical as well as symbolic, to a considerably greater degree than are found in the communication channels of superordinate groups.[3] Since a transcript is by and large implicit rather than explicit, it is chiefly of the sphere of Firstness. When a transcript is partly realized, it enters the sphere of extralinguistic action and reaction proper to Secondness. And when the practice of Secondness enters consciousness and interpretations and meanings emerge, Thirdness exercises its mediating role, and the semiotic triad is well on its way toward taking on the character of a full-blown linguistic sign. Thus the spheres of Firstness, Secondness, and Thirdness are one thing for the haves, but they are something else altogether for the havenots. In fact, differences between their perception and conception of the semiosic process within which they find themselves may be as great as that between salt water and fresh water, or between Tlöny, the inveterate hyperidealist, and Funy, the helpless and hopeless supernominalist. Tlöny and Funy simply stand no chance of seeing things eye to eye. They are on opposite sides of an unbreachable communication gap. Funy concretely sees everything there is for the moment and nothing but the moment, while Tlöny abstracts from all concrete seeing in order to make of his world what should be the case according to his elaborate preconceptions.

But . . . no . . . wait a minute. This would be the same as saying that the relation between the haves and the havenots is hardly more than dualistic, binary, oppositional, the product of something and something else that contradicts the first something. How can genuine triadicity be brought into this picture? We must look further, to the broad historical context that makes up Latin America.

Playing It by Ear, Then

Triadicity with respect to the Latin American scene is a question of the social conditions of Spain and Portugal before the conquest, and of European interrelations with Amerindians and with African Americans and interrelations between all of them and the future *mestizos* and *mulatos*.[4] In the first place, recent historiography no longer weeps torrents of crocodile tears over the so-called "black legend" and how it was used by the English and others to defame Spain and how Spain and the Spaniards were not quite as devilish as their billing had them. Light is now shed on Amerindian and African Americans' subversive activities rather than their suffering and passive, stoic subservience. As a result, the so-called subordinates are viewed as more lively and engaging in clandestine activities of rebellion and at times openly kicking against the pricks than was previously suspected.

Actually, when brushing the "black legend" aside and taking a good look at the Iberian Peninsula at the time of the conquest, it becomes quite clear that it did not genuinely sport that conspicuous medieval feature of the classic manorial "estate" with a landed gentry surrounded by presumably loyal serfs to the same degree that could be found in the rest of Europe. If this was so of the Peninsula, it was even more so of the colonies. During the conquest, subsidies or pecuniary assistance was granted to the King by many of the conquerors, especially from Spain, and their reward was in the form of land grants (*encomiendas* in the Spanish colonies, *capitanias* in the Portuguese colony).[5] Consequently there was hardly any King-Kingdom/colonies dualism in the order of the King-Kingdom/serfdom dualism and antagonism characteristic of Europe during the medieval era. The colonial powers, especially Spain, had much of pre-modern corporate character. Independently defined privileges and jurisdictions existed in hierarchical fashion, from the Spaniards (or *peninsulares,* as I will hereafter call them in reference to Spaniards born in Spain and residing in the colonies) downward to the *criollos* (Spaniards born in America), and then to the Amerindians, *mestizos, mulatos,* and African Americans.[6] This is a most important point. A manorial system customarily implies a common culture between lord and serfs and a traditional regime of mutual obligations. In Latin America this was not the case. There, the equivalent of European serfs were of *other* ethnicities and *other* cultures: they were literally and figuratively *other,* and there was hardly any commonality between the one and the *other*—somewhat, we might imagine, like the characters of our Borgesian dramatic absurdity, the polylogue.

Consequently in the Americas there was a pluralistic, though compartmentalized, society, with paternalistic lines of administration and human codependent interrelations. As a result, feudalism never really developed in the colonies. Rather, there was a relatively high degree of liberty and freedom of movement within the quasi-corporate system. Few colonists were bound to the soil, and society had a fluidity that saw little need of the surf's ties with their respective nobles; hence the common people's loyalty was more directly aligned with the king. For this reason, during later years, there was no massive creation of a conservative bourgeoisie in the order of Europe outside the Peninsula (Morse 1989:95–100). In other words, what we have consists of fundamentally the same types of signs in the colonies and in Europe regarding monarchical administration. But there are different interpretants, and hence differently perceived and conceived semiotic objects. What in Europe was one thing (a drawing as a "Rabbit"; the Earth as "center of the universe") in the Americas was something else entirely (a drawing as a "Duck"; the Sun as "center of the universe").

Since the *encomiendas* in the Spanish colonies and to an extent the *capitanias* in the Portuguese colony and the allocations of Amerindian labor that came along with them was quite unlike the medieval European manorial system, it is dubbed by

Mario Góngora (1951:183) "patrimonialism" rather than "feudalism." Or perhaps even more adequately stated, it was a "corporate patrimonialism" (Morse 1989:100). The conquerors, in addition to their desire for land in order to attain the coveted status as *hidalgos* (sons of someone of high social status), were bearers of royal authority. The state was considered a conglomeration of lands, tributes, grants, and honors belonging to the royal patrimony. That is, the conquerors themselves represented royal patrimony, since they had made the fruits of the conquest available to the crown. In this manner they became much of an extension of the crown itself. Not only that, but since the Church was in their eyes universal, it was conceived to have spread an umbrella over Spain and Portugal and the colonies alike.[7] Consequently, the colonies were not colonies in the Northern European sense. They were an ecclesiastical, royal, and territorial extension of the Peninsula. The colonies were more properly an "incorporation" into the crown as a "corporate body," all of which was a forerunner of the modern "corporate state." What we have, then, is different signs for different interpretants, as things should be (Morse 1989:100–01).

So the Peninsula was *both* medieval *and* it was not medieval, corporate *and* not corporate. The colonies were colonies, to be sure, but they were not exactly colonies *either* in the medieval *or* the corporate sense, and at the same time they were part of Spain and Portugal and yet something *other*. They remained at the periphery, close to the border, the border of borders: *neither* the one *nor* the other (as incomplete colonies within the sphere of Thirdness), yet *both* the one *and* the other (as inconsistent when viewed within the sphere of Firstness). That is to say, whether we take the same signs and slap different interpretants on them or change the signs so they might enjoy a better fit with their interpretants, the same semiosic flow inheres: the interpretants can be perceived and conceived as *both* one thing *and* another, or as *neither* one thing *nor* another, depending upon the inventive mind of the beholder, be she comparable to the likes of a Tlöny or a Funy or a Maggie or an Emmy or a Lönny or whomever.

Thus we have an *incongruous complementarity* within the trials and travails that abounded in America. Yes, America: fabricated rather than merely found, invented and hypothesized rather than simply seen. The Latin American condition during the colonial period was not merely a matter of powerful and powerless, exploiters and exploited, masters and slaves (in the sense of binary Secondness), but rather, a mediated "third term" (of the nature of Thirdness) was always there, often latent in a nonverbal sort of "hidden (albeit chiefly extralinguistic) transcript." In fact, there were many "third terms," occasionally raising their mocking, taunting faces. These "third terms," emerging from the ashes of conquest and devastation, were *neither* conquerer *nor* conquered, *neither* hegemonic *nor* subaltern, but something else that provided the semiosic flux keeping the entire socio-politico-economic system in motion. The "third terms" perpetually brought to light that virtually infinite range of possibilities for action and reaction to be found between the two horns of the set of dichotomies invented for this new cultural mix from above. Consequently, there was movement, flow, a vibrant dance of life, arising from that codepedent, interrelated, interactive precondition that makes all biological communities what they are, especially those of human qualities. In another manner of putting it, the American colonies were always in a process of becoming a pluralistic flux, an incessant exchange and interchange between subsidiary (tacit) and focal signs of public and private activities and of formal affairs and everyday life. That's the way it was, because that's the way it had been invented, constructed, fashioned.

Nevertheless, some observers continue to reduce the trajectory of Latin American cultures and civilizations to a dualistic *either/or* affair, a sort of Augustinian City of God and City of Man, Abel and Cain, Jerusalem and Babylon, a world of private dreams appropriate to the saints and the dog-eat-dog world of public life, and above all, civilization and barbarism.[8] A comparable form of dualistic thinking applies to male-female interrelations. Scholars often conceive of the male species generally gravitating toward the *macho* practices of public life. In contrast, the women usually, but not always, found comfort in their *mariana* role in the saintly image of the Mother of Christ, and at the same time they were compelled to act as mere passive repositories of the male's sexual fantasies and carnal urges. Yet the male evinced a tendency toward "dualistic man," in the somewhat sexist conception of Glen Caudill Dealy (1992). This characteristic is the product of a specifically peninsular Christian dualism that exacted the patriarchal and morally outstanding family man image in the home, but with license to engage in immoral practices outside the home and in the streets. While Protestant capitalism in its most stringent form demanded a righteous life both in the home and in public life—recent inquests regarding the immoral practices of our public servants testify to this—the Latin American male according to the dualist interpretation could live quite at peace with the contradiction between his self-serving public life and the moral principles that bound him to his family and his intimate circle of friends.

The split between private and public domains, saintly composure in the home and street-wise roguish conduct outside, the City of God image in conflict with the City of Man image, might lead to the assumption that the notorious maxim of the Spanish colonial period, "Obedezco pero no cumplo" ("I obey but I do not concord or comply, or, I pay homage and lip service to God, King, and Spain, but the sordid affairs of everyday life call for other, more practical measures"), is basically a binary affair. "I obey" brings along the baggage of the City of God image. "I do not comply" puts one in the cut-throat, in-your-face, City of Man environment. As we shall see in the following sections, however, things are not so simple. There is no genuine dualism in a socio-cultural milieu of multiplicity, pluralism, hybridity, nonlinear and asymmetrical hierarchization. Between *either/ors* of private life and public life, the home and the street, there is the *both-and* and the *neither-nor* offering an uncountable concoction of alternative responses many of which are forthcoming in daily practices whenever and wherever.[9] Consequently, interrelations inherent in the triadic concept of the sign engulf customary polarities (colonizer/colonized, lord/serf, private/public, home/street) with a "third term" lurking behind the scene at any moment willing and ready to make its appearance and disrupt the action, whether to a minimal or devastating degree. *Both* the one horn *and* the other horn of the oppositions used to account for the Latin American cultural scene are essential, for sure. Yet, *neither* the one *nor* the other can be absolutely prioritized. In the first place, the one term of the presumed binary needs the other one—they are codependent—and in the second place, a "third term," in fact many "alternative terms," can at any given point make their presence felt either explicitly or implicitly.[10]

This process is the case also of general sign processes. The representamen is what the semiotic object is not, but it enters into relation with the object through mediation of the interpretant in such a way that it becomes *incongruously complementary* with it. That is to say, both object and representamen *are* what the interpretant *is not;* yet they are complementary with it. At the same time they complementarily depend upon one another and emerge solely in response to this codependence. This is the case, because the three sign parts are to an extent interchangeable, as they perpetually emerge and resubmerge in the actions and consciousness of their respective collaborators, their semiotic subjects. So, as I suggested in the antecedent chapter, there is no Representamen/Object, Representamen/Interpretant, or Object/Interpretant dichotomy. Rather, each pair of the three terms are in interrelation with one another solely by the grace of an always present yet occasional subtly concealed "third term" (according to Figure 3). As a consequence of this interrelated interaction, every term, within the sphere of Thirdness where the condition exists for signs to take on a countenance that might previously have been alien to them, is *neither* exclusively the one thing *nor* the other. This is because all terms are always becoming something other than what they were in the process of becoming.

Moreover, since any of the three terms possesses, within itself, the possibility for becoming one of the other terms at another point down the semiosic stream, all three sign components are in a manner of speaking, and from the sphere of pre-Firstness that gives way to Firstness, *both* one thing *and* the other and at the same time *neither* one thing *nor* the other. The codependently interrelated sign and participatory interaction I allude to is not simply a matter of signs consciously and willingly made and taken. It also includes signs of tacitness, signs whose interpretants take on a subsidiary role while other signs rest within the central focus of attention.[11]

Dancing to a Different Tune

This character of semiosis with regard to the Latin American mind and heart during the colonial period and thereafter can be sensed in a lingering Thomist strain as outlined by the baroque scholastic, Francisco Suárez (1982). It is not so much that Suárez's philosophy was evoked, tacitly acknowledged, or even patterned in the everyday affairs of Latin America prior to and following the independence movement. It is a matter of the Spanish intellectual's synthesis striking a responsive chord in the sentiments and thought of peninsular people that continues to the present. We read from Richard Morse that:

> Although one can point to instances when Suárez was invoked at the start of the Spanish American independence wars, his significance for the subsequent history of the new nations does not depend on whether or not he provided a pre-Enlightenment precedent for contract theory and popular sovereignty. It lies, rather, in the fact that his fresh marshaling of Scholastic doctrines, in response to imperatives of time and place, encapsulated assumptions about political man and his dilemmas that survive in Spanish America to this day. (Morse 1989:102)[12]

Suárez's philosophy includes a distinction between natural law and the conscience of the people. Natural law is what it is. The people are fallible and often mistaken. But they can alter their course of action in order to get on track again insofar as that may be possible. Sovereign power originates in the people. They do not exactly delegate this power to their leader. Rather, the leader takes power on consignment with the understanding that she will pay it due respect. If she does not, the will of the people might take back what they believe is rightfully theirs. Consequently, she will find herself out of the picture. In this sense the leader is subordinate to the people, by the people's choice, and at the same time the people are at least provisionally subordinate to her. Once again, it is a *neither-nor* affair of heart and mind, of nature and culture, and it is a *both-and* affair when considering the myriad set of cultural possibilities of semiosis.

This is a crucial point. Latin America's problems of political development have been commonly ascribed to inadequate collective maturity or deficient schooling in the ways of Western democracy. The result has often been viewed as impoverished and unstable social conditions pervaded by an authoritarian ruler/ruled mentality, which pretty much falls in line with Dealy's "dualistic man" syndrome. However, more in tune with the Latin American psyche is the idea that Suárez's thought is symptomatic of a sixteenth-century concept of interactive, interrelated, codependent negotiation between individual, society, and government that has not quite been superseded in today's Latin America.[13] This is not foolproof evidence that Latin America is "underdeveloped" or "developing," because their dichotomies have not properly entered into a "disenchantment with the world" stage such that the capitalist-materialist incentives could play a role. No. It suggests that the continent has taken another, alternative route. The Latin Americans have not become entirely disenchanted with their world; yet they have partially embraced so-called modern practices. They continue to sport a few pre-Hispanic, medieval, and especially baroque signs; yet throughout history they have also to a degree embraced enlightenment thought, positivist philosophy, Marxist doctrine, dependency theory, modernization methods of import substitution, and more recently "neoliberal" policies, throughout their national period.

The "cultural logic" of Latin America, then, whatever it may be, is not simply a question of *types*—Medieval, Renaissance, Baroque, Augustinian, Thomistic, democratic, authoritarian, privatized, and so on. The instability that ensued after the colonial period cannot be explained away by the fact that, unlike genuine Western societies, they simply didn't have what it takes, and if they had had it, things would have been more Western. Typologies do not impart "logics" to socio-politico-economic and historical conditions. They may, however, reveal logics that have spontaneously emerged through human interrelated interdependency and interaction. This emergence throws pure types into disarray, and variants and transitions reveal tendencies that are sophisticated in their complexity and subtle in their manifestation. Alternate cultural logics never cease in their effort to subvert the "logical types" of standard intellectual practices. Subverting logical types is a violation of philosopher Bertrand Russell's recipe for proper thinking, of course. Russell tells us that a man is not tantamount to the class of all men, a map is not the same as the territory it maps, a university is not equal to a cluster of buildings. These particulars and generalities are of different logical types, and should not be mixed. If one takes a single African American's despicable behavior as characteristic of his entire ethnic group, if one clenches one's fists when viewing the photograph of a Ku Klux Klan rally, if one places a bomb in the Humanities Library because one received an "F" in analytical chemistry, all these acts in a certain manner of speaking, confuse "logical types."

However, in the pragmatics of everyday communication, this is the way we often think and act, in accord with our cultural "cultural logics." Whether we know it or not and whether we like it or not, we often play havoc with Russell's demand that we keep classes of things in their proper place and according to "logical typing," and we usually manage to get along in life. As a matter of fact, general statements the likes of "All complete sentences must sport at least one subject," "Latin America is a third world subcontinent," and even "All swans are white," should be prohibited if we were to take Russell's theory in its most stringent form: they consist of particular sentences that address themselves to presumed universals. There is, of course, no iron-clad guarantee that the universals entailed in these and other such sentences will stand the test of time, and there is always the possibility that at the next bend in the stream some of them will be up for alteration. Yet we could hardly engage in meaningful dialogue without using words alluding to universals as if they were valid for all time. That is the beauty and the bestiality of articulate mammals' ways of communicating (see Bateson 1972).

This variation and creation of differences regarding erstwhile generalities taken as "reality" is nowhere more evident than in the Baroque period in the Peninsula and in Latin America.[14] Hispanic and Luso conservatism, orthodoxy, and recalcitrance regarding change qualify a society that was bound by the Counter Reform at a time of religious experimentalism, scientific inquiry, and nascent industrialization. Pomp, splendor, and vanity existed alongside misery and suffering in the Peninsula and the colonies at a time when elsewhere capitalism was beginning to exercise its force. A tension between tradition and change in the Peninsula was concealed in themes and ideas embroidered with mosaics, lace, elaborate ornamentation, and metaphors and allegories. Language became convoluted, twisting and turning and doubling back upon itself in strange attractor form, portraying itself and hardly anything else. Curved, labyrinthine lines replaced parallelism, symmetries, harmonies, equilibrium, balance. Life became much of a theater, a farce, and the people often became hardly more than caricatures. After the profound Baroque period in Latin America, the Enlightenment dreams of reason—individualism, liberalism, secularism, and emancipation for all—made a scattering of incursions here and there. But there were few conclusive victories. Things did not exactly remain the same, for sure. They changed, but as the French language has it, the more they changed, the more they seemed to stay the same. There was *both* change *and* there was no change; there was *neither* change *nor* nonchange. With these inner conflicts, how can one talk of any "age of reason," following classical logical tenets? If Latin America is viewed as a black sheep within the Western United Club of Nations, it is more the consequence of an unwillingness to join the club than an incapacity to cram the continent into a stock set of typological pigeon-holes.

The upshot is that Latin America neither was nor is exactly *Homo hierarchicus* nor exactly *Homo democritus,* but something else. Louis Dumont's work (1980) erecting a hierarchy-holism/egalitarianism-individualism dualism pits the culture of India against Western cultures. That dualism, stretched to the breaking point even regarding India and the West, simply does not fly with respect to Latin America. For Dumont, like many others, there is West against the Rest. Latin America resists this dualistic thinking. Latin America is not the West, but neither is it exactly the Rest. Its languages are chiefly of the West, but not the West precisely as it is now, for the whole of Latin American history is incongruously, complementarily coexistent. The continent's cultures are of the Rest along with the West, but, like language, all is there all at once, in a kaleidoscopic, heterogeneous mix. Consequently, Latin America's particular cultural "cultural logics," as we shall see in chapter sixteen, dance to the tune of their own band of *marimbas, bongos, charangos, flautas,* and *guitarrones.* These "logics" are marvelously illogical and irrational, magically realistic and concretely pragmatic; they are "logics" that know no clearly demarcated boundaries and respect no rigid injunctions. They play fast and loose with any and all practices, whether in politics, aesthetics, business, school, or in the home. They are what Carlos Fuentes says of language, a "shared and sharing part of culture that cares little about formal classifications and much about vitality and connection, for culture itself perishes in purity or isolation which is the deadly wages of perfection." Language, and cultural "cultural logics," like "bread and love," are shared by all members of the community. They make up tradition. Without them there is no tradition, and without tradition, there is no creation. Nobody "creates from nothing" (Fuentes 1988b:27).

Is the Tune Hybrid?

Latin America's uncanny magic was in the air from the beginning—as we shall note with emphasis as the following chapters unfold. This magic is Western; yet it is distinctly non-Western—it is, so to speak, the result of subtle, extralinguistic as well as linguistic "hidden transcripts." In Latin American cultural logics, especially where Amerindian and African American cultures have exercised their influence, there is an obstinate, enduring "enchantment" of the world, that charming, seductive irrationalism, that magnetic, enticingly "illogical" way of knowing and of doing things. Latin American cultural logics encompass the sphere of vagueness, where incongruous complementarities soar with few fetters and impediments, where they can coexist comfortably without compunction or regrets.

To cite a scattering of examples—which will be discussed in more detail in the final chapters—that Andean dance, the *huayno,* persevered generation after generation and evolved into a hybrid musical form, the *chicha,* that can today be heard throughout Latin America and in New York and elsewhere. From the Peruvian *zamacueca,* the *zamba* and *cueca* emerged and thrived. In Chile the *cueca* became the national dance; in Argentina it took on the name of the *chilena;* in Perú the *chilena* eventually became known as the *marinera.* A rhythmic feature of this dance, in Venezuela the *joropo,* or the Mexican *son* or *huapango*—for example "La Bamba," which became the theme for a movie in the United States—consists of alternating or simultaneous bars of 3/4 and 6/8 time. Such rhythmic patterns, previously thought to originate in Spain, are also found in the cross-rhythmic patterns of the African drum, and in other combinations of African, Peninsular, and pre-Hispanic folk dances. Nineteenth-century salon dances (waltz, polka, *contradanse*), when introduced into Latin America, fused with folk and popular forms to become the Mexican *jarabe,* for example, performed by Mariachi ensembles. Cuba has been the fountain-head for numerous popular genres, for instance, the *habanera, bolero, conga, mambo, chá-chá-chá,* all with a pronounced Afro-Cuban syncopation. The Colombian *cumbia* has found its way into the nooks and corners of the entire continent and in certain sections of Europe. The *tango,* in part of African American influence, ushered in that international superstar, Carlos Gardel, and enjoys variations throughout the Western world, in spite of its tight choreographic structure, the mannerisms, and rigid movement of the dancing couple. The Brazilian Carnival would not be what it is without the *samba* and the *samba* could not continue to thrive as it does without the Carnival: an entire year's preparation by working class participants goes into the *samba* performance during the festivities. Brazilian *capoeira,* a ritualized martial art-like dance performance, is also a cult theme, almost a mystical religious form. And there are the Catholicism-African religion hybrids that have brought about the emergence of the *santería* in Cuba, *voodoo* in Haití, and *candomblé* and *macumba* and *umbanda* in Brazil (Carneiro 1986, Gonçalves da Silva 1994, González-Wippler 1989, Ribeiro 1994, Wafer 1991). *Latin America:* marvelously real, a prodigious reality.

This somewhat random scattering of illustrations might suggest *transculturation,* a term introduced by Fernando Ortiz (1974) in his anthropological study of the tobacco and sugar "counterpoint culture" in Cuba and made part of the Latin American critical vocabulary by literary scholar Angel Rama (1982; see also Pratt 1992). Ortiz believes transculturation more adequately expresses "the different phases of the process of transition from one culture to another" than Bronislaw Malinowski's term, *acculturation.* This is because transculturation:

> Does not consist merely in acquiring another culture, which is what the English word acculturation really implies, but the process also necessarily involves the loss or uprooting of a previous culture, which could be defined as deculturation. In addition it carries the idea of the consequent creation of new cultural phenomena, which could be called neoculturation. In the end, as the school of Malinowski's followers maintains, the result of every union of cultures is similar to that of the reproductive process between individuals: the offspring always has something of both parents but is always different from each of them. (Ortiz 1995 [1940])

The notion of transculturation is multifaceted, to say the least. It presents a scintillating, nonlinear, virtually chaotic mosaic of customs, art, trades, and general practices regarding extralinguistic and linguistic "hidden transcripts." The old idea of acculturation is unilateral, a one-way street ending in a blind alley: the subordinate culture ("Not-A," *other*) is absorbed, amoeba-like, into the dominant culture ("A"). Acculturation evokes the view of a melting pot of the three major ethnic groups of Latin America to produce *mestizo* culture. However, this is an oversimplified image of a happy-go-lucky mergence, and if not, an overlapping, of cultures (*"Both* A *and* Not-A"). The image is not entirely unfaithful, as far as it goes. But it doesn't go far enough. It only implies myriad possibilities, with nothing necessarily having been actualized.

Transculturation, in contrast to acculturation, gives a more satisfactory account of cultural give-and-take within what Mary Louise Pratt (1992) calls the "contact zone," where the havenots select and invent from whatever is imposed on them from the dominant culture. They engage in "cultural" guerrilla warfare and in the process go through the apparent motions of assimilating the dominant culture, but they adapt it to suit their needs. They put on a show implying "I obey," but they do not "comply," for they subtly subvert the system, in addition to whatever overt contestation and negotiation may be going on. But is this not the practice, mentioned above, of the *criollo*'s "I obey but I do not comply" with respect to the Crown? So it would seem. Does this not suggest that the practice was not simply a binary matter of subordinates and superordinates? Yes, I would suggest. Then transculturation must occur at all levels within colonial society. In the process there is *neither* dominant culture *nor* subservient culture but from top to bottom, something *other* is emerging. Perhaps the usual allusions to transculturation do not tell the whole tale.[15]

According to many scholars, the radically multifaceted Latin American scene could hardly be qualified by any term other than "magical." The problem is that "magical," as in "magical realism," brings along a load of neoromantic baggage. I would prefer the Weberian term "enchanted." Latin America remains with one foot caught in premodern "enchantment," and yet, it is at the same time "modern." During colonialism, the enchanted mind-set of the havenots constantly subverted the crown's designs, foiled the Church's monopoly of sacred images, found a way to flatten the rigid hierarchies by fusing sacred and secular practices, and frustrated the aristocratic class's every effort to exercise what it believed to be its full hegemonic rights. But, as reiterated in the preceding paragraph, this "cultural" guerrilla activity was not the sole dominion of the havenots: the colonist haves had their own sly ways as well. They operated within the interstices of the rigid hierarchical colonial system handed down by the crown, between respectful and tactical but loose-lipped manifestations of obedience and at the same time pragmatic evasionary moves that skirted the law. As the saying had it, I repeat: "Obedezco pero no cumplo" ("I obey but I do not comply").

As a result of this somewhat laid back, lax, pliable attitude, this loosening of inflexible rules and regulations, African and Amerindian religious practices found their way into everyday Catholicism. "Enchantment" merged with standard European traditions: many *criollos* took to using herbs, elixirs, and even drugs produced by African American and indigenous subordinates. When there were no specific rules and recipes for situations and conditions unique to the colonial setting, popular methods, streaked with non-European characteristics, were often adopted. As a result, the chasm between cultural incompatibilities diminished; contradictions were softened, and alternative possibilities between them rose to the occasion; customs became mutually interpenetrating such that they took on the nature of intricately and labyrinthinely intermeshed codependency, and novelty co-emerged from conventions. In short, there was heterogeneity in spite of efforts to impose homogeneity.

All that was the tacit, spontaneous, and more often than not covert response to the regime of order the colonial power attempted to exact. On a more overt basis *peninsulares* and especially *criollos,* with a wink of the eye, paid due respects to God, King and Country, and went about their affairs in partial disregard of the crown's wishes. Many laws—the reading of the *requerimiento,*[16] abolition of Amerindian slavery, stringent regulations regarding treatment of African American slaves and Amerindians in the *repartimiento* system—were looked upon as so impractical, even absurd, that it became impossible to put them into practice.[17] Much like the "blue laws" in the British colonies, colonists of the Spanish crown fudged on their compliance with rules and regulations. The crown, from the very beginning, and in part due to Bartolomé de las Casas's obsessive litigation in favor of more humane treatment of the Amerindians, enacted laws that carried the best of intentions.[18] But these laws were ideals that had hardly a chance of taking their place in the actual comings and goings of everyday affairs in the colonies. In other words, there was a distinction between formal institutions and laws, on the one hand, and everyday practices, on the other.

The laws were admirable and well-meaning documents, for sure. But they could hardly have functioned effectively in the rough and tumble of frontier and colonial life: the ideals rarely touched bases with "reality," for the two were by and large incompatible (much like our interlocutors in our polylogue). Hence it was so difficult to "comply" with the laws that there was "no genuine compliance" with the laws. The verb "to comply" was one thing for the crown, but another thing altogether for the colonists. This conflict between "ideality" and "reality" was actually quite in line with the ideal space of "America as invention" from the very outset. "I obey but I do not comply" collaborated with "America as invention," and *both* were taken into a liquid semiosic embrace by *neither*-the-one-*nor*-the-other- . . . *nor*-the-other- . . . practices that produced a unique cultural mix. "America as invention" of a combined Maggie-Tlön sort contradictorily complemented the devious "I obey but I do not comply," which combined the equally devious Emmy and the vacillating Funy with the presupposition-laden Lönny and T'sui's many worlds within bifurcating time. This affords the image of a Deleuze-Guattari *rhizome,* whose center is everywhere and nowhere. (Instead of Kant's [1983:45] saying *"Argue as much as you want and about what you want, but obey,"* in Latin America we might have "Obey, and argue as much as you want and about what you want, then comply, that is, if your practical affairs warrant it, and if not, don't.")

Hybridity, mentioned in passing, offers the image of the creation of new transcultural forms. It is the third "term," or better, it is extralinguistic and linguistic "cultural" guerrilla practice, that gives rise to heterogeneity where according to the haves' dictates homogeneity was supposed to be the rule. Hybridism dissolves the binaries, and the mother liquor gestates and interacts and condenses into something other than a mere concoction of the original ingredients. There is open organic synthesis that creatively engenders, out of conformity plus resistance, cultural offspring that are *neither* the one ingredient *nor* the other. There is Bakhtin's (1981) hybridity in this formulation (also Young 1995), and there is Bhabha's (1994) hybrid as the result of contestation and negotiation. There is also the third, "cultural" guerrilla practice that plays the final note of the linear binary fugue and breaks into a sophisticated polyrhythmic flow. In this vein, hybridism will be the name of the game in the following chapters.

The hybridization of Peninsular, African American, and Amerindian cultures is perhaps nowhere more evident than in the Guadalupe-Tonantzín image.[19] An Amerindian-featured Virgin of Guadalupe's appearance to Juan Diego in 1531 served to integrate Christian iconography and indigenous structures of belief, which by the end of the colonial period emerged as a significant icon representing Mexican nationalism. The important point is that this icon was not held solely by the Amerindian contingency: the *criollos* themselves took it up, fomented and propagated it, and transformed it into a cultural institution, the *guadalupana,* a marianist cult of profound implications. Indeed, the *guadalupana* cult can no longer be separated from Mexico as a social, political, and cultural entity. Guadalupe is so much a national symbol of Mexico that the nation would suffer an irreparable diminution without it. The border between Mexican nationalism and *guadalupana* has become so diffuse as to be rendered indiscernible. This annealment of the two symbols was solidified shortly before independence. In the annual homage to the Virgin of Guadalupe at Tepeyac in 1794, the *criollo* priest fray Servando Teresa de Mier suggested that the *Piedra de Sol* (Aztec calendar stone) bore living proof that the image of the Virgin had been indelibly pressed on the Amerindian Juan Diego's poncho by Saint Thomas, who had once visited the New World to preach the gospel to the Amerindian inhabitants.[20] While there, Saint Thomas had presumably revealed the importance of the Virgin Mary. However, the message later fell into the interstices of the pagan Amerindian religions that soon took hold. The message was later to be revealed once again by Saint Thomas through the Amerindian mediary, Juan Diego. Yet, Saint Thomas's sermons had not been entirely forgotten, since the Amerindians incorporated his presence in the Americas with the legend of their god with clear eyes, light skin, and a beard, Quetzalcoatl ("plumed serpent" in Nahuatl, the language of the Aztecs). Eventually Quetzalcoatl was fused and confused with Guadalupe in the minds of the native inhabitants' religious ceremonies to become a transcultural, hybrid form of worship (Maza 1955, O'Gorman 1989, Rodríguez 1994).[21]

Such fusion has been labeled "syncretism," and it is often left at that. *Syncretism:* the combination or reconciliation of variant to virtually mutually exclusive beliefs, of distinct cultural artifacts, practices or traits, or in linguistics the fusion of two different inflectional terms. The concept of syncretism doesn't quite do the trick, however.[22] It leaves one with the sneaky suspicion that it is the social scientists and cultural critics who see the juxtaposed and otherwise incompatible elements, while the practitioners themselves view their images in holistic form, with neither clear-cut distinctions nor juxtapositions. Well, then, one might counter that phenomena such as the Guadalupe-Quetzalcoatl and Thomas-Quetzalcoatl connections entail bridging, spanning, which implies at one and the same time trans-lation, trans-culturation, and trans-mutation (*trans-* = spreading across, over). But neither is that qualification adequately faithful to the cultural practice in question. There is also mutual interpenetration, interrelatedness, contradictorily complementary codependent emergence, of all tendencies in question, such that between them there is that elusive border of borders—elusive because it may be felt, though it is neither seen nor said. In other words, what I have dubbed the "border of borders" embraces the "vortex" of Figure 2, the effervescence of possibilities virtually any one of which might stand a chance of making its appearance at a given time and place.

Classical logic is of little consequence in practices involving mutual interpenetration, interrelatedness, and codependent emergence. It is of little consequence, for there is *both* suspension of disbelief *and* there is no suspension; and there is *neither* suspension *nor* nonsuspension of disbelief. What is sensed is believed, but the believers know it is not really what they profess it to be, yet it is believed, yet it is not really believed. No dishonesty is implied here, but rather, a lingering enchantment of the world in the face of creeping disenchantment. "America as invention" and "I obey but I do not comply" disseminate far and wide and take on many countenances and they engulf the entire cultural sphere in their semiosic tidal wave that breaks and embraces and then leaves things as they were, but not quite. One enjoys no possible escape, for one is within it, that is within semiosis, wherever one is.

On this note, let us take a walk through a selection of other Latin American cultural phenomena in the form of key terms and phrases and their rich meanings in search of a feel for the subcontinent's enchanting "cultural logic."

Notes

1.   This, we shall note in chapter seven, falls closely in line with the thought of Michel de Certeau (1984), and it is an eminently suitable concept that can be used to account for Latin America's nonbinary yet hierarchical socio-politico-economic culture.

2.   The term "poaching" is taken literally for Scott, just as it is figurative "poaching" with respect to Michel de Certeau's (1984) reader of the text, as we shall see below. I might make mention here of a variation on the theme of cultural "poaching" in Jenkins (1992) and on the related theme of cultural "appropriation" in Ziff and Rao (1997), all of which are related to the theme as presented within the covers of this book.

3.   This difference with respect to communication channels between the haves and the havenots becomes apparent in the studies of William Labov (1972) in Harlem and Basil Bernstein (1975) among working class families in England, which demonstrate that language among the haves is considerably less context-dependent than that among the havenots (for the distinction in regards to oral and literate cultures, see Ong 1977, 1982, 1991; with respect to rituals and conflict in Mexican popular culture, Beezley et al. 1994, and in Brazil, DaMatta 1991). This preordains the haves to greater success in our linear, logically oriented Western cultures, to be sure, but they suffer a loss in terms of their inability to participate in the overall semiosic process.

4.   *Mestizos,* as specified above, are generally considered a mixture of European and Amerindian; *mulatos* (*pardos* in Brazil) are a mixture of European and African American. The English word "mulatto" takes on an undesirable connotation in the U.S., but not to the same degree in Latin America, therefore I will use the Spanish *mulato.*

5.   The *encomienda* (like the *capitania* in Brazil) was a grant of authority over land and the Amerindians residing therein to an *encomendero.* It carried the obligation to Christianize and protect the Amerindians in exchange for their labor, an obligation that was both honored and abused, as would be expected.

6.   Actually, as Magnus Mörner (1967) reveals, racial mixture during the Spanish American colonial period became so complex and the Crown's attempt to maintain ethnic distinguishability by virtue of racial classification became so futile after a few generations had passed, that the cultural milieu was rendered virtually chaotic. Indeed, "chaotic" is an apt adjective, as it evinces the image of Latin America's poly- or multicultural qualities centuries before the idea became fashionable in Eurocentric cultural studies celebrating "postmodern" diversity.

7.   As is well known, the Spanish conquest was carried out in the name of *God, King,* and *Spain;* in this respect it can be said that the "religious conquest" hardly took a back seat to territorial and economic motives (Ricard 1966).

8.   The notion of the city in the context of the present narrative is important. Most particularly the Spanish Americans were city people, Thomists. For St. Thomas human beings are most naturally town and city dwellers. Therefore the Spaniards as Thomists, in the Peninsula as well as in Latin America, highlighted the role of the city, especially during the Baroque period, as Antonio Maravall (1986) argues convincingly.

9.   In this respect at least, it must seem that Roberto DaMatta's (1984, 1991, 1994) confidence in the *casa/rua* (home/street) pair of terms is binary, and that a certain structuralist bias comes through to mar his otherwise brilliant analyses of Brazilian cultural practices. However, a careful reading of DaMatta will reveal that his thinking is genuinely triadic (see especially Hess and DaMatta 1995; DaMatta 1995).

10.   In addition to Dealy's dualist interpretation, a perusal of Ménendez Pidal (1966), Inman (1942), and West (1957) would shed more light on the problem.

11.   This generality apparently goes against the grain of the customary set of dichotomies supposedly qualifying the Baroque as opposed to the Renaissance (see Wölfflin 1950, Coutinho 1969). The condition, in light of the present essay, is not merely dualistic but pluralistic, or better, *incongruously complementary.*

12.   See also Stoetzer (1979) and Hamilton (1963), of whom Morse, by the way, remains mildly critical.

13.   I'm sure it has become apparent by now that I place humans as semiotic agents within the same arena as the signs they make and take as if they were, themselves, signs among signs. And this is precisely the point: sign emissaries and interpreters are part of the same codependent arising as are all signs (for further, merrell 1995a, 1996, 1997, 1998a).

14.   See especially, regarding the Spanish Baroque, Maravall (1986), and with respect to Spanish America, Leonard (1966) and Sarduy (1974).

15.   My only reservation about transculturation is that the term, especially regarding Angel Rama's appropriating it for his literary studies, smacks of high modernism, elitism, and a certain anxiety regarding the unruly masses as seen from the eyes of a lettered vanguard. John Beverley (1999:44–49) puts forth the same reservation. In view of this reservation, hereafter I will most often use the term "hybridism" with respect to "third term," *both-and, neither-nor* practices in Latin America.

16. The *Requerimiento* or "requirement" was a document, presented to the Amerindian villages prior to the Spaniards' entering and conquering them. It was read in Spanish with a translator, when available. It demanded of the Amerindians that they lay down their arms, submit to the King of Spain, and embrace the Catholic religion. If not, the conquerors would not be held responsible for the consequences. Customarily read to incredulous Amerindians, sometimes in an unknown tongue and sometimes to an empty village since its inhabitants had already taken to flight, the *Requerimiento,* however drawn up with good intentions, took on absurd proportions when put into practice in the Americas—and it could easily have lent support to the "Obedezco pero no cumplo" syndrome. Bartolomé de las Casas once wrote that upon reading the *Requerimiento* he didn't know whether he should laugh or weep, so ridiculous it appeared to his eyes (see Hanke 1949).

17. The *repartimiento,* instituted when *encomienda* labor became scarce, consisted of a redistribution of Amerindians into dispersed communities for their consequent assignment as labor, principally in the mines and agricultural zones, and according to local needs (Hanke 1949).

18. One should mention, at the very least, that as a consequence of de las Casas's efforts, by 1537, for the "first time in history an imperialist nation initiated a critical ethnic questioning of its own colonial expansion" (Cevallos-Candau 1994a:6).

19. It is worthy of note at this juncture that the popular classes in Latin America have always nurtured a special relationship with images, for obvious reasons: in the absence of written texts, literacy enjoys much less importance than sound effects and optical images (Mignolo and Boon 1994, Mignolo 1997). These "extratextual" signs have been exploited to the hilt on TV, with their melodramas that evince kinship with oral traditions (Martín-Barbero 1993:108–16, 142–45).

20. Actually it was the Peruvian Antonio de la Calanaha who in 1639 first postulated the visit of Saint Thomas to the Americas. The story was later taken up by Mexican *criollo* Carlos de Sigüenza y Góngora, who metaphorized the connection between the Catholic figure and Quetzalcoatl, which was politicized by Teresa de Mier (see Aguilar Camín 1993:23–24; also, for a general historical account, Brading 1980).

21. See Teresa de Mier (1981:221–54) and a relevant discussion in Brading (1988:63–69); and for an excellent analysis of the Guadalupe-Quetzalcoatl connection, Lafaye (1976).

22. See Serra (1995) for a sympathetic critique of "syncretism" as the term is customarily used in Brazil. I might add that a growing number of Afro-Brazilian scholars, especially in Salvador, wish to abolish the term altogether, given its indelibly dualistic and hegemonic implications (Figueiredo Ferretis 1999, Conçalves Silva 1999, Marcondes de Moura 2000, Medeiros Espega 1999).

Chapter Four

Between the Devil and the Deep Blue Sea?

> The deep below, the deep above.
> The waters overflow.
>
> —Gloria Anzaldúa

> At each border, I found myself because I knew I belonged to none
> of them.
>
> —Marjorie Agosín

Personalismo[1]

The classical grandeur frequently displayed in Latin American oratory—at political rallies, poetry readings, conferences, banquets, weddings, and other ceremonies, and even in the classroom—bears witness to the importance of personal appearance, public demeanor, private composure, and occasionally to style and form at times to the sacrifice of content, to rhetorical aplomb over tightly structured argumentation, to the ways of the telling rather than the hows and the whys. This contrasts with the relatively demure, publicly silent, properly worded, and appropriately articulated delivery among the citizens of predominantly Northern European cultures. (Of course what I have written is yet another generalization, and generalizations, generalizations are: perhaps helpful tools but potentially dangerous instruments, sometimes good to think with and talk with, but only if there is mindfulness that, as generalizations, they cannot help but remain fuzzy, and at times inconsistent, and invariably incomplete.)

The Latin American individual's worth is at times gauged by words more than deeds, by speech more than action. There is hardly any "strong, silent" John Wayne type elevated to mythical status. The linguistic economy of Abraham Lincoln, the homey quipping of Ronald Reagan, the "give-em-hell" pragmatism of Harry Truman, would not command the same respect in Latin America, where intellectuals and writers, as well as dynamic men and women are the rule, and where the stoic Amerindian who became president of Mexico in the last century, Benito Juárez, is an exception. No recent United States president corralled such respect among Latin Americans as did John F. Kennedy. And for obvious reasons, in addition to his Catholicism. He had everything: education, intelligence, aristocracy, youthful image, lovely jet-set wife, charismatic demeanor, exceptional oratorical capacity, Camelot charm. He had what is called *personalismo*. If one has it one has it, and if not, not. It comes sort of naturally—it is in one's knowing how to do things tacitly and subsidiarily, as described above—and for this reason it is difficult to cultivate.

In Latin America, *personalismo* is for the most part a projection of one's public image, a public self—albeit a fluctuating, fluid self. In contrast, private and family life are another matter. In Anglo-America's individualistic, relatively more money-grubbing materialistic culture, the same apparent distinction is not as sharp between private and public life—though, as argued briefly above, the distinction in Latin America is not as clearly definable as some scholars would have it. The "let it all hang out" autobiographies of celebrities where no holds are barred and there is little to no respect for members of the immediate family are virtually unknown in Latin America. The Latin American family is largely a private affair, and nobody else's business. *Personalismo,* on the other hand, is the public *persona.* This is to say, in public life the person makes the position, not the other way round. The person embodies what she is given the empowerment to represent, and the same can be said for Latin America's institutions. The presidency *is* the president, the Church *is* the physical structure and the Virgins and Christs and all the saints that are contained within. *Peronismo is* coterminous with Juan Domingo Perón and perhaps even more so with Evita Duarte Perón. As goes Fidel Castro, so goes the Cuban Revolution. Zapatismo of the Mexican Revolution *is* inseparably incorporated in the figure of Emiliano Zapata. APRISMO (of the *Alianza Popular Revolutionario Americano,* a call for Pan-American solidarity) *is* coterminous with its father-figure, Peruvian intellectual Víctor Raúl Haya de la Torre. And so on. The person literally defines the office. It is very much unlike public office in the U.S., where the new arrival merely conforms to the "job description" that goes along with her taking a seat behind an oak desk. In Latin America, when one office holder goes, enter the next chief, and the personalized office is up for a radical change, because now somebody else *is* the office: the office is now condensed into the form of another human being. Consequently, there is an endless string of alliances, manipulations, fraudulent elections, appointments through nepotism, and palace revolts and coups, giving the entire Latin American area the image of endemic instability. This is by and large the outcome of a paternalistic, status-seeking order within which each person, flaunting her *personalismo,* maneuvers to take over the spotlight and impress the audience out there over her competitors. The heroine (or hero) is the person that gets her own way, come what may. The aloof, relatively detached, impassionate and impersonal individual hardly stands a chance in this arena of stars.[2]

The future is conceived to be in the hands of outstanding individuals, not in unseen and impersonal forces. History also owes its becoming to dynamic individuals; they make it and they hold its destiny in their grasp. The idea of an invisible hand extended by some *Zeitgeist* or other that pushed history and the collective whole of society along is discarded in favor of the energetically gyrating arms of the most charismatic and gregarious figure amongst the cultural giants that happen to be out there. What's important is this day, right here and now, when what is happening is happening; it is the present, and it is she who makes the present what it is, who creates time, gives expression to the community, molds history, forges visions of the future. This is evident in the political swings from right to left at some time or other in the Latin American nations. Conservatives and liberals, reactionaries and revolutionaries, all advance solutions to whatever problems might happen to be plaguing a given country. A swing in one direction or the other might indicate altered ideological sentiments, or it might be simply a show of force by the military. Quite often it is an indication of whoever was able most effectively to captivate an expectant audience. In our polylogue Averroës, according to most expectations, should have been endowed with a massive dose of *personalismo*. But he was not. Thus she thwarted the anticipations of all parties concerned, save for Hladdy who kept the faith come what may. In a real life Latin American context, Averroës would soon have become a fallen god: he simply didn't fit the bill. In this respect he was like Aztec emperor Moctezuma II of old, and like Francisco Madero who briefly became Mexico's president after the fall of Porfirio Díaz from 1911 to 1913. Their *machismo*, charisma, will to dominate, and their *personalismo* left much to be desired.

On the other hand, Cuba's Castro—or Castro's Cuba, however one wishes to cut the cake—is the living repository of *personalismo*. Cuba's Castro in the beginning was the epitome of confidence, of a capacity to move history at the same time that history bore testimony to his powers and his prowess, as was articulated in his "History Will Absolve Me" speech (Castro 1962). Castro's Cuba was a nation of people in search of a hero, and some of those remaining on the island still believe they found him—though their number is admittedly dwindling, many of the reasons for which are beyond Castro's control. For these people, leadership is of the most basic, the most fundamental, sort. Leadership is coterminous with the leader, the man himself. Theodore Draper (1965:9) hit the nail on the head almost four decades ago. Castro is more keenly in tune with the charismatic leader principle than to Marxism, communism, or any other ideology or doctrine or movement: Castro *is* his own ideology, doctrine, movement. He *is* his office; he *is* the Cuban Revolution; he *is* Cuba and Cuba *is* him—or perhaps I should put this in the past tense?[3]

In this sense, he who enjoys more than a moderate dose of *personalismo* is not necessarily the "rugged individualist" of the North American sort. The individual with *personalismo* is at the same time many and one. He is many not in the sense that the one and the many say "I wanna be like Michael Jordan" or "Sammy Sosa" or "Brad Pitt" or "I wanna be like "Madonna" or "Serena Williams" or "Gloria Estefan" or "Tina Turner," in reference to their favorite individual endowed with *personalismo*. Rather, it is the one and the many who pay due respect to their counterpart not simply because they want to be like or to identify with him, but because they realize that he is there and they are here due to some turn of events—a belief in some ill-defined destiny or a strange rather non-Unamuno "tragic sense of life"—that elevated him to that status.[4] But perhaps some day one person among them will have her chance. However, if luck happens to smile favorably on her, she will not simply become "like" someone else, some heroic icon—Michael Jordan or Tina Turner or whomever. She will continue to be herself—who is now another self, of course—on her own terms. So it isn't "rugged individual me" against the world in the dualistic North American sense, but "incongruously complementary 'me' and 'we'," where one from among the "we" can become another "me," and "I" will either pass on or take "my" place among the "we" once again. It entails incessant mediation between distinctions such that there are no rigidly distinguishable binaries at all. "Me" *is* "we" and "we" *is* "me"—*both-and* from the sphere of Firstness—and one of "us" will become "me" and in such event "I" will become someone else—*neither-nor* within the sphere of Thirdness (Fuentes 1971:9–42).

What I have just written must appear inordinately schematic and hopelessly vague. However, the apparent methodlessness of my madness is not to exhaust a topic, but to introduce a set of preliminary terms within Latin America's cultural semiosis and highlight their importance regarding "cultural logics." In this vein, I invite you to ponder over a few more distinctively Latin American character traits.

Machismo

The *personalistic* leader's qualities by way of tradition, especially if that leader is of the male variety, are by their very nature linked to an overpowering sense of *machismo. Machismo:* it is the manifestation of how a member of the male species is, how he feels toward himself and toward others, how he sees his world, in the sense of tacitness and subsidiary-focal perceiving and knowing as described in chapter two. He would like to see his world as subject to his will and his desire; he would like to relegate other men to subservience and all women to submission. He feels he must be master of his own ship, which includes as its crew his entire community. His power, fortune, fame, and sexual prowess are all legendary, or at least so he thinks. But what, more precisely, is the nature of this male trait called *machismo?*

Miguel León-Portilla (1963) offers a definition of Mexican *machismo* that antedates the conquest. Prior to the Spaniards' confrontation with American civilizations, the Spanish word denoted the male of the species, as well as he-goats and mules. Eventually, the meaning of "macho" merged with a comparable word in Nahuatl, whose passive form is pronounced "macho" (to be known) and refers to a place where bold and faithful warriors met after their death. Put "male" (whether virile or impotent) of an animal species with "warrior," and you have ambiguity worthy of the best Mexican-Spanish nouns. That is one interpretation, of which the ebullient and often hyperbolic Earl Shorris (1992:430–32) makes much rhetorical hay. What is for sure, the word "macho," an "exaggerated aggressiveness and intransigence in male-to-male relations and arrogance and sexual aggression in male-to-female relationships," quite belatedly made its way into Spanish dictionaries (Stevens 1973:90). The word as we now know it seems to have been more the work of journalists, poets, essayists, novelists, and social scientists than of philologists and lexicologists (Brandes 1979, Brusco 1995, Gilmore 1981).

Placing the word in a historical context, after the conquest and colonialization of Mexico had been completed, peacetime connotations of *macho* took the form of sexual aggression in addition to its characterizing one's ability to play the role of lord, person of stature, *hidalgo.* This bisexual clash became a sort of "spiritual *machismo,*" insofar as it was translated from the Spanish conqueror raping an Amerindian woman (*Malinche*) to the would-be *macho* melting before *Mariana* (from the "Marianist" Virgin of Guadalupe tradition).[5] The woman was taken as a sexual object and physically and mentally inferior to the *macho,* on the one hand, and placed on a pedestal as the repository of everything pure, of good will, and saintly—and hence superior to the *macho*—on the other hand. Male-female relations became packed into the stereotyped mold of a dominant-aggressive male and a submissive female, as the passive, self-sacrificing, obedient wife and mother who is of moral and ethical qualities superior to the male.[6] During the colonial period, since the *mestizos* as *neither* Amerindian *nor* European (*peninsulares*) were relegated to a cultural limbo and rarely enjoyed any royal road to power, respect, or *hidalguismo,* and since the *criollos* (Spaniards born in the Americas) did not enjoy quite the same privileges as the *peninsulares, mestizos* and *criollos* had hardly any recourse but to take on a role as something in the order of socio-political and cultural "eunuchs" (Schurz 1964:83). Their compensation for loss of political power and social standing evolved into the *macho-mariana* syndrome. The colonial haves, then, became specialists in the dominant-aggressive-male-stereotyped *macho* in contrast to the havenots, the submissive-feminine-stereotyped masses of Amerindians, African American, *mestizos,* and often even the *criollos.* This tense duality eventually evolved into the patron-client interrelations in the independent Latin American countries.[7] It isn't so much that the new lords of the independent Latin American republics sought power in order to retire to the good life on their estates, to become overpowering dictators, or to get rich from the fruits of their aggression. Rather, in however vainglorious or inept a fashion, they actively pursued supreme sovereignty for themselves and their entire community, where values were measured in terms of "manliness, personal valor, a capacity for imposing oneself on others" (Paz 1961:71 [1952]).

We have it from Mexican philosopher Samuel Ramos (1962 [1937]) that the conquest of Mexico—and by extension all of Spanish America—had as one of its principal themes the rape and exploitation of Amerindian women. The offspring of this violent union developed an "inferiority complex" as a result of the "original sin." The mother became somewhat devalued and subdued as a person, and the *criollo,* rather than a *hidalgo* or a person of merit, became dominant to the extreme. The *mestizo* son had little alternative other than to assume the role of his Spanish father: he was *neither* Amerindian *nor* European, yet he chose not to associate with the downtrodden and suffered perpetual frustration in his efforts to become European. Eventually, given his what Ramos terms his "sense of inferiority," his behavior took on neurotic proportions.[8] In this regard, Octavio Paz in *The Labyrinth of Solitude* (1961:82 [1952]) observes that it is "impossible not to notice the resemblance between the figure of the macho and that of the Spanish conquistador. It is the model—more mythical than real—that determines the images the Mexican people form of their men in power: feudal lords, hacienda owners, politicians, generals, captains of industry." This set the stage for three centuries of colonialism. After the paternal archstone of monarchism was violently rejected in Latin America roughly between 1810 and 1824, *machismo* emerged in reinvigorated form and has reigned ever since, giving vent to the institutions of *caciquismo* and *caudillismo*—to be discussed in the following sections—and aiding and abetting the patriarchal and paternalistic societies. The term later became an epithet used in conjunction with certain male behavioral patterns. It is this modern meaning of the word that becomes the focus of Octavio Paz's controversial essay, "The Sons of La Malinche" (1961:65–88).

Machismo: the cult of aggressive masculinity; that is its expression, its manifestation, its thrust, today. Sex is power, authority, domination, repression, aggression, violence. In one of the most grating definitions, it is the masculine ideal in Spanish American culture and society. Regardless of social standing, the *macho* is revered for his sexual prowess, his action-orientation (both physical and verbal), and his raw aggressiveness. Stridently masculine, he is outwardly and allegedly sure of himself, apparently conscious of his presumed inner worth, and prone to gamble everything on the self-confidence that he will in the end have things his own way. He may express his supposed inner confidence by overt action, in the event he is a *caudillo* or revolutionary, or he may do so verbally, in the event he is a leading intellectual, lawyer, or politician (Gillin 1955:493).[9]

According to tradition—a tradition that is admittedly waning in contemporary Latin America—a quite common assumption has it among Latin American males that there is a nondomestic inclination present in *machismo.*[10] This inclination is succinctly encapsulated in the attitude that the woman's place is the home and the church and the man's place is the street—carousing, with *compadres* or business associates, with mistresses, and so on. The celebrated and maligned Don Juan image of the male and his "pregnant in the summer and barefooted in the winter" mentality regarding the woman of the household is, of course, a stereotype that does violence to actual male-female interrelations, though, unfortunately, there seems to be a certain drop of truth to it. While the stereotype holds among many urban males, especially of the lower middle and lower classes, male-female relationships among peasants are more likely of a certain complementarity rather than merely dominance-subservience. This characteristic is in part one of necessity, since given scarce incomes and subsistence agricultural practices, both husband and wife must often engage in work on their minuscule plot of land and outside the home. Nevertheless, traditionally the wife has been excluded from political life, the husbands dedicate considerable time to ritual drinking—which the wives usually resent—and wife beating is unfortunately still quite common (Harris 1978). Moreover, the wife remains in a state of dependency, since the male member of the household is usually in charge of the financial affairs. Migration of males from Mexico to the United States without their families, which has increased since the economic crisis of the early 1980s, minimizes the role conflict stemming from *machismo.* Yet since the husband sends money back home, which is often the sole income of the family, the wife remains dependent on him. Moreover, it is even convenient for him, since he can more effectively abdicate any active role in the household, which supports the "woman in the home, man in the street" aspect of *machismo* (Rothstein 1983).

A problem arises as a result of *macho* mores that call for shirking household chores and general domestic affairs. The home becomes a matriarchal domain, especially in the father's prolonged absence; yet the assumption among males and females alike is that of male dominance. This causes a conflict among the offspring. What is a child to do? Honor the father and obey the mother, or vice versa?—a schizophrenic sort of oscillation of the "I obey but I do not comply" dictum (Careaga 1987). But if the father's *macho* behavior is undeserving of such honor, where does that leave the child? And if the father's role is that of dominance over the mother, then to what extent is the mother's word the last word on things? The mother often openly shows her disdain for the father's *machismo;* yet she is with almost equal frequency compliant with respect to his wishes and commands, and then, when the father is not around, matriarchy resumes its hold on the home. The father shows his disrespect for the matriarchal tendency in his home, and attempts to force an exaggerated authoritarian form of patriarchy if and when he is around. To aggravate this conflict, women often admire a member of the opposite sex who has manly good looks with a tendency toward *machismo;* this encourages the sons to fashion themselves to fit the mold. However, in the home these same sons sense contempt on the part of their mother toward the *macho* characteristics of their father. The vicious circle is unfortunately self-perpetuating (Brusco 1995:85–87).[11]

Yet, such apparent dualisms as I have outlined in the previous paragraphs are incapable of telling the whole story. Between *Malinche* and *mariana,* between the *macho* as superior and as inferior, there is no excluded-middle but a border, the border of a border, the "emptiness," crying out for some of the cultural riches therein concealed to be tapped. The fact of the matter is that the *macho* is in a manner of speaking and according to cultural stereotypes *both* superior *and* inferior to his counterpart. So contradictory terms can cohabit that same cultural sphere, no matter how tension-ridden and violent the union may be. The *macho* is in actual practice *neither* the one person *nor* the other one, *neither* superior *nor* inferior. For he is perpetually in the process of self-expression, of identity switching, of evincing yet another mask, which actually entails becoming what was his *other,* becoming some *other,* some hitherto unknown quality. As Octavio Paz once put it, the male of the species—and for that matter the female as well—is always on the cultural stage acting out some role or other, and hence he must at every moment re-invent himself. A more faithful expression of Peirce's concept of the self as the process of becoming something other than what it was could hardly be found.[12]

Speaking of the supreme actor and the consummate *macho,* we have that "man on horseback," the *caudillo.*

Caudillismo[13]

Spanish intellectual Eliseo Vivas points out that in contrast to the "black legend" painting the Spanish conquistador as a brutal and pathologically avaricious man, blinded by his lust for gold, riches were actually for him strictly a means. The end, considerable more significant than the means:

> was not economic independence conceived essentially in terms of body comfort and enjoyment but freedom from bondage to other men, freedom from servile relationships, spiritual autarchy, which is achieved only when you are able to say to another man, *a mí no me manda nadie*—no one bosses me; I am lord because I have land and gold and Indians, and I need not beg any favors from you or anyone else. (Vivas 1971:7–8)

Gold talked to the Spaniard, affording him not simply the temporal things he coveted, but more important still, the image of nobility, respect, honor, and esteem, an estate, the pleasure of vices, and the means for vengeance against all enemies. The conquest was carried out in the name of God, King, and Spain, to be sure, but the "I" did not trail along far behind, and in fact it often took precedence. That "I" was not a nascent precapitalist "I," however, but an "I" more proper to a pre-Renaissance Hispano-Arabic "I." Were it all simply a get-rich-quick matter in the sense of modern capitalism, the Spaniard would most likely not have engaged in so many apparently irrational quixotic quests.

Caudillismo, an institution that continues to highlight the "I," has its roots in the Spanish "I" and in *caciquismo* (*coronelismo* in Brazil), a local rather than national phenomenon. The term *cacique* purportedly comes from Taino-Arawak, a dialect from the Caribbean, and means "chief" or "boss" (*jefe*). During the twentieth century, the term "cacique," at times carrying pejorative connotations, has been put to use ordinarily to designate someone who exercises local hegemony. When a *cacique*'s sphere of influence expands to engulf the entire national scene, he takes on the countenance of a *caudillo.* What are the prerequisites for this *caudillo?* In order to lift himself up by his bootstraps along the social ladder of success, he must be charismatic, personalistic, a classical orator, able to present a captivating image of himself, and prepared to risk all in a violent *coup,* or a revolution.

First and foremost, he is a populist. He must at the drop of a hat be willing to shun the *criollo* elite and appeal to the working class. Later, when it becomes politically expedient to do so, he caters to the oligarchy. He can promise the sky to all those present at a middle class rally. The next day if he finds himself on a university campus, he is a champion of higher education. On the following week in the countryside with landless peasants, he can bring himself to tears when expounding on social injustices and the need for land reform. He does his damnedest to be all things to all people. These practices often call for strong-arm tactics when different power groups find themselves on a collision course. Such practices have motivated palace revolt after palace revolt by those wannabe *caudillos* in competition for the coveted presidential seat.

For example, Venezuela during the nineteenth century suffered from an apparently self-perpetuating stream of *caudillos.* First there was José Antonio Páez (1830–46), who was replaced by two brothers, José Gregorio and José Tadeo Monagas (1846–61), then Paéz (1861–63) decided he was ready for another try at it. After an interim, Antonio Guzmán Blanco (1970–87) pushed his way into the Presidential Palace, who was followed by Joaquín Crespo (1887–98), Cipriano Castro (1899–1908), and Juan Vicente Gómez (1908–35). Until the country became oil-rich, rarely had it remained free of the grip of *caudillismo.* The history of most other Latin American nations has followed comparable, though less spectacular, paths forged by the "will to power" of those who are most capable of getting their way.

Carlos Fuentes's *The Death of Artemio Cruz* (1964 [1962]) is a masterfully constructed picture of a *machista mestizo-mulato-caudillo cum* conqueror helping to forge postrevolutionary Mexico out of the ashes of destruction. Artemio Cruz's chief goals in life included wealth, but more than that, power, domination, authority, and the respect he felt he had earned but never received from the prerevolutionary *criollo* aristocracy. He shaped his destiny virtually from nothing. The son of a *mulata* mother and a landed *criollo* father in the tropical plains of Vera Cruz, he crossed the mountainous region to the high plateau, fought in the revolution, took advantage of men and women at every opportunity, became a member of the *nouveaux riches,* and obediently played out his role as what Octavio Paz dubbed a *gran chingón*[14] to the end of his life of corruption, subterfuge, and betrayal. This is a "will to power" Mexican style, and in general, Latin American style. It is the notorious road to *caudillismo* paved with the blood and sorrow of those who were sacrificed for the benefit of ends that remain more in the mind and in human relations than in sprawling mansions, lavish lifestyles, and money in foreign banks.

Caudillismo: it's a magical word, it's a magnet that by its very nature appeals to the sentiments. To repeat Juan Domingo Perón's generalization, the people don't think, they feel. One of Latin America's supreme *caudillo(a)s* should know. With a nod to Eva Perón, I now include the female gender in the term.[15] The individual fills the image of the *caudillo(a),* if s/he is capable of so doing. S/he makes the President the President, the CEO the CEO, the hacienda owner a lord. If money for the sake of consumption is not the all-consuming goal, neither is power for the sake of might which makes one the right kind of person. Rather, power is the avenue toward fulfillment of what is conceived to be a more noble goal: to be the person everybody else would like to be. Conscious pursuit of power takes the back seat to a desire for the esteem granted to her/him who is moving up the ladder economically and politically, and in many cases even more importantly, socially and culturally. Coming along with this esteem is the desire of everybody to emulate those who have risen to the upper echelons of society and culture. All folks admire the confident, dynamic, charismatic individual. S/he garners esteem, and by the force of her/his will, s/he usually exercises control over those who esteem her/him.

Control and *esteem,* those are the watchwords. If one is controlled one should, logically and rationally speaking it would seem, resent the source of that control. If one holds another individual in high esteem, it shouldn't be simply the result of that individual's control over the person granting the esteem. But that is not exactly the case regarding the *caudillo(a)* image: s/he who controls, is able to control precisely because s/he is esteemed, can grant favors and expects them in return, can dole out punishment as well as rewards, can cast into exile and place in comfortable offices, can give exuberant praise and knows how to receive it, and so on. S/he who controls, controls and can remain in control because s/he receives esteem, and s/he who esteems the esteemed does so with the hopes that the opportunity will present itself, someday, sometime, for her/his own ascension to a position of control. This condition might be unbearably oppressive were it conceived within the Anglo-American relatively more capitalist, consumerist, socio-cultural setting where almost everybody is in a do-or-die symmetrical competitive conflict. The Latin American condition is quite otherwise, however, and it must be considered on its own turf. Relations are more complementary and less symmetrical than in the U.S. In Latin America, those who are in power are esteemed more for who they are and for the hows, the whys, and the wherefores of their ascending to the position of their power. But were the esteemers to be given the chance, they would replace those in power at the first opportunity, and feel little remorse for it. It is not that they are bloodthirsty, but rather, the complementarity of weblike, nonlinear interrelations have taken a turn, and now the outs have found a way in and the ins are out and once again looking in. Perhaps at some future moment lady luck will once more smile on them, and opportunity will show its smiling face. Indeed, there is much of Antonio Gramsci's hegemony and power in the Latin American *caudillo* image.[16]

Controlling others and at the same time reaping their esteem: the "tragedy" and the "comedy" of *caudillismo*. It is potentially a virtuous rather than a vicious circle, but ofttimes, and unfortunately, it is a bizarre mixture of "comic" virtuosity and vicious "tragedy." In the final analysis, what, exactly, is a *caudillo(a)* anyway? The word "caudillo(a)" is much like the word "chicano(a)," as Cherrié Moraga (1983:90–144) bears witness. The daughter of a *chicana* mother and an Anglo father, she writes that she was not in tune with the meaning of the word until she felt it after a long series of painful experiences. "Chicano(a)," like "caudillo(a)," "macho," "personalismo," and other terms to be discussed below, such as the Brazilian "jeito-jeitinho," are words of the sort that if you have to inquire as to their meaning you wouldn't understand them anyway. So don't ask, just feel. A tall order indeed. To repeat, it's like getting a feel for a Zen koan. So how can I properly qualify *caudillismo* and *caudillo(a)s?* Once again, in large part, I can't, not really. That is, I can't in exclusively textual language, especially since I am neither *chicano* nor Latin American but a male Anglo-American looking inside from the outside while trying to feel in a vicarious mode from the inside without being able to get both feet in from the outside. However, I might suggest that if one happens to find oneself at that border of borders, that hairline that is everywhere and nowhere, perhaps, just perhaps, one may get a feel for what *both* is *and* is not, and *neither* is *nor* is not. Anyway, back to the scattering of effables regarding the topic at hand.

While more "primitive" *caudillo(a)s* spread havoc in the backlands during the nineteenth century, their more "sophisticated" counterparts, indoctrinated in French culture and certain aspects of other European cultures, were emerging in the palaces, cultural events, and salons found in the urban centers. Nonetheless, most *caudillo(a)* traits remained basically the same: the ability to eliminate enemies, win friends, and influence all newcomers. Historian Edwin Lieuwen writes that "nearly every *caudillo* tended to conform to that type." S/he was generally an army officer and a representative of the armed forces. S/he apparently possessed superior energy, courage, and self-confidence, and for this reason inspired a certain awe and respect in her/his followers. S/he believed in her/his inherited right and destiny to govern, as a person with a mission (Lieuwen 1965:23). Obviously, one's *macho* nature was a prerequisite toward becoming a *caudillo,* though this does not necessarily discount a woman's taking on the role of *caudilla*—Evita Perón, the most shining example—but usually in good Latin American matriarchal rather than patriarchal style. (Madonna, of course, was no Evita, and she never could have been. Neither could Jackie Kennedy or Barbara Bush or Hilary Clinton have played an effective Evita role in real political life. The fact is that, historically, Latin America in certain respects is capable of manifesting greater respect for a woman in politics than the United States.)

Spanish writer and historian Victor Alba sees the *caudillo(a)* as a natural evolution of the colonial *encomendero* and the nineteenth-century *hacienda* owner. The *caudillo(a),* "like the *patrón,* must be a just man (or at least appear to be so)." If a male *caudillo* is by nature severe and inflexible, he can also be amiable and paternal when the need for such qualities arises. He must be "a *macho,* a he-man, if he wants to enter politics," yet he is capable of moments of compassion (Alba 1969:349). Presidents during the latter quarter of the nineteenth century of the ilk of Mexico's Porfirio Díaz and Argentina's Julio A. Roca, and even to an extent Brazil's Dom Pedro II, personified the *caudillo-macho* bosses who established dictatorships of "Order and Progress," following the positivist slogan. They were a blend of *personalismo, machismo,* and authoritarianism to the hilt. As such, they never ceased to add a personal touch to their office, which ingratiated them with those who supported them. On the other side of the coin, as we noted above, revolutionary-reformist President Francisco Madero of Mexico proved timid, vacillating, and ineffective, and consequently he simply didn't satisfy the expectations of the public and was soon overthrown by Victoriano Huerta (Meyer 1972). The personification of a revolutionary *caudillo* awaited the entry of Pancho Villa on the scene. He possessed, to a considerably greater degree than Madero, all the attributes that characterize *machismo* and *caudillismo* (Aramoni 1961:149–50).

When Generalisimo Francisco Franco ruled Spain, coins were stamped with his image and the caption: "*Caudillo* of Spain by the Grace of God." But whose God? Why, the *caudillo's* God, of course. And where did the *caudillo* get his special dispensation? Why, from God, whether his granting of this privilege is stated outright or remains implicit. Thus we have a circle that was vicious from the viewpoint of the outside antagonists but virtuous from that of the inside adulators. Those who felt it were in tune to the rhythm of the beat, and those who did not fought it to the bitter end, or they acquiesced, went into exile, or exercised a rather passive form of resistance. I wrote what I wrote not in justification or exaltation of Franco and Franquismo, but rather to suggest that what is felt is felt and that's that, no ifs, ands, or buts. That is how the populace that esteems a *caudillo(a)* esteems her/him.

But how, ultimately, can the *caudillismo* phenomenon be explained historically? Here is one interpretation of which I am particularly fond. Up to the last few decades, historians tended to conceive *caudillismo* as a particularly Latin American characteristic. More recently it is seen as a particular Latin American expression of a general stage in the evolution of societies and polities throughout the globe. Whenever feudal or archaic systems lose their ability to maintain their hegemony in the name of monarchic legitimacy, local *guerrillas* emerge and instability ensues. In Latin America, at the close of the eighteenth century, urban *criollo* aristocrats were imbued with enlightenment ideals, but unlike European nations, the countryside retained a quasi-feudal, quasi-corporate character. Loyalty to the local *patrón(a)* as embodiment of patronizing authority that encompassed the source of one's livelihood, one's spiritual guidance, and one's identity with the community expanded by centrifugal force to include the nation itself. In a fluctuating mix of *caudillismo* and ideals of equality and freedom for all, the nation now evolved into a milieu in which the most adept *caudillo(a)* became more equal than everyone else, because s/he was now a national father or mother figure whose task was that of granting certain freedom to those who remained closest to her/him in the hierarchical chain of status, influence, and respectability. In a very *concrete* sense, the *caudillo(a)* was most effectively able to endow her/himself with the best—and unfortunately often of the worst—of *personalismo, paternalismo, machismo,* and patriarchy (Lambert 1969).

Yes. There must be a concrete, private yet public, individual yet collective, feel for the *caudillo(a)* (as a consequence of Firstness). S/he is felt, not merely cognized, sensed, not merely intellectualized, interpreted tacitly and subsidiarily without the need for willfully executed focal interpretants. In fact, there is a quality of Firstness about the *caudillo(a)* that gets one in the guts. The *caudillo(a)* is what s/he is without the need of saying what s/he is—which would be an impossible task anyway. Whatever meat and potatoes of Secondness and Thirdness there is to the *caudillo(a)*, they are masked by the sizzling spice of Firstness the *caudillo(a)* exudes at every moment. S/he is *neither* simply what s/he is *nor* is s/he not what s/he is; s/he is always becoming *something else,* because s/he has been capable of filling that "emptiness" that potentially defines the *caudillo(a)* as what s/he *might be* or *would be* or *should be* as long as s/he is able to exercise her/his god-given talent for captivating the people.

I cannot overemphasize these concrete interrelations within a *caudillo(a)* setting. This is far removed from the relatively abstract linkage of authority found in the U.S. The president of the U.S., of course, is an individual with his own personality and character traits, his own behavioral patterns and idiosyncrasies. But this individual is to a large extent coterminous with the nature of whoever may occupy the presidency at whichever time: he conforms to the "job description." The concepts of "president" and "presidency" in the U.S. are abstract terms. They correspond to an institution. Whoever happens to occupy the position and act out the necessary role is there now and of utmost importance when carrying out her/his duties acceptably, then s/he is gone tomorrow. In Latin America, in contrast, the *caudillo(a), El/La Presidente,* is who s/he is: s/he is *Presidente,* the living incarnation of the presidency, s/he *is* the presidency and the presidency *is* her/him. There is no clearly defined abstract category, but rather, the term takes on its meaning in accord with the *caudillo(a)* here and now. There simply is no line of demarcation between the term as abstract symbol and as concrete feeling and sentiment, on the one hand, and as iconic and indexical links that are most intimate to human interrelations on the other. In fact, during the culminating moment of a *caudillo(a)'s* career, she is tantamount to the fatherland/motherland itself. S/he does not simply fill a slot that could have been filled by one of a given number of other individuals: s/he is prior to that slot, and hence she *is* that slot, so it was never really "empty" for it was nothing until s/he made it what it is. In this manner, when s/he is no longer *caudillo(a),* no longer voice and embodiment of the nation, when someone else has displaced her/him, *Presidente* and presidency as concrete terms will never be the same. There is now another *caudillo(a),* and the old *caudillo(a),* a fallen god, exists only in collective memory.

Latin American *caudillo(a)s* desire to climb the social ladder with much the same obsession that North Americans customarily desire to ascend the ladder to wealth. The *caudillo(a)'s* social ladder brings status, fame, admiration, and emulation. The North Americans' economic ladder does too. The chief difference is that the social ladder regarding *caudillismo* calls for more political action and sacrifice of the *caudillo(a)*'s time and efforts to a cause, whether real or fabricated: in this regard *caudillismo* is an extension of the responsibility the colonial paternalistic-patriarchal lord ideally shouldered. The capitalist economic ladder, in contrast, is calibrated primarily by a pecuniary tape measure, and aggressive "rugged individualism" in the no-holds-barred marketplace, political arena, or wherever, is the wherewithal for going the desired length. Both cases exact calculated behavior, each to its own end, and both require carefully orchestrated moves. Thus it can be said that the Latin American way of the *caudillo(a)* brings economic motives to bear on the political arena, while the prime motivator of North American politics is increasingly becoming money. Consequently, the appeal of populism, which in spirit has a *caudillismo* tinge to it, is of relatively diminished importance in politics, U.S. style.

It bears mentioning, in summary, that in spite of certain characteristics found in all *caudillo(a)s* throughout history they have come in many countenances and many guises. Juan Manuel Rosas, who dominated the Argentine republic from 1835 to 1852, was athletic, charismatic, and he could ride with the best *gauchos* around. Doctor José Rodríguez Francia (1811–40) of Paraguay was a cultured aristocrat, while his contemporary, Antonio López Santa Anna (1828–44) of Mexico was a rich *criollo,* and Diego Portales (1830–37) of Chile was a wealthy entrepreneur. The Guatemalan Rafael Carrera (1838–65) was an illiterate Amerindian, Benito Juárez (1857–72) of Mexico, also of Amerindian roots, was in contrast an educated liberal politician who found it necessary to exercise *caudillo(a)*-like power. The Bolivian José Mariano Melgarejo (1864–71) was an illiterate *mestizo* alcoholic, while *mestizos* Andrés Santa Cruz (1829–39) of Bolivia and Rufino Barros (1872–95) of Guatemala were exceedingly cruel and barbarous military men, and Gabriel García Moreno (1869–75) of Ecuador was a professor and religious fanatic. Then there was Evita, offering a complementary matriarchal image that elevated her to the status of one of the greatest *caudillo(a)s* of them all.

Some *caudillo(a)s* were honest and forthright, while others were hardly more than thieves; some believed in and sincerely attempted to institute justice, while others arbitrarily meted out barbaric and vindictive punishment; some were of humble demeanor, while others suffered from delusions of grandeur. There simply is no stereotypical *caudillo(a),* yet all have a few loose and limber characteristics in common. Regarding Latin American *caudillo(a)s, either/ors* become fuzzy, borders fade, and *both-ands* and *neither-nors* emerge. This characteristic bears testimony to the flux and flow, the living semiosis of Latin American "cultural logics." I would suggest at this juncture that these Latin American cultural logics are of the nature of cultural logics the world over. The difference is that Latin America, given its screaming pitch of hybridity, brings these "logics" to the fore with greater aplomb.

On to consideration of a distinctively Brazilian phenomenon, which, I hope, will afford us a giant step toward an understanding of the topic at hand.

Jeito-Jeitinho

"Tem jeito ou não tem jeito?" ("Does she have that special 'knack' or 'cunning' about her or not?"). That is the question dividing the adroit, skillful, dexterous, sly, shrewd, subtle, clever, nimble, quick-witted, astute, perspicacious, ingenious, artful, adventuresome Brazilian from ordinary folks—whatever "ordinary folks" means, whatever "adroit, . . . etc." means. *Jeito* is, along with *saudade,* one of the most difficult words in Brazilian Portuguese to decipher (Prado 1962). The term is confusingly polyfaceted: "Dar um jeito" (= "To find some singular way, make do with what you have, bend the rules a little, pull a few strings"), "O jeito é . . ." (= "The singular, etc. way to do it is . . ."), "É o jeito" (= "It's the best or most subtly clever way"), "Ao jeito de" (= "In the particularly cunning style of"), "Daquele jeito" (= "In that uniquely sly way"), "De qualquer jeito" (= "Anyway"), "De jeito nenhum!" (= "No way!"), and so on (Levine 1997:80–110).[17]

A Brazilian who has the good fortune to have been born with the gift of *jeito* has that charming way about her. She always has a few tricks up her sleeve, in her creative, unorthodox, somewhat idiosyncratic way. She has that special style for communicating in a familiar, down-to-earth manner with people from all walks of life and according to what the particular situation calls for. She has a unique talent for getting things done, her way, through her verbal aplomb, and the apparent ease and spontaneity in her dealings with others. She is especially adroit in *jeitinho* practices (i.e., when engaging in "dar um jeito," as mentioned above). The unwritten, tacit custom of the *jeitinho brasileiro* entails methods for using and beating the system by subtle means almost always with a note of humor, a little irony, a wink of the eye, a knowing nod, and perhaps a dash of cynicism—all by use of subtle "hidden transcripts," of course. It is a means for avoiding bureaucratic glitches and authoritarian and institutional roadblocks, a way to get things done in the most expedient way possible. In the most positive sense, it is tightly linked to Brazil's national identity, it is a "symbol of our cordiality, street smarts, and conciliatory character" (Barbosa 1995:47).

Jeito-jeitinho: it is witness to untranslatable knots in the web of the Portuguese language. If ever there was living proof of philosopher Willard v. O. Quine's (1960) "untranslatability principle"—briefly to be discussed in chapter nine—this is it. The words simply cannot be said in English. Indeed, "O jeito, isso sim tem jeito" ("'Jeito' itself, yeah, it's really got 'jeito'"). The sign is its own sign, a sign of itself, so to speak. It doubles back on itself to evince a mirror-image of itself. At the same time it mirrors the whole of the way of being Brazilian, in all its complexity, in all its particularities (the sign's practice is proof of language and everyday life in terms of its being felt at tacit levels, the product of subsidiary know-how). Lívia Barbosa offers an entire volume on the word and what it entails. She writes that after beating her head against the wall for some time, she realized her confused state of mind had a bearing on her incapacity to comprehend that the negative, the "no," in Brazil, does not signify that which semantically we would ordinarily expect it to signify. She discovered that "no" is not the/a limit. Unlike laws, cultural codes of conduct and norms do not set down boundaries fixed for all time but remain to a greater or lesser degree flexible; that is to say, the "no" they imply is fuzzy. So also the "no" between the two "jeitos" in "Tem jeito" and "Não tem jeito" is exceedingly slippery (Barbosa 1992:2). The "no," in regards to "jeito" more than perhaps any other Brazilian vocable, means "No," and it also means "Not really no and not really yes," it means "Perhaps yes"; it means "By all means, yes"; it means "No, . . . but yes"; it means "No, . . . but, . . . well, just no"; it means *Both* yes *and* no"; it means *"Neither* yes *nor* no"; it means *"All* of the above"; it means *"None* of the above." In short, it means what it means, but not so very clearly and not so very distinctly, and at the same time it means what it does not mean, but at the same time. . . . And so on. Perplexing, all this.

Jeito-jeitinho can be conceived as a sort of move toward meritocracy, toward an egalitarian social setting—which flattens an otherwise hierarchical society—toward political stabilization. To the extent that in Brazil there are inequalities in the distribution of rewards, through the dialogical, egalitarian practice of *jeitinho,* resentment toward those who receive greater rewards by those who receive fewer rewards is less intense than we would expect. This is because justification of rewards is often offered on the basis of merit—she who is most adept at the *jeitinho* game—and not necessarily on the basis of tradition or social status. That is, privilege earned by merit in *jeitinho* culture somehow becomes morally and politically more acceptable to most people than privilege earned by inheritance. In nine words, *jeitinho* is in a manner of speaking "of the people," "by the people," and "for the people."

Barbosa interviewed a number of Brazilians for her study of *jeitinho* and found that they all recognize the term and know what it means; that is, they have a feel for its meaning (within the sphere of Firstness). One interviewee suggested that the word is used and put into practice by all Brazilians "from the office boy to the president" (Barbosa 1992:32). Obviously it is understood and put into practice quite differently by office boys and presidents. Yet everybody understands it and uses—and often abuses—it, each in her own way. *Jeitinho* at once implies the maximum of generality and the maximum of particularity. It's a general way of everybody's getting things done within particular circumstances and according to the ways of particular individuals. It's a unique way things get done with whatever is at hand and by creative individuals wherever and whenever. It's serious business, for one's survival is at stake, whether in the local market place, at knife's edge in the *favelas,* over a brandy discussing a million dollar business deal, or at the conference table while engaging in political decisions that will affect the lives of millions. It's the business of showing off one's ability to give a sly wink while distorting ordinary social, political, and economic customs and habits (compare to the "I obey but I do not comply" dictum as discussed above). It's straight talk, and it's talk peppered with irony, cynicism, sarcasm, mockery, parody, satire, and word play of all sorts. It's a carnival of words and of gestures, of interrelations and the codependent emergence of signs becoming more signs.

None of the characters of our polylogue practiced *jeitinho.* Not really. They were too wrapped up in themselves. They communicated, to a very limited extent, but didn't really communicate with *jeito,* because any given one of them could not comprehend the subtlety and complexity of the whole affair—though the composite of all the characters afforded a comprehensive grasp of it. In a certain stretch of the imagination, put all the characters together and you have a certain sense of *jeito.* No,

. . . no . . . that's not right, not really. Someone definitely constructed the polylogue. Borges and I, in this particular case. And for obvious reasons I, a mere Anglo-American guy, don't really and can't really have *jeito*. So the collection of characters cannot evince it. But, . . . wait a minute. I believe I do have considerable familiarity with Brazil, and with Borges and his characters, and with Beckett and waiting for something to happen but since it doesn't happen one just invents things to say and do—recall Pierre of the polylogue and Borges's "Pierre Menard, Author of the Quixote" (1962 [1944]) in this regard. Beckett's invention, Borges's heterogeneous mix of incompatible characters that found their way into our polylogue, and Brazil's contradictory complementary fusion and confusion of words and gestures. All this I know to a certain degree, or at least so I would hope. It seems that at least a tinge of *jeito,* and many other things as well, must have rubbed off on me, somehow. Perhaps. So in a loose sort of way I must know at least something of what *jeito-jeitinho* is, and at the same time I don't know what it is. Perhaps.

The subtitle of Barbosa's volume, "The Art of Becoming More Equal Than Everybody Else," is revealing. The individual who has *jeito* usually manages to get his way because there is that certain "way" about him. That "way" is as charming as it is repulsive, as attractive as it is revolting, as captivating as it is reprehensible. But it is the "way" of all who know how to become "more equal" than their fellow citizens. "More equal?" The very phrase incorporates the "illogical logic" of *jeito-jeitinho.* If some are "more equal" than others, then there is no equality, and if there is no equality, then some cannot be "more equal" than others. That is the beauty and the banality of the word and its practice. *Jeito-jeitinho* implies a continuous spectrum of "equality." In a manner of speaking, all Brazilians are born into the possibility of *jeitinho* "equally," but some soon find themselves chained by the *jeito* of others because they knew not how to cultivate their God-given talent for becoming "more *jeitinho* equal" than others.

This "democratizing" function of *jeito-jeitinho* may seem like a dubious cultural model. Privilege earned by inheritance has long been at least marginally acceptable to oppressed or marginalized peoples on the basis of mystical or fatalistic beliefs in an eternal order—the adverse effects of a lingering enchantment of the world. Such beliefs at least offer a certain sense of security. On the other hand, privilege earned because one person happens to be more quick witted, sly, shrewd, cynical, or poetically endowed than other people is a difficult pill to swallow. However, perhaps many of those souls who are—or think they are—scrambling up the ladder would like to believe in the saving grace of *jeito-jeitinho.* Yet the fact remains that, to reiterate, entering into the play of *jeito-jeitinho* can be advantageous for the person who has it, but it is neither a crutch nor a master key for the havenots: they play the game and for their efforts they might be the focus of a few smiles, laughter, an "Isn't she cute, quaint, a clown, or whatever," or she is tossed a coin in a nearby can or hat. One might come up with the rejoinder that just as nobody who is not a yuppie can love or admire a yuppie, on the other side of the coin we have the adage that only an adept *jeitinheur* can appreciate another *jeitinheur* and pay him due respect, and in the process both are dehierarchized. The other side of the coin, moreover, is just that: *other.* Princes may seem to be kindly father figures, and yuppies may be nothing but spoiled siblings. Their status came relatively easily for them. If they are nimble *jeitinheurs,* so much the better; and if not, they may still be able quite effectively to stay at the top or percolate toward the top: things are relatively cut and dried; everyone knows his place. A meritocratic *jeito-jeitinho* cultural hodge-podge, it hardly needs saying, is certainly one of the least stable systems imaginable. It is precisely because of this cultural fragility that racism and sexism and social class enter the picture, but *jeito-jeitinho* exercises its tendency to soothe wounds and salve bruised egos.

Barbosa constructs a three-term set of categories for depicting *jeito-jeitinho* culture. On the left side we have the "Favor," on the right side, "Corruption," with "Jeitinho" in the middle. Corruption is corruption, at whatever level, and after granting the term's polyvalence, I will assume we are all in some agreement regarding its meaning. But what is favor? This uniquely Brazilian slant on a universal Western practice calls for some qualification. Portuguese colonization of Brazil, based on monopolization of the land, gave rise basically to three social categories: lords, slaves, and "free men," who were in fact dependent upon the proprietorship of the lords. Relations between masters and slaves were relatively well defined. Relations between lords and "free men" were for the most part that of dominant and subaltern, to use current fashionable terminology.[18] Any benefit that might be forthcoming to the so-called "free man" was by way of some form or other of favor from those who wielded power.

Favor was the general form of social mediation, more appealing and more in line with the practices of *jeitinho* than slavery. It is understandable that the institution—we must call it an institution, so embedded in everyday practices as it is—has found its way into Brazil's literature, most notably in the works of Machado de Assis. Favor formed and gave flavor to the national life of Brazil, and it perseveres to this day. It is present everywhere, in politics, industry, commerce, professions, skilled and unskilled labor, and at the soccer stadium, in the restaurant, and in the home. Brazilian critic Roberto Schwarz writes that:

> Slavery gives the lie to liberal ideas; but favour, more insidiously, uses them, for its own purposes, originating a new ideological pattern. The element of arbitrariness, the fluid play of preferences to which favour subjects whatever it touches, cannot be fully rationalized. . . . Favour in turn implies the dependency of the individual, the exception to the rule, ornamental culture, arbitrary pay and the servility of labour. . . . [Favour] governed both patronage and gratitude. The symbolic compensation was perhaps a little out of tune, but not ungrateful. (Schwarz 1992:22–23)

Schwarz goes on to suggest that from the very beginning of Brazilian history favor falsely assures the weak that somehow they are not really slaves, in spite of their subservient position, and it assures the powerful that their position of superiority is secure. Each needs the other, both in their complicity recognize their place in the social game of make-believe-that-you-are-not-really-like-this, and the centuries of slavery are conveniently conjured away. Yet this "recognition sustains an extraordinary complicity, made even worse by the adoption of the bourgeois vocabulary of equality, merit, labour and reason" (Schwarz 1992:25).

Barbosa, to repeat, places favor at one extreme and corruption at the other, with *jeitinho* falling in the space between the two. Favor takes on a positive connotation with respect to corruption as the lesser of the two evils, so to speak, relegating corruption to negative connotativity. Favor at least implies reciprocal action, although it is understood that one party enjoys an advantage over the other. Corruption, in contrast, is ordinarily a one-way street: one party wins and the other one loses. Since *jeitinho* can be an *either/or* affair, but also either *both-and* or *neither-nor,* it can be *either* of positive *or* negative connotation, or *both,* or *neither.* There is a leveling effect in the *jeitinho* custom. In many cases there might not be a clear distinction between superordinate and subordinate; in others the distinction might be there but it becomes diffuse and cloudy during acts of *jeitinho;* in yet others the tables might be overturned with respect to superior/inferior categories. For these reasons *jeitinho* can to a certain degree take place between players of the game who hardly know each other, while favor is usually solicited solely among friends and relatives. Moreover, petition for a favor demands a relatively formal setting, while *jeitinho* can take place most anywhere: at home, at play, at work, in the street, restaurant, and so on.

The distinction between *jeitinho* and corruption might appear to be clearer than that between *jeitinho* and favor. But in practice, confusion ensues. *Jeitinho* is subtle and discreet. Corruption, though customarily an under-the-table operation, is relatively straightforward, in addition to the fact that it usually involves a larger sum of money, a greater infraction of the law, a more scandalous infringement of social conventions.[19] Consequently, corruption tends to widen the gap between haves and havenots, dominant and subservient, powerful and subalterns, while *jeitinho* often, though not always, brings about a move in the other direction. It has a flattening effect. The general attitude is: "Today he is more equal than I because his *jeitinho* was in better rhythm than mine, but tomorrow it may be my turn." *Jeitinho* is not the sole possession of some individuals and inaccessible to others. It is in a sense "out there," in constant flux, and for all to share. At any given moment the sharing is unequal, but in the long run of things *jeitinho* exercises an equalizing tendency. Barbosa concludes that although those who engage in favor, *jeitinho,* and corruptive interactions believe there is a definite line of demarcation between them, in actual practice the borders become fused and confused.

Barbosa also takes pains to distinguish—insofar as that is possible—between the person who has *jeito* and the *malandro* (scoundrel, rogue, rascal, a general badass). The *malandro* is street-wise and sly, and somewhat of a layabout, a scoundrel, and perhaps a con artist, though not necessarily a crook. The opportunistic *malandro* might be an idler, yet he is capable of furious activity if an opportunity presents itself and he believes an advantageous position can be gained.[20] There is a certain affinity between the *malandro* and the "pícaro," a trickster, rogue, or rascal, of the Hispanic tradition. Yet there is also somewhat of an affinity between the "pícaro" and he who has *jeito.* In general the difference between *malandragem* (roguish practices) and *jeitinho* is that the former lurks along the margins of legality, where one must constantly improvise, making do with what one has, while striving to subvert the system, perhaps merely for the sake of doing so, but preferably for some gain or other.[21] The latter, *jeitinho,* in part maintains the appearance of legality, but it often involves illegal activities, so it is *neither* legal *nor* illegal, it is in a manner of speaking "paralegal." While *malandragem* calls for constant improvisation, *jeitinho* allows for a greater degree of creativity; whereas *malandragem* requires a relatively fixed set of individualized acts during each moment of the life of the *malandro*, *jeitinho* entails process, ongoing individualizing acts in a series in which each successive act is something other than what any and all preceding acts were.[22] *Jeitinho* calls for a perpetual process of becoming someone other than what one had been in the process of becoming.

The art of *jeitinho* is not entirely absent in Spanish American cultures, where rogues and operators and charmers also abound. On writing this I actually have another aspect of *jeitinho* in mind, that of the "Cantinflas" sort (the character played by Mario Moreno in Mexican films). Both Pedro de Malasartes—a fictitious character and a sort of Brazilian Cantinflas—and Macunaíma—the protagonist created by Mario de Andrade, Brazilian writer of the "modernist" movement in his novella *Macunaíma* (1984 [1928])—each in his own way, embody *jeitinho* (Barbosa 1992:44–47). The verb "cantinflear," the adjective "cantinfleado," and the present participle "cantinfleando" imply a confusion and an evasion of reality by the indirect use of language as a weapon. Twisting and turning use and subtle abuse of language by means of "cantinfleadas" might enable one to take advantage of each and every situation, thereby becoming "more equal" than others, even than those that had been the "cantinfleador's" social, political, and economic superiors. But now they are not. They have been flattened to the level, or perhaps even below the level, of the wily "cantinfleador" who now happens to be in their midst.[23]

Intriguing as this topic may be, however, I must move along; the semiosic flow moves us along.

A Paradoxological Social Drama

No ethnography-etymology of *jeitinho* would be sufficient without reference to Roberto DaMatta's (1991, 1994) study of the social drama surrounding a commonplace expression that attempts to re-establish the hierarchization that *jeitinho* tends to flatten. This melodrama is condensed into the expression: "Você sabe com quem está falando?" ("Do you know who you are speaking to?").

Defiance, challenge, social distanciation, de-personalization, objectification of the subjectivized. The phrase is as complex as it is simple. In DaMatta's conception it highlights the perpetual conflict between *individual* and *person*.[24] The individual is product of Enlightenment egalitarianism according to which all people were born equal and stand on equal footing. The individual is in this respect a social atom, a body that fills a category, any body, anywhere, and at anytime. In contrast, a person is someone, tantamount to an embodiment of the original *fidalgo/a* (Spanish, *hidalgo/a*), a son or daughter of someone of social stature, someone important. "Você sabe . . .?" hierarchizes. *Jeitinho* and *malandragem*, complementary expressions in part evolving out of what Sergio Buarque de Holanda (1935) originally termed "o homen cordial" (the cordial individual), tend to de-hierarchize (Resende 2000). "Você sabe . . .?" in other words is in a sense the negation of *jeitinho* and *malandragem*. While *jeitinho* and *malandragem* are manifestations of "democratizing" tendencies, "Você sabe . . .?" reaffirms Brazilian authoritarianism. Social interaction at work, during negotiations in public gatherings or in the street, may evolve into a cordial give-and-take, a one-upmanship affair of *jeitinho*. But when the presumably subordinate "individual" of the verbal and gestural bantering unwittingly or intentionally steps beyond what the dominant "person" considers that invisible line of social demarcation, "Você sabe . . .?" may erupt to put him in his proper place.

"Você sabe . . .?" is somewhat comparable to that expression in the United States, "Who do you think you are?" The latter commonplace phrase, however, places sharper focus on the subordinate individual in an effort to shove him down to what is considered the proper social level; the former, in contrast, throws the spotlight on the dominant person and in the process elevates her appropriately. Nevertheless, "Who do you think you are?" is in Brazil somewhat the social counterpart of "Você sabe . . .?" In the United States the individual is all-important. Everybody is first and foremost an individual. He possesses an individuality that stands out above and beyond all other individualities insofar as its owner is capable of winning at whatever socio-cultural game is being played: to be "Número uno" is the name of the game, for one must triumph at all cost. In Brazil, a person is with much greater frequency a person by birth, or if not, by a long and successful series of *jeitinho* encounters, and now, she is surrounded by individuals who must pay her proper respect. In Brazil, when appropriate social distinctions are to be reaffirmed, the person must rise to the highest possible peak of the social terrain, in contrast to the United States, where the individual must find his place (Barbosa 1992:75–77).

In sum, unlike *jeitinho*, "Você sabe . . .?" makes use of the authoritarian base of Brazilian culture. It de-equalizes and re-establishes presumed social identity. It is a rite of separation or distinction, it re-fortifies symmetrical relationships, and above all, it negates, it says one cannot occupy the social pigeon-hole one is trying to enter, that one must not try to take leave of one's "inferior" standing. *Jeitinho*, on the other hand, is a matter of verbal and gestural negotiations, of indirect bargaining, of imposing one's will on others through amiable, informal, indirect and subtle nuances, by means of a large dose of word play. And all that without really taking things too seriously. "Você sabe . . .?" is a game with explicitly and implicitly defined rules, where the winner takes all; *jeitinho* is relatively ruleless play, perhaps apparently frivolous. Yet the *jeitinheur* always has a hidden and very important purpose in mind: ultimately to get the upper hand. Unlike "Você sabe . . .?" however, where ideally the winners are always the same winners, in the play of *jeitinho*, today's winner may be tomorrow's loser, and vice versa. "Você sabe . . .?" then, tends toward binary relations, tree structures, mannerist social labyrinths of bifurcating paths, and Deleuze and Guattari's (1983) molar, hierarchized "paranoia." *Jeitinho* tends toward *n*-ary relations, *rhizomic* nonlinear labyrinths, and Deleuze and Guattari's molecular, nomadic "schizophrenia."

To wrap things up, the terms I have introduced in these last sections illustrate, I would suggest, the *is* and *is not* and at the same time *both* the *is* and the *is not* and *neither* the *is nor* the *is not*. The *caudillo(a)*, can rise up chiefly by force. The *macho* becomes what he is in part by force also. These terms are of the more dualistic, of the "A or Not-A" sort, much like "Você sabe . . .?" *Jeitinho*, on the other hand, is more "democratic" and more pluralistic by nature. It approaches the ideal of "*Both* A *and* Not-A," and in the best of possible cases perhaps even "*Neither* A *nor* Not-A."

Spanish American *personalismo* may also make overtures toward *jeitinho,* often as derived from the "Você sabe . . .?" syndrome. But it never quite gets there. It never gets there, because no matter how close the ties of *personalismo* may be, they always remain short of the mark because of a social difference, which can at any moment lead to an eruption of the "Você sabe . . .?" sort. Since the difference remains, other possibilities from the border of borders, from that infinitesimal yet infinitely expansive chasm between the *neither* and the *nor,* can emerge. They emerge in interrelationship, in the incongruous complementarity and codependent emergence, with all other possibilities.

The stories of *personalismo, machismo, caudillismo,* and *jeitinho,* I would submit, are stories of general sign processes as they were outlined in Chapter Two. There is no dualism regarding the four terms in question, but rather, each term merges in semiosic, triadic fashion, via the border of borders, with its *other,* with all its *others,* and those *others* merge with the one. The rushing, gushing play of signs and nonverbal communication surrounding these key terms of Latin America's forms of life dance to the resonating rhythms of syncopated cultural beats, whose "logics" confuse inflexible minds that want everything in its proper place because everything should know its proper place. As far as these cultural "logics" are concerned, there is no "proper place" for all seasons and all reasons, for all that is is semiosis and all that is semiosis is process. So goes life in Latin America.

Perhaps it behooves us to pursue these strange "logics" a little further. In order to do so, I invite you to walk with me along a digressionary path.

Notes

1. This entire chapter will be a study of generalizations, that is, of stereotypes that border on the archetypal. These generalizations are in part the product of popular images and the behavior they elicit more than historical veracity, of cultural fabrications more than reality. I write this in light of Russell's warning against loose generalization and illicit use of "logical types," briefly discussed in chapter three. There, I also alluded to the impossibility of everyday communication without violating "logical types" along the way. While keeping in mind that stereotypes as generalities often do irreparable harm, for strategic purposes I recreate a few of them in this chapter for the purpose of illustrating certain facets of Latin America's cultures in preparation for the succeeding chapters.

2. Roberto DaMatta (1986:28–30), in this regard, places political legitimacy in the person, not the presidency, which thereby creates the "problem" of legitimacy in Latin American as seen through the eyes of many outside scholars (see Lambert 1969).

3. An excellent survey of the Cuban condition up to and including the Cuban revolution, and how Castro could have become such an overpowering, ubiquitous force is offered by Louis A. Pérez in *On Becoming Cuban: Identity, Nationality and Culture* (1999).

4. Reference of the phrase in quotes is to Spanish existentialist Miguel de Unamuno's (1954) philosophy.

5.   *Malinche* (the Spanish counterpart to the Nahuatl name, *Malintzín*) was an Amerindian who served as Cortes's translator, counselor and mistress, and, so the legend goes, she also helped Cortes get the psychological upper-hand in his engagement with the Aztec emperor, Moctezuma II. Thus she has gone down in history as an emblem of female transgression and treachery. In today's Mexico to be branded a "malinchista" is the height of insult; it is to indicate that one has turned one's back on one's own cultural heritage (for further, Alarcón 1989, Cypess 1991, Glantz 1995, Mirandé and Enríquez 1979).

6.   Yet Reyes Nevares (1970:15), writing of contemporary *machismo* in Mexico, argues that it is basically the flight of the male from underlying feelings of weakness, weakness *vis-à-vis* the *Mariana* image and as compensation a show of strength in confrontation with the *Malinche* image. This apparently inextricable element of *machismo* is not necessarily inherent to Catholicism. *Machismo* actually runs contrary to the traditional emphasis on a contrite, crucified, broken, and impotent Christ, a "macho turned inside out" (Nelson 1971:75). *Machismo* continues to evince this sacred-secular dualism, nonetheless, in spite of Spanish philosopher Miguel de Unamuno's (1958) effort to instill a "virility of faith" in Catholic males.

7.   The interrelationship was exploited to the maximum by the stereotypical Latin American *caudillo,* to be discussed in the following section.

8.   See also Díaz-Guerrero (1975) and Goldwert (1980), both of whom generally follow Ramos's thesis.

9.   I might point out that presumed *macho* tendencies are quite common throughout the Spanish speaking countries of the tropical areas, though they are less pronounced in Brazil (where there are wide regional distinctions); while in Argentina, Chile, and Uruguay, the situation is in certain ways more akin to Southern European cultures than to the rest of Spanish America (Andreski 1966:47).

10. Gutmann (1996) argues very convincingly how the *macho* tradition is waning in Mexico, given the demands of life in contemporary Mexico City where the women must take to the streets and work one and often two shifts. See also Brusco (1995) on how evangelist movements in Colombia bring about a tempering effect on *machista* tendencies.

11. It bears mentioning that Castro tried to root *machismo* out of the Cuban psyche. However, he conceded to a degree of defeat in 1971 with the observation that "we still have to fight it. Unfortunately there is machismo. Not as much as in Mexico, but there is still machismo here. It is something that exists and it will be a long fight to eradicate all those attitudes which are so deeply rooted in the mentality of some people" (Levinson and Brightman 1971:20).

12. Indeed, in the Peircean sense there is *both* a self (in the fluctuating sense) *and* there is no self (in the fixed sense). So from an orthogonal vantage point it can be said that there is *neither* a self *nor* is there not a self; there is just incessantly self-perpetuating semiosis (for more on Peirce's concept of the perpetually transient self, see Colapietro 1989).

13. As with *machismo,* I cannot hope to do justice to the term *caudillismo,* but rather, I attempt to give it sufficient qualification so as to provide for its relevance to the story being unfolded here. For more detailed discussion of the phenomenon of

caudillismo, see Barager (1968), Bushnell (1988), Finer (1988), Goldwert (1980), Hamill (1992), Lambert (1969), Lynch (1992), Nicholson (1969), Souchère (1964).

14. The noun *chingón* comes from the verb *chingar.* The meaning of this verb in Mexico is complex, and I make no pretentions of being able to clarify it here. In its most vulgar connotation it means "to screw" or "fuck." The chimerical *la chingada* is the mother image, not the mother of flesh and blood but a mythical figure, dating from the time of *Malinche* and the rape of the first Amerindian women by the Spanish conquerers. In contrast, the *gran chingón* is he who, by physical force, verbal manipulation, and the force of his will, is able to "screw" everybody else. In Paz's words, the verb *chingar:*

> has as many shadings as it has intonations, as many meanings as it
> has emotions. One may be a *chingón,* a *gran chingón* (in business,
> in politics, in crime, or with women), or a *chingaquedito* (silent,
> deceptive, fashioning plots in the shadows, advancing cautiously,
> and then striking with a club), or a *chingoncito.* But in this plural-
> ity of meanings the ultimate meaning always contains the idea of
> aggression, whether it is the simple act of molesting, pricking, or
> censuring, or the violent act of wounding or killing. The verb de-
> notes violence, an emergence from oneself to penetrate another by
> force. It also means to injure, to lacerate, to violate—bodies,
> souls, objects—and to destroy. (Paz 1961:76–77 [1952])

15. Evita, Juan Perón's wife, is the shining example of a *caudilla* in a quite positive light, whereas the cold, brutal "Doña Bárbara" of Rómulo Gallego's novel by the same name (1942 [1929]) is one of the best examples of a *caudilla* in a negative light.

16. In anthropology and communication theory Gregory Bateson (1972) and Anthony Wilden (1972) develop the idea of *symmetrical* and *complementary* relations, which bears some resemblance to the incongruously complementary scheme I am in the process of developing here. The resemblance breaks down, however, insofar as theirs remains binary, while in my own conception, symmetry/complementarity is itself incongruously complementary, which is to say that a third term, many alternative terms, can slip into the virgule, the border of borders, separating the presumed oppositions.

17. As I understand Lívia Barbosa (1995), *jeito* refers to that special ability for getting things done with a knack and an ingratiating twist of customs and of language; *jeitinho* ("little *jeito*") refers to the general practice itself. Hereafter, I will often hyphenate the two terms, *jeito* and *jeitinho,* in order to maintain the necessary distinction between them and at the same time link them.

18. "Subaltern," "subalternity," "subalternative," buzz-words within hegemonic scholarly circles these days, relate to an individual or individuals of inferior rank or range, people of a subordinate position. I have neither time nor place in this inquiry to provide ample discussion of the problematics inherent in the term as it emerged from within postcolonial work in the Indian context and its application to the Amerindian condition in Latin America. Subaltern investigator Ranajit Guha's (1988:8)

definition of the term might seem general enough to fit into any cultural milieu that might go by the name of postcolonialism. Yet, there is controversy. I simply make mention here of Mallon's (1994:1507) allusion to textualism and elitism among Latinamericanist literary scholars of subalternity, Beverley's (1999:85–88) labeling subalternity excessively binary in nature, and Mignolo's (2000:196) observation that the term as used in Indian Subaltern Studies is "from and by Indians," whereas in Latin America it is largely a *criollo* experience, hence quite distinct. I leave the final say on the matter to specialists on the issue.

19. For this reason the concept of "corruption" is proper to the United States's relatively "dualistic" and "binary" mind-set, while "jeitinho" remains as a strange, alien phenomenon (DaMatta 1984:43, Santos 1966). "Jeitinho" is more than binary, it is extra-binary, it always implies the *both-and* and the *neither-nor* at the same time that there is more explicit focus on the *either-or,* one thing and its antagonistic counterpart.

20. Rowe and Schelling (1991:138–39), allude to *samba malandro,* a response of the African American subculture to the harsh reality of exploitation and discrimination, which led to a "rejection of the work ethic and to a counter-cultural idealization of idleness and of the body as a source of pleasure rather than as an instrument of work." This interpretation, while revealing, is actually a variation of the more general theme of the "malandro" (for further, DaMatta 1991).

21. In this regard, *malandragem* goes hand in hand with that ritualistic-agonistic-rhythmic musical-dance activity, the *capoeira,* which will be briefly discussed in chapter sixteen.

22. There is a relationship between these two Portuguese terms and the Spanish "vacilar" (to "vacillate," "hesitate," "fluctuate," "stagger," but also to "trick," "elude," "jest," "simulate," and so on) which is also virtually untranslatable into English. Characteristic of the pregnant meaning of the word, an alteration, "vacilada," is a tongue-in-cheek, roguish, sly verbal act. It entails one's donning a *mestizo* mask consisting of a fusion of Amerindian irony and the Spanish picaresque, all of which is "baroqued" by a bit of fantasy.

23. Cantinflas and the act of "cantanflear" has recently been criticized on the grounds that Cantinflas, in his playing the role of the subaltern, portrays the poor strata of the cities of Mexico as helpless, hopeless, and passive—even idiotic—cogs in the social machinery (Pilcher 2001). However, I would take a more positive view, especially found in Cantinflas's early films (see in this regard Bartra 1992:123–29; Monsiváis 1988:77–96).

24. This, however, is not just another binary relationship. Like DaMatta's other apparent oppositions, ultimately it implies the *both-and* and the *neither-nor* in addition to the *either-or* (see Hess and DaMatta 1995).

Chapter Five

Paralogical Meditations

> The borderland, like the God of the Scholastic philosophers, will be everywhere and nowhere.
> —Alfred Mac Adam

> Our dreams would end up getting caught in the webs of the border.
> —Guillermo Gómez-Peña

It Is All Becoming What It Is Becoming

As was implied in chapter one, Karl Popper maintained that belief at its core has little respect for reason. The most respectable way of conducting one's affairs is to look for grounds for reasonable doubt, to disbelieve, and to give tentative reasons for one's disbelief in order to place in question one's erstwhile belief. In other words, one should play the Devil's advocate not by suspending disbelief but by suspending belief. Then, by creating an imaginary, contrary to fact situation—often called a "thought experiment"—one can postulate what would happen if certain conditions were to inhere. And, by putting this imaginary situation to a practical test, one can create better grounds for one's belief—a new belief that must now be suspended, and subsequently another hypothetical situation can be created. This is in part an endorsement of David Hume's notion regarding inductive arguments from the observed to the unobserved: no conclusion that is forthcoming from the observed is any iron-clad reason to believe without a shadow of a doubt anything in regards to hitherto unobserved phenomena. That is to say, the premise of an inductive conclusion is no necessary reason to believe in that conclusion. Inductive skepticism, then, plays havoc with the will to believe, and for obvious reasons.

That much said, for the purpose of the present volume I see no need to write any more on the matter. What is worthy of brief note is Peirce's suggestion that there are basically four methods for "fixing belief" (*CP*:5.358–77). (1) One can unthinkingly accept whatever the patriarchal voice of *authority* happens to hand down. This more often than not will get one nowhere, Peirce writes, for it might well be that there is little to no sense or sanity regarding authority's iron-hand or sleight-of-hand, whichever the case might be. (2) One can engage in that Cartesian practice of plumbing the depths of one's solitary *introspective* powers presumably to discover, *a priori*, the one and only Truth, and from that point erect one's epistemological edifice. But who is to say that one person is any more capable at this game than any other person? Who is to be the ultimate arbiter? Peirce rejects this method outright. (3) One can grab onto an idea and *tenaciously* cling to it for dear life, come what may. The problem here is that this procedure could turn into a solipsistic enterprise. This is for Peirce entirely unacceptable. (4) It is the *community* on which Peirce focuses his attention—which, I must add, evinces the idea of the interrelated, interactive, codependent emerging of all signs in the participatory universe of semiosis. We cannot live by individual belief alone. Rather, through a process of dialogical give-and-take, we and the entire community to which we belong can perhaps stand some chance of arriving at some quite plausible answers to at least a few of our questions. With these answers, hopefully we can best govern our affairs, at least until someone in the community unsuspends disbelief, which serves to open the dialogue once again. Then, after some affable bantering, hard-nosed debates, and perhaps even some verbal pyrotechnics, we may be able to arrive at another tentative and tenderly fallible answer to some problem or other. And life somehow goes on.

Now, what I am saying is that to say the answer to a question is "*Either* A *or* Not-A (or B)" and then to decide it is "A," take a leap of belief into it, and carry on into the distant horizon, is not sufficient. In many cases, the procedure is not necessarily and with respect to all possible circumstances of any more validity than assuming at the outset that the answer is "B." Neither is it of more validity than assuming that it is "*Both* A *and* B," or that it is "*Neither* A *nor* B."[1] At one time the Earth ("A") was the center of the universe, then it was the Sun ("B"). From an ahistorical vantage, juxtaposing "A" and "B" gives a syncretic package, "*Both* the Earth ('A') *and* the Sun ('B') are the center of the universe." The pre-Copernican tells us one thing; the post-Copernican tells us another thing. From the ahistorical perspective, they are both right according to their particular mind-set. From the historical perspective, neither of them is right, for today, we more properly enlightened souls believe that "*Neither* the Earth ('A') *nor* the Sun ('B') is the center of the universe, but the answer lies elsewhere" (in Einsteinian relativity). Each one of these possibilities constitutes a world, and the concoction of any of them or all of them, however *inconsistent* that concoction may be, is also a world. But no matter how many worlds we bring together as happy bedfellows or ruthless antagonists, the collection of worlds, however complex, will still not be tantamount to *The World*. The collection of worlds will remain *incomplete*. The upshot is that we are condemned to our particular world versions, and there is no absolutely foolproof method for arriving at the *Truth*. Perhaps the best we can do is engage in a relatively open dialogue with our neighbors in order to arrive at some better understanding of ourselves, of them, and of our surroundings, and hope for the best.

In light of my words in chapter two, our hoping for the best would entail the collective efforts of an entire interrelated, interactive, codependent community of individuals periodically altering their mode of seeing the world, seeing it *as* such-and-such, and seeing *that* it is so-and-so. Consequently, the community's tacit and subsidiary knowing is perpetually in a state of readiness for change such that the making and taking of signs is more adequately qualified as process rather than product. Moreover, this matter of incessant change, of process, would be null were it not for the border of borders and its accompanying "emptiness," as outlined above. What lies behind the transition-translation from "A" to "B"? How can we account for "*Both* A *and* B," and "*Neither* A *nor* B," unless by way of the "fourth" entity, the "nonsuch," the "emptiness," that gives rise to the semiotic whirligig as depicted in Figures 2 and 3? How could there be anything but a *plenum* of fixed signs were it not for the "vortex," around which the entire process spirals?

What I have suggested thus far in this chapter is in a roundabout way related to our dialogue. Belief in "A" or anything else because it is handed down by *authority* is Hladdy's way. Maggie the *tenacious* one is into her particular world, come what may, and nothing or nobody is going to change her. The presumptuous, supercogitating Lönny hypothetico-deductively *infers* his world, and blindly holds to it, only to be confronted by Scharlach's unexpected inversion of his world, which does him in. The subjective idealist, Tlöny, *re-constructs* his world at every turn, so it is nonessentially "*Both* A *and* B." Put Lönny and Tlöny together, and you have the makings of a solitary *introspectionist* whose world may or may not be genuine, and it may or may not be fixed; there's actually no way to tell. Emmy's world can also be at any given moment a syncretistic juxtaposition of *both* one thing *and* another thing, a "*Both* A *and* B" world: this can lead to Deleuze and Guattari's "schizophrenic nomadism." That is the down side. The up side is that Emmy can be regarded as a rough-and-ready "cultural guerrilla" out to subvert the system, for, heroine potentially of 1,000 masks that she is, she is capable of asserting "*Neither* A *nor* B but something else" (in his own way Tlöny is capable of a comparable feat). Funy is a sorry excuse for an *inductivist*, since he cannot jump to the level of generalities from his gush of particularities: his world cannot be more than a serial "Now A_1, Now A_2, Now A_3, Now A_4, . . . *n*." In contrast, that rather mystical gazer of the Aleph, Daneri, as well as Tzinacán of Borges's "The God's Script" (1962 [1944]), suggest a nonlinear grasp of the whole, which is forever beyond reach.[2] Now, put all these disconnected souls together into an unruly package, and you still have no complete and consistent image of a codependent, interrelated, interacting community of sign makers and takers in the sense of Peirce. Alone, they are simply individuals; the collection makes up a rather disparate polyvocal whole.

And yet, and yet . . . denying any of these souls is to deny them all. As a whole, they are of the nature of the Latin American cultural whole, that "river that sweeps [them] along"; but they are "the river." That cultural whole is a massive labyrinthine conglomerate of signs that might eventually destroy them; but they are that massive labyrinthine conglomerate of signs. This conglomerate is "a fire that can consume" them; but they are that fire. Their cultures, fortunately or unfortunately, are "real"; they, fortunately or unfortunately, are what they are, their cultural flow.[3] As was revealed in the polylogue, Borges *is* himself the river, an expression of Latin American multiplicity, difference, divergence, and diversification, *par excellence*. But this Latin American expression is not exactly *sui generis*. It is unique, to be sure, but it is also the product of *mimesis*, of imitation. After Latin America's independence and the repudiation of everything peninsular, there was a cultural vacuum to be filled, such filling coming chiefly from France. And the newly independent nations imitated supremely, that is, the oligarchies imitated, and as a result the entire subcontinent took on the trappings of yet a few more cultural countenances (Zea 1963). Roberto Schwarz puts the matter of imitation something like this. The Latin American cultures of imitation of the nineteenth century—imitation of can cultures of imitation of the nineteenth century—imitation of Enlightenment thought, French romanticism, symbolism, Parnassianism, and so on, and of U.S. political ideals, of positivism, of Herbert Spencer's social Darwinism—are actually cultures by elimination. There is either elimination of some aspect of a tradition with the replacement of an imitation, or there is the possible *sui generis* development of a genuine cultural expression accompanied by elimination of the tradition. Putting Schwarz in the framework of the present disquisition, it can be said that whatever professed nation building and sense of national identity and nationalism there may have been is artificial and spurious at best. It "is *and* it is not" the genuine product; it is "*Both* A *and* B," a fusion of tradition and the imitated. If this imitative and somewhat sham world is passively accepted, its acceptance is "as if" it were simply "A," no more, no less. If the imitated world is rejected outright, it is tantamount to "B." If, on the other hand, there is passive resistance, or even underground and implicit subversive activity, it serves to make life difficult for the imitated product. That is, if there is covert "cultural guerrilla" activity directed toward undercutting "A," then "*Neither* A *nor* B" is tacitly assumed (Schwarz 1992:1–16).

This situation might remind us of Richard Rodriguez's autobiography in *Hunger of Memory* (1983). The parents of a Chicano child moved into the middle-class and apparently assimilated the norms of that "imitated" culture. They evolved from "B" (Chicano) to "*Both* A *and* B" (Anglo *and* Chicano) and then presumably to "A" (Anglo)—thus fulfilling that dream of the U.S. conservative right and its solution to all ethnic, social, political, and economic problems. They became true-blue "American" and nothing but "American." Or so they thought, and to all outward appearance so most everybody else would think. But this ignores possibility of "*Neither* A *nor* B." After many swings and foul balls and outs and a few occasional hits, Richard managed to become middle-class, like all the other respectable white kids—or at least that's what he initially deluded himself into believing. But things could just as well have been otherwise. The transition could have been toward "*Both* A *and* B," toward "*Neither* A *nor* B," and hence perhaps even toward something else, something new. Richard now speaks, but not exactly in the sense of Gayatri Chakravorty Spivak's (1988) subaltern who "cannot speak." He speaks, but his speech is "as if" it were within "A." It is not Spanish, yet, mixed with a little Spanish syntax, a lingering tinge of an accent, and occasional strange meanings, it is not exactly the most genuine sort of English either. In this sense Richard's language is "*Neither* A *nor* B," whether he knows it or not and whether he likes it or not, yet there is nothing new on the horizon. So, he continues to inhabit that nowhere zone, that border of borders, between "A" and "B."

Poor Richard: *Tan lejos de Dios y tan cerca de los Estados Unidos* ("So far from God and so close to the United States"), as Carlos Vélez-Ibáñez (1996:226) puts it.[4] Richard's search for a place in the world is that of any Mexican-American. He is:

> a kindred soul, a brother, a likeness of ourselves, and a holographic presentation of ourselves, as genuine as any of us. His is the triple tragedy of class, culture, and unvalued physiognomy—the first giving him a sense of conscious exclusivity, the second largely captured and cocooned in the stereotypes of commodity,

and the third a constant unwanted reminder. All, however, push
him to seek out places and spaces; for these have created a dissatisfaction in him, which he did not and does not know how to resolve. (Vélez-Ibáñez 1996:226).

In other words, in the semiotic terms of chapter two, Richard's seeing *as* and seeing
that and his entrenched tacit behavior including focal and subsidiary awareness are
the products of acceptance or rejection and of *both* and of *neither*. He is a perpetual
conflict of tensions, tendencies and proclivities, of assertions and denials, of vacillation and reticences, of ancient habits and recently acquired habits, of public life and
private life. He is a monologue of bipolar conflicts. He has "constructed a two-
dimensional space of opposites instead of unfolding the multiple dimensions that are
part of all Mexicans of the American Southwest and of himself" (Vélez-Ibáñez
1996:232).

Rigoberta Menchú, Guatemalan Nobel Peace Prize recipient, is a much different
case. She comes off as a Deleuze and Guattari (1983) "deterritorialized" individual
who can to all appearances willfully, overtly, and often forcibly speak from the interstices, from within a "*Neither* A *nor* B" vantage point. Menchú's voice seems to
carry credibility, for she has been there, she has *sensed* and *felt* what was there, and
now she bears witness to what there was with her entire body, and her body is repository of her entire community. It is in her bones. She exudes a sense of the structural privileges history has conferred on certain social groups, and of the nature of
racism, sexism, colonialism, and imperialism. Thus she begins to enter directly into
relationship with the audience she addresses. And she talks. But this is not exactly
"subaltern talk," because she alters her ordinary talk and changes it as she sees fit in
order that it might be in tune with her audience. In this sense John Beverley
(1993:17–18) is correct in his estimation that, unlike Menchú, writers such as Pablo
Neruda, Nobel Prize laureate for literature, customarily speak to Latin America's
exploited classes "from above," while either explicitly or implicitly alluding to the
distinction between literate and oral cultures. This vertical view, "from above," simply does not command the desired element of feeling, of sensing first-hand, of visceral knowing, that is evoked by Menchú's words.

However, I must make passing mention of David Stoll's controversial book,
Rigoberta Menchú: And the Story of all Poor Guatemalans (1999). After comparing
Menchú's cult text with local testimony from her native village, Stoll claims he has
discovered that Menchú was not even present at some of the incidents she gives account of in her testimony, and that many of her personal stories were actually based
on experiences suffered by other members of her community that she picked up on.
Stoll charges "postmodern" scholarship with constructing an entire world around
simplistic images of victimhood by way of alleged testimonials from the mouth of an
individual supposedly speaking for her entire community to create a massive body of
discourse accounting for oppression among all the have-nots of the world. Stoll
writes: "When a person becomes a symbol for a cause, the complexity of a particular
life is concealed in order to turn it into a representative life. So is the complexity of
the situation being represented? Sooner or later, in one form or another, what the
legend conceals will force its way back to our attention" (Stoll 1999:xi). As would

be expected, a number of testimonial scholars were outraged, and there was even the charge that Stoll was the victim of cooptation by the U.S. Department of State (see Beverley (1999:65–84).

More on Rigoberta Menchú in chapter fourteen. For the moment, a question arises. I trust that in regards to the *either/or* and the *both-and* and *neither-nor* interrelationships and codependencies, the importance of Peirce's tripartite concept of the sign is becoming increasingly apparent. The sign's three components—representamen, object, and interpretant—are perpetually in the act of taking each other in, in a flowing, liquid embrace such that the *one* merges with and becomes the *other*, but by that time the *other* has merged with and become something else, and so on. In this manner, *either/or* dualistic pairs, thanks to the border of borders, phase into *both-ands* and *neither-nors* in the scintillating, shimmering, undulating, flowing semiosic process. But how does this aid in our understanding of the *other*, that is, the subaltern *other*, who as a sign (representamen) is the *other* (object) of the hegemonic sign (representamen) as *one*, who is the *other* (object) of the subaltern *other*? This interdependent, interrelated interaction between dominant and dominated is surely not as symmetrical as Peirce's philosophy of communication might imply. In search of an answer, let us consider the possible responses of the dominated *other* during the Spanish conquest and colonization of the Americas.

When Things Are Not as They Seem: Cultural Clashes

As far as Hernán Cortés was concerned, the religion, beliefs, rites, and in general the customs of the Aztecs were no less than abominable, practices of barbarians, evidence of the anti-Christ. It is significant that in his letters he tells of human sacrifices while referring to the Aztec temples as "mosques." In so doing he is implying that the wars with the Amerindians were an extension of the "Reconquest of Spain" against the Moors who invaded in the year 711, a "Reconquest" that finally culminated in the expulsion of the "infidels" in 1492, the very year Columbus disembarked in the Americas.

Christianity, in this and a host of comparable manifestations of the Spanish mind, presents itself as the ideological legitimation of the conquest that can justifiably impose itself on the indigenous cultures and religions. In large part, the march of feudal Europe toward capitalism realized its motivating force in the conquest and colonization of the Americas. The pillage of Aztec and Inca treasures, and later, exploitation of gold and silver deposits in Mexico, Peru and Bolivia; the dramatic rise in production of sugar cane, and other products of the soil; the increasingly lucrative slave trade; all these activities filled the coffers of the emerging capitalist nations, England, France, Italy, and Holland, more than they did those of Spain and Portugal. These countries remained for the most part mired in the relatively immobile hierarchy of quasi-feudalism—yet, as pointed out above, they sported a quite modern corporate monarchical system. According to one of the admittedly more negative reports, 18,000 tons of silver and 200 tons of gold were transported from America to Spain between 1521 and 1600. During the same period, it has been estimated that the indigenous population diminished by as much as 90% in central Mexico and 95% in the highlands of Peru (Beaud 1981:19). This dramatic reduction of raw labor stimulated an almost equally dramatic increase in the importation of slaves from Africa. As an accompaniment of this destruction of lives, there was an effort on the part of the colonizers to prevent the practice of indigenous religious customs. Nevertheless, while the Amerindians were converted to Catholicism, whether of their own accord or by force, they in turn converted the Catholic saints and Mary into pre-Hispanic deities and virgin-mothers. This is a supreme example of sign transformation. It is a matter of seeing signs *as* something other than what they were when handed down by the conquerors, of alternative tacit, subsidiary awareness of a newly invented semiotic world. One set of signs engendered another set of hybrid signs, all of which remain intimately interrelated, and "reality" was henceforth a mutual interpenetration and codependent emergence and merging of many "realities." In this sense, linear, asymmetrically hierarchized *either/or* interrelations exist alongside nonlinear *both-and* and *neither-nor* interrelations that are neither simply either symmetrical or asymmetrical but a complex mixture of the two.

This turnabout of Amerindian and European signs and practices can also be articulated in the manner of a "cultural guerrilla logic" in the style of Michel de Certeau (1984)—to be discussed in more detail in chapter twelve—as well as Scott's "hidden transcripts" as described above. According to the conquerors, the idea of culture and religion was a matter of two incommensurable systems: one is right and the other wrong, one is destined to become the norm, the other must surely vanish. It was to all appearances an *either/or* situation. Catholicism was God's way, so it must persevere; pre-Hispanic religious practices were heretical, hence they should go the way of all other manifestations of ungodliness. From the indigenous point of view, in contrast, "hybridization" became the rule. *Both* the one set of practices *and* the practices of the *other* were put into effect. For, according to the Amerindians' mindset, old practices were never entirely shed, while at the same time new practices were either willfully embraced or they were the product of imposition by skillful tactics or ruthless force. Yet, from a complementary perspective (of successive heterogenization), what eventually came about was something entirely new emerging from within what would otherwise have been regarded as the excluded-middle. This novel practice would be best termed *neither* the practice of hegemonic forces *nor* the practice of the *other*, but something else, something different, something novel.

Nevertheless, as far as the Spanish Crown was concerned, it was business as usual and full speed ahead. The religion of the conqueror operated on the basis of the theological, cultural, ethical and moral inferiority of the indigenous peoples. At the same time there was the necessity of fulfilling God's will by evangelizing the Amerindians and bringing them into the Catholic fold, thus rendering them vassals of the King, molding them into upright subjects either by loving inculcation or initially by the sword and later as a byproduct of ofttimes sadistic castigation for any evil doing. Indeed, José de Acosta wrote in *De procuranda indorum salute* (1984:392) that there are three classes of "barbarous nations," Eastern cultures (India, China, Japan), urban American cultures (Aztec, Maya, Inca), and those nomadic "savages, hardly different from animals," that roam the American continent. The heated polemic between Bartolomé de las Casas, defender of the Amerindians, and Ginés de Sepúlveda, imbued with Aristotelian thought and arguing that "inferior" peoples are "inferior" because that is their natural lot in life, brought some carefully hidden

Spanish presuppositions and prejudices out in the open (Zea 1992). Bartolomé de las Casas, a valiant precursor of modernity, proposed emancipation for all human beings: nobody is either superior or inferior to anybody else, but flaccid and even malicious thinking (and circumstances) can often appear to make it so. In other words, it is not a matter of Spanish ways replacing indigenous ways, whether by the cross or the sword. Rather, both stand on equal grounds at the outset, and now it is the charge of the Spaniards to show by their noble deeds and kind words that their ways are worthy of emulation (las Casas 1942). It might be said that las Casas won the debate. But, of course, nobody really wins in such encounters. Each side verbally flogs the other into submission, a decision is made, a few new laws are enacted, and it's back to many of the old abuses. To make a long story short, there were a few noble champions of the masses, but for the most part there were exploiters, systematic persecutors, and ruthless inquisitors for the next three centuries.[5] So much for the travails of human history.

The important point to be made regarding the present inquiry involves the subtle and nondualistic religious responses on the part of the *other*, "subaltern" peoples (Amerindians and African Americans), to the Spanish hegemony, the *other* of the *other*. In making this point as briefly and as succinctly as possible, I must resort to a few generalizations of the most general sort. Generalizations are generalizations, of course. For each and every generalization, exceptions invariably make their presence known. However, in order to get a feel for and to conceptualize culture, articulate mammals that we are, generalizations are pretty much unavoidable. So, please hold onto your hat, for they will come loose and fast.

By and large the Amerindians' and African Americans' responses when confronting the European newcomers shortly after the conquest depended on the human interrelations that were soon established. Chilean sociologist Christian Parker divides the various responses into four tendencies: (1) *either a violent or a nonviolent attitude of rebellion* accompanied by an attempt to revalidate ancient deities ("Not-A," that is, "Not-Christianity," but traditional beliefs), (2) a relatively *submissive attitude*, leading to an open embrace of Christianity ("A," "Yes, Christianity"), (3) *partial submission*, involving an outward show of accepting the Christian religion, but at the same time there is perseverance of ancestral beliefs and clandestine practices bringing about a fusion of Christianity and pre-Hispanic religions ("*Both* A *and* Not-A"), and (4) *active resistance* to the colonial order, often culminating in messianic movements that reject the colonists' ways and indigenous ways in favor of something else, something new ("*Neither* A *nor* Not-A"—but the emergence of something else, something new) (Parker 1993:26–38). Now, that's about as general as we can get. Nevertheless, Parker's division of behavioral traits may help us come to terms with the perplexing Latin American condition.

Allow me at the outset to suggest that things are not as clear-cut as we might like them. For example, (1) has the forces of colonizers' saying "A," but the subalterns say "Not-A." This might seem clear enough. But the boundaries between (1)–(4) become blurry. For example, response (1) may initially be that of conquered groups in the periphery of the colonial empire such as some of the Pueblo Amerindians of New Mexico, the Pima community of Arizona, and the Tarahumaras of Northern Mexico, who, in view of relatively sparse attention from their Catholic Fathers, quietly reverted back to many of their former practices, but without giving up all vestiges of Catholic practices (response 3). Among other Amerindian groups, while the over-powering force of the colonizer initially evoked outrage and negation on the part of the colonized, they were soon beaten into a state of resignation and compelled to adopt their victor's ways. They overtly submitted to Catholic ways, but in an act of rebellion they covertly returned to their previous form of life—(response 3). [6] This would also be the case of "idols" of pre-Hispanic vintage playing out their role be-hind Catholic "altars" in the Amerindian mind, as described by Anita Brenner (1929).

According to response (2), the conquered peoples, having been thrown into a sort of limbo, without identity or direction, gravitate by attraction or by force or co-ercion, toward "A." Attraction toward "A" was often the case of the "religious con-quest" by example and humility rather than by the sword, epitomized in the utopian ideals of Bartolomé de las Casas and especially Vasco de Quiroga and his work with the Tarascan Amerindians of Mexico (Zavala 1965). As an alternative to (2), shortly after the conquest of the Incas, *mestizo* chronicler Garcilaso de la Vega claimed to be a more authoritative voice than the Spanish chroniclers since he was intimate with the Amerindian way of life. Garcilaso sang praises to Inca knowledge, a hands-on empirical and practical knowledge that he considered in no way inferior to European knowledge at a time when the Aristotelian and Ptolemaic conceptions of the universe were in jeopardy. At the same time he held certain respect for the European ways and European theology. He advocated coexistence as the only feasible answer to cul-tural conflicts. This is quite comparable to response (3), the emergence of mixed re-ligious practices in the order of "*Both* A *and* Not-A," which ideally allows acknowl-edged apparent incompatibles to co-mingle in peace. There is no simple embrace of one practice and rejection of another one.

In contrast to Garcilaso, Felipe Guaman Poma de Ayala was an ethnic separa-tist. He believed the clash of European and Amerindian ways had produced an en-tirely new context within which *neither* the one *nor* the other could be adequately operative. Yet, he believed Christianity of a certain hybrid strain that could be con-ducive to the American milieu was the most feasible answer to both the Europeans and the Amerindians. Although members of each group would go their own separa-tist ways, Christianity would bring equality to all. Thus the Amerindians should eradicate their practices of idolatry, embrace the Catholic faith, learn to dress and eat and act like Spaniards, and in general carry out their role as good citizens. This attitude was quite unlike that of Garcilaso, who championed coexistence while main-taining that there were superior facets of the native culture that should be conserved. In other words, Guaman Poma basically called for "*Neither* A *nor* Not-A" but some-thing else. That something else would be more "A" than "Not-A," since at least a somewhat altered form of Christianity would retain the upper hand. This, then, is a mild sort of response (4), without the emergence of any vaguely defined alternative (Jara and Spadaccini 1992a:67–76).

An intriguing phenomenon evincing a double "Not-A" that culminates in a somewhat messianic "*Neither* A *nor* Not-A" is that of a rebellious group in Peru called the *taquiongos*, who formed a cult and practiced a heretical ritual of song and dance called Taki Onkoy. The central motif of this ritual was the Amerindian perception of the *pachacuti* (a "mother earth" image and an inversion of the world order), of the condition of the *other* as a result of the conquest's turning their world "upside-down." Taki Onkoy rejected both Inca and European dominance. The song was a glorification of the past and a rejection of the present Inca dominance, and the dance was of desperation and hopes, an effort to exorcise the foreign evil (Jara and Spadiccini 1992a:48–49).

During the colonial period, quite often, to the chagrin of the Spanish clergy, a rough sort of syncretic (3) eventually came to predominate. In contrast, (4), saying "*Neither* A *nor* Not-A" much in the order of the *taquiongos*, entailed a fanaticism that often took over in an attempt to fill the vacuum that inevitably remained. Fanaticism is fanaticism, however, and it usually solves few problems in the long run other than in the minds of a handful of opportunistic leaders. This response does, however, bring about a necessary subversion of the excluded-middle of classical principles. It thus introduces an element of underdetermination: to the same conditions there can be many possible responses, with none of them necessarily enjoying priority over any of the others, given the prevailing conditions.

The above range of possible responses from (1) to (4), any one of a number of which stands an outside chance of emerging at hardly a moment's notice, gives rise to ever-increasing generality concerning the range of any particular response. That is, the task of determining the range of customary applicability of a particular response is left to the pragmatic capacity of the Amerindian subjects of the response to negotiate a *modus vivendi* regarding the circumstances within which they find themselves. Thus their success depends upon their imagining how to cope with whatever circumstances that might pop up and upon their conceiving of new strategies. Conceiving of new strategies is not an everyday occurrence. It is especially difficult during hard times when the subservient Amerindians must toil from dawn to dusk and hence have neither the time nor the energy to hope new hopes and dream new dreams. Consequently, category (4) usually came into its own slowly, if at all, as the colonial period made its way through history. The *neithers* and the *nors* of this category also usually remained vague. The rebellion of Túpac Amaru of Peru during the final years of the eighteenth century presents an interesting case of this vagueness. The rebellion arose in reaction to generation after generation of abuses. However, it curiously accompanied a concomitant proclamation of Christianity rather than a return to ancient pre-Hispanic beliefs (Mires 1988:15–58).

Cultural hybridity, operating chiefly within (3), is what gives life to the other three sorts of responses.[7] Hybridity contains, within itself, *both* one possible response *and* another, . . . *and* possibly another, . . . *and* then yet another, and at the same time it is *neither* the *one* nor the other but something else. Thus it can get along quite comfortably with the inclusion of inconsistent alternatives to the same prevailing conditions. We find a paradigm case of this in the Virgin of Guadalupe of Mexico—as briefly mentioned in chapter three. Shortly after the conquest of the Aztecs, the Catholic Virgin mysteriously appeared to a humble Amerindian peasant, Juan Diego, at Tepeyac, ancient sanctuary dedicated to Tonantzín, Amerindian goddess of fertility. The profound significance of what later became known as the *guadalupana* myth consists of the combination of the Virgin Mary, Mother of God, and Tonantzín—or Earth Mother, who had the responsibility of comforting the Amerindians during the traumatic experiences suffered at the hands of the conquerors. The conquerors constructed a shrine dedicated to the Virgin of Guadalupe at the very site of the ancient sanctuary of Tonantzín. This brought the two traditions together into a codependently merging whole and gave sustenance to the *mestizo* or hybrid ethnic make-up of what became today's Mexican culture and society (Lafaye 1976). [8]

The *both-and* response (3), then, can be radically *overdetermined*. At least two and usually many and possibly an infinite number of responses, some of them mutually exclusive, are brought together in what evolves into a peaceful to not-too-peaceful coexistence. To complement this overdetermination, the *neither-nor* response (4) is primarily *underdetermined*. It keeps the door open to an indefinite number of possible future alternatives. Thus the atemporal sphere of (3), bringing together "*Both* one response *and* another, *and* another, *and* another, ... *n*" ("*Both* A *and* Not-A"), complements (4), which allows for "*Neither* one of a pair of mutually exclusive answers to a particular contextualized problem situation *nor* the other, but, over time, it may give a nod to *both* of them." Putting the whole package together, and the gamut from (1) to (4) can only be taken in one massive gulp, timelessly, as "possibly all the above"; so everything and anything enjoys a possibility of arising. At the same time, from the sphere of *underdetermination*, it is "not necessarily any of the above." All this leaves us with, . . . well, just "emptiness," the "border of borders" from which all possible responses can gush forth, according to how I tried to cope with these terms in the first two chapters of this inquiry.[9]

In short, we have a general, apparently "irrational" and "illogical" (at least according to Western "reason" and classical "logic") set of possible responses within the pragmatics of human conduct. Inferential processes are there, for sure, but they are tacit inferences rather than consciously devised strategies for coping. Thought is there, but it is "thought" from the gut, and almost instinctive, level, at the level of "deep culture." "Chiefly symbolic" signs are there, but so also are those extralinguistic iconic and indexical signs and the *others* to which they interrelate as well as signs that appeal most to the inner self, the self and its inner *other*. Since the baser signs play a prominent role in the pragmatic give-and-take of responses (1) to (4), an overriding element of unsayability pervades amongst symbolic signs—as is usually the case of signs of extralinguistic nature emerging through smells, tastes, touches, sounds, and sights. This is, essentially, "nonlinguicentricity" at its levelheaded best.

Then does it allow for *simulacra*? If the question refers to *simulacra* in the infamous order of Jean Baudrillard (1983a, 1983b), in a manner of speaking, yes. But if *simulacra* are taken merely as "*A*," there is always already the possibility of the emergence of complementary signs: "Not-A," "*Both* A *and* Not-A," and "*Neither* A *nor* Not-A." Is this not cognitive, rational, logical, and conscious and intentional employment of rigorous thinking? Yes again. But the same process is already flowing at tacit levels as well. Well then, is it not language as the index of what is a distinctively human semiotics? Most likely. But obsessive stress on language eventually evokes the hollow question, "Is that all there is?," which in turn provokes a solid "No!" There is everything that *is not* what there *is*. And other than that? "Emptiness" once again pervades.[10] It may be said in this regard, then, that the media is *in* the message and the message is *in* the media. At the same time, the message is *in* the making [11]and taking of signs, signs of whatever type, whether linguistic or not.

Hence the meaning of the signs is *in* their making and taking and interpreting, that making and taking and interpreting having emerged as no more and no less than so many more signs, whose making and taking and interpreting consist of yet more signs, and so on. Signs make themselves less vague in collaboration with their makers; they make themselves signs of more general application in terms of their entering into more intimate interrelations with other signs in collaboration with their takers.

This is the case, whether we are speaking of the colonized subaltern's response to the colonizer or vice versa. A linguistic message, a command, is in the air— assuming there is now a common language between colonizer and colonized. The addresser can comply, simply rebel, actively resist after an outward show of compliance, or covertly and clandestinely resist in the form of a fusion as a result of code-pendent mergence of what the addresser demanded and expected and what the addressee needed and desired. Or the addresser may hold all the options open as a set of possibilities for any and all future acts. Or he may embrace none of the above, which would be possible in death, coma or catatonia, or the most pure form of passive resistance. In its extreme form, this passive resistance could hardly be called "resistance" at all, for from within the sphere of such "resistance," there would be nothing against which that "resistance" could "resist." It would be simply resistance, without relation of similarity to anything (Firstness), relation to something as *other* (Secondness), or mediation of what simply *is* and its *other*, which gives rise to something else (Thirdness) (Chaui 1986). All this is, most properly speaking, of the nature of semiosis. It knows no suffocating predominance of linguicentrism, ocularcentrism, or bifurcation into dichotomies. Semiosis asserts binaries and simultaneously denies them; it includes them and simultaneously excludes them; it reveals them and simultaneously eludes them. Semiosis: possibly *both* any sign *and* virtually all signs and yet *neither* exclusively any particular sign *nor* all signs, *both* sign *and* nonsign and yet *neither* sign *nor* nonsign. To say what something *is* is to say what it *is not*; to say what it *is not* is to say at least in part what it *is*.

In order more properly to qualify this mind-bender, a look at it from a more general perspective might be helpful.

Beyond Colonialism?

Colonial and so-called postcolonial literatures are an exploration of a world at the boundary of "civilization," a world that has not (yet) been completely assimilated into the Western way of life. That world is therefore usually looked upon as uncontrollable, chaotic, unattainable, and ultimately evil. If brought together with European culture presumably as a syncretic whole, it is often taken to be virtual madness, the combination of contradictories, with no internal "logic." The multifaceted alterity appears at the outset incomprehensible. Therefore it is often rejected outright. It is the Lacanian "Imaginary" (possibly *both-and*) that must be brought in line with the "Real" (*either-or*). But this is impossible if contradictories are retained within the equation. So the colonizer must interpolate the equation into the "Symbolic," which is *neither* the one *nor* the *other*, but it is arbitrarily made tantamount to the one as prior to and privileged over the *other*. Then, and only then, can there be the one as the result of an *either/or* choice over the *other*.

Abdul JanMohamed (1985:84–5) writes in a Lacanian vein of two broad categories of colonialist literature, the "imaginary" and the "symbolic."[12] The "imaginary" text has the colonized functioning as an image of the imperialist self in such a way as to reveal its self-alienation. These texts fetishize a nondialectical Manichean allegory that plays on a radically abstracted dualism between colonizer and colonized. The European comes out as of high ethical values and moral principles while the native is evil incarnate. JanMohamed suggests that Rudyard Kipling's *Kim* is an attempt to find dichotomized solutions, "*Either* A *or* Not-A." At the same time it retains the prioritized and benignly holds onto alterity such that there is a sort of juxtaposed "A *and* Not-A." This class of novels overlaps in some ways with the "imaginary" text: those portions of the novel organized at the emotive level are structured by "imaginary" identification with its vestiges of the oral tradition, while those controlled by cognitive intentionality are structured by the rules of the "symbolic" order more typical of literate texts. Ironically, these novels—which are conceived in the "symbolic" realm of intersubjectivity, heterogeneity, and particularity yet seduced by the specularity of "imaginary" *otherness*—better illustrate the economy and power of the Manichean allegory than do the strictly "imaginary" texts. JanMohamed's type of fiction, pervaded by the "symbolic," is the thrust of novels by Joseph Conrad, Nadine Gordimer, and the likes. Here, "juxtaposition" and even "syncretism" are deemed impossible dreams within the power relations of colonial society because such a context traps the writer in what JanMohamed dubs the "libidinal" economy of the "imaginary." As a consequence, the narrative becomes reflexive by limiting itself to a rigorously detailed examination of the "imaginary," which is latent but occasionally rises to the surface of the colonialist mind-set. This type of fiction is able to free itself from the Manichean allegory by a process of affirmation and negation, by enunciating what things *are* and revealing that they *are not* what their appearances make them out to be (JanMohamed 1985:85). In this process the "symbolic" goes in the direction of *neither-nor* ("*Neither* A *nor* Not-A"). But it is incapable of actually getting there, for it tries to maintain a synthetic view.

A more faithful picture of this situation would take narrative a step further up the semiosic stream to articulate the equivalent of "*Not both* A *and* Not-A." That is to say, the move is in the direction of the border of borders, toward the "emptiness." It is within the border of borders (the dividing line of Figure 1) between the negated one and the negated *other*, that the true "otherness," the "emptiness," the "vortex" of the sign (Figures 2 and 3), can possibly be felt—though it can never be stated clearly and distinctly. Within this "emptiness," things are never as precise as we would like to make them from within the sphere of the genuine *neither-nor*. In the "imaginary" text, the idea of a subject is eclipsed by the narrative's fixation on and fetishization of the other: the self becomes a prisoner of the image projected on it by its hegemonic counterpart. Even though the colonized *other* is negated by the projection of the inverted image, his presence as the presence of an absence (as "*Not both* A *and* Not-A") can never be canceled. The colonist's desire serves to trap him in the dualism of the "imaginary" and foments a violent hatred toward the colonized *other*. A desire consequently emerges on the part of the colonizer to exterminate what are considered the subhuman, savage *other*, a desire that is thematized to become the underlying thrust of "symbolic" texts such as Joseph Conrad's *Heart of Darkness* and E. M. Forster's *A Passage to India*. These texts manifest their "symbolic" nature through the implicit "imaginary" texts they contain. The narrators relish in describing their mutilation of natives, but at another level the "imaginary" texts occasionally reveals themselves to evince the present absence of the *other* (JanMohamed 1985:86).

JanMohamed's indelibly Manichean allegory mirrors the epic of Western civilization, beginning with the initiation of its expansion five hundred years ago when it stumbled onto a "new" continent that it proceeded to "invent," and culminating with the industrial revolution. During this epic the West "invented" a destiny for itself. This destiny consisted of "civilization," Western style, endowed either with (1) the Catholic duty to bring the barbaric *others* into the Christian fold and transform them into legitimate vassals of God, King, and Country, or (2) the Protestant "white man's burden" of providing material and spiritual benefits to the hapless souls of the world. After the movement for independence in Latin America, this great dichotomization of the world's peoples was translated by the Latin American mind into "civilization," particularly Parisian style, and "barbarism" as what the American soil does to the unwary citizen who leaves the "light" of his European heritage and enters into a pact with the demons of "darkness," nature. The paradigm case of Latin America's "invention" of "civilization/barbarism" is found in Domingo Faustino Sarmiento's *Facundo, Or Life in the Argentine Republic in the Days of the Tyrants* (1960 [1845]). In this work, "civilization" is present among respectable people of Buenos Aires and "barbarism" is found in the riff-raff of the capital city, the unenlightened inhabitants of the provinces, and especially the *gauchos* of the pampa. Sarmiento "re-invents" the known—Western "civilization" (culture)—and translates the unknown—Latin American "barbarism" (nature)—into its antithesis in order to keep the demarcation clear and distinct. At least that was the professed goal.

What actually emerged was something else. A newly invented "reality" surfaced. This new "reality" consisted of a different culture, a culture that was at home in some of Sarmiento's bookish referents to a "barbarism," the concrete aspects with which he enjoyed little familiarity, and at the same time it was not exactly foreign to that strange "re-invented" form of Sarmiento's concept of "civilization." That is to say, Sarmiento occasionally revealed his latent and for the most part implicit (tacit, subsidiary) admiration for the subtle ways of the "barbarous" *gaucho*. The pampa and the *gaucho* gave rise to a new image from what had originally taken on the countenance of a cultural vacuum: it was not a matter of *either* "civilization" ("A") *or* "barbarism" ("Not-A"), but rather, of *both* the one *and* the *other* and at the same time of *neither* the one *nor* the *other*, but something else, something different, something hybrid. The one and indivisible whole of Argentina is a far richer cultural heritage than is the strictly defined "civilized" counterpart to "barbarism."

There is mimesis in *Facundo*, just as we saw in Schwarz's Brazilian texts. There is also "invention," a translation of the "symbolic" and the "imaginary" of which JanMohamed writes into something else. This something else can give rise to a heritage capable of producing a citizen of the world the likes of Borges, and many others as well, whose mind cannot remain at ease with simple pros and cons, but reveals more, much more. JanMohamed's "symbolic" is open to the *other* whereas his "imaginary" remains blinded by its refusal to look beyond Manichean poles of opposition. The unwary reader might be led to suspect that Sarmiento writes in the "imaginary" mode, while Forster's *Passage to India* more subtly brackets the values and bases of the colonizing culture and highlights those of the colonized culture and mercilessly satirizes the relations between them that produced the "imaginary" mode. Sarmiento's posture is actually quite unlike that of Forster, however. The Argentine writer has one foot simultaneously inside the *other*—whether he likes it or not—while looking out to the West, and he has the other foot inside the West—at least that is his desire—while looking inward to the *other*. Hence he engages in *both-and* and *neither-nor* "illogical logic." Quite often he seems momentarily to exist, so to speak, at the border of borders. He is actually neither a writer either of JanMohamed's "symbolic" or "imaginary" nor does he exist in "civilization" while remaining divorced from "barbarism."

Yet, over the long haul both JanMohamed's "symbolic" and "imaginary" and Sarmiento's "civilization" and "barbarism" are mediated by the "real." That is to say, they are mediated by the border of borders, that which can possibly arise from the interstices, as we have observed in previous sections, which offers the set of all possibilities for future becoming. When subcultures and cultures brush against each other like great clouds, given the uncertainty of incessant movement, there is a build up of electrical forces toward an unforeseen threshold at which point there emerges a sudden burst of energy giving rise to a clap and thunderous repercussion. It is all nonlinear. It is an apparent *homogeneity* of the masses but at the same time there is a *heterogeneity* of scintillating semiotic outbursts against those who are in control, outbursts resulting from differences of potential, differences that make a difference. This process involves movement and migration from country to country and from culture to culture and language to language, or within country, subculture, and language, through borders. Beyond the general images of "modernity," "postmodernity," "postcoloniality," and "capitalism," there is no single picture or frame, no overriding holographic pattern in three-dimensional luster. There are no privileged representations of reality, but only relations, and relations between relations. There are only swirls and vortices, incessant interplay of interrelations and codependent emerging, waves giving way to more waves, and flow, flow, flow. Culture, language, movement and multiplicities: in spite of the pressures of the would-be dominant forces to flatten everything to the same distinctless mass, the interstices that never cease their appearing here and there, offer new openings. They offer unrehearsed possibilities. Sameness can once again become differentiation such that what was previously at the borderlands, the periphery, the once marginalized, gains a toe hold, then a foot and a hand hold, then there is an opening, something visible, there. But what? Ah, that's it, the opportunity for some ordinarily illicit act, some activity that would otherwise be prohibited. Rootlessness finds a fissure where the terrain is open to penetration, and an anchor, fingers and tentacles dig ever more deeply, widening the rent. Between one world and another, one territory and another, one past and another past, past and present, present and future, and all those worlds and times and spaces, the difference widens. And . . . What do you know? . . . a new, hybrid form has been emerging, is emerging, will have been emerging.

The general concept I am striving to develop is not simply born from a refusal to propagate the poststructuralist idea of the play of texts, or of a unlimited, slightly differentiated flow filling the mixed multicultural bag. On the contrary. It is a refusal to give in to the obscure, the inscrutable, the unfathomable, and somnambulistically consume whatever catchwords are ladled out in the name of theory. It is born out of a mania for difference, for differentiation of the un-differentiated and the de-differentiated, for the shadows lurking there somewhere in the corners. It is resistance to closure, to the meaningless flux of simulacra, to hyperspatial images, to floating signifiers, to images of consumption voraciously and mindlessly exercised by consuming bodies. It is the realization that whatever yield there may be, it will nonetheless remain *incomplete*, and most likely *inconsistent*, quite unharmonious and rebellious. What was rooted with such pain and struggle is uprooted. What modicum of certainty that appeared to be at hand vanishes into thin air. Whatever was grasped slithers away like a greased pig at the County Fair. All was a pathetic dream, a hopeful illusion.

No, . . . wait a minute. I now read like just another one of our currently fashionable prophets of doom, I fear. Things surely can't be as gloomy as I seem to have implied. There must be some middle ground. This middle ground must exist between the *one* and the subaltern *other* and the *other* of the subaltern *other*, which is presumably the *one*. A further look at the very idea of a borderline behooves us.

Notes

1.   "A" and "Not-A (or B)" relate to the Principle of Noncontradiction, where something cannot be "B" if it is "A," and vice versa; the "A" and "B" relate to the Excluded-Middle Principle, according to which something must be either "A" or "B," with no possible of there being any third term between the two horns of the distinction. The first principle entails negation while the second entails a distinction that at least implies a weak form of negation. When there is the need for manifested negation, I will use the first form, when not, I will most often use the second form. (The relationship between the two principles in question will become evident in chapter six, where the first is included within the sphere of Firstness and *vagueness* and *inconsistency* and *overdetermination*, while the second is linked to Peirce's Thirdness and *generality* and *incompleteness* and *underdetermination*.)
2.   "The God's Script" is about an Aztec priest, Tzinacán, who believed he divined the universe's secrets in one of the spots on a jaguar's hide.
3.   It will have become evident to the Borges scholar that I have in these lines rephrased the ending ruminations found in "New Refutation of Time" (Borges 1962:234 [1944]).
4.   This phrase is attributed to Porfirio Díaz, "benign dictator" of Mexico from 1876–1880 and from 1884–1910, with respect to the relationship between Mexico and the United States: "Poor Mexico, so far from God and so close to the United States."

5.   For the context surrounding the las Casas-Sepúlveda debates, see Hanke (1949, 1959), Zavala (1964); for a general overview of the colonial period, see Burkholder and Johnson (1994), Gibson (1966).

6.   I should mention that in *The Vision of the Vanquished* (1977), Nathan Wachtel documents the other side of history with respect to Middle America and Peru by a pioneering use of historical accounts as a result of the oral tradition of the conquest in the form of popular plays, some of which continued to be performed well into the twentieth century. The problem is that Watschel overemphasized the destructive force of the Spaniards. The same type of study today of some cult hero would most likely produce comparable results, as it did in the case of that recent sanctuary of fanatics in Waco, Texas, the destruction of which was occasionally labeled a "holocaust" by those who sympathized with the antigovernment cause (see also, along these lines, Leon-Portilla's, *The Broken Spears* 1990, an account of the Conquest of Mexico as narrated by the vanquished).

7.   I am addressing myself to the term "hybridism"—about which more below—as chiefly propagated by Bhabha (1994) and García Canclini (1995). For a critique of the term, see Beverley (1999:85–132).

8.   I should mention that the situation in Brazil, given the greater concentration of African slavery and a somewhat more lenient colonial rule, differed from that of the Spanish colonies, especially outside the Caribbean area. Yet the nature of human interrelations bears similarities. Roger Bastide (1978:9–11) observes that in all the colonies there were slaves and ex-slaves who maintained separate cultures ("*Either* A *or* Not-A"), and those who assimilated to form other cultures "*Not-*(A or Not-A)." This is the side-by-side existence of one culture and another, of two worlds. Thus Bastide (1978:122) wrote: "The American Negro lives in two worlds, each with its own separate rules: while adapting to his social environment, he still—in another sphere of existence—maintains his ancestral religion." Yet, Bastide readily concedes that Brazilian left loopholes for new cultural patterns. Moreover, the African American way of life was not subsumed within a vast monolithic culture, but rather, there were many cultures (Bastide 1979:67–68). Thus, between European and African American the "logic" is not simply a matter of "*Either* A *or* Not-A," but of "*Both* A *and* Not-A" and at the same time of "*Neither* A *nor* Not-A." This could help account for Nina Rodrígues's (1900) and more recently Mario Aurélio Luz's (1995) contention that the African Americans of Brazil belonged to a wholly alien world, disconnected, far removed and by and large impervious to Western ideas, and that there was hardly any hope for their leaving their home cultures and becoming completely integrated into the *other* (it is also in line, I might add, with Price-Mars's [1983] work on the African Americans of Haiti).

9.   As mentioned above, the terms *underdetermination* and *generality* and *overdetermination* and *vagueness* will be the direct focus of discussion in chapter six.

10.   This conception of the possibility of something codependently emerging from the interstices renders account of the becoming of *criollo* consciousness in Spanish America, and most specifically in Mexico, since South American *criollos* were in general more fearful of the Amerindian and African American masses than were the Mexicans. This *criollo* sentiment was accompanied by the emergence of a *criollo* sense of nationalism. Intellectual and writer Carlos de Sigüenza y Góngora, for example,

considered himself to be *neither* Spaniard *nor* Amerindian, but *criollo*, yet on most accounts he remained rather in opposition to the *mestizo*. In general, the American experience was considered baroque, due to the inability to "rationalize" the world and the human conditions (Jara and Spadaccini 1992a:80–86).

11. It bears mentioning at this juncture—a point to be presented in more detail in chapter six—that the distinctively Peircean idea that it is up to the sign's maker to render a vague sign more specific for the benefit of the addressee, and that it is the responsibility of the addressee to further generalize a sign of generality handed to her by the addresser.

12. JanMohamed very conspicuously ignores the third term of Lacan's trio, the "real." I have my suspicions and perhaps an answer for this omission, but best I leave that matter for another possible time and place.

Part II

The relevance of Peirce's semiotics becomes paramount with further words in chapter six on overdetermination and underdetermination, vagueness and generality, inconsistency and incompleteness, and the contradictory complementarity of signs. These terms correlate with semiosis as signs interrelatedly, interactively, and codependently emerge in the practices of everyday cultural life. Chapter seven boots these practices to another level with stress on triadicity, mediation, and the "emptiness" of all signs that brings semiosis about in the first place. A new trio of concepts, homogeny, hegemony, and heterogeny, illustrates the inadequacy of certain prevalent views propagated in certain areas of "cultural studies," Marxist and non-Marxist alike. In short, hybridized difference becomes the watchword. A pilot case, that of Argentine women protesting against the military regime that lasted from 1976 to 1983, helps bear this out. It also discloses the problem of whether "postmodernism" really exists in Latin America, a problem that is foregrounded along with the prevalence of signs of complexity and ambiguity, at bodymind levels. When I write bodymind, we shall note, I mean to imply an abrogation of the grand Cartesian split that has kept Western thought in tatters for the past few centuries. I wish to imply that perhaps nowhere as effectively as in Latin America, given the area's vast cultural hybridization, can we find more dramatic examples of bodymind fusion. Chapter eight offers some suggestions regarding this problem in light of the interrelated, interacting, codependent emergence of cultural semiosis as illustrated through the Latin American scene.

Chapter Six

How Does Peirce Fit In?

> But the boundary between black and white is neither black nor white, nor neither, nor both. It contains the pairedness of the two.
>
> —Charles S. Peirce

> The First and Third worlds have mutually interpenetrated one another.
>
> —Guillermo Gómez-Peña

The Other "Logics" Again

The cosmic egg making up Figure 5 (a generalized form of Figure 1) is a concoction of at least two worlds separated by nothing more than a membrane, so fallible and so fragile. What is inside is separated by an even more delicate film of demarcation. This is a demarcation that hardly demarcates. Rather, it serves to de-mar at the same time that it mars and in this manner it de-mar-cates, making an exceedingly tenuous difference between one world and another world. It might seem intuitively obvious that the line separates "A" from "Not-A" and that within the egg anything must be either of one value or the other value, and never the twain shall meet.

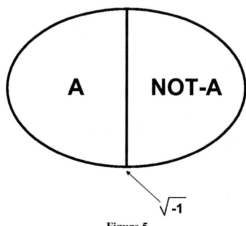

Figure 5

Not so, however. If I might be permitted to retrace a now familiar path, I might say that the line, no matter how flimsy it may appear, is nonetheless that which stalwartly lies between one thing and another thing. It is not "A," to be sure. But neither is it "Not-A." So it must be "A-lessness," for it is not "A." If this is the case, then it must also be "Not-A-lessness," for it is not exactly "Not-A" either. So it is "Not-A-lessness-A-lessness."[1] However, as "A-lessness" the line possesses something in common with "Not-A," since "Not-A" is also "A-less"; and as "Not-A-lessness" it shares a commonality with "A," since "A" is also "Not-A-less." In this sense it at one and the same time enjoys "A-ness" and "Not-A-ness," so it is "*Both* A-ness *and* Not-A-ness," and the Principle of Noncontradiction is given a devastating karate chop. It is also "*Neither* A-ness *nor* Not-A-ness," so the Principle of Excluded-Middle hits the canvas. The line of de-mar-cation, then, is in a manner of speaking "emptiness," yet it implies, within itself, the possible for the engenderment of every-thingness.[2] It is at once nothing and everything. Please keep this model in mind, for it has already had a bearing on much that has been written to this juncture and it will have a profound influence on all that is yet to be written.[3]

The rent or rend, the fissure or tear, the bare suggestion of an opening, then, is a hairline of identification, identification as a process of the one thing identifying itself insofar as it is a difference from another thing. However, just as that difference is always a different difference, so also identification is a process of becoming without the possibility of its being a having become. In an interview, Homi Bhabha declares in this respect:

> [I]dentification is a process of identifying with and through an-other object, an object of otherness, at which point the agency of identification—the subject—is itself always ambivalent, because of the intervention of that otherness. But the importance of hy-bridity is that it bears the traces of those feelings and practices which inform it, just like a translation, so that hybridity puts to-gether the traces of certain other meanings or discourses. It does not give them the authority of being prior in the sense of being original: they are prior only in the sense of being anterior. The process of cultural hybridity gives rise to something different, something new and unrecognizable, a new area of negotiation of meaning and representation. A good example would be the form of hybridity that *The Satanic Verses* represents, where clearly a number of controversies around the origin, the authorship and in-deed the authority of the Koran, have been drawn upon in the book. (Bhabha 1990b:211)

So there are not merely two original moments. A third pushes its way in through the interstices, a third space and a third time, which enables other positions to emerge. Bhabha (1990b:216) calls the emergence and assertion of this third term "transla-tion"—recall the translation of sign as outlined in chapter two. New sites are always being opened up; but they cannot be old flasks in which to put new wine or taken as new flasks to be filled with old wine. They are in the process of becoming something other than what they were becoming.

This is a far cry from the customary binary classifications deployed in the construction of order in terms of the haves and have-nots, those who exercise hegemony and those who are destined to remain in positions of subservience. There are now multivalent ambiguities. It is not merely a matter of the "*either* or the *or.*" Rather, it is a transition and transformation from a futile all-embracing attempt at "*Both* this, *And . . . And . . . And . . . n*" to a sly, roguish, and more subtle "*Neither* this, *Nor . . . Nor . . . Nor . . . n*" and then at some point in the interstices, something else, something different, something out of the ordinary. Taking the whole of these possibilities for the practice of everyday life into account—as if that were really possible, which it is not, of course—it might be said that there is no custom but customs, no fashion but fashions, no strategy but strategies, no rule but rules, no choice but choices. A choice, rule, or strategy over another choice, rule, or strategy, is largely binary. In contrast, when attempting to consider the whole of everyday life, choices, rules, and strategies are nonlinear, unpredictable, uncertain, for the most part *inconsistent*, and they evince qualities of virtual chaos and *rhizomicity*. Almost anything can in principle become virtually anything else (it is *overdetermined*). But when it comes down to the nitty-gritty of actual practices, multiple variegated choices, rules, strategies, lead to the engenderment of interrelated, interdependent, interactive, context-bound actualities that are invariably *incomplete*, for they could have been something other than they are and at some future time and place they will have become one of a spectrum of alternative possibilities (they are *underdetermined*).

All this goes to suggest that there is no priority of essence over existence and no priority of existence over essence. That is to say, what *is* could always have been *other than it is*, and it will have been one of the myriad possibilities of that *other*. What emerges in practice does not become what *is*, for there is no "is," that is, no "is" equal to what *is* that is not what *is not*. And regarding what *is* and what *is not*, there is nothing else that "can be." There is only process, the becoming of some nostalgic order of being, to be sure, but that being is nothing except that it is no more than the being of the becoming of what will have never become what it is and nothing but what it is. Traditional humanistic values seem to fall by the wayside, if they do not disappear entirely. Dissemination, dispersal, diaspora, deterritorialization and reterritorialization, and scintillating, effervescent, vibrant, rippling near-Brownian movement at the hairline or membrane: each actor on the flowing stage is a "vortex" in *n*-dimensional space and nonlinear time that can fly off in one of many directions (overdetermination), and whatever may have happened is no necessary indication of what will have happened in the future, for the future, as much as the past, resists closure (underdetermination). The idea of the subject also wanes, since there is no such fixed category and since it does not reside in some determinable space-time juncture. The category of the subject:

> cannot be established either through the absolutization of a dispersion of "subject positions," or through the equally absolutist unification of these around a "transcendental subject." The category of subject is penetrated by the same ambiguous, incomplete and polysemical character which overdetermination assigns to every discursive identity. For this reason, the moment of closure

of a totality, cannot be established at the level of a "meaning-
giving subject," since the subjectivity of the agent is penetrated
by the same precariousness and absence of suture apparent at any
other point of the discursive totality of which it is part. "Objectivism" and "subjectivism"; "holism" and "individualism" are symmetrical expressions of the *desire* for a fullness that is perma-
nently deferred. Owing to this very absence of a final suture, the
dispersion of subject positions cannot constitute a solution: given
that none of them manages ultimately to consolidate itself as a
separate position, there is a game of overdetermination among
them that reintroduces the horizon of an impossible totality. It is
this game which makes hegemonic articulation possible. (Laclau
and Mouffe 1985:121–22)

Now, I must add that such antagonistic pairs of terms the likes of "objectivism" and
"subjectivism," and "holism" and "individualism," do not any ordinary logic make,
nor do they provide any genuine stuffing for that mixed bag that goes by the name of
"hegemony." A term and its opposite, as Laclau and Mouffe point out quite effectively, is not the same in everyday practice as a logical contradiction. It may be no
more than the difference between contrariety ("A/B") and legitimate contradiction
("A/Not-A"). Both terms of the first retain their own form of positivity; the one and
only term of the second is met by the blank wall of its negation, and it can apparently
go no further. The first allows for interrelations, interaction, exchange, openness; the
second is characterized by immutable intransigence. The first belongs exclusively to
an ideal language of propositions without the flesh and bones of concrete living; the
second is organic, to be sure, but there is no individual "in here" against everything
else "out there," but rather, everything is codependently emerging and mutually interpenetrating, with nothing taking necessary or absolute priority over anything else.
The difference is not that of Hegelian oneness and its negativity and antitheses and
syntheses against a Marxian clash of many things all of which are determined by the
overriding force of economic history. No. There is neither classical contradiction nor
opposition in the binary sense of the terms. If a contradictory force arises out of the
wilderness, or if some opposite force is pitted against the reigning force, it is not a
matter of planes against planes, tanks against tanks, guns against guns, or even of a
policeperson's night stick brutally aimed at a cranium or rocks thrown at cars and
enforcers of the law behind protective shields. These are, most properly speaking,
just binaries. However, actually, if "A" and "Not-A" and/or "A" and "B" there must
be, at any rate there is never exclusively, *either* the one *or* the other: *both-and* and
neither-nor interdependent interaction is sure to inhere as well. There is no simple
timeless and spaceless linear logic of dominance/subservience, but a "logic" of codependent, interrelated interaction and exchange in time and space.

   What we have here is somewhat comparable to Bhabha's (1994:25) concept of
negotiation rather than simple negation or opposition, as is also patterned in Jara and
Spadaccini's (1992a) relationship between *criollos* and *peninsulares* in Spanish colonial society. Contradictory propositions are there, for sure, but they are not mere

antitheses that clash with their respective theses to bring about something else. On the contrary. All-out interaction sooner or later becomes caught up in *inconsistencies, contradictions,* and *paradoxes,* and in many cases there are no intransigent conflicts and clashes, no virulent antagonisms, no incommensurable discourses for which there is no solution in the sense of Kuhn and other theorists of incommensurability—the early Lyotard included. The name of the game is more a matter of making the best with what we have in the sense of de Certeau. In the process we come to live with inconsistencies and contradictions and paradoxes, often with quite remarkable aplomb, from within the sphere of Firstness, vagueness, overdetermination, which serves to hold together otherwise incompatible objects, acts, and events. During this process, each horn of the inconsistencies and contradictions and paradoxes is now here, now it is not, for the other horns have ephemerally pushed it aside. This *either/or* action-reaction activity is within the sphere of Secondness. Further down the semiosic stream, where Thirdness, generality, overdetermination, and incompleteness come to the surface, something different, something new, can potentially emerge from the interstices. It is like a trembling, vibrant combination of the sign "vortex" and the "cosmic egg hairline" of Figures 1, 2, 3, and 5 into a massive fluid, flowing semiotic gush from whence all possibilities give rise to all that is becoming. On the one hand, within the sphere of pure possibilities, myriad inconsistencies, contradictions, and paradoxes there can be. On the other hand, in the process of becoming, there is a concerted effort to separate the placid sheep from the bucking goats in order to keep control over the world.

How, then, can we account for the apparent impossibility, or at least the extreme discomfort, of embracing actual inconsistencies, contradictions, and paradoxes, and assimilating them into everyday affairs? We can't, explicitly. An account that cannot be exactly articulated but must be in large part felt is possible because the sheep and goats of each dilemma share something; at the interstices there is some commonality between them, at the "A-Not-A-lessness" of Figure 5. It is not a simple matter of "objective relations," for at the border of borders there are no relations. There is only the "vortex" and "hairline," the minuscule point and fissure: this "something" shared by two or more terms, this "emptiness" that is at the same time the possibility of everythingness. The problem is that "A" is ordinarily considered "A" and nothing but "A," in some fixed and firm and founded sense, and "Not-A" is what "A" is not, categorically, and make no bones about it. This testifies to the deeply entrenched Identity Principle in our thought processes. Yet, it seems reasonable to propose that we must somehow try to come to grips with the flowing coexistence of inconsistencies, contradictions, and paradoxes at the "vortex" and "hairline," for if not, we remain trapped within a world of binary Seconds, do we not?

What Is Really Between the Neither and the Nor?

According to the standard story, there is the dominant power whose presence is made evident by differences: of dress, skin color, language, customs. Many of these differences are within diverse cultural milieus stretched out until they become full-blown oppositions: "A/Not-A" (within the sphere of Secondness). It would appear quite simple. "A" is not "Not-A" and "Not-A" is not "A." Within such cultural mixes, however, there is concrete, interrelated, codependent give-and-take between the dominant and the subordinate: both groups do what seems necessary in order to survive in the best way they know how. It would appear, then, that the opposites are what they *are* in the process of becoming only insofar as they *are not*. In other words, the negative comes into a liquid embrace with the positive within what I have called "emptiness." Emptiness contains, within itself, the possibility for the emergence of virtually unlimited possibilities. The problem is that within cultural kaleidoscopes where clear-cut opposites presumably rule, everything must be *either* the one *or* the other pole of the binary structure. Let us look at all this another way, to mix things up a little.

The division in Figure 5 includes a distinction between the incongruously complementary pairs in the "imaginary number" ($\sqrt{-1}$). This number is in a process of becoming some, *either* the one ($+1$) *or* the other (-1) of the two alternatives in concrete living. But erstwhile differences cleaved into oppositions ($+$ or $-$) could not have been possible without the division, the hairline. This division maintains the one and the other in an undulating, effervescent, rippling sphere of pure possibilities; it also implies "0," "emptiness," the unnoticed, unpremeditated absence of everything. Emptiness precedes "$\sqrt{}$" as a sign with *neither* positive *nor* negative value. This sign is no more than a sign of possibilities that may begin their becoming. Emptiness, in contrast, just *is*: there never were, there are not, and there can never be, any oppositions within the realm of emptiness. There is only emptiness. From emptiness and then "$\sqrt{}$," we have incongruous complementarities in the overdetermined sphere (of Firstness) giving rise to *either/or* antagonisms in the sphere of the concrete lived world (of Secondness) as the product of minds and hands, of cuts and taxonomies, of perspectives and preconceptions and prejudices. Now, after the great bifurcation has transpired, mediary Thirdness can make its play. Let's hear from a few examples.

Edward Said (1978, 1993) writes extensively that power belongs to one side and the other side can hardly do more than remain powerless ("A *or* Not-A"). For Bhabha (1994), in contrast, there is a certain unity of the *one* and the *other* by the *other*'s contesting and negotiating with the *one* through a third force ("*Both* A *and* Not-A," with the *and* as the third term). As far as I have been concerned—and as I shall argue below in greater detail—in addition to emptiness, *both-and* within the sphere of Firstness, overdetermination, vagueness, and the *either/or* sphere of Secondness, there is that sphere where *neither* the one *nor* the other inheres ("*Neither* A *nor* Not-A," of mediary Thirdness, underdetermination, generality). To repeat my above example, viewed ahistorically and synchronically, the Earth is *both* the center *and* it is not the center of the universe. At a given space-time juncture it is conceived as *either* the center *or* not the center. On the other hand, from the historical or diachronic view, *neither* the one *nor* the other is absolutely the case, but something else, perhaps many something elses at an indeterminate number of times and places.

Take another look at Laclau and Mouffe's thesis, for instance. Their Gramscian view does not simply entail a positivity and a negativity, with a binary choice between the *either* and the *or*. Rather, "A" is taken for "A" and "Not-A" for "Not-A" by way of the negativities that each implies with respect to the other: "A" is *not* "Not-A" and "Not-A" is *not* "A." In other words, they are taken for something other than what they would be taken for under other circumstances. Consequently, an interrelation of negative equivalence absorbs all the positive determinations of the haves in negative opposition to the have-nots. This does not create a system of positive differential positions between the two: it dissolves all positivity. The haves are semiotically reconstructed as their opposite, the have-nots: the colonists are thus in a sense "anti-colonized."[4] The tables are overturned. The interrelation between the colonizers, that which gives rise to a tension-ridden "identity" between them, becomes purely negative. Such "negative identity" cannot be represented in a direct manner—i.e., positively. It can only be represented indirectly, through a stretched, vague, overdetermined, equivalence ("*Both* A *and* Not-A") between the range of all possible differential moments. Hence the ambiguity, the vagueness penetrating every interrelation of equivalence: two terms, to be in some form or fashion equivalent, must also be in some manner different—otherwise, there would be a simple identity. In this way, "the equivalence exists only through the act of subverting the differential character of those terms" (Laclau and Mouffe 1985:128). We do not have the simple binary case, then, of one pole defined as a "positivity" entering into a mortal struggle with its opposite, a "negative" pole. On the contrary. All the possible differential determinations of each pole have dissolved through one pole's negatively equivalent reference to the other pole, and in the process each one of them implies what it *is not*.

Now, this may appear reminiscent of Saussurean differentials, and indeed, Laclau and Mouffe remain with one foot mired in the Saussurean gravel pit of particulars sharply separated by means of their digitalized differences. They do not quite flow along that Peircean semiosic stream of smooth contours and folds and ripples and occasional processual eddies of negotiated conflict. Nonetheless, I would suggest that Laclau and Mouffe's use of Saussurean terms merges quite nicely with the Peircean conception of semiosis. We must bear in mind that the fluid embrace of complementary contradictories that include inconsistencies and incompatibilities and samenesses and differences are comparable to the nature of vagueness and overdetermination within the sphere of Firstness. Only when they have been actualized into the light of Secondness (customarily through "ocularcentric," "linguicentric" means and methods) can they be linked in binary fashion as Saussurean "differences" (and, by extrapolation, "oppositions"): "*Either* A *or* Not-A." Subsequently, they become prime candidates for sign engenderment into successively more finely differentiated differences that make a difference in a process of underdetermined generality that may approach, but never reach, continuity. This differentiational process occurs by means of new possibilities and probabilities and necessities perpetually pushing their way, or freely and smoothly emerging as it were, through the rather arbitrarily defined interstices between *either/or* terms. In short, Laclau and Mouffe's formulation must be properly "triadized" in order that it may be rendered viable according to the tenets of the present disquisition.[5]

In this fashion, to say that to be something is always not to be something else (to be "A" implies that it is *not* "Not-A") is to say that what possibly *is* can become what actually *is*. Hence what it *is not* otherwise *could have been*, and what it *is* always already stands ready to becoming something *other than what it is* in the next moment. Yet that "other than what it is" could always have been something *other than what it happened to be* in the process of becoming. This apparent banality is not dominated by binary thinking according to which *not being* something is simply the logical consequence of being *something else*. Positivity ordinarily dominates lingui-centrically conceived discursive practices. What is affirmed here is something quite different: signs, through their codependent cohabitation within Firstness, ignore positivity, though positivity must be taken into account within Secondness. Then, within the sphere of Thirdness, negativity once again comes into the interplay of semiosis.

In this regard, Laclau and Mouffe's (1985:129) dictum that the "impossibility of the real—negativity—has attained a form of presence" takes on heightened credibility. However, in the Peircean conception the negativity of Firstness is pure negativity, properly conceived. Like the "empty set" of set theory, it is a "noticed absence," a "pure" or "positive negativity," rather than the negativity of actualized signs of Secondness. So perhaps Laclau and Mouffe must have it all wrong after all. Pure negativity actually precedes their conception of negativity. Their negativity is "real," it is Secondness, it entails actualization of "*Either* A *or* Not-A." In my formulation, in contrast, the action begins with a suggestion of the noticed absence of the empty set, which is itself dependent upon pure "emptiness." In a manner of putting it, whereas Laclau and Mouffe stop at the equivalence of the empty set, I refuse to allow for the empty set without consideration of "emptiness."

The distinction I make here is crucial. If negativity exists through triadic rather than a dyadic and reciprocal interrelationships, then there can be no total equivalence and hence there is neither total identity nor total opposition nor differentiation that can be clearly and distinctly specified. There is only "emptiness," which makes for the possibility of noticed absence merely implying something that *is not*. Then there is vagueness and overdetermination, which give rise to possible opposition—or contradiction or inconsistency—and identity through the becoming of Firstness and its becoming as the engenderment of Secondness and the *either/ors* of standard logic. But all this cannot have been without the *neither-nors* of difference and generality and underdetermination within the sphere of Thirdness, which is invariably an incomplete enterprise. To their credit, Laclau and Mouffe (1985:129) assert that just as their so-called "logic of difference" never manages to make up a cleanly sutured self-contained and self-sufficient space, so also, neither can the classical logic of equivalence and identity and opposition ever achieve its professed goals. However, they hardly pay more than lip service to anything comparable to what is in this essay termed generality and incompleteness and vagueness and contradiction-inconsistency and underdetermination and overdetermination, all within the sphere of incongruous complementarity.

A tad closer to the tenets of this inquiry, as mentioned, is Bhabha's negotiation rather than merely negation. From overdetermination, contradictions, virtualities, *both-and* considerations, there is negation in terms of the empty set from which *either/or* imperatives arise at the level of Secondness. Negotiation, in contrast to mere negation, takes a detour; it becomes thoroughly dialogic. But it is not of the customary form of dialogic found in linguicentric talk. On the contrary. At heart it is a manifestation of the *neither-nor, avant la lettre*, before the sign exchange has entered into the light of day as full-blown Thirdness, that is, language. At heart it is of the nature of Firstness, of interrelations that make a detour around Secondness and take on the trappings of the *neither-nor* to enter directly into generalities, the under-determined, which themselves depend on binaries, that is, on oppositions of ordinary "A/Not-A" vintage. But they are much more than mere binary relations within Secondness: they always contain, within themselves, an element of subversion against that very Secondness of the sort found only in the *both-ands* of Firstness and the *neither-nors* of Thirdness. In this vein, when Bhabha talks of negotiation rather than negation:

> [I]t is to convey a temporality that makes it possible to conceive of the articulation of antagonistic or contradictory elements, a dialectic without the emergence of a teleological or transcendent History, and beyond the prescriptive form of symptomatic reading where the nervous tics on the surface of ideology reveal the "real materialist contradiction" that History embodies. In such a discursive temporality, the event of theory becomes the *negotiation* of contradictory and antagonistic instances that open up hybrid sites and objectives of struggle, and destroy those negative polarities between knowledge and its objects and between theory and practical-political reason. (Bhabha 1994:25).

If Bhabha argues against anything smacking of a primordial binary division of right or left, progressive or reactionary, and so on, he does so only to stress the fully historical and discursive *différance* between them.

To their credit also, Laclau and Mouffe (1985:68–70) take their Gramscian argument a small step further, alluding to chaos ordered from above by authoritarianism meted out by the hegemonic haves, and an entirely different form of order arising spontaneously from below at the hands of the have-nots. This latter order might appear at the outset to typify movements in Argentina and Chile organized by women during those countries' military dictatorships (Bouvard 1994; Hollander 1997; Yaeger 1994), community organization after the earthquake of 1985 in Mexico City and the role of "Superbarrio," a masked folk hero who goes to verbal battle against the rich and powerful in the name of the have-nots (Guillermoprieto 1994; Monsiváis 1987; Poniatowska 1988), and self-help programs in Peru (Soto 1989). Indeed, one interpretation of Antonio Gramsci as theoretician of "uneven development"—as applied to the particular case of Italy, given its industrialized North and its traditionally agrarian South, its Catholic tradition mixed with capitalism—would seem most appropriate to Latin America. However, Laclau and Mouffe perceive a basic ambiguity in Gramsci's thought regarding the contingent character of the working class struggle for equality and the necessary character of this struggle assigned to it by economic demands. We cannot have things both ways, they write. Economic pressures show how society can bend according to the ways and will of the people, and the people do not simply behave in a random and solely statistically determinable manner, but show some character and guts unrecognized by standard Marxist theory. But Gramsci, and to an extent even Laclau and Mouffe, remain within *either/or* imperatives. In other words, they commit what appears to be a subtle sin committed by Roberto DaMatta's overly stringent dichotomy between "individuals" and "persons" as discussed in chapter four. Actually, DaMatta takes pains to point out that there is not simply the one or the other but both the one in the other and the other in the one. Consequently, a consideration of *both-and* and -*neither-nor* modes of thought begin to emerge.

However, after all is said and done, Laclau and Mouffe are perhaps not so far off base as I might have implied. They loosely write of a "logic of equivalence" and a "logic of autonomy." At an initial, rather cross-eyed glance, the first "logic" would take its place in DaMatta's "individual's" behavior, while the second "logic" would suit the "person's" liking. Each "individual" is pretty much the same as every other "individual," so the classical Principle of Identity would apply. The "autonomous" person, in contrast, is presumably master of her own ship, hence there is "identity," but that "identity" is unique to each person, according to the "logic of autonomy." However, when antagonisms arise and democratizing struggles break out, then:

> The logic of equivalence, . . . taken to the ultimate consequences, would imply the dissolution of the autonomy of the spaces in which each one of these struggles is constituted; not necessarily because any of them become subordinated to others, but because they have all become, strictly speaking, equivalent symbols of a unique and indivisible struggle. The antagonism would thus have achieved the conditions of total transparency, to the extent that all unevenness had been eliminated, and the differential specificity of the spaces in which each of the democratic struggles was constituted had been dissolved. (Laclau and Mouffe 1985:182)

Only in the event that a struggle were to take place with each of the social groups operating within hermetical confines—which can never be the case—would the "logic of equivalence" and the "logic of autonomy" become pure contradictories, since the social identities would always already have been acquired and fixed.

In this respect, at least, Laclau and Mouffe are in line with the processual "logic" emerging in these pages with the general Latin American condition. There can be no pure identity or contradiction, given the sphere of overdetermination and vagueness, and there can be no clear-cut *either/or* imperatives, given the perpetually incomplete sphere of underdetermination. Thus the road to "democratic equivalence" is not completeable, for a certain element of vagueness there will always be, and total freedom to be oneself by exercising one's "logic of autonomy" will always meet with inconsistencies, since differences are differences only by virtue of the existence of some notion of generalities (identities, equivalencies) against which that "autonomy" can come about. So "the demand for *equality* is not sufficient, but needs to be balanced by the demand for *liberty*," that calls for consideration of a "radical and *plural* democracy" (Laclau and Mouffe 1985:184). Just as inconsistency and incompleteness, and vagueness and generality, and overdetermination and underdetermination are incongruous complementarities in addition to their being logical contradictories, so also with respect to autonomy and equivalence, and liberty and equality. In the final analysis, there is only incongruous complementarity of the *neither-nor* sort, a "logic of vagueness and generality." In every case, openness is preserved, without conceivable beginning or ending or center.

A Difference That Fakes a Difference

Where Firstness reigns, vagueness is the password. And for a very good reason. It is not that contraries and contradictories are simply fused, for there is really no all-out conflict in the first place. There is no more than what for lack of a better word might simply be dubbed *undecidability*. It is quite difficult to picture this condition. In fact, it cannot be "pictured" at all. Perhaps in part because of this resistance to pictureability, it has eluded the grasp of Western logocentric thought. Yet, Derrida (1973) writes in so many—perhaps too many—words that this condition lies at the core of Western thought, in the *aporias*, the binds, the twists of the Möbius strip, where a tragic flaw is found in any and all texts of sufficient levels of complexity.

Such signs as Derrida's *pharmakon* and *hymen* and *supplement* and *différance* are oblique expressions of these "flaws" of undecidability—and admittedly to say "flaw" is somewhat of a misnomer, for actually it is the saving grace of all texts, that which affords them their value, in spite of what their authors might have thought. *Pharmakon*—somewhat like $\sqrt{-1}$ of Figure 5—is *both* a poison *and* a remedy, *both* deadly *and* life-giving. The sign is looked upon as ambiguous. In technical terms, it would be charged with the misdemeanor of inconsistency, for it cannot simultaneously mean one thing and its opposite. Yet it incorporates both meanings. It is the immediate product of the Möbius strip twist: there is both "inside" and "outside," both "figure" and "ground," both "this" and "that." There simply are no binaries in the ordinary sense. If there were, once again, the prison-house of Secondness would suck us in. When we move from the sphere of Firstness and the Seconds actualized from it, Thirdness pushes its way onto the scene. The human semiotic animal, that pliable thinking reed, takes smug comfort in believing she has arrived at the finish line with her language, her signs of Thirdness. But there is no determination (provability is the Gödelian word) of this being so. There is no genuine knowing without a shadow of a doubt whether a given generality is either complete or incomplete. Presumptuous though fallible individuals that we are, we would like to persist in our naive belief that many, if not all, of our conceptions are quite complete. And we proceed to wrap them up in a tidy package. Yet we have no certainty regarding their validity, for our generalities remain perpetually open to new additions and deletions somewhere along the line.

Within the fuzz of Firstness, what we might call a "logic of *différance-temporality*" comes into play. According to orthodox logic, there is an infinitesimally thin line—the line of demarcation in Figures 1 and 5—between opposites. I argued above that a certain Peircean "logic of vagueness" would play havoc with logic of the classical sort. A disjunction of the set of all bald men and the set of all non-bald men does not exactly leave the "empty set"—for who is to draw the line between "bald" and "non-bald"? A line, if line there must be, can be no more than vague. When with age the hirsute man loses one hair, then another, then another, at what point can we say lo and behold with the loss of that hair there, he is now bald?

The deciding point is so blurry. For one person it is here, for another person it is there. The line of demarcation becomes smudgy. This dilemma reveals a virtual continuum of gradients between the one pole and the other of the supposed contradiction. This important point also plays the role of "guerrilla warrior" against cherished structuralist-semiological principles according to which Saussurean differences are stretched into whole-hog binary oppositions. Although Derrida lodged an all-out attack on binarism of the semiological sort, this war was indefatigably waged by Peirce almost a century before the venerated Gospel According to Derrida was written.

So, what is the answer? There is no clear and distinct, complete and consistent answer. Clarity and distinction must be a matter of Seconds that are what they are on no uncertain terms. The problem is that vagueness (of Firstness) lies outside the conception of any existent Seconds; and generality (of Thirdness) is alien also to the conception of Seconds in terms of its strictly defined binary logic. Unfortunately, the Western tendency is to beat the infinitesimal differentiations of Firstness into oppositions when entering the anteroom of Secondness. Then, when individuals begin to merge into the ranks of generals, the tendency is to fuse small differences into identities and divide large differences into oppositions. Nietzsche (1974:171) criticized this obsession "to treat as equal what is merely similar—an illogical tendency, for nothing is really equal—is what first created any basis of logic." And later Heidegger (1969:45) observed "the same is not the merely identical. In the merely identical, the difference disappears. In the same the difference appears, and appears all the more pressingly, the more resolutely thinking is concerned with the same matter in the same way." [6]

All this, to the chagrin of the purveyors of good taste and proper logic, seems to bear on that "irrational" Buddhist sort of "logic" of *both-and* and *neither-nor* rather than the *either/or* in the traditional Western way. The Master holds a stick above the apprentice's head and tells her: "If you say anything I will hit you with this stick; if you say nothing I will also hit you." The hapless youth appears damned if she does and damned if she doesn't. It's an *either/or* bind typical of linear, binary logic. But what if the apprentice enters the line of demarcation, widens it, grabs the stick from the Master, and hits him on the head with it? She has drawn something out of the erstwhile excluded-middle. She has actualized one of the many possibilities from the "hairline" in Figure 5. The beginning of her becoming somebody she was not follows the flow: "0" $\rightarrow$ $\emptyset$ (empty set) $\rightarrow$ "$\sqrt{\ }$" $\rightarrow$ ± 1 $\rightarrow$ $+1 \mid -1$ $\rightarrow$ CHOICE (and then *this* rather than *that*, or *that*, or …).

Physicist Max Planck once complained that a new scientific theory "does not triumph by convincing its opponents and making them see light, but rather because its opponents eventually die, and a new generation grows up that is familiar with it" (in Kline 1980:88). With time, the line opens into a pair of gaping jaws, and the prohibited, but yet possible in spite of the prohibition, gives birth into the world of actuals, of existents. Our apprentice, in contrast, made a flying leap into "emptiness" and emerged as someone becoming someone other than who she was becoming, all in the blink of an eye.

The upstanding logician's and the rhetorician's argument would have it that if the terms used in a proposition are strictly defined regarding a finite context and were complete in terms of their use (i.e., extension, "reference," hooking the terms onto actuals), then the Principles of Identity, of Noncontradiction, and of the Excluded-Middle hold true. However, over time, no context remains identical with itself, and no term reaches completeness to the extent that it will never allow for at least one more interpretation. The sentence "Bill Clinton is Bill Clinton" is not true if the former use of the term relates to Bill Clinton, October of 1997, and the latter use relates to him as of December of 1999. The assignment of signs to Bill Clinton puts both him and the signs incessantly in the process of becoming something other than what they were becoming.

One might wish to protest: my vagueness and generality (Firstness and Thirdness) are suspended in thin air, with no more than an imaginary thread to support them. Perhaps, then, I should bow down to the world of existents (Secondness) about which we can talk, and leave it at that. Within the world of existents, we would expect we could plainly see that what *is*, *is not* something else, and what *is not*, is excluded by what *is*. There's no more to the matter. However, regarding what we would like to take as existing objects, acts, and events, and the grounding for all knowledge of what there *is*, an opinion from the likes of Einstein, Louis de Broglie, Max Planck, Bertrand Russell, Wittgenstein, Quine, Goodman, Putnam, and Rorty might go something like this: *Insofar as logic and mathematics are connected to "reality," they are uncertain; insofar as they are absolutely certain, they cannot be indubitably connected to "reality."* And as a consequence of the metamathematical "limitative theorems," from the likes of Kurt Gödel, Alfred Tarski, Emil Post, Alonzo Church, Alan Turing, and Skolem, we might have: *If a sufficiently powerful and sophisticated set of signs is presumably complete, then there must be a tragic flaw, an* aporia, *an inconsistency, somewhere; if it is deemed consistent, then it cannot but be incomplete, for somewhere there is a lack, a deficiency, that calls for the addition, a* supplement, *of something from "outside."* The upshot is that our generalities (Thirdness) are invariably incomplete, and our perception and conception of particulars (Secondness) eventually land us in vagueness (Firstness) and inconsistency.

Classical logic, of course, will accept nothing less than brilliantly gleaming crystals of thought. Each thought is presumably embedded in static being, and it is distinct from all other thoughts by a strictly defined line of demarcation. Variations must be the imperfect realizations of this underlying truth of all things. This obstinate dream of standard logic places barriers before us barring any and all successive gradients between the two poles of the hopeful contradiction. The dream, however, is destined to send out its own death notice: it is invariably plagued with some element of vagueness. For nothing is absolutely *either* the one *or* the other, but thinking can often make the betweenness appear to disappear. Actual things are *neither* clearly and distinctly the one *nor* the *other* (underdeterminate), and merely possible things are *both* the one *and* the *other* (overdeterminate). How could it be otherwise? If quantum theory, relativity, and the limitative theorems might happen to be on the right track when they use such intangibles as i $(= \sqrt{-1})$ to compute the behavior of possibles that can be actualized into one of practically an infinite number of "realities," then we are forced to conclude that our physical existence and by extension our cultural existence are caught up in a complex tangle of incongruous complementarities.

In this vein, from our polylogue we learned that Funy's world of incessant rapid-fire becoming without fixity is without any beingness after the fact of becoming, much as is that of Tlöny, given his subjective idealism. As far as they are concerned, there are only Seconds. (Here, at least in Tlöny's case, we have a certain *jeitinho* streak, though it remains implicit.) Lönny, and in their own way Pierre and Hladdy, want fixity, as does Maggie from within her dream world. Their world would ideally be a utopian form of completed Thirds. (Here we find the makings of the would-be personalistic and rather utopian *caudillo* image, with a necessary tinge of nascent *machismo*, given the need for control.) T'sui, of course, admits to many worlds, to idealistic pluralism. Emmy's world is pluralistic also, but it is pragmatic through and through: she quite objectively becomes, for the time being, just what she needs to be, and no more. In the best of all worlds a T'sui-Emmy combination would bring Firstness in line with Secondness and a perpetually incomplete Thirdness. Yet we must put all the actors of the polylogue together, as I have suggested above, and we would have the whole bag at once stuffed with overdetermination and underdetermination, with vagueness, along with its inherent inconsistencies, and generality, incomplete generality. In a manner of speaking, we once again have everything and nothing, or better, in these nonexistent, imaginary characters, we have nothing more than a border of borders. We have "emptiness."

Notes

1.   This formulation is comparable to a Peirce "thought experiment" wherein he uses the example of an empty blackboard upon which a solitary mark—a border of borders—is deposited to separate one continuity from another continuity (*CP*:6.203–04).

2.   Allusion to Oriental philosophy becomes here more than ever quite obvious, I would expect. For an illustration of the "Cosmic Egg Principle" put forth in this inquiry and its relation to Buddhism, see Huntington (1989), Kalupahana (1986).

3.   You will have noticed the affinity between the paragraph you have just finished and Jacques Derrida's baffling and ubiquitous undecidables, words that "can no longer be included within philosophical (binary) opposition, resisting and disorganizing it, without ever constituting a third term, without ever leaving room for a solution in the form of speculative dialectics" (Derrida 1981:71). There is, for example, the *pharmakon*, the Greek generic term including both remedy and poison found in Plato's *Phaedrus* as a simile for writing. There is the *hymen*, indicating both membrane and marriage, the virginal distinction between "inside" and "outside" and its renting with consummation of the marriage vows. We also have the *supplement*, both an addition and a replacement, and the notorious *différance*, which is both time and space as a deferring and a difference and at the same time neither time nor space. In all cases the *either/or* is present, for sure, but the *both-and* and the *neither-nor* also manage to make their way onto the scene to create havoc with the usual classical logical principles. In this regard Augusta Dwyer (1994) writes of the

Mexican-U.S. border, and border mentality, which is like an oscillating dividing line, a quivering, trembling, border of neither here nor there, like the imaginary number and the hairline separating the two halves of the Cosmic Egg.

4.   My use of the term "semiotics" here includes the entire gamut of sign making and sign taking, both linguistic and extralinguistic. Laclau and Mouffe, in contrast, use the "linguicentric" term "discourse," which, as I have argued elsewhere (merrell 1997, 2000b), is a severely restricted conception of the whole of human interaction.

5.   Although admittedly, Anna Marie Smith's (1998) interpretation of Laclau and Mouffe is a move in the right direction.

6.   For a view of the *both-and* and its disruption of the Principle of Identity in feminist thought, see Irigaray (1985), Tavor Bannet (1993).

Chapter Seven

Triadomania Again

> I'm in-between. This identity, like exile itself, leaves me unprotected. Within this void, this fallen state, I develop a new identity.
> —Arturo Elizondo

> A border should be a meeting point, not a place of walls and separation.
> —Rudolfo A. Anaya

How about "Cultural Logic"?

What now? Where now? How now? I have addressed myself somewhat to the triadic nature of the Peircean sign, but there are still many holes. We have journeyed into the labyrinthine sphere of cultural differences, but everything remains tenuous, vague. There have been a few overtures in the direction of some conception of alternate "logics" as cultural "logics"—about which these days there is much mention without revelation, lip service with few tips suggesting what it is that is with such facility evoked—but there is nothing we can get a grip on. It is high time I either put up or shut up. So I must try to try again.

Laclau and Mouffe, in somewhat less cavalier fashion than is customary among most hard-nosed critics of and ecstatic navigators in that heaving, unpredictable ocean of poststructuralism and other "isms," summarily allude to a number of "logics." There are vague, unqualified allusions to a "logic of contingincy," of "necessity," of "difference," of "symbolic constitution," of "neo-post-capitalism," of "consumption," of the "other" or "alterity" or the "subaltern," of "detotalization," and, of course, of "hegemony," to mention only a few. Allow me to engage in my own rather summary placement of Laclau and Mouffe's allusions into three spheres: *contingency*, *hegemony*, and *socio-cultural necessity* (or in another way of putting it, Firstness, Secondness, and Thirdness). I must hasten to add that these pigeonholes are not fixed: they are rhythm; they flow along, as elusive as can be. For instance, "contingency" is not merely Firstness (chance, spontaneity, a Brownian movement of uncertainty). It is Firstness as the possibility of what might emerge at some space-time juncture, and it also includes the becoming of Secondness in terms of what happens to have just been actualized and is now happening. "Socio-cultural necessity" is not merely Thirdness (probability, what Peirce termed "habit"). It is an emerging of Secondness, what is-becoming and has-been-becoming, and of Thirdness, what should, would, or could be-becoming or will-have-been-becoming. And "hegemony" is not simply binary Secondness—which is what one might well take to be the case after a perusal of much literature on the issue. Rather, it is a fusion of Firstness and Thirdness in the coming and going of everyday life, which seems to take on all the trappings of what would ordinarily go by the name of Secondness.

That is to say, "hegemony" is not simply a matter of polarities. It contains, within itself, an implicate tendency, an implicitness, effervescent, scintillating presenting of the possibility of new tendencies on the part of the haves and have-nots and the possibility of emergent images, interrelations, and ideas giving rise to the possibility of renegotiation of norms and values. This is not a binary matter of pure Secondness; it intermittently highlights Firstness and Thirdness while subjecting Secondness to minor to radical alteration. A certain sense of "identity" may make its appearance during these exchanges, if it might be so fortunate. But if "identity" there be, it can be no more than ephemeral, transient, a barely distinguishable, minuscule area within the entire flow of things.

If you will, let "contingency" act as a counterpart to the possibility of a sign, or a representamen. Let "hegemony" play the role of the object of the sign, that is, its *other*. And let "socio-cultural necessity" constitute the makings of the sign's interpretant, the *other* of the *other* (while keeping in mind, of course, that the thin membrane between the terms is hardly more than the dynamic frontier delineating a small, temporary whirlpool from the entire movement of the river from within which it arose). Now, consider the sign as representamen, and the semiotic maker and taker as sign to be (1) in a swimming embrace with all its possible *others* as a matter of contingent happenings; (2) in apparent opposition to some actualized *other* as a matter of intransigent combat, dynamic struggle, rough-and-tumble agonistics; and (3) in intermediate, codependent interrelation with its *other other* as a matter of dialogic exchange, of renegotiation, and at times of happy consensus. Consider also a more general picture, including item (1) as *homogeny*, (2) as *hegemony*, and (3) as *heterogeny* (see Figure 6). *Homo-* qualifies the sphere of Firstness as a union of incongruent contradictories into a harmonious package in terms of sheer possibilities without any pair of presumed opposite terms having emerged to begin their mortal combat. *Hetero-* qualifies the sphere of Thirdness as sets of actualized terms that have either become bored or exhausted as a result of their incessant warfare and are now beginning a potential reconciliation of their differences. The suffix, *-geny*, indicates a manner of emergence, origin, organic becoming without reaching the stage of already having become.

All this might appear as so much taxonomic drivel, Grand Narratives at their totalizing worst. So I really must more adequately specify what I have schematically mapped out before going on. But first, if I may be so allowed, I would like to indulge a bit more by illustrating the Peircean importance of my scheme.

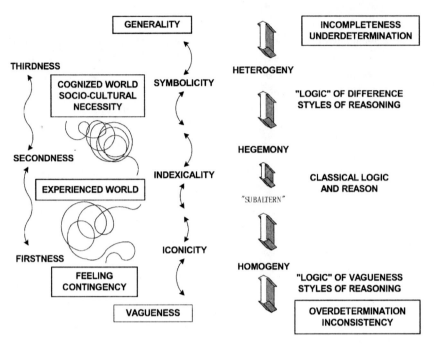

Figure 6

How Better to Qualify the Haves and the Have-nots, Perhaps

JanMohamed's hypothesis of "imaginary" and "symbolic" narratives rings a bell—in spite of his ignoring the "real." The "Imaginary" is a hopeful syncretistic union of opposites, of colonizer and colonized; the "Symbolic" entails recognition that syncretism is no answer, and takes a reflexive turn inward, evoking ambiguity, irony, skepticism, cynicism, and at times even nihilism. The "Imaginary" is in this sense somewhat comparable to Firstness; the "Symbolic" to Thirdness. The problem is that to all appearances JanMohamed formulates this pair of terms with Secondness (binarism) in mind. But Secondness alone cannot fill the bill. In order to fall in line with Firstness, the "imaginary" should include *both* a term *and* its opposite. And in order to cohere with Thirdness, the "symbolic" must evoke the idea that *neither* the one term *nor* the *other* either in isolation or paired can provide an answer to the pressing problems of socio-cultural struggle. Secondness alone simply cannot hope to account for all these characteristics.

Taking the injunction "A," handed down by those who rule as a code to be honored, come what may, we have Peirce's *authority* (as briefly described above regarding his "fixing of belief"), which, in his anti-Cartesian argument, was discarded as no guarantee whatsoever that it will put us on the straight and narrow path toward knowing. Taking "Not-A," we have Peirce's *tenacity*, the method of the rebellious upstart who goes his own way without any regard for authority or the helpful suggestions of anyone else in his community. This, for obvious reasons, will rarely lead to any legitimate answers. We can have the Cartesian *a priori* method of *introspection* by some presumably privileged individual who spreads the word about her having plumbed the depths of her consciousness, survived, and returned with the grounding bit of knowledge in hand. Peirce's anti-Cartesianism simply will not let this concept fly, however. There is no knowing, ultimately knowing, who is to be trusted and who is not. Why should we blindly place faith in anyone and abide by her counsel without questions or the opportunity for a good counterargument? Peirce's prescribed road to the best of all possible worlds of knowing rests in amicable conversation, banter, debate, kibitzing, and even agonistics when it becomes necessary. This, I have suggested, is the dialogic way toward knowing. It entails *neither* necessarily "A" *nor* necessarily "Not-A," but most likely something else. That "something else" is what emerges within the *community* out of dialogic give-and-take. During the dialogue, what is accepted becomes caught between the horns of some dilemma or other, and something must give. But upon giving, something else emerges, which is then put to the dialogical or practical test, and hopefully some general opinion will ensue.

Now, I invite you to take a wild flight of the imagination. In the twentieth century, quantum theory, especially when carrying the labels of Heisenberg's *uncertainty principle* and Bohr's *complementarity*, is brazenly, and apparently without remorse or regrets, ambiguous, and even inconsistent, depending upon "thought experiment." One of these thought experiments gave rise to the particle-wave complementarity. Is a quantum "event" a "particle" or is it a "wave"? To put the matter quite baldly, the only possible responses to such questions is "Yes, but no," "No, but yes," "Yes *and* no," "*Neither* yes *nor* no," and "*All* of the above" and "*None* of the above." Perplexing, to say the least.[1] In Galileo"s "Dialogue," Simplicio the Aristotelian disrespectfully asks Salviati: "So you have not made a hundred tests, or even one? And yet you so freely declare it to be certain?" Salviati responds: "Without experiment, I am sure that the effect will happen as I tell you, because it must happen that way" (Galileo 1967:145; in Brown 1991:2–3). This recalls Einstein's remark regarding Arthur Eddington's experiment designed either to verify or falsify Einstein's general theory of relativity. When asked his opinion about the possible outcome of the event, Einstein responded that if it appeared to refute his theory, then he was sorry for the dear Lord, because the theory was correct. A marvel of arrogance? Yes ... *and* no. Such declarations bear witness to the power of the mind and the confidence of she who dwells within it. It also testifies, I would respectfully submit, to the inextricable union of Firstness-Secondness-Thirdness, representamen-object-interpretant, iconicity-indexicality-symbolicity, and feeling-sensing-interpreting. This union can hardly be put to the test, like Galileo's thought experiments could have been. Yet Hume, Locke, and others, including Peirce, bear witness to the impossibility of one's observing oneself in the act of observing oneself in order to distinguish roughly between the equivalent of Peirce's categories. It's comparable to the quantum "event" just described.

It seems that, with respect to this mutual embrace of Peirce's intriguing triads, and in light of his anti-Cartesian posture, the counsel might be: never bow to *authority* unless it is deserving of your respect, do not blindly push forth come what may with paranoid *tenacity*, beware of those false prophets bearing tidings of their having been to the wilderness of their *introspective* mind where they saw the light of Truth, but pay your dues to the *community* of your choice, keep the dialogue open, and do the best you can. With respect to the triads themselves, we would have it that the imaginary thought-sign is the possibility of "A," a might-be from the sphere of "*Both A and* Not-A." In this regard, the semiotic object of the sign would be something other than "A." And the interpretant would be "*Neither* A *nor* Not-A," but since it brings "A" and its respective *other* into a three-way mediation, it potentially gives rise to the emergence of something different, something even possibly new. We can construct the now familiar tripod (Figure 7), with the "point" or "vortex" connecting each of the "sign" components. (I would respectfully ask that you mesh the implications of Figures 6 and 7 with the discussion of *personalismo, machismo, caudillismo,* and *jeito-jeitinho* from chapter four in order to get in the groove of the alternative "logics" slowly being presented. This input is, I would suggest, essential, since limited space does not permit further exposition here and since one should really experience these "logics" for oneself in order to reap a full harvest.)

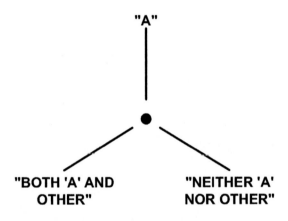

Figure 7

Recall that the "vortex" is the composite of all possible, but unactualized, signs. It is the sheer "emptiness" of anything and everything. It is as if we had "*Both* A *and* Not-A" and "*Neither* A *nor* Not-A" written on the two sides of a strip of paper and then we make of the two-dimensional sheet a Möbius-band in three-dimensional space to yield "*Both* of the propositions," and "*Neither* of the propositions." Moreover, the choice is not a choice between what is in no uncertain terms true and what is not true, between what exists and what does not exist, but rather, between what from some context or other might be possibly true and what might be possibly false, and what might possibly be neither true nor false because it not yet is. There is no more than our "tripod" plus the "vortex." This is a sort of combination of JanMohamed's (1985:83–85) "imaginary" and "symbolic," coupled with the "real," plus the pre-imaginary, which is tantamount to: $0 \rightarrow \emptyset \rightarrow$ "$\sqrt{}$" (of $\sqrt{}$-1). The pre-imaginary is, itself, *neither* positive *nor* negative; it is valueless. It is *just that,* or as Gertrude Stein would say, it is the *it-ness.*

This is not very clear, I fear. But what more can be said if what is to be said cannot explicitly be said? It only lends itself to a sort of feeling for what is on the tenuous cultural track of semiosis. There is no Cartesian clarity to be had at this extralogocentric, extralinguicentric sphere of vague and overdetermined possible signs where nothing is distinct and where there are no sharp lines of demarcation.

Back to a few more concrete examples, then.

A Picture Puzzle of N-Dimensions and Uncountable Pieces

Latin America today, it goes without saying, is a complex, virtually chaotic, "logic" of ethnicity and culture, conquest and postcolonialism, virtual identity and radical difference, imitation and distortion, conflict and co-optation, antagonism and reciprocity. Whoever surfaces to the top of the gush of ongoing cultural becoming in the beginning might appear to have gained the upper hand. But not necessarily. That is, unless he might have been able simultaneously to perch on the shoulders of all those below and maintain a paternalism-patronizing hegemonic relationship with them. He who happens to be of the haves at the top depends upon those have-nots below and they in turn depend upon him: incongruous complementarity, codependency, and codependent arising in perpetual fluid movement except when by force or by cajolery the process is fractured and temporarily frozen.

In the beginning, the forging of independent Latin America seemed to be the product of clear and distinct delineation. Answers were straightforward, and no further questions were asked. Or so it seemed to those at the upper levels of society who were in the process of nation building and in search of identity (for examples, see Sommer 1991). Today, almost two centuries later, nations are under construction and the cultural, political, social, economic, and ethnic kaleidoscope in these countries continues to defy "identity." Take a *mestiza* woman from Mexico—or the U. S. for that matter. Part of her heritage is Native American, another part perhaps African American, and another part Castillian, which is itself streaked with Arabic cultural presuppositions and propensities, perhaps along with a little Roman, Celt, and so on, influence. The matter of her cultural heritage, her identity, her proper posture *vis-à-vis* the pressures of today's neoliberal, postmodern consumerism become a mixed and confusing bag of tricks. One might tell her that she really should choose. She should choose who she is, what her attitude is with respect to herself, her background, her political inclinations, her behavior and relations with others in society, her role in the economic life surrounding her—what she will purchase and what she will be willing to do in order to purchase more, and how she will use it—and so on. Indeed, the choices are hers, and to decline exercising her right to choose is itself also a choice that will have its own effect on her. Whichever choice or set of choices she arrives at, she will remain separated and at the same time integrated; she will adopt and she will reject; she will embrace and she will resist; she will interrelate and become part of an interlocked concoction of conflicts and contradictions. Along these lines María Lugones writes:

> If something or someone is neither/nor, but kind of both, not quite
> either.
> if something is in the middle of either/or,

if it is ambiguous, given the available classification of things,
it is mestiza,
if it threatens by its very ambiguity the orderliness of the system,
of schematized reality.
if given its ambiguity in the univocal ordering it is anomalous,
deviant, can it be tamed through separation? Should it separate so
as to avoid taming? Should it resist separation? Should it resist
through separation? Separate as in the separation of the white
from the yolk? (Lugones 1994:459)

Yes, of course, *choice*. Lugones says in so many words that we are condemned to choose whether we know it or not and whether we like it or not. The choice exists between the *either* and the *or*, that is, between both the either and the or, or rather, what is between the either and the or. But no. Not that, I'm afraid. Not really, for there is nothing between the either and the or. But that's not right either. Not really. In a metaphorical manner of speaking, emptiness is between them: nothing and everything, as possibilities. The emerging mergence of both the one and the other is declaring "Both A and Not-A." Poking around in the interstices at the risk of falling into the very slightly, in fact infinitesimally, parsed mouth of emptiness, and one might perchance enter that never-never land where "Neither A nor Not-A" is the case, and there is a ray of hope that something novel might emerge—the self-organization of all things, all things as organism, as benign signs of ongoing resonance. It's all a process, a marvelous process, and she, that is, our enchanting and enchanted mestiza, is in it, as are all of us. What she is, is not what she is, and she both is and is not what she is, and she is neither what she is nor what she is not; and she is all of the above and she is none of the above. Riddles. They make shambles of our comfortable binary thinking.

Is there no way out? But who promised us a yellow brick road anyway? Who said there must be either discovery and knowledge or eternal darkness? A matter of dominating or of subservience? Of raping nature or living a sordid animal existence? Of razor-sharp binary choices between eithers and ors? Of course Galileo and Bacon and Newton and Locke and Descartes, and later Thomas Edison and Henry Ford and Bill Gates and many others, and a host of celebrities of various sorts in their own way, all give us an image of that machine-oriented, materialistic, consumerist good life. From another direction, a concoction of religious saints, seers, and assorted sinners also promise milk and honey. As do those who "discovered, conquered, and colonized" America, and Hitler and Mussolini and Stalin and a few Latin American revolutionaries and visionaries and populists who belong to the same crowd. Where did it all get us? Within the last century we have been warned by Nietzsche and Heidegger and Wittgenstein and Foucault and Derrida, and their critics and disciples that the promised paradise is a sham. And we have the limitations on our knowledge by way of Heisenberg and Bohr and Gödel and their counterparts in science, logic, and mathematics. Any and all answers to all questions eventually meet their others, and eventually there may be a happy meeting ground, or some alternative or other may pop up between the neither and the nor, and then it may be a matter of all of the preceding or none of it. Riddles.

What is for sure, binary thinking must go the way of the dinosaurs, for if not, it is most likely we who will follow them into oblivion. Yet, strange as it may seem, binaries continue to rule the roost in many quarters. Cultures are for some reason or other still seen as hardly more than oppositions between the powerful and the helpless. The idea generally has it that the powerful form a bloc; they are unified, quite stable, concordant, and allied toward common economic, social, political, legal, moral, and aesthetic goals. The weak, in contrast, are diverse, dispersed, diasporic, discordant. The haves are into structure, control, domination, manipulation; the have-nots are reduced to a diversity of interests, with no central organizing force (for example, Hall 1981). John Fiske (1989a) dubs the power-bloc homogeneous and the people heterogeneous. He compares the former to Bakhtin's centrifugal forces and the latter to centripetal forces, conceding that the opposition is actually more like the dynamic conflict between an occupying army and "cultural guerrilla" activity, following de Certeau (1984) and Eco (1986). The struggle, we read, is always a confrontation between legato or hegemonic forces of homogeneity and the unruly, staccato or heterogeneity of the people's weak and usually futile hits and misses. Yet, distinctions cannot be so clearly demarcated. As we have noted and will note with greater emphasis, the have-nots actually enjoy a "cultural guerrilla power" that invariably pushes new terms into the gaps between erstwhile opposites.

Fiske thinks he makes a move in this direction (1989b:1–21). He offers the jeans craze in support of his dualistic thinking. Regular jeans evoke the image of country, work, tradition, community, and relative classlessness and changelessness; designer jeans are upscale, bringing forth the idea of urban life, social distinction, leisure, contemporary "yuppie" values, and the transient. But, then, along come the natural-born rebels who, in a show of their contempt for society and its values, mutilate any and all jeans, fading them, tearing holes in them, putting patches and daubs of paint over them, cutting them off, wearing them more loosely than normal. In the next scene we have the late capitalist system manufacturing jeans that way and selling them at inflated prices as stylish, the way to dress like the in crowd. The moral to the story is that the hegemonic power mongers succumbed to rebel pressures, so the opposition was not as intransigent as it appeared at the outset. Hegemonic and homogenizing culture suffered change at the hands of the insolent upstarts from heterogenous culture (recall Figure 6).

All this is oversimplified, I would submit, even though the signs of rebellion are there and even though over the long haul such rebellion can bring about change in society. I would opt for an alternative, a less binary, homo-hetero-geny, model. Granted, those in power generally tend to put things in a straightforward way, simply providing the information and setting the machinery in place in order to reap profits. And the sober-minded somnambulistic folks tend to take what is ladled out to them by the power mongers with neither questions nor much creative input. However, the wily "cultural guerrilla-minded" nimbly catch the ambiguities of the system and use them to subvert it in the only way they are capable. According to the power-bloc, money talks, might makes right, and status is everything. That story is the power-bloc's favorite. Everybody is there to fulfill their respective role, and with a few constables around, the ship's order is maintained. This is a binary view, however: langue keeps tabs on parole, signifiers keep signifieds under cover, diachrony pays proper homage to synchrony, and syntagmatic chains allow only prescribed paradigmatic input. The other, nonbinary story has it that the orderly phalanx marching in step to the beat of the big band is to a greater or lesser degree constantly thrown into disarray by the "cultural guerrillas" for whom rules are made to be broken. The first story falls comfortably in line with the traditional hard-line view of science: what is of worth is that which is universal and unchanging, that which is solid and lasting; what changes is of ephemeral value and unworthy of serious attention. But, according to the recent view, originally pioneered by philosopher Karl Popper, science is good precisely because it is open to change, because there are always a few "guerrilla" scientists lurking around. In fact, it is at its best when in constant war with itself, and it progresses most effectively by revolutions and internal conflicts. Not only is science perpetually at war with itself, so also are many of our most cherished inductively derived beliefs (Agassi 1975). Well, then, does this mean that within science according to most onlookers the most sober and secure path to knowledge around is plagued with glitches here and there, and that we should never count our swans before they hatch. Perhaps the most succinct way to put the issue is by evoking what is known as the "paradox of induction," developed by Carl Hempel (1945).

In a nutshell, the tale goes like this. We could assume "All swans are white" and attend to our daily affairs quite effectively without ever becoming aware of any anomalies or alternatives. It is simply true to say "All swans are white" and false to say that "Some swans are nonwhite," and that's that: case closed. It is ideally an either/or binary matter. We have an ingrained feel (Firstness) for the whiteness of swans, and we could hardly feel otherwise, unless in some imaginary world. However, a certain explorer down under, namely, Captain Cook, once found—that is, sensed (via Secondness) and interpreted (via Thirdness)—some black swans. Henceforth the categorical borders suffered a change. It eventually became known that "Most swans, but not all, are white; those nonwhite, that is, black, swans can be found in a remote region of the globe, namely, Australia." Instances like these led Popper to declare that if you look for positive evidence for a general proposition you will almost always be able to beat the world into submission and "discover" your evidence. So looking for positive evidence is no big deal. What is important is looking for negative evidence that will change customary ways of thinking and of looking. In other words, you should expect to be surprised by the unexpected, and then you can give a nod of acknowledgment that you are not surprised that you are surprised when an expected unexpected event turns up. Consequently, you alter your expectations somewhat, and continue on your way expecting another surprise somewhere along the road that will thwart those newfound expectations. If you want to learn something, don't just see everything and say everything as repeats of what presumably was, is, and will be. Look for mistakes, differences, events that weren't supposed to happen.

In this manner, it should not be at all shocking that "All swans are white" did not withstand the test of time. In fact, it was to be expected. This goes to show that in the sphere of possibilities for all events, seeing and saying must imply the statement:

"Swans are white and they are nonwhite." One pole of this contradiction was held true during one period of human history, the other pole during another period. So if "Swans are white *and* they are nonwhite" is taken to be atemporal, then "*Either* swans are white *or* they are nonwhite" is atemporal in another, more limited sense, for, logically speaking—that is, in terms of classical logic—either one or the other is viewed as immutable, depending on the time and the place and the folks involved. However, we also have the implicit statement: "It is *neither* the case that all swans are white *nor* is it the case that no swans are nonwhite." That is to say, previously "All swans are white" was the case, but it is now the case that "Most swans are white." And it was previously the case that "No swans are nonwhite" but it is now the case that "Some swans are nonwhite, specifically, those that are black." From this rather unkempt sphere—where events, seeing, and saying are *neither* timelessly one thing *nor* the other but potentially something else, something different—we have temporality. Given our temporality, we have one thing at one time and another thing at another time, with both things thrown into the same bag as part of a vast ocean in constant self-organizing movement wherein it is perpetually becoming something other than what it is.[2]

So we have, at one extreme, (1) "*Both* white swans *and* nonwhite swans," at the other extreme, (3) "*Neither* exclusively all white swans *nor* no nonwhite swans," and in the middle, (2) "*Either* white swans *or* nonwhite swans; white swans, therefore not nonwhite swans." (1) is the atemporal sphere of unactualized possibilities in harmonious intermeshing, no matter how contradictory, (2) is the sphere of classical logic, and (3) is the sphere of emerging novelties between the *either* and the *or*. (1) is qualified as exceeding vagueness; it is fraught with contradictions any number of which can over time be actualized, hence it is overdetermined. (3) is marked by generalities arising from the particulars actualized from (1) and passing through (2); it is invariably incomplete, since there is no knowing when and where something new and different will emerge to take its place between two already actualized general conceptualizations, hence it is underdetermined. Given the above considerations, (2), the sphere of *hegemony*, is under most circumstances the dwelling place of binary practices as they are customarily articulated: there are *either* the haves *or* the have-nots, locked in an apparently eternal, timeless, synchronic struggle. (1) may be labeled *homogeny* (as discussed above regarding Figure 6). (3), then, is *heterogeny*, since between any two general terms or statements there always exists the probability somewhere and somewhen of something else emerging, hence the system is perpetually moving toward the completion of its own continuity without ever realizing that goal.

Now, allow your attention nomadically to wander over (1) and (3), and you begin to "resonate" with the tossing, rolling, heaving tide of semiosis, which includes "cultural guerrilla" strategies. You are also coming to an awareness of the unspecifiability of this "resonance." You can't clearly and distinctly say what you think about the *hegemonic* cultural milieu outright; at best, you can only feel it, empathize with it, bring it into rapport with your general understanding. Consequently, you might find yourself on the path of "cultural guerrilla" activities. I wrote, "find yourself." That's an overstatement, actually. From within your "cultural guerrilla" mode of bucking the waves, kicking at the pricks, swimming cross-stream, you will engage in your somewhat subversive activity because of your gut feelings and proclivities. Your behavior will be what it is because that is how you feel, often without your ability precisely to articulate your actions and reactions. It is as if you were a natural born "cultural" guerrilla.

Consider, in this light, a brief illustration, surrounding the question: "What makes Brazilians Brazilians?" In large part chiefly because of their "*jeito*," Roberto DaMatta (1984) tells us. *Jeito* and its broader complementary term, *jeitinho*, we now know, have no faithful translation in English. In a certain manner of speaking, it is an artful way of getting things done, a knack, a skill, a gift, bent, genius, a customarily ingratiating manner of getting what one wants, usually without alienating all people concerned. Yet the ways of *jeito-jeitinho* more often than not involve acts that are prohibited either by written laws and codes of ethical standards or tacit social mores and modes of behavior. But not necessarily. So *jeito-jeitinho* is bigger than any individual and bigger than life. Its ideal form might be something like a combination of Charlie Chaplin and Bill Cosby and Whoopi Goldberg and Tom Cruise and Clint Eastwood and Cary Grant and James Cagney and Humphrey Bogart and Cantinflas and Carmen Miranda and Jack Nicholson and Marlene Dietrich and Katherine Hepburn and Sean Connery, with a little Fred Astair and Ginger Rogers and Xavier Cugat and Ella Fitzgerald thrown in for good measure. The thought is exhilarating. It evokes a warm feeling and a grin and a scowl and a roguish wink and an in-your-face verbal slam and an ironic comment and a few subtle nuances and a desire to fight and love and voice a tune and move your body about. But, then, the feeling is all just wishful feeling. It isn't really *jeito-jeitinho*. *Jeito-jeitinho* is actually something culturally and tacitly assimilated and carried out in large part unthinkingly. If you got it, you got it, and if you don't, you don't. If you got it, you just do it and make no bones about it, for it is you and you are it. And if you know it implicitly, you can't thoroughly say it explicitly, so you know it *and* you don't know it, and at the same time you *neither* know it *nor* do you not know it. That is, you don't know it in such a way that you can say it, you can only show it in so many ways. At the same time, you know it but can't say it, you can only show it, so you don't know it. *Jeito-jeitinho* is obviously disconcerting to the social analyst; it is largely an ineffable knack for putting on a good Brazilian act.

Lívia Barbosa's (1992) concept of *jeito-jeitinho*, we observed, occupies a halfway house between corruption and favor as mentioned in chapter four. Corruption is corruption, enough said. Favor is a particular Spanish American and especially a Brazilian custom. It involves a little nepotism, a little of the "ole boys' school," a little "you owe me one," or an "I'll scratch your back and you scratch mine," and all this immersed in a paternalistic, patriarchal, patronizing society. Practices of favor are most tacitly acknowledged with a raised brow and a nod, or some other set of nonverbal cues, though DaMatta (1991, 1994) writes diatribes against them. In contrast, corruption, I would imagine, is of no account in anybody's book. *Jeito-jeitinho* can, at the level of the favor, be hardly more than friendly verbal bantering and quipping, with the understanding that by so doing someone is jockeying for a favor and someone else is about to give a favor in order that, in the future, payment of the debt may be forthcoming. *Jeito-jeitinho* can, in the worst of scenarios, also gravitate to the other extreme, where it threatens to become outright corruption. Roughly speaking, in this sense, if favor is considered as "A," then corruption would be in the most extreme cases tantamount to "Not-A." Put the two together and you would have "*Both* A *and* Not-A," the worst of all possible worlds, something like a cocaine kingpin president, or a charismatic, handsome, and energetic drug lord who is godfather to hundreds of kids in the slums and who lavishes millions on their parents. In the middle, you have *jeito-jeitinho*, "*Neither* A *nor* Not-A," where there is no telling what the wily fox is going to come up with next: he's a scoundrel, for sure, yet you can't help but like the forever amiable chap (Barbosa 1992:32–36). *Jeito-jeitinho* practice in this sense most effectively entails one's art of becoming "more equal" than other people. The general attitude is: today it's her/him at the top of the heap, but tomorrow it could be me, if I'm good enough at the game and happen to be in the right place at the right time. *Jeitinho*: what makes Brazil Brazil.

Back to our "swan" statements (1), (2), and (3) on page 123 and their counterparts in Figure 6 for a moment.

Little Signs within the Inconceivable Big Picture

Bringing about a happy emergence of (1) and (3), and of *homogeny, hegemony,* and *heterogeny*, we have either *inconsistency* or *incompleteness*, or perhaps both, by the good grace of Gödel's proof that spelled the limitations of logic and mathematics, and by extension the sciences, the humanities, and, in general, all human communication. The upshot is that we cannot help but spout out unexpected contradictions and occasional paradoxes, and no matter how much we manage to say about some particular aspect of our world, our saying will always be incomplete.

Sign processing within these limitations is a dialogical community affair. Peirce writes that whenever a sign is vague (inconsistent) it is up to the maker of the sign to render it a bit more precise, and in the best of all worlds hopefully to clear up the inconsistency. On the other hand, in order that the sign's nature as a generality may become properly acknowledged, the sign's taker must enter into the game, interacting with the sign, with its maker, and with the entire ambient, in order to bring the sign's meaning a tad closer to its completion—but, as pointed out above, the sign's meaning never stands a chance of completion in the genuine sense (Peirce, *CP*:5.505). Hegemony as a dualist practice of the sort we might expect to find in (2) could well culminate in the empowerment, the enfranchisement, of those who have the proper pull and know-how to engage in the most advantageous but ruthlessly aggressive practices. Such practices including paternalism, patriarchy, *machismo*, and patronage, however, compose a stark desert of dualistic values.

Dualism is a stringently limited view. Vagueness and overdetermination (implied by [1]) and generality and underdetermination (implied by [3]) from a broad cultural view paint another picture entirely. In order to put this picture in focus, consider, once again, Figure 6.[3] There is alternation from homogeny (1) to hegemony (2) and heterogeny (3). The scheme is neither linear nor progressive. It is radically nonlinear. I use reversible arrows of various sorts to emphasize the fluid character of all the categories involved. This is no indication of linearity or isotropic timeless time, however. The categories, usually coming in threes rather than twos, are placed at various levels to depict their fuzzy codependent interrelationships and their nonlinear, time-bound, self-organizing nature, though, I must hasten to emphasize, no hierarchy of dichotomous terms is implied here. The general movement is from signs of vagueness by way of a "logic of vagueness" or "inconsistency" toward acknowledgment of classical logic and varying "styles of reasoning," and then to a "logic of difference" by way of classical logic that ends in the construction of invariably incomplete generalities, universals, taxonomies, and hierarchies.[4] Inconsistency is abandoned for good, and progression upward is toward the fulfillment of those fond and familiar dreams of the good life, social justice, emancipation for all, and complete and consistent knowledge. Given the overdetermination-underdetermination factor, however, there is no utopia to be had. In other words, the plenitude of all things is a pipe dream, and customary fast-track ocularcentrism (sight), phonocentrism (sound), and Derrida's "myth of presence" (through kinesthetics, contact, touch), are no royal highway to the land of milk and honey. The "logics" of vagueness and difference are here and here to stay, whether we know it or not and whether we like it or not, thanks to homogeny-hegemony-heterogeny interrelations.

All this has further bearing on Peirce's categories. Firstness, as we observed in chapter two, is the mode in which something is as it is irrespective of anything else, such that it would not make any difference if nothing else existed, for it is self-contained and self-sufficient. This mode is apprehended not by intellect or as a result of sensations received from the big wide world out there, for, simply put, there is no other mode that could be perceived or conceived in relation to Firstness. There is only Firstness, vague feeling. Firstness is also without parts, for if there were parts there would be something other than the whole of the Firstness. The whole of the Firstness is a melding of everything that makes it up. It is without clearly delineable features; it is vagueness of the vaguest sort. Imagine a combination of vibrations in the air that according to Fourier analysis produce in their composite high $C^\#$. You hear the note and nothing else, you feel it, and this feeling is perpetuated, one second, two seconds, then many seconds and minutes, without its being related in any form or fashion to any other sounds. You simply feel it as it is, no more, no less.

Now imagine you are the subject and the sound is the object, and by listening to the high $C^\#$, by sensing it and perceiving it, you enter into it as a result of many years of your own musical appreciation and actual practice. Your recognition of high $C^\#$ as just that, high $C^\#$, is an act of reaction and interaction with something *other* than $C^\#$ and *other* than yourself. It is *otherness*, the *otherness* of Secondness, of indexicality. Everyday living is pervaded through and through with such action, reaction, and interaction with ephemeral items of our surroundings, with tokens, items as they pop up on the stage before us, the stage we are on. Thirdness, on the other hand, is a general matter. The high $C^\#$ note is recognized as such in terms of its being related to and distinguished from any and all other notes in the repertoire of your knowledge of music. It is now not merely this note here and now, but high $C^\#$ as a type, a general category. The note as a type is a modification of its feeling and of its perception *as* such-and-such an item from among a range of other items to which it is related. It is acknowledgment *that* the sound belongs to a general category that gives it its character insofar as that character is susceptible to an account by means of symbolic signs, words, language (recall seeing *as* and seeing *that* from chapter two).

Relating all this to our polylogue for a moment, we might suppose that Borges's Daneri, contemplator of the Aleph, is in resonance with his feeling of pure Firstness. Funy, in contrast, is capable of accounting only for Seconds in a myriad stream of particular signs that occur once and once only. Funy's world leaves him hopelessly lost in his perception of individuals as disconnected atoms. Tlöny also sees particulars, but from the vantage of a "subjective idealist." What he sees is what there is; his world is the figment of his mind's own making. Lönny's world is chiefly of Thirdness, as is that of his antagonist, Scharlach. They hypothetically deduce their world and try to cut it at its joints in such a way that it may conform to the Procrustean bed. Rorty's dialogic entails the initial moves of Firstness (the sphere of vagueness, or overdetermination) as a set of possibilities some of which make their way into the realm of Secondness. But as Seconds, they are not properly intelligible until given some form of meaning within the sphere of mediating Thirdness (of generality, underdetermination). This world of all our polylogeurs is hybrid: it takes a bit here, rejects something there, interjects something somewhere else and shaves off a few edges to yield a smooth contour, molds and kneads the concoction, and the process continues without end, for it is of the nature of semiosis, knowledge of which for us fallible souls is inexorably incomplete.

This hybrid view of knower and known is gradually coming into view. It is now taken for granted that Gramsci's concept of hegemony made it possible to move beyond the dualistic idea of power brokers imposing their values on helpless and hapless common people. This switch has been a long time in coming, however. Amongst leftist writers the dominant classes control and the popular classes are victims. In later years, especially given hegemony theory, the popular classes were looked on positively as a group with virtually unlimited resources and capacities to manifest their defiance and in the process provide alternatives to the stolid, stultifying ways of the dominants. Such obsessive focus on extremes in order to erect dichotomies is discomforting. The problem is that, in anthropologist Néstor García Canclini's (1984:51) words:

> there is so much insistence on the juxtaposition of the subaltern and hegemonic culture and on the political necessity of defending the independence of the subaltern culture that the two come to be thought of as two quite separate entities. With the presupposition that the task of hegemonic culture is to dominate and that of the subaltern culture is to resist, much research has had no other aim than to inquire about the ways the two distinct roles were carried out.

In this sense, obsession with *either* one *or* the other of the horns of the presumed opposition is binary thinking, in spite of the concession that the subalterns might enjoy more power to alter the system than was previously thought. This Manichean tendency is certainly not vintage Gramsci, for he resists facile dichotomies. There is not merely power, but also seduction, complicity, negotiation, subversion, and covert "cultural" guerrilla action.

Gramsci teaches that what meets the eye is often not as clear-cut as it appears. He ties the notion of popular culture to the subaltern condition and at the same time reveals the complexity of these ties. The dynamic interaction between subalterns and the dominant class, as pointed out above, makes for constant shifting of postures and strategies such that the interrelations are best qualified as process. There is no standing still; everything is in perpetual movement. Consequently, the subaltern's admission of hegemonic power is not necessarily an act of submission, and her rejection of that power is not necessarily resistance. All expressions from the haves are not always the manifestation of irresistible hegemonic forces, and the passive response of the subalterns is not simply a bow of the weak to the strong (Gramsci 1992). Nor is the exercise of hegemony merely a product of the inculcation of Pierre Bourdieu's *habitus* in the people such that they respond the way they respond because they can't really respond otherwise (Bourdieu 1990, Bourdieu and Passeron 1977). Creative responses on the part of the people, in de Certeau's (1984) conception, keep the social organism's heart pounding and lungs heaving. In the final analysis, popular culture is above all creative.

Given their creativity, what the people believe, buy, and consume cannot simply be subsumed within a binary logic of domination and subservience. The dominant rationality would have it, nonetheless, that the people behave and consume in such a way that they all become one homogenous soup (from homogeny, not homogeneity). It might appear that the subalterns gravitate toward homogeny, while the dominants move up slightly toward the world of heterogeny, in order to highlight their distinction from those *others* and to refortify their power. Yet the subalterns, given their de Certeau role as cultural guerrillas, or "poachers," create differences of their own upon expressing their contempt for their lot in life. They sweet talk their superiors and play up to them; at the same time they cheat a little, mix things up in order to alter them, bring spice to life, and subvert the motives of the hegemonic haves—all of which within the Brazilian context is of the practice of *jeito-jeitinho*. In so doing they are not simply liars, thieves, and rebels obsessed with overturning the system. They are engaged in practices on a small scale compared to the megalevels of lying, thieving, and subversion going on at the upper levels. They are simply doing the best with what they have, while carving out their own domain of heterogeneric differences (compare to Scott's function of "hidden transcripts" in chapter three).

But these cultural tendencies did not simply spring out of a vacuum. They existed in interrelated, interactive codependence within the sphere of homogeny, Firstness, wholeness. Within homogeny, there are parts, to be sure, but they are possibles, they are not (yet) actualized *for* a particular mind. The parts remain melded into one, that is, they make up a collection so vast that in terms of themselves as possibles there is no room for them to retain any form of distinction or individualism, so they are welded into one another, they are annealed. Firstness is the continuum of all that is possible. It is like a ring, with no conceivable beginning or ending and no middle. As Secondness emerges into the being of the becoming and the becoming of the being of signs, the ring is cut and severed, such that there is now one side and the other side and the border of borders in between. And the chain of Seconds has begun its becoming, the task of which then begets Thirds, and more Thirds. There is no conceivable end of semiosis, nor is there any conceivable beginning, or center.

Beverley (1999:62) writes that the "Chinese boxes' logic of subaltern identity points to a multiethnic and multicultural or culturally (and linguistically) *heterogeneous* sense of the natural, which is not dependent on a logic of transculturation (although it can incorporate it)." Granted, though he is falling into that faddish habit of playing loose and limber with the word "logic," Mignolo's "search of another logic" that never quite finds a home is another case in point. At least his notion of "border thinking" as *"thinking from dichotomous concepts rather than ordering the world in dichotomies"* (Mignolo 2000:85) mildly suggests a combination of homogeny and heterogeny as the concepts are developed here. Further, his "bicultural, bilinguing" mind as a fusion of local differences and the perpetual incompleteness of any totalizing happy meeting ground (patterned on heterogeny) plus the inevitability of enduring consistency at the global level (atemporally encapsulated within homogeny) gives much food for thought.

Mignolo laudably has no need of Hegelian dialectic logic in his call for an "other thinking" and an "other critique." An "other thinking" is no longer locked into either the one or the other of whatever actual alternatives might be at hand; a "double critique" knows no hierarchizing. Together they make up an "other logic," Mignolo writes. Indeed: "Border thinking could open up the doors to an other tongue, an other thinking, an other logic suspending the long history of the modern colonial world, the coloniality of power, the subalternization of knowledges and the colonial difference" (Mignolo 2000:338). But upon finishing Mignolo's exhaustive inquiry, one is prone to ask: "Is that all there is? Where's the punchline?" There's a build-up and then a letdown. One fills one's head with visions of answers to come but there is no delivery. (Of course, I have provided no "cultural logic" thus far, yet I have implied that if "cultural logic" there be, it is "extralanguaging"; it is a matter of corporeal feeling and sensing and at most vague saying [merrell 2001].)

Allow me to attempt at least an illustration of this self-perpetuating semiosis.

How Subverting Signs Emerge

In 1977 in the historic Plaza de Mayo of Buenos Aires and site of the presidential Casa Rosada, the women's sudden appearance was hardly noticed except by the secret police of the military government.

At first there was only a handful of women walking around in flat shoes and wearing kerchiefs over their heads. They appeared uncertain, even frightened (after all, Argentina was ruled by a repressive dictatorship that lasted from 1976 to 1983 and "disappeared" some 30,000 citizens and tortured countless more). They wore photographs of missing family members on their dresses. They came from every social class to fight the armed forces, the politicians, the clergy, the complacent press, everybody, in order to get some answers. The handful of women gradually grew to fifty, then hundreds, and then more than a thousand. Tourists began asking questions that embarrassed the state. But the women went virtually ignored by government officials. Their visits to the Catholic Church in search of support yielded no results: its complicity was obvious. The government continued to pay the women hardly any mind. Yet they persevered. As time went by, they became known as the *Madres y*

Abuelas de la Plaza de Mayo ("Mothers and Grandmothers of May Square"). While the 1978 World Cup soccer championship team was honored, the women protested. When progovernment youths, whipped into a frenzy, spat insults at them, they asked questions. Eventually, moral outrage ensued. In 1980 the Argentine human rights movement became involved, especially after Adolfo Pérez Esquivel was awarded the Nobel Peace Prize. In 1981, workers began protesting inadequate wages, working conditions, and housing. In 1982 they joined the protesting mothers, and in that same year the press took a more active role in criticizing the government. The humiliating Malvinas/Falkland war came and went. And finally, in 1983, the military brought out and dealt its last deck of cards. Elections were held, a civilian became president, and the military, as a final *coup*, granted itself amnesty from all human rights violations!

This train of events is perhaps one of the best examples of honest, sincere, patriotic subversion on the part of subalterns from among subalterns: women, taking on a role with few precedents. It is also living proof that the subalterns, by peaceful means, can create alternatives and impose them on the dominants. Subalterns interjected the homogeny of hegemony with a massive dose of heterogeny, and the system finally caved in. Iconicity raised itself to the level of indexicality by signs pointing toward the presence of absent individuals, and silent icons and indices proceeded in the direction of symbols, which were eventually forthcoming. Overdetermined Firstness engendered underdetermined Thirdness, subversive Thirdness, and the erstwhile hegemonic discourse of Secondness and Thirdness suffered the consequences. Persistent women, makers of alternative signs, gave vent to their signs of vagueness, brought them to their most supreme expression, and they were eventually interpreted by their signs in terms of generalities, and found the interpretation to be the alternative that demanded the most serious attention. Signs from the overdetermined sphere took their place between the otherwise excluded middle between existent dichotomies of an intransigent polity. The "Mothers and Grandmothers of May Square" and related movements in Latin America bear perhaps the most striking illustration of what DaMatta (1991) calls "relational society," where the whole follows a "logic" that the parts can choose to ignore. The "and" of "*Both* A *and* Not-A" fuses and confuses the mansions and the shanties, the powerful and the weak, the dominant and the subaltern.

However, DaMatta's concept of "relational society" is perhaps no more strikingly exemplified than in Latin American *mestizaje* (racial mixture). *Mestizaje* entails nonlinear interrelations. The *mestizo* of today, especially in countries like Mexico, Colombia, Peru, Venezuela, northeastern Brazil, and the Caribbean, is no simple mix of European and Amerindian or African and European or Amerindian and African. The mix is virtually randomly variegated. Moreover, *mestizaje* is not merely a racial fact, but in addition, it is the incorporation of the Latin Americans' way of life, their very existence, the becomingness of their being, the beingness of their becoming. *Mestizaje* is more than an abstraction, it speaks; it perceives, conceives, narrates; it becomes at once actor and spectator on the stage of everyday living. *Mestizaje* is also intimately linked to three of the four terms discussed in chapter four: *personalismo*, *machismo*, and *caudillismo*. While these three terms are by no means limited to the term "mestizaje," the *mestizo* is one of their most prototypical embodiments. *Caudillismo, machismo,* and *personalismo* are in this regard chiefly a matter of an inner need to dominate, control, to impose one's will. Anthropologist Eric Wolf (1959:240) writes of the *mestizo* male as "power seeker" *par excellence.*[5]

Mestizaje entails a different socio-politico-economic and cultural sensibility. In tales from the U.S. by way of James Fenimore Cooper, Mark Twain and others we have a pretty dire image of the African Americans, the Amerindians and the *mestizos* in the U.S. Harvard professor and scientist Louis Agassiz once painted a picture of the non-European ethnic groups and the *mestizos* of Latin America as physically and morally degraded people. The passing of time has unfortunately done little to temper the North American prejudice toward the *mestizo.* This is not surprising, given one of the basic differences between Anglo American and Latin American policies on territorial expansion. The Anglo American policy was fundamentally one of *exclusion.* It fixed limits beyond which the Amerindian should not venture; in fact, the native was looked upon as an encumbrance and should be cleared off, like the forests, the buffalo, and the wolves. The Latin American policy, in contrast, was chiefly one of *inclusion*—though, as one might expect, there are plenty of exceptions to the rule. Consequently, even though the *mestizo*'s place in society in the Latin American colonies left plenty to be desired, he fared considerably better there than in the U.S. Quite ironically, given the distinction between exclusionary and inclusionary practices, during the nineteenth century, travelers, businessmen, and diplomats from the U.S. to Latin America generally enthused over the cultured oligarchy in Latin America. On the other hand, they had few kind words for the *mestizo* class, which was often assumed to be no more than a bastard people (Pike 1992:144–51). In the 1930s historian Herbert Eugene Bolton (1939:98) saw the Spanish-Anglo borderlands as a "meeting place and fusing place of two streams of European civilization, one coming from the south, the other from the north." Had Bolton been keener on actual empirical studies of border cultures, however, he would have realized that long before development of his "borderlands" thesis, North American racism had taken its toll.

Nevertheless, I repeat, *mestizaje* entails an entirely different socio-politico-economic and cultural sensibility, and until and unless that fact is acknowledged by peoples of non-*mestizo* cultures, whether in the U.S. or Latin America, there will be little hope of understanding this hybrid mix, let alone of coping with it and merging with it. How so? It is an openness to institutions and realities of everyday living, to the subjectivity of the social actors and the multiplicity of loyalties, to the relations of patronage, paternalism, *compadrismo,*[6] *personalismo, caudillismo,* and so on, that operate simultaneously in Latin America. It is a constant weaving, unraveling, and re-weaving of intricate ties and relations and encounters and elbow rubbing. There are continuities of relations broken by frequent discontinuities, and reconciliations and renewed continuities. In this strange concoction, this hybrid mix of urban and provincial and rural, of European and *criollo* and African American and *mulato* and Amerindian and *mestizo,* multiplicity pervades, nonlinearity reigns, uncertainty is the tenuous rule, vagueness finds its way into every nook and cranny, and everything is always already in the incompletable process of becoming.

In spite of all this, the hard-line view of Latin America more often than not remains obstinately mired in bivalent logic, in a Manichean mind-set. However, as a new millennium begins, new "cultures of difference" are emerging in the West—which should by now, of course, be news to nobody. The nature of these new sensibilities, often going by the names of postmodernism and postmodernity, are trashing the monolithic "big narratives" with their pressure to homogenize people, commodities, institutions, and practices, in favor of "little narratives" of diversity, multiplicity, and heterogeneity. The prevalent rhetoric tosses the general, universal, and abstract, and replaces them with the specific, concrete, historical, contextual, pluralistic, and all this by highlighting the ephemeral, variable, tentative, perpetually flowing and changing.

But . . .

Is Latin America Really Disenchanted?

For some observers the present mix of the grave old world of modernism-modernity and its discontents and the brave new world of postmodernism-postmodernity and its reactionaries is in large part the outcome of what Max Weber called the "disenchantment with the world" to which I have alluded. "Modern" societies, politics, and economies, and science, theology, and the arts have revolved around diverse strategies for maintaining moral, religious, ethical, and aesthetic sensitivities, while accepting the disenchanted world-view as handed down chiefly by the sciences.

What is this disenchantment all about? At the root of science—and hence epistemology—it is basically a denial of Secondary Qualities of subjectivity, experience, feeling, and a reduction of nature to Primary Qualities of that which can be effectively theorized, measured, and described in abstract mathematical terms. Nature becomes a scurry of disinherited atoms without purpose in a colorless, tasteless, odorless, and silent universe, as Alfred North Whitehead (1925) so effectively articulated it. There is hardly any place for ideals, possibilities, feeling, sentiment, or passion, nor does a push toward some undefined end fit into the picture. Everything is a matter of unfeeling pushes and pulls. No intrinsic value can exist within nature; there is no value in the nature of the things themselves. Action at a distance as a result of magic, mystery, supernatural powers, or the unseen hand of God gave way to action at a distance described mathematically, yet still endowed with mystery, for no explanation was forthcoming—it is just the way the universal machine works.

Weber's term for disenchantment is *Entzauberung*, which literally means, "taking the magic out." But was the magic really eradicated, lock, stock, and barrel? I repeat, if we follow John Maynard Keynes, Newton was not of the age of reason but the last of the magicians. Nevertheless, Newton, along with Galileo and Descartes, presumably with great resolve initiated the disenchantment project of objectification, mechanization, and reduction. The inorganic universe was the first to go the way of this emerging world-view. Then biology caved in to mechanism. And finally, the mind became an epiphenomenon, a mere effect of physical machinery. Life ultimately became meaningless: nature was to be theorized, observed, and described, with no subjective human input. There was no truth of the matter but merely the facts of the matter. Behavioral psychology, paying homage to this mechanistic view, postulated that the mind must correspond to physical principles. Thus it lost its personal, subjective propensities and proclivities, and became completely subjected to its environment. Even time suffered the embarrassment of its being discounted altogether by scientists of the eminence of Albert Einstein, who said: "For us believing physicists, the distinction between past, present, and future is only an illusion, even if a stubborn one" (Hoffman 1972:258).

A countermovement has been underway for some decades, however. It is marked by a disenchantment regarding the mechanistic, deterministic, reductionistic world-view and a re-enchantment of the world. Some talk revolves around quantum theory's slam-dunk finale bringing about the demise of the Cartesian-Newtonian picture with a return to some mystical-magical views in the image of Taoism or Buddhism.[7] While some of these ideas are far-fetched, they are nonetheless part of the barometer reading of the vacuous nature of much Cartesian-Newtonian thought, and they indicate attunement with new sensibilities. These new sensibilities seem to be rejecting a science that provides only shadows and symbols of reality, and it is now pointing in the direction of the world as an interrelated, interacting, codependent, self-organizing whole the parts of which are not isolable without destroying their qualities. The view seems to be that of a Lönny-Pierre (Averroës) "methodological realism" coupled with a Funy-Hladdy-Maggie-Tlöny-T'sui "ontological idealism" to yield an Emmy-Peirce (Rorty) type of "objective idealism." In a nutshell, it is like the quantum physicist who does what she does best with a sense of interacting with the real. However, she knows quite well that she can't interact with that real without participating with it, without altering it somewhat, so she will never be able to know it just like it was/is/will have been. The world remains real in a pragmatic-dialogic manner of speaking, but it is quite ideal in a real way of speaking. Since what the world *is* becomes what it *is* after the physicist interacts with it, it is *now* becoming something other than what *it was* becoming. So time has also made its re-entry. Moreover, the age-old mind-body problem takes on a new face. Mind and body interact, just as does everything else in the universe. Mechanism, determinism, and reductionism, as well as any and all dualisms, become simply unintelligible, and the disenchantment or the world is undermined.

This talk of re-enchantment seems to be a tough swim against the current of disseminating, fragmenting, differentiating, postmodern discourse. And so it is, insofar as it has been portrayed thus far. Actually, modern life itself culminated in a maelstrom of unruly change, especially evident during Baudelaire's days as effectively illustrated in Marshall Berman's *Everything That is Solid Melts into Air* (1982). Yet, the notion that it all holds together in organic fashion survived in modern science, philosophy, and the arts. Not so, however, according to one strain of so-called postmodern thought. The most prevalent of the multiple interpretations of the postmodern launches a fierce attack on the notion of organic unity, completely dismantling the long-held venerated concepts of form, structure, and the whole as a totalized, complete and consistent, harmonious and well-wrought, whole. In the Derridean mold, the radically fragmented and pluralistic field is a "free play" of infinite substitutions by way of referenceless signifiers. Nothing, "either in the elements or in the system, is simply present or absent. There are only everywhere differences and traces of traces" (Derrida 1980:26).[8] This mainstream interpretation of postmodern-ism views its fragmented nature as an extension of Berman's modernism as culmi-nating in a maelstrom.

Yet, according to another, antagonistic interpretation, postmodernism is con-structive rather than deconstructive. It sees the universe as a vast interconnected web in the order of the emerging scientific view from quantum theory to chaos theory.[9] In this sense, one can "look through the shattered and disjointed fragments of our post-modern wasteland and see them all as one vast sum and unity of essentially interre-lated objects" (Shusterman 1989:108–09). The modern age had entirely overlooked this possibility of pluralism within a whole incessantly becoming something other than what it is by a bootstrapping, self-organizing process. This whole as a receding horizon is contrary to Hegel and more in line with Nietzsche in the sense that it will always remain incomplete and beyond the grasp of the knower who is, himself, just another part of the whole. Now, in this organicist, peripheral view of postmodern-ism, we have what I would suggest is at least the initial makings of a genuine re-enchantment of the world in contrast to the disenchantment of linear, corpuscular-kinetic, atomistic modernism-modernity.

In short, modernity had pushed vagueness under the rug as meaningless since hard-nosed logical reason must inhere, generality was a project to be fulfilled at some future bend in the road, and complete and consistent knowledge was to be had through meticulous and obsessive application of Cartesian reason. There was no overdetermination of theories, thought, and action, but simply what there is, in all its shining and fixed-for-all-time *Truth*. And the goal was determination on no uncertain terms rather than underdetermination; it was completeness once and for all rather than gravitation in some direction that will hopefully move us a bit closer to the fin-ish line without the possibility of ever having arrived. Postmodern inclinations took the low road rather than the presumed high road, with neither expectations nor posi-tive prospects.

In Latin America there has always been a vague sense of unity as an interre-lated, interactive whole of codependently emerging and submerging events. This falls quite closely in line with the view that in Latin America, postmodernism (a pos-sible re-enchantment of the world according to the organic, holistic view) did a leap-frog act over modernism (disenchantment, a fragmentary view *via* Berman) without having entered fully into the mainstream of Western modernism. In this sense Latin America has been, even during the heyday of modernism, postmodern *avant la lettre* (Yúdice 1992).[10] In other words, Latin America, as postmodern *avant la lettre*, sa-vored the alternative postmodernist re-enchantment view without ever having re-ceived a healthy serving of modernity's disenchantment, Western style—though for almost two centuries there were plenty of efforts to "modernize" Latin America. This has created an enigmatic hybrid fusion and confusion of tendencies and pro-clivities and cultural differences quite unlike anything else found in so-called "de-veloped" and "developing" societies.

The Trouble with Many Views of Latin America

But what is Latin America, really? A well-nigh impossible question. For, if the universe, and by implication, a given cultural universe, are conceived as a vast interconnected yet unfathomable whole, then the incessantly transmuting events and that whole in flux play havoc with the dream of identity of parts and of unity grasped in the ideal of some motionless instant.

The obsession during the present century in Latin America with the idea of identity was from the very beginning problematic. Given the thrust of the present inquiry up to this juncture, and as I will argue in greater detail below, there is no conceivable beginning or ending, nor can any center be specified, regarding culture. Culture consists of the perpetually shifting sands of tendencies and propensities and customs in time and space. If this very important characteristic of culture is not acknowledged, the notion of collective identity threatens to become the focus of an outright essentialist question for the soul of the nation. Culture, by its very nature, is a construct, and any knowledge of a culture we might be lucky enough to stumble upon is likewise an incessantly shifting construct. There is no such beast as a fixed cultural essence. Bhabha suggests so much (1990a). Bhabha is on course and holding a steady keel regarding culture as construct and the people as at the cutting edge between the power-bloc and specific discursive forces. His problem is that he falls victim to the linguicentric fallacy of reducing culture, elusive, slippery, slithering and undulating and flowing culture, to narration, discourse, language, a binary play of signifiers and signifieds devoid of flesh and bone subjects and divorced from concrete cultural contextualization.

Unfortunately, Amaryll Chanady's essay on the idea of Latin American identity, after discussing Bhabha, commits the same fallacy. She observes that no sooner than the idea of nation is constructed, it is deconstructed, "by the successive, and always complementary and substitutive, interpretations whose incompleteness and constant succession and mutual contradictions demonstrate the inexistence of any originary center" (Chanady 1994:x). Rather than culture as organic, we read that culture is an interplay of differences and heterogeneities, contentions and antagonisms, perpetual squabbling and alliances and ephemeral truce making: constant change. Chanady is on course here with respect to her rejection of no nonsense quests for the total picture in favor of the more humble effort to grasp a few bits and pieces of cultural differences among differences. I agree with her acknowledging the inevitable incompleteness of any and all constructive grasps of culture. I also find her parade of mutual contradictions between cultural bits and pieces to be proper for any viable to and fro navigation in an effort to acquire a feel for culture. Yet, Chanady, like Bhabha—and Mignolo, as we observed above—remains with a foot caught in linguicentrism. This is to be expected, I suppose, for after all, she is quite in line with the temper of her poststructuralist, deconstructive crowd, most of them linguicentrists to the letter.

It is all as if Chanady and her heroes, Derrida and Foucault, were dwelling exclusively within the upper echelons of Thirdness, symbolicity, language, heterogeneity, sights and sounds of phonemes, sememes, signifiers and signifieds, and, conceded, a dose of what I have called incompleteness and underdetermination (in this regard take another look at Figure 6). It is as if the other senses that so pervade cultural life were all reduced to language and nothing but language, a vast linear parade of linguistic "facts" to be gleefully deconstructed while one is in one's armchair and surrounded by texts and within the purview of that omniscient eye, the monitor. It is as if extralinguistic sights and sounds and smells and tastes and kinesthetics were really of no account, as if indexicality and iconicity were nothing if not dressed up in glib rhetorical garb, as if inconsistency and overdetermination were a matter of the virtual presence of words, words, words, with no place to go, as if Firstness and vagueness could enjoy a modicum of respect only after their elevation to the sublime level of articulation, the Nietzsche-Derrida interpretation of interpretation. All this, I hardly need write, consists part and parcel of remnants of modernity's thought.

On the plus side, according to the view of Latin America in an incessant quest for identity with which Chanady is imbued, monological discourse is criticized: there is no *latinoamericanidad, mexicanidad, argentinidad*, and so on, but homogenic-heterogenic, hybrid, multiply ethnic, transcultural plurivocal writing and debating and bantering and conversing and prattling.[11] After citing a diversity of studies on the Latin American cultural scene, Chanady's focus remains obsessively on literature, and chiefly on the linguistic evocations and implications therein. But to her credit, she does at least go on to suggest that Latin America's hybrid diversity is a giant step beyond "Bakhtinian polyphony or heteroglossia, and certainly beyond the appropriation or assimilation of various international Others in a strategy of textualizing the multifaceted culture of a country as a means of colonizing it symbolically and homogenizing difference in an institutional practice that consolidates dominant forms of identity construction" (Chanady 1994:xvi). Still, the problem with much narrative and discourse from the continent is that it remains mired in Saussurean-based or neo-Saussurean thought according to which the problem can be solved by the have-nots' integration into the haves' way of life rather than there being any engagement in legitimate dialogic exchange.[12] In other words, there needs be a de-struction—rather than merely a "deconstruction," as Chanady puts it—of "the traditional categories of Self and Other, Sameness and Difference, National and Foreign culture" (Chanady 1994:xvii).

This is no mean project of anthropophagizing the foreign in order to make things new. That was still part and parcel of modernism. Rather, it is a matter of something arising from within, from the border, the margin, the emergence of difference that makes a difference. There is no homogeneity, here, but uncountable differences: Latin America was "born in difference." Difference entails optimal multiplicity, numbing plurality, at its complex, hybrid best. It is Latin America as postmodern before the fact. It is radically different architecture and art and rites and rituals and other religious paraphernalia and in sum all cultural institutions and practices.

All this, and yet, the problem remains: most poststructuralist, deconstructive, postcolonial, and neocolonial parlance, as well as the discourse aligned with the various feminist and post-feminist and gay and queer and lesbian and minority philosophies and movements, focus almost exclusively on the upper echelons of Figure 6. Thus they are often guilty of runaway linguicentrism, plus a massive dose of properly dedichotomized, nondualistic language as a remedy for all ills. As amply evinced from within the dark lower corridors of Figure 6, language is no cure-all for the afflicted, no oasis for the weary cultural traveler, no panacea for the perplexed of mind. This is becoming increasingly evident through alternative solutions to cantankerous cultural dilemmas from Native Americans, Africans and African Americans, and other groups.

In actual cultural practice, I would submit that the sphere of Firstness takes no back seat to Thirdness, and neither one of them can be anything, any-*thing*, at all without the succession of signs engendered through Secondness. If disenchantment of the world occurred chiefly as a result of a divorce from Firstness (feeling) by the machinations of signs of Secondness (experience) and Thirdness (inference, cognition)—action and reactions, linear cause and effect series, conceptualization and abstraction and logic and reason and mathematics—then re-enchantment of the world cannot come about except by a return to Firstness, to feeling, sentiment, emotion, the heart in addition to the mind as the measure of all things. This implies the whole of the senses coming to bear on what is to be felt. What is felt is felt in terms of that homogenous sphere, an implicate sphere of possibilities, some of them incompatible with their neighbors, yet all of them there, in what appears to be peaceful coexistence. Here, there is no modernist or postmodernist fragmentation, no disintegration, no dissemination, no deterritorialization or territorialization, no presumed "big narratives," no "logic of difference." Nor is there anything to deconstruct, because there is nothing there at all. There is only the implicate, that which is merely possible, implicit. It cannot be said nor can it hardly be thought. It can at most only be felt, perhaps embraced by some sort of sixth sense. At any rate, it can't be conceived or sent through the high-tech communicative channels of Thirdness.

But how can I hope to give account of this feel if it is well nigh incognizable and ineffable? This is admittedly a dilemma. Allow me to throw a skewed glance toward the confusion this way. Chanady makes a diamond-in-the-rough allusion to the "colonized other," the "colonizing other," and the "hybrid." The first is a manifestation of Secondness for the colonizer, the second is Secondness for the colonized, and the third is the process of mediation between the first two and their mediation between themselves at the same time that they mediate the Third term. There can be the colonizer who interrelates and interacts with the *other* by gravitating from conceptualization to the transculturation process to embracing the *other* and virtually becoming one with the *other* at the same time that that *other* becomes the one.

Notable instances of this process are found in the tales of Cabeza de Vaca and Gonzalo Guerrero. Take the case of the latter. Prior to the conquest of New Spain, the Caribbean air currents suffered a mood swing, wrecked a Spanish galleon, and washed a few sailors to the shore of the Yucatan peninsula. All but a couple perished during their first years as slaves to the Amerindians. Of the two, Jerónimo de Aguilar gladly left with Cortés's crew when they arrived to the rescue, while Gonzalo Guerrero, with Mayan wife and *mestizo* kids and tattooed body, decided he was now more Mayan than Spaniard, and opted to remain. For Guerrero there had been a powerful cultural baptism of fire: he went under as a Spaniard and re-emerged as a neophyte Mayan. Jerónimo, in contrast, never found the wherewithal to shed his Spanish skin, and, along with *Malinche* (*doña Marina*), he provided an invaluable translating service for Cortés.

If we imagine cramming both Gonzalo and Jerónimo into the same cultural body, the distance between Spanish culture and Mayan culture becomes virtually nil—the hybrid cultural body becomes tantamount to the whole of Figure 1. There is still the Spanish side and the Mayan side, for sure. This enabled those immersed in Spain's traditions to see a Spaniard as a Spaniard and those immersed in Mayan culture to see one of their own. But between the two cultures, as in Figure 1, the border of borders, the hairline, the "emptiness," gives rise to the emergence of something new. The new is not exactly "hybridism" in the biological sense. Rather, it is the codependent emergence of what had been the excluded middle. It is more than an overlapping, syncretic intermeshing of both the one and the other, more than an acculturation with the one becoming coterminous with the other. The new, in addition to a recombination of what there is, brings something out that had been implicit, implicate, from the "black hole," the "singularity," where there had been just emptiness. As a composite whole, the new is *both* the one *and* the other, and it is *neither* the one *nor* the other. As was schematically given in the polylogue, there is *neither* "rabbit" *nor* "duck." Rather, there exists the possibility of a "dabbit" and a "ruck" and/or a "duback" and a "rabuck" and/or a "dubbit" and a "rack," and many things besides (recall such play on words from the polylogue *via* inspiration from Goodman and Putnam—to be given further discussion in chapter nine). From the border of borders, the sky's the limit, it would appear.

Unlike the Gonzalo-Jerónimo incongruous complementarity interrelationship accompanied by the codependent emergence of something new, the colonizer—either the Spaniard of old or the neocolonist of current times—can maintain a distance while initiating or at least entertaining the idea of a sort of "civil rights" movement in favor of the colonized, as in a manner of speaking did Bartolomé de las Casas. In such case, however, there is no genuine meeting of the cultures, no *bona fide* "hybridization." There is only the one and the *other* mediated by a third term without entry into Firstness in depth. This is the case in general of the "religious conquest" of the Americas (Ricard 1966). It is also the view of Alonzo de Ercilla y Zúñiga in his writing of the poem of epic proportions, *La Araucana*, or *The Araucaniad* (1945 [1569, 1578, 1589]). From another vantage, there can be the colonizer in a horn-lock with the *other*, with hardly a sign of interdependence or mediation. Such was the "conquest by the sword," and, quite notably, the case of the *bandeirantes* (literally, "flag bearers") of Brazil who made periodic forays into the backlands in search of gold and slaves, whichever happened to be more accessible (Morse 1989). This accounts for the difference between the postures of Amerindian rebels the likes of Túpac Amaru and Guaman Poma *vis-à-vis* the colonizers. In all cases there is a virtually infinite multitude of possible differences, different postures, all of the nature of process, all a matter of differences that make (or elusively fake) a difference. In all cases there is some nod, however faint, toward the depths of Firstness, feeling, a re-enchantment of the world, interrelated interaction between culture and nature, the one and the other, which gives rise to a codependent emergence of something else, from within the overdetermined, inconsistency laden sphere of vagueness—at the hairline in Figure 1.

The world of minimal differences becomes a world of virtual indiscernibles, unlike Funy's world: for him everything is discernible. In Tlöny's world we are in the same boat, from a strictly mentalist, idealistic framework. Unlike Funy and Tlöny, we take our differences, the differences we fashioned rather than merely found, for the sake of making a collection, a community, for the sake of rendering our world somewhat less heterogeneously confrontational and a tad more homogenous and interrelational.

Speaking of homogeny, we must for another moment get back to the Firstness of signs, to what genuinely makes semiosis semiosis.

Notes

1.   Brown writes in this regard that the "simple fact is that many thought-experimental situations, like the scientific theories they deal with, are outright inconsistent" (Brown 1991:94).

2.   The above is another way of putting Peirce scholar Charles Hartshorne's (1970) view that temporality begins to emerge within Secondness and comes into full bloom within the sphere of Thirdness.

3.   It bears mentioning at this juncture that I have often availed myself of the overdetermination-underdetermination and inconsistency-incompleteness and vagueness-generality scheme in various previous studies of our sensing, perceiving and interpreting signs (merrell 1995a, 1996, 1997). For further work on a "logic of vagueness" see Nadin (1982, 1983); for a "logic of inconsistency" see Rescher and Brandom (1979); for a "logic of difference" I find Deleuze (1990, 1993, 1994) quite helpful. Of course, articulation of these "logics" has not been forthcoming thus far. Given their very nature, articulation with respect to everyday cultural life can hardly be more than vague, evocative rather than precise, provocative rather than conclusive, suggestive rather than injunctive. Be that as it may, the following pages will afford a certain sense of these "logics" within cultural settings. At least that is my hope.

4.   The idea of "styles of reasoning" is from Hacking (1985).

5.   Wolf is admittedly overgenerealizing and exaggerating (if not to say excessively stereotyping). But a grain of credence must be allowed him, for he does reveal some of the chief characteristics of the *mestizo*, though exceptions abound and as the *mestizo* becomes more numerous his characteristics become more heterogenous and less homogenous. Moreover, the *mestiza* must also be given due consideration, and she has been since the time of Wolf's study.

6.   A *compadre* is a godfather. In Latin America the paternalistic, patriarchal "godfather" image aids and abets *machismo* and allows at least ephemeral legitimacy to *caudillismo* and *caciquismo*. *Compadrismo* is used here in reference to the "ole boys' club" mentality spawned by the *compadre* image (in Argentina the term goes much further, helping to define the male-oriented nature of early *tango* culture).

7.   See especially, in this regard, Capra (1975), Goswami (1993), Griffin (1988b), Hagen (1995), Hayward (1984, 1987), Siu (1957), Smith (1995), Talbot (1981), Zukav (1979).

8.   This notion of postmodernism in the Latin American scene as a disintegrating effect that renders the area open to the rape of disenchanted global economic

pressures that have resulted from disenchantment of the world and disenchantment of modernism-modernity is forcibly argued by Ribeiro (1995; from various alternative views see also Colás 1994, Hopenhayn 1995, Larsen 1995, Lechner 1995).

9.   For example, Bohm (1980), Bohm and Hiley (1993), Griffin (1988a, 1993).

10.   Also García Canclini (1995), Ortiz (1886, 1988), Teixeira Coelho (1995), Vianna (1999).

11.   Also in this regard see Ortega (1988), Martín-Barbero (1993), García Canclini (1995), Schwarz (1992), Rama (1982), Martínez (1979). The general thrust has it that national, cultural, and even group and individual identity are what dreams are made of; they are not realities that can be articulated. The notion of semiosis bears this argument out: the self is always something other than what it was, identity is a perpetually transient sea of ambiguity, inconsistency, vagueness and incomplete generalities; nothing is fixed.

12.   This observation also applies to Mignolo's general critique of subaltern studies applied to the letter regarding the Latin American postcolonial scene and his complaint that postcolonial theorizing is often confused with postmodern thinking (Mignolo 2000:201). Nevertheless, one of Mignolo's favorite metaphors, the modern/colonial not as one and other but as two sides of the same coin smacks of Saussurean binarism. We will recall that Saussure used a comparable metaphor: the signifier and signified as two sides of a sheet of paper. What's left out of the equation is the paper itself, that infinitesimally thin line between the one and the other, that "emptiness" that is *both* the one *and* the other and *neither* the one *nor* the other, that "emptiness" that is at once nothing and possibly everything—as illustrated in Figure 1.

Chapter Eight

Cultural Rhythms

> There is a third element in this discord, which is that this music is found neither in Spain nor in Africa. Cuban music is greater than the sum of its parts: it is a vision and an atmosphere where some people play and others listen, and, what is most important, where people dance. Even the bolero is made for dancing. In Cuba, music is or rather was everywhere, carried to all corners of the planet by Cuban musicians.
>
> —Guillermo Cabrera Infante

> My poetry is a border animal between night and day.
>
> —Alexis Gómez Rosa

This chapter will most likely appear to have taken such a radically tangential turn that it is completely out of sync with all that preceded it. That is not the case, however. Not really, I would hope. In the first place, the following paragraphs bear directly on certain important aspects of the polylogue initiating this inquiry. In the second place, my apparently paratactic, parasemantic, parapragmatic, and paralogical madness actually has a certain method to it; that is, the apparently illogical juxtapositions are illustrations of interrelated codependency, and flux and flow, characteristic of all cultures.

But first, some preliminaries.

On What There Can Be in Our World

What do we see? Or better said, what *can* we see?[1] Our pupil is but a minuscule porthole allowing a look at the vast sea of radiation. We can hardly see anything of this turbulent sea; we are more in the dark than basking in the light of knowledge.[2]

Our eyes respond only to the electromagnetic vibrations between about .00004 and .00007 centimeters in length. Yet we are constantly subject to a barrage of waves from as large as a mountain to considerably smaller than a solitary atom. Flip on the TV and you can see some of them. . . . No, that's not right. You can't really see them in the direct sense of seeing. You can only see the consequences of their having been converted into Boolean bits of information and those bits into a stream of light you can see. (Here, we once again confront the characters of our dialogue. We are—or at least I would hope that by now there is agreement in this regard—neither Tlönys nor Funys nor Maggies nor Lönnys nor Hladdys nor Daneris nor Emmies. Neither are we Borges's library rats nor are we his hapless lottery players. We are a diverese combination of all of them, and with a little Richard Rorty to boot, I would suspect. We never see—or better, sense, through all the channels—

absolutely all there is nor do we see all there is not; we are neither helpless dreamers nor are we hopelessly tied to the world's particulars; we are neither strictly hypothetico-deductivists nor do we simply go about recursively collecting data and inducting them into their proper pigeon-holes. The world will never be absolutely identical to what our mind makes of it nor is it forever exactly what it is—identical to itself—and autonomous of the mind. These most important points should become increasingly apparent as we move along to the rhythm of the sections that follow. We and our signs, that is, we and our world, interrelate, interact, and collaborate, in the self-organizing, co-dependent emergence, of what might be, is, or should be coming into being, of what is being becoming.)

Radiation is only one kind of information the grand whole of which we remain for the most part blind to. We are also deaf to most of the sounds around us; our chemical senses of smell and taste are extremely impoverished in comparison to other organisms; our sense of touch is torpid alongside a lowly cockroach's antennae; our sense of changing air currents and other atmospheric alterations are brutish in the eyes of the deer, the squirrel, and the puma. As far as experience goes, we are in possession of the tunnel-sensation of a mole or a hedgehog; at least we certainly lack the sophistication of the wily foxes, among other cleverly endowed members of the animal kingdom surrounding us. A spider lives in a two-dimensional universe of its own making. Within this habitat our arachnid friend remains quite oblivious to all the outside coming and going, yet she is remarkably sensitive to a fly's fluttering, a rain drop, a gentle breeze on her planar world. We live in an interconnected web too, a three-dimensional web. It is also by and large of our own making, rather than simply what there is. Like Columbus's America, it is more invented than discovered, more fabricated than found. It's not a matter of what you see is what you get, for what you see is largely what you want to see, which is to say that it could have been seen in any one of a vast array of alternative seeings.

The Mexico City of the 1950s Carlos Fuentes wrote about in *Where the Air is Clear* (1960 [1958]) was an "imagined city," just as was the Mexico City of the 1980s he wrote about in *Christopher Unborn* (1989 [1987]). Indeed, "we would know nothing of Balzac's Paris and Dickens's London if they, too, had not invented them" (Fuentes 1988b:26). Our own three-dimensional web we have spun from our imagination exists, our physicists tell us, in the unseen context of four-dimensional spacetime of which common folks are only beginning to become aware. Our ordinary perception is virtually limited to the objects, acts, and events of our immediate environment. We find inordinate difficulty in remembering collections of things that are greater than the "magic number seven, plus or minus two" (Miller 1956). Our manipulation of numbers is quite limited, unless we use pen and paper or a calculator, and our spans of time are limited to our own lifetimes, unless we consult history books and such. Projecting outside our immediate three-dimensional space and our limited one dimension of time demands enormous leaps of the imagination of the sort accomplished by Einstein, Pablo Picasso, Heisenberg, Wolfgang Amadeus Mozart, Bohr, Gertrude Stein, and Borges. And considerations of the whole of our abstract logical, geometric, and mathematical systems are limited to prodigies such as Georg Cantor, Bernhard Riemann, Kurt Gödel, and, once again, Borges.

As far as the spider is concerned, her fabricated universe is well nigh motionless. So is ours, at least from one of our most customary viewpoints. Galileo demonstrated that experiment alone cannot tell us whether we are moving or not. When inside the cabin of a large ocean cruiser in a calm sea, if you see a gnat flying around, if you bounce a ping-pong ball against the wall, if you ambulate around in your confined space, it is all apparently the same as if you were in the comfort of your own home. But the ship is moving, while you generally tend to assume your home is cemented to the earth. But our homes are also moving at the same velocity as the earth, and the earth's motion is computable in relation to the sun as a stationary object: it is whizzing around the sun with a speed of almost twenty miles per second. But the sun is moving as well with respect to the center of our galaxy at about 150 miles per second . . . and so on. What Galileo revealed was refined further by Einstein. In one of his many thought experiments, Einstein imagined himself in an elevator in empty space being accelerated at the rate of 32 feet per second per second, and concluded that his sensations would be the same as if he were subjected to gravity on the earth's surface. He went on eventually to convince the scientific world that the attraction of gravity is a matter of curvatures in space. The spacetime continuum blossomed forth. This was an imagined world, essentially no less bizarre than Cervantes's *Don Quixote*, or Menard's fragments of the same novel.

Our Strange World

Many things seem strange to us from time to time, and rightly so. A sense of strangeness is hardly more evident than in many of Borges's stories, or, I might suggest, the Borges-inspired polylogue. Take the inhabitants of that apparently bizarre planet, Tlön, as a case in point. The Tlönians, of "Tlön, Uqbar, Orbis Tertius" (1962 [1944]), were inveterate "subjective idealists" in the grand old Bishop Berkeley style. If the premises of Borges's tale are taken at face value, the Tlönians are in all likelihood solipsists—we learned that much from Tlöny. For example, some coins are lost. One person finds one of them in a place where they couldn't possibly have been lost. Another person finds one of them somewhere else. And so on, until all the coins are accounted for. To suppose the found coins are the same as the lost coins would be a heretical thought for the Tlönians. When they were lost, there were existent no more. Those who found the coins brought them into existence once again because they happened to take a gander at them—i.e., they urged them into existence by inventing or imagining them—at a particular spacetime juncture, which had nothing to do with the coins someone happened to lose. To each her own, I guess.

As far as we Earthlings are concerned, it's a more simple matter of "Finders keepers, losers weepers." The lost coins are the private property of whoever runs into them, for the coins, before their having been lost, while they are lost, and after they have been found, are the same coins, clearly and distinctly. If for the Tlönians the coins simply didn't exist unless they were in someone's consciousness, for us there are things that are not in our consciousness because they fall outside our ordinary capacity for creating an image of them or thinking about them. One of these things is the process of exponential growth. Another is asymptotic approximation. Regarding exponential growth, it is well-nigh impossible for us to get the idea through our stubborn heads that if a thin strip of toilet paper is folded upon itself a few thousand times it would be a few million miles thick. Incredible, but true. That's reason and mathematics for you, as bizarre as the strangest scene in a sci-fi novel. With respect to asymptotic approximation, it is difficult to concede that if Achilles wishes to run from one end of his city-state to the other, he must run half the distance, then half the remaining distance, and so on, without in his lifetime or ours being able to reach his destiny. If Zeno's logical trick appears so silly that we need pay it no mind, it's most likely because we know quite well that Achilles the fleet-footed can accomplish his goal in relatively short order. Yet, strictly from within Zeno's mighty logic, the paradox endures, even though a host of philosophers has claimed to resolve it.

In addition to the things we can't quite fathom, let alone see, there are the things we don't fathom or see because we choose to ignore them (in this vein recall focal and subsidiary awareness from chapter two). We have no need to see them, for in a manner of speaking we know them so well they are no longer worthy of our attention. Or perhaps we ignore them since they are unnecessary for our survival or our need to find and keep a mate, to find or make some shelter and eat and sleep, and even to win fortune and fame. At this moment, I am unaware of my lung heaves, my palpitating heart, my liver's cleansing act, my stomach's violent destruction of solid matter. My body knows how to do what it does without my active intervention, thank you. I was not at the moment giving any thought to a hurricane in the Caribbean, the approaching clouds overhead, the squirrels in the back yard hiding their black walnuts in preparation for a cold spell, the mound of mid-term exams I will soon have to tackle. The reasons for my omissions are obvious. We helplessly finite creatures can take in and think about only so much. Beyond that, there is just a lot of noise. Let too much light into your camera, and you get a lot of precisely that: white light, "noise," a combination of all the visible frequencies, which disallow those subtle variations that bring objects into the picture. Turn on three stereos, one playing rock, the second playing Bach, the third playing R & B, and it's hard to keep things in their proper place. The ears and eyes and other organs are equipped to send information to the brain, but within severely restricted limits. Their job is also to shut out most of the possible information.

Selecting useful information is the most important job of perception (this became quite obvious in our polylogue). The vast expanse of possible information that always lies before our waking experience is also a minefield of possible errors. Our now familiar "Rabbit-Duck" ambiguity can be interpreted in whichever way we wish. The Gestalt "Faces-or-Vase" diagram is another case in point. You see "Faces," and the "Vase" falls into the background, and vice versa. In other words, that which is not foregrounded is by and large ignored. It remains as possible information, that is, information that can at a moment's notice pop into the foreground with a concomitant backgrounding of the "Faces." Are these just simple examples? Yes. But actually not so simple. They are lessons that what we get used to falls into the implicit, tacit, nonconscious field of our passive awareness. I repeat, we can only take in so much. Were we so fortunate as that narrator in Borges's "Aleph" (1970 [1945]), Daneri, we would be able to take in massive chunks of information in one gulp. But we cannot. Much of our sensory atrophy is learned within the context of our culture and our conventions. Some of it, on the other hand, is the product of stupor. This consists of signals that fatigue our physical sensors to the point that we see what is not there or fail to see what according to our proper cultural upbringing we should see. One of the most common examples of this automatically induced stupor is found in everyday afterimages. Stare at a bright light, then look away at a white wall, and the opposite of the bright image, a dark patch, will meet your gaze. Concentrate on a red patch for a while, then look at the wall, and the color's complement, green, will appear. The afterimages are contrary to what should be seen because they correspond to the place in your retina where the sensors had been stupefied by the intensity or the sameness of the stimuli. That is, your sensors can no longer send the signal to your brain saying "White wall!" or "Red patch." The rest of your retina responds normally, but that part of the retina that had been the focus of your attention does not. You see in part what there is not in addition to what there is.

An example of seeing what there is not in spite of your cultural inculcation is that of the "Ames room." There is a room with a far wall one end of which is relatively close to the front wall and the other which is far removed. Yet the "close" side is connected to a low ceiling and the "far" side to a high ceiling due to the tapering upward as the eye moves from the "close" to the "far" side. However, the wall is so proportioned that, when the viewer looks through a peephole provided in the front wall, the back wall appears as rectangular as can be. If a child is placed at the "near" side of the wall and an adult at the "far" side of the wall, the child appears about 7'6" tall and the adult 3'8" tall, even though the viewer's brain knows it can't be so. The retina sends the brain the proper information, but the brain insists in imposing "rectangularity" on the "far" wall, because that's the way walls are supposed to be. The viewer sees what there is and what there is not in a contradictory mix of messages (recall the discussion surrounding Figure 4). Our ordinary culture-laden ways of seeing the world have suddenly become strange.

What is it Like to be Other Than What You Are?

What strange cultures, those of Tlöny, Funy, Lönny, Maggie, Emmy, etc.—and even Rorty—as revealed in our polylogue. One person's "green" can be another person's "blue," one person's violence, sex, and foul language can be another person's customary way of life, one person's "Gavagai" as a "bachelor" can be another person's "aging yuppie." Our interlocutors seemed to be completely out of tune with each other. Their messages did not resonate. That is because they had become so accustomed to making and taking their signs in the way they made and took them that they assumed there was no other way. Within our own culture, our own use and abuse of signs can become so habitual that they drop out of consciousness: our sensors fatigue of all the violence we see on TV such that it loses its impact, or they fatigue of four-letter words in the movie theater so much that they no longer have the shock value they once had, or they fatigue of sex in ads to the extent that it appears pretty much commonplace.

But at least a minuscule portion of that of which we are at some moment not conscious can stand a chance of leaping to our attention. Peirce calls it *abduction*, that which was possibly there but of which we were not aware until somewhere and somewhen we happened to notice it. Such was the case of a group of macaque monkeys in Japan who enjoyed an abundance of bad sweet potatoes humans dumped on the beach as waste for their consumption. But it was difficult to chew them with their acquired coating of sand until it suddenly occurred to one of the members of the tribe to wash the lump of food in the water nearby. Soon others were doing it, and then the next generation of macaques was taught the trick. The first enterprising monkey, like the ape-man of Stanley Kubrick's movie *2001*, became aware of some connection that had been there all along. But since all the monkeys were somewhat painfully going about their gritty munching as usual, none of them had made the lateral mental move in order to see what had ordinarily gone unseen. In less dramatic learning experiences, such as the human case of apprenticeship and entry into a profession as a master, we have the example in chapter two of philosopher of science Michael Polanyi. The apprentice learns in part by explicit instruction, but more importantly, by watching the master at work, by learning tacitly and corporeally through implicit processes. This more subtle form of learning is internalized in great part without the agent's maintaining conscious awareness of the internalization. With much sweat and practice she finally reaches a stage when she can carry out her task with much the same efficiency and the same confidence as her master. Now, it can be said that she just does what she does, without the need of being aware of the tacit acts of her doing. It is comparable to her relatively uncomplicated acts of riding a bicycle, driving a car, and spouting out grammatically correct sentences: she no longer has to think about it, she simply does it. When she is so performing, in a metaphorical manner of putting it, she is in tune with herself and with her environment.

Use of a metaphor in this context is not mere coincidence. Metaphor is by its very nature a remarkable instrument. We speak of being in tune with the times or out of tune with each other. We might even speak of "sympathetic vibrations" to use K. C. Cole's (1984) metaphor, and of being on the same "wavelength." We speak of ideas that "resonate" and of descriptions or anecdotes that "ring true." When we do so we are rarely aware of the fact that we are talking physics. Resonance is the physics lesson we all learned the first time we tried to pump ourselves on the playground swings. The trick, we soon learned, is in the timing. Pushing forward or leaning backward at the wrong place or time gets us nowhere. The thrust of the pump has to coincide with the natural rhythm of the swing. The key to the resonance lies in pushing or pulling in time with the way the swing naturally wants to go. It is the synchrony of many small periodic pushes that work in unison to add up to a much larger one.

Resonance. What is it, really? We might tend to lump it with other phenomena such as sine waves, oscillators, frequencies, and wavelengths of the sort that only physicists could have a feel for. But among physicists there are words for subatomic phenomena the likes of "quarks," from James Joyce's *Finnegan's Wake*, and "charm," "quark colors," "resonance," and other such terms that have their metaphorical attraction. Resonance exists at the lowermost state of the physical world, as the physicists know it. From there it moves up through molecules, life systems, our solar system, galaxies, and the entire universe. An interesting example of resonance in this regard is that of an occasional firefly phenomenon. Ordinarily, to the outside observer, a firefly's flash-dance might appear well nigh random with respect to the other flies' electrical display. However, this is mating season, and it is serious business. What actually happens is that flies with the same on-and-off flashings are becoming attracted to one another as they recognize the "matches" between them. Eventually a large number of them will become "mutually entrained" or synchronized. Then the entrainment will become more general, until finally, virtually the entirety of the community's intermittent flashing is in unison. Literally, resonance means to resound, or sound again: to echo. Clay doesn't resonate because it is too full of internal friction to vibrate; a falling leaf simply falls in somewhat random fashion due to its irregular folds and the invisible air currents. In order for something to resonate, it needs a force to pull it back more or less to its starting place and enough energy to keep it going. The trick is to have it resound again and again in a kind of continuing echo.

Clay and leaves aside, the universe as a whole is a remarkably springy and sprightly place. Galaxies and planets and atoms and almost everything else in between vibrate at one or more natural frequencies. When something else nudges them periodically at one of those frequencies, resonance results. Soldiers marching in step with the natural frequency of a bridge can cause it to collapse, which is why soldiers break step when crossing makeshift bridges. The ill-fated propjet Electra developed an unfortunate habit of falling apart when the rhythm of the rotating propellers matched the natural frequency of the winds. The same occurred to the early prototypes of the Bell helicopter. Recent studies suggest that giant icebergs can be splintered by the resonant force of gently lapping ocean waves. Such examples are relevant to what is today known as "chaos theory" and "dissipative structures" according to which there is the possibility, however remote, that a butterfly flapping its wings in Brazil can cause a typhoon off the shores of India. When resonance is thrown out of whack in a minuscule portion of the universe, the slightly out-of-balance behavior can be magnified manyfold, given the nonlinear properties of the entire system, such that catastrophes can ensue.

The power of resonance comes literally from being in the right place at the right time. Resonance, in other words, allows a lot of little pushes in the right place to add up to big results—or in the above example, the butterfly causes a bit of dissonance that can bring about disastrous results. Particle accelerators use this principle of a "kick in the pants," as one physicist put it, to nudge electrons and protons almost to the speed of light. But resonance is also a familiar phenomenon in everyday human existence. A lot of little pushes in an already angry crowd can lead to a full-scale riot. A lot of little daily digs over the dinner table can eventually lead to divorce, alcoholism, neurosis, or homicide. A few otherwise insignificant failures at a low point in someone's affairs can lead to depression or even suicide. Sometimes clever politicians exploit this property in order to play on the public's natural dissatisfaction with inflation, taxes, public institutions, or customary behavior—and get a large resonant response with a very small input of energy or new ideas. From the devastating ideology of an Adolf Hitler to the naive homespun philosophy of a Ronald Reagan, and from the "I have a dream" of Martin Luther King to "Ask not what your country can do for you" of John F. Kennedy, what appears to be at the outset a little information, delivered in the right way at the right time and by the right person, can go a long way. All is a matter of information. Giving your dog the command to grab a Frisbee between his teeth involves little energy: vibrating vocal chords, a pointing finger, some sound patterns in the air, the twitting of an eardrum. It can, however, bring about the release of quite a bit of physical activity from your canine friend.

Information is much more than the physical force and energy behind it. With very little information, rather than physical change, the entire system can be thrown out of kilter (Martin Luther King's words), and a new form of order stands a chance of emerging. Resonance, then, is far more than a brutal amplifier. It can also be music to our ears. The opera singer's performance is an ode to resonance; each pure tone that fills the opera house is the tiny vibration of a vocal cord amplified by the shape of her chest and throat. The same pure tone, of course, can shatter a crystal glass, it can provoke a stray dog to howls, or it can grate on the ears of a person out of tune with opera culture. A violin bow slips along the string, catching it imperceptibly at precise intervals that push it at the proper time to keep it vibrating. To play a flute, you set the air inside resonating at many different frequencies, depending on how far the sound waves travel between the mouthpiece and the finger holes. The holes are so placed as to pick out those tones that correspond to the standard musical scale—but how you blow determines whether your flute will resonate with the notes that are purest and loveliest.

In this sense, resonance can provide a good metaphor for the process of learning. It often takes a lot of little pieces of information to add up to a deep understanding, and a lot of little insights to add up to a great idea. But these little bits and pieces need to come at the right time and strike you in the right way. If the information comes along before you are prepared to offer feedback, the input simply dissipates, like a playground swing when pumped the wrong way. Adding energy without timing gets you nowhere. If you pump at the wrong time on a swing, you are opposing the natural pattern—bucking the current, so to speak. You sap energy instead of adding it. The flute player who sets the air vibrating at a frequency not natural to the flute doesn't get a note at all, but so many different frequencies that the result is an amorphous, irritating hiss.

Becoming Other and Falling Out of Sync

Being "out of tune" with things is always irritating because the energy you put into your efforts doesn't seem to get you anywhere. It goes against the grain instead of with it. It steals your harmony and leaves you with noise. You can be in or out of tune with yourself—like the flute and the violin—or in or out of tune with others. Two flutes played beautifully but slightly out of tune with each other can be much more unpleasant than one flute played badly. Partners in a marriage who are perfectly in tune with their professional or personal lives can be badly out of tune with each other, too. Members of different generations often find it difficult to stay in tune with both their peers and the other members of their families, and it is rare to find yourself on the same wavelength with the same people at home, at work, and on vacation. People from different cultures can be so out of sync with one another that at every juncture communication falters, yet somehow a remarkable degree of harmony can occasionally be reached apparently with the greatest of ease.

Resonance also plays an important function in our relationship with our physical environment. Resonant absorption colors everything from sports cars to begonias. The pigment molecules in the skin of a McIntosh apple absorb the parts of sunlight that vibrate harmonically in the frequencies we see as blue and green; the rest of the light is reflected, and we see red. Chlorophyll molecules in green leaves vibrate to the tune of red and blue and absorb them, reflecting the leftover green; the same leaves absorb green and reflect autumn colors in the fall. Gaze at a deep red rose. The combination of frequencies making up the red light bounce off the petals, enter your retina, excite and resonate with the rods and cones, which send signals to your brain, and you enjoy one of nature's miracles to the fullest. You see red because the blues, greens, and yellows were absorbed into, that is, they resonated with, the surface of the rose's petals. The energy of these waves of light tingles around in the petals for a moment and then race out in the form of radiant energy. Resonance gives us the world we see—and smell and taste and touch and hear as well. In collaboration with your conventionally held filters, it lets some things through, stops others in their tracks for your inspection, determines what will be perceivable and what not, what will be transparent and what opaque, what audible and what silent, what untouchable and what not, what odorless and what pungent, what bland and what tart or sweet, and so on (Cole 1984:272).

But we are ordinarily oblivious to most or virtually all of this. We get on with life within the big picture as if we knew what that big picture were all about, whereas we actually know virtually nothing about it, and we are certainly ignorant regarding most of the resonance around us, from subatomic to galactic levels. The differences between Einstein's laws and Newton's laws are truly very small—all but imperceptible, for that matter, except at speeds close to the velocity of light. You never notice that time slows down on a trip across the country, or that everyone in the plane gets very slightly heavier during the flight. You could never notice the difference between gravity as a Newtonian force and as an Einsteinian curvature of space. Yet the significance of those small differences is enormous. Einstein's laws made Newton's laws only a little bit wrong, but philosophically, they are completely out of sync with one another. This is very peculiar. The slightest change in our view of the world can orchestrate profound changes in our ideas. Small differences that Darwin noticed in species of turtles and birds and iguanas led him down the path toward evolutionary theory. Even today, confidence in evolution is continually bolstered by such small irregularities as Stephen Jay Gould's (1980) now well-known Panda's Thumb—a thumb that is really an appendage rigged out of an overgrown wrist-bone. Nearly perfect design is not good evidence for evolution, Gould argues, because it would more likely be the handiwork of a nearly perfect Creator. Rather, he tells us, oddball arrangements and bizarre solutions are the proof of evolution. Such oddball arrangements, one would suspect, are not the path a sensible God would tread. Yet they seem to be the natural process, constrained somewhat by history.

In human cultures it takes at least two to play the game of resonance because one must feed energy to the other. Two partners in a business feed each other ideas and energy at just the right times and places to get the best results. Or the escarpment of a watch lets the spring go just enough and at just the right time to give the pendulum (or crystal) the push it needs to keep it going. However, three can play the game considerably better than two. The game is played if the third partner in the sense of Peircean semiotics is capable of mediating the first two partners and at the same time bringing about a mediation between herself and each of the first two partners in the same way that she orchestrates a mediation of the first two partners. The three-member affair gyrates and twirls and whizzes along the semiosic stream, but with each turn, unlike the ordinary symmetrical, linear setup between two binary pairs, the asymmetrical, nonlinear relations between the semiotic trio is always already something other than what it was. In short, binary principles are largely those of classical logical imperatives. Triadic principles, in contrast, make a play for differences. They follow a vague "logic of difference," of nonlinearity, of asymmetry. It hardly stands a chance of moving along the stream in the symmetrical, *either/or* order of binary logic. It learns to swim by each partner's entering into resonance with all the other partners. Yes, resonance. It's chiefly what keeps semiosis in motion.

All this might be interesting, but how can we relate it to the plurality of cultures in Latin America? How can we relate it to differences within cultures and between cultures? How are resonance and nonlinearity and asymmetry related to themselves? In a further effort to come to grips with these issues—and perhaps to the unwary reader's chagrin—I will embark on yet another digression. I wish to turn to some of the most bizarre twists with respect to misunderstanding and language traps and cultural dissonance that have come out of philosophy in this century. I believe they will offer keen insight into our search for alternative and subversive cultural "logics."

Notes

1. I write "see," but, I must emphasize, hopefully without ocularcentric biases, and simply for parsimony of articulation. What I mean by "see" is "to perceive" in its broadest possible meaning, "to perceive" with any and all the senses, as I have generally used the word elsewhere.

2. Regarding the following discussion—for which I owe a debt to K. C. Cole (1984)—recall also the words on "seeing," "seeing *as*," and "seeing *that*" from chapter two.

Part III

Chapter nine calls on the aid of philosophers Nelson Goodman, Willard v. O. Quine, and Hilary Putnam in cutting and honing a key with which better to comprehend communication across cultures and between individuals within the same culture. The use of language as that which makes us distinctively human enters center stage, but not without duly acknowledging the importance of those baser signs of the body. This story prepares the ground for chapter ten, which focuses on the two Mexicos as described by Guillermo Bonfil Batalla: that of the "imagination" as imposed by the dominant culture and "México profundo" of the subservient culture. The used and abused Shakespearean trio of Prospero-Ariel-Caliban then comes to the fore further to illustrate the need of a triadic rather than the stringently limited and limiting binary view of culture. Chapter eleven continues this message while throwing the spotlight on: (1) the work of two Brazilian writers: Euclides da Cunha and Gilberto Freyre, (2) recent corruption, violence, and political intrigues in Mexico, and the escalating cynicism of its people, and (3) the bizarre events surrounding the impeachment of Brazilian President Fernando Collor de Mello in 1992. Then, in chapter twelve, passage of NAFTA and the uprising of the Zapatista Liberation Army (EZLN) in Mexico make their way through the interstices. Signs of subversion by the "cultural" guerrillas, the dispossessed people of Mexico, suggest how culture is an ongoing process, and that there is always resistance to the either/ors in favor of both-ands and neither-nors.

Chapter Nine

Rules? What Rules?

> [A] border wasn't an abyss but rather a beginning, a point of departure, and the possibility of experiencing another kind of happiness. As a result, my poetry became a vast borderland.
>
> —Marjorie Agosín

> In my secret life I wasn't Puerto Rican. I wasn't American. I wasn't anything. I spoke every language in the world, . . . and could be understood by everyone.
>
> —Esmeralda Santiago

Green with Envy or Just Singing the Grues?

Here, I introduce some problems from Anglo-American philosophy in an attempt more adequately to account for the cultural practices that have often found themselves in the spotlight in previous chapters. These practices revolve around sign making and taking within the ongoing flow of everyday life, which is to say that signs revolve around signs becoming something other than what they were becoming. Nothing remains the same; in fact, nothing remains at all, for everything is always on the go. I begin, then, with Nelson Goodman.

To the question "What *can* we see?" Goodman's "New Riddle of Induction" (1965) offers an unexpected response. Goodman's conundrum goes something like this.[1] Any upstanding English speaker ordinarily believes the statement "Emeralds are green" is beyond doubt true. Supposing that all the emeralds she has examined before a given time are "green," she is quite naturally confident that "Emeralds are green" will always be confirmed, for according to her observations, emerald *a* on examination was "green," emerald *b* was "green," and so on. Now suppose she meets someone from Netherworld and discovers that his perception of things is apparently unstable from her perspective and that his use of predicates is radically distinct from her own. In other words, Ourworlder and the Netherworlder are out of sync with each other. They simply don't resonate—much like our polyloguers.

Among other oddities, Netherworlder's language contains the following two terms which Ourworlder, after a few hits and misses and some excruciating soul searching, learned to translate in stumbling and out of sync fashion into her language thus:

> Grue = examined before the temporal "reference point" t_0 and is reported to be "green" or is not examined before t_0 and reported to be "blue." (t_0 is apparently an otherwise arbitrary moment of time that is not in the past.)

> Bleen = examined before the temporal "reference point" t_0 and
> is reported to be "blue" or not examined before t_0 and
> is reported to be "green."

Before time t_0 for each of Ourworlder's statements asserting an emerald is "green," Netherworlder has a parallel statement asserting that it is "grue." And as far as he is concerned, his observations that emerald a on examination is "grue," that emerald b is "grue," and so on, adequately confirm his own hypothesis. It will obviously appear to Ourworlder from the standpoint of her language and her normal color taxonomy that Netherworlder's sensory images change radically after t_0. But actually, from Netherworlder's perspective, the glove is turned inside out: as far as he can tell, it is Ourworlder's taxonomy that is time-dependent—in a sort of radical Funy fashion, we might expect. That is, Netherworlder's translation of Ourworlder's color scheme would result in the following report:

> Green = examined before t_0 and is reported to be "grue," or not
> and is reported to be "bleen."
> Blue = examined before t_0 and is reported to be "bleen," or is
> not and is reported to be "grue."

From the perspective of each translator, then, the other's inductive process is zany. Apparently, the two interlocutors are totally out of each other's groove, for there is hardly any resonance at all with respect to "green" and "grue." On the other hand, if the two perspectives are taken together as an atemporal whole, they are apparently quite symmetrical; but when taken separately as self-sufficient wholes, they are asymmetrical with respect to one another (Gärdenfors 1994, Rescher 1978). In a manner of speaking, Ourworlder and Netherworlder possess their own "metaphysics of presence" with respect to their conception of their own world, though from the other's complementary world, this "metaphysics of presence" is easily demythified. [2]

In this light recall Tlöny's play on "grue" and "green" and Funy's distortion of "Gavagai." Their perception and radically ephemeral conception of things are not irrelevant to Goodman's riddle. Tlöny is an inveterate "idealistic, a mental nominalist," and Funy is a hopeless "physical nominalist." Tlöny conceptualizes and universalizes each and every mentally constructed grasp of the world he makes and takes at each second, though those universals are no more than arbitrary, and they suffer refutation at every subsequent moment. Funy sees what he sees, apparently quite clearly and distinctly, though he is incapable of bringing any group of his bundles of perception together into a general conceptual package. Goodman's nominalism is certainly a far cry from that of both Tlöny and Funy. Yet, like Tlöny, Goodman's world is fashioned not found, by and large mentally fabricated not physically given, and like Funy, the only "reality" is that of particulars: there are no generalities in the world "out there."

In fact, we have experienced this phenomenon often in the above examples. Columbus's finding that what was supposed to be "salt water" was actually "fresh water" could be relabeled "fralt water" from an alternative perspective according to which there was no change from before t_0 to after t_0. In like fashion, the Virgin

Mary, after her apparition to Juan Diego—the Amerindian imbued with his native Tonantzín theology—could well be "Guadalupe" as distinguished from "Tonantzín" before t_0 and after t_0 for the Catholic fathers. But for the Amerindian community, the EarthMother-MotherofChrist could have been tantamount to "Guadantzín" (or "Tonalupe"). The two images were fused, confused, and hybridized such that something new emerged from within the erstwhile excluded-middle. In comparable fashion, the Spanish American colonial dictum, "I obey but I do not comply," could conceivably involve a transmutation from "Obey" and "Comply" before t_0 to "Obly" and "Compey" after t_0, while as far as the Crown was concerned, "I both obey and comply" was the norm. Examples abound.

A Certain Mark of Distinction

If we relate Goodman's thought experiment to Peirce's vague concept of a time-dependent "logic," there is more than initially meets the eye. We recall that from the perspective either of Netherworlder or Ourworlder, the other's perception appears "schizophrenic." That is, each presumes s/he exists in a broader frame with respect to the other, which is actually not the case.

This situation is relevant, I would submit, to Peirce's ruminations on his proposed "logic of continuity," or "vagueness." In order to develop a feel for this "logic," we are asked to imagine a blackboard as a vague range of possibilities. If we make a mark on it, a discontinuity is produced. This discontinuity is itself a continuity complementary with the continuity of the blackboard—that is, it consists also of an infinite continuum of points. But the chalk mark is not really the line, for a line ideally is of infinitesimal thickness, and hence invisible. The visible mark is actually a narrow plane, a white strip that severs and displaces a segment of the black surface:

> Thus the discontinuity can only be produced upon that blackboard by the reaction between two continuous surfaces into which it is separated, the white surface and the black surface. The whiteness is a Firstness—a springing up of something new. But the boundary between the black and white is neither black, nor white, nor neither, nor both. It is the pairedness of the two. It is for the white the active Secondness of the black; for the black the active Secondness of the white. (*CP*:6.203)

The generality of the clean blackboard, then, is viewed as analogous to geometrical continuity. This original generality is broken by the first mark. The mark, however, is the product of an arbitrary act, for it could have been drawn in an infinity of different ways. But once it has been drawn, it separates one side from the other. This line of demarcation between the blackness of the blackboard (a continuum of possibilities) and the whiteness of the line (a complementary continuum of an equal—infinite—number of possibilities) is itself neither black nor white. It is the "pairedness of the two." With respect to the black continuum, the line of demarcation is something *other*; it is a Second manifested by the whiteness (a generality) of the (actual) white. And with respect to this white continuum, the line of demarcation is also something *other*; it is a Second manifested by the blackness of the black. As *neither* black *nor* white, the line of demarcation between the blackness and whiteness remains underdetermined, if for no other reason than that of its "schizophrenic" oscillation from whiteness to its *other* (blackness) and from that other as blackness to its own *other* (whiteness), and back again. But from another perspective the line of demarcation is not really *both* blackness *and* whiteness (i.e., overdetermined possibilities), for as an actual (Second), it is something, though that something is destined to remain indeterminate. Of course, we have seen all this before, in our discussion of the hairline dividing the cosmic egg in Figure 5, and of the border of borders and "emptiness."

What has this to do with Goodman's paradox and "cultural logics"? Allow me to suggest that it is this: between "green" and "blue" and "grue" and "bleen," there is, *a priori*, no fixed border. Once a border is tentatively, and, more often than not, arbitrarily, established, it could always have been something else, and in the future it invariably will have been something else. Hence any and all inferred generalities in the form of predicates regarding some semiotic object, and the taxonomies constructed from them, are inexorably underdetermined. And, given the entire range of possible predicates, past, present, and future, there is no absolutely determining what may be actualized at some moment from the sphere of underdetermination. There is no complete and consistent determination of underdetermination. This is because a sign of underdetermination (heterogeny) is never entirely free, given the interrelated codependency of all signs and of the vagueness and overdetermination of semiosis. In other words, within the sphere of possibilities of overdetermination (homogeny), emeralds can be contradictorily *both* "green" *and* "grue." Within the world of dualistic Secondness (where hegemony rules), they must be *either* the one *or* the other from some particular perspective. And within the sphere of underdetermination (heterogeny), they can determinately and for all time sport *neither* the one attribute *nor* the other, but one of an indefinite array of other possible attributes. The crux of the semiosic flux lies in the plurality of possible "cultural logics" all of which make up one "logic" in incessant flow, from top to bottom and vice versa, from right to left and vice versa, and in all directions and back again simultaneously on the map presented in Figure 6.

Lönny hypothetico-deductively constructed a set of signs with which to solve the crimes that had been committed. But his signs were radically underdetermined, for there was an alternative to them, namely, Scharlach's alternative, from a broader vantage point. This alternative emerged from the exceedingly vague sea of possibilities within the sphere of overdetermination at the border of borders. Pierre Menard dug into his nonconsciousness and emerged with a few fragments of prose identical to some passages from Cervantes's masterpiece. But the expected reception of his efforts was not forthcoming, for the literary critics contextualized the two texts and gave Menard's text a reading from within his early twentieth-century setting: whatever interpretations might arise, they could not help but remain plagued by underdetermination, for some unexpected happening always stood a chance of popping up. The upshot is that in the concrete situation of our polyloguing interlocutors, there is no foolproof certainty whether what one person says will not fall on the deaf ears of another person, or whether that person will completely misconstrue the words and make them out to be something entirely different than what the addresser had in mind. Such was our polylogue. The problem is that some of the interlocutors dwelled inordinately on vagueness, given their dream-like existence; others remained caught in a world of presumably determinate generalities, due to their inability to imagine any alternatives to their world; still others lived in a jungle of Seconds, whether physically (Funy) or in a world of their mind's making (Tlöny). Vagueness, then, must be brought into relation with generality, and both must be interrelated with Secondness. How so?

A quick turn to Willard v. O. Quine may help.

Rabbits, by Reason, Ruse, or Re-Cognition?[3]

Using examples so modest they appear sanguine and at times even absurd, Quine believes he demonstrates that, like our polyloguers, you can never actually know what I am talking about and I can never really know what you are talking about—contrary, it would appear, to Rorty's hopes, and the hopes of many others as well. This would mean that there is hardly any possibility of our completely resonating with one another. But it doesn't necessarily matter anyway, Quine would retort. As long as we make gallant pretenses at communicating, and insofar as we are at least successful enough to meet our own demands for satisfaction, for practical purposes it can be said that more often than not we know with some degree of approximation what each other is talking about.[4]

To cite Quine's notorious example (1960), suppose a field linguist without any knowledge of a native language overhears "Gavagai!" from one of her "informants" when in the presence of a fleeing rabbit. "Gavagai!" could possibly be construed as a holophrastic sentence such as "rabbit," or it could be the equivalent of "There goes a rabbit," "Yonder, a fleeing ruminant," "Grayness penetrating a background of brownness punctuated by intermittent greenness," "Ambulating becoming amongst diverse botanical becomings," or some other alternative. The common noun is *translated* into other parts of speech and thereby it presumably becomes meaningful within the context of the utterance. The fact that the "informant" uttered "Gavagai!" in this particular occasion attests to the fact that on this and other such occasions he is "seeing gavagaily" in a manner comparable, the linguist might assume, to her in her own language "seeing rabbitly" when uttering the holophrastic sentence "Rabbit!"

Quite conceivably, the sensations experienced by both the linguist and her "informant" are virtually equivalent, those sensations consisting of the presence of "rabbitness" and "gavagainess" respectively. But there can be no absolute guarantee that this is so. From within the Peircean framework, "rabbit" (as a term or word) is used potentially to indicate an entire set of propositions (sentences), "That is a rabbit," etc., from which an argument (text) can then be engendered. The term is in this sense a condensed sign whose interpretant must carry an overload, serving in multiple capacities (as if it were a composite icon). On the other hand, within the distinct framework of term and interpretant, there is no absolutely determinate meaning, translation, or "reference." There is no way of knowing without a shadow of a doubt that "Gavagai!" "refers to" a concrete, individual thing in English we call "rabbit," hence a mistake always stands at least an outside chance of emerging.

Quine calls this uncertainty of meaning the *inscrutability of reference*. It stipulates that the "reference" of general terms or terms of divided "reference" in an alien language cannot determine how the world is otherwise sliced up into patterns, or how scattered portions of it are combined—recall my reservations about "reference" in chapter two. From one language to another, the world may be cut up in widely varying ways that lead to radically divergent translations between the two languages, depending on how far one is willing to make compensating adjustments in the translation of terms in question. In Quine's hypothetical native language, "Gavagai!" may be tentatively correlated with the term "rabbit." If a rabbit happens to be in the vicinity when the two terms are used supposedly as synonyms, a set of "Undetached rabbit parts" and a "Temporal stage in a rabbit's space-time development" can also be present. So there is no certainty that "Gavagai!" translates into "Rabbit!" or to something else. Thus the theoretical uncertainty concerning translation of "Gavagai!" into "Rabbit!" stems from the radical impossibility of knowing absolutely that "Gavagai!" relates to "Rabbit!" and not to "undetached rabbit parts" or "rabbit stages"—that is, it relates to "Slices out of the space-time continuum." In this manner, the linguist's deciding upon "rabbit" or "rabbit slices" depends upon her particular vantage. However we wish to slice the cake, when we translate from one language to another or when we try to understand the way another language cuts up the world as illustrated by the Goodman examples, uncertainty is sure to inhere.

Quine seems to imply that, at home in our own language when conversing with other members of our speech community, we usually make the tacit assumption we are communicating, do the best we can, assume everyone else is doing the same, and hopefully get along swimmingly. As far as "reference fixing" goes, we simply say in so many words, by guesswork, and by implication, that "this" is a proof, "that" a formula, and "that" a number, or in Peirce's vocabulary, "this" is an argument (text), "that" a proposition (sentence), and "that" a term (word), or, perhaps, "this" is a "rabbit slice," "that" a "rabbit," and "that" a set of "rabbit parts." This network of sentences and terms is our "frame of reference"—to use Quine's jargon. Relative to this system, we can and do communicate, usually meaningfully to a remarkable degree. But once we begin to contemplate the overwhelming range of alternatives to our customary use of language, or what we ordinarily conceive to be the denotation of our words, we begin to appreciate how slippery language can become (Quine 1969:48).

It would seem, then, that Rorty's amiable chit-chat in our polylogue might get us nowhere if we take Quine at face value. But then again, we might be able to argue and in general kibitz to the satisfaction of all parties concerned. Regarding other aspects of our polylogue, the prospects are quite dire. Hladdy's talk with Averroës was ignored by everybody, Averroës was obsessed with what was for virtually everybody else utter trivia, Daneri's moment of Aleph-gazing insight that for the life of him he could not forget was so much Greek to Funy, and Funy's particulars were of no consequence for Daneri. Emmy the rather talented "cultural" guerrilla warrior was taken as a bimbo and could get little respect from her companions, and Maggie lived in a world of her own. Lönny's downfall was as inconceivable for Tlöny as it was for Maggie, and Pierre's mimetic talents went unappreciated by Hladdy. And so on.

Our polylogue, I would suggest, illustrates Quine's *inscrutability of reference* and *indeterminacy of translation* dilemmas at their best or at their worst, however we wish to take them. But actually, we should be grateful, for without these dilemmas, the third term between dominant and subservient, and all other binary pairs, would stand nary a chance of emerging from the border of borders into the light of day. There would be only the *either* or the *or*; we would have no "cultural" guerrillas; here would be no novelty, nothing to be surprised over, nothing but a dull and drab existence.

Cats and Cherries and Other Things

Quine's thought experiment is bizarre. But Putnam (1983a) does him one better: he leads us by the hand to the brink and playfully giving us a gentle nudge.

Putnam's story tells how minds can be the same though their signs are entirely different, or conversely, how signs can be the same but minds entirely different. In either case, radically distinct "semiotic realities" are yielded—as if taking the differences between our interlocutors' languages to their extreme form such that incommensurability inheres. It has to do with ordinary notions of "reference" apparently gone mad: I talk about "cats" and "mats" but you take me to mean "cherries" and "trees," and you talk about "cherries" and "trees" but I think "cats" and "mats." If we somehow manage to keep things honest, and at the level of first-order predicates, it is entirely possible that we may get along fine with the belief that we are communicating groovily. But here, as in all forms of communication, there is no determinably knowing we are on the same frequency and resonating at all. In fact, there always exists the possibility that we are talking about different things altogether. This is not merely Quinean confusion regarding whether you are thinking "rabbit" or "A space-time slice of rabbithood" when I say "rabbit," but rather, the same sign (representamen) relates to two entirely incompatible "semiotic objects," and hence their respective interpretants (concepts) are equally incompatible.

To be more specific, Putnam shows that, all contexts being equal regarding two radically distinct nouns, "A cat is on the mat" can be reinterpreted in such a manner that "cat" for one interlocutor relates to *cherries* for another, and "mat" for the one relates to *trees* for the other. All this, without affecting the "truth"-value in each case of "A cat is on the mat." Putnam then designates "cat" and "mat" for some *cat* and some *mat*, and "cat*" and "mat*" for some *cherries* and some *trees*. Suppose that when you say "A cat is on the mat" you mean that there is some *cat* such that it is on some *mat*. Good enough. However, I, by some quirk of the imagination, construe your sentence to mean that there is (are) some *cat** (*cherries*) such that it is (they are) on some *mat** (*trees*). You don't know what I take your words to mean and I don't know what you mean by your words. In this manner, if I reinterpret your sign "cat" by assigning it the "intensional" framework you would ordinarily assign to "cherries" (and I to "cat*"), and in the same semiotic act I reinterpret "mat" in terms of what you would ordinarily assign to "trees" (and you to "mat*"), then we have reciprocally translated two signs into two other signs. Yet phonemically and orthographically, "cat" is the same as "cat*" and "mat" is the same as "mat*." Although we may believe our communication has us congenially resonating along the same channel, our meanings are at cross current with one another: ordinary lines of communication have suffered a complete meltdown.[5]

Supposing you utter "cat" and "mat" and I construe your signs as "cat*" and "mat*," then structurally and interrelationally "A cat is on a mat" would for you mean virtually the same as "A cat* is on a mat*" for me. The only difference is in what is taken to be the object of "reference" of our respective signs and what interpretation they are given—a difference that is a crucial one. And this, Putnam swears, would fall in step with our well regimented habit of assigning "truth" to "A cat is on a mat," or any other string of signs for that matter, in every possible world—i.e., within the realm of vagueness. As Peirce might be prone to put it, when vagueness pervades the scene, maintenance of noncontradiction can at times become a futile enterprise. "Cat" and "cat*" can live in blissful coexistence as long as their interpreters do not catch onto their ontological and semantic confusion. And insofar as the contradiction remains merely possible, the interlocutors may continue to swim along in blissful ignorance, oblivious as to the communication chasm between them. The upshot is that "The cat is on the mat" or "The cat* is on the mat*" can be taken either as intensional or extensional.

Putnam's conclusion could conceivably apply to any domain of individual items of experience, whether *cats* and *cherries*, *mats* and *trees*, or any nonexperiential domain for that matter—"unicorns" and unicorn pictures, "quarks" and quark equations, or "square circles" and square circle talk. Regarding any of these items, all of which come in signs of one sort or another, in spite of whatever we may conceive as meaning or "truth," unintended (unexpected) situations can always stand a chance of emerging from the overdetermined sphere. If they do so, they may taunt us and throw our confidence-building programs, beliefs, conceptual schemes, and general views from within the underdetermined sphere for a loop. You intended "cat" to be *cat* and I took it to be *cherries* ("cat*"). Or one person takes "lightning bolts" to be "spears thrown by Jove" and another sees them as nothing but "electrical discharges." Or the "Earth" as "static" becomes the "Earth" as "revolving about the Sun." And so on. The total range of possibilities is virtually beyond imagination, I would expect. In fact, an image of the Virgin Mary in a Spanish American colonial setting could be "María" (Guadalupe) as far as the priest is concerned, but the Amerindian peasants see "María*" (Guadantzín, or Tonalupe), and each party interprets the image as it sees fit. Or the Crown could read "comply" as just that, "comply," whereas the colonists meant "comply*" (= "compey," and "obly," as a hybrid of "comply" and "obey").

Now, "cats" and "cats*" are radically distinct, one sign referring to *cats* and the other to *cherries*. So even though "There is a cat on the mat" and "There is a cat* on the mat*" are logically and structurally equivalent, it would seem impossible to conceive of their being fused together in such a way that their divergent referents will not immediately become apparent. At least, so it would seem. Putnam effectively counteracts this assumption, however. He reminds us that if the number of *cats* and the number of *cherries* available to a given pair of interlocutors just happens to be equal—an unlikely affair one must admit—then it follows that "cats" in relation to *cats* and "cats*" in relation to *cherries* demands a shift of the entire set of lexical items in "cat" language and in "cat*" language. Given such a shift, the two languages as wholes become radically distinct. The sentences of each language remain unchanged regarding their "truth"-value, while at the same time the extension of "cats" and "cherries" (i.e., "cats*") is drastically altered.

This is basically the same as to say that within my "cat language" I speak past you and from within your "cat* language" you speak past me; yet as far as our respective "languages" go, our "semiotic worlds" appear as stable and as resonant as can be. What is more, from within the range of all possible spatio-temporal contexts, "cats" for *cats* and "cats*" for *cherries* are equally permissible, as possibly are "cats" for "bats," "rats," "blatz," "quacks," "quarks," "sharks," "aardvarks," or virtually any other combination for that matter. Each interpretation is distinct, yet all interpretations are equally admissible from some perspective or other. In fact, "there are always infinitely many different interpretations of the predicates of a language which assign the 'correct' truth-values to the sentences in all possible worlds, *no matter how these 'correct' truth-values are singled out*" (Putnam 1981:35). Putnam concludes that nature does not single out any one "correspondence" between signs and the furniture of the world. Rather, nature "gets us to process words and thought signs in such a way that sufficiently many of our directive beliefs will be true, . . . but this leaves reference largely indeterminate" (Putnam 1981:41).

This perturbing radical indeterminacy of "reference" and of "interpretation" might remind us once again of the strange case of Pierre Menard and his writing a few passages identical to some passages in *Don Quixote*. Ironically, as was previously mentioned, Menard's critics totally recontextualized his text, claiming the replica was actually a great improvement over the original. It was the product of creative endeavors not of a Golden-Age Spaniard but of a twentieth century Frenchman ignorant of the time of which he wrote. They considered Menard to have:

> enriched, by means of a new technique, the halting and rudimentary art of reading; this new technique is that of the deliberate anachronism and the erroneous attribution. The technique whose applications are infinite, prompts us to go through the *Odyssey* as if it were posterior to the *Aenid*. . . . This technique fills the most placid works with adventure. (Borges 1962:44)

Placing Borges's "thought-experiment" within the context of Putnam's quandary, Menard's fragments could be taken by one reader as Menard's text and by another reader as Cervantes's text, or vice versa, and virtually incommensurable interpretations would ensue. In one interpretation, the Menard text might contain allusions to Nietzsche, William James, Russell, Proust, Dickens, and others, while the Cervantes text would be relatively impoverished. And in another interpretation the Cervantes text might be rich in the cultural lore of early seventeenth-century Spain, which would be diluted considerably in the Menard text. What is virtually the equivalent of "cat" for one mind can be tantamount to "cat*" for another. In another way of putting it, nothing is either "cat" or "cat*," but mind can often serve to make it so. As long as minds do not or cannot genuinely meet at some point or other, there is little hope of effective communication. Menard's text or Cervantes's text, or "cat" or "cat*," consists of the same signs in terms of their pure possibilities (of Firstness). But upon their being actualized (into Secondness) and endowed with interpretants (Thirdness), they relate to different "semiotic objects" whose respective interpretants are radically distinct, even well nigh incommensurable.

But there's the other, complementary problem: if different signs relate to the same "object," cannot their meanings in the best of all possible worlds be for practical purposes the same? In order to address this question, allow me to indulge in a little . . .

Hedging at the Edges

The notion of radically distinct interpretations drawn from the same set of signs of vagueness presents a problem for customary notions of language, "reference," and meaning. Logician Gottlob Frege often expressed his contempt for vagueness. It was for him a defect. It played havoc with orthodox logical principles and should be eradicated at all cost in order to make way for clear and distinct thinking. That opinion became gospel for logical positivism. The idea that the existence of vagueness might require a special form of logic was apparently never seriously entertained.

However, vagueness is not simply the product of frizzled thinking. It is a possible way out of the linguicentric morass within which we find ourselves. Vagueness is not merely surface opaqueness. It goes to the core of language and of signs; it is of the very essence of thought. In fact, without vagueness (Firstness), there would be no thought (Thirdness) in the first place. Solely by way of vagueness can artificial borders and domains be erected. That is, vagueness is not a breakdown of clear-cut borders and domains; it is necessary for their very existence. The so-called "sorites paradox," a dilemma emerging from the existence of fuzzy boundaries, is relevant to the notion of vagueness. Consider the distinction between ignorance and knowledge. If a child learns by internalizing disparate bits of information, at some point she will pass, we would like to think, from wide-eyed innocence to enlightenment. But suppose it is decided by the Committee for Epistemological Respectability that the dividing line between her ignorance and knowledge is henceforth $n \pm 10^3$ bits of information. If at some point our young lady has internalized $n \pm 10^3$ minus 24 bits, will she still be steeped in ignorance? With the addition of a dozen or so more bits, will she all of a sudden become knowledgeable? No, we might wish to respond. Ignorance is not necessarily transformed into knowledge nor knowledge into ignorance by the mere addition of a few more bits. Then what is the answer, precisely? There is no precise answer. "Ignorance" and "knowledge" cannot but remain vague: the dividing line between them is a cloud (Wright 1976).

On the one hand, the realm of vagueness forces an indefinite number of unexpected interpretations on us. On the other hand, the realm of generality allows for an indefinite number of alternative interpretations, each of them with the potential for equal accountability. Our hand is perpetually forced, but between each pair of cards, others potentially arise to give us the promise of winning the pile of chips in the long run. However, since such images are what dreams are built on, we can never know for sure whether our signs are faithfully telling us what is "real" or whether we have the hand that will at long last give us a win.

At any rate, if we put into concert the entrenched vagueness residing within Emmy, Maggie, and Pierre, the particularities within physicalist Funy and the mentalist Tlöny, and the chronic generality within Lönny, and in his own way within T'sui, we would vaguely have the makings of Figure 6. "Green" for Funy and Tlöny can quite conceivably become at one of any given number of expected moments "grue." Any interpretation of "Gavagai!" made by Lönny would be a shot in the dark. And what might be taken for a "cat" in Maggie's world could well be taken for "cat*" in Emmy's or Pierre's world according to how they might be interpreted. All the interlocutors are perpetually on a roll, though there is always the element of chance, of the unexpected, of the world and its presumed knowers happening to show another of their many faces.

In light of these quandaries of reference and misreference, interpretation and misinterpretation, and words and counterwords, all bearing witness to the problems of communication and of knowing our world and the cultural spheres within which we happen to find ourselves, how in the world can we more effectively make our way back to Latin America? Perhaps by way of a few vague ruminations on "alternate cultural logics."

Notes

1. If I might add, in merrell (1997) I have developed this theme with more specific focus on Peirce's semiotics.
2. I must emphasize once again that I am now portraying the strong view of Goodman's conundrum stipulating symmetrical relations between Ourworlder and Netherworlder. This view would be that of the sphere of overdetermination wherein what would in dualistic (Secondness) thinking consist of incommensurable schemes enjoying no hierarchy of values but atemporally flattened to the same level. The other, less robust interpretation falls within the sphere of underdetermination: complementary views can be equally confirmed, but not at the same time; it is a matter of now this interpretation, now the other one, hence temporality, irreversibility, and asymmetry enter the scene—to be discussed in the next chapter. Yet, when taking into account either Ourworlder's or Netherworlder's view of her counterpart as "schizophrenic," symmetry relations between them in the overdetermined sphere give the promise of temporality to come, for from one "schizophrenic oscillation" to a successive "oscillation," a certain increment of time has transpired in the mind of the onlooker.
3. In the schematic summary that follows, I do not wish to do violence to Quine's elaborate philosophical thesis. My aim is, rather, to illustrate how it is germane to the general cultural view I am attempting to present for your consideration.
4. The hypothesis is that by communicating in the Quine manner, all concerned parties will eventually be comfortable with their world. This is somewhat comparable, I might point out in passing, to Donald Davidson's (1984) appropriation of what is called the "principle of charity" (for further, Evnine 1991, Norris 1985).

5.   It bears mentioning at this juncture that Putnam's thought experiment is inspired by what in logic is called the "Löwenheim-Skolem theorem" demonstrating that in formal language, specifically first-order logic, a finite model opens itself up to an unforeseen number of possibilities, some of them mutually incompatible. The formal details are not necessary here since Putnam transfers the theorem from formal language to natural language (see, for example, Lakoff's [1987] rendition of Putnam's thought experiment with respect to everyday language use).

Chapter Ten

Feeling, Form, Fallibilism

> The border is the sea
> Blue, deep, dense
> Transparent, mysterious, deadly
> Shark infested
>
> —Luis Cruz Azaceta

> I'm Mexican, but also Chicano and Latin American. On the bor-
> der they call me *chilango* or *mexiquillo*; in Mexico City I'm a *po-
> cho* or *norteño*; and in Europe I'm a *sudaca*. Anglos call me
> "Hispanic" or "Latino," and Germans have at times taken me for
> a Turk or an Italian.
>
> —Guillermo Gómez-Peña

The "Popular"

Unfortunately, much of today's parlance in the humanities has it that identity arises
out of the contradictory struggle of power and resistance to power. This agonistic
duality is couched in a discourse of *otherness*. One side negates the other side, and
vice versa, in an eternal, dualistic set of fakes and feints and moves and counter-
moves and jabs and hooks, and if a rare knock-out punch is delivered, the winner
then confidently goes out in search of another antagonist (Laclau and Mouffe
1985:125).

This is a simple enough logic, a binary one-on-one affair, it would seem. But it
is a far cry from a genuine "logic of difference" capable of expanding binary logic
into a field of increasing complexity (Laclau and Mouffe 1985:130). Binary logic is
a necessity, however. Without division of the overdetermined sphere of undivided
vagueness (Firstness, homogeny—from Figure 6) into something and something
else, there could hardly be anything at all. But there is always at least something,
from the very moment in history when the first cell set itself apart from what it was
not: the entire remainder of the universe (Maturana and Varela 1980). Then comes
the agonistic duality (Secondness, hegemony); then comes successive differentiation
(Thirdness, into the underdetermined, general, incomplete sphere, heterogeny),
where, given the dispersal of differences, adjustments must constantly be made in
order to allow for the integration of complexity. When this complexity becomes so
inordinately labyrinthine, so unbearably stupefying, that a critical mass is reached
and the whole concoction implodes into proliferating overdetermined cultural manifestations, then the initiary binary act can once again come into play, and the familiar
game of comfortable "logical differences" recommences.

Regrettably, even this process is often taken as a play of binarism. Granted, this "agonistic logic" is in the beginning a "specular logic" of one thing and its respective *other*, which is constructed as inversion, bilateral symmetry, a reciprocal action-reaction scheme. If left at that, there would be no more than a Secondary master/slave struggle. The subservient party would fantasize counteridentification with the dominant party, and if the tables were turned, then what was at the bottom would now be at the top and what was at the top would now be at the bottom, and the agonistics would go on much as before. A populist program thus provides pseudorepresentation of the have-nots with the haves, which can give the appearance that all is fine with the world (much as was the case of Reaganism and Thatcherism during the 1980s). Ernesto Laclau's (1977) forming years in Argentina included Peronism, populism Latin American style, which is considerably less predictable and unstable. Laclau attempts to redefine Peronist complexity by distinguishing between one form of populism from the perspective of the haves and another populism from the perspective of the have-nots. There is as a consequence no genuine middle ground, no place for alternatives of the "grue," "gavagai," "cats*," "Guadantzín," "compey," or any combination of a virtual infinity of other alternatives sort. There is no legitimate overdetermined vagueness or underdetermined generality.

By way of this sort of thinking, Laclau and Mouffe, and indeed, I fear, many scholars of the Birmingham school of cultural studies, conceive of society in terms of relatively fixed class relations. The overdetermined sphere in a sense tends to become superdetermined upon its division into a hierarchically edified set of dualisms. Yet, these dualisms can take on superdetermination chiefly because they are predicated on an avowed nonessentialist doctrine of class as an abstraction or generality that has lost its footing in the semiotically "real" world of polylogical, differential give-and-take. According to this give-and-take, every move can be negotiable and is often negotiated, since it is by its very nature polyvalent.[1] A Michael Jordan T-shirt worn by the peasant of Michoacán, Mexico selling his wares by using broken English to tourists in the marketplace is in strict binary terms an index of cultural imperialism. But at one and the same time the T-shirt is also a promise of modernity, a fusion of proclivities and tendencies that distort and alter the very practices of imperialism and modernity without the peasant's necessarily nurturing a single rebellious thought in his head. His concrete semiotic acts are not necessarily any more binary nor are they any less over- or underdetermined than the linguicentric act of taking emeralds as *either* "green" *or* "grue," as *both* "green" *and* "grue," or as *neither* "green" *nor* "grue" but something else. As far as the peasant is concerned, he is simply going about his daily play of differences with no further ado. He doesn't need to think the differences. He feels them, and acts accordingly. Whether or not he can tell us who Michael Jordan is, is of hardly any consequence. Michael Jordan is most likely for him just a vague icon (overdetermined, inconsistent) that indexes his entry to the marketplace, and all the tacitly produced differences (generalities that are underdetermined and incomplete) become whatever they may become, according to the context and whatever happens to be happening.

In this manner there is no difference that makes an absolutely determinate difference between imperialism and subalternity, haves and have-nots, dominant class and popular class, or even "high" culture and "low" culture (the difference, like the border of borders, is subject to the "sorites paradox"). Rather than binarily definable difference, there is just culture, with neither uppercase "C" nor lowercase "c," but rather, with a somewhat highlighted "c" that testifies to culture's processual, flow-like, intricately complex, perpetually transient character.[2] The untenable concept of popular culture, then, in John Frow's words, is:

> its structural opposition to high culture: a binarism which at once unifies and differentiates each domain. The category of popular culture has a unitary form, however, only as long as it is derived from a singular entity, 'the people'; otherwise it breaks down into a bundle of very heterogeneous forms and practices. Its appearance of unity is reinforced by the privileging of certain key examples: in the folkloric tradition it is the practices of song, dance, speech, and storytelling occurring outside commercial mediation that take this privilege; in cultural studies it is youth subcultures, which in practice means an exclusive focus on urban, public, and. . . male cultural forms" (Frow 1995:81–82; see, for a comparable view, McRobbie 1980, 1984).

An exclusively binary focus, in short, is a product of the incapacity or unwillingness to acquire a genuine spirit of difference.

And Its "Logic"

The upshot is that all signs point in the direction of some "alternate logic" regarding culture, and if I may say so, especially the cultures of Latin America. And this, in spite of the fact that many, if not most, interpretations of Latin America tend toward dualist thinking. For example, it appears that for Guillermo Bonfil Batalla (1996), to be Mexican is to be dualist. There is mainstream culture, the "imaginary" Mexico, which is pretty much an invention, the Mexico of modernity-modernism, the Mexico desired by the Porfiristas and by the post-Revolutionary *nouveaux riches*.[3] And there is "México profundo," the genuine Mexico, which is marginal. "México profundo" has no history; that is, its history is conveniently pushed under the rug. Since "México profundo" is considered to be "nonculture," its past is "nonhistory." National culture is the only culture worthy of its salt, according to "imaginary" Mexico. However:

> What has been proposed as national culture at different moments in Mexican history may be understood as a permanent aspiration to stop being what we are. It has always been a culture project that denies the historical reality of Mexican social origins. And it does not admit the possibility of building the future on the basis of reality. It is always a substitution project. The future is somewhere else, anyplace other than here, in this concrete, daily reality. Thus the task of constructing a national culture consists of imposing a distant, foreign model, which in itself will eliminate cultural diversity and achieve unity through the suppression of

what already exists. In this way of thinking about things, the majority of Mexicans have a future only on the condition that they
stop being themselves. That change is conceived as a definite
break, a transformation into someone else. It is never conceived
as bringing up to date through internal transformation, as liberating cultures that have been subject to multiple pressures during
five centuries of colonial domination. (Bonfil 1996:65)

This posture, Bonfil argues, is "schizophrenic." It has led to a fictitious state from
whose norms and everyday practices the majority of the population is excluded.
Otherwise, how can we explain the egalitarianism insisted upon by the nineteenth-
century liberals, which led directly to the consolidation of indentured servant relations on the *haciendas*? How do we explain anticlerical legislation converted into
fictional dead-letter laws, followed by a tacit agreement with the Church that negates
the spirit of the laws? We must admit to the existence of a great dominating fiction.
If not, how do we explain a system of democratic elections based on the recognition
of political parties as the only legitimate vehicles for electoral participation in a
country in which an absolute majority of the population does not effectively belong
to any party or exercise its right to vote? This "schizophrenic fiction" has had grave
consequences for Mexican life and culture that do not seem to worry the proponents
of the "imaginary" Mexico.

In the first place, it produces marginalization of the majority, of the "real" not
the "imaginary." The wealthy and powerful citizens of the Mexico that ought to exist
(Thirdness), but does not, have always been a minority. They have created their own
"imaginary" Mexico. The *others*, the "real" Mexico (Secondness repressed within
the sphere of Firstness as mere possibility) have always remained excluded by de-
cree. The proponents of "imaginary" Mexico do not recognize the existence of this
"real" Mexico but rather, they have set themselves the task of inventing their own
concept of the *others* of the "real" or "México profundo," and in a bogus, fictitious
way they put themselves at the service of these artificially fabricated *others*. Hence
the Mexican upper crust, "imaginary" Mexico, pays lip service to "México profundo," to the nation's pre-Hispanic past and the remnants of it carrying over into
the present. Yet they do their best to ignore it when engaging in the important matters of accumulating power and wealth and influencing friends and vanquishing foes.

A second consequence is that upon inventing "imaginary" Mexico, it becomes
well nigh impossible to recognize, appreciate, and stimulate development of the di-
versified cultural patrimony that history has placed in Mexican hands. Archaic colonial blindness regarding this patrimony remains, and it ignores the *other* Mexico,
"México profundo." If the *other* Mexico is to be avoided, an alternative culture (the
dominant Mexico) must be invented as a surrogate for the existing nonculture (of
dominated Mexico). The elements that ought to constitute the core of this new invented culture are not present in nonculture. It is a question, then, of "substituting for
reality instead of transforming it" (Bonfil 1996:67). Hence invented culture becomes
an imitation of European models, and "México profundo's" cultural patrimony
passes into oblivion in the minds of those who inhabit invented culture. "México
profundo" is considered useless, of no account. It is as if generation after generation

of people had taken a mistaken path, and as if their entire history, in the eyes of invented or "imaginary" Mexico, were no history at all. It was an aberration, something irrational and illogical. And now, it is dead weight that must be thrown off in order that Mexico can become modernized.

"México profundo" of the have-nots is the vagueness that has become actualized, but it is not really actualized. That is, it is not considered "really real" by the haves. It is a virtually silent, virtually invisible, yet omniscient reminder of that which according to the haves should be pressed out of the national life of the country. It is there, yet it is not there, or at least it shouldn't be there. It is Secondness, but a Secondness that is ignored, hidden away in the closet in hopes that diplomats, CEOs from the U.S. and Europe, and tourists from all over the globe will not notice it—except for those exotic representatives in the shops weaving sarapes and making other quaint items for tourist consumption. In contrast, the "imaginary" Mexico—the presumed modern Mexico—is what should be or ought to be, according to the haves. It is generality made "real," that is, it is made "more real than the real." It is an artificial and hollow Secondness raised to a screaming pitch of generality as an "imaginary" or invented, not an actual, construct. It is Thirdness without the supporting cast of characters and the props of Secondness, but rather, it is like a Samuel Beckett virtually empty stage that the audience must create by a sheer act of imagination. This is no genuine Thirdness but sham Thirdness, a merely imaginary Firstness that was conjured up while refusing to accept the Firstness of the genuine article, Mexico's cultural heritage. That imaginary Firstness was then jump started as Thirdness by an alien model—via modernism-modernity—that bore little resemblance to the genuine article. There is, in this manner, a convenient attempt to snuff out genuine Secondness ("México profundo"). In a manner of speaking, this genuine Secondness is seen, but it is not really seen, it is not seen *as* the *other* Mexico nor is there any seeing *that* it has such-and-such a set of attributes. "Imaginary" Mexico supposedly *is* the one and only Mexico. Hence, in a manner of speaking, invented Mexico, the fabricated *others*, becomes what is "real" on no uncertain terms, as if to say, "swans" *are* "white" and nothing but "white," "gavagais" *are* for certain "rabbits," emeralds can under no circumstances be *anything but* "green," "cats" *are* "cats," and that's that. There are no possibilities other than those dictated by "imaginary" Mexico, which has pushed its way to the surface to become a sham "reality," artificial Thirdness.

"Imaginary" Mexico is definitely the product of modernity's disenchantment of the world. It is an abstract (imaginary forced into a bogus "reality") prioritization of the ocular; it is linear, symbolic, and metaphorical in the order of inscription and textuality; it is an obsession with mind over body; finally, it is an attempt to force heterogeny into a homogenous mold. In other words, it is diametrically opposed to "México profundo," which has persisted with a greater or lesser degree of success in its enchantment of the world. This Mexico, in contrast to "imaginary" Mexico, is concrete. It entails incorporation of signs of chiefly iconic and indexical nature, with a larger share of the spotlight allowed all the senses instead of the obsessive linguicentric, ocularcentric view of "imaginary" Mexico. It gives Firstness its deserved time by way of signs of the body, of homogeny. Unfortunately, the tendency toward legitimate heterogeny has been reduced to hegemony as a result of the pressures of "imaginary" Mexico. "Imaginary" Mexico is chiefly an *either/or* affair, while "México profundo" is *both* the one *and* the other and at the same time *neither* the profundo" is *both* the one *and* the other and at the same time *neither* the one *nor* the other, except when the hegemonic bullies of "imaginary" Mexico force it into its silent, disappearing act. "México profundo," I would suggest, is much like what Deleuze (1978) has to say of the minority as "woman becoming"—recall Tlöny's opening words—or what Deleuze and Guattari (1986) conceive as "minor literature." The dominant group is a hierarchical and relatively fixed system consisting of symmetrical relations of binary forces and counterforces. The minority—that is, numerically speaking, the majority—on the other hand, is nonhierarchical, heterogeneous, transient, asymmetrical, and *n*-ary or *rhizomic*. "Imaginary" Mexico is the dominant, what has been actualized as a result of something distinguished from something else; the minority is perpetually in the process of becoming, without the distinctions that make the "imaginary" the "imaginary." "México profundo," in this respect, is the becoming of that which is prevented from having become; it is the always already transient; yet in this respect it is always the same, for it cannot have already become. The idea of the majority does not entail the majority as majority in quantity, but in terms of the standard presumably to be emulated. The task of "México profundo," in the eyes of the quantitatively minute upper crust—which considers itself the majority, for those of "México profundo" aren't really Mexicans—is to modernize, become *gente de razón* (people of reason). They need to become respectable and dress and eat and talk and work and play like the modernized West. The minority is in a sense a sham borderless border, a placeless place of becoming; it is a crossover, a *neither-thisness-nor-thatness* of culture.

The *other* Mexico, "México profundo," the virtually silent and invisible, the marginalized majority-minority, the "real" in contrast to the "imaginary," or the nondisenchanted of the world, is incorporation more than inscription, bodymind rather than an imperious mind exercising hegemony over body and world. To tell their story, the citizens of "México profundo" must "resist deep-seated habits of mind and systems of authenticity."[4] They must "be suspicious of an almost-automatic tendency to relegate non-Western peoples and objects to the pasts of an increasingly homogeneous humanity" (Clifford 1990:162). In other words, non-Western peoples live in the *now, their now*, which incorporates their past and their assimilation and perhaps at the same time their "guerrilla" subversion of *our now*—recall the Michoacán market vendor sporting a Michael Jordan T-shirt. In this regard, James Clifford tells the tale told by Anne Vitart-Fardoulis, curator at the Musée de l'Homme in Paris, of the grandson of one of the Indians who had been in Paris with the Buffalo Bill entourage. There was an intricately painted animal skin probably originating among the Fox Indians of the United States, which was now used to educate aristocratic children who were told that they should admire it for its curious aesthetic qualities. They were to learn that its ethnographic importance rests in its combination of masculine and feminine graphic styles and their role in specific ceremonies. The grandson, of the native North American culture, was visiting Paris in an effort to locate the skin his grandfather had been forced to sell to pay his way back to the United States when the Buffalo Bill circus collapsed. Vitart-Fardoulis narrates:

> I showed him all the tunics in our collection, and he paused before one of them. Controlling his emotion, he spoke. He told the meaning of this lock of hair, of that design, why this color had been used, the meaning of that feather. . . . This garment, formerly beautiful and interesting but passive and indifferent, little by little became meaningful, active testimony to a living moment through the mediation of someone who did not observe and analyze but who lived the object and for whom the object lived. It scarcely matters whether the tunic is really his grandfather's. (in Clifford 1990:163)

Clifford goes on to tell us that whatever happened in this encounter, two things are definitely *not* happening. The grandson is not merely replacing the artifact in its "authentic" cultural setting, which belongs to a history long past and for the most part irretrievable. His encounter with the skin is a recollection in his present situation, which includes chiefly iconic signs as well as whatever indexical and symbolic signs are necessary to convey, however vaguely and however poorly, a linguistic and analytic articulation of what there was before him.

Moreover, the painted tunic is not taken as an aesthetic object; that is, it is not inscribed, symbolized, and linearized, in order to authenticate it within a modern context as a relic. No. It is enmeshed in family history, in ethnic memory. It is incorporated, and chiefly iconized; it retains its nonlinear qualities; it becomes charged with sentiment, Firstness, body meaning; it is no longer an inscribed aesthetic object, no Firstness as *simulacrum* without the proper accompanying feel. It is, in all its vagueness, authentic, not general. It is its own type of sign, not a sign that has been symbolically relegated to a certain category along with other signs, each to its own. There is an identity, a very personal and personalized identity, but no difference that makes this identity an identity only insofar as it is individualized and properly categorized in an artificial and partly arbitrary (symbolic) way and (indexically) set apart from other signs categorized in the same manner. The tunic became for the grandson an engendered sign, to be sure (the present of his ancestors had become future). But its engenderment was the product of sign de-engenderment re-engendered (which includes history, time), and then and only then could it have been properly felt. If it had been solely an engendered sign of symbolic inscription it could make its way into textbooks and museums. But the proper feel for it would not be there. Clifford concludes that:

> the dominant, interlocking contexts of art and anthropology are no longer self-evident and uncontested. There are other contexts, histories, and futures in which non-Western objects and cultural records may "belong." The rare Maori artifacts that in 1984–85 toured museums in the United States normally reside in New Zealand museums. But they are controlled by the traditional Maori authorities, whose permission was required for them to leave the country. Here and elsewhere the circulations of museum

collections is significantly influenced by resurgent indigenous communities. (Clifford 1990:163)

Here also, Gárcia Canclini's (1993, 1995) message springs to mind: Amerindians making sarapes for tourists in the curios marketplace, and the "authenticity" of the items and what they mean for the Amerindians and what they mean for the tourists (something to hang on the wall or place on the mantel to show off to guests in their home). The "authentic" item proudly displayed in a strategic spot where it will be seen by all is hardly more than a bastardized form. It is now, I'm sorry to say, comparable to a Baudrillard *simulacrum* taking its place among other *simulacra* in countless homes in the U.S., Europe, and Japan. It has been properly postmodernized. But actually, as such it is a rape of meaning. Ralph Coe's *Lost and Found Traditions* (1986) reflects this rape of meaning in Western cultures of temporally pregnant artifacts. His *tour de force* reveals that Western knowledge discovers "genuine" tribal art, which might once have been genuine, but is now something else. It has been hierarchized, homogenized, dichotomized. Hundreds of photographers visualize, historians historicize, archaeologists archaeologize, and it all ends up in trading shops, museums, and relatively affluent homes. Yet, all may not be entirely lost, Coe tells us. He questions the common notion that tribal art is disappearing, and he is skeptical of the means and methods for judging purity and authenticity. He shows how traditional kachina, totem poles, blankets, and plaited baskets that have retained a degree of authenticity can be found alongside skillfully beaded tennis shoes and baseball caps, decorated attaché cases, and other articles developed specifically for the curio trade. Clifford, also in this vein, points out that resourceful Native Americans "may yet appropriate the Western museum." Some of their old objects may again participate in a tribal present-becoming-future (Clifford 1990:164).

In this manner the Native Americans—including "México profundo" as discussed in the above paragraphs—can and should become "benign cultural guerrillas." They can mimic and at the same time they can mock. Bhabha (1994:86–87) writes that the colonized can take to mockery and virtually nothing but mockery. In such case they are hardly more than the *other* of the hegemonic binary sort. In contrast, if along with mockery there is mimicry, things become ambivalent. Mockery can be taken as mimicry, but from an alterior or subaltern position; mimicry can be taken as mockery, but from that nonalterior position. It might seem that we have no more than another binary. Not so, however. In their composite, mockery as mimicry is not what mimicry was but it is now something else, and the same can be said of mimicry as mockery. So the binary has been re-iterated by the $\sqrt{-1}$ function—from the border of borders—and it loses its binarity. Then it is re-iterated again, and again, and it becomes heterogenous plurality. The increasingly finer differences begin subverting the object, and the project—whatever it may be—always remains incomplete. In other words, we began in Firstness, the vagueness of the overdetermined, with mimicry—but not without an implicit tinge of inconsistency, and we entered Secondness with acknowledgment of the *one* and its *other*, then we found ourselves centrifuged toward Thirdness, the general as successive differences, the underdetermined.[5]

So, on speaking of our now quite familiar terms, let's return to the idea of an "alternate logic," which will eventually show itself to be, I would hope, preferable to what we have had to put up with all these years.

As an Alternative to the Alternatives

"Alternate cultural logic"? Perhaps it sounds provocative, even excessively so. Perhaps not. Perhaps at this stage you would like to toss this volume in the trashcan. Perhaps not. Either way, I would suggest that we really should unpack and finally relegate to the circular file the very notion of a monolithic good-for-all-reasons "singular binary logic," with a "singular mode of analysis," "style of reasoning," and a "set of norms" for all peoples and all cultures at all times and all places.

Let me begin this way. Cultural historian John Docker (1994:126) talks of "fields of force," somewhat reminiscent of Martin Jay's (1993) "force fields." This is a sort of "Janiform" two-face logic, which does violence to our customary logical categories. The problem is that the alternative for Jay and the Frankfurt School is, as one would expect, dialectical logic (Jay 1993:26–27). This entails contradictions for which there are noncontradictory syntheses at higher levels. Consequently, Jay argues against Rodolphe Gashé's (1986) Derridean analysis and Paul de Man's (1979) Nietzschean-Derridean interpretation of the aporetic function of language according to which contradiction exists at the level of nonlogical infrastructures that include traces, *différance, supplementarity, pharmakon, dissemination*, and so on, and so on. At these levels (the sphere of vagueness and overdetermination in conjunction with the sphere of generality and underdetermination) contradictions are inevitable. This entails, according to Jay, mutually exclusive points of view: "A is A" and "Not-A is Not-A," and never the twain shall meet, for the tain of the mirror of identity is inevitable. Jay and other critics of poststructuralist *aporias* and postmodernist hype are not willing to toss caution to the wind and boldly enter something comparable to Firstness and Thirdness as they have been presented in this inquiry. Embracing the implications of Firstness and Thirdness, and Secondness as well, we find ourselves engulfed in that now familiar—and frightening for some observers—semiosic cascade: we are hard pressed to avoid swirling eddies and whirlpools and get around jutting rocks and try, often futilely, to negotiate re-entry into the mainstream. However, this is, I would suggest, a quite genuine image of the process of "culturing"—I insist on "culturing," which includes *all* aspects of semiosis, in contrast to Mignolo's linguicentrically limited "languaging." It is more dynamic, more open, more nonlinear and asymmetrical, than any and all binary billings have had it.

Unfortunately, there is still, among many humanists and social scientists, a lingering incapacity to shed traditional modes and methods and eschew some of the fetters of modernity. If we could just learn to take a back seat to some turn of the century philosophers and mathematicians the likes of Pierre Duhem (1954) and Henri Poincaré (1952), we might see our way to tenuous yet mentally and socially liberating terrain. Duhem and Poincaré were in general agreement that virtually an infinity of different and at times mutually exclusive perspectives, geometries, and physical laws can be made to account for the same set of presumably objective facts. And one of these perspectives, geometries, and laws is capable, within its particular context, of laying as just a claim to the title of "truth" as any other perspective, geometry, or law. Moreover, Niels Bohr reiterated time and again that the universe, when taken as a whole, cannot but show a Janiform countenance: it is radically inconsistent, or in the terms I have occasionally used, it is incongruously complementary. Quantum theory since the time of Bohr serves to bear him out (Folse 1985, Honner 1987). It is all a strange extrapolation of the Einstein dictum: things in motion dictate how space-time must curve; curved space-time dictates how things must move— somewhat metaphorically like Mavrits Escher's hand drawing a second hand that is drawing the first hand. It is Heraclitus's saying about the road which goes either up or down; it all depends upon which direction you decide to take. There might be some truth to relativity after all. I write this not in regard to a sort of Einsteinian relativity that is predicated on the most absolute of absolutes, the velocity of light. Rather, I allude to the inevitability of taking the road to relativity once one contemplates the nature of thought and of the universe, of the mind and of the body, to a sufficient degree (see Margolis 1991). After such contemplation, customary logical imperatives and the idea of one and only one legitimate mode of analysis and style of reasoning simply break down.

Allow me to encapsulate this breakdown with a lemma: There's virtuality, virtuosity, and virtue in the possible middle term between the horns of every dilemma. That is to say, the middle term emerges from the border of borders to throw neat pigeonholes into disarray. But this middle term itself contains the wherewithal for its own disintegration into many terms, and hence its demise. First there is the virtual, the vague, the overdetermined, and possibly the radically inconsistent and contradictory element of Firstness. Then, for better or for worse, there is virtuosity (Secondness), the exercise of dichotomous imperatives, the construction of twin towers of hierarchized value-laden oppositions. And finally there are the whirlpools of virtue through difference, which entail generality, underdetermination, and complementarity, that is, Thirdness. And all this by the judicious use of technique, style. This entire package, which includes the vague and the inconsistent and the general along with difference, is destined in a world of fallible semiotic subjects to remain incomplete. Thus rather than undying faith in eternal "truths," smug certainties, unlimited power, and arrival at the end of the epistemological rainbow—delusions all!—we have acknowledgment of finitude, fallibilism, limitations, temporality, uncertainty, the ever-not-quite arriving, the ubiquitousness of struggle.

With this in mind, I'll push hopefully on the path toward an alternate conception of cultural things.

Tempestuous Times

Chilean artist Roberto Matta made a move from surrealism to more cerebral art and a search for a style of reasoning that might reason the unreasonably new, or in the terms of this inquiry, a search for a "logic of vagueness and difference." In particular, *Storming the Tempest* (1982), a series of drawings based on William Shakespeare's *Tempest*, depicts Latin America's relationship with the West's modernity, from the time of the conquest and colonialism. Matta reveals that the presumed opposition between the European Prospero and the Native American savage, Caliban, or between Caliban and his indigenous counterpart, Ariel the otherworldly dreamer, or between Prospero and Ariel, loses its definition in that cultural mish-mash we call colonial Latin America (Baddeley and Fraser 1989:107–08).

The cultural importance of Shakespeare's work has been duly acknowledged among Latin American intellectuals, especially since the appearance of José Enrique Rodó's *Ariel* (1948 [1900]). Decades before Rodó's day, Latin American intellectuals, in directing their attention to the area's problems, blamed the cycles of anarchy and tyranny in their newly independent nations on Hispanic influences. Writers of the particular mold of Domingo Faustino Sarmiento, influenced by social Darwinism, also diagnosed many of the evils of their countries as a product of the "melting pot" consisting of variegated mixes of *peninsulares*, *criollos*, Amerindians, African Americans, and *mestizos* and *mulatos*. One of the most common solutions was to encourage racial miscegenation in order to "whiten" society. Rodó, foremost intellectual of Uruguay, the most European ("white") of all Latin American nations, completely turned the tables. He argued that the problem was not Spanish America's Hispanic heritage at all. Rather, it was due chiefly to the influence of that Colossus of the North, the United States, whose rampant materialism should be shunned in favor of the morally superior spiritual and intellectual values the Hispanic tradition had to offer. Availing himself of Shakespeare's *Tempest*, Rodó cast Prospero the colonizer in the role of United States materialist values, and that cloudy soul for whom life is a dream, Ariel, as the prototype of Spanish American cultural values. Now Sarmiento's "barbarism" becomes the U.S., and "civilization" remains in the hands of Spanish Americans. That is, "civilization" remains in the hands of the cultured (imaginary?) minority of Spanish Americans, those who had not yet been transformed by the subcontinent's "barbarous" physical reality. And North Americans become a counterpart to the *gauchos* and provincial tyrants of Sarmiento's *Facundo*, "materialist barbarians." It was hoped that cultural independence, if not economic independence, had finally come to the subcontinent.[6]

It perhaps bears mentioning that Rodó had a kindred spirit in Waldo Frank of the U.S. Frank believed the materialist strain in this country was not morally uplifting but inherently corrupt and corrupting, and argued against the influence of purely economic incentives. Frank's portentous, hyperbolic writing style and his inflated vision of himself did not exactly ingratiate him with his North American audience, though it did with a considerable number of admirers south of the border. His book, *The Re-Discovery of America* (1929), was by no means a best seller in the U.S., but, after the onslaught of the Great Depression when Frank turned increasing attention to Central and South America, it was quite widely read there. If serving no other purpose, Frank's strange story gives evidence that not all was of the nature of Prospero in the United States. Perhaps most of it was, and as an Arielist himself, Frank was closer to the Spanish American mind-set than to that of his own compatriots, which helps account for his popularity there and his inability to capture the lime light here (Pike 1992:149–56, Stabb 1967:67–78).

More recent writers have stressed that there are plenty of historical precedents for the Caliban image instead of the Ariel image regarding the colonized, exploited, brutalized, Native American, the displaced African, and the *mestizos* and *mulatos*, that is, the *others* of Latin America. What in current jargon goes by the name of alterity, the *other*, was, during the time of the conquest and colonization, looked upon as those *others* whose membership to the human race was at the outset questioned. Later, these *others* were classified in opposition to the *gente de razón*, the Europeans. Moreover, they were often placed in linguistic pigeonholes that shared an affinity with epithets depicting monstrosity. The *other* became "monstrous," that is, like the invention of America, the Amerindians' and African Americans' "monstrosity" was invented, imagined. The image of the "monstrous" became the image of America and Americans, from the very beginning. This went hand-in-hand with Columbus's and other discoverers' and explorers' inventing Cyclops, mermaids, Amazons, half-human and half-animal beasts, and above all, the despicable cannibal: that is, Caliban, alias the anthropophagic "monster," the Cannibal (Baudot 1996:15–41).[7] This is precisely Roberto Fernández Retamar's (1989 [1972]) celebrated and at times maligned re-interpretation of Rodó's dichotomy after taking inspiration from Cuban writer and revolutionary José Martí's "Nuestra América" ("Our America") (1977 [1891]). Sarmiento and his gang and Rodó with his turnabout were all cop-outs, we read in Fernández Retamar's essay. The genuine Spanish American symbol is not Ariel at all, but Caliban.

In this interpretation, Caliban was the colonized and enslaved and Prospero was the colonizer, whether in the form of the Peninsular empires or the Colossus of the North, the United States. That, more precisely, is the image that depicts the many generations of political and economic exploitation and racist social policies. However, this revised interpretation plays havoc with the nineteenth-century Latin American intellectuals' attitude. In terms of their dislike of literary realism, European style, it would be either as if they were like Caliban looking at himself in the mirror and seeing his own face or like Ariel looking at himself in the mirror and not seeing his own face. In light of their dislike of literary Romanticism, European style, it would be as if they were Ariel looking at himself in the mirror and not seeing his own face or Caliban looking at himself in the mirror and seeing his own face. Either way, the Caliban image wins hands down, and Ariel disappears in the mist. (Isn't this amazing? Talk about "green" emeralds becoming "grue," "cats" becoming "cats[*]," "Guadalupe" becoming "Guadantzín," "Gavagai" taking on many possible meanings, and other quandaries! Talk about the plurality of seeing, seeing *as*, and seeing *that*, and of focal and subsidiary awareness! Talk about the passively violent, the violently passive, ebullient, effusive, scintillating activity at the border of borders! Talk about the codependent emerging of myriad multiplicities from "emptiness"! Pluricultures like those of Latin America have known about all this all along. They are the spitting image *of* it, they *live* it, they *are* it.)

One problem with this revised view of the Shakespearean trope is that it plays loose and fast and dangerous with the Latin Americans' stereotype of the United States, which is epitomized by the aristocratic Don Fermín in Vargas Llosa's *Conversations in the Cathedral* (1974:259 [1969]), who says of the North Americans: "I'll never understand the gringos, don't they seem like little children to you? . . . Half-savages besides. They put their feet on the desk, take off their jackets, wherever they are." As far as Don Fermín is concerned, the *gringos* need a massive dose of etiquette. It is they who are the barbarians, Caliban incarnate. The Spanish Americans—the cultured ones, of course—are Ariel. But this is typically the view of the *gente decente*, those whose culture is respectable, imported from Europe. There are also the *others* (including "México profundo" and its counterpart in other Latin American countries), whose culture, whatever that may be, is "barbarous." On the other side of the coin, the U.S. had its own Arielist turn during the early part of this century in the form of Waldo Frank and others (Pike 1992:193–220).[8] Another problem is that José Martí, Sarmiento, Rodó, Fernández Retamar, and the likes to a degree remain imbued in dichotomies, in the dipolar thought of classical (Aristotelian-Eurocentric) logic, reason, and thought. All of which cannot help but end in stereotypes. Sarmiento, Martí, and the earlier proponents of civilization/barbarism and Ariel/Prospero remain with a foot caught in a Rousseau-style romanticism. In contrast, the likes of Fernández Retamar and one of his leading spokespersons, José David Saldívar (1990, 1992), as well as Niel Larsen (1991) and others, are either taken in by some form of dialectical materialism, binarist hegemony theory, or one of various other dichotomizing or quasidichotomizing schemes.

Actually, a reading of *The Tempest* by Dominique O. Mannoni's *Prospero and Caliban* (1956) reveals that the play, written when England was beginning to take an interest in the exotic lands overseas, depicts the theme of colonialism. It becomes evident that Prospero is no benign philosopher-king in the mold of other plays of the time. He is a paranoid colonial ruler who is threatened by every overture suggesting that his authority is something less than total, and that the "cultural" guerrillas may ultimately have their way. Consequently, his frail daughter Miranda, and the good slave Ariel and the bad slave Caliban, must constantly render him complete submission. Caliban is the brute he seems to be because he is seen through the eyes of Prospero, and Ariel is the noble and faithful servant as seen through those same eyes. Richard Morse even goes so far as to suggest:

> We have simply assumed that [Caliban] is uneducable, that he must hew wood forever. Perhaps, though, he already has no education of a "native" sort. Perhaps he did not try to rape Miranda but was the victim of Prospero's incest fantasies. We realize with a start that we do not really *know* Caliban. In the new version Prospero becomes the prosperous United States (with Ariel the magic wand of technology?), and Latin America becomes Caliban, the Caliban whom nobody knows, with whom Prospero loses patience, and whom he legislates to be an "undeveloped" brute. As in *The Tempest*, Prospero pities Caliban, takes pains to make him speak, teaches him "each hour one thing or another." (Morse 1989:170) (brackets added)

In other words, Caliban can be read as the monster-slave, the grotesquely deformed African made over into a slave in America. He can also be read as the monster-native, the brutalized Amerindian, and the half-breed offspring of the Spanish conquerors and colonizers and both of the *other* races. However, that was the Caliban invented and then transformed by Prospero. It was not, we now suspect, the real Caliban. Caliban once told Prospero: "You taught me language." But actually, Prospero couldn't—or at least wouldn't—have lowered himself to have conversed for long with his unruly slave without first imposing his own language on him, for the language of that unkempt *other* he considered barbarous, monstrous, inadequate, and incompatible with proper reason and logic. In this manner, the injunction is: "A! (language 'A,' my language, and you'd better learn it, for it is the only viable language, the language of culture)." This creates a conflict: is there really another (an *other*) language? Does Caliban-Latin-America really have a culture? To ask such questions, Fredric Jameson (1989:x) observes, is to already have "recognized the cultural superiority of the colonizer." How, he asks, could Caliban know anything but how to curse in this strange language imposed upon him?

However, that does not tell the whole tale. Caliban's words to Prospero, "You taught me language" and "I know how to curse," implies opposition or contradiction. It also implies "culturally guerrillerized" speaking against that which has been forced upon one. At the same time it implies difference, the difference of successive generalization of the antagonisms such that they become not contradictions but finer and finer differences finally to become complementarities, incongruous complementaries. The *tempest* brought about as a result of the West's disenchantment of the world and the utopian image of progress and prosperity (Prospero) reaped its havoc on Caliban's ecologically balanced but natural sphere of existence, which was due to its very nature considered "barbarous" and even "monstrous." The naturally enchanted order is ritual, tribal knowledge, fetishism, and magic. In contrast, the culturally disenchanted order is reason, technological knowledge, manufacturing, and marketing. The one is logical—according to classical tenets—and it is purportedly governed by the only viable reason; the *other* is an illogical style of reasoning. The one is predominantly linguistic, signs of symbolicity, morphophonemic and syntactic and semantic; the *other* is radically extralinguistic, hence it can lend itself to "guerrilla" activity. But this activity is suppressed insofar as that may be possible. This is revealed in Caliban's remark that his dubious gain was that he was taught language, Prospero's language. However, in the process of learning Prospero's language, he suffered the loss of signs of Firstness and of extralinguistic Thirdness, signs of soma, of the body, whose knowing is coterminous with the mind's knowing. These are signs of bodymind: bodymindsigns.

Caliban's extralinguistic posture, in Houston Baker's conception, consists in:

> *superliteracy*, it is a maroon or guerrilla action carried out *within* linguistic territories of the erstwhile masters, bringing forth *sounds* that have been taken for crude hooting, but which are, in reality, racial poetry. . . . [It invades] the linguistic territories of traditional . . . "masters" . . . What rises before Caliban is not a cursed status but rather a realization that his situation in a simple iconography forestalls a just reading of his "natural" situation. (Baker 1985:394)

But, of course, Prospero is also a magician. Like Newton, he is one of the "last of the magicians." His magic is also like the ice and other marvels of culture and technology introduced by those magicians of nature, the gypsies, into Macondo in García Márquez's *One Hundred Years of Solitude*. Prospero is in the eyes of Ariel and Caliban a magician proper, but the modern Prospero is not doing magic at all. At least he thinks his activity is far from the primitive innocence of magic. As far as he is concerned, he is doing science. Thus there is no real Ariel-Caliban polarity: both are Prospero's slaves. Ariel is the creature of the air, the dreamer, the child-intellectual trapped within his ethereal prison; Caliban is the deformed one whose island is forced from him and he is enslaved. Nor is there any real Ariel-Prospero or Caliban-Prospero duality: all are in their own right magicians of sorts. Codependent with and enchanted with the signs of their world, they are interrelated with them, and they interactively participate with them. They are all products of their signs and their signs are of their own invention.

There are, then, no legitimate dichotomies in our trio of characters, but rather, signs of incongruous complementarity, signs of myriad differences, of vagueness becoming actuality becoming generality, of overdetermination becoming incompletely realized, but not without a dash of inconsistency. They are all in that unfathomable sea of semiosis together, and cannot know which way is up and which way down, which is forward and which is backward, or where the beginning or where the ending is. In comparable fashion, Spivak (1985:264) reminds us that we pompous cultured folk of the intelligentsia have a little of Caliban in all of us, as well as our having cultivated a touch of Ariel. This is to say that we are, all of us, within the hallowed halls of academia, and in one way or another whether we like it or not, coparticipants with the world, as is Prospero.

Prospero's Caliban is a cannibal and Caliban's Prospero is the proprietor, to be sure. But Prospero is also there to be "culturally guerrillerized." Caliban was limited by Prospero's language and was thus in large part reduced to *balbuceos* (stammering, stuttering, mumbling, tongue-tied faltering, and hesitation). Caught up in this linguistic straitjacket, he could hardly hope to become Prospero's equal. He could never say in Prospero's language: "Not-A! (language 'A,' your language, is not the only viable language, it is the language of *your* culture but not of *my* culture)." So he was destined to inferior status, to his being colonized, whether by Prospero or some other disenchanted "magician" (Zea 1988:27–35). And yet, Prospero and Ariel and Caliban, though unequal regarding language, are equals in the sense that, as I have suggested, they are all suspended within semiosis. Classical logic simply does not prevail here. It does not prevail, in the first place, because Prospero and Ariel and Caliban are incompatibles inconsistently thrown into the same semiosic mess of Firstness. In the second place, Caliban is, implicitly, in the sense of the "México profundo" image, *both* what he is *and* he is not what he is. So it is *neither* the case that he is what he is *nor* that he is not what he is. The *Both-And* and the *Neither-Nor* are there, and they are not there, they are suppressed within the sphere of overdetermination, Firstness. The same can be said of the *other* side of Prospero and Ariel. It can be said of our trio of actors on the flowing stage of semiosis, because they are perpetually in the process of defining themselves. They are already becoming somebody else. They are radically transient. Consequently, the interrelated trio is codependently emerging at each and every moment.

In another way of putting it, if Prospero is the sign having emerged from the *other*, the "real," then Caliban is that *other* that made it possible for Prospero to be Prospero, and Ariel is of the nature of Caliban for they are both slaves. But Ariel is also of the order of Prospero, for he is a good slave and properly mirrors his master—at least in the master's eyes. It might appear that Ariel the vague is First and Caliban the dichotomized is Second and Prospero the intervening mediator is Third in terms of the semiotic variations taken as metaphors. However, put them into spiraloid movement, and the semiosic whirlpool gyrates down the stream a bit. And, . . . what do you know? Caliban has now become the model for which Prospero is an image. For Caliban as a "cultural" guerrilla has given his master a quick jab in the ribs with a cynical twist but with an ingratiating smile which for a fleet moment wins the favor of the master, in spite of himself. Re-enter Ariel who now displaces Caliban, and as the good slave, it is soon he who basks in the light of the master's favorable nod, while Caliban is for the moment relegated to the background. Then attention is turned to Prospero once again, who barks out an order to Caliban that he conform to the master's every wish. And so on. Secondness (semiotic object) becomes Firstness (representamen, sign) and Firstness in turn becomes Secondness (object), which with a whorl translates itself into Thirdness (interpretant), then in the blink of an eye Thirdness (interpretant) gyrates toward and merges once more with Firstness (representamen) upon pushing Firstness (representamen) once again to Secondness (object). That is to say, "A" is what it is and it is "Not-A," and it is "*Both* A *and* Not-A," and it is "*Neither* A *nor* Not-A." This is tantamount to "grue" and "green" and "Gavagai!" as timelessly many things and "cats" that are "cats*" and so on and so on all over again, and again.

How can we find our way out of this labyrinth? In desperation I turn to a few more words on the nitty-gritty of Latin American cultural history.

Notes

1.   With due respect, Laclau and Mouffe (1985:3) point out that a "logic of hegemony," if such a logic there may be, must surely be tantamount a "logic of incongruous complementarity," much in the way I have used the term here. It would be a "logic of necessity," to be sure, but not a "logic of determinacy." It would focus on indeterminacy, spontaneity (and here, their break with orthodox Marxism) (Laclau and Mouffe 1985:3, 25, 36–7). In short, we read that if society "is not sutured by any single unitary and positive logic, our understanding of it cannot provide that logic. A 'scientific' approach attempting to determine the 'essence' of the social would, in actual fact, be the height of utopianism" (Laclau and Mouffe 1985:143). John Docker (1994:116–18) writes of Jameson's totalizing and essentializing the social in his view of the postmodern breakdown of high/low cultural distinctions. However, I have problems with this and comparable armchair speculation which can so lightly make a distinction between van Gogh's peasant shoes of referentiality and Warhol's nonreferential "diamond dust" shoes among other "floating signifiers." This is much like the omniscient eye of Baudrillard: he seems to know, from the detached confines wherein he is privy to a God's-eye perspective, everything there is to know about the "consciousness" of the masses of postmodern humanity. Even Mattelart and Dorfman (1975) can be accused of comparable presumptions (see Ernest Gellner's [1992] elaborate argument).

2.   Even Mikhail Bakhtin is guilty of essentializing binary practices (Lodge 1990:89–90) (however, see Allon White [1993:8–10] on selected nonbinarist aspects of Bakhtin).

3.   The "Porfiristas" were those who supported Porfirio Díaz, president from 1876 to 1880 and from 1884 to the outbreak of the Mexican Revolution in 1910.

4.   In this sense the story of "México profundo" is much in the order of that of testimonial literature which has recently entered the spotlight of academia, a few examples of which will be presented in chapter fourteen.

5.   I should at this juncture point out that my conception of overdetermination as nary, rhizomic, as pure possibility, with all the inconsistencies implied, is quite unlike the relatively binary notion of overdetermination in Althusser (1990) and Balibar (1991). Yet insofar as they allude to the interrelationship of inconsistency, indeterminacy, and overdetermination, they move in the direction of an alternative to the usual binary imperatives (see also Reed 1996).

6.   Ironically, as Frederick Pike (1992:314–16) argues, President John F. Kennedy was so popular in Latin America for, among other reasons, his and Jackie's "Arielist" nature embodied in the "American Camelot" image that went completely against the grain of Rodó's stamping the U.S. with a "Prospero" image.

7.   In this respect see Beverley's (1993:1–22) cute word play on Lacan and Caliban and Cannibal, which, while offering a few moments of linguistic charm far from the dirt and sweat of the actual physical world, does not deliver the expected food for thought regarding Latin America.

8.   There were also the English exiles, epitomized by D. H. Lawrence's grand utopian regeneration of the world and Malcolm Lowry's infatuation with México mágico.

Chapter Eleven

When the World Is Not What It Is

> When I think of my own people, the only people I can think of as my own are transitionals, liminals, border-dwellers, "world" — travelers, beings in the middle of either/or.
>
> —María Lugones

> The U. S.-Mexican border *es una herida abierta* where the Third World grates against the first and bleeds. And before scab forms it hemorrhages again, the lifeblood of two worlds merging to form a third country—a border culture.
>
> —Gloria Anzaldúa

On What Has Become What It Is Not

Perhaps no two Brazils have been more fashioned than found, more a matter of im-position than an internalization of what there is, than the accounts put forth in Euclides da Cunha's masterpiece, *Rebellion in the Backlands* (1944 [1902]), and Gilberto Freyre's *The Masters and the Slaves* (1946 [1933]), from among other of his works.

Rebellion in the Backlands affords an image of a Darwinian dog-eat-dog world where the fittest, those of modern Brazil, wreak destruction on what they consider the "barbarians," the dispossessed *others*, immersed in their atavistic, fetishistic, fa-natical, marginalized way of life. These are the *sertanejos*, who inhabit the hinter-land of the state of Bahia in northeastern Brazil. The uncertainties of this part of the country, with its periods either of torrential rains or no rain at all, allow a precarious life-style at best. The people's stark existence cultivated a natural propensity for a group of them to flow along with the ravings of a maddened buffoon, "Prophet" Antônio Conselheiro. The Prophet's apocalyptic vision soothed insecure minds and gave them hope of eternal rest beyond the pain and suffering of this world. He led his people to the promised land where they found their City of God, Canudos. Canu-dos was no more than a chaotic disarray of mud huts surrounding a grotesque church, where the people were destined to engage in mortal combat against what they conceived as Babylon, that sinful worldly republic, Brazil, which was certainly condemned to fire and brimstone. The Brazilian army, after many setbacks, finally managed to annihilate this ethnic and racial concoction of Europeans and Amerindians, with a tinge of Africa, as part of a ruthless campaign inspired by the positivist philosophy of Auguste Comte. The young Brazilian nation thus presumably succeeded in rooting out those "primitive" elements within its very soul so as to make way for modernization, Western style. The army's destruction of Canudos was total, recalling the original Spanish demolition force wreaking havoc on the Aztecs' Tenochtitlán according to the Amerindian testimonials in León-Portilla's *The Broken Spears* (1962 [1959]). "Civilized" Brazil on the coast became a delirious mob taking on the countenance of a carnivalesque atmosphere when they greeted the puffed, severed head of the Prophet, a trophy the army brought back as testimony of the "superior" forces of Western material development. Yes, progress and modernization, at whatever cost.

Freyre's *The Masters* is a neo-romantic appraisal of idyllic Brazilian sugar plantation life, of the Big House and the minuscule shanties (slave quarters). In Freyre's view, the patriarchal lord is a father figure to the African, literally as a result of his lustfully ravishing the young slave girls and figuratively through the benign paternalistic and hierarchical relations between him and those who were, in his conception, born to serve. The amorous liaisons and patristic human interaction engendered a hybrid new world in the tropics, a civilization such as the world had never before experienced. We are given ribald tales of masters "whitening"—and therefore in their conception "improving"—the race of the servants and taking their *mulato* offspring in as their own in huts separate from the regular slave quarters to initiate a racial spectrum of successively finite differentiation. In this manner, the inevitable sadomasochistic relation between master and slave is buffered by the former's deep sense of compassion for those who allow him the wherewithal for realizing his dreams of becoming a lord, a person of respect, of authority, and someone upon whom other lesser human beings depend and to whom they owe their very existence. The customary antagonisms and cruelty found in slave societies throughout history become, for Freyre in Brazil, a culture of conciliation and tolerance, of inclusion rather than exclusion, of mutual understanding rather than conflict, of harmoniously complemented cultural tendencies and proclivities rather than simply the imposition of the dominant culture and an attempt to emasculate the subordinate culture. Freyre seems to believe Brazil achieved a genuine "racial democracy," "one of the most harmonious unions of culture with nature and of one culture with another that the lands of this hemisphere [and indeed, the nations of the world] have ever known" (1956:xii) (brackets added).

Da Cunha's Brazil is a brutal juggernaut, confrontational and violent. There needs be the destruction of the subservient, who are ill suited for "order and progress," by the dominant. An inevitable furious clash of races follows. Ethnocentricities arise from a conflict of values and ways of life. Passions are raised to a screaming pitch in an eternal dualistic conflict between intransigent cultures with horns irremediably locked—as if they inhabited incommensurable worlds of the cat/cat* or green/grue mold. It is a matter of unequal contingencies that can neither mix with nor decipher one another, so one must be either absorbed or it is destined to disappear altogether.[1] Freyre's Brazil is a fertile, consonant amalgam, the product of a conciliatory, peace-loving people who have forged a "racial democracy" out of the cultural wilderness. There is a harmonious state of conviviality, with everybody working, copulating, dancing, and feasting together when social mores so permit, and when not, in separation but with a harmonious, empathetic nod toward one another.

When at its best it is an idyllic Dionysian frenzy of passions that are satiated in a meeting of the sexes and of ethnicities. This is a union of unequal counterparts who cannot avoid each other but who can merge to find mutual understanding. All told, in Freyre's neo-romantic view it is a *both-and* interrelationship in contrast to the *either/or* of da Cunha. But overall, the whole affair becomes *neither-nor*: there is in the final analysis *neither* the one culture *nor* the other, but something else entirely.[2]

The positivist Brazilian regime following the Auguste Comtean positivist slogan of "Order and Progress" proudly displayed on the national flag saw the adversaries of Canudos who blindly followed the Counselor as barbarians counteracting reason, as primitive peoples impeding the inevitable march of modernity. Rather than pursuing the progressive ideal of private property, they practiced communal ownership of land; rather than erecting a well-oiled social machine, they were an unconscious brute mass the individuals of which were without specialized functions. They continued to grow, with neither rhyme nor reason, rather than evolve in orderly fashion. Each period of growth was hardly more than an unruly juxtaposition of successive layers in the manner of a polyp. It was spontaneous, purposeless growth, from the view of Darwinian, biological positivism. It was without evolutionary principles and impossibly rationally or logically to account for, hence it must be expunged from the official organ like a "malignant disease" (Cunha 1975:149). Da Cunha sees the action as the product of madness on the part of the government, a madness that can be seen only as the obsession with annihilating that which does not fit into the Comtean-Brazilian mold. Canudos was inconsistent, paradoxical, unkempt, unruly, chaotic. It couldn't be ignored, for it was a cancer feeding on society, not feeding literally, but psychologically. According to rational, binary modes of explanation, if it could not be incorporated into the system, it should be eliminated to make way for modernity and civilized life.[3]

Freyre, as mentioned, propagated the myth of "racial democracy." He did this by transforming the *mestizo* and *mulato*, both of whom were previously seen as tainted by African American blood, into a positive member of the nation. The concept of cultural hybridism, which had been mired in the ambiguities of racial theories, could now be carefully cultivated so as to flower into a respectable cultural alloy. It could be ritually celebrated in everyday relationships and in the great public events such as Carnival and soccer. Class borders would be transcended, "whitening" would bring about an erasure of all binaries, and utopia would surely be at hand.[4] Afro-Brazilian playwright and activist Abdias do Nascimento argues that if Freyre's utopia had become reality, or if the industrialization of Brazil had absorbed the Afro-Brazilian contingency into a work force in the best tradition of modernity, the result would have been the same. His people would nonetheless have suffered a loss of ethnic singularity. The modern scheme of acculturation and assimilation would have become so vague that it would give a favorable nod to sexual exploitation of women and physical exploitation of men while reducing Afro-Brazilian culture to an imperceptible blur (Nascimento 1989).

What actually happened according to Nascimento and other scholars is this. The slave trade emasculated and destroyed clans, villages, and lineages. During this destruction, groups from diverse civilizations merged and settled along the Western

half of Africa. After the slaves became the original victims of displaced homelessness in the Americas, forest peoples found themselves living with farmers, matrilin-
eal cultures with patrilineal cultures, members of kingdoms with members of tribes
and totemic clans. All were reduced to a single, nightmarish common denominator:
slavery. Original forms of ethnic solidarity having been destroyed, it was now impossible faithfully to reproduce African cultures in this strange new cultural world.
Residual and new configurations developed along the cracks and fissures that
popped up in the dominant slave society, that is, along the border of borders, along
the interstices in the new social system through which black cultures found, . . . —
no, that's not right; they invented—a home out of homelessness. As a result, African
cultures became a hybrid mixture making up African American cultures with exceedingly vague definition, and as a result they became something quite other than a
collection of individual cultures: it was a matter of the whole becoming more than
the sum of its parts and at the same time of the parts making up more than the whole.
The African American hybrid cultures as a heterogenous whole thus became subordinate to the superordinate class governing a larger slave society, a slave society that
took on increasing heterogeny but with nary a chance of completing the process of
emergence as a smooth homogenous master- or megaculture (Bastide 1971:72–88).
This nature of Brazilian and Caribbean, and to an extent, all of Latin American cultures owes thanks to the "cultural" guerrillas among them, as briefly discussed
above. Consequently, there was a grand hybridization of *both* the one side of culture
and the other, but *neither* the one *nor* the other became absolutely dominant;
rather, something else from the erstwhile excluded middle came into a process of
becoming.[5]

In sum, da Cunha was a reluctant, somewhat disenchanted proponent, even with
a tinge of skepticism, of late nineteenth-century utopianism, materialist modernism.
Freyre the neo-romantic *novomundista* (new-worldist, a view of the Americas as different and unique), saw material progress as the root of all Brazil's evils. Brazil, today, is, quite fortunately, *neither* the one *nor* the other, but something in the process
of becoming something else. After the ideals of Brazil as materialist modernism and
as a racial democracy waned, the days of Brazil as social classes according to which
ethnic and racial dynamics were subordinated to class reductionism came and went.
The dynamics of ethnicity and race in Brazil is now in the process of transformation,
and all is intertwined with political and economic processes, in a movement, I hope,
toward democratization. Ethnic movements are alive and well: there is questioning,
debating, protesting, and at times there is violence. The process is energized. "The
genie is out of the bottle. No racist elite will be able to contain it again" (Winant
1992:108). As in the case of Prospero and Ariel and Caliban, there is neither binary
symmetrical give-and-take between opponents nor a three-way tie among the triad of
competitors on the semiotic field. Rather, there is everything and a little of something else
besides, there is always already something other than what there was/is/will be.

What I am suggesting is that one interpretation of Brazil is of the nature of
"green" and another interpretation is comparable to "grue," with a host of alternative
interpretations besides. It is almost as if one Brazil were "cat," another Brazil were
"cat*," another Brazil, "cat$^\Psi$," and yet another Brazil, "cat$^\#$," and so on. The differences at times seem to become that great. Brazil is seen *as* two and more totally

different Brazils; and the seers see *that* Brazil is such-and-such and so-and-so in radically distinct ways. Each seeing has its focal and its subsidiary facet; each seeing is guided by a certain element of tacit knowing. It is a sort of jumbled composite of Maggie dreams, Hladdy fictions, Pierre pseudofictions, Emmy invented worlds, of Tlöny's mind-dependent "reality" plus Funy's trembling particulars, and all that, jam-packed into a Lönny-style hypothetico-deductive world that sets itself up only with the possibility of becoming demolished, perhaps by some neoliberalizing, opportunistic Scharlach who has been waiting around for the proper moment. All this, thanks to that fine line, that border of borders separating nothing from nothing, that is itself nothing but "emptiness." It's an uncertain world, to be sure, charmingly, yet disturbingly uncertain.

Now for a radical shift of focus to a couple of contemporary cultural-political scenarios in Mexico and Brazil for further illustration of this processual nature of cultural becoming.

Who's Wearing What Mask?

Alma Guillermoprieto writes in the *New York Review* (1996) that during the proceedings regarding recent political assassinations in Mexico, there was the discovery of a gap of approximately $100 million between Raúl Salinas's estimate of his own wealth and his actual worth.[6] This discovery was made when Salinas, in dire need of cash, sent his wife and her brother to Switzerland with a pair of suitcases to withdraw a significant portion of the $83 million he had previously deposited there. The accounts were frozen, and Mrs. Salinas suffered the embarrassment of a few days in a Swiss prison. Guillermoprieto records one of the key points in a subsequent interrogation of her husband, Raúl:

> *Question number ten*: What were your principal sources of income during the years 1988–1995? *Answer*: . . . On the private side, those related to licit business activity, and, on the public side, the salaries and benefits I was paid [as a government official, which he was, until 1992] and, lastly, my own savings and rental income. . . . At the beginning of 1994, as a reference, the total would have been around $10 million. (Guillermoprieto 1996:32) (brackets added)

Following this interrogation, at the request of Mexican officials, all Raúl Salinas's known accounts throughout Europe were frozen. Journalists calculated that $300 million would be the lowest realistic estimate of his wealth. Meanwhile, Citibank, which handled Raúl's money in the United States, including the transfer of the $50 million loan to a Cayman Island account, retained Robert Fiske, the former independent prosecutor in the Whitewater investigation, to represent it in whatever legal complications might arise from the case. A media report of these transactions and litigations took on an ethereal image of pure fantasy: beside the report, there was a photograph of a *pepenador* (scavenger at the garbage dump), bare feet bleeding, hands submerged in filth, with intense concentration on his face, as he searched for a morsel of food or some item he could exchange for a few *centavos*. Strange. A dreamy juxtaposition, and most likely a frightening image, of neoliberal things to come.

If the justice system had worked, the trials of Raúl Salinas de Gortari—for murder and "inexplicable enrichment"—could have revealed the changes in Mexico over the last decade or so that transformed the country from a paragon of authoritarianism into an unruly society in which the ruling elites take out contracts on each other. It could also have revealed Carlos Salinas de Gortari's role in the bizarre turn of affairs in the country with respect to which he had helped create what had seemed to be a positive image or order and progress—neopositivist style, with "técnicos" in place of Porfirio Díaz's "científicos." At one time it appeared that Carlos Salinas had accomplished a transition from authoritarianism to a multi-party electoral system. After all, he had handed over his virtually dictatorial power to opposition governors in three states, and in 1994 he presided over the first elections in which presidential candidates of opposition parties had somewhat of an outside fighting chance against the candidate from PRI (Institutionalized Revolutionary Party), the party in power since 1929. Carlos Salinas had also taken significant steps to modernize the economy. He sold off hundreds of state enterprises, thus easing the burden of these white elephants on a poor and overgrown and hyperbureaucratized state. He had opened Mexico to world trade through GATT and the grounds he prepared for NAFTA, and he had renegotiated a vast foreign debt, and revitalized the peso. That is at least what appeared on the surface, what Salinas wanted the monolithic TV complex, *Televisa,* and the powerful newspaper, *Excelsior*, to reveal to the public—and what he wanted from these extensions of the official ruling party he was accustomed to getting. All that, however, was by and large an invented Mexico, the "imaginary" Mexico.

In contrast to this Mexico, Guillermoprieto asks us to imagine an alternative scenario, a sort of "imaginary imaginary" Mexico. Perhaps Salinas had ordered the electoral ballots destroyed after the 1988 election so that no one could know how many votes were actually fixed in his favor. He might have covered up the fact that his competitor, Cuauhtémoc Cárdenas, actually won—which he did in the seat of power and 1/5 of the population of the entire country, Mexico City. Salinas could conceivably have persuaded—whether with money or with threats—the conservative presidential candidate in the 1994 elections, Diego Fernández de Cevallos, and briefly a front-runner, to stop campaigning once it was clear that his old enemy on the left, Cuauhtémoc Cárdenas, had no hope of winning. His brother Raúl might have been involved in rigging the bidding for state enterprises so that a few of Salinas's cronies could buy them at enormous profit. Carlos Salinas might have dug in his heels, obstinately refusing to pay the political price of a long-overdue devaluation of the peso. This would leave the dirty work to his successor and lead to an economic debacle; especially in light of the guerrilla skirmishes in Chiapas at the very moment NAFTA arrived on the scene hopefully to offer Mexico membership to the exclusive club of developed nations (about which more in the next chapter).

Yes. Guillermoprieto's presumably invented or "imaginary" scenario was actually more credible to many cynical Mexican onlookers than the so-called "real" one: the invented scenario, which was quite faithfully "real," more "real than the real," product of prefabricated *simulacra* (Guillermoprieto 1992:132). Strange indeed.

(Mexico is Mexico, of course, and emeralds are emeralds and cats are cats. But there is no preventing Mexico from becoming "Mexistroika"—as Carlos Fuentes [1988a] once put it—for some disgruntled onlookers. Perhaps it could have even become "Mexotitlán" for citizens of "México profundo," and "Northaméxico" and "Gringotéxico" for those pseudo-patriotic citizens dreaming of their dollars safe and sound in Houston banks and Wal-Marts and McDonalds south of the border. These alternatives would imply divergent predicates attached to Mexico as variously interpreted, in somewhat the manner in which emeralds can be *either* "green" *or* "grue" [see Ross 1997]).

As one speculative but pervasive and provocative rumor had it, Raúl himself ordered the murder of his former brother-in-law, José Francisco Ruiz Massieu. A rumor of this caliber would have been met with shock or disbelief a few scant years ago. But it was now coolly and cynically received, according to polls, by millions of Mexicans. In fact, the Mexicans had come to expect such antics from their politicians. For months following the event Salinas-like characters were featured ordering assassinations in some of the top-rated *telenovelas* (soap operas), and hardly a week went by without some prominent citizen declaring that the former president must be brought to trial. In one of the most widely circulated versions, a variation of which is cited in Andres Oppenheimer's book, *México en la frontera del caos* (1996), the story circulated that Salinas had ordered the murder of his former brother-in-law, and even that of his own successor as well. The motive? He believed both of them stood in the way of his plan to revise the constitution in order that he could be re-elected in the year 2000. The problem with this interpretation, of course, is that it goes against a profound grain in the Mexican psyche: the doctrine of no-reelection was abused many times over by Porfirio Díaz prior to the revolution, and the last ex-president who had tried to become re-elected in 1928, Álvaro Obregón, was assassinated for his efforts. Enough said. The upshot is that when cynicism prevails, as it does in Mexico, innocence has long since passed into oblivion. It is somewhat like the loss of innocence of the North American public when John F. Kennedy's closet womanizing was revealed, the behind-the-scenes maneuvering during the Vietnam War, Richard Nixon and Watergate, Reagan and Bush and the Iran-Contra affair, and Clinton and Whitewatergate and his alleged illegal fund raising and Paula Jones and Monica Lewinsky, and all the other scandals compacted into one single event and then magnified a few times over.

Cynicism: one's mind-set when one becomes skeptical, suspicious, doubtful, of another's motives and professed virtues, when one is contemptful of and scorns another's actions, when one holds that those actions are not *either* worthy *or* unworthy of one's attention, but rather, they are *both* worthy *and* unworthy of one's attention, for one can *neither* completely ignore *nor* give unmitigated, rapt attention to the *other's* actions. Consequently, those actions are *neither* worthy *nor* are they unworthy of one's suspension or unsuspension of belief. If one completely unsuspends belief in the *other*, then one risks being deluded and duped and ensnared by the trap the *other* has set. And if one completely suspends belief in the *other*, then one has nothing to go on, for one is within the socio-cultural context one is within, which includes that *other* as self-proclaimed superordinate in contrast to which one is presumably the subordinate. So one can *neither* suspend *nor* unsuspend disbelief, and at the same time one *both* suspends *and* unsuspends belief, for there could be no cynicism unless there were the acknowledgment of some possibility and some prior actuality of belief. If such possibility and actuality did not exist, there would be no cynicism, but merely naiveté, or pure innocence. Innocence (unscience) can exist in dichotomous relation with knowledge (science). Cynicism, in contrast, resists *either/or* imperatives: there must be at least a tinge of *both* belief *and* disbelief, and there can be *neither* purely belief *nor* disbelief. There is suspension between suspension and unsuspension *both* of belief *and* of disbelief. Indeed, this is a genuine illustration of the border of borders, the betwixt and between, "emptiness," where everything is possible and nothing is actual. So also with other comparable incongruously complementary terms concocted into one term.[7]

We must look for further illustrations of our bizarre cultural "logics," in Brazil.

When Jeitinho *Loses Its Charm*

On Tuesday, December 29, 1992, Fernando Collor de Mello became the first Brazilian president to suffer the embarrassment of impeachment. He was accused of having stood by with yawning nonchalance while his "éminence grise" fleeced the impoverished population of millions of dollars on his behalf.[8] There had been a lengthy investigation, and the Senate voted to remove him from office after a raucous wave of protests by thousands of citizens who took to the streets obviously threw a bit of fear in them. One might conclude that Fernando Collor's congressional indictment represented *either* a move toward democracy *or* yet another failure, *either* a euphoric empowerment of a people fed up with reckless arrogance of their leaders *or* a depressing watershed in the country's search for an honest government. But actually, it was *neither* the one *nor* the other, for Brazil's future hung in the balance at the border of borders separating the *either* from the *or*.

Collor's impeachment brought much of the student and professional class of the larger cities of Brazil out in the streets for a carnivalesque celebration. On the other hand, many Brazilians, and particularly the working class populace of Rio de Janeiro, were too distracted to pay much attention to the history being made in spite of their nonchalance. For, less than twenty-four hours before the final Senate vote deciding the President's fate, a *telenovela* starlet was found dead at the side of a road in the outskirts of Rio de Janeiro, with sixteen stab wounds distributed throughout her body. This was the news that was most effectively capable of galvanizing much of the nation. Daniella Perez, 22, though quite attractive, could well have been just another of some 4,000 victims of homicide in Rio every year. There was nothing really extraordinary about her, outside the fact that she was seen by some 40 million Brazilians on their favorite *telenovela*, *De Corpo e Alma* ("Body and Soul"). Daniella was not even the star of the series. She had a role in one of the multiple subplots used to keep the story going and the people glued to their seats. In the *telenovela* the "real life" Daniella was Yasmin, an innocent young ticket puncher on a Rio bus line, who had an obsessively jealous boyfriend, Bira, the bus driver. The bus driver in "real life" was Guilherme de Pádua, a moody, second-rate actor, who confessed within hours to having been Daniella's killer, that is to his having killed Yasmin as the jealous Bira. No, . . . wait a minute. Bira killed Daniella, . . . or was it Guilherme who killed Yasmin? The whole scenario became fuzzy. Fortuitous conjunctions, incongruous complementarities, between "reality" and melodrama! So much for one's grounding in the "real."

The strained romance between Bira and Yasmin had served as light comic relief for the main plot of the *telenovela*. (Or was it Guilherme and Daniella who served as the main plot for the comic relief to buffer Collor's release from the presidency of Brazil?) Daniella's mother, as it turns out, was the scriptwriter for *De Corpo e Alma*, and it was she who paired Guilherme with Daniella, creating the conflictive relationship between the two in the "fictive world," which somehow became interpolated into the "real world." Or was it the other way round? Yes? Perhaps? No? Guillermoprieto (1994a:289) writes that a friend told her regarding this tragic comedy, this comic tragedy: "Brazilians discovered virtual reality years ago. They never know when they are entering the screen and when they are leaving it." "Virtual reality," more "real" than the "real," as Baudrillard would put it.

At any rate, the outrage over Daniella's murder was astronomical. As far as popular culture went, the Senate's impeachment of the President was pushed into the background. Yet the media tried their best: newscasts blared, headlines were prominently highlighted, and foreign correspondents scrambled to get a piece of the action. On the Sunday following the impeachment the largest newspapers published special sections on this historical event. However, in Rio, many of them ended in the circular files, in the streets, and on the beach, trashed in order to get to the important issues: Daniella and the sports page. After all, Collor was just a politician. They don't get much respect these days in Latin America. The fury over Daniella, in contrast, reached a screaming pitch, especially in Rio. In Guillermoprieto's (1994a:289) words: "The blurry confusion in the public mind between reality and fantasy when it came to the murder scandal . . . turned into full-fledged delirium at Daniella's funeral. It took place the day after the murder, just hours after Fernando Collor de Mello submitted his resignation, and on the kind of sweltering day when everyone in Rio who can afford the bus fare is normally at the beach." Virtually the entire TV company showed up at the funeral. The public had come to mourn, but when the surviving stars of the *telenovela* appeared, one by one, there was applause, autographs were signed, people climbed over the gravestones to get a better look, people knocked each other down, and they knocked gravestones down. Photographers were everywhere, security police were scarce, the Rio heat was sweltering.

The homicide was on a Monday. It was reported on the same day as Collor's impeachment and resignation, on Tuesday. Daniella was murdered, Collor resigned, Guilherme confessed, and Daniella's funeral had turned into a brawl, all within a few short days. The nation's emotional reserves were drained as a result of the sorrows and horrors. But the story does not end there. It was soon rumored that the murderer might not have been Guilherme at all but his pregnant teen-aged wife. It really happened this way, according to one of the alternative interpretations. Guilherme testified in the court proceedings that Daniella-*cum*-Yasmin had sought a "real-life" relationship with him, Guillerme-*cum*-Bira. He suggested that she had even threatened to use black magic on him if he didn't jump in bed with her. Giving in to Daniella's incessant erotic pressure, he finally consented to see her to talk things out. During the meeting, according to Guilherme's story, he once again resisted her approaches. She became hysterical, and in the skirmish that followed, she was killed. Guillerme claimed that his wife, Paula, was nowhere near the scene at the time of the crime. He had dropped her off at a nearby mall, where she did some casual window-shopping for six hours, pregnancy and all. Then, after having committed the crime, Guilherme picked her up and they went home.

The prosecution had yet another story: it was Paula who was jealous of Daniella just as Bira had been jealous of all the men who gave more than a passing glance at Yasmin. According to this version of the tale, Guilherme drove Paula to a strategic spot on the side of the road in order that she could witness how Guilherme was going to reject Daniella. The plan backfired. Paula went into a rage, jumped out of the car, and ran over and murdered Daniella. Paula had been incapable of distinguishing between her husband's amorous scenes with Yasmin on TV and "real life," taking the passionate kisses between the two in front of millions of onlookers as the "real thing" and a betrayal of their own vows.[9] It might appear that the "simulated real" had become "more real than the real" and that what was "really real" had been pushed into the background and it gradually faded away. The "more real than real" consisted of signifiers and nothing but signifiers, while the "real," erstwhile signifieds now having taken a back seat to these *prima donna* upstarts, had been relegated to forgetfulness.

This might appear to involve, once again, the equivalent of "cats" and "cats[*]" and "green" emeralds and "grue" emeralds in the strict dichotomous sense. Such conceptualizing, however, is also unfortunate, for it bears no account of that which is most important: the border of the borders, that nonplace place, the *both-ands* and the *neither-nors*. There, the two horns of an opposition are actually in an intimate embrace, and at the same time neither of the horns is capable of giving witness regarding what there *is*, for what there *is* takes a back seat to what there *is not*, but can possible emerge. *Both* the one horn *and* the other one as possibilities not actualities (in the sphere of Firstness) are absolutely essential, for without the possibility of the one there is no possibility of the other. At the same time, *neither* the one *nor* the other can take necessary priority or enjoy necessary privilege over the other (in the sphere of Thirdness). There can be no hierarchization; priorities, hierarchies, and all those products of dichotomous thinking are of the nature of a Secondness that suffers from the partial absence of its companions, Firstness and Thirdness. Both Firstness and Thirdness are essential for there to be any Secondness in the first place, in order that there be any "real" that can be displaced by some form or other of the "irreal." Umberto Eco's (1976:6–8, 1984:177–82) observation that human semiotics is erected upon the foundationless premise entailing the capacity to lie is *a propos*. It implies what I have been trying to articulate: that there must have been at least *something* for the sign maker and taker before there could have been *nothing*, but that *something* (Secondness) must have emerged from the infinite range of possibilities (Firstness) before some particular possibility could have been tapped, at the border of borders (within Thirdness), to emerge as *something* that that previous *something* was not.

Thus, Daniella could not have become Daniella without the becoming of what she *was not*, Yasmin, and the same can be said about Guilherme. And taking the entire *telenovela* into account, alongside "real" Brazil, the "irreal" could not have become what it was without the becoming of the "real." Between the one term and the other of the incongruously complementary pairs, there is the border of borders, that vibrating, scintillating, pulsating, eternally dynamic yet static, perpetual motion each increment of which is canceled out by an equal but opposite increment that is always already somewhere else. Daniella, Yasmin, Guilherme, Bira, *De Corpo e Alma*, Brazil, the *other* Brazil, the *other other* Brazil, all are *both* what they are *and* they are not what they are; they *neither* are what they are *nor* are they not what they are but they are something else. This is no simple picture of superordinates and subordinates, haves and have-nots, powermongers and subalterns, "real" and "irreal." It is not as if there were Team A against Team B on the turf surrounded by a hundred thousand screaming fans. On the contrary. It is as if the playing field, the athletes, the audience, the entire stadium, are all codependently intertwined in the same effervescent, fluctuating, flowing play of semiosis.

It must be said, to keep things honest, that half of the Brazilians are chronically hungry. They can't afford movies, the Carnival parade, or even an occasional soccer game. All those activities are for ѡhe less poor of the poor, the middle-class, and tourists. But many of the poor in Brazil are able to buy or at least watch their neighbor's TV, for this is Brazil, where there are more TVs than refrigerators. Roberto Marinho, creator of *Globo*, and still center of the largest and most professional *telenovela* production in Latin America, has given the Brazilian public their daily soaps about "real" Brazilians, while the other countries of Latin America must resign themselves to dubbed series from the U.S. These lavishly produced melodramas are by Brazilians, about Brazilians, and for Brazilians, and they never fail to strike a responsive chord, vicariously fulfilling the dreams of their viewers in one form or another. TV in Brazil is thus an escape, perhaps even more so than in the U.S. (Kottak 1990, Teixeira 1995). In the soaps, the poor find jobs and eat; the evil are often redeemed; the good life can be there for all. And above all, the murder of Daniella Perez, which created an eerie resemblance between what appeared on screen and what appeared elsewhere, was uncanny proof that "reality" can at the most unexpected moment take a back seat to the sham "irreal" universe of the *telenovela*.

Fernando Collor de Mello became a miniseries; Daniella and her world became the "more real" Brazil. Daniella became a tragic heroine; Collor became a national disgrace and a scapegoat. His removal from power should have been celebrated as the successful outcome of a national crusade. But it was not, not really, at least among the popular classes. Especially in Rio, it was shoved aside by Daniella's world—though middle-class politically-engaged Brazilians danced in the streets over Collor de Mello's removal from office. Some time before Collor's impeachment, he had been a hugely popular, good-looking, karate-black-belt, skiing, scuba-diving, car-racing, jogging, made-for-TV icon who promised to bring Brazil into the twenty-first century as a shining example of progress and prosperity. He had all the makings of a charismatic figure endowed with a liberal dose of *personalismo* that could legitimately take his place in the long line of premier Latin American *caudillos*. But he did not. The media ate him alive during the latter months of his presidency, and he never recovered. He simply couldn't compete with the other "irreal" TV celebrities. Before he became president, he was a politician from Alagoas, a state in northeastern Brazil with the size and the poverty index of the poorest of the Central American countries, where most of the families don't even own televisions. Ironic. Fernando

Collor de Mello came from "nowhere," that is, he emerged from the interstices as it were. As president, he quickly cometed into the astrosphere, and then he fizzled, and fell back into "nowhere."

Guillermoprieto once interviewed Maria Tereza Souza Monteiro, of TV *Globo*, who said regarding why the TV public had been captivated with Daniella's murder and remained nonchalant regarding Collor's impeachment: "They followed the impeachment proceedings, but the technical ins and outs of the actual legal process were extremely difficult to understand. It was much easier to understand Daniella's death, and less frightening. People believed that it was their protests that led directly to Collor's departure, and that was scary: they thought, Oh my God, I can overthrow a President." (Guillermoprieto 1994a:316). Collor actually became the "irreal" villain of a *telenovela*. Like Guilherme de Pádua, he was merely a scoundrel. Once he walked off the set, that is off the "real" to enter into oblivion, he was back to "normal," as a human being rather than a fallible soul trying to play the role created by the Brazilians' image of that gallant, charismatic man on horseback, a *coronel* or *caudillo*. He is now just a guy, despised by most but still in favor with some of his former cronies. He enjoyed considerably more than his allotted fifteen minutes of fame and glory and must now remain content with his status as a fallen eagle.

Sex, Blood, Doubts, Diversion

But the story doesn't even end there. While president, Collor had appointed Paulo César Farias as his campaign treasurer. After he became president, he then asked Farias, or "PC" as they called him, to serve as liaison between the government and the rich entrepreneurs.

It later became known that during the Collor presidency, PC was on the take, extorting incredible sums of money from major Brazilian corporations. After Collor's impeachment PC was living a life of luxury in his northeastern state. It all came to a close, however, on June 23, 1996, when he was found dead with one of his lovers, Suzana Marcolino, in bed, a bullet hole strategically placed in each body such that they in all probability died instantly. The story soon told was that PC, a widower, from among his lovers, had decided to stick with the fair-haired, blue-eyed, light-skinned Cláudia Dantas from a respectable local family, and get rid of Suzana. Suzana, an attractive *mulata* with whom PC had made contact while in jail, had recently purchased a .38 revolver, which turned out to be the instrument used in the crime. She had plenty of motive for killing PC, for he planned to ditch her for Cláudia. According to interpretation A, she did so, then committed suicide at his side in bed. End of case. Now enter interpretation B. How could Suzana have so effectively located the precise spot in her lover's rib cage as well as her own to inflict instant death? Why was the pistol at the foot of the bed? How could she have contorted her hand at such a bizarre angle in order to pull the trigger of the weapon and send the slug into her own body? Most likely, this was a political assassination and a cover up. Case becomes fuzzy.

Various photographs were available of Suzana and PC, both dead, in bed, he half covered, she dressed for snooze time and with legs spread amply for the cameras posing at the foot of the bed. These shots, from various angles, appeared daily in each of the major newspapers and on the TV newscasts. During this time, as it turned out, in addition to PC, Suzana had at least two younger lovers. Cameras and reporters immediately converged on them, and their interviews preoccupied the media for the next week-and-a-half or so. Attention frequently focused also on Cláudia, as well as even on Zara, an English psychology student with whom PC had an affair in London when he was there hiding from the police. Meanwhile, back in Tahiti, the self-exiled Collor was living a life of luxury that would be the envy of any jet setter. On the cover of the July 3, 1996 edition of *Veja*, a weekly publication consisting of a mix of tabloid journalism and reporting of the *Newsweek* variety, we find a shot of PC's mug that almost covers the entire page. This portion of the page is tinged with deep red. In the upper left hand corner there is a small "real life" color shot of Suzana. In the bottom right hand corner there is another one of Collor, with a flowered wreath on his head, a drink in a coconut shell in his hand, and a cynical smile on his face—and all this above a caption reading "Sex, Jealousy, Blood." Politics had been shoved aside; the "real" had become *telenovela* big-time.

Such point-counterpoint maneuvers on the part of the media, public attention, political and amorous intrigues, would have been the envy of Tlöny, would have severely taxed the reasoning powers of Lönny, would have brought tears to Emmy, would have extended beyond Maggie's wildest dreams. Daneri would never have believed it had he seen it with his own eyes in the Aleph, Funy would have been driven to schizophrenia, Rorty would have shaken his head with pity, and Hladik would have wondered why he never thought of such a "more real than the real" plot. Who was the "real" PC?—i.e., was he "cat" or "cat*"?, "green" or "grue"? What kind of monster had the media created? How far could the important issues be skirted before the public began screaming out in a rage? Indeed, when Secondness falls to pieces, chaos erupts, certainty is zilch, and everybody is reduced to semiotic homelessness. But binary Secondness is neither the boon nor the bane of semiosis. All is not necessarily lost. Re-emergence is always possible, life can go on. And so it is, in Brazil, "enchanting" land of parrots and piranhas and interminable jungles and beaches and carnivals and skyscrapers and *favelas* and sex and jealousy and blood. [10] The difference now, unfortunately, is that favor and corruption are openly flaunted. There's no beating about the bush, and the subtle ins and outs and the hints and nuances of *jeitinho* practices have lost their charm—recall Lívia Barbosa on favor, corruption, and *jeitinho*. [11]

As an extended footnote to the Daniella episode, we have recent more developments with respect to *Nada Personal* ("Nothing Personal"). I allude to a Mexican *telenovela* produced by *TV Azteca* about amorous and business and political intrigues in which rich politicians wax cynical over the deplorable condition of Mexico and the merely wealthy take on airs of undeserved self-importance. Ironically, the billing had it on the subway walls that the soap was *La Realidad Vuelta Telenovela* ("Reality Transformed Into a Soap"). Then there were some unexpected "real" world intrigues. Two weeks before the filming of the *telenovela* was to be completed, Ana Colchero, the screamingly popular actress playing the part of Camila de los Reyes, simply quit. Her reason? The script had begun denigrating Camila, and she, Ana, that is Camila, no, perhaps I was right in the first place, Ana, wanted to maintain her integrity (integrity she wanted?, the *telenovela* was about corruption and sleaze and grime, for God's sake). She claimed she had signed a contract on the basis of one script, and then it had been changed against her will. All she wanted, in her way of putting it, was a "dignified ending" for her character (Colchero 1996:18). Ana herself had apparently begun taking the soap to be of the same stuff as "reality," her view of what that "reality" should be. But what, actually, was the "real reality" of the Mexican condition? Intrigues, favor, corruption, deceit, subterfuge. *Nada Personal*, its fluid script and its production, was as close or closer to "reality" than the invented "reality" Ana had envisioned. What she wanted was something more "real" than the "real," that is, she wanted the "real" of her imagination and not that of the "reality" surrounding her, which was actually quite in tune with that "reality" of *Nada Personal*. (Equally ironically, the final episodes of the soap were taped without Ana, while on the subway walls one could now read: ¡*Ha Vuelto la Realidad*! ["Reality has Returned!"]).[12]

Speaking of "reality," if I may return to Figure 6 for a moment, notice that the experienced world, the "real" of Secondness, of indexicality, of the haves and the have-nots, the powerful and the weak, the dominant and the subordinate, is a pale reflection of the entire field of semiosis represented by the whole figure. Both homogeny and everything possible at one whack and heterogeny and everything differentiated to becomes less and less easily distinguishable envelop Secondness in their apparently mad rush that fuses and confuses minds and hearts, and the brainy making of signs and gutsy taking of signs. That of which we are at a given space-time juncture aware and that which we can effectively articulate is but a minuscule spot on the Figure 6 map, whether we wish it or not.

On to other, Mexican intrigues.

Notes

1.   This scenario, reminiscent of many incidents of extermination of the Amerindians in the U.S., was not entirely uncommon in Latin America. Shortly before the turn of the century Argentine president General Julio A. Roca waged a campaign against Amerindians and *gauchos* in order to make way in the pampa for progress. During approximately the same period Porfirio Díaz, dictator of Mexico, reduced the rebellious Yaqui Amerindians of Sonora to virtual slavery in the distant Yucatan peninsula. Yet da Cunha sees the somewhat comparable episode of Canudos as an act of madness on the part of the Brazilian government only understood as a need to control the otherwise uncontrollable and then to explain the unexplainable, justify the unjustifiable. This message comes through loud and clear in Vargas Llosa's narrative account of the Canudos massacre in *The War of the End of the World* (1984 [1981]).

2.   That is at least Freyre's view in more or less his own words. In contrast, see Mota (1978) and Bastos (1986) for the counterargument that Freyre's Lusophile patriarchal-aristocratic mentality is incapable of breaking the bonds of dualism; also Skidmore (1974) who has for a quarter of a century argued against the Freyre-inspired "racial democracy" idea. However, for a recent tempered and sympathetic critique of Freyre, see Reis (1999).

3.   Collectively, Canudos is comparable to Caliban, and the "civilized" coast of Brazil is Caliban having evolved into Ariel pursuing the image of the erstwhile colonizer, Europe-Prospero. On the other hand, Freyre's Master is Prospero transformed by the tropics and hybridized by the Slave consisting of Amerindian and African American cultural phenotypes, those phenotypes themselves having been transformed by the Master to produce a grand synthesis, a "Cosmic Race" in the words of José Vasconcelos (1925).

4.   With due respect to Freyre, it bears mentioning that shortly before his death he became aware of the inconsistency of his grand vision, especially with the coming industrial revolution during the Getulio Vargas years in Brazil (1930–45) that played havoc with his idyllic image of Brazil as a plantation culture (Mota 1978:60).

5.   A note of clarification: I've been using the term "hybrid" in the sense that dissolves elite/subaltern and kindred dichotomies (see also Beverley 1999:123–25). Hybridity as I use it is not simply a fusion of the many into *both-and* harmonious, homogenous oneness. It is also incessantly in the process of becoming *neither-nor* heterogeny (in this light see Mignolo's [2000:170] critique of the customary meaning of hybridity; also Kraniauskis [2000]).

6.   Raúl Salinas is the brother of Carlos Salinas de Gortari, President of Mexico from 1988 to 1994.

7.   As the Mexicans might say, as explanation of an event, *No es ni verdadero ni falso, sino todo lo contrario* ("It is neither true nor false, but something else entirely"). This in certain contexts can be the epitome of cynicism. It makes shambles of standard logical and rational standards of binary thought and of conduct (for excellent essays on the creeping cynicism in contemporary Mexico, I would suggest that at your leisure you consult Agustín 1990, 1992, 1997, Campos 1995, and Florescano 1995, in addition to the other works published during this decade I have herein cited).

8.   For a recent account of corruption during the Collor de Mello years, see Figueiredo (2000).

9.   Actually, according to some critics *De Corpo e Alma* was one of the worst *telenovelas* Brazil had produced up to that time. It continued for two months after Daniella's murder, during which time she was often morbidly presented in flashbacks, in bad taste, and with a large dose vulgarity. Nevertheless, the soap went out with a bang, a screaming success.

10.   In fact, there might yet be a resurrection of Collor politics. In an interview for *Veja* of June, 1997 he mapped out his strategy for a come-back, which included his launching a campaign for the presidency in the upcoming 1998 elections. Incredible. Even more incredible, Collor de Mello, still a fallen eagle and very rarely even given mention by the media in the polls regarding the Brazilian presidential elections for 1998, gave an interview to a group of university students in which he openly admitted, "I am not a saint, and neither is anybody else, I made a few mistakes." Later, to the question, "Do you sleep well knowing that 150 million Brazilians hate you?," his response was a curt: "Don't exaggerate." Understandably, the question was applauded, the answer was not (Collor de Mello 1998). (It bears mentioning that the elections came and went, Fernando Henrique Cardoso won handily as the first Brazilian President to be conceded a second term in recent times, and Collor was given

little notice.) To top it all off, in 2001, guess who was a candidate, and a hopeless long shot at that, for the upcoming presidential election? Collor de Mello!

11. It also bears mentioning that as of June of 1997 the intrigues were still surfacing and the deceased PC still managed to garner a share of the media spotlight once in a while. To top it all off, upon arriving at Salvador, Bahia, May 16, 1999, I picked up the local newspaper, *A Tarde*, and would you believe it? I was treated to the fifth installment of a new series on the intriguing contradictions surrounding the "PC Case." The article sported Suzana and PC, in the same post mortem scene in the same bed that had appeared in newspapers and magazines countless times in the past. It seems that suicide was now discounted, and the enigma was once again blown open.

12. Interestingly enough, Brazil's and Mexico's soaps made the cover story of *Time* magazine (Epstein and Padgett 1997) as the region's most powerful entertainment vehicle, which has grown bolder and sexier, serving as an effective sounding board for volatile social issues.

Chapter Twelve

Semiosic Undertows: The Mexican Scene and Signs of Our Time

> For the state itself the border is a necessary fiction. More a staged event than a particular place, the border is *put forward* as a theatre of purity and legitimacy, a kind of semi-permeable membrane whose gauze is woven by the officers and apparatuses of State surveillance who are at once the instruments of centrist control and the agents of documentary identity.
>
> —David Avalos and John C. Welchman

> I live in a political and economic system in which the known and accepted borders have become phantasmagoric; others, apparently nonexistent, have come to replace them.
>
> —Silvio Martínez-Palau

> The border is all we share.
>
> —Guillermo Gómez-Peña

Shifty and Elusive

In view of the previous chapter, one must be compelled to remark: how shifty, that process they call semiosis! It whisks us along while patronizingly allowing us the deluded notion we know what it's about. Then, without any warning signs we find ourselves tumbling down a cataract, our flimsy craft capsizes, and perhaps we survive the unexpected event more by luck than by management. We have lived to give the rapids another shot in another day. But the scenario repeats itself, again and again. And life becomes increasingly precarious. Perhaps the best we can hope to do is go with the gush, try to maneuver our way about, and get on with life however we can. (Which is, by the way, what I try to do in this chapter: place contemporary Mexico, that is, the Mexico of early years of the North American Free Trade Agreement [NAFTA] and the Zapatista Army of National Liberation [EZLN] movement within the general context of semiosis, with an eye toward the work of Michel de Certeau.)

So, How Do They Do It?

The enigmatic question is: how do *they* do it? The people of Mexico, that is. How do they cope with semiosis, where life is virtual chaos at every moment? No, . . . what am I saying? Actually, for them it isn't chaos, not really, but merely the way things are, no more, no less. If what one sees as chaos throws a bit of fear in one, for them it is everyday life. So they cope. Regarding cultural phenomena, order and chaos are somewhat relative terms anyway.

As we saw in chapter two, Peirce's basic trio of signs consists of icons, indices, and symbols. Purely iconic signs are signs of Firstness. But since there is no absolute purity in our blemished cultural worlds, icons are always tinged with Secondness (hegemony) and Thirdness (heterogeny). Secondness is highlighted in the one-thing-and-its-other characterized by indexical signs, signs enjoying relationship with something other than themselves in their road toward becoming full-blown signs. In symbols, both the signs and their objects reach what Peirce would consider their most "genuine" expression: *language*. After all, language is what makes humans most distinctively humans. There is a potential pitfall, however. Obsessive fixation on language, and linguicentrism can threaten. I bring up this topic once again in order to illustrate the complexity of semiosis, especially regarding cultural phenomena in general and in particular the current scene in Mexico, that hotbed of semiotic activity and one of the most ebullient manifestations of semiosis around. The important point is that there are no clean lines of demarcation between iconic, indexical, and symbolic signs. What we need to keep in mind is that the areas in Figure 6 have no clearly distinguishable silver linings, but rather, they merge into and interpenetrate one another.

Undertow: I should place the term with which I label this chapter in the spotlight. An undertow is the current beneath the surface that sets seaward when waves are breaking upon the shore. The low lying current goes against the tow, the thrust; it goes against that familiar rush of breakers onto the beach and over McDonald's wrappers and beer cans and other assorted trash and a few semi-naked and half-baked bodies and a little kelp and a dozen or so stalwart crabs. The undertow of semiosis is comparable to this seaworthy image: signs going against the grain of the rush toward such disordered complexity and corruption as to render them virtually meaningless, going against the grain toward who knows where and who knows when. But these signs of the undertow are usually ignored, while focus lies solely on the surface. One would expect that chiefly symbolic signs of the surface should be the organizing force behind cultural interaction. But in these so-called postmodern days, they are not. They often become so self-contradictory, hypocritical, and absurd that chaos threatens to overtake them. Chiefly indexical signs in any self-respecting semiotic world should point the way along that labyrinth we call the universe. But ordinarily they do not. Rather, they have, themselves, lost their way about and are capable of offering no cogent set of directions. Chiefly iconic signs are hardly any consolation. They are just there, perhaps smiling provocatively and beckoning that we come forward. But they offer hardly any hopes and few promises. Not at all comforting. All this appears, perhaps unfortunately, quite in line with Jean Baudrillard (1983a, 1983b), among others.[1] But, as I shall argue, it is not. And what about those undertow signs? They are more often than not conveniently ignored, or they are

shoved under the rug with hopes that the guests will not sniff them out. Yet they refuse to stay out of sight for long. They move up through the interstices eventually to
surface once again and reveal that all was not simply surface kitsch and pastiche, but
rather, that there was some real quality to the signs after all.

Yes. *Quality*, above all, *quality*. Signs of quality are signs whose Secondness
and Thirdness must take a back seat to their Firstness. They are signs of flow in the
coming and going of everyday life, of that part of life that moves along without our
need for awareness of their existence, signs that whiz by as we catch ourselves ro-
botically driving our car, unthinkingly eating our evening meal, mindlessly dressing
in the morning, passively walking from A to B while at work, automatically greeting
our associates with a nod, a smile, a slight grimace, or whatever (recall Polanyi's
tacit knowing from chapter two). They are signs of the body more than signs willfully engendered by the imperious mind's control. They are signs of bodymind:
bodymindsigns. These are the signs that reveal our cultural idiosyncrasies at their
deepest level. They are the sort of interrelated, interactive, codependently emerging
signs of Mexican cultural flows that make Mexico Mexico. In fact, let's go directly
to Mexico.

Above the Table and Below the Table

Mexico awoke from its dream of a utopian rite of passage from "third world" to
"first world" status on New Year's Day, 1994, shortly after NAFTA went into effect,
with a vengeful "I told you so, you sons of bitches!" EZLN had begun its campaign,
which, shortly thereafter in a *communiqué* to the newly elected president of Mexico,
offered the defiant interdiction: "Welcome to the nightmare." With NAFTA having
become reality, Mexico was supposed to start looking like Texas. Instead, it looked
more like El Salvador (Guillermoprieto 1994b; also Katzenberger 1995).[2]

Unlike uprisings in Central and South America during the 1960s and in the state
of Guerrero and elsewhere in Mexico thereafter, the EZLN was no ragtag band of
aggrieved landless peasants. "Subcomandante Marcos" was the focus of attention
toward which all eyes were turned and in the direction of which an army of international correspondents converged.[3] But things went strangely awry from the very beginning. Actually, a certain "Comandante Felipe," not Marcos, was supposed to have
been the top dog. In fact, Marcos was only fourth in command. Marcos became the
leader through default by a bizarre twist worthy of a postmodern comedy. The truth
is—if we wish to be a little cynical about the whole affair—that Marcos appeared to
fit the bill better than any of the other candidates: he was a little lighter of skin,
taller, and of more impressive stance, he pensively smoked a pipe, and he articulated
himself more effectively, with wry irony and ingratiating humor. It seems that
shortly after the insurrection broke out, Marcos was talking with some tourists, for
he was concerned over their concern over what was occurring. A flood of correspondents soon engulfed him, he was interviewed, and he became an overnight celebrity,
a mad faxer at home with the electronic media, which pleased the news hawkers. Before long, T-shirts appeared with the image of Subcomandante Marcos to take their
place beside Che Guevara and other revolutionary tourist items. With that impressive
precedent, who could possibly deny Marcos his moment of fame? Rather than "cats"
taken for "cats[*]" or "green" emeralds for "grue" ones, we have no mistaken identity

but a selection of that which fits more conveniently into high tech media methods and modes. In other words, what we have is the invention of a "reality," a "reality" that is capable of ingratiating itself with the post-Cold War, postmodern mood considerably more effectively than the Maoist "Shining Path" of Peru and other comparable groups.

And why Chiapas? That southernmost and poorest state of the nation had received little attention since the time of the Mexican Revolution of 1910–1917. However, it became evident in the early 1990s that the radically unequal distribution of wealth in Chiapas mirrored that of Mexico in general: the poorest state of the union was symptomatic of the whole. Besides, though the fact had been rather hidden over the centuries, Chiapas was actually one of the country's richest states in natural resources. In 1994 it was providing for almost 60 percent of the hydroelectric power of the entire country, 47 percent of the natural gas, 21 percent of the oil, and it was one of the chief producers of lumber, coffee, and beef. Nevertheless, one third of the houses had no electricity and one half had no running water or sewage facilities. In some of the provincial cities the Zapatistas occupied, for example Ocosingo, 70 percent of the houses had no electricity. What is more indicative, the state of Chiapas had recently suffered corruption on a minor scale, but of such an absurd nature that it could hardly be taken without a bit of humor.

Pulitzer Prize recipient Andres Oppenheimer (1996) tells an interesting tale regarding these corrupt political practices. He arrived at the airport of Tuxtla Gutiérrez, capital of the state, after a two-hour delay at the Mexico City airport, in hopeful anticipation of an interview with Marcos. From the local Chiapas airport he found that a 35-kilometer taxi ride through the hinterland was necessary to reach the small provincial capital. Why the delay in Mexico City and why was the airport not constructed closer to Tuxtla Gutiérrez? After some inquiry he discovered that the delay was because the Tuxtla airport is usually enshrouded in a mist and they were awaiting the signal to take off from the capital so they could arrive in Chiapas at a time when the fog had temporarily cleared. The inordinately long taxi ride was due to the fact that, in spite of recommendations to the contrary due to the unfeasibility of a landing site in that area, the airport had been constructed in 1979 at precisely this spot because the land had belonged to an ex-governor of the state, which he had sold at a handy profit. The high plains where the airport stood were called "Llanos San Juan" ("San Juan Prairie") but it had been jocularly rebaptized "Ya no se ve" ("Now it can't be seen," which, in Spanish, alliterates with "Llanos San Juan"). The airport was such an embarrassment that no governor since that time wished to have his name associated with its inaugural. So it was never inaugurated. But the tale doesn't end there. In 1992 the then governor of the state, Patrocinio González, made a deal with the army to use a more convenient military airport close to the city for civilian flights. This permission, however, was granted only to one airline, Aviacsa, which was in competition with the other airline, Mexicana, which continued to use the remote and usually inaccessible airport. As would be expected, one of the chief stockholders of Aviacsa was the same Patrocinio González. The convenience of using Aviacsa put the Mexicana flight virtually out of business. (Rather than Brazilian-style *jeitinho* practices, we have bald-faced *corruption* and *favor*.)

In regards to the vast gap between the haves and the have-nots, as well as such rampant corruption, Chiapas is a microcosm, albeit in radical form, of the national macrocosm. As such, a more symbolic seat for the peasant outcry in the name of revolutionary leader Emiliano Zapata could hardly have been found.

Undertow Semiosis as "Guerrilla" Warfare

The flow of signs, of Mexican semiosis, of business and patronage, politics and patronage, haciendas and patronage, all went about as usual in the mode that had become entrenched over the centuries since the time of the conquest. The serious business and the political rhetoric on the part of the haves, and the irony, the sarcasm and cynicism, the wit and the droll humor on the part of many of the have-nots, all these signs, to be sure, are most properly symbolic signs. These are signs whose combination, function, and meaning are all relatively explicit. Little should be left with an open question mark; things should be said and said like they are. Consequently, the indexical signs, when implicit rather than explicit, are customarily met with a knowing nod, for everybody—that is, everybody who is anybody—should know what the message is all about, should properly process the signs, and should carry on with their role with due respect.

However, the winks, the sly grins, the gesturing hands and eye-brows and nodding and wagging heads and know-it-all looks: they all belie other signs, many other signs, signs of the undertow, signs that usually remain below the surface but are at some of the most inopportune moments ready and willing to leap out and show their disrespect, take a gracious bow before their raucous, ribald, boisterous audience, and then disappear back into the onrushing tide. These are signs of iconicity (and they are signs potentially of the nature of Brazilian *jeitinho* and other "cultural" guerrilla tactics). They are not signs of lesser, but in certain respects, of greater importance than those other, supposedly more developed signs whose existence would vanish were they not perched on the robust shoulders of their predecessors, the signs of quality, feeling, sensing, sentiment, emotion, signs of tacit knowing and doing. Yes. The Mexican people, that is, the have-nots, those of "México profundo," usually know their signs well, though out of apathy, passivity, or perhaps fear, they do not carry them to the next integer and make of them signs of greater complexity. What is the nature of these insubordinate signs?

The assumption often has it in cultural studies that there is a dominant culture and a subservient or popular culture, and that the former exercises hegemony over the latter.[4] This assumption is flawed in ways that are becoming increasingly evident, especially in light of Michel de Certeau's (1984) contention that the would-be dominant group of capitalist societies are perpetually subjected to contestations and negotiations by the guileful ruses, subversive trickery, and "cultural guerrilla tactics" of the so-called subaltern groups. In de Certeau's conception, the dominant classes are powerful, but they are also laden with bureaucratic baggage; they are overweight, and sluggish. In contrast, the underprivileged are lean and mean, nimble and flexible, creative and mobile. The powerful construct the fortresses of capitalist might: shopping malls, schools, parks, stadiums, and public monuments. The weak make their own space in and leave their mark on those memorials to the virtues of capitalism: graffiti, shoplifted goods, defaced shrubs, signs, windows, and painted surfaces. In order to do so, however, the weak must be constantly on their toes; they must remain vigilant, and seize the proper moments to engage in their subversive acts whenever and wherever they can. There are numerous ways of altering standard procedures and methods that characterize the subtle, and stubborn resistance of the have-nots. Since they lack their own space, they have to get along in a network of already established forces and representations. They have to make do with what they have. In their "cultural" guerrilla stratagems, they take a certain pleasure in getting around the rules of a constraining space (Certeau 1984:18).

Making do with what one has. Strategies for survival when one is of the have-nots. This entails improvisation, constant improvisation, from trivial levels up to the top. As an exercise in "cultural" guerrilla triviality, shoplift an item worth $10.00 and buy a pack of gum and you've doubly manifested your contempt—often in large part implicit—for those that wield power. Take a couple of tools from the auto repair shop where you work, and soon you'll have a well-equipped workshop of your own. You may never belong to the power elite, but you'll give them enough pricks in their buttocks when their back is turned to help make life miserable for them.

Of course these are petty "I obey but I do not comply" tactics. However, if your friends and co-workers adopt these and similar strategies to throw monkey wrenches in the works at all levels, then collectively the have-nots may eventually have their way of getting even with and occasionally even taking sweet revenge on the haves. They are all doing things their way, in spite of what the rich and the powerful think they are doing. They aren't all producers of cultural artifacts, nor are they full-blown consumers according to the ideal social image. They are somewhere in between. That is precisely the art. The dominant culture must have everything given either in blacks or whites. But the have-nots are superior to such oversimplified binary imperatives. In a rather tacit sense they know everything is either *neither* the one thing *nor* the other, or it is *both* the one thing *and* the other, take your pick. That is to say, they *neither* exclusively buy *nor* do they exclusively not buy, when they shoplift and purchase some gum. They engage in another activity entirely. They *do* buy, but they *don't* buy everything they take; they buy a portion of it, however small. And they *do not, not* buy, for much or most of what they take remains unpurchased. From another, complementary perspective, they *both* buy *and* they don't buy. Put the two possible incongruous activities together, and we have the makings of Firstness and Thirdness, to complement the overriding Secondness of the dominant culture's *either/or* imperatives.

According to classical logic, we should simply have the powerful and the weak, those in control and those who have no say, the dominant and the subalterns. It is an *either/or* proposition. According to "cultural guerrilla logic," in contrast, it is possible to don a different mask for each occasion. One can be intermittently *both* one thing *and* the other: buying a little and stealing a little, showing civic responsibility by throwing trash in the proper receptacle and later that night strewing the contents of that same receptacle along the sidewalk, catering to the boss in the morning and stealing from the company in the afternoon. In fact, one can be virtually all things to all those who are in control. Concomitantly, one is, like a picaresque anti-hero, a *jeitinheur, neither* the one thing *nor* the other on a permanent basis, for there is always the possibility of engaging in some act that falls *neither* within the *neither nor* the *nor*: it is something else entirely, emerging from within the interstices. So between the *either* and the *or* one always seems capable of finding something to fill in a portion of the excluded-middle, thus bringing it into the equation.

All this is to say that the ordinary concept the haves hold with respect to popular culture, folk culture, or "guerrilla culture" of the de Certeau sort or of the EZLN variety, is that of a teeming cauldron of aesthetically senseless, intellectually trivial, morally bankrupt, and virtually chaotic semiotic activity. But this is an impoverished notion. Popular culture, and so on, actually present themselves not as a monolithic mass of faceless dough but as a radically heterogeneous, ongoing flux, of humanity and cultural artifacts. This renders them thoroughly contradictory, and they are always in transition, with no readily apparent purpose or direction. In their composite they make up "guerrilla culture," which is anything but reducible to any set of descriptive features. "Guerrilla culture" is in a manner of speaking identityless; it lacks identifying features; it eludes every effort conceptually to pin it down. Yet there *is* identity. It is, I would suggest, like the Peircean self, forever transient. It is, in a word, *process*. It defies all labels and all definitions. Once it has been labeled, it contradicts that very label; once it has been defined in terms of what it is, in contrast to what it is not, it has already altered itself to the extent that it is neither the *is* nor the *is not* but now something else.[5]

How to be a Good "Cultural" Guerrilla

Many of the marginalized groups within contemporary societies can enjoy little of the hotly pursued good life outside the most essential furniture, a beat-up car, a TV set, a few CDs, fast-food restaurants, a movie once in a while, small-change video games, a few pieces of clothing—and the vast majority of the world's populace cannot even afford these barest of amenities.[6]

Their consumption of what little they can afford is often converted into subversive acts. They engage in a carnival of "cultural guerrilla tactics," following their whims, vague wishes, desires, intuitions, inclinations, and feelings (i.e., Firstness, body, and the "irrational" in contrast to Thirdness, mind, and the "rational," of the power elite). For those in power, following the entrenched strategies, "time is money" and must be used judiciously, for both time and money are instruments of control. Those of the subaltern, the *other*, buy what they can, but they do not merely consume what they buy and then leave things as they were. The marketplace is there for their pleasure, for their leisure (wasting time is no problem), for their rebellion. As a prime example from hyperconsumerist culture, the video palaces in the malls are precisely the spot where the marginalized (youth, most of them of minority groups in the cities) can exercise their own degree of power and control. There, the video player can become the Emperor of the Emporium. They are in charge of that alternate world in front of them which, with practice, they can manipulate at will (Turkle 1984, also 1995).

It is in such everyday life of postmodern Western societies that the contradictions inherent in capitalist systems allow for incessant negotiation and contestation. It might appear at the outset that the power elite has all the cards stacked in its favor. However, the powerful and their institutions are lumbering giants. They drag cumbersome baggage along with them; they are conservative, slow to learn new

ways, and tend more often than not to resist all forms of change. They construct public places in order to set their power in concrete and keep the common folk under
their surveillance. Their control comes in the form of rules and regulations—the
law—exercised in terms of set-in-stone strategies designed to control by instilling
desires, drives, and compulsion for commodities of consumption. To make matters
worse, they constantly carry out their customary "objective studies" in order to discover better means for manipulating the public.

The presumably weak *other*, the subalterns, however, have their own ways that
do not conform to the motives, means, and methods of the strong. They travel light;
they are mobile, wily, full of tricks, and creative. They carve out bits and pieces of
territory within the malls, schools, and other public places designed by the powerful
to control them, and, engaging in hit-and-run "cultural guerrilla tactics," they find
ever-newer ways to subvert the rules and regulations placed before them. They must
make do with what they have, much in the fashion of *bricoleurs*. They do not simply
and passively consume the signs around them, they put them to use for their own
purposes, and they abuse them whenever they can do so and thereby manifest their
contempt, whether explicitly or implicitly, of the system (recall the "hidden transcripts" hypothesis in chapter three). De Certeau observes that this practice has been
around for quite a while. He evokes as a paradigm case that of the Amerindians
shortly after the conquest and colonization by the Spaniards. The victory of the colonizers over the colonized:

> was diverted from its intended aims by the use made of it: even
> when [the Amerindians] were subjected, indeed even when they
> accepted their subjection, the Indians often used the laws, prac-
> tices, and representations that were imposed on them by force or
> by fascination to ends other than those of their conquerors; they
> made something else of them; they subverted them from within—
> not by rejecting them, or by transforming them (though that oc-
> curred as well), but by many different ways of using them in the
> service of rules, customs or convictions foreign to the coloniza-
> tion which they could not escape. They metaphorized the domi-
> nant order: they made it function in another register. They re-
> mained other within the system which they assimilated and which
> assimilated them externally. They diverted it without leaving it.
> Procedures of consumption maintained their difference in the very
> space that the occupier was organizing. (de Certeau 1984:31–32)
> (brackets added)

The strategies of the conqueror were by design—one need only take a look at the
original symmetry of a Spanish colonial plaza—and ideally carried out by the rigid
protocol of the colonial guidelines set down by the Spanish crown. The Amerindians' tactics, in contrast, were amorphous, a matter of incessantly altering, alternating, and self-organizing semiosis. The example of the Amerindians, de Certeau assures us, is by no means extreme. To a degree, the same processes can be found in
the everyday life of our contemporary milieu, "in the use made in 'popular' milieus

of the cultures diffused by the 'elites' that produce language" (de Certeau 1984:32; see also Eco 1986).

Now, in the manner of Peirce's semiotics, to subvert a sign is to translate it into another sign. In order for this to occur, a sign, let's say a symbol, must travel the path toward the barest of iconicity, the field of possibility, where it can discard its worn luggage and grab a new satchel of meaning. It is then back to Firstness, to imagery and the imaginary, tacit signs, signs of sense and feeling and quality, signs of the body more than the mind, signs of desire more than convention, intuition more than logic and reason. In fact, there must be a plunge into the abyss where everything is possible before anything novel can stand a chance of emerging. As composer John Cage put it, between one and another word there is a vacuum, a moment of silence; the same can be said of any and all boundaries. Once the field of possibilities has been reached and sign translation is in progress, the sign, if it is to attain the status of symbolicity once again, must make its way along the stream and catch up with its former self in order that the translation may become manifest.

"Cultural guerrilla warfare," the semiosic process of signs incessantly becoming other signs, signs turning around and showing another face on their backside. The "guerrilla" is a warrior in the morning and in the afternoon she takes on the role of an innocent peasant. The graffitist in the local high school receives his diploma with a knot of emotion in his throat. The evening drug dealer is an amiable employee at the corner drug store. The shoplifter becomes a neutral bystander when confusion erupts. The Native American of New Mexico enters into the community corn dance during the week, and Monday morning he dons a suit and tie and is off to Sandia Base where he is employed as an engineer. The North African living in Paris creates a little Africa in the low-class neighborhood that is imposed on her due to her race and her background. The Mexican slum dweller buys a *hotquek* (pancake) on the street, and rolls it up and eats it like a taco. The blue-collar worker leaves the factory with his lunchbox full of nuts and bolts and wire and tools. The white-collar employee takes a handful of diskettes in his attaché case. And Subcomandante Marcos and the EZLN engage in their wily, unpredictable subversive tactics. From minuscule and relatively unimportant to sweeping and all-important, the examples are inexhaustible. All "cultural" guerrillas, whether petty or revolutionary, rebellious or benign, and whether in minor or major leagues, are engaged in playing both sides of the court. First they are honest Johns and Janes, then they are pilferers and poachers, and then it's back to their previous roles—activities almost worthy of an experienced *jeitinheur*, one might add. For the boss they are either one thing or the other: honest until they get caught and contemptible when their two-faced practice is revealed.

De Certeau's example of *la perruque* (the wig), is apropos in this regard:

> *La Perruque* is the worker's own work disguised as work for his employer. It differs from pilfering in that nothing of material value is stolen. It differs from absenteeism in that the worker is officially on the job. *La Perruque* may be as simple a matter as a secretary's writing a love letter on "company time" or as complex as a cabinetmaker's "borrowing" a lathe to make a piece of furniture for his living room. . . . With complicity of other workers . . .

he succeeds in "putting one over" on the established order on its home ground. Far from being a regression toward a mode of production organized around artisans or individuals, *la perruque* reintroduces "popular" techniques of other times and other places into the industrial space (that is, into the present order). (de Certeau 1984:25)

Thus, the very success of the commodity-consumerist oriented commercial system, and the making and selling and using of the objects of production, have created the means of, and even invited its subversion. From the view of the established order, "cultural" guerrillas are laudable laborers until their practices become known. Then they are canned. It is an *either/or* logical and rational affair. From the field of Firstness, on the other hand, the "guerrillas" are *both* honest *and* crooks, and whichever side of them that happens to surface depends on the context and the situation. From the "guerrillas'" own point of view, they are *neither* entirely honest *nor* are they entirely crooks; they are simply and without regrets doing what they can or what they want to a system that in their opinion has done them no favors. They do not necessarily have any truck with the boss they work for, the struggling owner of a franchise at the mall they frequent, the good-natured underpaid and overworked teacher at their high school, the local cop who sometimes prefers to look the other way. They are "guerrillas": subverting the system as a whole in their own small way.[7]

Indeed, de Certeau addresses himself to an "alternative logic." The problem is that it is linguicentric through and through; in fact, it is hyperlinguistic—the same old story over again. This characteristic, endemic in French thought, does not, nevertheless, reduce the importance of de Certeau's argument, that is, if we include all signs up to symbols, signs of language use. If so much is taken for granted, de Certeau's implicit alternative logic is context-dependent rather than context-free in the order of classical logic and Chomskyan natural language. We read that a "rich elucidation" of this sort of alternative logic is found in Sun Tzu's *Art of War* (1963) and in the *Book of Tricks* (Khawam 1976) of the Arabic tradition. But, de Certeau continues, we need not look that far abroad, for all societies contain, within themselves, the seeds of this "subversive logic," which emerges itself somewhere from the formal rules of daily practices. However, there is a problem:

[W]here should we look for [these practices] in the West, since our scientific method, by substituting its "own" places for the complex geography of social ruses and its "artificial" languages for ordinary language, has allowed and even required reason to adopt a logic of mastery and transparency? Like Poe's "purloined letter," the inscriptions of these various logics are written in places so obvious that one does not see them. (de Certeau 1984:22) (brackets added)

I find de Certeau's line of thought compelling, in spite of its obsessive, linguicentric focus on language and virtually language alone, especially in his reference to the "purloined letter" as a counterpart to the tacit dimension to which I have alluded in this inquiry. Expanding the field of de Certeau's account to include the whole of Peirce's semiotics, I would suggest that what we have is the four-fold set of possibilities for an alternative logic. This four-fold way at one and the same time overthrows classical logic and contains classical logic: "A," "Not-A," "*Either* A *or* Not-A," "*Both* A *and* Not-A," and "*Neither* A *nor* Not-A." [8]

However, we have heard this story before, so in an attempt to avoid boredom, let's return for a moment to Mexico.

Mexican Masks Par Excellence

At the outset it appeared that the Chiapas rebels (insofar as they are an *invented* "reality" as defined above) were quite unique. Unlike peasant uprisings of earlier years, EZLN was led by an outsider who had over the past decade taken up the Amerindians' way of life. He spent over ten years learning their language and doing things their way while at the same time gaining their confidence and informing them of centuries of wrongdoing and how things could be made right. If not an "Army of National Liberation," at least EZLN was an "Army of Indigenous Interests in Favor of Local Liberation." Clearly, most of the rebels did not carry weapons as modern and powerful as those that were proudly displayed on TV during the initial days of the movement. Yet the several thousand fighters were part of a coordinated plan, with a single command that articulated a consistent message. Their organization, logistics, communication, and public relations revealed years of preparation.[9]

EZLN's appearance was an immediate problem for Mexico and especially the then ruling PRI.[10] There had been persistent rumors of the uprising from the daily *La Jornada* and the weekly magazine *Proceso*, but the party machine paid them little mind, since it was almost inconceivable that several thousand peasants would be capable of launching an effective insurgency campaign. Yet, the rumors turned out to prove correct those critics who had been insisting since 1988 that the course followed by President Carlos Salinas de Gortari (1988–94) would some day lead to a major crisis. President Salinas's "Solidarity" program, designed to invest token pesos in the countryside in order to win back lost rural support for PRI, had been a failure: it had little public appeal, its prime mover lacked *personalismo* and populist appeal, and it was bloated with bureaucratic molasses flow protocols and government corruption—indeed, this "solidarity" is not exactly what Richard Rorty (1989) had in mind with his brave new utopia. As a case in point, much money was spent in the state of Chiapas itself in the name of "solidarity," but the region's authoritarian, corrupt social and political structure remained intact, and even strengthened. Hospitals and schools were built, but they lacked furniture, equipment, and personnel. The ex-governor of the state liked basketball, so hoops were placed throughout the peasant villages, even in places where the people knew nothing of the game. All the while the people themselves remained completely outside the decision-making process. Resentment became rampant. For this reason the rebellion could hardly have come at a more opportune moment: it ironically followed on the heels of NAFTA, and it marked the climax of peasant discontent.[11]

The rationale for a movement that otherwise might have appeared suicidal was actually quite laudable. The EZLN manifesto, as expressed in the original "Declaration from the Lacandón Jungle," included:

> TODAY WE SAY ENOUGH IS ENOUGH!
> TO THE PEOPLE OF MEXICO:
> MEXICAN BROTHERS AND SISTERS:
> We are the product of 500 years of struggle: first against slavery, then during the War of Independence against Spain, then to avoid being absorbed by North American imperialism, then to promulgate our constitution and expel the French empire from our soil; later the dictatorship of Porfirio Díaz denied us the just application of the Reform laws and the people rebelled and leaders like Villa and Zapata emerged, poor men just like us. We have been denied by our rulers the most elemental conditions of life so they can use us as cannon fodder and pillage the wealth of our country. (EZLN 1995:311)

And later, in a *communiqué* of January 11, 1994: "We believe that a genuine respect for the liberties and democratic will of the people are indispensable requisites for the improvement of social and economic conditions among our country's dispossessed. That is why, just as we brandish the banner of improvement in the Mexican people's living standards, we also demand political liberty and democracy" (EZLN 1994).

The tactic was not to take power or defeat the Mexican government but simply to become a mouthpiece of the people. Dignity for the Amerindians, democracy, justice: soberly reformist rather than wild-eyed, violent revolutionary goals, which were also what Octavio Paz (1970a [1969]) attributed to the student movements of 1968 that ended in the October 2 massacre at Tlatelolco. The mysterious masked spokesman, Subcomandante Marcos, apparently did not have revolution on the agenda (Castañeda 1995:79–86). On the other hand, Oppenheimer (1996:58–61) claims the movement had from the beginning been the arm of a radical Marxist movement based in Mexico City. It was not until Marcos had ingratiated himself with the correspondents and intellectuals throughout the West and until the movement gained the reputation of a unique *sui generis* operation that the charismatic, wisecracking leader made an about face and denied any Marxist leanings. At any rate, by February of 1994 the importance of EZLN had become apparent. This was definitely not just another skirmish. It was soon lauded and slandered, but in whichever case it was generally acknowledged as the world's first postcommunist revolution—to complement the Mexican Revolution of 1910–17 as the first profound social movement of our century.

According to Oppenheimer, among others, Marcos was unmasked early in 1995 and his name was said to be Rafael Sebastián Guillén, a Professor of Graphic Design at the Universidad Autónoma Metropolitana at Xochimilco. President Ernesto Zedillo (1994–2000) immediately put "Operation Rainbow" on the board, and a surprise attack was set to catch the wily Marcos and thus repeat the infamous ambush of the revolutionary hero Emiliano Zapata in 1919. The operation was a fiasco. EZLN, enjoying high-tech communication facilities in the middle of the Lacandón jungle, got wind of the countermovement, fled more deeply into the jungle, and the Marcos mystique was perpetuated. The nimble peasant leader continued popping jokes about the lumbering giant, PRI, and Mexican bureaucracy, while picking fun at the world's press and international opinion. A master at word play, tragicomic inversions, and quick mental maneuvers, he continued to outwit his plodding PRI antagonists.

All in all, the Chiapas rebellion epitomizes the de Certeau image of limber "guerrillas" constantly eluding the creaking bones of the plodding power structure. While Marcos was practicing his rhetorical moves, Byzantine debates in the capital city by archaic Stalinist methods beat about the bush with generalizations and without addressing the real issue. Sharp remarks from EZLN were met with stuttering, hesitation, and denials; quick *communiqués* were addressed by the president's acolytes parroting canned responses; the monolithic *Televisa* network, a right-arm of the government, silenced the important events while repeating the usual slogans about "Solidarity." It seems that the attitude was simply: "Who does this guy think he is?"[12] Other than that, Marcos's name and the movement were avoided whenever possible, and penetrating questions went unasked. (Obviously, EZLN, as Mignolo [2000:149] points out, was creating a new discourse, that is, a new "style of reasoning"; see also Mignolo and Schiwy [2002].)

If the Zapatista rebellion is not exactly revolutionary, neither was it, strictly speaking, an armed movement. It was reformist, yet it created the image on the part of the Mexican middle-class as revolutionary. There were arms, but there were actually more guerrillas than guns. The rebels were politically and economically motivated, yet there were few aspirations outside the local environs of the Lacandón jungle. There were attempts to change domestic social policies, yet there were no political designs and no attempts to engage directly in politics. Here we have a masterful case of signs that are simultaneously *both* one thing *and* another and yet they are *neither* the one thing *nor* the other. Binary thinking breaks down. There is not any simple this or that, no sign and *other*, no simple Secondness. Rather, there was the vagueness of Firstness, with all its inconsistencies, and the incompleteness of any and all generalities within the sphere of Thirdness, all rushing along the same semiosic stream. The semiotics of EZLN is as elusive with respect to binary analysis as is EZLN itself with respect to the official government body.

In this respect, Mignolo (1997a:338–39) quotes Marcos in an interview revealing that Zapatismo "is and is not Marxist-Lenist. The Zapatismo is not fundamentalist or milenarist indigenous thinking; and it is not indigenous resistance either. It is a mixture of all that, that crystallizes in the EZLN." Commensurate with these words, and from the perspective embraced in this inquiry, Marcos avails himself of extra-linguistic subversive "guerrilla" signs of the *both-and* and *neither-nor* sort. Indeed, as Beverley (1999:42–43) put it:

> Historians like Florencia Mallon are given to preserving and nurturing the written record, whereas peasant rebels, such as . . . the Zapatistas in Chiapas today, often want to destroy it, for example, by burning down the municipal archives (as the Zapatistas did).

They understand that the written record is also the record of their legal conditions of propertylessness and exploitation.

I need to be more specific in this respect. So . . .

How is it Possible to Keep Tabs on Those Radical Upstarts?

Sandinista rebel Tomás Borge Martínez once remarked in a *Playboy* (1983:198) interview:

> Perhaps I could say that I was led to the revolutionary life by reading an author named Karl May. Karl May, not Karl Marx. May was a German who wrote novels about the Wild West in the United States (without ever visiting America). . . . In the May westerns the heroes were archetypes of nobility—courageous, audacious, personally honest. I wanted to be like them. But since in Nicaragua we didn't have the Great Plains of the North American West, and since the injustices we were facing were different from those in Western novels, I decided to confront Nicaraguan injustices.

Marcos's and Borge Martínez's remarks are *apropos*. Both are Gramsci organic intellectuals, "cultural" and "socio-political" guerrillas. They are ironic, honest, and into nonlinear *both-and, neither-nor* thinking. Too often, and perhaps unwillingly, theorists of culture slip into the idea that (1) cultures must have some center that can be divined by some master plan the omniscient academic theorist brings to the scene, that (2) the plan is organized around some presupposed *either/or* imperatives, and that (3) the role of the theorist-now-turned-critic is that of analyzing what she sees with the detachment worthy of a scientist during the heyday of positivism.

Unfortunately, a center, a master plan made up of binary imperatives, and scientific detachment are all pipe dreams. But this doesn't deter some self-proclaimed cultural prophets, even from the most unexpected sources. Theodor Adorno (1973) and others of the Frankfurt School made observations from on high regarding the culture industry and the enlightened deception of the masses; Roland Barthes (1972) wrote about bourgeois myths presumably from some supreme outside vantage point; Michel Foucault (1970) was supposedly capable of sensing the nature of any and all broad culture-laden *episteme*; Jean Baudrillard and only Jean Baudrillard (1989) could possess the perspicuity of vision to see all that is wrong with North American postmodern culture after a quick trip through some of the tourist spots and a few academic settings in the United States, and so on.[13] It is as if they were culture dictators in the control rooms pushing whichever buttons happened to strike their fancy, and culture had no alternative but to respond accordingly. They seem oblivious to the fact that there is no God's-eye view from which the whole of culture can be surveyed. The idea that there is no central control room is quite unlike the image portrayed by Kafka or Dostoyevsky or Orwell or even Althusser's ideological state apparatus or Foucault's Panopticon. And it is quite unlike that of Foucault's *epistemes* or Thomas Kuhn's paradigms or Michael Polanyi's post-critical science, for there is no single voice of authority that is tantamount to the viewpoint of some homogenous community. Rather than some individual or social group at the control buttons, there is a heterogeneous mix of partly interdependent and partly autonomous subcommunities doing the best with what they have within their particular enclaves. There is no monolith but many irregular stones with no hope for their getting collected together to make up a foundation.

The dictum "There is no God's-eye grasp of the whole" goes against the grain of our customary belief in the power of symbolic signs. These signs are passed off as supreme signs of the mind, signs with which the haves can exercise a remarkable degree of control over the have-nots. These signs are considered signs of reason, of linear, bipolar logic, of well-tempered semiotic practices. Yet, we should not, we cannot, ignore signs of indexicality and especially of iconicity. These are signs of nature and of the body: nonverbal, nonlinear, "irrational," "illogical," *rhizomic* rather than tree-like, and prone to disorder, which subverts our taste for balance, equilibrium, harmony. Put the three classes of signs together, and we have integrating semiosis of bodymind, a continuity of signs of interrelated, interactive, coparticipating, codependent emergence: semiosis. In human cultural settings, the haves and their imperious symbols are invariably confronted by the "cultural" guerrilla activities of the have-nots and their subversive indexical and iconic as well as symbolic signs. The have-nots engage in puns, mockery, ridicule, satire, parody, and occasional violence—"cultural guerrilla" tactics. In so doing, they counter the haves' high culture with kitsch, pastiche, sycretisms, and illicit acts of a numbing variety of sorts. They elude their pursuers; they don a new mask for every occasion; they are everybody and nobody according to the circumstances; they remain indexically and iconically vague through their allusions, subtle nuances, elusive hints, sly gestures, and self-denying moves. Consequently, symbolic generalities constructed by the have-nots tumble, as new have-not self-contradictory identities slip through the fissures presumably holding the vacuum of excluded-middles.

Once a *communiqué* was issued over the internet in response to whether the Zapatista leader was gay, as per a recent rumor. A portion of it appeared in issue number six of *City Lights Review*, published in San Francisco. It read:

> Marcos is gay in San Francisco, black in South Africa, an Asian in Europe, a Chicano in San Ysidro, an anarchist in Spain, a Palestinian in Israel, a Mayan Indian in the streets of San Cristóbal, . . . a rocker in the national University, a Jew in Germany, . . . a Communist in the post-Cold War era, an artist without gallery or portfolio, a pacifist in Bosnia, a housewife alone on a Saturday night in any neighborhood in any city in Mexico, a reporter writing filler stories for the back pages, a single woman on the subway at ten P.M., a peasant without land, an unemployed worker, a dissident amid free-market economics, a writer without books or readers, and, of course, a Zapatista in the mountains of south-east Mexico.

With machine-gun cadence iconic images indexically emerge from the included middle to leave a vague, ambiguous symbolic muddle. What are self-respecting signs to do when there is no apparent rhyme or reason to their unruly mix? This is a supreme example of Gilles Deleuze and Félix Guattari's (1983) "schizogenesis." It is verbal "cultural" guerrilla tactics at their de Certeauean best: it is border of border thinking. The "paranoiac" remains within the system, caught in a one-dimensional stream of binary choices; there is no way out and no retrievable center. In contrast, the "schizophrenic" does an orthogonal sidestep that places her "outside." This is no transcendental quantum leap, mind you. Rather, it entails awareness of the binary wave-train head on: it is as if everything were there all at once, which endows her with the characteristics of everybody and at the same time nobody.

Deleuze and Guattari's schizophrenic is also a *bricoleur, par* excellence. She is in command of a hodgepodge collection of signs of related characteristics with a general but always transient rule of thumb for their use, and she goes about rearranging them in continually novel and different patterns and configurations: her language is a word-salad relating to a junkyard of semiotic objects. As a consequence, she remains indifferent toward the methods of production and the product, or the overall result to be achieved. What is of most importance is the doing, the process.

Enough jawing about activities of a general type, and another return to that most concrete of worlds: Mexico.

Back to Normal, that is, Chaos?

Death haunts Mexico. I don't refer to that special Mexican magnifying-mimicking-mocking familiarity with death. That characteristic Mexican attitude toward death blows it up into what is taken by the outside observer as a monstrous macroimage or sign (of Firstness)—most typically exemplified in the graphics of José Guadalupe Posada—which evoke mimicry (by the other, Secondness) and at the same time mockery (by bringing sign and other into interrelationship in such a way that they become the object of derision from another vantage, Thirdness). I allude to death in the brute physical sense of the term, by way of murder, political assassination.[14]

The government never satisfactorily solved the murders of Cardinal Juan Jesús Posadas Ocampo in May, 1993, presidential candidate Luis Donaldo Colosio in March, 1994, and José Francisco Ruiz Massieu, general secretary of the PRI in September, 1994. Meanwhile, back in the secluded quarters where the politicians meet, it was business as usual, with government lacking a genuine image of legitimacy—even after the National Action Party (PAN) candidate Vicente Fox won an unexpected victory of the PRI candidate in 2000. Jorge G. Castañeda (1995) suggests that the assassinations are the result of struggles for money and power within Mexico's elite, which includes the PRI, the nation's great capitalists (often of the PAN hierarchy), the drug lords, and even, to an extent, the church—although on paper there are no ties between Church and state; that is to say between Church and PRI; Vicente Fox and his party have altered that equation considerably. The entire sordid business has become the subject of the Mexican soap opera mentioned above, *Nada Personal*, which depicts the country's political leaders as a cynical and malicious caste of characters.

The struggles among the ruling elite are hard-driven by the international economy and Mexico's entry into NAFTA, which marked leaner and meaner modes of production—*maquiladoras* or sweat shops, downsizing at all levels, severe cut-backs in social programs, wages that fall behind inflation, and higher unemployment. Traditionally, the ruling party played a corporate, paternalistic-patriarchal role. More recently, it was pushed and pulled by the bloated bureaucracy of the one-party state, sham labor unions and peasant leagues, and increasingly by foreign and domestic capital and powerful drug lords. The technocratic leadership became a giant step removed from the close personal ties (*personalismo*) it had maintained up into the 1960s, and, especially after the massacre at Tlatelolco in 1968, it began moving toward a cold and impersonal bureaucratic-technocratic machine (Botz 1995). As a consequence, President Ernesto Zedillo and other party and government leaders seemed out of touch with the reality of Mexican life. The distant, humorless, straight-laced Zedillo lacked charisma, oratorical capacity, and personal charm. While president, he was unable to strike a resonant chord with the people. The official ruling family up to year 2000 seemed to have lost its tact for co-opting its opponents with enticing carrots. It apparently no longer had the wherewithal to apply the stick—it would most likely not dare do so even if it could, fearful of the outcry from international sources. The party became like Sisyphus trying to scale a sulfur belching Popocatapetl: he fears reaching the cauldron at the top, and at the same time he cannot remain perched on the slippery slopes for long. (Under the charisma and personal charm of the garrulous Vicente Fox, promises of change have been forthcoming, but only time will tell the tale.)

As the gap continues to grow between the haves and the have-nots, politicians and people, cities and countryside, the existence of a vacuum becomes increasingly evident. Wealth and power, like nature, abhors a vacuum. Something must emerge. So the Mexican army, it appears, is slowly stepping forth to fill the empty spots. Generals and colonels have begun to take things into their own hands in some of the rural areas. Military checkpoints exist along highways, travelers are hounded constantly and soldiers invade rural villages where guerrilla activity is seen as a threat. Torture, rape, and murder are occasionally the inevitable consequence. Mexico is unfortunately beginning to resemble other Latin American countries during the 1960s and early 1970s, when the military took over Argentina, Uruguay, Brazil, Chile, Bolivia, and Perú.

The high voltage behind the changes in Mexico, and for that matter, elsewhere in the world, is expressed in the current buzzwords: multinational corporations, globalization of capital, worldwide web, information super-highway, neoliberalism, privatization. These shifts of eddies and whirlpools and major alterations of the main current and periodic flood stages and occasional destruction of check-dams below are radically changing economic life, social classes and alliances, and political forces. In Mexico, as elsewhere, the turn has been toward something comparable to the classical liberal economic policies of the late nineteenth and early twentieth centuries when big government as we now know it from the time of F. D. Roosevelt to Ronald Reagan and Bill Clinton was virtually unknown. These new policies received a massive injection with the passing of NAFTA. At first there was panic and then disaster, as the peso was devalued by nearly 50 percent and the Mexican stock market crashed. Since then the story has it that the Mexican economy has begun its road to recovery. The question is: recovery for whom? Granted, the gross national product grew by 7.2 percent during the second trimester of 1996, and it continues to grow by leaps and bounds. But the growth was basically due to increased production of made-for-export commodities in the manufacturing sector. This growth has been accompanied by Mexico's continuing austerity program. Budgets for health, social security, and education are still being cut, workers' wages are virtually frozen, and unemployment is still on the increase. It is boom for some and bust for those who have yet to experience any kind of boom at all.[15]

But I have done little more than put a few statistics on the monitor and lament the current condition of the Mexican people. In so doing, have I really been able to take a grasp of the whole map of the socio-politico-economic situation? How can I say what I say if I cannot know the whole? If I can somehow sense the whole, how can I know I can sense it? What are the problems inherent in my assumption that I can know it? My problem is the general problem of postmodern learned ignorance, as we shall see.

Only a Map that Contains Itself Can Be Complete

The idea of a map and the term "mapping" reminds us of Fredric Jameson and his fashion of postmodernism. The "map" is a sort of shorthand for rendering comprehensible terrain that has otherwise become virtually incomprehensible by the tide of postmodern culture. Despite its currency, the term is slippery. A clue to Jameson's use of the term comes from Kevin Lynch, who in *The Image of the City* (1960) coined "imageability" with respect to urban space. Jameson expanded this idea as general "cognitive mapping," which is an extrapolation of the "image" to the "mental map of the social and global totality we carry around in our heads in variously garbled forms" (1988:353). The conundrum that inevitably ensues, Jameson writes, is that of finding one's place in one's "cognitive map" with the "great global multinational and decentered communicational network," which can only be accomplished with some radically new aesthetics capable of "mapping" the flow of multinational capital. To our chagrin, he offers us nary a hint as to how this task may be carried out.

Now, this talk about images and maps might be well and good, as far as it goes. The problem, especially in Jameson's case—and he is not alone in this regard by any means—is that the images and maps turn out to be "linguicized," they are the product of linguicentrism, in addition to their totalization and their ocularcentrism.[16] In order adequately to come to grips with imageability and mappability, one must give the terms a major overhaul. The radical incompleteability of the image and the map must be acknowledged, so forget about totalization. The image and the map are, in the combination of their parts and in their function, "schemes" (comparable to what Peirce dubs "diagrams"), in addition to their nature as "pictures," hence they are indexical in addition to their possessing iconic characteristics. And since they are neither completeable nor totalizing, they are not surveyable in one fell swoop. Hence they cannot be *said*, but only *shown*. If they lend themselves to incomplete and partial *showing*, then there is the possibility that they can at least be tacitly known through iconic signs. These are gut-level signs of touch, taste, smell, and nonverbal sight and sound, to be sure, but more germane still, they are signs of visceral feels and sensations through kinesthetic, somatic, motilic, proprioceptive means and modes (merrell 1998b). This is Michael Polanyi's (1958) celebrated *tacit knowing*, Norwood Hanson's *patterns of knowledge* (1958), signs of Pierre Bourdieu's *habitus* (1990), of Wittgenstein's (1953) *forms of life*, and, above all, of the nature of Peirce's *habits of thought* (Boler 1964).

The trouble with these formulations is that they remain in part or almost entirely linguicentric. Take Wittgenstein, for example. His "forms of life," "family resemblances," "language games," and other metaphors, as well as his general philosophy of meaning in use, seem ripe for liberating themselves from the tyranny of symbolic signs. Yet they remain linguistic through and through. This is nowhere more evident than in his observation and his saying that "Our language can be seen as an ancient city: a maze of little streets and squares, of old and new houses, and of houses with additions from various periods; and this surrounded by a multitude of new boroughs with straight regular streets and uniform houses" (Wittgenstein 1953:18). Robert J. Ackermann goes on to observe and say of Wittgenstein in this regard that one of the problems of sorting out this complexity is that "some of the areas of the City—languages of mathematics, science, emotion, and so forth—are seemingly polyglot, embracing a motley of language games whose relationship is obscure. We cannot assume that areas of the City are always clearly marked out by horizons or that ordinary-language categories will coincide with the horizons that are marked out in philosophical surveys" (Ackermann 1988:13–14). The borders of language are the borders of the city and the borders of sections within it that separate all the language games. Awareness of the borders enables effective use of language games, and by playing the games effectively, one knows one's way about in the city. The assumption has it that all is a matter of language and language is all: linguicentrism.

That is one problem. Another problem bears once again on the idea of totality. Who is qualified to do the mapping anyway? Jameson seems to conceive of the map as a vast unfinished project that can nonetheless at some point in the future be packaged, signed, sealed, and delivered. For Samuel Weber (1987:46–58), a Jameson map is a story of epic proportions waiting to be told once and for all by the proper shaman. The very idea of *saying* the story about an image or map that *shows* the weary traveler her way around confuses the *saying* and the *showing*. To *say* the *shown* would be tantamount to creating, in words, an image of the image, a map of the map, and if the creation is faithful, that map of the map would be so minute of detail that it would mirror itself, and that mirror image would in turn contain its own self, and so on. A sentence that presumably mirrors itself and at the same time talks about itself was of some concern in mathematics for the biggest part of the twentieth century, and is found in Gödel's celebrated proof. The verdict is that such mirroring and saying is either incomplete or it is inconsistent or it is both, and that verdict is often acknowledged in logic and the sciences, as especially witnessed in Douglas Hofstadter's (1979) masterful display. That's a rather vulgar way of putting it, but that's the way it is in a nutshell. To presume in the humanities and social sciences that mirroring and *saying* can be brought to completion is a totalizing, utopian dream. Either the world and our cultural world can be rendered completely comprehensible by an image or map in some sort of "metalinguistic" fashion, or it is a numbing rush of swirling bits and pieces the proper combination of which is undecidable. Given the current opinion of a jury of mathematicians, logicians, and physical scientists, surveyance is both visually and verbally impossible. There can be neither panopticism nor a voice from on high in our finite world. We have access to no more than fragmentary visual, auditory, tactile, olfactory, gustatory, and kinesthetic signs, and if we put any collection of them in some sort of order, it is because we fashioned them as a result of our dependency upon our semiotic world and its dependency upon us.

In order to avoid linguicentric and ocularcentric biases, then, are we to take Nietzsche at face value when he writes that the great thinkers think with their bodies, in dance, gyrating with oscillation, uncertainty, vacillation, twitching, spasms? The idea is attractive, even for us ordinary folks. But surely we cannot toss discursive thought into the trashcan and expect to find any answers by wordlessly dancing our way through life. Even Nietzsche himself had plenty to say on the matter, albeit often in a vague and evasive metaphorical mode. Are we inexorably reduced to making a choice between one thing and the other? Must our posture exclusively be a matter either of what Thomas Nagel (1986) labels a disembodied "view from nowhere" or of Rudolf Arnheim's (1969) obsession with "visual thinking"? Or must it be either semiology's priority of language (Lévi-Strauss 1963), the deconstructionist's biased "grammatological" primacy of writing (Derrida 1974), or some other fixation? Are there no viable alternatives between the *eithers* and the *ors*?

It might behoove us briefly to return to Peirce.

A Mediary Way?

Peirce's semiosis, by its very nature, is neither exclusively subject nor object, mind nor matter, inner nor outer, but a collapse of the poles of the oppositions into a whole, while at the same time each term maintains its identity by way of its complementary relationship with its companion term.

Descartes saw the mind as inner subjective consciousness that in the best of all circumstances contains ideas that mirror the world. Peirce, in contrast, was willing to concede to the vagueness and inconsistency and incompleteness and indeterminacy of semiosis. Peirce did not fall victim to what Richard Bernstein (1983) dubs "Cartesian anxiety" (i.e., *either* we have foundations, *or* darkness, anarchy, and chaos will surely prevail). That is because he ultimately found comfort in foundationlessness, placing the quest for knowledge in the same arena as all other walks of life. She who remains plagued by "Cartesian anxiety" must have things either one way or the other. Her way must be the right way, she supposes, and if something doesn't go to the tune of her band, it must be categorically discarded. Peirce's philosophy, as suggested throughout this study, entails interrelated, interactive, codependent emergence of feelings and "images" (Firstness), ideas and conceptual schemes or "maps" and their "saying" (Secondness and Thirdness), and actual experience. Peirce is aware that theoretical reflection, like the activities of everyday living, should not simply be mindless, detached, and disembodied. Reflection demands the act of becoming coupled with mindful awareness *of* that which might otherwise go undetected. But this mindfulness is at the same time, so to speak, mindlessly mindful. It entails mindful awareness at a level virtually exempt from the Faustian need to remain detached from the world, actively and aggressively controlling, manipulating, using, and abusing it.

An example, comparable to those of chapter two, is in order. When a child prodigy is given a violin and taught how to use it, she must first actively think through the moves explicitly imparted to her by her tutor and follow the examples she is given. After much practice and perhaps many tense moments, her talent begins to take over, and her moves become fluid. Now, her fingers and hands do what they do spontaneously, her body sways in rhythm to the sounds spilling forth, and all this without her mind having to give hardly any active, detached thought to what it is she is doing at the moment she does it. Body and mind (bodymind, as the term was used above) act in concert. No longer is there any subject here and musical object there, with the one imposing itself on the other in order to squeeze the desired product from it; there are no longer any inner/outer, mind/body, here/there distinctions. One might wish to say, within the framework of Cartesian terminology, that her violin playing has become mindless. Her activity has, in the Cartesian sense, become mindless, yet she is mindfully aware of her every move, of the whole of all her moves. She is not simply playing the violin, but rather, she and her instrument are in concert "violining." There is no mind here and body there, subject here and violin there, silence before and music now. There is a process of interactive becoming. In this sense, the very idea of mindlessness can lead one astray, especially in light of the general view of things slowly unfolding itself throughout the pages of this chapter. The prodigy's activity is now mindful in the most literal sense, for her mind has become inseparable from her body. She is not the subject as violinist who extracts music from her object, the violin, consisting merely of a few slats of wood held together by glue and some gut strings. No. The violinist is in the process of becoming a violinist only in concert with the violin's truly becoming a violin by its being played; the music is becoming music only in the company of both the violinist and the violin, and violinist and violin depend on the music for their becoming violinist and violin.

So it is not simply a matter of our violinist putting the violin to use. The violin also puts the violinist to use, and the music puts both of them to use as they put it to use, while they make their way along the semiosic stream in harmony with each other as signs among signs. It's a perpetually shifting three-way affair. Just as there is no sight without seer and that which is in the process of seeing becoming, no dance without dancer and what is dancing becoming, no painting without painter and what is painting becoming, no science without scientist and what is science-in-the-process-of-becoming, so also there is no sign without an interpreter (interpretant) and that which is sign becoming. And—to get to the meat of the issue—there is no meaning without a semiotic agent or interpreter and that which is in the process of becoming meant. The mutual interaction between signs, sign engenderers, and meanings to which I allude could quite easily create the notion of putting to use as chiefly of linguistic nature, if not exclusively enshrouded in symbolic signs. This is simply not so, however, that is, if we reject our linguicentric tendencies. The crises of the last half of this century—in physics, biology, linguistics and the social sciences, philosophy and philosophy of science, history, criticism and theory, and in the arts—have incessantly bared the conspicuous limitations of the vernacular as well as technical language. Despite the profusion of technical terms, the wine of new meanings poured into the bottles of old terms, and the onslaught of neologisms at work and at play, language has remained incapable of the task asked of it regarding the vast expanse that lies beyond common experience. Language is even notoriously deficient regarding the mundane matters of everyday life. In a word, there are situations, events, acts, and objects on all levels of experience to which language, whether ordinary or technical, simply does not and cannot apply. This is where visceral, corporeal feels, sensations, sentiments, inclinations, notions, and intuitions come into the picture, inextricably to link mind and body, to compose bodymind.

I would suggest that the Mexican people excel in the everyday affairs of bodymind knowing what needs to be known and acting on it through tacit channels. My odd collection of allusions to Mexico, Peirce's signs, images and maps, ocularcentrism and linguicentrism, tacit feelings and explicit knowing, "cultural" guerrillas and control, and totalizing and undecidables might appear to be itself no more than a disconnected set of fragments without rhyme or reason. On the contrary, I would suggest. These fragments are intimately interrelated. You can't have one pole of any of these complementarities without the other: they are codependent, and their nature as signs in flux in turn depends upon their codependency. Thus all signs in agonistic struggle exist by virtue of the interrelations with all other signs and by way of mediation. Mediation lies outside the purview of that classical logic most often playing the major role in analytic semiotic enterprises. In fact, any complete logical account of this ebullient gush of semiosis is out of the question, for we are in it, and in it we will remain.

In this regard, perhaps the Mexicans have it right. If we always already find ourselves living in/with semiosis, our best bet is to go with the flow, and get on with life however we can. As they put it: "Aguántate, mujer/hombre" ("Grin and bear it," "Persevere," "Tough it out," "Cool it," "Take things as they come," "Be patient," "Bend with the wind," and all of the above, simultaneously and contradictorily).[17] If it seems that this would put one in a bind, not to worry: it's all of the nature of semiosis, knowledge of which, as far as our feeble, fallible, finite minds go, is radically incomplete, and somewhere along the line bloated with inconsistencies, in the extralinguistic undertow, where iconic and indexical signs are doing their becoming. I would only hope that, after tossing my own rather dry cynicism to the wind, the Mexican people's ability to persevere might finally win out, given the promise of honest, sincere, down-to-earth measures enacted by president-elect Vicente Fox (2000–06).[18]

In order perhaps to get a better feel for the semiosic process of becoming, I now exercise another tangential leap into hitherto relatively unmarked territory the nature of which might appear bizarre at the outset, but I trust, once again, that the message will eventually come clear.

Notes

1.   I say "perhaps unfortunately" due to my critique of this aspect of Baudrillard in merrell (1995a, 1996), regarding which limited space does not permit divulgence here.

2.   Articles and book-length analyses, reviews, and commentaries on the EZLN uprising abound. From diverse views, see Benjamin (1996), Botz (1995), Castañeda

(1995), Harvey (1998), Marcos (1995), Ross (1997), Simon (1997), Warnock (1995), Womack (1999); see especially Ponce de León (2001).

3.   For an *avant garde* view of recent Mexican history and the events leading up to the 1994 uprising, see Aguilar Camín (1988), Aguilar Camín and Meyer (1989), Botz (1995), Careaga (1992), and Meyer (1992).

4.   For the notion of the dominant culture's control over the subservient culture, see Said (1993); for a critique of this view, see Bhabha (1994).

5.   This is the sort of "guerrilla" qualities with which Che Guevara is most effectively endowed according to Ileana Rodríguez. It is also characteristic of difference in the female sense: inquisitive, yet gentle; placid yet vibrant; trenchant yet serene; forceful yet supple. It is far removed from the customary male obsession with *either-or* dominance, control, power (Rodríguez 1996:49–61).

6.   Indeed, at the Habitat 2 Conference at Turkey during the summer of 1996, Fidel Castro observed in his wildly applauded speech that the very idea of the so-called "consumer culture" of our times is hypocritical, for it excludes roughly 4/5 of the world's population, and that this hypocrisy is given testimony by the fact that not a single representative from the seven richest countries of the world was present.

7.   For marvelous examples of "guerrillerismo" in the *maquiladora* workplace on the U.S.-Mexico border, see Peña (1997), Ruiz (2000).

8.   I was in Mexico at the time of the terribly tragic attack on the World Trade Center and the Pentagon, September 11, 2001. Once back in the U.S., I began going through this manuscript for the penultimate time. I had no more than picked up the manuscript when it suddenly occurred to me that the West could well be seen as what I have called the plodding giant and certain Islamic terrorists could be seen by their sympathizers as sly "cultural" or "religious" guerrilla heroes. It's a matter of who does the constructing and from what perspective. Needless to say, this troubled me, and it still does. Rules and strategies are changing in ways that defy comprehension. I certainly don't have the answers, but I continue to sense that if any answers can be forthcoming, they will emerge from incongruously complementary combinations rather than from the stock logic of Enlightenment dreams (or, of course, from ethnocentrists or religious fanatics).

9.   See especially the article by Régis Debray (1996) in the weekly magazine *Proceso*.

10.   The "official" party, PRI, had its beginning with President Plutarco Elías Calles, who organized it in 1929 as the *Partido Nacional Revolucionario* (PNR), its name was changed by President Lázaro Cárdenas in 1938 when it was baptized as the *Partido de la Revolución Mexicana* (PRM), then it was changed for the last time by President Miguel Alemán in 1946 and given its present label, the *Partido Revolucionario Institucional* (PRI). Under the three names, whether cleanly or by fraud, it never lost a presidential election and held the reins until 2000, when swashbuckling jeans-clad PAN (*Partido de Acción Nacional*) candidate Vicente Fox Quesada, labeling his PRI opponent a "wimp" (*Time*, 2000), won the Mexicans' confidence.

11.   For an overview of this period in Mexico see Orme (1996) and Warnock (1995), for a polemical reporter's account, Ross (1997), and for an excellent book in Portuguese, Fuser (1995). It has recently been the opinion of many that NAFTA is

now in its post-puberty stage and is beginning to flex its muscles (Chaffin 1996). Its long-range effectiveness, however, remains to be seen.

12. This attitude bears similarity with Roberto DaMatta's "Você sabe com quem fala?" (from chapter two), the chief difference being that DaMatta's example is principally between "persons" and "individuals" and in the present case it is between the governing body and a group of dissidents.

13. For a critique along these lines of the Frankfurt School, see Swingewood (1977); for a critique of Barthes, Foucault, Baudrillard, and the social sciences in general, see Fay (1996), Sless (1986), and perhaps merrell (1995a).

14. I must add, however, that that other particularly Mexican attitude toward death pervades many of the pages of this inquiry (for an overview see Carrión 1952, Ochoa Zazueta 1974, Paz 1962, Westheim 1971).

15. According to Issue #502, Sept. 12, 1999 of the Nicaragua Solidarity Network Weekly News Update of the Americas, workers in Mexico's maquiladora sector "have seen their wages fall 23 percent in the five years since the North American Free Trade Agreement (NAFTA) went into effect in 1994," and that "maquiladora workers in Mexico are now being paid one-tenth what US workers would make for the same work."

16. Even the antilogocentrist poststructuralists and deconstructors are often guilty of linguicentrism insofar as they tend to focus on language and language alone (merrell 1997; for further on ocularcentrism, Jay 1993; for the perils of confidence-building totalizing programs, Lyotard 1974).

17. I would recommend Shorris (1992) for a discussion of the implications of "aguantar" in Mexican and Mexican-American cultures.

18. Significantly enough, the Associated Press (printed in Lafayette, IN, *Journal and Courier* [Dec. 2, 2000, B-1] has Zapatista leader Marcos hunkered down in the jungle of southern Chiapas state sending a *communiqué* to Fox that reads: "The nightmare ends today. Another could follow, or it could be a new dawn." Fox followed him in a speech a few days later, assuring him: "Today a new dawn begins for Chiapas." Unfortunately, the dawn continues to wane.

Part IV

The preceding chapters bear chiefly on colonial Latin America and current social, political, and economic trends and tendencies. In chapter thirteen the tenor now changes to that which underlies these processes, that is, to resonance and dissonance, harmony and disharmony, symmetry and asymmetry, equilibrium and disequilibrium, and above all, rhythm and syncope, from biological to cognitive to broad cultural levels. Chapter fourteen emphasizes an unexpected element of openness in the strangely dialogic nature of the contemporary Latin American scene, particularly regarding extralinguistic signs. Consequently, the feeling, gradually emerging throughout this inquiry, now begins to assert itself: the Latin Americans, and to an extent all people, do not merely talk, they sing, they do not walk, they dance, they do not react like atoms in an enclosed chamber, they interrelatedly, interactively, and codependently emerge as a whole, as cultures incessantly becoming other cultures. In other words, the Latin Americans are supreme examples of bodymindsigns in virtually perpetual motion.

Chapter Thirteen

Spaces, Syncope, Synchrony

> To come from elsewhere, from 'there' and not 'here,' and hence to be simultaneously 'inside' and 'outside' the situation at hand, is to live at the intersection of histories and memories, experiencing both their preliminary dispersal and their subsequent translation into new, more extensive, arrangements along emerging routes.
>
> —Iain Chambers

> The border: a zone of chiaroscuros.
>
> —Alfredo Villanueva-Collado

> Border culture is a polysemantic term.
>
> —Guillermo Gómez-Peña

Figure 6 embodies the interrelated, interactive codependence of vagueness and signs of imagination, of feeling, of Firstness (Maggie's world at its dreamiest), of the experienced world (of Funy and Tlöny, each in his own way), and of generality, of thought, of Thirdness (Lönny's hypothetico-deductive construct at its best). We run the gamut from iconicity to symbolicity, from body signs to mind signs and their union in bodymindsigns, from overdetermination to underdetermination, from inconsistency to incompleteness, and the dream of noncontradiction dissolves and the excluded-middle ideal is in shambles—all of which we noted in the above tales from Brazil and Mexico.

But, . . . ! . . . I fear I'm still caught up in excessive abstraction. How can one get down to the brass tacks of concrete language? How can one really say what one feels and senses? Articulate that with which one is in resonance? Express what is impressed on/in one's body? How can one get what one has penned up inside out in the open? In other words, what is it that I am trying to say anyway? Perhaps the key is to attend more closely to *rhythm*. After all, rhythm is, I would expect, how "green" can become "grue," "cats" can become "cats[*]," "Guadalupe" and "Tonantzín" can become "Guadantzín," and how "Gavagai!" can be variously interpreted, and all that and many more instances of language change and general sign change, and change of change, with neither fixity nor finality. This is a problem, stemming from Alfred North Whitehead's "fallacy of misplaced concreteness," that provokes a call for Peirce's "concrete reasonableness."

So, rhythm.

It's All in the Beat

In living organisms, spontaneously rhythmic oscillations can in nonlinear fashion lock onto nearby rhythms in the process of what is called "mutual entrainment."[1] This nature of nonlinear rhythms to entrain, synchronize, and resonate is a function of their time-dependent sensitivity: disturbances at different times will alter previous rhythms such that they become resonant with rhythms of the present.

For example, the heartbeat can be accelerated or slowed by altering the rate of stimuli rhythms. During this process the "phase space" of the heartbeat is reset, and the breakdown of rhythmicity can lead to arrhythmia and eventually to a disintegration of the heart's periodicity. Death can result. However, this and other comparable phenomena are more complex than we might suppose. Arthur Winfree (1987), after years of laboratorying, theoretical reasoning, and philosophical speculating, offers a brilliant treatise on the spatio-temporality of biological rhythms. He depicts the heart's rhythms as a topology of wave patterns. A wave can be illustrated as a one-dimensional line on a two-dimensional sheet of graph paper. This wave is indicative of a rhythm in three-dimensional space coupled with vortices in one dimension of time. Time is a wily trickster, however. It lends itself to no faithful depiction on the printed page or in a graph or other figures and diagrams. It can, nonetheless, be patterned as a fourth spatial dimension. That is Winfree's own trick in his attempt to hog-tie time. He avails himself of a chemical process called the Belousov-Zhabotinsky reaction, discovered in 1951 and one of Ilya Prigogine's most important models illustrating his theory of "dissipative structures." This is likely the first experimentally observed case of spontaneous pattern formation by "dead" matter. "Live" matter evinces rhythm, which keeps things alive and kicking. Inorganic or "dead" matter, outside of mechanical subnuclear, atomic, and molecular oscillations, was supposed to be entirely inert and incapable of self-organization. The Belousov-Zhabotinsky reaction does a slam-dunk in the face of the organic/inorganic and life/nonlife dichotomies.

The term "dissipative structures" evokes the apparently contradictory image of disintegration and chaos along with its opposites: structure, balance, harmony, equilibrium. And contradiction it is: the process entails far-from-equilibrium conditions containing forces and elements in a constant struggle with one another, then at some unforeseeable point they erupt into self-organizing wholes that are capable of maintaining their identity by remaining open to the flux and flow of their environment. Migration of inorganic chemicals and functions of living organisms collaborate to bring about order from far-from-equilibrium, fluctuating, virtually chaotic, situations. The second law of thermodynamics stipulates that in a closed system, entropy will increase and islands of organization will dissolve; the system will eventually settle down to a tensionless sameness. Open dissipative structures, in contrast, incessantly expel entropy into their environment so as to create order and organization and at the same time stave off the onslaught of entropy build up. There is a constant input of matter and energy that is organized from within, and there is an expulsion into the environment of chaotic matter of lesser organization. A warm-blooded animal maintains constant body temperature in spite of wide variations of temperature outside. It does so by creating flows within that ingest matter and energy, using them to produce flows of heat, and emitting flows into the environment. All is process, nonlinear movement, constant exchange, interaction. The watchword is now nonlinear flow, and rhythm. Linear laws of cause-and-effect break down in far-from-equilibrium, nonlinear situations. In nonlinear systems, rather than a tunnel-minded singular focus, there is a multiplicity of possibilities at each juncture. Rather than one response to virtually every problem situation that presents itself, there are many possible answers to each problem situation. Rather than a race of the knife-edge "now" from past to future, the weight of the past is always present, and both past and present collaborate and contrive to pattern the future. It is rhythm evolving into complex polyrhythm.

And it is time. That slippery customer. As if the hairlines in Figures 1 and 5 were sliding from East to West, and then back again, all so rapidly that we cannot follow them either with the eyes or the mind. Nothing is present, at least as far as consciousness is concerned, but rather, everything is becoming something other than what it was becoming. Nothing is ever here and now and laid out in an array for our inspection. We are always at least a half beat behind the march of time. Winfree (1987:45) refers to the "narrow window of time between two successive beats" that, when subjected to the right stimulus, can reduce future beats to chaos. Comparable off-beats wrought in time, these syncopic moments, are common to us all: a sneeze, a hiccup, an asthma or panic attack, a heart palpitation, the shock of a new idea or premonition, a moment of creative insight, a fainting spell or near-death experience, a vertiginous feeling, sexual orgasm (Clément 1994). Then, in most all cases, syncrony, resonance, entrainment, resume their course. That is to say, the "periodic attractor" brings things back to "normal." The "phase space" is reset. If not, widespread turbulence can break out and chaos ensues.

Winfree gives an enticing example. Traveling along the circumference of a color wheel, we move from red to yellow to green to blue and back to red again. Simple enough. But if we begin spiraling inward, the bands become shorter and shorter until finally at the center we reach a hueless point, which can be none other than a combination of black and white; that is, it is gray. This is a color of uncertain hue that can become any color or no color, according to the context and the perceiver's dispositions. This hueless center can be exemplified by a soap film filling up the space within a tiny wire ring. The soap film cannot shrink out to the edges of the circle unless some interior point is pricked. If the center is pricked, then the soap film moves away from that point and, by the capillary action of the liquid, it clings to the wire along the circumference of the circle. The soap solution now makes up a thin torus around the wire. Like all surfaces, some central point must be retracted before that surface can expand out to its borders. In this sense the point where the soap film was penetrated is comparable to what I have alluded to above as the border of borders or the borderless border. The soap film's border exists at the extremity of the circle, one would expect. But the borderless border exists potentially at any point except one of the infinite number of points along the circumference. When this borderless border is removed, then the two-dimensional space ceases to exist, and all we have is a one-dimensional line doubling back on itself to form the wire-thin torus. The border was a "nothing," an "emptiness" so to speak, that made for the possibility of the entire space containing the soap film—or, by analogy, the entire spectrum of colors on the color wheel. When the "emptiness" that made for the possibility of anything and everything is negated, then within the two-dimensional space there is not something but "nothing," pure "emptiness." Yet there is something, an infinity of things, namely, the points on the circumference of the wire along a one-dimensional space. From any point along the circumference one can travel along finally to reach one's point of departure. This change occurs over time, of course.

Winfree's hueless point at the center of the color wheel is a "phase singularity," a "black hole," or a metaphor of "emptiness," if you will. It can be defined as a point in real three-dimensional space or in an imaginary space in which nothing is changing and there are no differences, yet the "singularity" is the author of all change. It is like the eye of the hurricane, the spoke of the Buddhist's wheel, the imaginary point on the soap film, the "vortex" in Figures 2 and 3. In this sense it contains everything collapsed to a point, much in the order of the Aleph Daneri witnessed.

Outside Looking In?

Now what is the gist of my strange and unexpected digression? A soap film as metaphor of the color wheel: how vain and supercilious! And yet, if one contemplates the image sufficiently, one cannot help but get a feel for and even acquire a reverence for its relevance. For, when comparing the soap film and its final state, an infinity of soap-points along a self-returning curve, with Figures 1 and 5, we have a "point-singularity," a "black hole," at once containing nothing and anything and everything, that "emptiness," which, when pricked with a pin, begins to expand.

As this grayness expands it reveals tenuously vague points, some of them black and some of them white; and as it continues to expand toward its destination, the population of black and white points increases and the vagueness takes on increasing complexity: colors of all sorts spew forth. This is comparable to imagining that the hairlines in Figures 1 and 5 are stretched out in both directions until they become identical to the circle that once contained it. It is like one of those Escher prints consisting of a circle from the center of which black and white demons are generated, and as they continue to be generated in a move toward the circumference of the circle, they become smaller and smaller until at the outer extremity they are infinitesimal. That is to say, metaphorically speaking, in our finite world of finite things there can be neither precise center nor precise circumference, neither Aleph nor Funy's world of mere particulars without generals, neither Zahir nor Tlöny's mentally nominalistic world of things that are now here, now there, now somewhere else. Yet it all exists as vagueness, as vague images and vague concepts.

The point is at the singularity of the color wheel where we have the continuous possibility of everything there in absolute homogeny (once again, from Figure 6). The point is at the extremity where all possible actualized colors fuse into one another to form a continuum where we have heterogeny. In between, there is continuity as well. However, just as we will never know the center nor the rim in anything but an ideal, theoretical way as in the image of the color wheel, so also we will never perceptually or conceptually grasp pure homogeny or pure heterogeny. Yet, perhaps we may be able to get a feel for them. And just as everything in between is melded into a continuum, we will never know it precisely. Yet, we are capable of exercising a massive series of artificial and partly arbitrary cuts and distinctions at some presumed set of joints, in order to construct a world, our world, from the infinite field of all possible worlds. If the distinctions become too numerous and/or too vague, chaos and gravitation toward undifferentiatable smoothness threaten. If the distinctions become too few and/or too abstract such that they are taken at face value and as eternally true, a hegemonic mind-set, fanatical dyadophilic (dualistic) thinking, threatens to take a firm stand and rule the roost. We can't have on a permanent basis that lazy and hazy oceanic feeling, and we had best resist the tendency to give in to dyadophilism. We should strive for a happy medium, a smooth rhythm. But the rhythm must maintain a certain syncopation so as to ward off boredom, a syncopation that often threatens to fly off along a disoriented and perhaps even chaotic tangent. The trick is to maintain the rhythm at a steady enough pace to keep things under control, to keep the beat going on, while avoiding the onslaught of chaos, and with enough syncopated rhythm to make life life and to prevent purely mechanical re-iterations.

The beat, syncopation, rhythm. Ultimately, it all comes down to a matter of "singularities" as borders that are borders of borders. In the words of physicist John A. Wheeler, ultimately everything begins with "0" ("emptiness") and ends with "0" ("emptiness"). There is "emptiness" and then there is what we might dub Derridean *différance*, then a proliferation of spatiotemporal differences that make a difference, and finally it's back to "emptiness." So we have the equation: "0 = 0" (Wheeler 1980). The idea is more properly topological than mathematical; it is conceptual rather than substantive; it is process rather than product; becoming rather than being; pragmatics rather than syntax; fluid verbs and adjectives rather than crystallized nouns; a legato of becoming rather than a staccato of things. The things and the actors change, but the processes in topological interrelated, interactive, codependent becoming remain. Winfree writes that circadian rhythmicity, at variance from species to species and from individual to individual and cell to cell, will nonetheless topologically be virtually the same. All these processes will undulate around singularities. They will be subject to perturbations as a result of outside stimuli; they will at certain junctures be threatened with symmetry breaking and dissipation and dissemination and eventually the eruption of chaos; then they will all make moves to reestablish their rhythm. They will all carve out trajectories mappable as a line on a two-dimensional graph in the most abstract sense. But those trajectories will have transpired in three-dimensional space and within one dimension of time that can itself be considered another dimension of space, for time will appear to have been broken down. From figure eights to Möbius strips to scroll rings in the form of a torus, all processes will lend themselves to vague topological images, to paradoxical language use. But the processes will continue to be just what they are, and as such they will continue to resist any and all crystal clear conceptions and descriptions.

We must remember that a point on a line is just that, a point. For a Linelander inhabiting a line-world, however, an antagonistic point can be a barrier, a border, preventing further advancement. If that line-world passes through part of a two-dimensional sheet, the Flatlander can with the greatest of ease go around it; it presents no limitation in the least. From an orthogonal view, in the third dimension, a line on Flatlander's world is just a line, to be sure. But for Flatlander it is a barrier. If it were to cut entirely across and bisect a two-dimensional plane, Flatlander would not be able to pass from one side to the other, for that "other side" would remain beyond the boundary, beyond the borders of her world. However the Spherelander, inhabiting a world of three dimensions, would have no trouble going over or under or to one side or to the other of it, and easily make his way to the "other side," whatever that might be. However, he would be hard pressed to penetrate the outer extremities of the outer limits of his world, for there is no "other side." However, "Dr. Burgerstein," an imaginary four dimensional being, could readily see the "one side" and the "other side" and leap from one to the other with no further ado. It's all topology, whose dimensions can ideally go on and on, there are no outer limits.

(This notion of topology and progression through dimensions and in and out of time is comparable to Funy's and Tlöny's perception and the Zahir as one-dimensional spin-outs of physical and mental things and events and signs relating to them; it is Lönny's two-dimensional topological solution to the homicides set down on a map of the city, and then Scharlach, within his three-dimensional world, complete with a time-line, saw Lönny's every move and easily set a trap for him; it is Daneri's timeless four-dimensional view of the entire universe within that marvelous "singularity," the Aleph, where there were no longer any time-bound rhythms but everything is always already there. A step in science or the arts is initially only a timeless dream without substance, an imaginary hook, line, and sinker in search of an unwary fish. Then, in time, this step is given expression of one sort or another and displayed for all to see: a Cézanne or Picasso or Jackson Pollock painting, the Belousov-Zhabotinsky reaction, a Mozart or John Cage piece, Virginia Woolf's or Samuel Beckett's prose, a Gertrude Stein line, all are in their own way tiny models of the universe.)

Whichever the case, as far as we are concerned our posture is as if we were on the outside looking in. At least that is what we most often like to believe, as if we were privy to some objective, neutral, detached perspective. Yes. We would always like to see things from "our" position, which is the most sublime position, at least for us. But topologically speaking, whatever our position, whether a line, a plane, a sphere, or a hypersphere, we are within it, and within we shall remain. We can smugly and imperiously construct our *either/or* categories, and, after we have chopped process up into static blocks, we foray out into the world, ready to conquer any and all antagonists. But, topologically speaking, the *both-ands* and *neither-nors*, along with time the trickster, will somewhere reveal our sham world for what it is.

But, . . . good grief! I remain mired in abstractions! Fleshless, gutless abstractions! Somehow I must impart a *feeling* for what this is all about. Perhaps a quick voyage through a few Caribbean tropes and topologies might help me more effectively portray what I mean by cultural rhythms and resonances.

The Ultimate in Mangled Topologies

Antonio Benítez-Rojo's *The Repeating Island* (1992) draws rather disparately from Deleuze and Guattari and chaos theory to arrive at the picture of the Caribbean as a bridge, an other *other*, the *other* as difference that makes a different difference. The Caribbean consists of a discontinuous conjunction, a disjunctive continuum, a complementarity of agonistics, a fluctuating hodge-podge of subalterns—all of the above in a contradictory mix—evinced by perpetually opposing forces. It is a mess of "unstable condensations, turbulences, whirlpools, clumps of bubbles, frayed seaweed, sunken galleons, crashing breakers, flying fish, seagull squawks, downpours, night-time phosphorescences, eddies and pools" (Benítez-Rojo 1992:2). It is of radically uncertain signification and significances. The entire area repeats itself again and again, in an ongoing, obstinate series of recursive loops.

This combination of all re-iterations makes up a monstrous "strange attractor," where self-repeating hurricanes have for eons gyrated about the Bermuda Triangle, causing the unexpected huffs and pitches that capsized galleons in olden times and have devastated ramshackle sprawls of poverty in modern times. If Zeno's ideal world consisting of simple re-iterations along a line, a one-dimensional labyrinth, lands us in a paradox—those four infamous paradoxes of the philosopher of Elea— then I leave your imagination to wrestle with the infinitely more complex labyrinth Benítez-Rojo's Antilles throws at us. Each return of a line, any line wandering through the Caribbean, potentially ends up every-where and no-where pointing in an infinity of directions toward every-*thing* or perhaps no-thing at all. Yet it consequently turns back on itself to continue along the tired irreversible push toward some undefined and undefinable end. The Gulf of Mexico, sporting its strategically placed emerald gems of tropical lush, has weathered the devastation of time, of geological, meteorological, and ecological catastrophes, and of repeated Western World interventions. Yet, in spite of the downturns and disappointments, the unfilled promises and shunted dreams, the area has remained vibrant, a superposition of sand, soil, rock, and delicate life, and of languages and cultures. It evinces a titillating, scintillating, shimmering, effervescent flutter of activity, like the glimpse of a hummingbird poised in mid-air while inspecting one of the gala array of flowers offering themselves up to it. It is a flux of virtuality in expectation of some-thing that never quite comes to pass, that always lurks in the uncertain future, that remains beyond the receding horizon.

Benítez-Rojos's Antilles knows of no forbidden contradiction in the sense of classical logical principles. What is *A*, here and now, is sure to be not-*A*, there and then, or perhaps vice versa. All is a cascade, a continuous outflow, a vertiginous rush, of semiosis. Nor does the excluded-middle principle manage to wield its terrible swift sword: choices of all or nothing, this or that, we or them, I or Other, are never exactly an *either/or* affair, but they are a matter of either *neither-nor* or *both-and*, and at the same time of *neither* the *neither nor* the *nor* and *both* the *neither and* the *nor*. Catholicism or Afro-Cuban *santería* (a vibrant mix of African religions and Catholicism)? Mysticism or magic? Synthesis or syncretism? Juxtaposition or fusion? French or Creole? Bourgeois capitalism or socialism or paternalism? Anglo-American or Puerto Rican? Or Hispanic or French or English or Dutch or Afro-Caribbean? The marvelously and uncannily irreal or hard-nose reality? It is not a matter of the one or the other, but of a continuum of shades without borders or clear divisions. Whatever ephemeral borders there may be, they are the product of human minds, hearts, and hands. There is tension, for sure, which intermittently erupts in violence. Yet there is a certain free-flow harmony perhaps unknown elsewhere in the world. There is dissymmetry with a vengeance, yet fearless symmetries manage to prevail as well. A move toward equilibration is always present, yet dynamic far-from-equilibrium processes perpetually maintain the entire region open to well nigh every-thing and any-thing. Smooth lines and surfaces reveal, upon closer inspection, the fissures and cracks, nooks and crannies, broken edges and punctuated contours, of myriad fractal cultures. The Antilles could well be intuitively viewed as living proof of Ilya Prigogine's "physics of complexity."

The situation is compelling regarding the remainder of Latin America as well.[2] There are important differences between the Caribbean and the continent, to be sure. The Caribbean was the first to suffer violation by the cross and the sword of European outsiders, most often motivated more by dogmas and grand designs than by their experience of the immediate surroundings, more by lust and power than by compassion and understanding. And it was first to taste the bittersweet glory of a successful independence movement, in Haiti, 1804. At the same time, some areas of the Caribbean were last to gain independence from their colonial exploiters: Cuba, Puerto Rico, Trinidad, Jamaica. The similarities between the Antilles and continental Latin America outweigh the differences, however. The product of the initial assault was, in the beginning with the union of the originary couple, archetypal of which is that of Malinche and Cortés, the *mestizo* (of mixed blood), incorporating both the Cain and the Abel making up Latin America's cultural prototype, in all its complexity. The effect of this union continues to be felt to the present day whenever one ponders over the continent's history.

The peoples and cultures—I put the terms in plural, for there can be no singularity here—do not and cannot enjoy any stable form of identity, for they are one of the most pluralistic, if not the most pluralistic, of cultural conglomerations in the history of the human species. It is not simply a matter of the customary dualistic labels: Amerindian/Spaniard, African/Spaniard-Portuguese, America/Europe, country/city, civilization/barbarism, nature/culture, and so on. Between Aztec and Mayan and Quechua and Guaraní and a host of other sedentary and nomadic cultures there are commonalities. But there are also differences greater than those between Greek and Roman and Moorish and Spanish and Germanic and Saxon. What is the Latin American? Native America in its multiple forms? But native America is itself of mind-numbing diversity. Is it part African? What part? Bantú or Sudanese or something else? Is Latin America a product of the Renaissance, or of a Spain and Portugal still mired in Medievalism and streaked with Arabic cultures? Or is it more a product of the postcapitalistic, postindustrial era? What is the future of the area? Back to the Pre-Hispanic roots? To European civilization? Or forge ahead toward the grave new world of postmodernism, whatever that ultimately may be? The Latin Americans thrive in a cultural milieu of hybridized conglomerations, they breathe it, they consume it, they expel it.[3] This rather nomadic, multitangential digression has been, I would suggest, more necessary than whimsical. For I believe it implies, and may access a feel for, a most compelling point: Latin American cultural complexity. The meaning of the message is in the feel not the form, in kinesthetic meanderings not precise mental constructs, in a language of vagueness not of that pristine logic making up a security blanket to which under many circumstances we need desperately to cling.

But, . . . now I fear I have digressed inordinately. I suppose I digress because, quite frankly, regarding the topic that I've thrown into the spotlight, I cannot simply say what is on my mind, for it is not a matter of simplicity at all, but complexity of the most complex sort. Well, then, . . . allow me to try, one more time, with renewed focus on specific Latin American issues.

Notes

1.   A dramatic case of mutual entrainment occurs when, as described above, fire-flies converge on a particular area and seem to eventually begin synchronizing their off and on flashes.

2.   Throughout the entire Latin American area, in a diversity of ways, that dreamy dichotomy between the so-called "third world" and "developed world" has remained inordinately cloudy. Actually, languages, cultures, and economic development have presented a confusing picture. Few cities are more cosmopolitan and European than Buenos Aires; few cities are further from Western Enlightenment ideals and suffer more from human degradation than Haiti's capital, Port-au-Prince. Latin America obstinately resists any and all neat classificatory schemes. It is complexity taunting the crystals of taxonomic simples, virtual chaos somehow maintaining itself in a dynamic balance in spite of the overwhelming odds against its so doing (see Zea 1963, 1969, 1992).

3.   While the term "pluralism" is most common to postmodern parlance, many Latin-Americanists are more comfortable with "hybridization," brought to prominence especially by Néstor García Canclini (1993, 1995), and "transculturation," coined by Fernando Ortiz (1947) in his seminal study of the Cuban sugar economy, and in recent years put to use by Angel Rama (1982).

Chapter Fourteen

The Labyrinth of Denial and of Acceptance

> The psychological borderlands, the sexual borderlands and the spiritual borderlands are not particular to the Southwest. In fact, the Borderlands are physically present wherever two or more cultures edge each other, where people of different races occupy the same territory, where under, lower, middle and upper classes touch, where the space between two individuals shrinks with intimacy.

> —Gloria Anzaldúa

> We are a culture that inhabits a place that pretends to be occupied by another culture.

> —Armando Ramírez

A Perfusion of Signs of All Sorts

Bakhtin's concept of dialogic entails border perforation, border diffusion, border effacement: trans-linguistics, the separating of linguistics and linguistic notions of phonology, syntagmatics, paradigmatics, meaning, and culture at large, and a move away from the Saussurean structuralist wedding between stylistics and Russian formalist poetics.

This, in a post-Bakhtin setting, is tantamount to forgetting linguicentrism by eschewing strictly language-based textualism, poststructuralism, deconstruction—of the narrow-minded variety—in favor of a genuinely triadic conception. Dialogism, polyphony, heteroglossia, Carnival, centrifugal forces, and perpetual openness are the watchwords: when at their best they exercise a nimble leap out of linguicentric textualism and into the arena of bodymindsigns, which includes the whole of Figure 6. Here, there is no "To be or not to be?" but rather a very tentative and tenuous becoming of the being of semiosis, that is, signs doing their thing, which is made possible by the being of the becoming of semiosis. Nothing ever simply is, in a fixed sense. It "ises," that is, there is a process of "ising" going on. Likewise, nothing ever thinks, but rather, we can only say that "thinking" is going on, like rain is happening or wind is blowing or sea is violently waving. Dialogic interplay is not engaged; there is just dialogic becoming, happening. Things happen; they have been happening; they are happening; they will have been happening. Happening happens to happen happeningly. What more can be said?

What more can be said? What more can be said is that what is possible cannot continue to be ignored. That from the Saussurean-structuralist-semiological signifier and the petrifaction of the signified into formal linguistic discourse and from the poststructuralist-deconstructive opening of the signifier to a delirious free play while shunting the signified aside, there is a genuine opening out of all aspects of the sign. This opening out includes the possible, the actual, and a decentering, dispersal, dissemination of actuals in their flow toward that long lost fullness or oneness of things, with no chance of arriving except in the theoretical long run, that is, at the infinite stretch.[1] This semiosic, processual flow includes not only experience and the ordinary Western modes of logic and reason (Secondness, indexicality), but also the vague, overdetermined, inconsistent qualities of feeling (Firstness, iconicity), and the general, underdetermined, perpetually incomplete character of thought and conceptualization, the more formal affairs of the mind (Thirdness, symbolicity).

It is to be expected that over the past few decades, theory, and more recently cultural studies, have been dominated by the so-called "logic" of modernism-modernity. That is to say, classical logic, with a little difference, dissemination, and so on brought in for good measure. Occasionally there may also be some overtures to a Hegelian logic of negativity that presumably incorporates the *other* to make up a happy family. In the first case, a logic of bivalence or binarism prevails; in the second case, the *other* remains enshrouded in a negative aura and its possibility as positivity remains unrealized: it is still excluded from the self yet in a negative way constitutive of it. What is worse, the deeply entrenched idea of progress in modern thought brings with it some variation or other of Hegelian totality that over time finally comes to its completion. Time is seen as a string of empty boxcars careening down the rails of progress, and they are to be successively filled at the temporary stops. The present is of relatively no account; it is only the future that really matters, for at history's end, if everybody has carried out her/his task properly, emancipation and the good life are there and waiting for all. Ah, the good life, that of us professors, of course. Passing the day surrounded by the polished, smiling faces of credulous young students, passing the evening with a good book and a glass of sherry after a scrumptious meal, and then making preparations for passing a few more clouds of intellectual gas in the classroom on the following day. Yes, we are wonderfully enlightened and emancipated, aren't we?

However, when taking the whole of Figure 6 into our purview, we must concede that what seems to be the case could always have been becoming something *other*, and at some future moment it will have been becoming something *other* than what in the present it seems to be becoming. Nothing is unchanging and nothing is guaranteed; nothing is intrinsically identical to itself; there is nothing essential about any contextualized cultural practice. Modern theories of meaning held undying faith in identity, essentialism, reference, and correspondence, with context deemed of hardly any account regarding the hard-nosed, rigorously formal conceptions of language. The various ramifications of structuralism-semiology and poststructuralism-deconstruction have given up on much of this nonsense arising out of classical physical science, to be sure. But they often remain caught up in their own limitations. They whittled down the robust classical theoretical monument. And what were they left with? Language. So they ended up in linguicentrism, while virtually ignoring everything extralinguistic that allows language to become language.

In another way of putting it, most recent theories exclude the *other other*, the border of borders. A big mistake. In order to remedy this problem, shrewd observers have at times concluded that nothing but the *other* is of much worth. Granted, on this account the *other* is positivity instead of negativity. Yet the tables have merely been turned, for this positivity is now defined in contrast to its negative, which was the erstwhile self, previously a positivity in contradistinction to the negative *other*. Little has changed. We look at the beast from the frontal view, then from the dorsal view, then we stand on our head and look at it from a cross-eyed view, and it is still the same beast. The neo- or post-Gramsci work of Stuart Hall, Chantal Mouffe, and Ernesto Laclau, and that of Michel de Certeau and Pierre Bourdieu, among others, represents a heroic effort to account for the complex multidimensional, nonlinear, intricately interrelated, *rhizomic* nature of the contemporary cultural milieu. Yet something is still missing. All these stories are chiefly of full-blooded to fleshless Secondness with a comfortable and nonthreatening dash either of Firstness (Deleuze and Guattari) and/or Thirdness (Foucault). But Secondness, whether of the modern, Saussure-structuralist-semiological variety or of the flavor of later vintages, is prioritized in one form or another. This is unfortunate. Culture is semiosis; it is linguistic and nonlinguistic and extralinguistic all in one package. It is continuous interaction and agonistics the result of which is the codependent emergence of more signs, of more culture, but of a somewhat different countenance with the surfacing of each new eddy in the stream, however minute and however ephemeral. The shifting waters at the surface bear witness to the myriad, virtually infinite, possibilities contained within the undertow, and they give way downstream to general, albeit ill-defined, maneuvering, and negotiating flows within the current. I repeat: nothing is fixed for more than a few fleeting moments.

According to the thrust of this inquiry, entrenched logic and reason (of Secondness) in conjunction with the "logics" of difference and vagueness (of Firstness and Thirdness), as well as various and sundry "styles of reasoning" broaden the outer extremities of the sphere into distant horizons. Customary categories wane, as a consequence. Syncretism breeds a lingering tendency toward binarism. Conceded, the pair of images, terms, or practices is held together such that both the one and the other are there, somehow, somewhere. Yet there are two, or perhaps more than two, that come in what are customarily conceived as contradictory pairs. What we need is a diffusive, profusive, yet vague, sense or feeling of the possibility or virtuality of many things, a mind-numbing multiplicity of things. This is more than Bakhtinian heteroglossia or polyglossia, as it is more than transculturation, which sort of spreads an umbrella over everything without really or necessarily bringing about the interpenetration, the codependency of all signs, extralinguistic as well as linguistic, arising into the light of day. So, where to now? What is for sure is that whatever will have been happening is now beginning to happen. The best we can do is try to navigate the flow.

It behooves me to try to become more concrete on this issue, I would suspect. In an effort to do so let me turn to yet another concrete Latin American dilemma.

What Happens When There Is Resistance to the Flow?

Mexico's cultural diversity began, it would appear, with the antagonistic tale of two civilizations. The contradictions between Aztec and Spanish seem total and clearly distinguished. After the conquest, the situation doesn't appear to have changed much: there is the oligarchy on the one hand and the Amerindian communities on the other. Today, the modern descendants of the old oligarchy have apparently not changed much in terms of their mind-set and the Amerindians have preserved much of their own identity.

Or so it might seem. But not so, however, not exactly, that is. Guillermo Bonfil Batalla (1996) argues extensively that in general today's peasants do not ordinarily think of themselves as "indios," though their customs retain a predominantly Amerindian flavor. And the old elites as well as the new upper and upper middle class are into boutiques, chic restaurants, nightclubs, sunny beaches, and jetting around the world when they can. At the same time their attitudes toward the lower classes have not changed substantially from those attitudes held by many generations in the past. The subordinate urban groups are by no means culturally homogeneous. Some keep ties with their rural communities. Others take on the trappings of consumer society, apparently having forgotten who they were. Still others are in cultural limbo, fluctuating between their urban present and their rural past, between misery when things go bad and middle-class self-absorption when luck smiles favorably on them—then they often squander it all and end up in virtual misery again. The middle classes do not have their own middle-class sense of belonging and usually even prefer to consider themselves something other than middle-class. Then what are they? They are not of the aristocracy, nor would they suffer the insult of being relegated to the lower echelons of society; by some "mistake" they just happen to have drifted toward the middle, and there they are, consuming foreign cultural products as if there were no tomorrow.[2] Bonfil's estimation of the problem of "national culture" is that the cultural diversity of Mexico is not a question of different cultural levels. That is to say, the cultural diversity:

> is not a matter of expressions that differ among themselves according to the position that each group or social segment occupies, in terms of their greater or lesser access to the resources and practices of a common culture. This phenomenon—cultural differences related to social stratification—is no doubt present in the cultural dynamics of the country. However, it is not the factor that explains the cultural diversity of our society. Much deeper than such situational differences, at bottom, what explains the absence of a common Mexican culture is the presence of two civilizations that have never fused to produce a new civilizational program. Neither have they coexisted in harmony, to each other's reciprocal benefit. (Bonfil 1996:61)

According to Bonfil, in Mexico's strange version of Western modernism-modernity and postmodernism-postmodernity, there is no convergence of social groups into successive differences, as is presumably the case of the so-called "developed" West. There is only an antagonistic conflict of opposite, intransigent forces. It is the same old story: the winning minority takes almost everything and the losing majority is left holding an empty bag. Contradiction remains largely the name of the game. It is usually a matter of *either* the hegemonic powerbloc *or* the under-dog way of life. Unfortunately, this story has pervaded Mexican history since Inde-pendence. Faithful to attitudes emerging out of colonial life, positivist liberalism during the latter half of the nineteenth century, and postrevolutionary programs, the general opinion among middle and upper-class groups has it that the Amerindians are a drag on society and an obstacle to progress and should fade away as soon as possible. From the colonial period to the present, when Amerindians kept their noses clean and showed themselves to be good subordinates, they were kept around as a labor force. When not, they were occasionally exterminated, or as in the case of the Yaqui group in Sonora during the Porfirismo, they were transported to another area—Yucatan—and reduced to virtual slavery. Zapatismo during the revolution and in the EZLN guise of the NAFTA years under Subcomandante Marcos is a possible alternative, according to Bonfil. They defend the villages, given their agrarian orien-tation and their affirmation of traditional life patterns. The problem is that their dis-semination throughout the rest of Mexico can hardly be forthcoming, for they are more local than national. In other words, there has been no general movement of the APRISMO variety envisioned by Víctor Raúl Haya de la Torre.

The powerbloc ("imaginary" Mexico) has pigheadedly continued promoting Western schemes of modernity instead of encouraging growth of the cultural capaci-ties that exist among the majority of the Mexican population—outside recent cultiva-tion of arts and crafts as a tourist attraction and as a buffer for chronic unemploy-ment. The obstinate, tunnel-minded vision of modern life of the Occidental variety tends to conceal a systematic ignorance of the reality of the Mexican condition. There is, in Bonfil's (1996:65) words, "a permanent aspiration to stop being what we are, a cultural project that denies the historical reality of Mexican social origins." Ef-forts to construct a national culture consequently entail imposition of distant, foreign models that tend to eliminate cultural diversity and achieve unity, to shunt het-erogeny aside and give priority to a sham form of homogeny, through repression of what actually exists. Consequently, "México profundo" is submerged into the sphere of increasingly remote possibility, this *other* Mexico that still manages to make its presence felt in times of crisis such as the October 2 massacre at Tlatelolco in 1968 (Paz 1970a). The majority of the Mexicans have a place in the sun only on condition that they cease being what they are, that they properly don a mask and take on somewhat of an alien role. These social and cultural pressures have culminated in a "schizophrenic posture" that has created the various and sundry fictions of progress (for example, nineteenth-century liberal dreams of individualism and egalitarianism ended in an indentured servant system during the Porfirismo). Mexico the dominant has aided and abetted the real marginalization of the majority of the citizenry such that the actual members of this majority constitute a collapsed minority. The *other* Mexico, in contrast, remains as nothing more than a possibility. It is the genuine homogeny that could flow toward a heterogenic flowering of differences and unique cultural expressions (from Firstness to Thirdness). Unfortunately, there is on the surface only dualistic Secondness in the image of Western modernization that is destined to end in a schizophrenic, oppressive sameness (at Thirdness).

That's politics for you. In contrast, let's take a look at a few other voices within Latin America.

And When the Flow is Acknowledged?

Oral literature and testimonials have recently entered the academic marketplace with much fanfare. I cannot shed the sneaky feeling that they are too convenient: they allow us all-too-comfortable armchair participation with so-called subalterns. But that is another issue.

What is at stake here is consideration of the testimonial regarding the haves-havenots and high-low culture dichotomies. Texts of literate cultures entail the author's, narrator's, and autobiographer's "I" as just that: the "I." However loose and fast it shifts from here to there and from then to now, it presents itself as an individual entity in good Western fashion. The "I" of testimonials, in contrast, is customarily collective. John Beverley (1993:83) suggests that the testimonial "I" takes on the grammatical status of a "shifter," a linguistic function that can ideally be assumed by anyone and everyone in the community. I would rather consider the "I" much like the "empty set" of "set theory." It can be ephemerally, indeterminately, and incompletely filled by some member of the community during which process it creates its own function from among a variety of possible functions. It is not Borges's Funes (Funy), who, like Proust's hero, remains trapped in a Humean rush of "I" or self-becoming that never becomes because it doesn't stick around long enough to do so. It is more akin to Emma Zunz (Emmy), whose "I" fills the empty box and invents a function for pragmatic or survival purposes, then she can go on her way, perhaps much better for the experience, perhaps not. Emma, one of the few women characters in Borges's fictions, however underdeveloped as a literary figure she may remain, gives us memory through a filter. She speaks for herself and at the same time for all women. Emmy, a variation of Borges's Emma, is unique only insofar as she stands for her gender. The function of her "I" in the polylogue oscillates between that of Borges's short story and of various female types: she is now a bimbo, now an aggressive woman of red-neck vintage, now in motherly fashion defending the rights of others, and so on. She gives us the image of a woman forced into her customary role, but at the same time capable, in "cultural" guerrilla fashion, of subverting that role for the purpose of her self-realization.

The Latin American testimonial lays claim to no identity apart from the community from within which it found its voice. Rigoberta Menchú, for instance, unlike EZLN leader Subcomandante Marcos's estimation of himself, speaks with her own voice, for sure. Marcos would like to convince his audience that his "I" remains much like the "empty set" of set theory. There is no such individual "I" that presents itself to the public; there is only the "empty set" that is filled by the communal "I" of the Mayan descendants of Chiapas. Like Marcos, Menchú also speaks for her community, not merely for herself (and therein the problem with Stoll's Menchú, briefly pointed out in chapter five). Were her testimonial to lose its function as a communal voice, it would become autobiographical—though it could retain implied relations to the community. Latin American autobiographies come in a spectrum of sorts, from

Cabeza de Vaca's *Adventures* (1961 [1542]) and Euclides da Cunha's *Rebellion in the Backlands* to Miguel Barnet's "testimonial-novel," *The Autobiography of a Runaway Slave* (1968 [1966], the edited autobiography of Esteban Montejo), to Che Guevara's *Episodes of the Cuban Revolutionary War 1956–58* (1968 [1968]), and Omar Cabezas's *Fire from the Mountain* (1985 [1983], reportedly the faithful transcription of taped verbal exchanges), to Richard Rodriguez's *Hunger of Memory* (1983, the struggle of a Chicano for identity and entry into middle-class status). It can be pseudo-testimonial, as Beverley puts it, like Manlio Argueta's world of a peasant woman of El Salvador in *One Day of Life* (1983 [1981]), or Luis Zapata's *El vampiro de la Colonia Roma* ("The Vampire of the Roma Neighborhood") (1979), chronicled narrative such as García Márquez's *Chronicle of a Death Foretold* (1982 [1981]), or Mario Vargas Llosa's *The Real Life of Alejandro Mayta* (1984 [1986]), or narrative texts mixed with testimonial accounts such as Elena Poniatowska's *Until We Meet Again* (1969 [1987]). Or it can come in the name of ethnographic life stories such as Ricardo Pozas's *Juan the Chamula* (1962 [1952]) and Oscar Lewis's *The Children of Sánchez* (1961).[3]

If in the genuine testimonial the "I" is disseminated, the process of dispersal, deterritorialized, the Deleuze and Guattari "schizophrenic" self that is at once all selves, then there exists the possibility of not one sign but many signs the collection of which is one sign, a composite possible sign. This composite possible sign is at the outset within the sphere of the vague, the overdetermined and radically inconsistent: if there is any form or fashion of identity regarding the "I," it is a self-contradictory identity, or better, an identity of incongruous complementarity. How so? If one speaker speaks for all speakers, then the message is a radical form of the "open work." It presents the possibility of virtually unlimited interpretation on the part of the interpreters, for the self or "I" of the work remains radically unspecified and unspecifiable in any determinate way. As one self or sign, that sign is a sign of particularity having been actualized from the composite sign of radically overdetermined and vague possibility. Signs of vagueness will remain as vague as they are insofar as their maker does not add a few more actualized particulars from the unruly hodge-podge of overdetermined signs. But signs are inordinately vague, and vague they are destined to remain unless their maker gives them a bit more specification. In regard to testimonials, the speaker is in control of vague signs, for she tells us what she warts to tell us (which is often what she thinks we want to hear) and that's that.

Menchú begins: "My story is the story of all poor Guatemalans. My personal experience is the reality of a whole people." (Menchú 1984:1 [1983]). Her concluding words are: "I'm still keeping secret what I think no one should know. Not even anthropologists or intellectuals, no matter how many books they have, can find out all our secrets" (247). In between we read: "[W]e have hidden our identity because we needed to resist, we wanted to protect what governments have wanted to take away from us" (170), and, "For the Indian, it is better not to study than to become like *ladinos*" (≈ *mestizos* in Central America) (205). There is a multiplicity of particularities, the whole of which is one voice, ideally at least. Yet we the readers are limited by the vagueness of the sign, in the absence of the utterer, since the testimonial as a published text is read from the pleasant bookish smell of some study somewhere, and it has been worked around with by some rather bookish editor whose motives must always be up for certain questioning. Context would help. But there is none. There is only the text. So the text remains quite vague and overdetermined. In other words, the oral tradition as written text can appear so unbearably overdetermined precisely because there is no context of the telling, with no subtle nuances, voice inflection, gestures, body positioning, audience participation, and so on. There is no bodymind united with the text, no bodymindsign, but only the text as lifeless black marks on white that are ordinarily taken to exist "out there," ready for the intervention of the all-knowing disembodied mind.

Indeed, Beverley is on the mark, I believe, when he writes that Menchú as subaltern, like all subalterns by definition, are a "component of their own personal identity, . . . and cannot be adequately represented by literature or in the university," for, "that literature and the university are among the practices that create and sustain subalternity" (Beverley 1999:71). The academy begins with the subaltern, and then canonizes *I, Rigoberta Menchú*, and it loses its subalternity; yet it is analytically dissected and reconstructed as if it were the spitting image of subalternity. What is taken for subalternity is thus invented (Secondness streaked with hopeful Thirdness). As discursive invention, it remains bodyless, lifeless. What would be actually and concretely subaltern cannot be captured by academic discourse because the subaltern is *neither* subaltern *nor* is she not-subaltern. She is becoming something other than what can be caught in the net of pompous academic assumptions and practices.[4]

Bodyless, lifeless, discourse. Signs of many possibilities but with hardly any chance of genuine interhuman interaction, of codependent emergence within the community and by way of the context of the telling, of a sense of feeling, experiencing, or of knowing what was, is, and will be known. It is up to the reader, the interpreter, to render the discourse of the text evincing overdetermined vagueness somewhat more determinate. A difficult task, if not impossible. So we read and interpret the text in one of many possible ways—"Yes, here is this testimonial voice that must surely be real, . . . real?, how can it be real if so radically overdetermined, like a fiction? And if fictitious, then how can it bear more than a modicum of verisimilitude? How much meddling went into the editing? How much buffering of the testimonial voice in order to cater to some imagined audience? How can I willingly unsuspend my unwilling suspension of belief to take a leap of faith into the mind of this remote, quite foreign voice? Whose voice is it, really?" Inordinate doubt remains, for the text perpetuates its radical underdetermination, its resistance to any and all fixed interpretations.

Since the text was at the outset radically overdetermined, no matter to what length the interpreter takes her interpretation, and no matter how complete she may think it remains, it is nonetheless radically underdetermined and incomplete, in spite of the level of generality it might have taken on. Beverley (1993:14) writes that Rigoberta "*uses* the possibility of producing a text already established as a literary genre to address a reading public constituted in large part by university-educated people, without succumbing to an ideology of the literary generated and maintained by the university, or, what amounts to the same thing, without abandoning her identity as a member of her community." This is to imply that she is not wholly within her community in the oral tradition, for she is now hobnobbing with the university crowd. But neither is she of the literate university-educated community, for one foot remains in her tradition. I repeat: she is *neither* the one *nor* the other. This is like labeling literate culture "A" and oral culture "Not-A," and their fusion "*Both* A *and* Not-A." But Rigoberta is *neither* of the one culture *nor* of the other, *nor* is she a composite or fusion of the two. She is something else, "*Neither* A *nor* Not-A." She is a vague yet absent representamen that functions like an index indicating, implicitly pointing out, the object of the text, which is absolutely necessary, given the lack of a context, in order that the account may be taken as a roughly to faithfully genuine testimonial.

Given this absence of the witness, the textualized and decontextualized and edited testimonial or pseudotestimonial necessarily highlights the word, the subject of an utterance (the simplest form of a symbolic sign). In addition to the highlighted word, there are implications of indexicality, that is, relations toward the object or predicate of the sign, which is the "semiotic," not the "real," object. Yet the word or subject remains relatively devoid of adjectivization and verbalization. There is an absence of a predicate and some concomitant detailed, relatively complete, and fleshed out sentence, text, narrative, description and explanation, or argument (the most complex of symbolic signs). In other words, there is the subject, the word, as absent bodymindsign that would otherwise incorporate the sign indicating its respective context revealing the sign's attributes by way of its predicate, to make up a text implicitly contained within that same bodymindsign. But the bodymindsign as text is absent, and all we have is fleshless text, with few determinate signposts. We have no alternative but to grope about in the dark, creating our own interpretants, which remain radically indeterminate. In another way of putting it, an implicit, imaginary spotlight is thrown on the semiotic object, which cannot but remain enshrouded in vagueness. The sign could be made less vague by the utterer within some respective context. But that is virtually an impossibility.[5]

Further specification of the testimonial sign, then, depends upon the interpreter. His task is daunting, however. For there is hardly any well-rounded text, since what is at hand is still caught up in the oral tradition. If the interpreter would like to conceive of what he has before him as an argument or a relatively replete and complete narrative or text, it is of some "logic of vagueness" (within the sphere of Firstness), and is now available through a radically diverse "logic of difference" (within the sphere of Thirdness) and numbingly variable "styles of reasoning." That is to say, if some satisfactory symbolic sign is to be forthcoming on the part of the interpreter's efforts, the Secondness of the interpretant remains quite underdetermined. And if some fashion of a genuine, relatively complex symbolic sign is up for grabs, it can be nothing more than radically underdetermined. The situation is like one in which what for one interpreter is "green" for another interpreter is "grue," what for one is "Guadalupe" for the other is "Guadantzín," and what for one is a "Cat" for another is a bunch of "cat[*]." Signs can be swirled that far apart, I would suspect. The confusion rests in the relative importance of the semiotic object in testimonials that complexifies the issue in comparison to ordinary fictions—or dreams, hallucinations, and lies—the semiotic objects of which are usually, though not always, of less importance. Whereas in fictions the sign can become virtually that of the Saussurean freeplay of signifiers related only to other signifiers—which gives poststructuralists and deconstructors wild flights of the ecstatic imagination—the testimonial sign must be to a degree grounded in whatever might be taken by a particular individual or a community at some given time and space slice as the "real." This is why Emmy's world appears to be considerably more "real" than those of Maggie, Tlöny, Lönny, Hladik, and Funy, though that appearance can be quite deceptive.

Yet binaries continue to linger. It is still to a large extent "us" against "them," the haves and the havenots. It is like Bonfil's account of the testimony of an Amerindian from Villa Alta, Oaxaca. He tells the story of his village, where "before, things did not change, . . . everything was always the same." Now, however, "things are very different." From the colonial period through the nineteenth century to the present, "outsiders" have brought pressure to bear, and things could not help but change. Traditional monuments and customs went the way of the forests and the animals, and the village became something entirely different than what it was. Then the push of the eroded, unproductive countryside and the pull of city lights depleted the village's population, and it is now hardly more than a ghost town. But the narrator realizes that the destruction has not been unilateral, they have also had a hand in destroying themselves: "What happened to us is what happened to the bird we call *yase*. When someone touches its nest, even without hurting the eggs, the female destroys the nest and goes away. What we do not know is who came near and touched our nest. Practically speaking, that has been our history. We have spent our lives destroying ourselves" (Bonfil 1996:142). The relationship is n-linear, asymmetrical, multi-dimensional, and unpredictably chaotic, for sure. And the product has been tragic, for sure. In a sense it also remains dualistic, a matter of either the one possibility or the other, either acquiescence to the forces that be or resistance.

What, then, are the genuinely open alternatives? An EZLN response with Subcomandante Marcos as mouthpiece providing the presence of a bodymindsign in the absence of witnesses? Marcos, whose nimble word play allows precious drops of memory and meaning to fall into that semiotic space where the haves are in eager anticipation? Yes. That is one alternative, among all the "cultural" guerrilla possibilities: passive resistance and fusion and concealment of subversive signs and subtle linguistic nuances and open rebellion whenever and wherever it is feasible and always waiting, waiting for opportunities, for the wait has persevered over 500 years and it will continue for the next 500 years if the haves continue to resist change. The alternatives seep through the border of borders with the capacity to disseminate far and wide.

So much for testimonials.[6] We must really look further, in the direction of rhythm, . . . and music. That's where the border of borders is felt.

Notes

1.   I allude to Peirce's occasionally maligned notion of the asymptotic or approximative advance of a community of investigators toward truth (see merrell 1991a).

2.   In this regard I would recommend Guadalupe Loaeza's (1988, 1992) mordent accounts (also Mejía Prieto 1980).

3.   Around a decade ago there was a rich outpouring of analysis and commentary and applause and critique of testimonial literature. For further, see Beverley (1983),

Beverley and Achugar (1992), Campa (1999), Yúdice (1988), Foley (1986), Sklo-dowska (1992), Vidal and Jara (1986), Gluck and Patai (1991), and Spivak (1988).

4.   Beverley goes on to tell us that Menchú "is an intellectual in a sense clearly dif-ferent than what Gramsci called the traditional intellectual—that is, someone who meets the standards and carries the authority of high culture, philosophy, and sci-ence—and a sometimes explicit hostility to intellectuals, the state education system, and the authority of book-learning is one of the leitmotifs of her testimony" (Bever-ley 1999:71). Menchú, of course, is just who she is (Firstness), and when she speaks, it is the academy that to an extent imposes discourse (Secondness and Thirdness) on her words and places them in neat desiccated pigeon-holes and textualizes them and publishes them with Verso (or Duke, Minnesota, or whatever press), in order to per-petuate the academic power-elite's hegemony.

5.   This becomes especially problematic in the event that a testimonial is edited to the extent that it becomes a pseudotestimonial, such editing having remained victim-ized by binary imperatives of a "hidden transcript" sort as described above (see Sklodowska 1994).

6.   Among some observers the idea has it that the testimonial "fad" has reached its prime and is now on a downhill slide (for example, Gugelberger 1996). I would rather doubt that testimonial literature is destined to pass into oblivion, even though it has not lived up to its original billing, given faith on the part of many theorists of testimonial literature in the outmoded concepts of essentialism, representation, and truth. On the other hand, I would expect that this subgenre will never become part of the traditional canon, since the very idea of "traditional canon" has also outlived its usefulness.

Part V

Music, rhythm, dance. Resonance and syncope. Signs of iconicity and indexicality, of bodymind, bodymindsigns. Signs of tacitness more than straightforward explicitness. The importance of that "sixth sense," kinesthetics, allowing for the body to do what it does best. Chapter fifteen initiates the rhetorical, existential, phenomenological turn with a wave and a weave and a sly wink, which introduces in chapter sixteen the hybrid, complex nature of Latin American music, dance, and the persistence of the Baroque, with special emphasis on Brazilian Samba and Bossa Nova. Chapter seventeen reintroduces "emptiness" and the triadic nature of the incessantly mediating sign to a screaming pitch. Here, it becomes most apparent that within cultural dynamics there is constant subversion of classical logical principles, as bodymindsigns codependently emerge to complement abstract linguistic, mental, cogitating signs. This is culture at its most expressive, and nowhere, I would suggest, is it better exemplified than in Latin America, where anything and everything can be found and felt and sensed and interpreted and at least in part intellectualized, where human cultures are condensed to a massive, fluid vortex of proclivities and propensities and tendencies and interactivities, where cultures are magnificently seen for just what they are, the flux and flow of signs of heart and mind, of the gut and of cogitation.

Here, then, is the final episode of my story. If its reading proves a mere fraction as gratifying as did its writing, then I expect the experience will have not been entirely in vain.

Chapter Fifteen

From "Emptiness," Rhythm Is Born

> Reporter: If you love our country as much as you claim, why do you live in California?
>
> Guillermo Gómez-Peña: I'm demexicanizing myself in order to mexiunderstand myself better.
>
> Reporter: And what do you consider yourself?
>
> Gómez-Peña: Post-Mexican, Pre-Chicano, Pan-Latino, Trans-Territorial, Art-American . . . It all depends on the day of the week or the project I'm working on.
>
> My writing went nowhere for over 20 years until I returned to the border after a long absence.
>
> —Rolando Hinojosa Smith

It's in the Bodymindsign

Music. It has both horizontal and vertical components. The horizontal aspects are those that go on during a certain period of time such as melody, counterpoint (or the interweaving of simultaneous melodies), and rhythm. The vertical aspect comprises the sum of what is happening at any given moment: the result is either notes that sound against each other in counterpoints, or, as in the case of a melody and accompaniment, of the underpinning of chords that the musician gives to the principle notes of the melody. As a rule of thumb, then, harmony is primarily vertical, melody is primarily horizontal; melody and rhythm can exist without harmony, but the inverse is hardly the case.

Music can be profoundly moving by means of resonances that are in the process of their being set between tone-stress and ideal motion and nervous tension and diverse impulses. But music, it would appear, is not in possession of any power within itself. It has no necessary effect on the body as a consequence for social action, unless its sounds and circumstance can be related to a coherent set of ideas about self and *other* and body feelings and their interrelationships with the world and the codependent emergence of the world-*other* and body and mind: of *bodymindother*. There is surely no direct connection (of one thing and its *other*: Secondness) between musical sounds and one's emotional response to them. Rather, sounds and emotions are united (as one: Firstness). But that is not all. Sound and response need some *other* of the world that evokes the response, and the response is possible only with respect to the interrelated interaction and codependent emergence of both sound and *other*. The

247

Thirdness of music emerges from its Firstness, but that Firstness, to be genuine Firstness, depends upon Thirdness for its emerging as music, and both depend upon Secondness.

There is, in conjunction with music—and its companion, dance—a certain "sixth sense," which may well be the most fundamental and hence the most important of them all: *kinesthetics*. This sense is quite different from the standard five senses: it is neither itself nor anything else. Like the other senses, it cannot stand alone, for it is integrated. It overlaps and merges with the other sensory modes. Unlike those complementary senses, it has no identity of its own, but takes a bit here and another bit there, from the other senses. Its playground is the area of overlap, the liminality or border between and the fuzzy lines of mergence, present in the interrelationships between the five sensory modes. In a word, kinesthetics consists of the natural complements shared by all the senses. So it complements them and at the same time it is its own complement: it is the complement of complements, it is incongruously complementary. Language contains hardly more than the barest suggestion of this form of complementarity. Language is laced with all the senses and all the senses are closely interrelated within language. A term can express one sense, albeit vaguely, incompletely, and quite inadequately, and at the same time it contains, within itself, vestiges of another sense. Originally to look and to see were based on a root that meant both to see and to say; to touch is based on the echoic representation of a knock; taste originally meant to touch. So much for trivial examples. The important point is that we tend to think of language as chiefly visual (discrete marks against a background: ocularcentrism) and auditory (ripples in the air: phonocentrism)—the principle senses in Western discourse—whereas it actually involves all the senses. So much also for linguicentric biases. Let me begin this chapter in earnest, then, with a tale of two *motilities*.

The story must begin with the essence of what some scientists consider the most profound nature of twentieth-century physics: Niels Bohr's *complementary principle*—of course, we have been hearing much of this throughout these pages. Complements are a far cry from opposites, dichotomies, or binaries, for they add up to more than the sum of their parts. They are like day and night, which also include dawn and daybreak and sunrise and aurora, on the one hand, and on the other, sunset and twilight and dusk and afterglow. They are like male and female, each of which, genetically speaking, contains something of the other and both of which are contained within either one of the two terms and at the same time are themselves and nothing but themselves. The category "human organisms," for example, contains all females plus that part of them that is shared with males, and all males plus that part of them that is shared with females. What they share is neither exactly male nor female nor is it either nonmale or nonfemale: it is, in a manner of putting it, female-male-lessness. In regard to female-lessness there is something of maleness, and in regard to male-lessness there is something of femaleness. In other words, the two terms are terms of interrelatedness, mergence of one into the other, codependence.

What has this to do with kinesthetics? Actually, it has everything to do with kinesthetics. That is to say, it has to do with rhythm and harmony and symphony and syncope and above all with resonance—as we saw in chapter eight. The whole shebang is like the complementary *Yin-Yang* melody-harmony: ☯. It is anything but static: it is a flux of undulating, palpitating, rhythmic movement. There is resonance, to be sure, plenty of it. Without the resonance there could be no complementarity, and without the complementarity there could be no movement. The sound of music, any music, as well as the wind whipping through the yellow pines along southern Colorado mountain slopes, the Pacific waves seen from a distance along California's Highway 1, a dust devil in the Mojave desert, a flash flood along Arizona's Gila River, Pueblo Amerindian chants experienced in New Mexico, all this, and outward, to spiral galaxies millions of light years removed, none of this would exist without resonance.

Resonance is resound, rebound, vibration, reiteration, echo, all, more often than not, with a to and fro sort of imbalance: *syncope*. Something begins movement, but it is pulled back by something else, that pulling back compelling the first something to reciprocate with a pull of its own, and the give-and-take goes on, without conceivable end: resonance is also an example of elegant agonistics, the Heraclitean cosmic struggle of the elements. Resonance at times also becomes synchrony. A tuning fork puts others in the vicinity in motion to the same tune. Each member of a swirl of fireflies at some point gets its turning on and turning off in rhythm with other members, and the phenomenon of "mutual entrainment" is in effect. A basketball combo at the NCAA tournament gets a certain rhythm it has experienced a few times during the long season, and it becomes literally invincible. The list is inexhaustible, of course, but I trust the point has been made, once again. Resonance in the proper tune allows for all parties involved to expend a minimum of energy and realize a maximum of payoff. Out of tune resonance can be no more than a wheel-spinning affair, and in the worst of circumstances it can turn into veritable chaos. A gentle nudge with a nightstick by a police officer at a peaceful demonstration might end in a riot and much blood and perhaps a few deaths. In contrast, Martin Luther King's "I have a dream" was capable of bringing many minds into convergence along the same wavelength. *Resonance*. It is the stuff of life and the staff by which the universe is measured, from subnuclear particles to galaxies.

Kinesthetics is resonance manifested. The manifestation does not, indeed it cannot, make a clear-cut distinction between resonator-resonated, that is, between subject-object. Manifestation of resonance is like a paraphrase of Merleau-Ponty on perception, especially his notion of the "reversibility" of perceiver-perceived (or sensor-sensed as I have been using the terms in this chapter):

> [T]he idea that every perception is doubled with a counterpercep-
> tion . . . , is an act with two faces, one no longer knows who
> speaks and who listens. Speaking-listening, seeing-being seen,
> perceiving-being perceived circularity (it is because of it that it
> seems to us that perception forms itself *in the things themselves—
> Activity = Passivity*). (Merleau-Ponty 1968 VI:264–65)

What we have here is tantamount to the interrelatedness, the codependent arising, of "dancer-dance" during a performance, that is, the act of dancing. The dancer is virtual presence (Firstness), doing the dance, which is actually just now pastness (Secondness) in the process of being presented in the here-now (that is, the here-now for some observer), and both come together in the act of dancing, which is future oriented (Thirdness). Dancer and dance are interrelated. They merge into one another, and at the same time they are codependent: they are complementary. Thus they reciprocate, interacting in terms of the action of one on the other is reversed such that the other interacts on the one. This interaction is what is actually seen as dancing, dancing that is a rhythmic, undulating flow as a result of the reversings of dancer into dance and dance into dancer. This reciprocation, interaction, reversion of roles, however, is not completeable, for Thirdness must remain as an unfinished symphony insofar as finite semiotic agents go. Reversibility is always incomplete, and never realized in its totality. Neither of the two sides of the complementary equation completely becomes the other such that there is identity or absolute parallelism. Rather, there is always some interruption, some hiatus, something lacking in the interaction: that's what the function of the syncopic flip-flop is all about. Perfection is not realizable in our fallible world.

However, if the experience of two processes of becoming is never such that the processes can exactly overlap or coincide, this is no indication that the experience is for that reason blemished, or that the experience is incapable of bringing about a wedding of the two processes. That is the beauty of experience and its value for us in a world of constant change. Experience of syncopic resonance is comparable to an e. e. cummings-like resonating line, "He danced his did danced he." It almost contains a mirror-image symmetry, but not quite, that is, not really. "He danced" is the "dancer" dancing the dance. Once "He" as the dancer "did" it while in the act of carrying on with the dance, the act became a past act overlapping with the act that is now present. But this is not really the case, for before the act enters into the awareness of the "dancer," it is now almost-but-not-quite-immediately-past. So "danced he" preceded "he danced," though not by much. Yet "danced he" follows "he danced" along the syntactic string, hence it is neither prior nor posterior, but interrelates and interacts in reciprocity, all making up the "dance" of past performances, the present performance, and all future performances. There is a chiasmus, a "crossing over." During this process, one side does not exactly translate into the opposite of the other side. Both retain their uniqueness at the same time that their codependency becomes evident *to* experience *within* the consciousness of the sign interpreter. That is, the consciousness of the experiencer arises in codependency with the sign in order that there can be an interpreter, in order that the sign can construct the interpreter and the interpreter the sign.

For there can be no subject-object, inner-outer, here-there. These images are intellectually Cartesian and they are spatially Euclidean. The proper model, to use Merleau-Ponty's example, and with invocation of the above section on Winfree, is topological. Like the Möbius-strip or the Klein bottle, there is no inside-outside or two-, three-, or four-dimensional space, but always something in between. In all these cases space is like a fabric with continuous folds in extraspatial dimensions, which allow for an interpenetration of folds. Such is the nature of the dancer, a surface consisting of contours and folds and cavities and twists and turns in space of the Möbius-strip sort, and at the same time it is interrelated with the dance in terms of codependence and mutual interpenetration. The dancer (present, Firstness) is there for the seeing, hearing, and in certain special dancing events even the smelling and feeling if the observer is close enough—especially if that observer is her partner(s). But the dance (past, Secondness) is never exactly either here or there. It is a past unfolding that was then enfolded and is now in the process of once again becoming unfolded as a nonempirical presentness-becoming in interrelation with the dancer who is in the now—that is never exactly now but always the product of anticipation and necessity that is in the process of receding into the past—dancing (Future orientation, Thirdness) the dance, which is neither here nor there but always already somewhere else.

How in the world can we more adequately account for this process? Perhaps we can't; that is, I can't, at least in ordinary language and classical logic. Just as we cannot see our seeing, think our thinking, know our knowing, when engaged in the very acts of seeing, thinking, and knowing, so also the dancer cannot dance her dancing. It is a three-way process. Rather than saying, "The 'dancer' is 'dancing' the 'dance'," better said, "*It* dances." This is like saying, as I suggested in the previous chapter, "*It* rains," or in another sense perhaps "Live *it* up" or "Just do *it*," for there is no identifiable subject, no gender. . . . but . . . No. . . . That's not quite it either. There remains an unidentifiable subject that we really should do away with entirely. So what about "There is rain going on"? But . . . of course that is not what we're trying to get at either. Where, or what, is the "there"? There can be no "there." And to where is it "going on"? How can there be any purpose, any goal, any direction? There can't be. Not really. So how do we say *it*? We can't. That is, unless we have some sort of temporal and nonmodal "logic" and some sort of "logic" devoid of "identity" and capable of embracing terms that happen to appear in the middle ground between contradictories (it seems that we haven't taken so much as a baby-step beyond our conception of the absent subject of the testimonial).

Let us try to begin anew, then. Our dancer is to some extent and to a greater or lesser degree subject to sensory data of the standard five classes: *visual, auditory, olfactory, tactile,* and *gustatory*. While being seen, the dancer plays the role of the Secondness of signs, the becoming of "sign-events out there." The dance itself, in contrast, is nonempirical. Yet it is in a way subject to past experience of the same sort as dance performance. At least, we would suspect, in regard to the dance there are anticipations governed by expectations regarding what might or should transpire—there is, then, a certain goal, however vague, regarding human semiotic activity. This involves *quality*: emotions, feelings, sensations, evoked by inclinations, wishes, desires, beliefs, customary ways and means of doing things. With the evocation of quality we are now in the domain of the Firstness of signs, what "has not yet become but might be in the act of becoming"—this, definitely, is purposeless, goalless. The actual becoming of the dance which involves the act of dancing toward the realization of some wished for, desired, expected performance as the result of "mind-signs in here," is of the province of the Thirdness of signs. Now, finally to get to the meat of the matter insofar as that may be possible, it is this Firstness of things that is most appropriately kinesthetic, if indeed it is possible to place kinesthetics in any category at all. Kinesthetics is "in" the body but it projects "outside." "Within" the body, of course, there are natural rhythms and flows: the brainmind engenders wave patterns, muscles expand and contract, cells subdivide, the heart beats, the lungs heave, the guts undergo peristalsis, the bladder inflates and deflates, the liver does its garbage disposal act, and so on.

Of the five customary sensory channels, for obvious reasons touch is most closely related to kinesthetics. With respect to touch, Merleau-Ponty scholar Sue Cataldi writes that it is:

> the mother of the senses; and our skin is the oldest, largest, and most sensitive of our sensory organs. Our sense of touch was the first to develop and through it we acquired knowledge of a vast array of textures—from the scratch of wool to the sleekness of satin, from the slipperiness of soap to the goo of glue, from the scrub of a beard to the down of a feather. Through touch we are also sensitive to pressure; differentiations in shape; variations in weight and thickness; fluctuations in fluidity, aridity, and tem-perature; and distinguishable styles of movements. (Cataldi 1984:125)

Tactile sensations—and in an exceedingly more specialized way gustatory sen-sations—are unique insofar as there must be an object body in actual contact with the subject body. But it is ambiguous also, since, as Merleau-Ponty argues in great detail, there is no absolute distinction between the touching body and the body touched. The right hand touches the left hand. But wait. Could it not be the other way round? What is touching and what is being touched? A hand caresses a cat; the cat arches its back so as to push against a hand that happened to appear, and begins purring. A hand holds a flower; the flower comes in contact with a hand in terms of something that can possibly aid it in its reproductive process. A hand picks up a stone on the beach; the stone comes in contact with a hand in such a way that its concrete existence at this space-time juncture becomes manifest before its general essence as merely a stone among stones makes its way into a universe that was, is, and will be just what it is. In every case the touched interacts with the toucher just as the toucher presumably exercises its hegemony over its universe of the touched. There is interrelated, interactive reciprocity, a reflexivity, a reversibility, that is not in effect to the same degree in seeing, hearing, and smelling, since concrete physical contact is not as pronounced—of course gustatory sensations usually involve physi-cal contact, but it is limited to a specialized, and relatively small, portion of the body's kinesthetic surface (Merleau-Ponty 1962, 1968).

More than Merely Tactile

However, there is more to the issue than merely touch with regard to kinesthetics. There is *haptic* perception, which is chiefly tactile, and it also includes certain as-pects of all the sensory modes. Haptic perception is the touched environment, for certain. But the touching also includes a spatio-temporal sense of the environ-ment in terms of its possibilities for being seen, heard, felt, smelled, and tasted. Haptic perception is intimately related to the body while visual perception is closer to the affairs of the mind—though actually, there is no mind/body distinc-tion here. If the West has come increasingly to prioritize mind over body, and as a logical consequence the visual over the haptic, language over other communicative media, propositional knowledge over schematic and imagistic knowledge, and symbolicity over indexicality and iconicity, perhaps the time is ripe, I must repeat, for a more balanced conception. This balance is most effectively forthcoming through a bodymind interrelatedness, interactivity, and codependency. The bodymind complementarity pervades all levels, from inner to outer and from biological to psychological to phenomenological.

Touch involves haptic sensations, and haptic sensations are intimately involved in kinesthetics, especially since the time and space of affectivity regarding the entire bodymind are most apparent in the time and space of tactility. There is more overlap between the touched and the touching than between the seeing and the seen, the hearing and the heard, and so on. The felt object is never entirely divorced from the act of feeling, which projects out into the environment and at the same time draws inwardly: there is proximity and at the same time distance; there is a there and at the same time what is there is here; there is an unfolded outside that at the same time enfolds with the enfolded bodymind inside that is unfolding in order to sense the unfolded outside (Merleau-Ponty 1962:316). This oscillating there-here, outside-inside, touched-touching is a continual shifting, a vague, rhythmic dynamic of ambiguous reversibility of experience. In touching, there is movement that touches and movement that is touched. What is apparently now the "outside" of the Möbius-strip is the "inside" from another view. So depending on the view, any spot on the strip is either one or the other. However, cutting a hole in the strip provides access from outside to inside and vice versa, and the one is enfolded into the other while it unfolds out to the other in order to sense it. Topologically, there is no absolute priority of either "outside" or "inside," "enfolded" or "unfolded," "here" or "there," "now" or "then." Everything is connected with everything else in an interrelated, mutually interpenetrating, codependently emerging, and complementary way (Merleau-Ponty 1968:256).

While this characteristic is most evident regarding tactile sensations, it is by no means absent in other sensory modes. You are, for example, struck by the brilliant array of an Arizona sunset, a rendition of Beethoven's Ninth Symphony, the smooth tang of a fine wine, and the aroma of a freshly cut rose. You are apprehending the phenomena and they are taking hold of you; you feel them and they are the *felt* that is entering you; you are enfolded in them and they enfold themselves in you; they are the "outside" that is becoming "inside" and you are the "inside" that projects "outside." You are affected, touched, but not tactually or tactically. You are touched, but touched haptically, kinesthetically, both "inside" and "outside." Your entire past condenses into this affectivity here-now; the entirety of your surroundings converges into your being touched now. You make a mark, a distinction, between some aspect of your surroundings and everything else, and you indicate (index) it as such-and-such; that which was distinguished and indicated is in turn that which makes of you a distinction and an indication setting you apart from your surroundings. Your "I"-*other* distinction, however, is artificial. The "I" before the distinction is what it is (icon), just as the *other* is what it is (icon). As repositories of Firstness, they converge and merge with one another, they mutually interpenetrate each other, they are interrelatedly codependent, such that any distinction remains exceedingly vague unless a somewhat arbitrary line of demarcation is made.[1]

Maurice Merleau-Ponty believed the painter during her act of painting comes into a heightened haptic awareness of herself with respect to the object of her painting—which is crucial, I would suggest, to an understanding of bodymind. Merleau-Ponty was a great admirer of Paul Cézanne. Both he and Cézanne challenge the West's inner/outer and subject/object and mind/body dichotomies like few painters and philosophers. Merleau-Ponty writes "quality, light, color, and depth that are there before us are there only because they awaken an echo in our body and because the body welcomes them" (Merleau-Ponty 1964:22). And he tells us of Cézanne: "we cannot imagine how a mind could paint. It is by lending his body to the world that the artist changes the world into paintings" (1964:16). In this manner, sensing, genuinely sensing—I must continue to write "sensing" rather than "perceiving," "seeing," or some other term in order to avoid the customary stereotypes and premises—is a matter of "sensing" from the "inside," which is really not "inside," for the "inside" is everywhere. And that which is "sensed" is "outside," but there is really no "outside" in the traditional manner of speaking: it is nowhere for it knows no limits—limits of which we can be aware, that is—and it is everywhere, for it is "inside" and at the same time it is elsewhere.

Merleau-Ponty also cites Paul Klee, for whom the painter does not simply sense the world, but, in reciprocity, the world senses the painter, and the painter's act of painting is a breaking out from the "inside," which is to say that the "outside" breaks into the "inside" (1964:31). There is no Lacanian or Foucauldian "gaze" here, nor is there merely sensor and sensed. Rather, it is a process of "sensing happening," a "happening of sensing," a simultaneous enfolding and unfolding of some "here happening" and some other "there happening." But there is really neither "here" nor "there." There is just "sensing happening"—please relate this, if you will, to the act of dancing as discussed above. To give my language a Deleuze-Guattarian (1983, 1987) slant, the bird-watcher's binoculars give him visual sensing capability approaching that of the keen-eyed exotic bird, and they meet, they interrelate, interact, interpenetrate, they are codependent, they are happening, they are becoming-events. The bird-watcher happens to become who he is becoming because of the bird's becoming; the bird is becoming because of the bird-watcher's becoming. Their becoming is codependent with the becoming of their immediate surroundings, their remote surroundings, the continent, the oceans and other continents, the Earth, the Planets and the Sun, the Galaxy, the Universe. An apparently quite insignificant becoming is all-becoming.

More adequately stated, perhaps, it is all a matter of rhythm-becoming, music-dance becoming. A sense of rhythm-becoming is as instrumental in breaking down customary habits of thought as is the inside/outside-subject/object dissolution. From the sheer intellectual force of Bach's recreating the Pythagorean harmony of the spheres to so-called "primitive music" and the likes of jazz, which, according to Theodor Adorno (1973), is evoked by a desire to transcend reason and surrender to the body, from Plato's exclusion of music of the body—of women, slaves, teenagers—and St. Augustine's suspicion of music of all forms, to the guttural outpourings at a rock concert, the same tension exists. It is a tension between what should be—ideal perfection, the mind's imposition on nature—and what might be—natural rhythms, the body in tune with itself. This tension is hardly anywhere more evident than in the scandal caused by early New World music and dance, in part of Native American and African origin, upon its introduction to repressive Old World practices during the seventeenth century. The *chacona*, for example, of Peruvian Amerindian and perhaps also of African American origin, was introduced into Spain at the turn of the century, and shortly thereafter it sparked a dance craze in Italy and throughout much of Europe. For example, Susan McClary writes of the *chacona* (or the Italian *ciaccona*) that:

> On the one hand, it was celebrated as liberating bodies that had been stifled by the constraints of Western civilization; on the other, it was condemned as obscene, as a threat to Christian mores. But most sources concurred that its rhythms—once experienced—were irresistible; it was banned temporarily in 1615 on grounds of its "irredeemably infectious lasciviousness" [Bianconi 1982:101]. Nor was social pedigree a sure defense against contamination; even noble ladies were said to succumb to its call. Like soul music at a later historical moment, the *ciaccona* crossed over cautiously guarded class and racial boundaries. Whatever the *ciaccona* signified in its original contexts, it quickly came to be associated in Europe (by friends and foes alike) with forbidden bodily pleasures and potential social havoc. (McClary 1995:87) (brackets added)

What seems to be most disconcerting in the *chacona*, the *zarabanda*, and other music and dance imported to the Old World from the Americas is, to re-evoke the term, syncope. These rhythms are a dance between hesitation and assertion, affirmation and denial, stability and instability, continuity and discontinuity, regularity and unsuspected breaks, motion and suspended animation. The body experiences tentative hoverings, a disequilibrium, a reestablishing of stability, an unanticipated detour through one beat and into another one, a bold entry of a new cadence and delicate nuances. This sort of music, as would be expected, met resistance at the pens of the Pythagorean purists of Enlightenment ideals. But the bulges and cavities, the somewhat symmetrical but flawed contours and the flows of the body, resisted the crystalline purity of stodgy musical forms. McClary concludes her essay with the observation that relocating music in the body is the most adequate way of understanding music history. Music:

> can only maintain its Pythagorean purity if we erase the bodies it shapes and that shape it. To be sure, studies based on contingencies such as the highly mutable body are bound to seem messy in comparison with the mathematical charts we like to flaunt. But they also promise to make visible and audible the power music has exercised in the social world. And because of the extraordinary specificity of musical artifacts, such work also can contribute heavily to projects seeking to reconstruct the history of the body. (McClary 1995:101)

The *body, bodymind.* Flows and folds. Function and form. Series and breaks. Continuities and fissures. The seat of rhythm, vibrations "in here" in sympathy with vibrations "out there." Once again, ultimately it's a matter of resonances, and unbalanced syncopated ones at that. During the humdrum of everyday life we are hardly aware of the resonances surrounding us. The earth and moon are resonant with the sun and the entire solar system, which is resonant with other systems within our galaxy, which is resonant with other galaxies. Chlorophyll molecules in plants vibrate to the tune of red and blue light and absorb them, reflecting the remainder, consisting of the green frequencies. These same plants absorb green and reflect other colors during the autumn season. The colors of white light pass through countless droplets of water to spread out into a prism that is magnified into a rainbow. Ultraviolet light vibrates in harmony with the molecules of glass that allows only visible rays to get through; suntan lotion absorbs that same ultraviolet light before it gets to the skin, thus preventing painful sunburn. Electrons in one state resonate with electrons in another state of the same atom provisionally to keep it in harmony with its surroundings. From the microscopic to the cosmic, resonance rules.

But as pointed out in chapter eight, during our daily existence we tend mindlessly and blissfully to go about, assuming things are just as they should be, unaware of most of the violent Heraclitean struggles of the universe. Mindfulness is the exception rather than the norm, it would appear. The trick, however, is to enhance mindfulness and minimize mindlessness. How so? Let us eventually return to Latin America, albeit by an indirect route by way of Pierre Bourdieu.

Bodymindsigns

Bourdieu's (1977:94) observation that when revolutionary societies seek to remold mind and signs by deculturation and reculturation they stress what the body knows and does. Bodies must be dismembered to forget what they remembered and did by habit and remembered in order that they begin the long road of doing by different habits. This focus is found in millenarian movements and cults as well (see also Comaroff 1985, 1992, Wilson 1973, Turner 1968).

Bourdieu uses the term *habitus* in alluding to a set of dispositions formed by the process of in-formation. By this Bourdieu means that there is an in-forming into the body of social practices that are eventually remembered. Consequently, the body is remembered as a result of the in-forming, and hence it becomes em-bodied such that what it does it does because that is what most genuinely qualifies the body's becoming (Bourdieu 1990). When scholars take this to mean the "inscribed" body, they are more often than not falling victim to linguicentrism, or if not, they run the risk of being misinterpreted in linguicentristic ways. I would rather use the term "in-form" rather than "inscribe." "In-form" is spatial and temporal and topological and processual, not merely written and willingly giving itself up to static conceptions. The human form is definitely not a *tabula rasa* in the sense of anthropologist Marcel Mauss (1973). Neither are any of its parts or the parts of animal forms "good to think with" as Claude Lévi-Strauss (1963) would have it, nor does it simply compose a set of physical oppositions (Needham 1973). Those are all linguicentric modes of thinking. In contrast to these modes, the body is a construction by convention, and as such it is an ongoing whole in perpetual flow toward somewhere else and into something that it at present is not. The body has been in-formed and it is in-formation in such a manner that it exudes the becoming of an in-forming process (in-formation that is always already process and never completed product). At the same time, the body in-forms itself by means of a complementary process from that which is at least at the moment something *other* than the body. This interactive, codependent emergence of in-formation is a process wherein that which has been in-formed as *other* than the body can in-form the body and what has been in-formed as the body can in-form the *other*. This undulating, syncopated, dynamic process is like a ski ride along Möbius slopes where there is no telling where in-side is and where out-side is not. All binary distinctions have been dismembered with hardly the possibility of any rememberment. There is no "logic of consumption" here, no rational capitalistic gains and losses, no economic determinants. All that comes later. At the ebb and flow of bodymindsigns, there is only space and time and topology and process. There is only that which is just-now-beginning-to-emerge from the interstices, the border of the border, from "emptiness." But as soon as it emerges to become "logic," rationalism, economy, it has been dis-membered, disformed, mutilated, and shattered into bits and pieces making up inscriptions and texts and classes and categories: Secondness.[2]

That is the problem with Bourdieu. He accounts for what came after what was/is/will-have-been becoming. He cannot account for habitus as bodymindsigns, but rather, he offers a tale about signs of the body having been subjected to mind. His theory of habitus remains enshrouded in linguicentrism to a considerably greater degree than the post-critical philosophy of tacit knowing through focal and subsidiary means of Polanyian vintage as discussed in chapter two. Thus Bourdieu cannot effectively account for the alternative "logics" this inquiry seeks. How can we talk about a "logic of difference" without addressing ourselves to the "undifferentiated" that gives rise to "differences" that can then enter into the process of their "dedifferentiation" toward their returning to "undifferentiation"? How can we allude to any "logic of dissemination" if we care not a whit about the "undisseminated" from whence "dissemination" emerged and toward which it can begin a return? What would be a "logic of consumerism" or of "postcapitalism" or of "postmodernism," or of whatever, were there no consideration of the flux and the flow that made them possible?

I would tend to agree with Bourdieu's idea that habitus is "a product of history" that:

> produces individual and collective practices—more history in accordance with the schemes generated by history. It ensures the active presence of past experiences, which, deposited in each organism in the form of schemes of perception, thought and action, tend to guarantee the 'correctness' of practices and their constancy over time, more reliable than all formal rules and explicit norms. . . . The genesis of a system of works or practices generated by the same *habitus* . . . cannot be described either as the autonomous development of a unique and always self-identical essence, or as a continuous creation of novelty, because it arises from the necessary yet unpredictable confrontation between the

> *habitus* and an event that can exercise a pertinent incitement on
> the *habitus* only if the latter snatches it from the contingency of
> the accidental and constitutes it as a problem by applying to it the
> very principles of its solution: and also because the *habitus*, like
> every 'art of inventing,' is what makes it possible to produce an
> infinite number of practices that are relatively unpredictable . . .
> but also limited in their diversity. (Bourdieu 1990:54–55)

The chief problem I continue to have, however, is with Bourdieu's use of mechanistic terms such as "product, "generation," and "deposited" instead of "process," "engenderment," and "in-forming." But that is a problem of nomenclature, not of the feeling, sensing, and thinking behind the words.

The flow of habitus at the post-critical, "a-logical," "a-rational" level of feeling that is always already emerging into sensing and thought and language is revealed in Richard Rodríguez's words:

> I grew divorced from my body. Insecure, overweight, listless. On
> hot summer days when my rubber-soled shoes soaked up the heat
> from the sidewalk, I kept my head down. Or walked in the shade.
> My mother didn't need anymore to tell me to watch out for the
> sun. I denied myself a sensational life. The normal, extraordinary,
> animal excitement of feeling my body alive—riding shirtless on a
> bicycle in the warm wind created by furious self-propelled mo-
> tion—the sensation that first had excited in me a sense of my
> maleness, I denied. I was too ashamed of my body. I wanted to
> forget that I had a body because I had a brown body. (Rodríguez
> 1990:271–72) (recall in this vein what was written of the *mestizo*
> above)

The signs of which Rodríguez writes are felt, they don't have to be thought or spoken: they are signs of iconicity of the most basic sort, signs of feeling, quality, sentiment. They are during the coming and going of everyday life intimate signs of tacitness that are never focal but remain subsidiary, until the moment they receive the full heat of the spotlight, then they can be thought and spoken. If Rodríguez can now speak of them, it is with hindsight and a more contemplative mind. But now the signs are not the same signs. To a degree, they are now subject to the will and effective control of their maker and taker. The signs are those of the indexical and chiefly symbolic variety.

Rodríguez's world within which he was previously immersed was a cultural dreamland wherein the signs of his thinking belied the signs of his feeling. The iconic signs of quality were there, but the logical, rational signs of his culture suppressed them. Dreams shadow waking life, which avoids dream at all cost, for proper appearances must be maintained—must avoid the sun, must avoid showing too much brown skin, must look down when walking and away when talking to someone who is "white." The dream, like the shadow, doesn't go away. When the lights are bright and the room is illuminated from all angles, it fades out. But it is still there, at the unseen border of borders, ready to make its appearance when least expected. It is a rhythm of the shadow's re-informing and re-membering the body and hence perhaps eventually the mind and bodymindsigns. In this manner the shadow is a symptom. The mind ordinarily prefers to forget it, to dis-member it, relegating it to the invisible. But if a symptom is a means for forgetting, it is also a means for preservation and re-membering, for it is always present in its absence. It is a way back home. Richard Rodríguez re-traced his steps while re-membering all the way, and he revived his shadow, and re-invented his place in the world (compare to Bonfil's concept of "México profundo").

This process of in-forming signs, signs of habitus, of entrenched semiotic propensities and proclivities, is feeling at the heart of socially constructed cultural practices. It is the basis for sensing and understanding cultural life. Cultural life is the way it is because that's the way it feels. It feels the way it feels because that's the way cultural life is. This feel is what gives quality, tone, texture (Firstness all) to living. The feel is in the flow, the rhythm, the arrhythmia, the syncope. Which is where we should look, that is, where we should get a feel for the process through the only media I have available to me: words, words, and more words. How absurd, all this! So self-defeating. If I could just leave language aside and sing or dance or mime or paint or compose what I sense is what we need to know, I would. But, of course, I can't, within the covers of a book. So I must push on, I suppose.

Where There's a Feel, There's a Way

Perhaps to get a better feel for what I believe this inquiry is about, take jazz pianist David Sudnow (1978), who writes a fascinating book on focal and subsidiary feeling, sensing, and knowing, though without using the terms in quite the same way I use them here. He narrates how his teacher provided explicit instructions on such matters as chord production and constructional rules that could be mechanically obeyed, but which contributed virtually nothing toward the teaching of jazz.

After having received the proper litany of linguistic instructions, and after having made a few exemplary moves, the young Sudnow tried to play jazz. During this time his teacher offered advice, but it fell on partly deaf ears, for it was inordinately vague and of little use or comfort. The apprentice wanted explicit guidelines. But they were not, nor could they have been, forthcoming. Following the counsel to "get the phrasing more syncopated," he fumbled and faltered. It was as if he had been told to go out in the world and speak Chinese after he had been given a few grammar rules and a handful of words. Then the master showed him how it was done with a little of his own improvisation. His fingers flew over the keyboard, and the student saw how it was done, but he couldn't do it. After a particular move by the master a question was asked: "What was that?" The master was puzzled: "What was what?" The apprentice: "What you just did." The master: "Nothing really, you just do it." Do what? There was no what, no that, no how. There was just doing, and in the doing, a little bit of vague showing. There was no jazzist here and fingers there in contiguity with a piano and melody that emerges and extends out somewhere else. There was only "jazzing," which in its jazziest form consists of fingers, piano, melody, and the entire context. As Sudnow learned, little bits and pieces of jazzing were picked up tacitly during the process of his jazzing becoming genuine jazzing. The little bits and pieces slowly showed themselves to him, in-formed him, and dis-membered him so as to allow for re-membering. Jazzing is an integrated practice, interrelating code-pendent facets of the jazzist's entire bodymindsigns in such a way that the sounds emerge. Thus Sudnow could write that: "To *define* jazz (as to define any phenome-non of human action) is to *describe* the body's ways" (Sudnow 1978:146). But, of course, to describe the body's ways is to engage in the process of jazzing, or cycling or tennising or driving or thinking or writing or talking while at work or at play. Jazzing becomes sort of an extensional self-consciousness, like the blind person us-ing a cane to feel her/his way about.

Sudnow reports that he can now sit himself at a piano and he is immediately oriented, ready to engage in jazzing. Before, he had to begin by shuffling himself around in his seat until he found the right spot, roam the keyboard with his fingers, and get his mind properly attuned to the task at hand. Now he just does it, like the accomplished speaker who before an audience has a vague idea in mind and opens her mouth and begins speaking, confident that the most appropriate words will spill forth, making up the sentences as she goes along. But jazzing took years to learn. It was not a simple matter of learning the chords and then listening to a few jazz pieces and then felicitously sitting down to improvise. There were years of listening, years of chording, years of roaming about with the fingers, before jazzing began emerging. Sudnow writes that when he first began jazzing with a combo, he was within jazzing but couldn't keep up. He was "a bucking bronco of my own body's doings, situated in the midst of these surrounding affairs. Between the chord-changing beating of my left hand at more or less 'regular intervals' according to the chart, the melody movements of the right, and the rather more smoothly managed and securely pulsing background of the bass player and drummer, there obtained the most mutually alien-ative relations" (Sudnow 1978:30). His hand jumped around from place to place. He felt there was little coordination, little flow, little continuity, only fits and starts and stops.

Then, at some point, he began jazzing, genuinely jazzing. He eventually found himself singing to himself as he was jazzing, talking to himself, dialoguing with himself. He found himself, that is, he found his fingers, carrying out various tasks simultaneously. His fingers were singing, talking, dialoguing. As the conversations with himself began taking form, he found himself:

> looking down at these hands of mine, their ways, my ways of em-
> ploying them, seeking practically useful terms for conceiving 'my
> relationship to their ways,' reflecting upon how I could employ
> them, and what it meant, as manageable practices at the keyboard,
> to 'employ them' for this music to happen—a thoughtful scrutiny
> over such matters, and over the very consequences of the thought-
> fulness itself, became a central part of what practicing the piano
> now came to involve. (Sudnow 1978:84)

His hands have become, are still in the process of becoming, jazzing hands. He is familiar with the sight of these hands, but not in the way he was before. Then, he had to will them to move along the keyboard and as a consequence things often came out wrong. He tried to get them right, but to no avail. It was like the aspiring Buddhist monk trying to try not to try. Things just didn't come spontaneously.

Finally they did. Now, his hands have their own way, of which he is in large part unaware and control over which he has no desire. He watches them do what they do, his hands, and he is often surprised that he is not surprised that what they do is of their own accord, without any prompting or reprimanding or correcting on the part of his willful mind. The bodymindsigns just emerge, as if out of the clear blue sky. It all comes naturally. The nonjazzist who one bright day decides to do some jazzing may think she is producing jazz. But Sudnow knows better. He knows that the piano, the hands, the conscious and nonconscious self, the emerging sounds, are all jazzing. No single thing is in control. In fact, there is no control. There is just jazzing. Jazzing is going on. When it is happening it is happening because it was happening, it is happening, it will have been happening.

> From an upright posture I look down at my hands on the piano keyboard during play, with a look that is hardly a look at all. But standing back I find that I proceed through and in a terrain nexus, doing singings with my fingers, so to speak, a single voice at the tips of the fingers, going for each next note in sayings just now and just then, just this soft and just this hard, just here and just there, with definiteness of aim throughout, taking my fingers to places, so to speak, and being guided, so to speak. I sing with my fingers, so to speak, and only so to speak, for there is a new 'I' that the speaking I gestures toward with a pointing at the music that says: It is a singing body and this I (here, too, so to speak) sings. (Sudnow 1978:152)[3]

And on, and on, all reminiscent of Borges and his *other* of "Borges and I" (1962 [1944]). Sudnow's "so to speak" testifies to the impossibility of articulating this process. It affords a feeling for Daneri's infinitely more complex gaze upon their entire universe's process of self-organizing becoming.

It also subtly turns our head toward the offbeat, so common to jazz improvisation, most characteristically qualified as syncope.

A Pause That Can't Relax

Syncope: we are now familiar with the theme in light of Arthur Winfree's work as briefly yet broadly outlined in chapter thirteen and thereafter. Here, in regards to feeling and sensing and knowing, I will try to take the theme a step further.

Syncope is the mother of dissonant rhythm, of hesitation, indecision, uncertainty, vacillation, irresolution. It applies not only to music and arrhythmia, but also to such unexpected occurrences as sneezing, laughing, asthma attacks and epileptic seizures, as well as near-death experiences and orgasm. There is discord in the harmony, then a collision comes about, a fragment of the beat disappears, and from this disappearance into the border of borders, rhythm is born anew. Syncope is a gap, a fissure, a temporary lapse, when there is a certain loss of absence. It can be a brief fainting spell, a cerebral eclipse, a swooning or loss of consciousness, a break-down in the heartbeat, de-emphasis of a musical note followed by emphasis on the succeeding note, a grammatical elision, poetical enjambment. If the gap is narrowed to a line, it becomes tantamount to the hairlines in Figures 1 and 5. It is the border of borders, where "emptiness" resides; it is tantamount to $\sqrt{-1}$; it is the invisible line of the Möbius-strip that separates "inside" from "outside"; it is scotoma, an area of pathologically diminished vision or a blind spot; it is *neti, . . . neti*, the "not this, . . . not this" or "neither, . . . nor," of Eastern metaphysics. So that's why the West has pushed it under the rug since the very beginning! It is chaotic, disheveled, unruly; it cannot be beaten to a pulp and distributed into a neat set of pigeon-holes; it cannot be controlled; it mocks and taunts our every effort to apprehend it and stash it away in the prison-house of language; it resists any and all rational accounts.

A couple is dancing, dancing . . . the tango . . . the tango. Bodies are stiff, stiff as they glide across the floor in what appears to be mechanical, mechanical movements, movements are almost jerky, jerky but smooth. He takes her waist, her waist. He bends her at midbody, midbody . . . the pivotal point, the point from whence the body sweeps downward to the left and downward to the right, the left and the right. Then . . . suspense. Suspension of time, time breaks down, it's down and out, for a fleeting moment . . . a moment fleeing so rapidly it is hardly noticed . . . noticed hardly at all. She is there, arm high, arm low, leg stretched, leg bent, she is there, there . . . then quickly and nimbly off again . . . after the suspense. "There is no dance without syncope—without syncopation" (Clément 1994:2). Especially regarding the tango. There is undulating rhythm, and then there is a violent pause of orgasm, of suspense, then a pause that does not quite relax, then more rhythm. We can understand why the Church prohibited the tango and why prudes the world over despise it.

Physical, mechanical time never stops. But biological time breaks down. This we learned from Arthur Winfree. And dance, music, and poetry exploit time for their own purpose: biological-bio-alogical-antilogo-rhythm. Syncope is able to accomplish the impossible. It short-circuits the coming and going of billiard ball particles in classical isotropic time and space, fuses space and time and things and events into an irregular topology, reveals the gap nobody wants to see or know about, because it appears as that awful void, it is the end, death. But without syncope there is no life, no life without death, no death without life. Without it there is no movement, no change, no time as we feel it and sense it. Without it there is neither pleasure nor pain, joy nor sorrow, good nor evil, black nor white, no differences that make any difference. Without it the universe is scentless, colorless, tasteless, soundless, senseless. Without it all the *simulacra* some postmodernists gloat over would actually become genuine *simulacra*, crystallized into a block. Syncope is a genuine revolt against the crystal, against symmetry, equilibrium, balance, sameness, and identity. It is symmetry breaking, disorder, dissonance, fluctuation, dissipation, bifurcation, dispersal, dislocation, diaspora.

The sphere of overdetermination (Firstness) can live quite comfortably with contradiction, inconsistency, anomaly, paradox. There is no dissonance, no discord, no offbeat, for there is really no time. There is no time for there is no separation—at least not yet—of something into something else: everything is one and the one is everything. The coming of Secondness, of division, of that hopeful symmetry of the universe, brings with it the possibility of syncope, when symmetry becomes dis-symmetry. But syncope cannot live within Secondness alone. The new rhythm, through discord, dissonance, the offbeat, toward new concordance, consonance, harmonious resonance, is available solely within the mediating sphere of underdetermination, of Thirdness. Within overdetermination, *both* the one *and* the other is second nature. Secondness demands—though it does not always get—*either* the one *or* the other. Thirdness, perpetually underdetermined Thirdness, potentially ushers in what is *neither* the one *nor* the other, but quite possibly something else: a new rhythm. This Thirdness can occur when the fissure, the hairline, makes itself felt. It is the tightrope walker precariously balanced between the line stretched between one stable point and another, pole in hands at a 90° angle with respect to the line, teetering now toward the one side, now toward the other side. The line is *neither* the one *nor* the other and at the same time it is *either* the one *or* the other and *both* the one *and* the other. Suspended, there, where there is *neither* up *nor* down *nor* right *nor* left *nor* forward *nor* backward. Suspended, in the middle, which is everywhere and nowhere, and everywhen and nowhen. A wrong move and death: the hairline is expanded to infinity.

Tight roping through life is not so precarious, however. The suspension comes and goes: syncope. The heart beats, the lungs heave, the legs weave, the vocal chords wave and waft, the tongue wavers and waffles. The mind vacillates, hesitates, then at some unexpected moment it moves on, a new thought came from "nowhere." Creativity in the arts, and the sciences and mathematics as well, is supreme when thinking and sensing and feeling take off on tangential and orthogonal paths. The most adept ballet dancers, musicians, actors, and performance artists in general are those who always seem to be able to come up with the unexpected, that is, after that brief moment of suspension, after syncope. The most adept basketball and tennis and football and soccer players are those who always have a surprise up their sleeve: you never quite know what they're up to, they're *jeitinheurs*. This is to say that tight roping through life is a matter of reaching the point of suspension, then there is a bifurcation point, and a new path, in fact, an infinity of possible new paths, open themselves up, and one must "let go." It is the Buddhist advice: letting go of the past and the future and what is between them and taking a leap toward somewhere and somewhen. But this is not a nihilistic leap toward annihilation. Life goes on, and if it doesn't, then death, which is not so tragic, for afterward, life is renewed. After the syncope and the leap there is almost invariably some new rhythm, ecstasy, epiphany, euphoria. The bipolarity between "yes" and "no" is annulled. Something emerges between them.

This something is the result of the simultaneous repulsion and attraction, the fear and the desire, of the *either* and the *or* that becomes, is in the process of becoming, *both-and* and *neither-nor*. It's like the hiccup or the sneeze: you fear it and you want it, you dread it, but when it comes, . . . oh, that brief moment of ecstasy, it feels so good. Contrary to what Catherine Clément says of syncope as a Hegelian dialectic between repulsion and attraction, this is akin to a Peircean process of mediation between the one and the other without there existing the possibility of any synthesis, for the process is just that: *process*. It propels the dance, the music, the rhythm of a Jackson Pollock painting, the revelry of a James Joyce or a Virginia Woolf page, the indecision of Samuel Beckett's *Molloy*, *Malone Dies*, and *The Unnamable*, or of Brazilian writer Clarice Lispector's *The Passion According to G. H.* (1988 [1964]), all of which never end, that is, they can't end even though they end, for they must go on, they have no alternative but to go on. Authors and performers die, the canvas and the pages have edges, the music stops, but they all nonetheless go on, from one day to the next, from one lifetime to the next. For Hegel, logic eventually disappears and along with it dialectical movement. And that's it. The curtain draws to a close, a hand thrusts forward at the fissure; there is a wave to the audience in delirious applause, then a disappearing act, and nothing. The audience remains spellbound, rapturous, static and ecstatic, crystallized. There is no tomorrow. Peircean semiosis, in contrast, is perpetual movement toward who knows what, and who knows where and when. The fun is in the run, not crossing the tape where and when the camera stops the action for all time. Clément, nevertheless, hits the bull's-eye when she writes:

> Syncope deceives death. In all ways. By delaying the weak beat, excessively prolonging time, and by making it disappear subjectively, it pretends to delay progress toward the biological conclusion. By crossing the limits of consciousness, it anticipates immortality. I leave the world, and then I return to it. I die, but I do not die. I am placed between the two, between life and death, exactly in the between-the-two, refusing one and the other. And that is how I dupe not only death but the difficult exercise of *the end of life*. . . .
>
> To delay, to anticipate, to provoke dissonance, and to resolve it. Syncope is an act of rebellion against the natural deterioration of the aged body, against the living decomposition that alters the imago of one's own body as real time moves on. Better to melt into nature before one's time, better to dissolve, better to topple intentionally into a weakness agreed to in advance . . . better to die than to die. (Clément 1994:260–61)

Mocking death is that marvelously real, that charming, Mexican respect and disrespect for death, which is in itself a syncopic posture, always in the between, always putting off a decision and a natural closure, just a little longer. This prolongation is also of the nature of the border, the Mexican-U.S. border, articulated thus:

> I am a nomadic Mexican artist/writer in the process of Chicanozation, which means I am slowly heading North. My journey not only goes from South to North, but from Spanish to Spanglish, and then to English; from ritual art to high-technology; from literature to performance art; and from a static sense of identity to a repertoire of multiple identities. Once I get "there," wherever it is, I am forever condemned to return, and then to obsessively reenact my journey. In a sense, I am a border Sisyphus. (Gómez-Peña 1996:i)

So much for offbeat philosophy. But, . . . no . . . I really should interject a few more words from our unforgettable polyloguers. Maggie's and Hladdy's timeless, mythical state of creation doesn't fit in the same bag with syncope. Funes gives a more faithful rendition of the phenomenon, with his hesitation, his stuttering and stammering, his indecision. But these moments are tenuously ephemeral. What we need prior to their suspension is the confidence building acts, however fake, of Emmy and Lönny: in Borges's story Emma Zunz was forced to prostitute herself in a patristic society in order to get the job done, and Lönnrot of "Death and the Compass" evinced that in-your-face control of the situation that would be the envy of the Newt Gingrichs and Dennis Rodmans and Howard Sterns of the world, but in the long run his ambition spelled his own undoing. We learned from Tlöny that after the act of re-cognition, of re-membering, of re-construction, the mind always experiences something different, something new, from T'sui's infinite array of possible pathways shooting out from an infinity of bifurcations. Put them all together, and Averroës and Rorty and all the others as well, and we have rhythm and syncope and more rhythm. But there is little communication. Why? Because something is missing, the glue that could mend all the actors into a cohesive community of interlocutors whose interdependent interaction bootstraps them into genuine dialogue.

More on this later.

Notes

1.   Along comparable lines, see the work of Birdwhistell (1970), Condon (1971, 1974), Hall (1973), and regarding dance kinesthetics, Laban (1960).
2.   If you are so inclined you might take a look at merrell (2003), where I highlight the importance of topological form to bodymind awareness.
3.   Igor Stravinsky has some comparable words: "Fingers are not to be despised; they are great inspirers and in contact with a musical instrument, often give birth to unconscious ideas which might otherwise never come to life" (in Copeland 1939:25).

Chapter Sixteen

From Rhythm (Semiosis):

Music and Dance (Signs) Are Born

> At the still point, there the dance is, . . .
> Except for the point, the still point,
> There would be no dance, and there is only dance.
>
> —T. S. Eliot

> . . . music heard so deeply
> That it is not heard at all, but you are the music
> While the music lasts.
>
> —T. S. Eliot

When Dance Is Not Just Dance

Music. Dance. You are *it* and it is *you*, as long as the rhythm goes on. Dance is hardly anything at all without music and music is not what it is without dance. That much really needs no saying. A cultural phenomenon that cries out for articulation, in view of all that has been written in the preceding chapters, includes dance . . . yet it is nondance, and it includes music . . . yet it is nonmusic. That is the nature of what in Brazil goes by the name of *capoeira*. *Capoeira* is dance to the beat of music and it is martial arts to the rhythm of dance and it is musical background for an excuse to rumble and it is dance for the purpose of defense. Throughout four hundred years of persecution and prohibition, *capoeira* has persevered up to our time—now recognized and practiced throughout Brazil and in many parts of the world.

The history of *capoeira* sports three epochs: *slavery, marginalization, academy.* Slavery period *capoeira* was a clandestine form of martial art in preparation for defense against the whites, for an offense in case a rebellion were to break out, or to be better prepared if and when the time for an attempted escape might arise. The activity was disguised as dancing, singing, and playing, activities deemed by the landowners as quite fit for the slave folks. After the abolition of slavery in 1888, *excapoeira* practicing slaves had no place in the new society, and they either went under cover or became *marginalized.* Then, during the 1930s and the *Estado Novo,* that quasi-socialist state under Getulio Vargas, prohibition of *capoeira* was revoked, and the first academies were established in Salvador, in the state of Bahia. It had now come out of the dark corners of the cultural closet and entered the light of day.[1]

Capoeira properly performed is beauty to behold. The action takes place to a background of throbbing percussion instruments, especially the *berimbau,* a musical bow of Congo-Angolan origin consisting of an open gourd resonator, which is held against the chest, and the instrument's string is tapped with a stick. Both men and women engage in the game-contest-match-dance-play (labeling it is not easy). They move in, circle one another with legs flailing, raise an eyebrow and feign a kick and a nudge, withdraw, fake an attack by leaping high in the air with legs cocked, gyrate with a quick twist of the torso, dodge a jab by swinging the head close to the floor with legs wide, give a head-fake and move in rapidly with arms swinging. This activity occurs to the accompaniment of trembling chords and tautly stretched skins of the drums. And all the while there is hardly any actual contact at all! Contact is feigned; it is not as it appears, it is *both* contact *and* noncontact, it is *neither* contact *nor* noncontact.

Capoeira is dance, it is performance, it is song, it is play, it is fake combat and combat in earnest, it is a "guerrilla game," it is *all* of them, . . . and it is *none* of them. At times it has been nonverbal *jeitinho*, a composite of sly and roguish acts, of conning and cunning, of contemptful in-your-face bad-ass taunts and challenges typical of *malandragem* (street-wise talking and acting). At other times it has been a spontaneous and carefully calculated, a playful and ployful, a charming and charading spectacle for the enjoyment of all present.[2] It has been a ritual, a dance with quasi-religious connotations, and it has been a brutal clash of gladiators, a means of mentally—if not physically—abusing an opponent. It has been *all* that, . . . and it has been *none* of that, but rather, something else. The *capoeirist*: an artist and an athlete, a soldier and a poet, a charismatic crowd-pleaser and a scoundrel, a rogue and a humorist, serious and a clown, comic and tragic.

> The Orient has its Zen.
> Europe developed psychoanalysis.
> In Brazil we have the Game of Capoeira (Capoeira 1992:106).

That is to say, *capoeira* can be looked upon as a way of living, a serious yet ludic philosophy of life, as therapy and cure for the mind and body caught up in the neurosis of contemporary rat-race society. That is how the author of *Capoeira: Os fundamentos da malícia* (*Capoeira: The Fundamentals of Roguery* [*Cunning, Cleverness*]), with the pseudonym, Néstor Capoeira, bills it (also Capoeira 1981, 1985). *Capoeira*, in addition to its combining agonistics, street fighting, dancing, gaming, playing, performing, and clowning, is a tool for survival in a world where the have-nots have an inordinately hard row to hoe. It is a survival kit for the person who knows the ways of *jeitinho*, of *malandragem*, of conning while ingratiating, of winning favors while pretending to give other favors in return, of getting one's way more often than not while bringing as little harm to others as possible. To enter into *capoeira* as a student is to enter the school of life, much in the sense of the martial arts and T'ai Chi Ch'uan. At one and the same time it is to learn cynicism and sincerity, tact and barbarisms, irony and simple slapstick, comedy, poetry and vulgarity, virtue and vice, tenderness and violence, reason and absurdity. Opposites meet and fuse into one, into *capoeira* living.

Paradoxical, all this? Of course it is! That's why it's *capoeira*. It thrives on paradox, which is no defeat but a rewarding nod for one's ability to join opposites. *Capoeira* is not simply strapped by a rigid code of ethics or aesthetics like samurai and some of the martial arts which have evolved from relatively more hierarchical societies. It is open, fluid, a flux of bodymindsigns that complement their linguistic counterparts found in *jeitinho*. *Capoeira* is a special way of looking at life and learning to live it. Life is rhythm, music, dance, play, struggle, strife, opposition. It is gaiety and laughter and it is blood, sweat, and tears. Above all, it contains, at each and every moment, the seeds of syncope, as we read from Winfree on biology and Clément on Eastern and Western thought. It is, in short, of the nature of the overdetermined and the underdetermined spheres more than of the nature of mere Secondness. It is extralinguistic through and through, with primacy placed on the hum, the rhythm, and the beat of life. It is in the body, after countless hours of practice when one gets a tacit feel for what it is that needs to be done, as we learned from David Sudnow. It is semiosis at its iconic and indexical best, with nary more than a tinge of symbolic signs.

Our hapless interlocutors of the polylogue had little of it, for they were articulate animals *par excellence*. Such is the case of most of Borges's characters anyway. They are hardly more than talking heads, mouths that flap and minds that cogitate. They live in fear, it would appear, of the extraverbal. There is no rest for those wary but tongue- and brain-weary souls. But let's forget our polylogue for now and focus a moment longer on the extralinguistic.

What Is Behind Nondance Dance and Nonmusic Music?

According to current Western scientific accounts, fifteen or twenty billion years ago the singularity that contained the possibility of the entire universe exploded. Sound and rhythm and everything else came later. According to ancient Eastern knowledge, in contrast, it all began with noise, then there was rhythm, patterns changing through time, rhythm breaking and remaking. Babies are fascinated with racket, any racket; then more subtle appreciation for rhythm emerges; the mind comes into increasing attunement with the rhythm of time, the dance of life.

When the rhythm is right, it is felt haptically and kinesthetically; it is not yet either smell or taste or touch or sound or sight. Nor is it mind. All that comes later. For now, it is signs of iconicity, beginning with pure quality and then undulating out and emerging into signs of indexicality and finally of symbolicity, all of which carry within themselves the rhythms of their past. There is no fighting the rhythm, when it's the right rhythm, whether in the sign or the mind or the body or a combination of them—all of which are signs of varying degrees of complexity and sophistication. The rhythm is propelled. It is a self-propelling sign. It propels itself in time, but for the sign—human, animal, or otherwise—that is doing the feeling—in tune with, and codependently emerging with the rhythm—time loses itself in that rhythm. But rhythm is time and time is rhythm. If the feeling sign happens to be a human signer-object, sign-representamen, interpreter-interpretant, if that sign is barely a sign of feeling and no more than that, then the mind is disengaged. But body is mind and mind is body and both are signs. The rhythm flows from some point of "emptiness" nowhere and everywhere within the body and ripples outward through the arms and legs. The body feels light. It dances, it flies, it is bodymindsign, when the rhythm is right.

Body and mind and sign are living rhythm. A stone is to all appearances frozen rhythm, but deep down, at molecular and atomic and nuclear and subnuclear levels, it guards the secrets of the entire universe's rhythm. From the stone's subnuclear levels to cosmic levels, rhythm simply cannot be denied. Musician David Sudnow knew it through jazz, philosopher Maurice Merleau-Ponty knew it through motility and kinesthetics, aesthetician and feminist Catherine Clément knew it through syncope, biologist Arthur Winfree knew it through biology and topology. In fact, all painters and poets and musicians and dancers know it through what they do. And C. S. Peirce knew it through semiosis. Yet, our polyloguers could hardly know it, for they were obsessive talkers, not feelers. If the most fundamental nature of matter is vibration, and if all vibration is sound, then perhaps the Pythagoreans had it right after all: the universe is music, rhythm (Berendt 1988). We are much too torpid to get in rhythm to the dance of atomic and molecular life, and life is much too short to dance to galactic rhythms, unless we lay claim to Nietzsche's Zarathustra capacities. Yet, it is becoming increasingly evident that there is a link between microlevel vibrations and biological processes and macrolevel cosmic cycles: they are all interrelated, interactive, and codependently emergent. One of the most telling tales of this interrelatedness lies in what was dubbed above resonance, and resonance owes its life to what is labeled entrainment, synchronization.

Entrainment: the "groove," as they put it in the 1960s. Synchrony of heart and soul, body and mind, self and everything else. A rhythm is felt but it can't quite be thought. It is just vaguely felt, but since it is not thought, it is not genuinely felt, or at least that is the feeling. But actually, it is neither genuinely felt nor is it not genuinely felt. At its most basic levels it is just felt. Thinking the feeling is like trying to clap with one hand, chase your own shadow. To think it and say it might be possible solely by an Einsteinian leap into some formal equation or other. To create it would be like writing a Bach or a Beethoven score. To play it would be the act of a jazz combo or the entire Tito Puente or Machito band or the New York Symphony Orchestra. Impossible, for mere mortals. Yet when we are at our best we can feel it, somehow, at the gut level of Firstness. The feeling is in time and time is in the feeling, but since the feeling is timeless, there is not really any time. There is only rhythm. That is to say, there *is* time, nontime time.

Mickey Hart, once drummer for the Grateful Dead, writes that when he is drumming, he likes to get as close to a trance state, that of a shaman, as possible. Yet, he goes on:

> I also know that I can't let myself go completely because if I do, my drumming will deteriorate and I will quickly lose the state. There have been many times when I've felt as if the drum has carried me to an open door into another world, yet if I let myself pass through that door I can no longer drum and that yanks me back. Perhaps this is why the shaman has an assistant who takes over drumming as the trance deepens.
> When the shaman reaches that door, he sings his songs and the spirit allies come, often taking up abode in his drum, . . . Percussive noise might be helpful in inducing trance, but it was rhythmic

entrainment that enabled the shaman to actually move into this
spirit world. (Hart 1990:176)

There is a ripple in time—a door, a line, the hairlines of Figures 1 and 5—that
keeps timelessness from overtaking the rhythmer. It is the fine line between the line
and itself, it is the border of borders, an entry to emptiness, which is everythingness,
which is to say, it is chaos.

What are perhaps the Grand Masters of all time with respect to this sort of
rhythm come from Africa. As far back as 1928 Erich von Hornbostel wrote an article
suggesting three criteria for qualifying African drum rhythm: (1) *antiphony* (call-
and-response) (hegemony, Secondness), (2) *polyphony* (two or more voices that
harmonize though they are independent of the melody) (heterogeny, Thirdness), and
(3) sophisticated *rhythmic flow* that is "syncopated past comprehension" (homogeny,
Firstness). The flow of a group of drummers is for the novice Westerner at first dis-
orienting. It seems like a violent clash of rhythms at cross current. They collide, and
the subsequent ripples rush out in many directions simultaneously, apparently without rhyme or reason. There can be three or four of these processes going on at the
same time, which strikes one's ears as hopelessly disordered. It seems virtually beyond comprehension. Actually, there is not simply one beat one can *feel* and with
which one can get entrained. There is a subjective rhythm, which must come from
within, somewhere, somehow, at that centerless center of the body when the point of
"emptiness" is. There, the "hidden rhythm" is found, and from there the beat
emerges and bonds with other beats at the surface (Waterman 1948). This is no
"hidden transcript" sort of thing, mind you: it has nothing to do with our linguicen-
tric-logocentric banalities and biases. The hidden rhythm cannot be said; it cannot
even be felt if by feeling we mean something that began as mindsigns that by habit
became embedded, entrenched, automatized bodysigns. This "rhythm from the
crypt" of the music of the body finds its way to bodysigns that cannot be anything
other than that: bodysigns. At the core of bodysigns the mind has no recourse but to
drag along behind, hoping to get a piece of the action.

So perhaps the only way to get in tune with a complex set of polyrhythms is
from the "inside" out, with full realization that there is no all-out distinction between
"inside" and "outside," yet that's perhaps the best way to put it in language. This
"coming out" of the "inside" and the "in-forming" of the "outside" is when at its best
the culmination of a life-long process. John Blacking (1995:127–47) observes that
among the Venda of South Africa, when children begin hitting something with
something else to make noise, adults or older children begin tapping out a counter-
beat to create a polyrhythm. The kids soon catch on. Eventually they engage in the
same play amongst their peers and with the smaller tots. Polyrhythm is for these
people a biological and cultural thing from the very beginning. When in Africa a
drummer begins his drumming, he becomes a self-contained, self-reflexive, self-
sufficient percussion "machinic organism," in the sense of Deleuze and Guattari's
"schizogenesis." He listens to himself and only to himself. What is more, as a supreme example of his "enchantment of the world," he lives with his drumsticks: especially if they have belonged to a master drummer, he takes them wherever he goes,
he eats with them, defecates with them, copulates with them, sleeps with them. With

this interrelationship, this interaction, this codependence, practice goes on for years until the hopeful drummer reaches a level of proficiency, when instrument and body become one. Then, much like Sudnow I would expect, he does what he does without having to think about the fingering or count the beats. Then the mind is free for other matters involving style, variations, distinctiveness (Chernoff 1979:1–23).

The young Nietzsche wrote that music—and dance for that matter—lies behind rational thought and understanding: it is in tune with the subtle and supple Dionysian mysteries and contradictions of everyday living of which hard-nose *macho* Apollonian logic cannot render account. At the circumference of music and dance, the inquirer "realizes how logic in that place curls about itself and bites its own tail, [and s/he] is struck with a new kind of perception: a tragic perception, which requires, to make it tolerable, the remedy of art" (Nietzsche 1956:95) (brackets added). In Nietzsche's view, art is a necessary complement to rational thinking. His *Birth of Tragedy* was an effort to show the relationship between engaged Dionysian art and detached Apollonian reason, between the ebullience of music and the relatively fixed nature of philosophy, the combination of which is destined to end in a sense of tragedy. Tragedy, for words cannot *say* what music and the arts can *show*. Thus, Sudnow's autobiographical work.

I doubt that any musical tradition is more Dionysian than that which is found in, once again, Africa. Many of us Westerners encounter difficulties with the African musical mind-set. To some it is boring, monotonous, and seems only to dull the senses. Others who look for patterns can make neither heads nor tails of the complex polyrhythms. Still others have sensed that their moral values have been challenged by the sensuous nature of the rituals and dances that accompany the music. Yet some Westerners seem to take to African rhythms like ducks to water. They give up trying to understand the beat and just give in to it and let themselves feel it any way they can. They allow themselves to admire and enjoy it for what it is, a spontaneous, emotional creation, a dynamic expression of vitality. There is no sense in emphasizing the incomprehensible, awesome gap between Western logic, reason, and aesthetic norms and African sensibilities. The most profound sense is accompanied by the feel, by letting go, giving up one's analytical propensities and proclivities and forgetting what is ordinarily deemed most dignified and proper (Blacking 1995).

If one wishes to pronounce the Apollonian dictum regarding the African Dionysian frenzy of rhythm and sounds that "This is not music" one is *both* right *and* wrong. The music is a different form of music because it is entirely different from music, "our" music. Hence it is not music. But if one carefully places this music within the African socio-cultural context, one eventually comes to realize that it is music. It is music, just as for the Netherworlder emeralds are "green" up to a certain point in time and "blue" thereafter, or just as for one person "gavagai" means one thing and for another person it means something altogether different. On the other hand, she who says, "This is not music" is *neither* right *nor* wrong. It is *neither* music affirmed *nor* music denied, for it is something other than what is considered music and yet it does not contradict, nor is it contrary to, music. It is something else along orthogonal lines rather than along equal but opposite lines of force. A Westerner who desires to appreciate and understand African music "must begin with a recognition of his own fundamental attitudes about music so that he may adjust to a fundamentally different conception" (Chernoff 1979:33).

Getting into the groove of African music can thus become a key to understanding the meaning of profound cultural differences. A feeling for the cultural world within which a musical tradition exists is knowledge of the pliability of human beings in general. This is especially the case with respect to African music, because it makes up the foundation of all cultural activities and attitudes and beliefs and behavioral patterns to a considerably greater extent than Western music and even the music of most other traditional societies. Rhythm is secondary in emphasis and complexity to melody and harmony in Western music, but it is the other way round in African music. A classical piece of Western music progresses in terms of a series of chords and tones, and the rhythm often, though not always, plays a subordinate role. In African music this sensibility is virtually reversed. The melody and harmony—if and when it can be said that there is any—are usually clear enough, though they may appear quite strange to Western ears. The complexity ensues by virtue of the fact that there are two and often more consonant or dissonant and syncopated and heterogenously mixed rhythms going on, and there seems to be no way to know which rhythm is dominant and which subordinate. All this is disconcerting, to say the least. Even the most accomplished Western musicians have been baffled when they first come across new African music. One rhythm defines another, and that one another one, and the last one serves to define the first one. Cross rhythms are at war with each other, and parallel rhythms play elusive games of hide-and-seek or they coax each other in new directions. How do we go about getting inside this irregular, nonlinear, effervescent flow? We try and fail. Then we try again, and again, and finally we sense we have a feel for it, but it lithely slithers out of our grasp. We should never garner false confidence. Chernoff warns us in this regard that:

> we must beware of misinterpreting the meaning of what we are told or what we see and hear according to our own ways of thinking about music and enjoyment. If four untrained Westerners were given drums and asked to make some African music, they would not hesitate to start pounding away. On the other hand, if a Westerner who has learned all the possible variations for a master drum is put in front of a fired-up group of musicians, everybody might still become bored. In either case, two little African boys playing on bottles could probably do much better. Obviously there is a special kind of sophistication to the ways that rhythms work in African music. What would be at issue would be a difference of sensibility, the whole orientation to music and to life which defines the significant dimensions of excellence within the total configuration of a musical event. In this chapter, as we try to think our way into an appropriate aesthetic perspective, our foremost concern will be to attempt to judge the music on its own terms, to try to get an idea of what dimensions of musical performance and participation will make the occasion "very, very sweet." (Chernoff 1979:92)

Keeping two beats going, three on one side to two on the other, and sustaining it, while bringing in a vocalized tune that caters now to one side, now to the other, is just as normal for the people of these cultures as a couple of synchronized beats are for us. Our two-dimensional rhythm might be as natural as can be for us; their alternating two three-dimensional rhythms, and even more, is just as natural for them. Since the time they were babes in their mothers' arms they were charmed and soothed to these offbeats. The rhythms became the individual and the individual became them, and both the rhythms and the individual were one with the flow of the entire community: all became one massive harmonious dissymmetry, one syncopated whirl, of cultural activity. This is indeed sophisticated rhythmic flow. It is syncopated past comprehension. It is certainly beyond binary antiphony, and it is more complex than most of the intricate polyphony found in Western harmonious ways. It is a move toward homophony in the most genuine sense. A rhythm could be a "hidden rhythm" or "transcript" and she who remains outside the culture flow from which it emerged would stand nary a chance of deciphering it.

Understandably, the African slaves and their ancestors have been some of the most adept de Certeau-style "cultural" guerrillas ever known.

Surely There Is More, Is There Not?

Dance, music. Both are life, and life is both. Susan Foster tells how choreographer, dancer, and dance instructor Deborah Hay's dance performances take place in imaginary times and spaces, creating a harmonious ambient: they create a world of grace, rapport, equanimity, charm. The performance engulfs dancers, musicians, audience, and the entire setting: all dances, and dance is all, *it* dances, dance dances.

Deborah Hay is able to create this mood, according to Foster, because each and every minute of each and every day is dance. The world sings and the song is dance and the dance is the world. Movement is everywhere—in the tree leaves caressed by the wind, in the cars lumbering and dancing by, people gliding along the sidewalks and pausing and shifting and continuing, birds landing on the rooftops, clouds creeping along as they gradually change their form. Fluctuation, ebb and flow, the universal order dances. Hay's life is a dance, a living dance, of which she never ceases trying to become aware, while sipping coffee, reading the morning newspaper, on her way to the studio, in the subway, at the local delicatessen. Her attitude toward life and dance is due in part to her inspiration from Asian religions and the art form, T'ai Chi Ch'uan. She wishes to create a Taoist vision of the universe through dance (Foster 1986:7–8). She is in this manner quite properly of a mind-set to get inside African music and dance, or Latin American music and dance for that matter.

Speaking of Latin America, nowhere is dance and music exalted more than during Carnival time. In fact, life in that part of Latin America closest to its African roots—the Caribbean, the coasts of Colombia and Venezuela, and especially, the northeastern coast of Brazil—lives dancing. In these areas, the people exude pride, gaiety, and ebullient rhythm, no matter how sordid their physical existence might appear to us. Whole residential neighborhoods hold a rakish charm. It is as if there were something in the air, something electric, an essential energy somewhat unlike anything found in other parts of Latin America. There's no understanding it or saying it. It is just displayed and felt and sensed. The characters of Brazilian author

Jorge Amado's novels live it; João Guimarães Rosa's style patterns it; Clarice Lispector's hypersensitivity drills to its core. But the outsider must be engulfed by it, and if she is lucky, there may someday, somehow, be a tender, tenuous, and excruciatingly vague and indescribable feeling. During everyday coming and going in the neighborhoods of Salvador, largest city of the state of Bahia in Brazil, though there may be no music to be heard, each body has a rhythm, a pitch, and all bodies flow to the resonant, syncopated concert in the process of unfolding. The people do not walk, they flow; they do not jerk themselves up and down the streets and stairways, they float; they don't simply sit, they poise; they do not abruptly open and slam doors, the doors place themselves in their hands and proceed to glide back and forth; they do not engage in a staccato of talk, their voices embrace each other in a legato chorus.[3] This vibrant rhythming is brought to its delirious best when everybody is carnivaling. This is a time of magic, when rhythms entirely absorb the public. Everybody sings and sways, as they never do during any other occasion. They all dance; dance dances them and they dance dance; dance dances dancingly.

Roberto DaMatta writes how the epithet occasionally applied to Anglo-Saxon culture, "Tough guys don't dance," is, to a certain degree also characteristic of Brazilian and Latin American *machista* mentality. But not during carnival time, when all men, prototypical *machos* and homosexuals and cross-dressers alike, give in to the beat and begin rhythming like the women in their midst (DaMatta 1994:64–69). The involvement is holistic to the extreme. It is pansemiotic. This is no time merely to listen to music or to ambulate or eat or copulate or get in out of the heat and the rain. The entire body and spirit are immersed in a shared felt and sensed and shown and said delirium virtually without borders and with few limitations. Nobody listens to the music. They live it through swaying and leaping and singing and seeing the collective consonance and sensuously touching one another and smelling the perfume and the bodily olfactory elixirs and occasionally even passing a few morsels of food. For a few days, samba is carnival and carnival is samba. They are vibrant rhythms of life itself. The whole world is a stage on which everybody participates; there are no detached spectators in the respectable modernist tradition.[4]

Roger Bastide (1971) relates Henri Bergson's "memory-as-recollection" and "memory-as-habit" to African culture throughout Latin America. The body contains internalized, implicit, tacitly engenderable signs, which are just as much a part of memory as those traces etched on the brainmind. Realization of these signs of the body is never entirely divorced from the mind, however. They are bodymind signs. They are signs of life, which "has its reasons, which reason does not know" (Bastide 1971:223–24).[5] Signs of bodymind memory make up collective memory. It consists of corporeal, visceral, signs of all the senses, in addition to cerebral signs. Memory is actualized more in motor sequences than in words and images—which in our times are inextricably caught up in linguicentrism and ocularcentrism.[6] They are set in movement by physical gestures, vocal rhythms, dancing, and cultural quasi-ritualistic practices rather than by intellectualized memories. Regarding African influences in Latin America, the slaves often found themselves against their will in socio-cultural and environmental contexts radically different than that to which they were accustomed. Somehow they had to find a way to cope. And they did. They did, by taking a bit of the masters' customs and religion and ways of feeling and sensing and saying and mixing it with their own form of life. The product of this activity has often gone by the name of "syncretism," as mentioned above. Actually, it is more than that. It is "cultural" guerrillism as the result of the codependent emergence of hybridized cultural practices. These practices are ongoing: there is no product, only process; and there is not simply a combination of cultural atoms into a hodge-podge collection of careening molecules. Something new emerged, which was *both* European *and* African and at the same time *neither* European *nor* African. As Bossa Nova artist Antônio Carlos Jobim once put it, *O Brasil não é para principiantes* ("Brazil isn't for beginners"). The same could be said of African America in general (Levine 1977, Roberts 1972, 1979).

Nowhere is this transforming process, this transculturing, this "cultural" guerrillism, this hybridizing, subtler than when those people participating in emerging African American cultural life are dancing. Dance was an art form that simply could not be erased from the Africans slaves' memory, primarily because it was so deep, visceral. And it could be practiced in silence, in solitude, and even when bound in chains. The body was memory that could remind the stupored mind of what had been and what could still be, in spite of stringent limitations. The body breaks into a dance and the conscious, willful mind is hard pressed to bring up a distant rear. The brief moment between action and thought all but disappears, and body and mind for a moment become bodymindsign. The body becomes mind; it is mind becoming; it takes to the air before the conscious mind is aware that it is soaring at ever-greater heights. The conscious mind is taken for a ride, and where it will land it cannot foresee. It now belongs to the body, to bodymindsign. It has become rhythm, of a reason and logic it does not know.[7] The inner rhythms of the slave were exteriorized in ways the master did not censure. The rhythms, the dances:

> did not appear in any way dangerous. They were not a manifestation of paganism, but simply a form of amusement. The Negroes were therefore left to enjoy themselves in their own fashion, without interference (whereas the *candomblés*, *changó*, and such things as Myelism or Voodoo were persecuted). Indeed, far from being dangerous, these dances actually served a useful purpose during the slave era. Their erotic nature, the whites hoped, should rouse those who performed them to a high pitch of sexual excitement; and this, in turn, would lead to the birth of numerous [offspring], a future source of slaves that would have cost their masters nothing. (Bastide 1971:172)

So the rhythm survived, by a supreme form of "guerrilla" resistance (Roberts 1977:56–59, and especially Fryer 2000). And it continues to survive. In fact, it has found its way into mainstream culture quite effectively.

The Looser the Meter, the Better

Music: especially that of Latin America. Its fluid architecture unfolding in time, can express social attitudes and even biological, cognitive processes, for sure. This music is effective only when it is in the process of being heard and felt by ears and bodies that share a particular musical form as well as an entire set of cultural experiences. Once again, this receptivity is the product of habit. In this sense music confirms what is already present in cultural patterns and activities. What it adds is patterns of sound.

This sound is not the lurid limericks that appear during commercial breaks sandwiched between athletic events on TV. It is not some of those booms provided by a Walkman background while one is studying or ambulating down the sidewalk or riding in the subway. It is not the racket of parades and formal festivities. It is not even the so-called "easy listening" some people drone into their heads in elevators or when they have nothing else to do or when engaging in pop psychology or New Age meditative practices. It is music, Latin American style. During the process of its unfolding, the sound patterns of genuinely shared African-Amerindian-Latin rhythms exercise an effect on the bodies and minds of each individual within the community. This process is what makes Latin American music music. It is the process, the emergence (Firstness) of music into sound (Secondness) that brings about its characteristic effect (Thirdness, through habit) that is of most importance at present.

Granted, one might counter that consonance and dissonance are a matter of acoustics, and that music in terms of raw physical sounds is an artificial concoction, not a natural process, hence music is learned, clearly and distinctly (Zuckerhandl 1956). But this would be music as nothing but sound (Secondness) and as learned or the product of habitual response (Thirdness). Sound and response as such are essential, to be sure. Yet they would hardly be more than the equivalent of a computer's hardware taking software input and outputting information on the monitor and through the speakers: it would process what it received in the only way it knew how, and it would spit out a canned product that unless something went haywire could not have been anything other that what it was. Music becomes music when a couple of ears begin picking up some noise and the brainmind begins processing it as exciting because of cultural experiences. In the process brainmind makes distinctions between music and noise, order and chaos, and consonance and dissonance. This is the process of creating forms from within the border of borders, from Firstness, where there were no necessary forms in the form in which they are being creatively formed. It is the general process of all art in the forming (Fischer 1963). In the final analysis what is happening is that forming is going on without there being any closure of the forming process. While the music happens there is forming; when the music stops the forming slips ever-so-slightly below the surface. There is no simple sound (Secondness), nor is there any bringing about of a characteristic effect (Thirdness). Yet the forming is still there, a virtually rippling process as pure possibility, slightly below the surface of whatever collective cultural happenings are happening.

Above all, making music is communicating, especially on the Latin American scene. Music communicates through rhythm and tone stress, which is a purely physical state in the process of emerging, a self-reflexive, self-contained sign of Firstness, a sign of itself. It communicates as a sign of a socio-cultural phenomenon that can be accompanied by dance or by words: it becomes Secondness, it takes on the semiotic object in the process of its becoming what itself as a sign is a sign of, and it takes its place among other signs, chiefly of symbolic and kinesthetic nature. Enter the musical sign's interpretant, and it communicates as a pattern of sounds combined to evoke feelings, sentiments, emotions, kinesthetic responses, and ideas, thoughts, and memories. A relationship is in the process of becoming between "outer" signs and "inner" meanings. Even if the music has neither words nor any apparent purpose or connection with cultural life other than its simply emerging among people, it may still touch various levels of consciousness among all participants to evoke a collective array of responses. Certain intervals, melodic patterns, harmonic variations, contrapuntal techniques, the coming and going of multiple rhythms, may bring about extramusical behavior because that's the way of the community's tacit knowing. That's the way they feel, feel as, and feel that, that's their way of life, and that's that (Blacking 1995:31–53).

This combination of feels and sensations and thoughts and sounds and kinesthetics and words is hardly anywhere more intertwined, I must reiterate, than during carnival time. New World carnivals, I repeat, owe their uniqueness to an intensive African-American-European mix. These are the areas where slavery was most intensively practiced. The slaves' effort to squeeze a bit of enjoyment out of life gave rise to a profusion of rhythms and dance styles. When this activity became so raucous as to annoy the Europeans, it was often limited to the public square during festival days. Popular celebrations were thus African Americanized with respect to music, dance, costumes, and instruments (Roberts 1972:49–51). As a consequence, today, carnivals and various festival occasions are perhaps the most visceralized cultural manifestation found on the Latin American cultural scene. These are the times when body, or better, bodymindsign movements come to the fore. They are displayed and flaunted with few inhibitions; they become tender, sensuous, provocative, aggressive, and violent; there is flirting, touching and dancing, lovemaking, pushing and shoving, and fighting and occasionally killing. All this is through the expressive purpose of music and its identification with the body movements that generated it, in individually and collectively coordinated ways. There are endless possibilities of coordination, of unlimited experimentation, all of which create ways in which the music and the dance can be felt. This feeling of the body through kinesthetic movement and musical rhythms is perhaps as close as one can get to resonating, genuinely resonating, with other people (Blacking 1973:89–116).

Perhaps the most effective way of feeling the transcultural element of Latin American music and dance is through getting a feel for polyphony and polyrhythms. Rhythm is the manner of dividing musical time into intervals of relatively short and long duration, into movement toward or away from stressed and unstressed beats, into the regular and irregular patterns by which the direction and flow of the movement is determined. Rhythm coheres with and supports the melodic line, regulates it, and eventually brings it to a close. Virtually the same can be said of rhythm in dance. Both motional and emotional changes in music and dance come about through variations in rhythm. Since rhythm is so germane to the way of feeling music and dance, it lies at the heart of resonance between sound and sight and kinesthetics—and, as mentioned above, during carnival time smells and tastes even come into play. Many techniques are employed by composers and choreographers and performers to insure rhythmic variety with the proper cadences and transitions and duration of each movement. Frequent stresses and accents can render a rhythm lively and stirring, infrequent ones can provoke a sense of nostalgia and tranquility. Excessive regularity creates monotony; too much irregularity becomes confusing. There must be a happy meeting ground of satisfied expectations and surprise. A shift of accent from the expected to a surprising beat or stress is syncopation. Combining two or more rhythms or movements in dance creates polyrhythm. A combination of sounds yields polyphony. All these elements are exploited to the maximum in Latin America, along with a peculiar dose of counterpoint to complement polyphony.[8] Counterpoint is the art of combining different melodic lines in a musical composition. When it occurs with polyphony, it consists of the combination of two or more different melodic lines at the same time that the lines are counterpointed in terms of their handling.

Cuba and Brazil provide the best laboratories for the Latin American beat, bar none. However, their contributions to the world of rhythm are quite distinct. After a casual listening to the music from the two traditions, one is struck by the intensive, hard-driven quality of the Cuban beat in contrast to the more suave, laid-back Brazilian style. Brazilian melodies are by nature smooth, flowing, gentle, and replete with offbeat syncopated accents. These differences are uncannily patterned in the difference between Brazilian Portuguese and Caribbean Spanish. The first is of the nature of the tuba, the baritone, the French horn, and the xylophone and kettledrums; the second is of the more harsh sound of trumpets, blaring trombones, raspy saxophones, and the cadence of the snare drums. I do not wish to imply that the Spanish language is rough and grates on the ears while Portuguese is smooth, melodious, and more pleasant. Both are equally melodious and equally charming. The difference is that the Spanish cadence is more straight ahead, while spoken Portuguese tends more toward swings and wavers, vacillations and hesitations, in addition to its less direct nuances. The drumming styles of the Samba schools of Rio de Janeiro emphasize swinging, springy rhythmic patterns, and sudden leaping, in contrast to the more intensive, in-your-face beat of Cuban percussion instruments (Roberts 1972:12–13).

In Cuba, *habanera, son, danza cubana, bolero, mambo, conga, rumba,* and *chá-chá-chá* evince all-pervasive African American elements of syncopation and polyrhythm. The same can be said of *salsa,* of New York and Puerto Rican origin, and of Colombian *cumbia* and Dominican *merengue.* The Argentine *tango* has its origin in the Cuban *habanera,* in music from Andalucía, Spain, and in the *milonga* of the River Plate region developed within the African American slave culture during the nineteenth-century. But taken as a whole, Cuban music offers the most intricate mix of any national tradition in Latin America, except perhaps Brazil. This is a harvest of the African influence in Cuba's religious practices, folkloric tradition, and in general popular culture, brought to our attention especially in the work of Lydia Cabrera (1986). The hybrid blending of rhythms, lyrics, and the dance moves they elicit are a result of Spanish and a tinge of European and Yoruba and Congolese and the Abakwá secret society of Nigerian origin is of rich profundity found rarely around the world.[9]

The pirouetting eddies in the flow of Cuban music most commonly take on a $^3/_2$ and at times a $^2/_3$ rhythmic pattern called the *clave* ("key"). It spreads an umbrella over two measures and takes them for one. This serves to produce what appears to be a discrepancy between the melody and the rhythm. They engage in a struggle with each other that can be annoying to untrained ears, but the Cubans and Latin Americans easily take it in their stride (Grenet 1939). It consists of a first part that calls and a second part that answers, quite common to African and African American music, and it has directly affected North American jazz.[10] This call-and-response is actually typical of music throughout the Latin American subcontinent. The technique renders the music difficult to get a handle on, since it characteristically involves, in addition to musical rhythm, dance and instrumental styles and lyrics many times with a theme that can be either amorous or folkloric or politically engaged and subversive. The multiplicity of it all is confounding to the newcomer, and it taxes even the most experienced non-Latin observer.

The most widespread pattern in Latin American music of African influence consists of the seemingly off-beat, ♪♪♪ ♪♪, with a number of variations. Da-dah-da-dah-dah. It is basic to the Cuban *habanera*, the Argentine *tango*, the Dominican *merengue*, and many other musical expressions, and it is also typical of ragtime in the United States. It sort of catches you off-guard at the outset, then you are abruptly shoved into another mode, then there is a momentary lull, then it grabs you once again. You try to pin it down but can't, not quite, but you can sort of sway to it, then suddenly you realize you're not in sync with the beat, so you wiggle the torso a little while you place one foot down, and there, . . . no . . . yes . . . that's it! . . . isn't it? . . . no . . . not quite, . . . and you give up in frustration. It is like Alma Guillermoprieto (1990:36) reports of the Brazilian African Americans during the carnival:

> One of the subtler forms of amusement for blacks at carnival time is watching whites try to samba. White people have had nearly the whole century to work it out, and most of them still can't quite get it right. It's not that blacks mind; that whites look clumsy while they're trying to have fun is a misfortune too great to be compounded by mockery, but it's also a fact that can't be denied. Whites are certainly given points for trying, though, and in the Samba Palace the ones who got up to dance seemed to be much more warmly regarded than those who tried to maintain their dignity.

Brazilian musicologist Oneyda Alvarenga (1946) has found thirteen major Africanisms in Brazilian music. Many more are certainly lurking behind the composite of Caribbean rhythms. These Africanisms include variations on the standard rhythm phrase described above, ♪♪♪ ♪♪, which is the call-and-response sequence common to virtually all African American regions.

Now for some specifically Brazilian aspects of music in search of a mix that will enable a peek at what might be meant by "alternative cultural 'logics'."

Better Loose and Communal than Abstruse and Formal

In John Chernoff's (1979) comparison of Western and African music, the first is metronomic: its time pushes inexorably toward a distant moment, some goal, teleological or otherwise. African music, on the other hand, invites participation between "composer"—whoever she may have been, for she is most likely anonymous and her music is part of collective memory—musicians, and audience. The audience consists of individuals each of which must engender a personal rhythm that resonates with all other personal rhythms. Each musician also has her own rhythm that flows along in concert with that of the other musicians. The original maker of the music is no romanticized solitary genius at all in the Western sense. Rather, she merges into the collective whole much as if the entire community was condensed into a single bodymindsign.

Western music harmonizes different notes into chords that exist as static blocks on the written score, with terms such as *rubato, accelerando, arpeggio, glissando*, having to do with the tempo and the style of the passage from one note to other notes: the sound pushes on, now relentlessly, now slowly and playfully, now gracefully, now in racehorse fashion, now tentatively, now confidently, and so on. African-based music consists of beats that emerge from relations between rhythms with apparently no dominant pattern, no superordinate and subordinate linear developments. Rather, there is a flow of interchangeable nonlinear currents and subcurrents and crosscurrents. There are hardly any formal strictures; alternatives remain alive and well at all moments, ready to make their play and move lithely off along a tangential path in nonlinear fashion. All alternative currents remain loose, offering themselves up amenably, acquiescently, and even docilely and submissively, when another current emerges. There is no clear-cut dominant current that has its way come what may, but many currents that slither in and out and give way to their successors for the moment hopefully to make their own play in another day. It is apparently rigid chronometric linearity in contrast to what appears to be fluid synchrometric nonlinearity, determinacy and necessity in contrast to uncertainty and a virtually infinite number of equal possibilities.

But appearances deceive. The first case is not as tense, fixed, and unyielding as might be expected and the second case is not as "democratic" as we might wish. The first can allow for token representation of all sounds concerned and the second, while appearing pliable, breaking into ripples according to the ways of the wind, can actually be a subtle way of the subcurrent that dominates for now to maintain its hegemony while giving the appearance of patronizing benevolence: reminiscences of Gilberto Freyre's neo-romantic "racial democracy," but not quite. If music can in any form or fashion be a metaphor of culture at large, it could be here. Western music—outside its African and other influences—would appear relatively rigid in rules of composition and structure. African and African American music—including jazz, blues, and such in the United States—are in comparison relatively supple. But just as African rhythms in night clubs in New York, Paris, Rio de Janeiro, or the Havana of old bring about hardly any more consciousness raising and subversive provocation than providing amusement for affluent patrons, so also Latin American "democratic" governments, dictatorships, and military regimes can assimilate, co-opt, and otherwise force, subordinate subcurrents into peripheral flows and keep them there because they are good folks and know their place. And just as the rules and regulations of Western music are relatively fixed, misunderstood and misfit romantic geniuses can always manage to stand out by bringing about a rebellious eddy in the stream thereby causing the flow to become something other than what it would have been in the process of becoming. What I mean is that the first case can be relatively more "democratic" in spite of its apparently inflexible austerity, and the second case can be more inflexibly stratified no matter how elastic it might seem. *Rhythm, music,* and *dance*, then, make up my sensuous, off-beat, hesitating, ever-tenuous, syncopated, virtually ineffable "metaphor" of Latin America.

Although well nigh unsayable, the metaphor in part bears on four terms discussed in chapter four: *personalismo, machismo, caudillismo,* and *jeitinho*. The first three terms are most typical of Spanish America—though Brazil has its own form of charismatic charm, patronage, *machismo,* and *coronelismo*—and the final term is Brazilian through and through. That *jeitinho* has its expression in song and dance must certainly be a foregone conclusion. The subtle lyrics giving an indirect jab to the ribs of a friend, associate, boss, lover, another artist, a bureaucrat or policeman or soldier of a military or the government, is hardly anywhere more suggestive than in Brazil. The syncopated moment of pause, the unexpected move, the surprise, is of *jeitinho* vintage. *Jeitinho* through dance is, as would be expected, most significant of all. It can be seen in the *lundu*, a song and dance of Angolan origin, which was introduced to Brazil and Portugal in the sixteenth century, and immediately censured by the Church due to its lascivious nature. It involves the *umbigada*—an invitation to dance by bouncing off each other's navels—and a succession of provocative hip movements. Mother to much Brazilian poetry, two other dance steps, the *batuque* and *maxixe*, later evolved into the samba in the latter part of the nineteenth-century and the beginning of this century during which time it lost some of its African characteristics and embraced elements from other sources. A variation of this dance comes by way of the European polka that was introduced into Brazil in 1845 and soon became a screaming success. Its transformation in Brazil due to African American influences include the characteristic *jeitinho* hip movement, which, when used, became a dance form called the *polca-maxixe*, which also evinces some elements of the modern *samba*. It is set to the customary off-beat, the syncopated and now familiar, ♪♪♪ ♪♪, with its hop-skip-jump, its tension, its disturbance, its sensuality. This is comparable to what David Appleby (1983:80) terms the "delay factor" in the performance of the temporal ellipses. The "minute differences" in application of the delay factor "give each dance its specific individual quality." They provide an almost "imperceptible suspension, a languorous breath, a subtle syncopic pause," which is difficult for the unaccustomed ear to capture. They are a "little bit of nothing" so typically Brazilian (Appleby 1983:83).

A little bit of nothing, a little bit of syncope, an oxymoron characteristic of the notion of "emptiness" presented in the initial chapters of this inquiry. It is much like André Hodier's (1975:207–08) characterization of syncopation in North American jazz: decomposition, disintegration, noncontinuity that, nonetheless, holds together as if it were a coherent package. Unlike European music, there is hardly any relaxation after the tension, for everything is present simultaneously, in the little bit of nothing, in the "emptiness" between one note and another syncopated note. This little bit of nothing, this climax or orgasm, this "little death," the pause that almost refreshes and rejuvenates, this palpitation or murmur, this arrhythmia, this zero sign, is the crux of the flux, the center of the Buddhist wheel, the "vortex" in Figures 2 and

3, the $\sqrt{-1}$ factor that sets a series off along one of an infinity of orthogonal paths. This is not the product of a solitary meditator sitting and waiting for a bolt of inspiration from the clear blue in the Western sense. It is of the process of actual experience, not by each and every individual as a windowless monad but of the entire resonating, vibrantly mutually entrained, community. It is culture in effervescent motion rather than a fixed world.

In short, it is of the nature of the *samba-canção* ("samba song") as metaphor.

Samba Takes Five and Returns Like a Rose by Another Name

By the mid-point of the present century Brazilian samba had become institutionalized and virtually synonymous with *Carnaval* and well on its way toward become a commercial affair attracting hordes of tourists. And then Bossa Nova appeared, which modified samba with a virtually unlimited number of possible alterations.

Bossa Nova did not replace samba but became the source of its evolution into what was in the process of becoming neither samba nor non-samba, but something else. One of the prime movers of this change was guitarist and songster João Gilberto. After a few years of the most intensive concentration imaginable, Gilberto released *Chega de Saudade* (roughly, "The Arrival of Nostalgia") in 1959, which came to be known as the "Bible of Bossa Nova" (Medaglia 1993:75). Antônio Carlos Jobim, another innovator, tacked the label, Bossa Nova, to this new tendency. *Bossa* in local slang is a special skill, a knack, a particular and peculiar way of doing things, it is a sort of *jeitinho*. But it was not easy to come by. Ruy Castro in his book entitled *Chega de Saudade* (1990), a quasi-epic history of the movement, writes of Gilberto's painful process of coaxing samba into existence. Gilberto had to learn how to sing in a whisper and through his teeth, to use his nose more than his mouth, to listen to his guitar more than himself singing, to pay no attention to what his guitar was doing and listen to himself, to shut himself up in his small tiled bathroom in Rio in order that the sounds might resonate better and he could get in tune with himself, with his guitar, with the music, . . . no, . . . that's not it: he had to learn how to get out of tune while appearing to be in tune, . . . no, to be in tune while seemingly out of tune, . . . and to sing slightly ahead of his guitar, . . . to sing slightly behind his guitar, . . . to sing as if he were a neutral spectator of his guitar's doings, . . . and to play his guitar as if someone else were singing instead of him, . . . and to sing as if the guitar were not really there, . . . and to sing as if he were merely talking, . . . and to talk singingly, . . . he had to do *all* of the above simultaneously, somehow, . . . and he had to do *none* of the above, somehow (Castro 1990:147–49).[11] Hour after hour the solitary apprenticeship continued, until death, insanity, or success might happen to make its way around. It was, I would expect, something like David Sudnow trying to learn what he learned but virtually from scratch, without teacher and without examples. (There is the popular anecdote about Gilberto's cat that would customarily take its afternoon sunbath on the balcony of his apartment high above the street in Rio; one afternoon the cat became so fastidiously neurotic over the incessant slightly-less-than repetitious variations that it let out a screech and leapt to its death on the concrete below, supposedly preferring suicide to the interminable creative torture.)

Bossa Nova. Altered stylistic parameters, liquid mergence of melody, harmony, and simplified rhythm while the voice virtually fades out, complexity of syncopation rather than the binary, repetitive samba beat, lyrics so simple as to appear trivial and even silly (such as *peixinhos com beijinhos* ("little fish with little kisses"), or *bim bom bim bom, é só isso o meu baião*, ("bim bom bim bom, this is all there is to my 'baião' [a type of song of the Northeast]"). These lyrics pay particular attention to individual words and word clusters with an almost total absence of passion, emotion, or any tragic sense of life. They consist of playful words and their combination into a whisper and a mere suggestion in colloquial tones, apparently frivolous rhythms and their concoction into a stuttering and stammering and hesitation and uncertain lapse. This is the *samba-canção*. Dualism is rejected outright. There is an emerging counterpoint; there is abandonment to a mixture of chords in consonance and dissonance. It is mixture and fusion and hybridization, not dualism, which entails a profusion of emerging tendencies that seem never to materialize but give in to newly emerging tendencies. It entails a Dyniosian play with maximum concentration on minute details, while relinquishing meaning. Yet it integrates particularities and peculiarities of popular music in characteristically universal means and modes. It is not regionalism, but a religion that cannibalizes ("anthropophagizes") universal trends and traditions (Campos 1986). And all this apparently without prejudices or preconceptions insofar as that is possible. Jazz, especially "cool jazz," is transformed and dovetailed into it, as are elements from Italian, French, Spanish, North American, Central American and Mexican, and Argentine trends. There is no obvious attempt toward iconoclasm, no hostility toward other musical periods, but good will toward all and to all some equal time. Pauses, brief interludes of silence, are coveted. A pause is a structural element, as in Ravel and Debussy and the impressionists, thus popular music finds itself comfortable with trends in high culture, especially in the work of Antônio Carlos Jobim (Brito 1993:21–27).

Brazilian "concrete poetry" plays a part in bossa nova. The musical style also bears a relationship with contact improvisation dancing and free dance. There are also relations, most of them implicit, between bossa nova and expressionism and Pablo Picasso cubism and "found" art, as well as between bossa nova and artistic paradoxes of the Mavrits Escher sort and art of the nature of Paul Klee and Jackson Pollock and Mark Rothko and Wassily Kandinsky.[12] Above all, a hyperconscious sense of melody, harmony, syncopation, rhythm, and lyrics is evident in pieces like *Samba de uma nota só* ("One Note Samba"), and *Desafinado* ("Slightly Out of Tune"). These pieces, in lyric and beat, are a self-referential commentary on themselves, on bossa nova, and on music in general. This is the cold, logico-rational, impersonal level of the movement, a sort of popular musical counterpart to composer Héitor Villa-Lobos's *Bachianas brasileiras* in the sense of an intellectual mixing of musical genres, movements, styles, and traditions. This is the semiotic level of Thirdness in much the manner of Bach, but without divorcing that level from Firstness, the most concrete, sentimental, emotional, and sensuous level of musical expression. After all, this is music. But the alterations and variations are an intellectual exercise at the level of Thirdness, hence is doesn't seem so strange—when considered intellectually that is—since it is divorced from feeling insofar as that is possible (Medaglia 1993:88–89).

Samba canção. But it is considerably slower than the customary *samba* rhythm. There is a certain note of nostalgia combining Brazilian *saudade* ("nostalgic long-ing," "re-memberment of something undefined and undefinable") with the Cuban-Mexican *bolero*. This is sensed in frequent syncopation and unexpected chord switches without any dominant or hegemonic chord, without finished counterpoint but with a constantly emerging counterpoint that never quite comes into its own. Like semiosis, the rhythm is always already in progress. It is process, without the possibility of finished product (Campos 1993:1–10). It is almost like a "catatonic" means of making music and singing. Instrumentalist and vocalist are both obliged to twitch and jerk and stutter and voice pure uncertainties. As such, it is jazz and it isn't jazz, for it is "modern samba." It is song and it isn't song, for it is sung so quietly it is hardly worthy of the name; it is quietly and passively spoken more than sung with gusto and force and emotion and vibrato. It is style and it is antistyle, for it is no more than style in the making without the possibility of that making becoming de-terminately made. It is a "state of mind," it is bodymindsign. It is who the songster is at this moment and who everybody is in the past, in the present, and in the future. As such it is *neither* old *nor* new, *neither* Brazilian *nor* non-Brazilian, *neither* popular *nor* high-brow, *neither* sentimental *nor* nonsentimental, *neither* intellectual *nor* non-intellectual. And it is *all* of the above and *none* of the above. It is a "third sex," a "state of becoming," which is virtually unintelligible unless one listens to it sixty times or so (Castro 1990:227–37). It is well-nigh nothing and it is a little of every-thing; it is everybody and nobody; it expands out to the stars and it collapses to a point. It is intense pragmatism and free spirited idealism. Poet Torquato Neto writes of Gilberto Gil, one of the most adept and talented survivors of the 1960s, that: "There are many ways to sing and to make Brazilian music; Gilberto Gil prefers all of them" (Perrone 1989:91). Gil's sounds and lyrics evince a mystical sense of space and time:

> In my spiritual retreats
> I discover certain things are so normal
> Like sitting in front of something and staying
> For hours on end with it
> Beautiful Barbara, TV screen . . .
> Playing an unconnected game
> That crazy people like to play
> What's more, I'd say it's no more
> Than the initial spiritual signs of this song (Perrone 1989:113)

It was during the latter 1960s that Gilberto Gil and Caetano Veloso came into their own, above all in 1968 with their LP entitled *Tropicália*, a veritable running al-legory of the Brazilian cultural experience including the world-wide youth move-ment coupled with the military takeover of Brazil in 1964 (Veloso 1997). It is a po-etic-musical construction of a world and a nation caught in a maze of contradictions, with references to music and art and society and politics and economics in Brazil and the world over. It juxtaposes modern popular Brazilian music (bossa nova) and sor-did peasant life in the interior and the *favelas* in Rio, modernist consumerist hoopla and those poor citizens who cannot buy much of anything, freedom and dictatorship, affluence and suffering, urban sprawls and rural underdevelopment, English lines and Brazilian popular lyrics, modern architecture and archaic structures, Batman and macumba rites, and on and on. Tropicália, part and parcel of the "tropicalismo" movement in Brazil and Latin America since Brazilian "modernism" of 1922, is anthropophagia to the nth degree, a nonlinear array of infinite possibilities any dozen or so of which might pop up at the most unexpected moment (Campos 1993:199–207). This surfaces nowhere more gushingly and rushingly than in a Caetano Veloso piece:

> Over my head the aeroplanes / Under my feet the trucks and trains
> And point out the highland plains / Is my nose
> I organize the movement, too / I lead the carnival, I'm who
> Inaugurates the monument in the midwest of a country in a pose
> Long live the Bossa-s-s! Long live the str-stra-straw huts!
> The monument is crepe paper and silver / The "green-eyed mulatta"
> Hides the "backland moonlight? with her hair behind the forest
> The monument has no door / An entrance is an old crooked narrow street
> And on its knee a smiling ugly dead child sticks out his hand
> Long live the forest la-la-land! Long live the mulatta-ta-ta! …
> Sunday the "Best of Bossa" is on / Monday is blue Monday for him
> Tuesday he's down on the farm, however / The monument is very modern
> It didn't say anything about the pattern of my new suit
> "To hell with everything else" my dear
> Long live "A Banda" da-da! Carmen Miranda-da-da
> (Perrone 1989:57–58)

And so it was, that is, was happening, was in the process of happening, continues to happen, will have been happening, in Brazil.

Notes

1.   Leticia Vidor de Sousa Reis (1997) argues quite effectively, however, that capoeira was taken up during the latter half of the 1900s by a number of Europeans as a pastime, for physical conditioning, and as a sports event. So capoeira wasn't quite an exclusively Afro-Brazilian practice before the Vargas years.
2.   Technically speaking, there are two types of capoeira, Angolan capoeira, which remains close to its original form as developed in Africa, and regional capoeira, a "modernized" art form integrating aspects of the martial arts and developed with an eye toward "middle-class" Brazilian tastes and tourist appeal (for the original capoeira, Rego [1968], for regional capoeira, Almeida [1986], for a comparison and contrast, Lewis [1992], Renato Vieira [1995], for capoeira in relation to general aspects of Brazilian cultural life, Bruhns [2000]).
3.   See Cornel West (1988) for comparable words on the African American youth of the inner cities in the U.S.

4.   For a first-hand account of the function of samba in the carnival, see Browning (1995), Guillermoprieto (1991), Vianna (1999), for a general Bakhtin view of carnival the world over, White (1993), Stallybrass and White (1986).

5.   Much in this regard, George Brandon (1993:129-63) attributes how societies remember to four memory types: personal, cognitive, habit, and social or collective. Habit memory is of the body, and the habit memory of all individuals in the community becomes social or collective memory, much in line with Bastide's thesis.

6.   Music is tied to culture in a way in which the descriptive capacities of language are not, such that music "can reveal the nature of feelings with a detail and truth that language cannot approach" (Langer 1948:191). All discourse about music "presents a philosophical problem, . . . because it belongs to a realm of discourse that is different from the subject of enquiry: 'music,' 'musical' discourse is essentially nonverbal, though, obviously, words influence its structures in many cases; and to analyze nonverbal language with verbal language runs the risk of distorting the evidence. 'Music' is therefore, strictly speaking, an unknowable truth, and discourse about music belongs to the realm of metaphysics" (Blacking 1995:226).

7.   John Blacking (1973) writes how music is a synthesis of cognitive powers and the human body, both of which are tacit in cultural processes. The forms music takes, and its effect on the citizens of a community, pattern the social experiences of bodies and minds in particular cultural environments, and it expresses these environments at a profound level that is perhaps inaccessible to the other arts. Through Blacking's studies of music among the Venda people he senses that learning music is at the deeper levels by osmosis; it is a tacit, implicit act, a learning by example and by doing. In contrast, in European cultures, "many formal changes . . . come about as a result of attempts by composers to make people more aware of social disharmony and inequality" (Blacking 1973:100).

8.   Blacking points out that polyphony in early European music is quite comparable to polyrhythms in much African music. In both cases performance consists of many people holding separate parts within the framework on a metric unity. The difference is that the principle is applied "vertically" or "synchronically" in polyphony and "horizontally" or "diachronically" in polyrhythms (Blacking 1995:47-48). The first is a combination of harmonies and chords, the second is a combination of melodies; the first is a grouping of many rhythms into one rhythm to yield a sense of homogeny, the second is a grouping of linearly developing sound strings over time to produce a sense of heterogeny. Put the two together and, as we learn from Alejo Carpentier (1980) during his musicologist moments, we have the best of two worlds and the best of Latin American music, though it remains more polyrhythmic than polyphonic.

9.   See José Piedra's (1990) study of Cuban rhythms in language and in music commensurate with the "illogic" of the culture in general, that is, of how Cuban culture resists being jam-packed into the mold of Western binary logic, to be the focus of our attention below.

10.   Recall Hornbostel's antiphony or the call-and-response method, which, along with polyphony and rhythmic flow, compose the three basic characteristics of African drumming.

11. When Frank Sinatra took a liking to Bossa Nova and sang a few pieces, he is reported to have remarked that "The last time I sang so quietly was when I had laryngitis" (Castro 1990:415).

12. In this regard see especially chapter three in Roskill (1992). Moreover, in this regard, the charge has often been made that Bossa Nova is the product of an affluent group of upper-middle-class white lads and few women who were making music for notoriety and pecuniary purposes and for export to the United States. With respect to this controversy, Charles Perrone writes:

> From a musical point of view, the condemnations . . . are difficult to sustain. In his sociological analysis Tenhorão [1969] regards Brazilian musicians' use of altered chords as nothing more than an emulation of the North American jazz idiom; he does not take into account the desire of educated musicians anywhere to diversify their work or to put new compositional ideas into practice. In a sarcastic response, Jobim pointed out that flat fives and sharp nines are not the exclusive domain of jazz composers, that Bach also used them. Furthermore, given its various stylistic parameters, Bossa Nova cannot ultimately be simplified as the crossing of samba and jazz, which is itself a fluid musical concept. That Brazilian musicians had contact with jazz is undeniable, but the results of this contact are purely Brazilian, a unique synthesis of rhythmic, harmonic, melodic, and performance-bound qualities. (Perrone 1989:xxvi).

Chapter Seventeen

Where's the Bossa, and Other Bossas?

I, like other queer people, a two in one body, both male and female. I am the embodiment of the *hiero gamos*, the coming together of opposite qualities within.

—Gloria Anzaldúa

At first it was hard to stay
     on the border between
the physical world
     and hers.
It was only there at the interface
     that we could see each other.

—Gloria Anzaldúa

"Emptiness," Again

Music is its own object; there is not necessarily any external semiosis to which a musical sign must relate. Inner (kinesthetic) relations are thus of utmost importance. They create echoes in the mind the interrelations of which evoke feelings and sensations and thoughts that are of the nature of the sign in its most simple and at the same time its most complex form. Gustav Mahler once remarked that he felt the urge to express himself in music only when *"indefinable* emotions made themselves felt" (Bonavia 1956:204). *Indefinable emotions*: they emerge, from somewhere; they are what they are and at the same time they bring premonitions of something else.

All this might seem to strike a responsive chord these days, even though Mahler is commonly labeled a "modernist": postmodernism tells us we can know no beginning, center, or end. That's not what I have in mind, however. What I have in mind is the hairlines of Figures 1 and 5 and their counterpart in Peirce's line drawn on a blackboard example. It has to do with drawing a line of distinction, a "cut," separating something from something else. This is a crucially important concept of African American music. We have Peirce's (CP:4.512) "cut" in his logical "book of assertions," G. Spencer-Brown's (1972) "mark" of distinction that sets one thing off against many other things, the Dedekind "cut" so named after mathematician Richard Dedekind, which consists in exercising a "cut" somewhere at an arbitrarily chosen spot along the continuum of rational numbers (Dantzig 1930). With respect to music, nowhere is the idea of a "cut" more evident than in African American influenced polyrhythms. The "cut" has its initiation in repetition. A sign begins by repeating itself. First there is the Peircean interrelationship. The sign includes Firstness,

Secondness, and Thirdness, that is, if it is what Peirce called a "genuine" sign. Upon repetition, it begins a new spiral around its focus, its central axis, the "vortex," the "emptiness," the hairlines or $\sqrt{-1}$ of Figures 1 and 5, the border of a border. I repeat, as John Cage once put it, between a word and a word, or a sound and a sound, there is an almost infinitesimally small lapse, a moment of silence, where "emptiness" reigns.

African American rhythms place special emphasis on the "cut." With each "cut" you pick the beat up again, but after a more abrupt lapse. There is a return to the "beginning," to "emptiness," and then it's as if the sound were engendered for the first time, but it isn't the first time since it is a repetition, but it isn't really repetition, for what is now becoming is other than what was then becoming. There is no apparent goal, no obsessive future orientation, and no cumulative development. Sounds just happen, again, . . . and again. This sort of music, it would seem, is destined to play second fiddle to Western cumulative, progressive ways and means. If there is apparently no purpose or reason, then surely it must be a fruitless exercise, so why bother? Do something that will yield a profit, whether in wealth or in the aesthetic satisfaction that everything has been taken to its logical end and there it came to a close.

Yet, in Latin America, the African American beat has not taken a back seat but has entered the mainstream. It is an important facet of the rhythm of music and of dance and of cultural life. The African American beat emphasizes dynamic polyrhythms that organize melody in an interweaving of lines of different metrical characteristics. There is improvisation. Every new beginning follows an almost imperceptible hesitation, then there is freedom to do what has not been done. There is much syncopation. Starting anew after a "cut" is more enticing if there is an unexpected accent: there is electricity in the move, it heightens excitement, your body can't help breaking into action. There is call-and-response. The group becomes involved, there is dynamic give-and-take, with each transferal of the voice following a brief lapse. In all cases, after the hesitation, at the silent spot, the "vortex," there is yet another "cut." This process is not exactly *metronomic*. That would be the linear way of music Western style. Rather, it is polymetric, as James Snead defines it:

> The typical polymetry of black music means that there are at least two, and usually more, rhythms going on alongside the listener's own beat. The listener's beat is a kind of *Erwartungshorizont* (to use a term taken from a quite different area) or "horizon of expectations," whereby he or she knows where the constant beat must fall in order properly to make sense of the gaps that the other interacting drummers have let fall. Because one rhythm always defines another in black music, and beat is an entity of relation, any "self-consciousness" or "achievement" in the sense of an individual participant working towards his or her own rhythmic or tonal climax "above the mass" would have disastrous results. (Snead 1990:221).

The individual does not stand out above and beyond the group, for the poly-rhythm is a community affair. All individuals will undulate and sway and swing and sing together, or they will fail together. The unexpected, the disturbance, the "cut," draws attention to itself with no apparent rhyme or reason, no apparent purpose, no goal. It just happens. It is a minuscule and tenderly ephemeral eddy in the river of semiosis, interconnected, interrelated, and dependent upon the whole. But from within the spot where it swirls around, that whole is unfathomable.

The "cut" shifts back to the sphere of overdetermination where unlimited possi-bilities present themselves (recall Figure 6). Something emerges, makes its play, gy-rates about for a while along with its companion signs, then it immerses itself back into the soup from whence it came. It enjoyed brief existence as an actualized sign, as a Second. While dancing around with other actualized signs, there were many possibilities and probabilities of interpretant signs, of interpretations, some of them coming into actualization, some of them not. Between any two interpretations of contradictory, contrary, or even equal and opposite force, there could always have emerged a third interpretation to take its rightful place among all other signs, in this, the underdetermined sphere. As we have noted above on various occasions, in the overdetermined, the Principle of Noncontradiction puts its mighty bifurcating sword in the sheath and withdraws; in the underdetermined the Principle of Excluded-Middle becomes lethargic, impotent. Only in the realm of Secondness, of actuals, can the *either/or* Principle of Identity hold down the fort, in this world of dualisms, of accumulated wealth and knowledge, of hegemony and subservience, of haves and havenots, of power brokers and food stampers. The "cut" is the prime benefactor al-lowing for a leveling of all actor-participants, with all holds barred and without su-premacy of any signs, for all signs could have been something other than what they are and in future moments they will always have been something other than what they were. This flattening is a Cézanne painting from the artist's walking around the objects and presenting it from many angles. It is a Picasso cubist depiction of a three-dimensional object on a two-dimensional plane by a view from many three-dimensional views. It is Dadaism, a return to hesitation, stuttering, and apparent simplicity. It is, in short, nonlinearity, perspectivism of a radical sort.

The "cut" is a return to paradise, to the tree of life. Paradise needs a serpent, au-thor of sinewy, undulating, unstructured, unformed movement. The squiggles are an ever-changing line, a border of borders separating good from evil, life from death, blissful pleasure from sweat-of-the-brow toil and suffering, knowledge from igno-rance, time from eternity. But that, of course, is the Biblical Paradise and the Biblical serpent: irremediably dualistic. The nondualist paradise is something entirely differ-ent. There, to evoke the concepts developed in chapter nine, it is not a matter simply of "green" or "grue," of "Guadalupe" or "Tonantzín" or "Guadantzín," of "cats" or "cats*," or of "Gavagai!" with either one meaning or the other. There can be "gruo" and "grua" and "gue" and "guo" and "gua" and "gruau" and so on—this, of course, we saw in our polylogue. "Green" Samba and cool jazz and Baião, and folklore and concrete poetry becomes the "grues" of Bossa Nova. There are no "cats-cats*," no mere binary distinctions, but just "cat," which can take on an indefinite variety of re-lations with the furniture of the world depending upon changing contexts. One repre-sentamen or predicate can come into relationship with something "out there," thus becoming a semiotic object and it can engender a meaning or interpretant which can then in its own turn become another sign or representamen. With each alteration, however slight, there is a return to the "vortex" and another "cut." With each "cut" there is a new beginning and a new sign or set of signs.

This image taken to the extreme is Tlöny constructing a new world at every step. It is Maggie in the wildest of her dreams. It is Pierre repeating to infinity the same text each of which is a radically different text. It is Lönny caught up in a nightmare of staccato shifting solutions to ever-changing situations, and he finally becomes a cross-dresser in an effort to emulate Emmy's talents—he might even go so far as to consider a sex change. It is Emmy becoming herself and someone other than herself at the drop of a hat and as she wishes, and at long last, she finds peace of mind. Funy, of course, is in his element: everything is already new under the sun such that ultimately there is nothing new under the sun. And Averroës, of course, remains more confused than ever. After all has been said and done, by inclusion of the "vortex" in the equation, radical nonlinearity is the key. At one end, contradictions are no problem, and at the other end, between any two signs there is always the possibility of another sign, and then another one, . . . and another one.

There is still no rest for the weary, it seems.

The Message Is Mediated

Consider Figure 8, if you will. The terms homogeny, heterogeny, and hegemony have been given ample discussion, I trust. Harmony, derived from the Greek *harmonia* ("concord, proportion, joint") is basically musical consonance, sound in tune with itself, an adaptation of various chords to each other, agreement between parts to make up a coherent design. Harmony is simultaneity, synchrony. If melody moves through space and time horizontally, as suggested above, harmony occurs vertically and all at once. It comes in blocks, each one succeeding the other, whether the succession is viewed as accumulation and progress in the Western way or as stops and starts in the non-Western way. In this sense homophony and homorrhythmicity (from the Greek, *homo-* or "the same" and *-phonos* or "sound, tone") can be conceived as a grouping of different sounds held together in harmony, a series of boxlike units as opposed to the twisting and contorting strands of melody.

Polyphony or heterophony (from the Greek *poly*, "many," and *hetero-*, "different") consists of a set of relatively independent variations interweaving themselves with the melody as it proceeds along the horizontal plane in time and space. Like strands of a rope, each is of little strength. It has no hope of being able to bear the load by itself. If all strands were entirely independent, there would be no collective effort but each strand would go its own way. When the strands interweave, in contrast, they make up a whole of codependent parts whose strength is greater than the sum of the strength of its parts. But this musical trope is no ordinary rope. It is a flow of strings in multi-dimensional space and nonlinear time; it is an undulating flow of binding yet caressing pressure that engulfs and captivates and motivates. Antiphony, corresponding to hegemony, on the other hand, entails pairs of opposites in head-bashing conflict with no apparent resolution. This, in more free-flowing musical semiosis, would be the call-and-response technique, were it to stand alone, but it does not, for it is always accompanied by homophony and heterophony, hence fluidity self-perpetuates, around the "centerless center," the "vortex," the "emptiness." All this, to the now familiar beat, ♪♪♪ ♪♪.

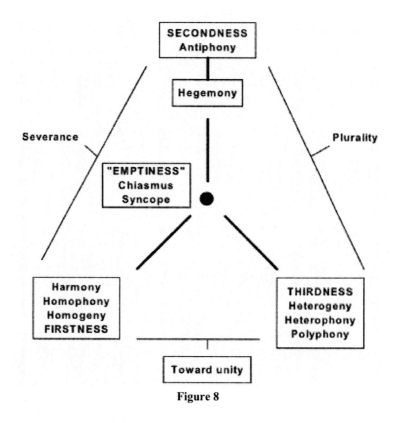

Figure 8

But let's not jump to conclusions. There is no sharp line of demarcation between homophony and heterophony and antiphony. Their border of borders allows for enough overlapping to frustrate the neatest of theoretical blueprints. The "categories" are only a matter of degree. Virtually no rhythm or voice may stand out, in which case homophony dominates, at least for the moment. Then, when least expected there is a swirl and some sounds emerge and bump you into a new movement and ephemerally heterophony rules, and later, the accent having retreated into the continuum, a most brief calm of homophony enters. Then it is back to a fleeting moment of the first process. Thus dissonant elements are held together. Syncope holds them together: a *conjunctionis oppositorum* always ready to burst from the central "vortex" when least expected. Putting all this in another way, homophony is the relatively undifferentiated, antiphony is linear differentiation, and heterophony is increasingly finer staccato differentiation along multiple, nonlinear lines toward the legato of the dedifferentiated or undifferentiated, without the possibility of finally having arrived, in the finite Kingdom of this Finite World.

In his reflections on Buddhism and Western phenomenology, Steven Laycock cites a sort of "call" and "response" by two masters. They are as follows:

> Body is the Bodhi Tree,
> The mind a stand of mirror bright.
> Take care to wipe it continually,
> Allowing no dust to cling.

And,

> There never was a Bodhi Tree,
> Nor bright mirror-stand.
> Originally, not one thing exists,
> So where is the dust to cling? (Laycock 1994:1–2)

The first lines allude to the mind-as-mirror-of-nature dream, which Richard Rorty gleefully and notoriously demolishes. This is the world of Secondness, of actualities "out there" and the mind's reduplicating them "in here," the "picture which holds traditional philosophy captive" (Rorty 1979:12). This picture garners high hopes of the completeness of Thirdness for all time, a Grand Unified Theory free of all falsifying possibilities. The second lines are a celebration of "emptiness," which can give rise to Firstness and Thirdness as a perpetually incomplete enterprise, and which defies a world and a mirror-as-mind mirroring it and blemishes in the mirror—since there is nothing to blemish. But when a mirror image is seen, in the world of Seconds, light has been born out of the "vortex." It has been transmitted through its medium—it was mediated—and in interrelationship and interaction and its codependency with the things of the world, it is refracted and reflected and in general "bent" by the mediating action of its medium upon taking on Thirdness. And it is seen. That is, the image it creates is seen, not the objects and not the mirror and not the light, but the image, however bent and distorted. Then the light is reabsorbed into the "vortex," it "dies," to remain there until semiosis beckons once again so that it can spring into action anew.

But all this is a local phenomenon. I write "local phenomenon" because it is just that. We see it here and now, because we are ready to see images in such a way, bringing with us a few expectations and memories and possible interpretations. We should harbor no illusions of being able to see the overdetermined global process—this we learned from chapter eleven. Nor can we be aware of all the virtually infinite number of possibilities the future holds in store within the underdetermined. We are just fallibly here and now. We can hold a little antiphony in our hands, we would like to think. But the whole of heterophony, which include times past and times future and many variations in spatial contexts, remains beyond our reach, to say nothing of the infinite possibilities hitherto unactualized for our self-conscious selves in the overdetermined sphere of homophony.

An example may help. Take a strip of paper, twist it at one end and connect the two extremities to form a Möbius-band, a fascinating topology that falls to the curse of undecidability. What I mean to say is that there is undecidability in a local view of the strip. Rotate the twist around the band in whichever direction and however far you wish, and wherever you happen to stop, draw a "cut," that is, a vertical line bisecting the band. Is the line on the "inside" or the "outside"? It is definitely *either* one *or* the other, according to your whims, for at each and every point on the band there can be an arbitrarily established bipolarity. Now draw a horizontal line along the entire length of the band such that it connects up with itself, and consider the band from this global perspective. Is the line "inside" or "outside"? To say it is *either* one *or* the other is absurd, for the bipolarity is no more. The line is *both* "inside" *and* "outside" and *neither* "inside" *nor* "outside," according to how we wish to cut the cake. The line was extended until it began eating its own tail without there ever existing any question of "inside" or "outside." There is simply no contradiction, no inconsistency, no opposition, and no binarity. At the local level, dualism exercises its force; at the global level it is of no consequence. At the local level there is arbitrary decidability, Secondness; at the global level, that of Firstness and infinitely extended Thirdness, decidability is a long lost dream. By the same token, homogeny or homophony has no truck with oppositions, contradictions, inconsistencies. The local level has them but it hardly pays them any mind, since they seen to be quite harmless. However, bisect the band with a vertical line, then choose another spot and bisect it again. No matter which pair of spots you choose, there always exists the possibility of a third line's emerging between them. This is the level of heterogeny or heterophony, which is neither local and dualistic nor global and holistic but differential (the product of differences), according to the nature of Thirdness.

So much for Möbius quandaries.

Do One, Duality, and Three Actually Make Four?

Consider the Dominant and Subaltern of Figure 9 to be the product of a split term. They make up a Janus-faced dualism of terms qualifiable by *either/or*. This is the contrast between the haves and the havenots, hegemony and the disempowered: Secondness, antiphony. Firstness, homophony, is oxymoronic: *both* one damned thing *and* the other, a happy coexistence of otherwise contradictory terms, a baroque-like conjunction of antagonists that would under other circumstances enter into mortal combat. Thirdness, heterophony, or *neither-nor*, is ironic (from *eiron*, dissembling).

Saying what something *is* while depicting it as something it *is not* covers much ground. Thus we see once again that the empowered and the subaltern meet, in the arena of Secondness. The slave notices that his master has had a slight twitch during the last few days. But, then, a twitch is just a twitch, nothing to worry about. No? No. A twitch can also be a subtle "wink" that can be roguish or friendly or a warning or a threat or a clue that advantage is being taken of somebody or that there has been an invitation to engage in illicit activity and many other things as well. A twitch-*qua*-"wink" is given at the level of Firstness, as a similarity to something else. If the sign taker is curious, adventuresome, or if the "wink" maker is her boss, then the intrigue may continue on. That same twitch-"wink" at the level of Thirdness as mediated risks becoming a parody, a response with the daring implications that what is being parodied is of no account.

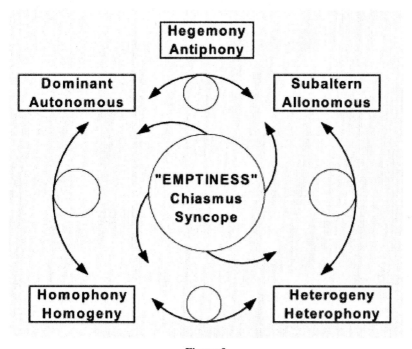

Figure 9

So in Figure 9 we have four terms when bifurcating the masquerading character of Secondness into two terms of undecidability, dominant and subaltern. The relationship between the two manifestations of Secondness, dominant and subaltern (as well as autonomous and allonomous), are that of "A" and "Not-A."[1] Homogeny, all-encompassing, is "*Both* A *and* Not-A," and heterogeny is "*Neither* A *nor* Not-A." We have thus run the gamut of possibilities of "alternative cultural 'logics'." But not quite. Taking Figure 9 as a whole, and we must have "All of the above," and "None of the above." The dominant is relatively autonomous and the subaltern is relatively allonomous. I must write "relatively" for there is no autonomy in the absolute sense: everything is thoroughly interrelated with and codependent upon everything else. If the one is "relatively autonomous," that is because it is more independent than the other and customarily "gives the orders." If the other is "relatively allonomous" that is because it is more dependent upon the "relatively autonomous" elements since it must customarily take what is given as a relatively passive recipient.[2]

The dominant actor puts on a mask of control and the subservient actor a mask of the controlled. The combination of the two makes up formal *either/or* relations metaphorically characteristic of parades, inaugural ceremonies, weddings, graduations, and the likes, where the hierarchy is virtually cut in stone and roles are ritualistically carried out. On the other hand, unforeseen events of the nature of "cultural guerrilla activity" on the part of the subordinate as described above can always threaten to upend the applecart. When this occurs, homophony and/or heterophony can threaten to emerge. Homophony is, metaphorically speaking, carnival: a prince becomes temporally a pauper, a man a woman, a bureaucrat a thief, and illicit sex becomes prescribed, intoxication is the norm, and so on. There is an inversion, to be sure, but with recognition that things are not what they seem but are what under ordinary circumstances they would not be. Yet they are in a sense *both* what they seem *and* what they otherwise would be. It is the "black sun" of semiosis, in the sense that "black" and "sun" are not taken for what they would ordinarily be but their meaning remains in limbo, as yet unactualized, a possibility for emerging into the light of day. When the Firstness of the oxymoronic pair has emerged to become actualized, then there can be oscillation between the *either* and the *or* of Secondness. Heterophony, on the other hand, is metaphorically a masquerade ball. A mask is worn, as in hegemonic interrelations. But there is acknowledgment that what is seen is not what there is, and what there is is not seen so it is for the moment out of the picture and of no consequence: there is *neither* the one *nor* the other.[3] The dissembler, pretending she is not what she is, is Nixon saying "I am not a crook," Reagan confessing "I don't remember," Father Bush claiming "I didn't know about the Iran-Contra affair," or Bill Clinton confiding "I might have done it, I don't recall, but if I did do it, I apologize." Almost everybody sees through the act. Finally, the chiasmus of Figure 9 is the crossover from one mode to another one by way of the "vortex" in Figure 8, the border of borders, $\sqrt{-1}$, "emptiness."

Chiasmus is what holds disparate, conflicting, antagonistic, contradictory, anomalous elements together as if they belonged together. It is the fountain of the rabble-rousing, carnivalesque yet "real life," the formal yet commonplace, the dissembling yet straight-faced, the "cultural" guerrilla mix-up of possibly and virtually everything. It is where the action begins; yet it is nowhere. It is when everything converges into a black hole of vibrant, brash, high-spirited nonactivity, yet there is nowhen. It is the engenderer of all hybrids, yet it is neither semen nor egg and it bears no spark of procreation, for it is mere "emptiness." It provokes a feeling for what lurks behind the baroque *horror vacui*. The baroque abhors empty space, nothing where there could be something: all space and all time should be full, a plenum depicting the fullness of all times and all places. Quite understandably, it has often been said that to say Latin America is to say "baroque" or at least "neo-baroque."

In sum, in the hegemonic interrelations we would have Lönny (Lönnrot) and his presumed control of Scharlach's destiny and then the inversion of the formula, or Emmy (Emma Zunz) turning the tables on the man indirectly responsible for her father's demise who makes him out to appear as her accoster. But this isn't really the whole story. In each case the switch contains a bit of metaphor and a bit of metonomy and a bit of oxymoron and a bit of irony, depending upon the vantage point and how the characters are taken. Funy (Funes the Memorious) would appear to be a good servant. His attitude is that of quietism. He realizes he cannot bring about any changes in his world so he passively accepts his lot in life. He is indifferent, he expects nothing and is therefore never surprised that he is never disappointed by what happens to happen. His will and his ego shrink virtually to a point; they are virtually nonexistent. That is one story regarding Funy. The other has him in an oppressively time-bound world where what now is is now something else, so it *both* is *and* is not what it is. Time is virtually his chiasmus: it jerks him into a persistent staccato of comings and goings without end, where everything can be everything and where nothing cannot be nothing but must be something and something can be everything. There is apparently no salvation for poor Funy. The worlds of Maggie (the Magician), Daneri (of "The Aleph"), and Averroës (of "Averroës' Search"), if and when completed for all time, would be Hegelian dreamland, Totality. But alas, they must live in their actual world of *eithers* and *ors*, and cope with the reality of underdetermination and the inconsistency and/or incompleteness of whatever might be at hand. There are not even any ultimate answers for our nimble-minded Tlöny (an inhabitant of the planet Tlön), who is capable of calling up any world he wants when he wants it. But in the final analysis whatever bed he happens to have feathered must be his resting place, for it is the bed he has made by the machinations of his own mind, however ephemeral and tenuous it may be. Latin American neo-baroque: mutual interpenetration of all our interlocutors, of conflicting and contradictory elements held together by the elusive glue of "emptiness," the border of borders, the borderland where everything is and nothing is, oxymoronically and ironically. There is a twitch that means nothing except that it is a twitch. But wait! It is a wink that perhaps means one of many possible things; but then, a wink is just a wink; but it is always more than just a wink, it is a twitch-wink, *both* a twitch *and* a wink and *neither* a twitch *nor* a wink. *Latin America*: What, really, is the meaning of this hybrid mix?

At your leisure you might contemplate Figure 8 and 9 further. Interrelate them with the characters of our dialogue, with all the figures that preceded them, with my obsessive ruminations on the Latin American scene, with the bodymindsign that is you, while attending to the intriguing and unthinkable feeling of the rhythm, . . . to the compelling sense of the rhythm, . . . to the unsayable rhythm, . . . to the rhythm, . . . the rhythm, . . . rhythm. . . .

Logically Illogical or Illogically Logical?

As we have observed, one response to an apparently incomprehensible and undecidable world is to use logic to show that what you have present to your rigorously analytical eye is illogical, and admittedly so also is your very analysis: by community consent we are all in a manner of speaking solipsists. Another response is to maintain blind faith in customary ways: tradition gives us truth all in one basket. Another response has it that some gifted soul among us can divine the ultimate truths and save us all: one solitary solipsist an entire community makes. But actually, she cannot an entire community make. Community is dialogue, interrelations, interaction, codependency. If hope there might be for any of us, therein it lays, in the *whole* of the community, in the *hole*, that is, the *chiasmus*.

Emily Hicks, shrewd observer of border writing, makes a move in the right direction, I suspect. After discounting "analytic logic" and "dialectical logic," she opts for a third kind of logic, "holographic or multidimensional logic." From this multidimensional perspective, "there is no necessary identity between form and content. Rather, there is a relation of incommensurability" (Hicks 1991:49). The point is well taken, at least up to Hicks's mention of the term "incommensurability." There, the trouble begins. "Incommensurability" implies two or more terms that have nothing in common upon which to make a comparison. It is intransigence. There is no dialogue. Interlocutors talk past one another using the same words with incompatible meanings and different words with much the same meanings. It is an invitation to chaos, or to silence when each party has talked itself into oblivion. It is the work of Paul Feyerabend, Thomas Kuhn, and others that booted the "incommensurability" debate in philosophy of science to a screaming pitch during the 1960s and 1970s. Arguments for and against it were hurled with fire and brimstone across the great "incommensurability" divide that separated them. On the one side were those who sought to preserve their coveted values of rationality and progress (of tradition) and defend the concept of epistemology and correct methods in science to the hilt. On the other side were those upstarts with a flair for detecting the metaphysical and occasionally the mystical even in the most sober of (individual, solipsistic) scientific pursuits, and who reveled in the chance to put down the nobler rationalist beliefs in logic and reason and experience as the tried and tested roads to truth. The debate has subsided somewhat. And for the better. If hard-line "incommensurability" were the case, we could hardly communicate a whit. Even a softer approach to the problem leaves us mumbling incoherent phrases that go in one ear and out the other without taking effect, and things are left pretty much as they were. In other words, if "incommensurability," then no change, and if absolutely no "incommensurability"—that is, if we understand each other to the letter—then no change either. We can't have things absolutely *either* one way *or* the other, they are *both* and *neither*.

Hicks comes close to implying so much when she argues:

> the notions of the border and the holographic interference pattern, unlike the analogical and the homological, allow for a description of the mediations of a logic of nonidentity. An "identity" that does not exclude differences characterizes the "sameness" of the holographic relation. Thus, form rather than content is emphasized by rejecting the notion of the identity between form and content; in this way, difference, most readily apparent in form . . . may be apprehended. (Hicks 1991:49).

The analogical and homological are of the nature of linear logic. The holograph metaphor implies nonlinearity. This is a quite worthy image. It is Karl Pribram's model of the brain-mind, which physicist David Bohm once used as a model of the "holographic universe" (Pribram 1971, Wilber 1982). The hologram is a two-dimensional infolding of a three-dimensional object. It contains that object as an overdetermined set of possibilities (Firstness) none of which are actualized. When laser light is bounced off the image in the proper way the three-dimensional object is actualized (into Secondness), and it now exists as an undetermined entity (Thirdness). Fair enough.

But however enticing all this may be, I must report that I do not believe Hicks goes far enough. She alludes to Arnold Schönberg's nonlinear twelve-tone series and to Julio Cortázar's multiple possible nonlinear readings of his novel, *Hopscotch* (1996 [1963]). But, in addition to the indelibly linguicentric, textualist nature of her exposition, in spite of her allusions to multidimensionality, Deleuze and Guattari's *rhizome* metaphor, and such, there is something lacking. I see in Hick's disquisition the "was" of Secondness as the "now" past that was sensed, but when consciousness becomes mediately aware of it as the "is," it no longer is. I see in Hick's concept the "might be" of Firstness as the holographic possibility for the actualization of myriad Seconds. I see the would be (Thirdness), as that sphere of underdetermination a portion of which at a given space-time juncture is most likely destined to become actualized according to the nature of the holographic image. I do not, however, see the "will have been" as a counterpart to the "might be," that sphere of overdetermination, the scintillating embrace of all possibilities within the border of borders, without which nothing "would be" or "would have been" becoming. Without the entire package, Hicks's model remains impoverished. It is as if we amputated the entire left-hand side of Figure 8, as if we rubbed out the lower three boxes in Figure 9. In other words, to ask the questions "Illogically logical?" and "Logically illogical?" is to miss the point; it is to remain within binary imperatives, "linguicentric" thinking. Genuinely taking the whole into account, including the *hole*, is a matter of embracing *both* "logic" *and* "illogic" and *neither* "logic" *nor* "illogic," and at the same time of embracing *both* imperatives, and *neither* imperative, quite painstakingly and hopelessly paradoxical though it all may seem.

Now, after this mild critique of Hicks, I must say that I harbor no illusions of clairvoyance or of any privileged insight, nor do I nurture much confidence in my ability to write what it is that needs to get written. I can do hardly more than write a few loose and vague words and raise a brow and give a wink or a grimace and perhaps offer a little clumsy body language and hope for the best. That much said, as a wrap-up of this volume, here goes my stuttering, stumbling, and not very grand but quite nonbland finale, for better or for worse.

Cultural "Logics": Holding It All in a Liquid Embrace

> *Flower of Latium Sambadrome*
> *Lusamerica powdered Latin*
> *What does this language want!*
> *What can it do!*
> —Caetano Veloso

> I like to feel my tongue brush
> Against the language of Luis de Camões
> I like being and to be
> And I want to dedicate my flush
> To creating confusions of prosody
> And a profusion of parodies
> —Caetano Veloso

Modernity-postmodernity, progression-digression, accumulation-conglomeration, enchantment-disenchantment-re-enchantment, linearity-simplicity-nonlinearity-complexity, patronizing-ingratiating. Gaunt, silent faces screaming hunger alongside high-tech consumerism. Centuries of ragged servitude beside gleaming affluence equal to the best found in Europe and the United States. Upward mobility that repeatedly topples, in Sisyphus fashion, before arriving at the pinnacle of success. Decrepitude below that has never before known any socio-economic mobility at all. Popular art pirated by high brow artists that bask in the international jet-set spotlight. Throughout it all: consonance and dissonance, resonance and syncope, rhythm and arrhythmia, *macho* strutting and supple swaying and swinging in-your-face power moves and subtle *jeitinho* maneuvers. And so on, and so on.

What do you do when it is all there all at once? What do you do when you find bananas and artichokes mix after all? What do you do when something done once is never enough and it must all be done over and over again, yet it is never the same after each and every doing? What do you do with that marvelously real, that profoundly irreal marvel, they call Latin America, and many other things besides? That loquacious, ebullient, exhilarating, undulating, hyperactive mix of *samba* and *tango* and *salsa* and *lambada* and tequila and rum and *pisco* and *cachaça* and cultural guerrillas and *caudillos* and carnivals and minifundia and latifundia and sweatshops and street vending and capital intensive factories and slums and towering apartments and many other things besides? That multidimensional, virtually chaotic, numbingly complex mix of old and new and futuristic and every color and ethnicity that was and is and will have been? That seat of paradise and utopia and purgatory and hell and the source of dreams and idealistic visions and images of the apocalypse? Tell me, please, what do you do? What can you say? How can you say it? How do you cope with what has been called a "veritable logical disaster"? (DaMatta 1994:125).

Nineteenth-century Latin America had its Auguste Comte and Herbert Spencer and others to rationalize and logicize things and bring "Order and Progress." The twentieth century has seen its Marx and Mao and Che and more recently the Chicago school of economics (the "Chicago Boys") and Latin American graduates from the Harvard school of business and and many other heroes and their programs in an attempt to get things on the straight and narrow once and for all. At the same time all the havenots, the disenfranchised, the wretched of the Latin American soil and the *favelados* and all the urban poor, and in addition, all the nimble and subtle cultural guerrillas and wannabe cultural guerrillas, never cease to do their thing, whether passively or subversively. Yet their lot in life remains basically the same, yet worse. Latin America the bad and the beautiful and the fearless and the frightening. It evinces a lingering enchantment of the world and simultaneously a sense of "the horror, the horror," those inscrutable words from the gut by Kurtz in Joseph Conrad's *Heart of Darkness*. Latin America attracts and repels, lures and jilts, mirrors and mocks, patterns and parodies. It is ineffably awesome, awesomely real, mysteriously ethereal, brutally mysterious, and it is incredibly down to earth. It's living paradox.

As far as logic of the venerable Occidental tradition is concerned, what is *is*, and what is not *is not*, and there can be no middle ground. I believe I have provided enough examples to leave you with the sense of cultural "logics" and their subversion of Noncontradiction and the Excluded-Middle. So, Latin America: "living museum" of customs and styles and languages and dialects and ethnicities and races. We have São Paulo that is no longer "hallucinated" as Mário de Andrade (1968 [1922]) once had it, but a gleaming, anomalous fortress of modernism and a nightmare regarding what postmodernism threatens to become. We have once beautiful

Mexico City that is no longer "where the air is clear" in Carlos Fuentes (1960 [1958]) words, following Alfonso Reyes and earlier Alexander von Humboldt, but one of the most nightmarishly congested spots on the planet and a lift of the veil to give a terrifying glimpse of things to come for all cities of the world. One cannot help falling in love with it all and at the same time fearing for the destiny of the entire human species. John F. Kennedy once said that as goes Latin America, so also will go the world. History might yet prove him right.

The absence of linearity in the area's social and institutional make-up, in its people's behavioral patterns, in the variegated manifestations of its culture, in the way its languages are spoken, all this thrown together in a heap with an absurdly singular label attached to it, *LATIN AMERICA*, defies all standard logic and all respectable forms of reason and all history and all the coveted ideas of cumulative advancement, progress, and the good life for all. This tale of three "races," Amerindian, African, European, is a tale of boundaries dissolved, the dissolution of distinctions of physical features and cultural practices and social, economic, and political institutions. If distinctions are completely dissolved, what remains should be virtual homogeny, yet we sense the screaming pitch of heterogeny. And the border of borders, which makes way for the emergence of everything that is, the border of borders, that "emptiness," the zero sign before there is anything at all. This border of borders in Latin America gives rise to a nonlinear "logic" of inclusion more than the customary linear, binary logic of exclusion.

Of course there are plenty of exceptions to the rule. To cite one case, Bonfil's "imaginary Mexico," the Mexico of nineteenth century liberalism, post-Revolutionary practices from the presidency of Plutarco Elías Calles (1924–28) to that of Miguel Alemán (1946–52) and beyond, and the neoliberal practices of Carlos Salinas de Gortari (1988–94) and Ernesto Zedillo (1994–2000) to Vicente Fox (2000–2006). The Mexico of modernization Western style, is exclusionary with a vengeance. "México profundo" is hidden away in the closet by "imaginary Mexico," except insofar as its folk art can be used for the tourist market. Just as nineteenth-century liberals made a gallant effort to interpolate positivism, a strictly philosophical prescriptive doctrine, into the Latin American scene and thus render it a descriptive doctrine, so also in post-Revolutionary Mexico there has been a concerted attempt to ape Western postmodern, neocapitalist consumerist societies and even outdo them whenever possible.

Yet, the inclusionary tendency persists. "México profundo" and all of "América Latina profunda" engage in cultural guerrilla tactics, and other than that they remain there, just below the surface, ready and willing to make their move when the opportunity presents itself. However, the cultures of nineteenth-century liberalism and present-day neoliberalism are far from pure and unadulterated and free of foreign agents. Rather, they are themselves a strange hybrid mix of liberalism and capitalism and corporativism and socialism and feudalism and Thomism and Augustinianism and Marxism and Keynesianism and statism and privitizationism, and many other "isms" besides. There is no relatively simple Louis Dumont hierarchical society nor is there any homogeneous form of egalitarianism. There never was and there never will be any simple dualism of social classes, political institutions, and economic practices, but rather, there is a multiplicity of quite cynical parodies of Western, non-Western, and ancient social, political, and economic programs.

What we have is a nonlinear, *n*-ary set of alternative "logics." "A" or "Not-A" gives way to *Both-And* and *Neither-Nor* and to everything and nothing. I must repeat: it is Funy and Daneri and Maggie and Emmy and Lönny and Tlöny and so on and so on all wrapped into one. It is semiosis at its fluid best. It is like that cultural hybrid of hybrids, the indomitable Caetano Veloso, who somehow gives a sense of the entirety of Brazil's jungles and rivers and parrots and jaguars and anacondas and cities and ultra-modern architecture and baroque monuments and beaches and carnivals and heteroglossia and ethnicities and races condensed into a solitary drop that at every moment threatens to become a black hole and anthropophagically devour the entire planet in one massive gulp.

In the first aphorism that opened this section we have allusion to a Parnassian poem by Olavo Bilac, a text in which the mother tongue is called "the last flowering of Latium," which appears satirically beside "Sambadrome," where the Rio Carnival is commercialized to the hilt. "Powdered Latin" reduces the Portuguese language's roots, Latin, to dust, which is blown about in the wind at random (Perrone 1989:84). What does this language want? What can it do? Everything and nothing. There are no limitations and there is nothing but limitations. It offers itself up, passively, to the caresses of its most attractive lover, and then it turns around and brutally and ruthlessly controls him when given the slightest chance.

In Latin America two and more and still more ethics and ethnicities, as well as multiple aesthetics and multiply contradictory socio-politico-economic policies, can coexist. You can rise from your mat in your adobe and straw hovel as an Amerindian in your local village in the morning, and by evening you can be donning shoes and typical tropical attire and you can easily be taken for a *mestizo*. You can be a rabble-rousing socialist rebel during your college days and fifteen years later a multimillionaire government functionary. You can be a liberal and a socialist and a conservative, as the occasion demands. You can be Catholic and you can belong to a *santería* or *candomblé* or *umbanda* community and you can be an agnostic, whatever happens to be most convenient. You can be patronizing and a cold-hearted capitalist, paternalistic and egalitarian, democratic and authoritarian and dictatorial, dedicated to your family and a jet setter and carouser. You can be all of those things and none of them. It's an extrapolation of "I obey but I do not comply" to the *n*th degree. It's like Jorge Amado's Dona Flor in *Dona Flor and Her Two Husbands* (1969 [1966]) whose first husband—who died but continues to visit her—Vadinho, is a roguish, adventuresome, unpredictable, terribly sinful and terribly exciting, *machista* character. Her second and present husband in the flesh, Teodoro, is polite, proper, and pragmatic; there is for him "A place for everything and everything in its place." Which of the two should she choose? Her phantom but terribly exciting husband, or her rather droll flesh and blood husband? She chooses not to choose. She opts for the two of them and lives a life of contradiction, . . . no, that's not quite it, . . . they become fused in her mind, . . . a hybrid, . . . so, she must realize a synthesis, no? . . . Heavens no!, . . . Never! Then what is it? It's by and large indescribable. It's a "logical disaster," a scandal of reason, a rape of the senses, a slaughter of what would ordinarily go as good taste. It's multiple times and spaces and everything causing and bringing about the emergence of everything else: Kantism gone mad! Repulsive but irresistible. Frightening but appealing.

Since the "logics" by means of which this semiosic process unfolds are radically nonlinear, *rhizomic*, there is always already a new beginning, somewhere, where there is no beginning, no center, and no ending: at the border of borders. Philippe Schmitter (1971:376–77) once observed that the Brazilian situation was virtually impossible to analyze, given its "illogic." The same can pretty much be said of Latin America in general. Marshall Sahlins (1976) writes on the challenge "cultural reason" poses to "practical reason," concluding that it takes on its most powerful form in anthropology, where customary dualisms the likes of mind and matter and realism and idealism become problematic and a *tertium quid* is always lurking around close by and ready for an attack. That *tertium quid* is, precisely, culture, that slayer of those separators of the sheep and the goats of the scientific and philosophical and philological and historical traditions. "Cultural reason" simply refuses to be jam-packed into the inflexible mold of "practical reason," to say nothing of "well reasoned logic." This generalization would appear to be more generally attributable to the Latin American scene than virtually any other cultural milieu on the globe during our times. The ordinary categories of Western thought and practices just don't fly, in spite of the fact that latinamericanists continue to read the entire socio-politico-economic and cultural scene in terms of the right or the left, neoliberalism or statism, nationalism or imperialism, consumerism or conservationism, capitalism or socialism (which remains a viable alternative in many minds in spite of the turns and twists in recent history), and so on. Nevertheless, linear "bourgeois logic" still manages to prevail, in spite of the odds: that supreme odd-couple, "bourgeois logic" and Latin America, that "logical disaster."

Masquerades and carnivals and even everyday life in Latin America are enough to blow this "bourgeois logic" to smithereens. Of the Carnival in Rio tourists ask why all the show of luxury and the afterwaste in a country where there are so many poor people. In terms of standard logic and reason, there is no viable answer. DaMatta gives the enigmatic response that the Carnival exists precisely because there are so many poor people. For a brief period, they can forget, dream, dance and sing, make love, fight to the death. It is the havenots' moment of ritualistic revenge against the haves. Why dwell on misery 365¼ days of the year? Become something that you are not for a while, to remind you that we are all always becoming something other than what we are so our lot in life is not fixed for all time but there is the sneaky hope that somehow, somewhere, somewhen, something else, something better, might lie in store. DaMatta (1994:144) reports on a remark by Joãozinho Trinta, an ex-member of the Samba School of Rio: "Only the intellectuals dwell on poverty, the poor prefer luxury." Carnivals and masquerades are all-inclusive: rules fall by the wayside, virtually anything goes, you can not only be all you can be but also whatever you would like to be. And, it bears mentioning, a few months after Joãozinho Trinta's observation, a military parade staged by the "benign dictatorship," the *dictabranda* ("soft dictatorship") as it was often called, brought national pride, fatherland, patriotism, order and progress to the surface, in a solemn and formal ceremony of *eithers* or *ors* to counteract the *both-ands* and *neither-nors* of the carnival.

Jorge Amado's Dona Flor reveals a fundamentally irresolvable paradox in classical logic and practical reason when she decides to embrace both husbands and thus create the best of all possible worlds, in deciding not to decide, choosing not to choose. This is itself a decision and a choice, of course. But it remains a problem only insofar as linear binary thinking is concerned. Nonlinear, *n*-ary feeling and sensing and becoming can live quite well with such trivial puzzles of the mind, for they follow a "logic" the subtleties of that the mind knows not, . . . that the mind has no chance of knowing, . . . really knowing, . . . or really saying for that matter, . . . for these subtleties are of the body, that is, of bodymind, . . . they are bodymindsigns at their scandalous, bad-ass, in-your-face, disrespectful best, . . . thank you, . . . *Bye, Bye Brazil, Bye Bye Tenochtitlán,* . . . and all the rest of you, . . . at least for now, . . . and have a nice day.[4]

> A borderland is a vague and undetermined place created by the emotional residue of an unnatural boundary. It is in a constant state of transition.
>
> —Gloria Anzaldúa

> The border sites constitute zones of perpetual motion and translation, confrontation of languages and cultures.
>
> —Azade Seyhan

> We're on the border between a land that has forgotten us and another land that doesn't understand us.
>
> —Arturo Islas

> As in mathematical physics, there is an actual physical phenomenon called "the border" that divides Texas from Mexico. Once an imaginary line, "the border" is today often visibly marked by barbed wire and concrete.
>
> —Patricia Seed

Notes

1.   An *autonomous* entity is self-controlled, self-perpetuating, and self-organizing, with no outside help; an *allonomous* entity is just the opposite: it needs some outside controlling agent in order for its function to be carried out (for further, merrell 1996). A living organism is in this respect at least autonomous; a laptop PC that organism is manipulating is allonomous.

2.   I wish to assert at this juncture that the four key terms in Figure 9 do not embody that celebrated and denigrated, that used and abused, Greimassian "semiotic square." The figure is slapped on a flat plane in order for its presentation in book form. However, three dimensions are implied. If we stretch the figure out, twist one end, and connect it with the other end to construct a Möbius strip such that the connection evinces the equivalent of the hairline, the border of borders, the "emptiness,"

between one sphere and another sphere, we have a more faithful picture of what is going on in the fluctuating, flowing arena of semiosis, which includes the swirling triad: homogeny (Firstness), hegemony (Secondness), and heterogeny (Thirdness).

3.   For an anthropological qualification of formal ceremonies, carnival, and masquerade balls as they are described herein, see Leach (1961).

4.   *Bye Bye Brasil* is an allusion to the movie of 1979 directed by Carlos Diegues; *Bye Bye Tenochtitlán* (1991) is the title of a novel by Armando Ramírez, native of Tepito. Tenochtitlán, at the site of present-day Mexico City, was the capital city of the ancient Aztec Empire.

References

Abram, David 1996. *The Spell of the Sensuous: Perception and Language in a More-Than-Human-World*. New York: Vintage.

Ackermann, Robert John. 1988. *Wittgenstein's City*. Amherst: U of Massachusetts P.

Acosta, José de. 1984. *De procurando indorum salute*. Madrid: Consejo Superior de Investigaciones Científicas.

Adorno, Theodor. 1973. *Negative Dialectics*, trans. E. B. Ashton. New York: Seabury.

Agassi, Joseph. 1975. *Science in Flux*. Dordrecht-Holland: D. Reidel.

Aguilar Camín, Héctor. 1988. *Después del milagro*. México: Cal y Arena.

———. 1993. *Subversiones silenciosas*. México: Aguilar.

Aguilar Camín, Héctor, and Lorenzo Meyer. 1989. *A la sombra de la Revolución Mexicana*. México: Cal y Arena.

Agustín, José. 1990. *Tragicomedia mexicana 1: La vida en México de 1940 a 1970*. México: Planeta.

———. 1992. *Tragicomedia mexicana 2: La vida en México de 1970 a 1982*. México: Planeta.

———. 1997. *Tragicomedia mexicana 3: La vida en México de 1982 to 1988*. México: Planeta.

Ainsa, Fernando. 1977. *Los buscadores de la utopía*. Caracas: Monte Ávila.

———. 1986. *Identidad cultural de Iberoamérica en su narrativa*. Madrid: Gredos.

———. 1989. "The Invention of America: Imaginary Signs of the Discovery and Construction of Utopia." *Diogenes* 145, 98–111.

———. 1995. "Identidade e utopia na América Latina." *Tempo Brasileiro* 122/123, 89–105.

Alarcón, Norma. 1989. "*Traddutora, Traditora*: A Paradigmatic Figure of Chicana Feminism." *Cultural Critique* 13, 57–87.

Alba, Víctor. 1969. *The Latin Americans*. New York: Praeger.

Almeder, Robert. 1980. *The Philosophy of Charles S. Peirce*. Totowa: Rowman and Littlefield.

Almeida, Bira. 1986. *Capoeira: A Brazilian Art Form—History, Philosophy and Practice*. Berkeley: North Atlantic.

Althusser, Louis. 1990. *For Marx*, trans. B. Brewster. London: Verso.

Alvar, Manuel. 1992. "Fantastic Tales and Chronicles of the Indies." In *Amerindian Images and the Legacy of Columbus*, R. Jara and N. Spadaccini (eds.), 163–82. Minneapolis: U of Minnesota P.

Alvarenga, Oneyda. 1946. "A influencia negra na música brasileira." *Boletin latino-Americano de Música* 6, 357–407.

Amado, Jorge. 1969. *Dona Flor and Her Two Husbands*, trans. H. de Onís. New York: Knopf.

Andrade, Mario de. 1968. *Hallucinated City*, trans. J. E. Tomlins. Kingsport: Vanderbilt UP.

———. 1984. *Macunaima*, trans E. A. Goodland. New York: Random House.

Andreski, Stanislav. 1966. *Parasitism and Subversion: The Case of Latin America.* New York: Schocken.

Appleby, David P. 1983. *The Music of Brazil.* Austin: U of Texas P.

Aramoni, Aniceto. 1961. *Psicoanálisis de la dinámica de un pueblo.* México: UNAM.

Arens, W. 1979. *The Man-Eating Myth: Anthropology and Anthropophagy.* Oxford: Oxford UP.

Arguedas, José María. 1971. *El zorro de arriba y el zorro de abajo.* Buenos Aires: Losada.

Argueta, Manlio. 1983. *One Day of Life,* trans. B. Brow. New York: Vintage.

Arnheim, Rudolf. 1969. *Visual Thinking.* Berkeley: U of California P.

Baddeley, Oriana, and Valerie Fraser. 1989. *Drawing the Line: Art and Cultural Identity in Contemporary Latin America.* London: Verso.

Baker, Houston A., Jr. 1985. "Caliban's Triple Play." In *"Race," Writing, and Difference,* H. L. Gates, Jr., ed., 381–95. Chicago: U of Chicago P.

Bakhtin, Mikhail. 1981. *The Dialogic Imagination: Four Essays,* trans. C. Emerson and M. Holquist. Austin: U of Texas P.

Balibar, Etienne, and Immanuel Wallerstein. 1991. *Race, Nation, Class: Ambiguous Identities.* London: Verso.

Barager, Joseph R. 1968. *Why Perón Came to Power.* New York: Knopf.

Barbosa, Lívia 1992. *O jeitinho brasileiro: A arte de ser mais igual que os outros.* Rio de Janeiro: Campus.

———. 1995. "The Brazilian *Jeitinho*: An Exercise in National Identity." In *The Brazilian Puzzle: Culture on the Borderlands of the Western World,* D. J. Hess and R. A. DaMatta (eds.), 35–47. New York: Columbia UP.

Barnes, Barry. 1996. *Scientific Knowledge: A Sociological Analysis.* Chicago: U of Chicago P.

Barnes, Barry, and David Edge, eds. 1982. *Science in Context.* Cambridge: MIT.

Barnes, Barry, David Bloor, and John Henry. 1996. *Scientific Knowledge: A Sociological Analysis.* Chicago: U of Chicago P.

Barnet, Miguel, ed. 1968. *The Autobiography of a Runaway Slave.* New York: Pantheon.

Barthes, Roland, 1972. *Mythologies,* trans. A. Lavers. New York: Hill and Wang.

Bartley III, William M. 1984. *The Retreat to Commitment,* 2nd ed. LaSalle: Open Court.

Bartra, Roger. 1992. *The Cage of Melancholy: Identity and Metamorphosis in the Mexican Character,* trans. C. J. Hall. New Brunswick: Rutgers UP.

Bastide, Roger. 1971. *African Civilisations in the New World,* trans. P. Green. London: C. Hurst.

———. 1978. *The African Religions of Brazil: Toward a Sociology of the Interpretation of Civilizations.* Baltimore: Johns Hopkins UP.

Bastos, Eliade Rugai. 1986. "Gilberto Freyre e a questão nacional." In *Inteligência brasileira,* R. Moraes, et al., eds., 43–76. São Paulo: Brasiliense.

Bateson, Gregory. 1972. *Steps to an Ecology of Mind.* New York: Chandler.

———. 1979. *Mind and Nature.* New York: Bantam.

Baudot, Georges. 1996. *México y los albores del discurso colonial*. México: Editorial Patria.

Baudrillard, Jean. 1981. *For a Critique of the Political Economy of the Sign*, trans. C. Levin. St. Louis: Telos.

———. 1983a. *Simulations*. New York: Semiotext(e).

———. 1983b. *In the Shadow of the Silent Majorities*, trans. P. Foss, J. Johnston, and P. Patton. New York: Semiotext(e).

———. 1989. *America*. London: Verso.

Beaud, Michel. 1981. *Histoire du capitalisme de 1500 à nos jours*. Paris: Seuil.

Beezley, William H., Cheryl English Martin, and Willian E. French, eds. 1994. *Rituals of Rule, Rituals of Resistance: Public Celebrations and Popular Culture in Mexico*. Wilmington: Scholarly Resources.

Benítez-Rojo, Antonio. 1994. *The Repeating Island: The Caribbean and the Postmodern Perspective*. Durham: Duke UP.

Benjamin, Thomas. 1996. *A Rich Land, A Poor People: Politics and Society in Modern Chiapas*, rev. ed. Albuquerque: U of New Mexico P.

Berendt, Joachim Ernst. 1988. *The Third Ear: On Listening to the World*. New York: H. Holt.

Berman, Marshall. 1982. *All That is Solid Melts into Air: The Experience of Modernity*. New York: Viking.

Berman, Morris. 1981. *The Reenchantment of the World*. Ithaca: Cornell UP.

Bernstein, Basil. 1975. *Class, Codes and Control: Theoretical Studies Towards a Sociology of Language*. New York: Schocken.

Bernstein, Richard. 1983. *Beyond Objectivism and Relativism: Science, Hermeneutics, and Praxis*. Philadelphia: U of Pennsylvania P.

Beverley, John. 1993. *Against Literature*. Minneapolis: U of Minnesota P.

———. 1999. *Subalternity and Representation: Arguments in Cultural Theory*. Durham: Duke UP.

Beverley, John, and Hugo Achugar, eds. 1992. *La voz del otro: Testimonio, subalternidad y verdad narrativa*. Lima: Latinoamérica Editores.

Bhabha, Homi. 1990a. "DissemiNation: Time, Narrative, and the Margins of the Modern Nation." In *Nation and Narration*, H. Bhabha (ed.), 291–322. New York: Routledge.

———. 1990b. "The Third Space: Interview with Homi Bhabha." In *Identity: Community, Culture, Difference*, J. Rutherford (ed.), 207–21. London: Lawrence and Wishart.

———. 1994. *The Location of Culture*. New York: Routledge.

Bianconi, Lorenzo. 1982. *Music in the Seventeenth Century*, trans. D. Bryant. Cambridge: Cambridge UP.

Birdwhistell, Ray L. 1970. *Kinesics and Context*. New York: Random House.

Black, Max. 1937. "Vagueness, an Exercise in Logical Analysis." *Philosophy of Science* 6, 427–55.

Blacking, John. 1973. *How Musical is Man?* Seattle: U of Washington P.

———. 1995. *Music, Culture, and Experience*, R. Byron (ed.). Chicago: U of Chicago P.

Bloom, Allan. 1987. *The Closing of the American Mind*. New York: Simon and Schuster.

Bloor, David. 1976. *Knowledge and Social Imagery*. London: Routledge and Kegan Paul.

———. 1983. *Wittgenstein: A Social Theory of Knowledge*. New York: Columbia UP.

Boelhower, William. 1988. "Inventing America: A Model of Cartographic Semiosis." *World and Image* 4 (2), 475–509.

Bohm, David. 1980. *Wholeness and the Implicate Order*. London: Routledge and Kegan Paul.

Bohm, David, and B. J. Hiley. 1993. *The Undivided Universe: An Ontological Interpretation of Quantum Theory*. New York: Routledge.

Boler, John. 1964. "Habits of Thought." In *Studies in the Philosophy of Charles Sanders Peirce*, E. C. Moore and R. S. Robin (eds.), 382–400. Amherst: U of Massachussetts P.

Bolton, Herbert Eugene. 1939. *Wider Horizons of American History*. New York: D. Appleton-Century.

Bonavia, F. 1956. *Musicians on Music*. London: Routledge and Kegan Paul.

Bonfil Batalla, Guillermo. 1996. *México Profundo: Reclaiming a Civilization*, trans. P. A. Dennis. Austin: U of Texas P.

Borge, Tomás Martínez. 1983. "The Sandinistas." *Playboy* 9 (September), 57–68, 140, 188–200.

Borges, Jorge Luis. 1962. *Labyrinths, Selected Stories and Other Writings*, D. A. Yates and J. E. Irby (eds.). New York: New Directions.

———. 1964a. *Other Inquisitions, 1937–1952*, trans. R. L. C. Simms. Austin: U of Texas P.

———. 1964b. *Dreamtigers*, trans. M. Boyer and H. Morland. Austin: U of Texas P.

———. 1970. *The Aleph and Other Stories, 1933–1969*, trans. N. T. de Giovanni. New York: E. P. Dutton.

———. 1978. *The Book of Sand*, trans. N. T. di Giovanni. New York: E. P. Dutton.

Botz, Dan la. 1995. *Democracy in Mexico: Peasant Rebellion and Political Reform*. Boston: South End P.

Bourdieu, Pierre. 1977. *Outline of a Theory of Practice*. Cambridge: Cambridge UP.

———. 1990a. *The Logic of Practice*. Cambridge: Polity.

———. 1990b. *In Other Words: Essays Towards a Reflexive Sociology*. Cambridge: Polity.

Bourdieu, Pierre, and J.-C. Passeron. 1977. *Reproduction in Education, Society and Culture*. London: Sage.

Bouvard, Marguerite Guzman. 1994. *Revolutionizing Motherhood: The Mothers of the Plaza de Mayo*. Wilmington: Scholarly Resources.

Brading, David A. 1980. *Origen del nacionalismo mexicano*. México: Era.

———. 1988. *Mito y profecía en la historia de México*, trans. T. Segovia. México: Vuelta.

Braidotti, Rosi. 1991. *Patterns of Dissonance: A Study of Women in Contemporary Philosophy*, trans. E. Guild. New York: Routledge.

Brandes, Stanley. 1981. "Like Wounded Stags: Male Sexual Ideology in an Andalusian Town." In *Sexual Meanings*, S. Ortner and H. Whitehead (eds.), 216–39. Cambridge: Cambridge UP.

Brandon, George. 1993. *Santeria from Africa to the New World: The Dead Sell Memories*. Bloomington: Indiana UP.

Brenner, Anita. 1929. *Idols Behind Altars*. New York: Harcourt, Brace.

Brito, Brasil Rocha. 1993. "Bossa Nova." In *Balanço da bossa, e outras bossas*, A. de Campos, ed., 17–40. São Paulo: Perspectiva.

Brock, Jarrett E. 1979. "Principle Themes in Peirce's Logic of Vagueness." In *Peirce Studies I*, J. E. Brock, et al. (eds.), 41–50. Lubbock: Institute for Studies in Pragmaticism.

Brown, James Robert. 1991. *The Laboratory of the Mind: Thought Experiments in the Natural Sciences*. New York: Routledge.

———. 1994. *Smoke and Mirrors: How Science Reflects Society*. New York: Routledge.

Browning, Barbara. 1995. *Samba: A Body Articulate*. Bloomington: Indiana UP.

Bruhns, Heloisa Turini. 2000. *Futebol, carnaval e capoeira: Entre as gingas do corpo brasileiro*. Campinas: Papirus.

Bruner, Jerome. 1956. *A Study of Thinking*. New York: Wiley.

———. 1986. *Actual Minds, Possible Worlds*. Cambridge: Harvard UP.

———. 1987. *Making Sense: The Child's Construction of the World*. London: Methuen.

Brusco, Elizabeth E. 1995. *The Reformation of Machismo: Evangelical Conversion and Gender in Colombia*. Austin: U of Texas P.

Burgos-Debray, Elisabeth, ed. 1984. *I, Rigoberta Menchú*, trans. A. Wright. London: Verso.

Burkholder, Mark A., and Lyman J. Johnson. 1994. *Colonial Latin America*. New York: Oxford UP.

Bushnell, David. 1988. *The Emergence of Latin America in the Nineteenth Century*. New York: Oxford UP.

Butler, Judith, Ernesto Laclau, and Slavoj Zizek. 2000. *Contingency, Hegemony, Universality: Contemporary Dialogues on the Left*. London: Verso.

Cabezas, Omar. 1985. *Fire from the Mountain: The Making of a Sandinista*. New York: Crown.

Cabrera, Lydia. 1986. *El monte, igbo, finda, ewe orisha, vititi nfinda: Notas sobre las religiones, la magia, las supersticiones y el folklore de los negros criollos y el pueblo de Cuba*. Miami: Chicherekú.

Cabrera Infante, Gabriel. 1971. *Three Trapped Tigers*, trans. D. Gardner and S. J. Levine. New York: Harper and Row.

Campa, Román de la. 1999. *Latin Americanism*. Minneapolis: U of Minnesota P.

Campos, Augusto de. 1993. *Balanço da Bossa, e outras bossas*. São Paulo: Perspectiva.

Campos, Haroldo de. 1986. "The Role of Anthropophagy: Europe under the Sign of Devoration," trans. M. T. Wolff. *Latin American Literary Review* 14 (27), 42–60.

Campos, Julieta. 1995. *¿Qué hacemos con los pobres?* México: Aguilar.

Capoeira, Néstor. 1981. *O pequeno manual do jogador de capoeira*. São Paulo: Ground.

———. 1985. *Galo já cantou*. Rio de Janeiro: Arte Hoje.

———. 1992. *Capoeira: Os fundamentos da malícia*. Rio de Janeiro: Record.

Capra, Fritjof. 1975. *The Tao of Physics: An Exploration of the Parallels Between Modern Physics and Eastern Mysticism*. Berkeley: Shambhala.

———. 1996. *The Web of Life*. New York: Anchor.

Cardoso, Fernando Enrique, and E. Faletto. 1979. *Dependency and Development in Latin America*. Berkeley: U of California P.

Careaga, Gabriel. 1987. *Biografía de un joven de la clase media*. México: Océano.

———. 1992. *La ciudad enmascarada*. México: Cal y Arena.

Carneiro, Edison. 1986. *Candomblés da Bahia*. Rio de Janeiro: Civilização Brasileira.

Carpentier, Alejo. 1957. *The Kingdom of this World*, trans. H. de Onís. New York: Knopf.

———. 1980. *Ese músico que llevo dentro*. Habana: Letras Cubanas.

Carrión, Jorge. 1952. *Mito y magia del mexicano*. México: Obregón y Porrúa.

Casas, Bartolomé de las. 1942. *Del único modo de atraer a todos los pueblos a la verdadera religión*. México: Fondo de Cultura Económica.

Caso, Antonio. 1941. *Positivismo, neopositivismo y fenomenología*. México: Centro de Estudios Filosóficos de la Facultad de Filosofía y Letras.

Castañeda, Jorge G. 1994. *Utopia Unarmed: The Latin American Left After the Cold War*. New York: Random House.

———. 1995. *The Mexican Shock: Its Meaning for the U.S.* New York: The New Press.

Castro, Fidel. 1962. *History Will Absolve Me*. London: Jonathan Cape.

Castro, Ruy. 1990. *Chega de saudade: A história e as histórias da bossa nova*. São Paulo: Schwarcz.

Cataldi, Sue L. 1993. *Emotion, Depth, and Flesh: A Study of Sensitive Space*. Albany: State U of New York P.

Certeau, Michel de. 1984. *The Practice of Everyday Life*. Berkeley: U of California P.

Cevallos-Candau, Francisco Javier. 1994a. "Introduction." In *Coded Encounters: Writing, Gender, and Ethnicity in Colonial Latin America*, J. J. Cevallos-Candau, et al. (eds.), 1–11. Amherst: U of Massachusetts P.

Cevallos-Candau, Francisco Javier, and Jeffrey A. Cole, Nina M. Scott, and Nicomedes Suárez-Aráúz, eds. 1994b. *Coded Encounters: Writing, Gender, and Ethnicity in Colonial Latin America*. Amherst: U of Massachusetts P.

Chaffin, Joshua. 1996. "Nafta Grows Up." *US/Mexico Business* 3, No. 7 (Dec.), 54–60.

Chanady, Amaryll Beatrice. 1985. *Magical Realism and the Fantastic: Resolved versus Unresolved Antinomy*. New York: Garland.

———. 1994. "Introduction." In *Latin American Identity and Constructions of Difference*, A. Chanady, ed., i–xlvi. Minneapolis: U of Minnesota P.

Chaui, Marilena. 1986. *Conformismo e resistência: Aspectos da cultura popular no Brasil*. São Paulo: Brasiliense.

Chernoff, John Miller. 1979. *African Rhythm and African Sensibility*. Chicago: U of Chicago P.

Classen, Constance. 1993. *Worlds of Sense: Exploring the Senses in History and Across Cultures*. New York: Routledge.

Clément, Catherine. 1994. *Syncope: The Philosophy of Rapture*, trans. S. O'Driscoll and D. M. Mahoney. Minneapolis: U of Minnesota P.

Clifford, James. 1990. "On Collecting Art and Culture." In *Out There: Marginalization and Contemporary Cultures*, R. Ferguson, et al. (eds.), 141–69. Cambridge: MIT P.

Coe, Ralph T. 1986. *Lost and Found Traditions*. Seattle: U of Washington P.

Coelho, Teixeira. 1995. *Moderno PósModerno*. São Paulo: Iluminuras.

Colapietro, Vincent. 1989. *Peirce's Approach to the Self: A Semiotic Perspective on Human Subjectivity*. Albany: State U of New York P.

Colás, Santiago. 1994. *Postmodernity in Latin America*. Durham: Duke UP.

Colchero, Ana. 1996. "Ana Colchero explica por qué dejó *Nada Personal*." *TV Notas* 67, December 27, 17–18.

Cole, K. C. 1984. *Sympathetic Vibrations: Reflections on Physics as a Way of Life*. New York: William Morrow.

Collor de Mello, Fernando. (Interview). 1998. "Collor diz que vota em Lula no segundo turno." *Folha de São Paulo*, June 9, 2–8.

Comaroff, John L. 1985. *Body of Power, Spirit of Resistance: The Culture and History of a South African People*. Chicago: U of Chicago P.

Comaroff, John L., and Jean Comaroff. 1992. *Ethnography and the Historical Imagination*. Boulder: Westview.

Condon, William S., and W. D. Ogston. 1971. "Speech and Body Motion Synchrony of Speaker-Hearer." In *Perception of Language*, D. L. Horton and J. J. Jenkins (eds.), 150–73. Columbus: Charles E. Merrill.

Condon, William S., and L. W. Sander. 1974. "Neonate Movement Is Synchronized with Adult Speech: Interactional Participation and Language Acquisition." *Science* 183, 221–35.

Copeland, Aaron. 1939. *What to Listen for in Music*. New York: McGraw-Hill.

Coronil, Fernando. 1989. "Discovering America Again: The Politics of Selfhood in the Age of Post-Colonial Empires." *Dispositio* 14 (36/38), 315–31.

———. 1996. "Beyond Occidentalism: Toward Nonimperial Geohistorical Categories." *Cultural Anthropology* 11 (1), 52–87.

Corrington, Robert. 1994. *Ecstatic Naturalism: Signs of the World*. Bloomington: Indiana UP.

Cortázar, Julio. 1966. *Hopscotch*, trans. G. Rabassa. New York: Random House.

Costa, Newton C. A. da. 1974. "On the Theory of Inconsistent Formal Systems." *Notre Dame Journal of Formal Logic* 15, 497–510.

Coutinho, Afrânio. 1969. *An Introduction to Literature in Brazil*. New York: Columbia UP.

Cumberland, Charles Curtis. 1952. *Mexican Revolution: Genesis under Madero*. New York: Greenwood.

Cunha, Euclides da. 1944. *Rebellion in the Backlands*. Chicago: U of Chicago P.

Cypess, Sandra Messinger. 1991. *La Malinche in Mexican Literature: From History to Myth*. Austin: U of Texas P.

DaMatta, Roberto. 1984. *O que faz o brasil, Brasil?* Rio de Janeiro: Rocco.

———. 1986. *Explorações: Ensaios de sociologia interpretativa*. Rio de Janeiro: Rocco.

———. 1991. *Carnivals, Rogues, and Heroes: An Interpretation of the Brazilian Dilemma*, trans. J. Drury. Notre Dame: U of Notre Dame P.

———. 1994. *Conta de mentiroso: Siete ensaios de antropologia brasileiro*, 2d ed. Rio de Janeiro: Rocco.

———. 1995. "For an Anthropology of the Brazilian Tradition, Or, 'A Virtude está no Meio." In *The Brazilian Puzzle: Culture on the Borderlands of the Western World*, D. J. Hess and R. A. DaMatta, eds., 270–91. New York: Columbia UP.

Dantzig, Tobias. 1930. *Number: The Language of Science*, 4th ed. New York: Free Press.

Davidson, Donald. 1984. *Inquiries into Truth and Interpretation*. Oxford: Clarendon.

Dealy, Glen Caudill. 1992. *The Latin Americans: Spirit and Ethos*. Boulder: Westview.

Debray, Régis. 1996. "Régis Debray subraya la advertencia del 'profeta' Marcos." *Proceso* 1019 (May 13), 6–16.

Deleuze, Gilles. 1978. "Philosophie et minorité." *Critique* 369, 154–55.

———. 1990. *The Logic of Sense*. New York: Columbia UP.

———. 1993. *The Fold: Leibniz and the Baroque*, trans. T. Conley. Minneapolis: Minnesota UP.

———. 1994. *Difference and Repetition*. New York: Columbia UP.

Deleuze, Gilles, and Félix Guattari. 1983. *Anti-Oedipus: Capitalism and Schizophrenia, I*. Minneapolis: U of Minnesota P.

———. 1986. *Kafka: Toward a Minor Literature*, trans. D. Polan. Minneapolis: U of Minnesota P.

———. 1987. *A Thousand Plateaus: Capitalism and Schizophrenia II*, trans. B. Massumi. Minneapolis: U of Minnesota P.

DeLong, Howard. 1970. *A Profile of Mathematical Logic*. New York: Addison Wesley.

Derrida, Jacques. 1973. *Speech and Phenomena, and Other Essays on Husserl's Theory of Signs*, trans. D. B. Allison. Evanston: Northwestern UP.

———. 1974. *Of Grammatology*, trans. G. C. Spivak. Baltimore: Johns Hopkins UP.

———. 1980. *Positions*, trans. A. Bass. London: Athlone.

———. 1981. *Disseminations*, trans. B. Johnson. London: Athlone.

Díaz-Guerrero, Rogelio. 1975. *Psychology of the Mexican: Culture and Personality*. Austin: U of Texas P.

Dobbs, B. J. T. 1975. *The Foundations of Newton's Alchemy*. Cambridge: Cambridge UP.

Docker, John. 1994. *Postmodernism and Popular Culture: A Cultural History*. Cambridge: Cambridge UP.

Draper, Theodore. 1965. *Castroism: Theory and Practice*. New York: Praeger.

Duhem, Pierre. 1954. *The Aim and Structure of Physical Theory*, trans. P. P. Wiener. Princeton: Princeton UP.

Dumont, Louis. 1977. *From Mandelville to Marx: The Genesis and Triumph of Economic Ideology*. Chicago: U of Chicago P.

———. 1980. *Homo Hierarchicus*, trans. M. Sainsbury et al., rev. ed. Chicago: U of Chicago P.

———. 1986. *Essays on Individualism: Modern Ideology in Anthropological Perspective*. Chicago: U of Chicago P.

Dussel, Enrique. 1998. "Beyond Eurocentrism: The World-System and the Limits of Modernity." In *The Cultures of Globalization*, F. Jameson and M. Miyoshi (eds.), 3–30. Durham: Duke UP.

Dwyer, Augusta. 1994. *On the Line: Life on the US-Mexican Border*. Nottingham: Russell Press.

Eco, Umberto. 1976. *A Theory of Semiotics*. Bloomington: Indiana UP.

———. 1984. *Semiotics and the Philosophy of Language*. Bloomington: Indiana UP.

———. 1986. *Travels in Hyperreality*. London: Picador.

Engel-Tiercelin, Claudine. 1992. "Vagueness and the Unity of C. S. Peirce's Realism." *Transactions of the Charles S. Peirce Society* 28 (1), 51–82.

Epstein, Jack, and Tim Padgett. 1997. "Breaking Taboos." *Time* (149, June 2), 36–40.

Ercilla y Zúñiga, Alonzo de. 1945. *The Araucaniad*. Nashville: Vanderbilt UP.

Evnine, Simon. 1991. *Donald Davidson*. Stanford: Stanford UP.

EZLN. 1994. "Versión de Propuesta del EZLN para que se inicie el diálogo." *La Jornada* (11 January), 10.

———. 1995. "Declaration from the Lacandon Jungle." In *The Postmodern Debate in Latin America*, J. Beverley, M. Aronna and J. Oviedo (eds.), 311–13. Durham: Duke UP.

Fann, K. T. 1970. *Peirce's Theory of Abduction*. The Hague: Martinus Nijhoff.

Fay, Brian. 1996. *Contemporary Philosophy of Social Science*. Oxford: Blackwell.

Fernandes, Florestan. 1958. *A etnologia e a sociologia no Brasil*. Spain: Anhambi.

Fernández Retamar, Roberto. 1989. *Caliban and Other Essays*, trans. E. Baker. Minneapolis: U of Minnesota P.

Feyerabend, Paul K. 1975. *Against Method*. London: NLB.

Figueiredo, Luis. 2000. *Morcegos negros*. Rio de Janeiro: Record.

Figueiredo Ferretti, Sérgio. 1999. 'Sincretismo afro-brasileiro e resistência cultural'. In *Faces da tradição afro-brasileiro*, C. Caroso and J. Bacelar (eds.), 113–30. Rio de Janeiro: Pallas.

Finer, Samuel E. 1988. *The Man on Horseback: The Role of the Military in Politics*. Boulder: Westview.

Fischer, E. 1963. *The Necessity of Art*. Harmondsworth: Penguin.

Fischer, Roland. 1990. "Why the Mind is not in the Head but in the Society's Connectionist Networks." *Diogenes* (151), 1–28.

Fiske, John. 1989a. *Reading the Popular*. New York: Routledge.

———. 1989b. *Understanding Popular Culture*. New York: Routledge.

Flanagan, Owen. 1992. *Consciousness Reconsidered*. Cambridge: MIT.

Florescano, Enrique, ed. 1995. *Mitos mexicanos*. México: Aguilar.

Foley, Barbara. 1986. *Telling the Truth: The Theory and Practice of Documentary Fiction*. Ithaca: Cornell UP.

Folse, Henry J. 1985. *The Philosophy of Niels Bohr: The Framework of Complementarity*. Amsterdam: North Holland.

Fontana, Benedetto. 1993. *Hegemony and Power: On the Relation between Gramsci and Machiavelli*. Minneapolis: U of Minnesota P.

Foster, Susan Leigh. 1986. *Reading Dancing: Bodies and Subjects in Contemporary American Dance*. Berkeley: U of California P.

Foucault, Michel. 1970. *The Order of Things: An Archaeology of the Human Sciences*. New York: Pantheon.

Frank, Andre Gunder. 1967. *Capitalism and Underdevelopment in Latin America*. New York: Monthly Review P.

Frank, Waldo. 1929. *The Re-Discovery of America*. New York: Charles Scribner's Sons.

Freyre, Gilberto. 1946. *The Masters and the Slaves*, trans. S. Putnam. New York: Knopf.

Frow, John. 1995. *Cultural Studies and Cultural Value*. Oxford: Clarendon.

Fryer, Peter. 2000. *Rhythms of Resistance: African Musical Heritage in Brazil*. Hanover: Wesleyan UP.

Fuentes, Carlos. 1960. *Where the Air is Clear*, trans. S. Hileman. New York: Farrar, Straus and Giroux.

———. 1964. *The Death of Artemio Cruz*, trans. S. Hileman. New York: Farrar, Straus and Giroux.

———. 1971. *Tiempo mexicano*. México: Joaquín Mortiz.

———. 1976. *Cervantes: O, la lectura de la crítica*. México: Joaquín Mortiz.

———. 1988a. "Bienvenidos a la mexistroika." *Cambio 16* 878 (Sept. 26), 58–64.

———. 1988b. *Myself and Others: Selected Essays*. New York: Farrar, Straus and Giroux.

———. 1989. *Christopher Unborn*, trans. A. MacAdam. New York: Farrar Straus Giroux.

———. 1990. *Valiente mundo nuevo: Épica, utopía y mito en la novela hispanoamericana*. México: Fondo de Cultura Económica.

Furtado, Celso. 1970. *Economic Development of Latin America*. Cambridge: Cambridge UP.

Fusco, Coco. 1995. *English is Broken Here: Notes on Cultural Fusion in the Americas*. New York: The New Press.

Fuser, Igor. 1995. *México em transe*. São Paulo: Páginas Abertas.

Gadamer, Hans-Georg. 1975. *Truth and Method*. New York: Crossroads.

Galileo Galilei. 1967. *Dialogue Concerning the Two Chief World Systems*, trans. S. Drake, 2nd ed. Berkeley: U of California P.

Gallegos, Rómulo. 1942. *Dona Barbara*. New York: Appleton-Century-Crofts.

García Canclini, Néstor. 1984. "Gramsci con Bourdieu." *Nueva Sociedad* 71, 45–62.

———. 1992. "Cultural Conversions." In *On Edge: The Crisis of Contemporary Latin American Culture*, G. Yúdice, ed., 29–44. Minneapolis: U of Minnesota P.

———. 1993. *Transforming Modernity: Popular Culture in Mexico*, trans. L. Lozano. Austin: U of Texas P.

———. 1995. *Hybrid Cultures: Strategies for Entering and Leaving Modernity*, trans. C. L. Chiappari and S. L. López. Minneapolis: U of Minnesota P.

García Márquez, Gabriel. 1970. *One Hundred Years of Solitude*, trans. G. Rabassa. New York: Harper and Row.

———. 1983. *Chronicle of a Death Foretold*, trans. G. Rabassa. New York: Knopf.

Gärdenfors, Peter. 1994. "Induction, Conceptual Spaces, and AI." In *Grue! the New Riddle of Induction*, D. Stalker, ed., 117–34. LaSalle: Open Court.

Gasché, Rodolphe. 1986. *The Tain of the Mirror: Derrida and the Philosophy of Reflection*. Cambridge: Harvard UP.

Geertz, Clifford. 1973. *The Interpretation of Cultures*. New York: Basic Books.

———. 1983. *Local Knowledge: Further Essays in Interpretive Anthropology*. New York: Basic Books.

———. 2000. *Available Light: Anthropological Reflections on Philosophical Topics*. Princeton: Princeton UP.

Gellner, Ernest. 1992. *Reason and Culture: The Historic Role of Rationality and Rationalism*. Oxford: Blackwell.

Gibbins, Peter. 1987. *Particles and Paradoxes: The Limits of Quantum Logic*. Cambridge: Cambridge UP.

Gibson, Charles. 1966. *Spain in America*. New York: Harper and Row.

Gillin, John. 1955. "Ethos Components in Modern Latin American Culture." *American Anthropologist* 57 (3), 488–500.

Gilmore, Margaret M., and David D. Gilmore. 1979. "Machismo: A Psychodynamic Approach (Spain)." *Journal of Psychological Anthropology* 2/3, 281–99.

Glantz, Margo. 1995. "La Malinche: La lengua en la mano." In *Mitos mexicanos*, E. Florescano, ed., 119–37. México: Aguilar.

Gluck, Sherna, and Daphne Patai. 1991. *Women's Words: The Feminist Practice of Oral History*. New York: Routledge.

Goldwert, Marvin. 1980. *History as Neurosis: Paternalism and Machismo in Spanish America*. Lanham: University Press of America.

Gómez-Peña, Guillermo. 1996. *The New World Border*. San Francisco: City Lights.

Gonçalves Silva, Vagner. 1999. 'Reafricanização e Sincretismo: Interpretações Acadêmicas e Experiências Religiosas'. In *Faces da tradição afro-brasileira*, ed. C. Caroso and J. Bacelar. Rio de Janeiro: Pallas.

Gonçalves da Silva, Vagner. 1994. *Candomblé e Umbanda: Caminhos de Devoção*. São Paulo: Ática.

González-Wippler, Migene. 1989. *Santería: The Religion, A Legacy of Faith, Rites, and Magic*. New York: Harmony.

Góngora, Mario. 1951. *El estado en el derecho indiano: época de fundación (1492–1570)*. Santiago: Instituto de Investigaciones Histórico-Culturales.

Goodman, Nelson. 1965. *Fact, Fiction and Forecast*. Indianapolis: Bobbs-Merrill.

———. 1978. *Ways of Worldmaking*. Indianapolis: Hackett.

Goswami, Amit. 1993. *The Self-Aware Universe: How Consciousness Creates the Material World*. New York: G. P. Putnam's Sons.

Gould, Stephen Jay. 1980. *The Panda's Thumb*. New York: W. W. Norton.

Gramsci, Antonio. 1992. *Prison Notebooks*, trans. J. A. Buttigieg. New York: Columbia UP.

Greenblat, Stephen. 1991. *Marvelous Possessions: The Wonder of the New World*. Chicago: U of Chicago P.

Grenet, Emilio. 1939. *Popular Cuban Music*. Havana: Ministry of Education.

Griffin, David Ray. 1988a. "Introduction: The Reenchantment of Science." In *The Reenchantment of Science: Postmodern Proposals*, D. R. Griffin, ed., 1–46. Albany: State U of New York P.

———, ed. 1988b. *The Reenchantment of Science: Post-Modern Proposals*. Albany: State U of New York P.

Griffin, David Ray, *et al.* 1993. *Founders of Constructive Postmodern Philosophy: Peirce, James, Bergson, Whitehead, and Hartshorne*. Albany: State U of New York P.

Guevara, Ernesto. 1968. *Episodes of the Cuban Revolutionary War 1956–58*. New York: International Publishers.

Gugelberger, Georg M., ed. 1996. *The Real Thing: Testimonial Discourse and Latin America*. Durham: Duke UP.

Guha, Ranajit. 1988. "Preface." In *Selected Subaltern Studies*, R. Guha and G. Spivak, eds. New York: Oxford UP.

Guillermoprieto, Alma. 1991. *Samba*. New York: Random House.

———. 1994a. *The Heart That Bleeds*. New York: Random House.

———. 1994b. "Zapata's Heirs." *New Yorker* (70, May 16), 52–63.

———. 1996. "Mexico: Murder Without Justice." *The New York Review,* October 3, 31–36.

Guimarães Rosa, João. 1963. *The Devil to Pay in the Backlands*, trans. J. L. Taylor and H. de Onís. New York: Knopf.

Gutmann, Matthew C. 1996. *The Meanings of Macho: Being a Man in Mexico City*. Berkeley: U of California P.

Hacking, Ian. 1985. "Styles of Scientific Reasoning." In *Post-Analytic Philosophy*, J. Rajchman and C. West (eds.), 145–65. New York: Columbia UP.

Hagen, Steve. 1995. *How the World Can Be the Way it Is*. Wheaton, IL: Quest Books.

Hall, Edward T. 1983. *The Dance of Life: The Other Dimension of Time*. New York: Doubleday.

Hall, Stuart. 1981. "Notes on Deconstructing 'The Popular.'" In *People's History and Socialist Theory*, R. Samuel (ed.), 227–40. London: Routledge and Kegan Paul.

Hamill, Hugh M. 1992. *Caudillos: Dictators in Spanish America*. Norman: U of Oklahoma P.

Hamilton, Bernice. 1963. *Political Thought in Sixteenth-Century Spain*. Oxford: Clarendon.

Hanke, Lewis. 1949. *The Spanish Struggle for Justice in the Conquest of America*. Philadelphia: U of Pennsylvania P.

———.1959. *Aristotle and the American Indians*. Chicago: U of Chicago P.

Hanson, Norwood R. 1958. *Patterns of Discovery*. Cambridge: Cambridge UP.

———.1969. *Perception and Discovery*. San Francisco: Freeman, Cooper.

Harris, Olivia. 1978. "Complementarity and Conflict: An Andean View of Women and Men." In *Sex and Age As Principles of Social Differentiation*, J. S. LaFontaine, ed., 21–40. New York: Academic Press.

Hart, Mickey (with Jay Stevens). 1990. *Drumming Magic: A Journey into the Spirit of Percussion*. New York: HarperCollins.

Hartshorne, Charles. 1970. *Creative Synthesis and Philosophic Method*. LaSalle: Open Court.

Harvey, David. 1989. *The Condition of Postmodernity: An Enquiry into the Origins of Cultural Change*. Oxford: Basil Blackwell.

Harvey, Neil. 1998. *The Chiapas Rebellion: The Struggle for Land and Democracy*. Durham: Duke UP.

Hastrup, Kirsten. 1995. *A Passage to Anthropology: Between Experience and Theory*. New York: Routledge.

Haya de la Torre, Víctor Raúl. 1948. *Espacio-tiempo histórico*. Lima: La Tribuna.

Hayward, Jeremy W. 1984. *Perceiving Ordinary Magic*. Boulder: Shambhala.

———. 1987. *Shifting Worlds, Changing Minds*. Boston: Shambhala.

Heidegger, Martin. 1969. *Identity and Difference*. New York: Harper and Row.

Hempel, Carl. 1945. "Studies in the Logic of Confirmation." *Mind* 54, 1–26 & 97–121.

Hess, David J., and Roberto A. DaMatta. 1995. "Introduction." In *The Brazilian Puzzle: Culture on the Borderlands of the Western World*, D. J. Hess and R. A. DaMatta, eds. New York: Columbia UP.

Hesse, Mary. 1966. *Models and Analogies in Science*. Notre Dame: U of Notre Dame P.

———. 1969. "Ramifications of 'Grue'." *British Journal of the Philosophy of Science* 20, 13–25.

———. 1980. *Revolutions and Reconstructions in the Philosophy of Science*. Bloomington: Indiana UP.

Hicks, Emily D. 1991. *Border Writing: The Multidimensional Text*. Minneapolis: U of Minnesota P.

Hodier, André. 1975. *Jazz: Its Evolution and Essence*. New York: De Capo.

Hoffman, Banesh. 1972. *Albert Einstein: Creator and Rebel*. New York: Viking.

Hofstadter, Douglas. 1979. *Gödel, Escher, Bach: An Eternal Golden Braid*. New York: Basic.

Holanda, Sérgio Buarque de. 1935. *Raízes do Brasil*. Rio de Janeiro: José Olympio.

Hollander, Nancy Caro. 1997. *Love in a Time of Hate: Liberation Psychology in Latin America*. New Brunswick: Rutgers UP.

Honner, John. 1987. *The Description of Nature: Niels Bohr and the Philosophy of Quantum Physics*. Oxford: Clarendon.

Hookway, Christopher. 1985. *Peirce*. London: Routledge and Kegan Paul.

Hopenhayn, Martín. 1995. "Postmodernism and Neoliberalism in Latin America." In *The Postmodernism Debate in Latin America*, J. Beverley, et al. (eds.), 97–109. Durham: Duke UP.

Hornbostel, Erich M. von. 1928. "African Negro Music." *Africa* 1, 30–62.

Howes, David. ed. 1991. *The Varieties of Sensory Experience: A Sourcebook in the Anthropology of the Senses*. Toronto: U of Toronto P.

Huntington, C. W., Jr. 1989. *The Emptiness of Emptiness*. Honolulu: U of Hawai'i P.

Inman, Samuel Guy. 1942. *Latin America: Its Place in World Life*. New York: Harcourt Brace.

Irigaray, Luce. 1985. *That Sex which is not One*. New York: Cornell UP.

James, William. 1950. *The Principles of Psychology*. 2 vols. New York: Dover.

Jameson, Fredric. 1984. "Postmodernism, Or, The Cultural Logic of Late Capitalism." *New Left Review* 146, 59–92.

———. 1988. "Cognitive Mapping." In *Marxism and the Interpretation of Culture*, C. Nelson and L. Grossberg, eds., 347–57. Urbana: U of Illinois P.

———. 1989. "Foreword." In *Caliban and Other Essays*, by Roberto Fernández Retamar, *vii–xii*. Minneapolis: U of Minnesota P.

JanMohamed, Abdul R. 1985. "The Economy of Manichean Allegory: The Function of Racial Difference in Colonialist Literature." In *"Race," Writing, and Difference*, H. L. Gates, Jr., ed., 78–106. Chicago: U. of Chicago P.

Jara, René, and Nicholas Spadaccini. 1992a. "The Construction of a Colonial Imaginary: Columbus's Signature." In *Amerindian Images and the Legacy of Columbus*, R. Jara and N. Spadaccini, eds., 1–95. Minneapolis: U of Minnesota P.

———, eds. 1992b. *Amerindian Images and the Legacy of Columbus*. Minneapolis: U of Minnesota P.

Jay, Martin. 1993. *Force Fields: Between Intellectual History and Cultural Critique*. New York: Routledge.

Jenkins, Henry. 1992. *Textual Poachers: Television Fans and Participatory Cultures*. New York: Routledge.

Johnson, John J. 1958. *Political Change in Latin America: The Emergence of the Middle Sectors*. Stanford: Stanford UP.

Kalupahana, David J. 1986. *Nagarjuna: The Philosophy of the Middle Way*. Albany: State U of New York P.

Kant, Immanuel. 1983. *Perpetual Peace and Other Essays*, trans. T. Humphrey. Indianapolis: Hackett.

Kapleau, Philip. 1979. *Zen: Dawn in the West*. Garden City: Anchor.

Katzenberger, Elaine. 1995. *First World Ha! Ha! Ha!: The Zapatista Challenge*. San Francisco: City Lights.

Kellman, Steven G. 1991. "Translingualism and the Literary Imagination." *Criticism* 33 (4), 527–41.

Khawan, R. K., ed. 1976. *Le livre des ruses. La Stratégie politique des Arabes*. Paris: Phébus.

Kline, Morris. 1980. *Mathematics: The Loss of Certainty*. Oxford: Oxford UP.

Koertge, Noretta. 1998. *A House Built on Sand: Exposing Postmodern Myths about Science*. New York: Oxford UP.

Kosko, Bart. 1993. *Fuzzy Thinking*. New York: Hyperion.

Kottak, Conrad Phillip. 1990. *Prime Time Society: An Anthropological Analysis of Television and Culture*. Belmont, CA: Wadsworth.

Kraniauskis, John. 2000. "Hybridity in a Transnational Frame: Latin American-ist and Postcolonial Perspectives on Cultural Studies." *Nepantla* 1 (2), 111–37.

Krige, John. 1980. *Science, Revolution, and Discontinuity.* Atlantic Highlands, NJ: Harvester P.

Kuhn, Thomas S. 1970. *The Structure of Scientific Revolutions.* Chicago: U of Chicago P.

Laban, Rudolf. 1960. *The Mastery of Movement.* London: MacDonald and Evans.

Labov, William. 1972. *Language in the Inner City: Studies in the Black English Vernacular.* Philadelphia: U of Pennsylvania P.

Laclau, Ernesto. 1977. *Politics and Ideology in Marxist Theory: Capitalism—Rascism—Populism.* London: Verso.

Laclau, Ernesto, and Chantal Mouffe. 1985. *Hegemony and Socialist Strategy: Towards a Radical Democratic Politics.* London: Verso.

Lafaye, Jacques. 1976. *Quetzalcóatl and Guadalupe: The Formation of Mexican National Consciousness, 1531–1813.* Chicago: U of Chicago P.

Lakoff, George. 1987. *Women, Fire, and Dangerous Things: What Categories Reveal about the Mind.* Chicago: U of Chicago P.

Lambert, Jacques. 1969. *Latin America: Social Structures and Political Institutions,* trans. H. Katel. Berkeley: U of California P.

Langer, Suzanne. 1948. *Philosophy in a New Key.* New York: Mentor.

Larsen, Niel. 1991. *Modernism and Hegemony: A Materialist Critique of Aesthetic Agencies.* Minneapolis: U of Minnesota P.

———. 1995. "Postmodernism and Imperialism: Theory and Politics in Latin America." In *The Postmodernism Debate in Latin America*, J. Beverley, et al., eds., 110–34. Durham: Duke UP.

Lash, Scott. 1990. *Sociology of Postmodernism.* New York: Routledge.

Latour, Bruno. 1987. *Science in Action: How to Follow Scientists and Engineers Through Society.* Cambridge: Harvard UP.

———. 1993. *We Have Never Been Modern,* trans. C. Porter. Cambridge: Harvard UP.

———. 1999. *Pandora's Hope: Essays on the Reality of Science.* Cambridge: Harvard UP.

Laudan, Larry. 1996. *Beyond Positivism and Relativism: Theory, Method, and Evidence.* Boulder, CO: Westview P.

Laycock, Steven W. 1994. *Mind as Mirror and the Mirroring of Mind.* Albany: State U of New York P.

Leach, Edmund R. 1961. *Rethinking Anthropology.* London: Athlone.

Lecercle, Jean-Jacques. 1990. *The Violence of Language.* London: Routledge.

Lechner, Norbert. 1995. "A Disenchantment Called Postmodernism." In *The Postmodernism Debate in Latin America*, J. Beverley, et al., eds., 147–64. Durham: Duke UP.

León-Portilla, Miguel. 1963. *Aztec Thought and Culture.* Norman: U of Oklahoma P.

———. 1990. *The Broken Spears: The Aztec Account of the Conquest of Mexico,* trans. A. M. Garibay K. Boston: Beacon.

Leonard, Irving A. 1966. *Baroque Times in Old Mexico: Seventeenth-Century Persons, Places, and Practices*. Ann Arbor: U of Michigan P.

Lévi-Strauss, Claude. 1963. *Structural Anthropology*, trans. C. Jacobson and B. G. Schoepf. New York: Doubleday.

————. 1966. *The Savage Mind*. Chicago: U of Chicago P.

Levine, Lawrence W. 1977. *Black Culture and Black Consciousness: Afro-American Folk Thought from Slavery to Freedom*. New York: Oxford UP.

Levine, Robert M. 1997. *Brazilian Legacies*. London: M. E. Sharpe.

Levinson, Sandra, and Carol Brightman, eds. 1971. *Venceremos Brigade*. New York: Simon and Schuster.

Lewis, J. Lowell. 1992. *Ring of Liberation: Deceptive Discourse in Brazilian Capoeira*. Chicago: U of Chicago P.

Lewis, Oscar. 1961. *The Children of Sanchez*. New York: Random House.

Lezama Lima, José. 1981. *Imagen y posibilidad*. La Habana: Letras Cubanas.

Lieuwen, Edwin. 1965. *Arms and Politics in Latin America*. New York: Praeger.

Lispector, Clarice. 1988. *The Passion According to G. H.*, trans. R. W. Souza. Minneapolis: U of Minnesota P.

Liszka, James. 1989. *The Semiotic of Myth: A Critical Study of the Symbol*. Bloomington: Indiana UP.

Loaeza, Guadalupe. 1988. *Las reinas de Polanco*. México: Aguilar, León y Cal.

————. 1992. *Compro, Luego Existo*. México: Alianza.

Lodge, David. 1990. *After Bakhtin: Essays on Fiction and Criticism*. London: Routledge.

Lotman, Yuri M. 1990. *Universe of the Mind: A Semiotic Theory of Culture*. Bloomington: Indiana UP.

Lugones, María. 1994. "Purity, Impurity, and Separation." *Signs* 19 (2), 458–77.

Lupasco, Stéphane. 1947. *Logique et contradiction*. Paris: Presses Universitaires de France.

Luz, Mario Aurélio. 1995. *Agadá: Dinámica da civilização africana-brasileira*. Salvador: SECNER.

Lynch, John. 1992. *Caudillos in Spanish America, 1800–1850*. New York: Oxford UP.

Lynch, Kevin. 1960. *The Image of the City*. Cambridge: MIT.

Lyotard, Jean François. 1984. *The Postmodern Condition: A Report on Knowledge*, trans. G. Bennington and B. Massumi. Minneapolis: U of Minnesota P.

Magasich-Airola, Jorge, and Jean-Marc de Beer. 2000. *América mágica: Quando a Europa da Renascença pensou estar conquistando o paraíso*, trans. R. Vasconcellos. São Paulo: Paz e Terra.

Malachowski, Alan R., ed. 1990. *Reading Rorty: Critical Responses to Philosophy and the Mirror of Nature (and Beyond)*. Oxford: Basil Blackwell.

Mallon, Florencia E. "The Promise and Dilemmma of L A Subaltern Studies: Perspectives from Latin American History." *American Historical Review* 99 (5), 1491–1515.

————. 1995. *Peasant and Nation: The Making of Postcolonial Mexico and Peru*. Berkeley: U of California P.

Man, Paul de. 1979. *Allegories of Reading: Figural Language in Rousseau, Nietzsche, Rilke, and Proust*. New Haven: Yale UP.

Mannoni, Dominique O. 1956. *Prospero and Caliban: The Psychology of Colonization*, trans. P. Powesland. New York: Praeger.

Mansfield, Victor. 1995. *Synchronicity, Science, and Soul-Making: Understanding Jungian Synchronicity through Physics, Buddhism, and Philosophy*. Chicago: Open Court.

Maravall, José Antonio. 1986. *Culture of the Baroque: Analysis of a Historical Structure*, trans. T. Cochran. Minneapolis: U of Minnesota P.

Marcondes de Moura, Carlos Engênio, ed. 2000. *Candomblé: Religião do corpo e da alma*. Rio de Janeiro: Pallas.

Marcos, Subcomandante. 1995. *Shadows of Tender Fury, The Letters and Communiqués of Subcomandante Marcos*. New York: Monthly Review Press.

Margolis, Joseph. 1991. *The Truth about Relativism*. Oxford: Basil Blackwell.

Martí, José. 1977. *Our America by José Martí: Writings on Latin America and the Struggle for Cuban Independence*, trans. E. Randall, P. S. Foner, ed. New York: Monthly Review P.

Martín-Barbero, José. 1993. *Communication, Culture and Hegemony: From the Media to Mediations*, trans. E. Fox and R. A. White. London: Sage.

Martínez, José Luis. 1979. *Unidad y diversidad de la literatura latinoamericana*. México: Joaquín Mortiz.

Mattelart, Armand Q., and Ariel Dorfman. 1975. *How to Read Donald Duck: Imperialist Ideology in the Disney Comic*. New York: International General.

Maturana, Humberto, and Francisco J. Varela. 1980. *Autopoiesis and Cognition: The Realization of the Living*. Dordrecht-Holland: D. Reidel.

Mauss, Marcel. 1973. *Sociologie et anthropologie*. Paris: Presses Universitaires de France.

Maza, Francisco de la. 1955. *El guadalupanismo mexicano*. México: Fondo de Cultura Económica.

McClary, Susan. 1995. "Music, the Pythagoreans, and the Body." In *Choreographing History*, S. Foster, ed., 82–104. Bloomington: Indiana UP.

McGirk, Tim. 2000. "The Bionic Candidate." *Time*, July 3, 38–40.

McRobbie, Angela. 1980. "Settling Accounts with Subculture: A Feminist Critique." *Screen Education* 34, 37–49.

———. 1984. "Dance and Social Fantasy." In *Gender and Generation*, A. McRobbie and M. Nava, eds., 130–61. London: Macmillan.

Medaglia, Júlio. 1993. "Balanço da bossa nova." In *Balanço da bossa, e outras bossas*, A. de Campos, ed., 67–123. São Paulo: Perspectiva.

Medeiros Epega, Sandra. 1999. 'A volta à África: na contramão do orixá'. In *Faces da tradição afro-brasileiro*, C. Caroso and J. Bacelar, eds., 159–70. Rio de Janeiro: Pallas.

Mejía Prieto, Jorge. 1980. *Nosotros los cursis: Un análisis divertido, valiente y documentado*. México: Diana.

Melhuish, George. 1967. *The Paradoxical Nature of Reality*. Briston: St. Vincent's Press.

Menénez Pidal, Ramón. 1966. *The Spaniards in Their History*, trans. W. Starkle. New York: W. W. Norton.

Merleau-Ponty, Maurice. 1962. *Phenomenology of Perception*. London: Routledge and Kegan Paul.

———. 1964. *L' œil et l'esprit*. Paris: Gallimard.

———. 1968. *The Visible and the Invisible*, C. Lafort, ed., trans. A. Lingus. Evanston: Northwestern UP.

merrell, floyd. 1985. *Deconstruction Reframed*. West Lafayette: Purdue UP.

———. 1991a. *Signs Becoming Signs: Our Perfusive, Pervasive Universe*. Bloomington: Indiana UP.

———. 1991b. *Unthinking Thinking: Jorge Luis Borges, Mathematics, and the "New Physics."* West Lafayette: Purdue UP.

———. 1992. *Sign, Textuality, World*. Bloomington: Indiana UP.

———. 1995a. *Semiosis in the Postmodern Age*. West Lafayette: Purdue UP.

———. 1995b. *Peirce's Semiotics Now: A Primer*. Toronto: Canadian Scholars' Press.

———. 1996. *Signs Grow: Semiosis and Life Processes*. Toronto: U of Toronto P.

———. 1997. *Peirce, Signs, Meaning*. Toronto: U of Toronto P.

———. 1998a. *Simplicity and Complexity: Pondering Literature, Science and Painting*. Ann Arbor: U of Michigan Press.

———. 1998b. *Sensing Semiosis: Steps Toward the Possibility of Alternative Cultural "Logics."* New York: St. Martins.

———. 2000a. *Signs, Science, Self-Subsuming (Arti)facts*. Dresden: Thelem.

———. 2000b. *Tasking Textuality*. Berlin: Peter Lang.

———. 2003. *Sensing Corporeally: Toward a Posthuman Understanding*. Toronto: U of Toronto P.

Meyer, Lorenzo. 1992. *La segunda muerte de la Revolución Mexicana*. México: Cal y Arena.

Meyer, Michael C. 1972. *Huerta: A Political Portrait*. Lincoln: U of Nebraska P.

Mignolo, Walter D., 1989. "Colonial Situations, Geographical Discourses and Territorial Representations: Toward a Diatopical Understanding of Colonial Semiosis." *Dispositio* 14 (36/38), 93–140.

———. 1997a. *The Darker Side of the Renaissance: Literacy, Territoriality, and Colonization*. Ann Arbor: U of Michigan P.

———. 1997b. "Espacios geográficos y localizaciones epistemológicos o la ratio entre la localización geográfica y la subalternización de conocimientos." *Diseño* 3, 1–18.

———. 2000. *Local Histories/Global Designs: Coloniality, Subaltern Knowledges, and Border Thinking*. Princeton: Princeton UP.

Mignolo, Walter D., and Elizabeth Hill Boone, eds. 1994. *Writing without Words: Alternative Literacies in Mesoamerica and the Andes*. Durham: Duke University Press.

Miller, George A. 1956. "The Magical Number Seven, Plus or Minus Two: Some Limits on Our Capacity for Processing Information." *Psychology Review* 63, 81–97.

Mirandé, Alfred, and Evangelina Enríquez. 1979. *La Chicana: The Mexican-American Female*. Chicago: U of Chicago P.

Mires, Fernando. 1988. *La rebelión permanente*. México: Siglo XXI.

Monsiváis, Carlos. 1987. *Entrada libre: Crónicas de la sociedad que se organiza*. México: Ediciones Era.

————. 1988. *Escenas de pudor y liviandad*. México: Era.

Mörner, Magnus. 1967. *Race Mixture in the History of Latin America*. Boston: Little, Brown.

Morse, Richard M. 1989. *New World Soundings: Culture and Ideology in the Americas*. Baltimore: Johns Hopkins UP.

Mota, Carlos Guilherme. 1978. *A ideologia da cultura brasileira (1933–1974)*. São Paulo: Atica.

Nadin, Mihai. 1982. "Consistency, Completeness and the Meaning of Sign Theories." *American Journal of Semiotics* 1 (3), 79–98.

————. 1983. "The Logic of Vagueness and the Category of Synechism." In *The Relevance of Charles Peirce*, E. Freeman, ed., 154–66. LaSalle: Monist Library of Philosophy.

Nagel, Thomas. 1986. *The View from Nowhere*. London: Oxford UP.

Nascimento, Abdias do. 1989. *Brazil, Mixture or Massacre: Essays in the Genocide of a Black People*, trans. E. L. Nascimento. Dover, MA: Majority Press.

Needham, Rodney. 1973. *Right and Left: Essays on Dual Symbolic Classification*. Chicago: U of Chicago P.

Nelson, Cynthia. 1971. *The Waiting Village: Social Change in Rural Mexico*. Boston: Little, Brown.

Neville, Robert Cummings. 1992. *The High Road Around Modernism*. Albany: State U of New York P.

Nicholson, Irene. 1969. *The Liberators: A Study of Independence Movements in Spanish America*. New York: Praeger.

Nietzsche, Friedrich. 1913. *The Complete Works. the Will to Power II*, vol. 15, O. Levy, ed. Edinburgh: T. N. Foulis.

————. 1956. *The Birth of Tragedy Out of the Spirit of Music*, trans. F. Golffing. Garden City: Doubleday.

————. 1974. *The Gay Science: With a Prelude in Rhymes and an Appendix of Songs*, trans. W. Kaufmann. New York: Vintage.

Nina Rodrigues, Raimundo. 1900. *L'animisme fetichiste des nègres de Bahia*. Bahia: Reis.

Norris, Christopher. 1985. *The Contest of Faculties*. London: Methuen.

Núñez Cabeza de Vaca, Alvar. 1961. *Cabeza de Vaca's Adventures in the Unknown Interior of America*. Albuquerque: U of New Mexico P.

Ochoa Zazueta, Jesús Ángel. 1974. *Muerte y muertos*. México: Sep/Setentas.

O'Gorman, Edmundo. 1961. *The Invention of America: An Inquiry into the Historical Nature of the New World and the Meaning of Its History*. Bloomington: Indiana UP.

————. 1989. *Destierro de sombras*. México: UNAM.

Ogden, C. K., and I. A. Richards. 1923. *The Meaning of Meaning*. New York: Harcourt, Brace and World.

Omre, Jr., William A. 1996. *Understanding NAFTA*. Austin: U of Texas P.

Ong, Walter J. 1977. *Interfaces of the Word*. Ithaca: Cornell UP.

———. 1982. *Orality and Literacy*. New York: Methuen.

———. 1991. "The Shifting Sensorium." In *The Varieties of Sensory Experience: A Sourcebook in the Anthropology of the Senses*, D. Howes (ed.), 25–30. Toronto: U of Toronto P.

Oppenheimer, Andres. 1996. *Mexico en la frontera del caos: La crisis de los noventa y la esperanza del nuevo milenio*. Buenos Aires: Javier Vergara.

Ortega, Julio. 1988. *Crítica de la identidad: La pregunta por el Perú en su literatura*. México: Fondo de Cultura Económica.

Ortega y Gasset, José. 1964. *El tema de nuestro tiempo*. Madrid: Espasa-Calpe.

Ortiz, Fernando. 1995. *Cuban Counterpoint: Tobacco and Sugar*, trans. H. de Onís. Durham: Duke UP.

Ortiz, Renato. 1986. *Cultura brasileira e identidade nacional*. São Paulo: Brasiliense.

———. 1988. *A moderna tradição brasileira*. São Paulo: Brasiliense.

Ortner, Sherry B., ed. 1999. *The Fate of "Culture"*. Berkeley: U of California P.

Pacheco, José Emilio. 1991. *You Will Die in a Distant Land*. Coral Gables: U of Miami P.

Parker, Cristian. 1993. *Otra lógica en América Latina: Religión popular y modernización capitalista*. México: Fondo de Cultura Económica.

Paz, Octavio. 1961. *The Labyrinth of Solitude: Life and Thought in Mexico*, trans. L. Kemp. New York: Grove.

———. 1970a. *The Other Mexico: Critique of the Pyramid*, trans. L. Kemp. New York: Grove.

———. 1970b. *Claude Lévi-Strauss: An Introduction*, trans. J. S. Bernstein and L. Kemp. New York: Grove.

———. 1987. "El romanticismo y la poesía contemporánea." *Vuelta* 11 (127), 26–27.

Peirce, Charles Sanders (1931–35). *Collected Papers of Charles Sanders Peirce*, C. Hartshorne and P. Weiss, eds., vols. 1–6. Cambridge: Harvard UP (reference to Peirce's papers will be designated CP).

———. 1958. *Collected Papers of Charles Sanders Peirce*, A. W. Burke, ed., vols. 7–8. Cambridge: Harvard UP (reference to Peirce's papers will be designated CP).

Peña, Devon G. 1997. *The Terror of the Machine: Technology, Work, Gender, and Ecology on the U.S.-Mexico Border*. Austin: U of Texas P.

Perez, Louis A. 1999. *On Becoming Cuban: Identity, Nationalism, and Culture*. Chapel Hill: U of North Carolina P.

Perrone, Charles A. 1989. *Masters of Contemporary Brazilian Song: MPB 1965–1985*. Austin: U of Texas P.

Piedra, José. 1989. "The Game of Arrival." *Diacritics* 19 (3/4), 34–61.

———. 1990. "Through Blues." In *Do the Americas Have a Common Literature?*, G. P. Firmat, ed., 107–29. Durham: Duke UP.

Pike, Fredrick B. 1992. *The United States and Latin America: Myths and Stereotypes of Civilization and Nature*. Austin: U of Texas P.

Pilcher, Jeffrey M. 2001. *Cantinflas: The Chaos of Mexican Modernity*. Wilmington: Scholarly Resources.

Plotnitsky, Arkady. 1994. *Complementarity: Anti-Epistemology after Bohr and Derrida*. Durham: Duke UP.

Poincaré, Henri. 1952. *Science and Hypothesis*, trans. F. Maitland. New York: Dover.

Polanyi, Michael. 1958. *Personal Knowledge*. Chicago: U of Chicago P.

Poniatowska, Elena. 1987. *Until We Meet Again*, trans. P. Hughes. London: Allison and Busby.

————. 1988. *Nada, nadie: Las voces del temblor*. México: Ediciones Era.

Popper, Karl R. 1963. *Conjectures and Refutations: The Growth of Scientific Knowledge*. Oxford: Oxford UP.

Portella, Eduardo. 1995. "O testamento da utopia." *Tempo Brasileiro* 122/123, 133–39.

Pozas, Ricardo. 1962. *Juan the Chamula*. Berkeley: U of California P.

Prado, Paulo. 1962. *Retrato do Brasil: Ensaio sobre tristeza brasileira*, 6th ed. Rio de Janeiro: José Olympio.

Pratt, Mary Louise. 1992. *Imperial Eyes: Travel Writing and Transculturation*. New York: Routledge.

Pribram, Karl. 1971. *Languages of the Brain*. Englewood Cliffs: Prentice-Hall.

Price-Mars, Jean L. 1983. *So Spoke the Uncle*, trans. M. W. Shannon. Washington, D.C.: Three Continents.

Putnam, Hilary. 1976. "How to Think Quantum-Logically." In *Logic and Probability in Quantum Mechanics*, P. Suppes, eds., 47–53. Dordrecht-Holland: D. Reidel.

————. 1981. *Reason, Truth and History*. Cambridge: Cambridge UP.

————. 1983a. *Realism and Reason: Philosophical Papers, Volume 3*. Cambridge: Cambridge UP.

————. 1983b. "Is There a Fact of the Matter About Fiction?" *Poetics Today* 4 (1), 77–82.

————. 1985. "Is Logic Empirical?" In *A Portrait of Twenty-Five Years: Boston Colloquium for the Philosophy of Science 1960–1985*, R. S. Cohen and M. W. Wartofsky, eds., 75–100. Dordrecht-Holland: D. Reidel.

————. 1990. *Realism with a Human Face*, J. Conant, ed. Cambridge: Harvard UP.

Quine, Willard van Orman. 1960. *Word and Object*. Cambridge: MIT.

————. 1969. *Ontological Relativity and Other Essays*. New York: Columbia UP.

Rabassa, José. 1993. *Inventing A-M-E-R-I-C-A*. Norman: U of Oklahoma P.

Rajchman, John, and Cornel West. 1985. *Post-Analytic Philosophy*. New York: Columbia UP.

Rama, Àngel. 1982. *Transculturación narrativa en América Latina*. México: Siglo XXI.

Ramírez, Armando. 1991. *Bye Bye Tenochtitlan*. México: Grijalbo.

Ramírez, Santiago. 1961. *El mexicano: psicología de sus motivaciones*. México: Pax-México.

Ramos, Samuel. 1962. *Profile of Man and Culture in Mexico*. Austin: U of Texas P.

Redhead, Michael. 1987. *Incompleteness, Nonlocality, and Realism: A Prolegomena to the Philosophy of Quantum Mechanics*. Oxford: Clarendon.

Reed, Joel. 1996. "Nationalisms in a Global Economy." In *Reshaping the Shape of the World: Toward an International Cultural Studies*, H. Schwarz and R. Dienst, eds., 30–49. Boulder: Westview.

Rego, Waldeloir. 1968. *Capoeira angola: Um ensaio sócio-etnográfico*. Salvador: Itapuã.

Reis, José Carlos. 1999. *As Identidades do Brasil: De Varnhagen a FHC*. Rio de Janeiro: Funcação Getulio Vargas.

Renato Vieira, Luiz. 1996. *O jogo da capoeira: corpo e cultura popular no brasil*. Rio de Janeiro: Sprint.

Rescher, Nicholas. 1978. *Peirce's Philosophy of Science*. Notre Dame: U of Notre Dame P.

Rescher, Nicholas and Robert Brandom. 1979. *The Logic of Inconsistency: A Study of Non-Standard Possible World Semantics and Ontology*. Totowa, NJ: Rowman and Littlefield.

Resende, Beatriz. 2000. "Braziliam Modernism: The Canonised Revolution." In *Through the Kaleidoscope: The Experience of Modernity in Latin America*, V. Schelling, ed., 199–216. London: Verso.

Reyes, Alfonso. 1960. *Ultima Tulé*, in *Obras completas*, Vol. IX. México: Fondo de Cultura Económica.

Reyes Nevares, Salvador. 1970. "El Machismo en México." *Mundo Nuevo* 46, 14–19.

Ribeiro, Darcy. 1995. *O Brasil como problema*. Rio de Janeiro: Francisco Alves.

Ribeiro, José. 1994. *Mágico mundo dos Orixás*. Rio de Janeiro: Palias.

Ricard, Robert. 1966. *The Spiritual Conquest of Mexico*. Berekeley: U of California P.

Roa Bastos, Augusto. 1986. *I The Supreme*, trans. H. Lane. New York: Knopf.

Roberts, John Storm. 1972. *Black Music of Two Worlds*. New York: Praeger.

———. 1979. *The Latin Tinge: The Impact of Latin American Music on the United States*. New York: Oxford UP.

Rochberg-Halton, Eugene. 1986. *Meaning and Modernity: Social theory in the Pragmatic Attitude*. Chicago: U of Chicago P.

Rodó, José Enríque. 1920. *Ariel*. Boston: Houghton-Mifflin.

Rodríguez, Ileana. 1996. *Women, Guerrillas, and Love: Understanding War in Central America*, trans. I. Rodríguez and R. Carr. Minneapolis: U of Minnesota P.

Rodríguez, Jeanette. 1994. *Our Lady of Guadalupe: Faith and Empowerment among Mexican-American Women*. Austin: U of Texas P.

Rodríguez, Richard. 1983. *Hunger of Memory: The Education of Richard Rodríguez*. New York: Bantam.

———. 1990. "Complexion." In *Out There: Marginalization and Contemporary Cultures*, R. Ferguson, et al., eds., 271–72. Cambridge: MIT.

Rorty, Richard. 1979. *Philosophy and the Mirror of Nature*. Princeton: Princeton UP.

———. 1982. *Consequences of Pragmatism*. Minneapolis: U of Minnesota P.

———. 1989. *Contingency, Irony, and Solidarity*. Cambridge: Cambridge UP.

Rosaldo, Renato. 1993. *Culture and Truth: The Remaking of Social Analysis*. Boston: Beacon P.

Roskill, Mark. 1992. *Klee, Kandinsky, and the Thought of Their Time: A Critical Perspective*. Urbana: U of Illinois P.

Ross, John. 1997. *The Annexation of Mexico: From the Aztece to the IMF: One Reporter's Journey through History*. New York: Common Courage P.

Rothstein, Frances. 1983. "Women and Men in the Family Economy: An Analysis of the Relations between the Sexes in Three Peasant Communities." *Anthropological Quarterly* 56, 1–23.

Rowe, William and Vivian Schelling. 1991. *Memory and Modernity: Popular Culture in Latin America*. London: Verso.

Ruiz, Ramón Eduardo. 1992. *Triumphs and Tragedy*. New York: W. W. Norton.

———. 2000. *On the Rim of Mexico: Encounters of the Rich and Poor*. Chicago: U of Chicago P.

Sacks, Oliver. 1970. *The Man Who Mistook His Wife for a Hat, and Other Clinical Tales*. New York: HarperCollins.

Sahlins, Marshall. 1976. *Culture and Practical Reason*. Chicago: U of Chicago P.

Said, Edward W. 1978. *Orientalism*. New York: Pantheon.

———. 1993. *Culture and Imperialism*. New York: Random House.

Saldívar, José David. 1990. "The Dialectics of Our America." In *Do the Americas Have a Common Literature?*, G. P. Firmat, ed., 62–84. Durham: Duke UP.

———. 1992. *The Dialectics of Our America: Geneology, Cultural Critique, and Literary History*. Durham: Duke UP.

Santos, John F. 1966. "A Psychologist Reflects on Brazil and Brazilians." In *New Perspectives of Brazil*, E. N. Baklanoff, ed., 234–51. Nashville: Vanderbilt UP.

Sarduy, Severo. 1974. *Barroco*. Buenos Aires: Sudamericana.

Sarmiento, Domingo Faustino. 1960. *Life in the Argentine Republic in the Days of the Tyrants: Or, Civilization and Barbarism*. New York: Hafner.

Savan, David. 1987–88. *An Introduction to C. S. Peirce's Full System of Semeiotic* (= Monograph Series of the Toronto Semiotic Circle 1). Toronto: Victoria College.

Schmitter, Philippe C. 1971. *Interest Conflict and Political Change in Brazil*. Stanford: Stanford UP.

Schurz, William L. 1964. *This New World*. New York: Dutton.

Schwarz, Roberto. 1987. "Nacional por subtração," 29–48. In *Que horas são? Ensaios*. São Paulo: Schwarcz.

———. 1992. *Misplaced Ideas*. London: Verso.

Scott, James C. 1990. *Domination and the Arts of Resistance*. New Haven: Yale UP.

Sebeok, Thomas A. 1976. *Contribution to the Doctrine of Signs*. Bloomington: Indiana UP.

Sejourné, Laurette. 1957. *Pensamiento y religión en el México antiguo*. México: Fondo de Cultura Económica.

Serra, Ordep. 1995. *Aguas do Rei*. Petrópolis: Vozes.

Shanker, S. G. 1987. *Wittgenstein and the Turning-Point in the Philosophy of Mathematics*. Albany: State U of New York P.

Shorris, Earl. 1992. *Latinos: A Biography of the People*. New York: Avon.

Shusterman, Richard. 1989. "Organic Unity: Analysis and Deconstruction." In *Redrawing the Lines: Analytic Philosophy, Deconstruction, and Literary Theory*, R. W. Dasenbrock, ed., 92–115. Minneapolis: U of Minnesota P.

Simon, Joel. 1997. *Endangered Mexico: An Environment on the Edge*. San Francisco: Sierra Club Books.

Siu, R. G. H. 1957. *The Tao of Science*. Cambridge: MIT.

Skidmore, Thomas E. 1974. *Black into White: Race and Nationality in Brazilian Thought*. New York: Oxford UP.

Sklodowska, Elzbieta. 1992. *Testimonio hispanoamericano*. New York: Peter Lang.

———. 1994. "Spanish American Testinomial Novel: Some Afterthoughts." *New Novel Review* 1 (2), 32–41.

Skolimowski, Henryk. 1986. "Quine, Adjukiewicz, and the Predicament of 20th Century Philosophy." In *The Philosophy of W. V. Quine*, P. A. Schilpp, ed., 463–90. LaSalle, IL: Open Court.

———. 1987. "The Interactive Mind in the Participatory Universe." In *The Real and the Imaginary: A New Approach to Physics*, J. E. Charon, ed., 69–94. New York: Paragon House.

Sless, David. 1986. *In Search of Semiotics*. New York: Barnes and Noble.

Smith, Anna Marie. 1998. *Laclau and Mouffe: The Radical Democratic Imaginary*. New York: Routledge.

Smith, Wolfgang. 1995. *The Quantum Enigma: Finding the Hidden Key*. Peru, IL: Sherwood Sugden.

Snead, James A. 1990. "Repetition as a Figure of Black Culture." In *Out There: Marginalization and Contemporary Cultures*, R. Ferguson, et al., eds., 213–30. Cambridge: MIT.

Sommer, Doris. 1991. *Foundational Fictions: The National Romances of Latin America*. Berkeley: U of California Press.

Soto, Hernando de. 1989. *The Other Path: The Invisible Revolution of the Third World*, trans. J. Abbott. New York: Harper and Row.

Souchère, Elena de la. 1964. *Explanation of Spain*. New York: Random House.

Spivak, Gayatri Chakravorty. 1985. "Three women's Texts and a Critique of Imperialism." In *"Race," Writing, and Difference*, H. L. Gates, Jr., ed., 262–80. Chicago: U of Chicago P.

———. 1988. "Can the Subaltern Speak?" In *Marxism and the Interpretation of Culture*, C. Nelson and L. Grossberg, eds., 271–313. Urbana: U of Illinois P.

———. 1990. *The Post-Colonial Critic*. New York: Routledge.

Stabb, Martin S. 1967. *In Quest of Identity*. Chapel Hill: U of North Carolina P.

Stallybrass, Peter, and Allon White. 1986. *The Politics and Poetics of Transgression*. Ithaca: Cornell UP.

Stein, Steve. 1980. *Populism in Peru*. Madison: U of Wisconsin P.

Stevens, Evelyn. 1973. "Marianismo: The Other Face of Machismo in Latin America." In *Female and Male in Latin America*, A. Pescatello, ed., 89–101. Pittsburgh: U of Pittsburgh P.

Stewart, Ian. 1989. *Does God Play Dice? The Mathematics of Chaos*. Oxford: Blackwell.

Stewart, Ian, and Martin Golubitsky. 1992. *Fearful Symmetry: Is God a Geometer?* London: Penguin.

Stoetzer, O. Carlos. 1979. *The Scholastic Roots of the Spanish American Revolution*. New York: Fordham UP.

Stoll, David. 1999. *Rigoberta Menchú: And the Story of All Poor Guatemalans*. Boulder: Westview.

Stoller, Paul. 1989. *The Taste of Ethnographic Things: The Senses in Anthropology*. Philadelphia: U of Pennsylvania P.

———. 1997. *Sensuous Scholarship*. Philadelphia: U of Pennsylvania P.

Suárez, Francisco. 1982. *Suarez on Individual Action*. Milwaukee: Marquette UP.

Sudnow, David. 1978. *Ways of the Hand: The Organization of Improvised Conduct*. Cambridge: Harvard UP.

Swingewood, A. 1977. *The Myth of Mass Culture*. London: Methuen.

Talbot, Michael. 1981. *Mysticism and the New Physics*. New York: Bantam.

Tavor Bannet, Eve. 1993. *Postcultural Theory: Critical Theory after the Marxist Paradigm*. New York: Paragon House.

Teixeira Coelho, José. 1995. *Moderno Posmoderno*. São Paulo: Iluminuras.

Teresa de Mier, fray Servando, ed. E. O'Gorman. 1981. *El heteroxodo guadalupano: Obras completa, vols. I–III*. México: Fondo de Cultura Económica.

Tinhorão, José Ramos. 1969. *O Samba que agora vai: A farsa da música popular no exterior*. Rio de Janeiro: JCM.

Todorov, Tzvetan. 1984. *The Conquest of America: The Question of the Other*, trans. R. Howard. New York: Harper and Row.

Toulmin, Stephen. 1982. *The Return to Cosmology: Postmodern Science and the Theology of Nature*. Berkeley: U of California P.

———. 1990. *Cosmopolis: The Hidden Agenda of Modernity*. New York: Free Press.

Turkle, Sherry. 1984. *The Second Self: Computers and the Human Spirit*. New York: Simon and Schuster.

———. 1995. *Life on the Screen: Identity in the Age of the Internet*. New York: Simon and Schuster.

Turley, Peter T. 1977. *Peirce's Cosmology*. New York: Philosophical Library.

Turner, Victor W. 1968. *The Drums of Affliction: A Study of Religious Processes Among the Ndembu of Zambia*. Oxford: Clarendon.

Turner, Norman. 1996. "The Semantic of Linear Perspective." *The Philosophical Forum*. 27 (4), 357–80.

Tzu, Sun. 1963. *The Art of War*, trans. S. B. Griffith. Oxford: Clarendon.

Unamuno, Miguel de. 1954. *The Tragic Sense of Life*. New York: Dover.

———. 1958. "La virilidad de la Fe." In *La agonía del cristianismo*, of *Obras Completas*, vol. 16, 498–508. Barcelona: Vergara.

Valenzuela, Luisa. 1983. *The Lizard's Tail*, trans. G. Rabassa. New York: Farrar, Straus and Giroux.

Varela, Francisco J., Evan Thompson and Eleanor Rosch. 1993. *The Embodied Mind: Cognitive Science and the Human Experience*. Cambridge: MIT.

Vargas Llosa, Mario. 1965. *The Green House*. New York: Harper and Row.

———. 1974 *Conversations in the Cathedral*, trans. G. Rabassa. New York: Farrar.

———. 1986. *The Real Life of Alejandro Mayta*, trans. A. J. MacAdam. New York: Farrar.

———. 1985. *The War of the End of the World*, trans. H. Lane. New York: Farrar.

Vasconcelos, José. 1925. *La raza cósmica*. Madrid: Espasa-Calpe.

Vélez-Ibáñez, Carlos G. 1996. *Border Visions: Mexican Cultures of the Southwest United States*. Tucson: U of Arizona P.

Veloso, Caetano. 1997. *Verdade tropical*. São Paulo: Editora Schwarcz.

Vianna, Hermano. 1999. *The Mystery of Samba: Pop Music and National Identity in Brazil*. Chapel Hill: U of North Carolina P.

Vianna Moog, Clodomiro. 1964. *Bandeirantes and Pioneers*. New York: Braziller.

Vidal, Hernán, and R. Jara, eds. 1986. *Testimonio y literatura*. Minneapolis: Institute for the Study of Ideologies and Literature.

Vidor de Sousa Reis, Leticia. 1997. *O mundo de pernas para o ar: A capoeira no Brasil*. São Paulo: FAPESP.

Vieira, Renato Luiz. 1995. *O jogo de capoeira*. Rio de Janeiro: Sprint.

Villegas, Abelardo. 1960. *La filosofía de lo mexicano*. México: Fondo de Cultura Económica.

Vivas, Eliseo. 1950. *The Moral Life and the Ethical Life*. Chicago: U of Chicago P.

Wachtel, Nathan. 1977. *Vision of the Vanquished: The Spanish Conquest of Peru through Indian Eyes, 1530–1570*. New York: Barnes and Noble.

Wafer, Jim. 1991. *The Taste of Blood: Spirit Possession in Brazilian Candomblé*. Philadelphia: U of Pennsylvania P.

Walker, Evan Harris. 2000. *The Physics of Consciousness*. Cambridge, MA: Perseus.

Warnock, John. 1995. *The Other Mexico: The North American Triangle Completed*. Cheektowaga, NY: Black Rose.

Waterman, Richard Alan. 1948. "'Hot' Rhythm in Negro Music." *Journal of the American Musicological Society* 1, 24–37.

Weber, David J. and James M. Rausch, eds. 1994. *Where Cultures Meet: Frontiers in Latin American History*. Wilmington: Scholarly Resources.

Weber, Samuel. 1987. *Institution and Interpretation*. Minneapolis: U of Minnesota P.

West, Cornel. 1988. "Interview with Cornel West." In *Universal Abandon?*, A. Ross (ed.), 269–86. Minneapolis: U of Minnesota P.

West, Morris. 1957. *Children of the Shadows*. New York: William Morrow.

Westheim, Paul. 1971. *La calavera*, trans. M. Frenk. México: Era.

Wheeler, John Archibald. 1980. "Beyond the Black Hole." In *Some Strangeness in the Proportion: A Centennial Symposium to Celebrate the Achievement of Albert Einstein*, H. Woolf, ed., 341–75. Reading: Addison-Wesley.

White, Allon. 1993. *Carnival, Hysteria, and Writing*. Oxford: Clarendon.

White, Michael. 1999. *Isaac Newton: The Last Sorcerer*. New York: Perseus.

Whitehead, Alfred North. 1925. *Science and the Modern World*. London: Macmillan.

Wilber, Ken, ed. 1982. *The Holographic Paradigm, and Other Paradoxes*. Boulder: Shambhala.

Wilden, Anthony. 1972. *System and Structure*. London: Tavistock.

Williams, Raymond. 1961. *The Long Revolution*. London: Cox and Wyman.

Wilson, Bryan R. 1973. *Magic and the Millenium: A Sociological Study of Religious Movements of Protest Among Tribal and Third-World Peoples*. New York: Harper and Row.

Winant, Howard. 1992. "'The Other Side of the Process': Racial Formation in Contemporary Brazil." In *On Edge: The Crisis of Contemporary Latin American Culture*, G. Yúdice, J. Franco, J. Flores, eds., 85–113. Minneapolis: U of Minnesota P.

Winfree, Arthur T. 1987. *When Time Breaks Down: The Three-Dimensional Dynamics of Electrochemical Waves and Cardiac Arrhythmias*. Princeton: Princeton UP.

Wittgenstein, Ludwig. 1953. *Philosophical Investigations*, trans. G. E. M. Anscombe. New York: Macmillan.

———. 1974. *Philosophical Grammar*, trans. A. Kenny, R. Rhees, ed. Oxford: Basil Blackwell.

Wolf, Eric. 1959. *Sons of the Shaking Earth*. Chicago: U of Chicago P.

Wölfflin, Heinrich. 1950. *Principles of Art History: The Problems of the Development of Style in Later Art*. New York: Dover.

Womack Jr., John. 1999. *Rebellion in Chiapas: An Historical Reader*. New York: The New P.

Woolgar, Steve. 1988a. *Knowledge and Reflexivity: New Frontiers in the Sociology of Knowledge*. London: Sage.

———. 1988b. *Science, The Very Idea*. New York: Tavistock.

Wright, Crispin. 1976. "Language-Mastery and the Sorites Paradox." In *Truth and Meaning: Essays in Semantics*. G. Evans and J. McDowell, eds., 223–47. Oxford: Clarendon.

Yeager, Gertrude M., ed. 1994. *Confronting Change, Challenging Tradition*. Wilmington: Scholarly Resources.

Young, R. J. C. 1995. *Colonial Desire: Hybridity in Theory, Culture and Race*. London: Routledge.

Yúdice, George. 1988. "Marginality and the Ethics of Survival." In *Universal Abandon? the Politics of Postmodernism*, A. Ross, ed., 214–36. Minneapolis: U of Minnesota P.

———. 1992. "Postmodernity and Transnational Capitalism in Latin America." In *On Edge: The Crisis of Contemporary Latin American Culture*, G. Yúdice, J. Franco and J. Flores, eds., 1–28. Minneapolis: U of Minnesota P.

Zadeh, L. 1965. "Fuzzy Sets." *Information and Control* 8, 378–53.

———. 1975. "Fuzzy Logic and Approximate Reasoning (In Memory of Grigore Moisil)." *Synthese* 30, 407–28.

Zapata, Luis. 1979. *El vampiro de la Colonia Roma*. México: Grijalbo.

Zavala, Silvio Arturo. 1964. *The Defense of Human Rights in Latin America, Sixteenth to Eighteenth Centuries*. Paris: UNESCO.

Zea, Leopoldo. 1955. *La filosofía en México*. México: Libro-Mex.

————. 1963. *The Latin American Mind*. Norman: U of Oklahoma P.

————. 1969. *La filosofía latinoamericana como filosofía sin más*. México: Siglo XXI.

————. 1970. *Nuestra América*. Madrid: Revista de Occidente.

————. 1976. *Filosofía y cultura latinoamericanas*. Caracas: Centro de Estudios Latinoamericanos Rómulo Gallegos.

————. 1988. *Discurso desde la marginación y la barbarie*. Barcelona: Antropos.

————. 1990. *Descubrimiento e identidad latinoamericana*. México: UNAM.

————. 1992. *The Role of the Americas in History*, trans. S. Karsen. Savage, MD: Rowman and Littlefield.

Ziff, Bruce, and Pratima V. Rao. 1997. *Borrowed Power: Essays on Cultural Appropriation*. New Brunswick: Rutgers UP.

Zukav, Gary. 1979. *The Dancing Wu Li Masters*. New York: William Morrow.

Zuckerhandl, Victor. 1956. *Sound and Symbol: Music and the External World*. London: Routledge and Kegan Paul.

Index